Edexcel A level Further Mathematics

Core Pure Mathematics
Book 2

Series Editor: Harry Smith
Authors: Greg Attwood, Jack Barraclough, Ian Bettison, Lee Cope, Alistair Macpherson,
Bronwen Moran, Johnny Nicholson, Laurence Pateman, Joe Petran, Keith Pledger,
Harry Smith, Geoff Staley, Dave Wilkins

P Pearson

Published by Pearson Education Limited, 80 Strand, London WC2R 0RL.

www.pearsonschoolsandfecolleges.co.uk

Copies of official specifications for all Pearson qualifications may be found on the website:
qualifications.pearson.com

Text © Pearson Education Limited 2018
Edited by Tech-Set Ltd, Gateshead
Typeset by Tech-Set Ltd, Gateshead
Original illustrations © Pearson Education Limited 2018
Cover illustration Marcus@kja-artists

The rights of Greg Attwood, Jack Barraclough, Ian Bettison, Lee Cope, Alistair Macpherson,
Bronwen Moran, Johnny Nicholson, Laurence Pateman, Joe Petran, Keith Pledger, Harry Smith,
Geoff Staley, Dave Wilkins to be identified as authors of this work have been asserted by them in
accordance with the Copyright, Designs and Patents Act 1988.

First published 2018

21 20 19 18
10 9 8 7 6 5 4 3 2 1

British Library Cataloguing in Publication Data

A catalogue record for this book is available from the British Library

ISBN 978 1 292 18334 3

Printed in the UK by Bell & Bain Ltd, Glasgow

Acknowledgements

The authors and publisher would like to thank the following for their kind permission to
reproduce their photographs:

(Key: b-bottom; c-centre; l-left; r-right; t-top)

123RF: 170, 196r, Cobalt 77, 93r, **Alamy Stock Photo:** NASA Photo 52, 93cr, **Getty Images:**
SteveDF 1, 93 l, **SCIENCE PHOTO LIBRARY:** Andrew Brookes, National Physical Laboratory 31, 93cl,
Shutterstock: Tyler Olson 100, 196l, Spacedrone808 119, 196cl, Tatiana Shepeleva 147, 196cr.

All other images © Pearson Education

Contents

Overarching themes

The following three overarching themes have been fully integrated throughout the Pearson Edexcel AS and A level Mathematics series, so they can be applied alongside your learning and practice.

1. Mathematical argument, language and proof

- Rigorous and consistent approach throughout
- Notation boxes explain key mathematical language and symbols
- Dedicated sections on mathematical proof explain key principles and strategies
- Opportunities to critique arguments and justify methods

2. Mathematical problem solving

- Hundreds of problem-solving questions, fully integrated into the main exercises
- Problem-solving boxes provide tips and strategies
- Structured and unstructured questions to build confidence
- Challenge boxes provide extra stretch

The Mathematical Problem-solving cycle

specify the problem

collect information

process and represent information

interpret results

3. Mathematical modelling

- Dedicated modelling sections in relevant topics provide plenty of practice where you need it
- Examples and exercises include qualitative questions that allow you to interpret answers in the context of the model
- Dedicated chapter in Statistics & Mechanics Year 1/AS explains the principles of modelling in mechanics

Finding your way around the book

Access an online digital edition using the code at the front of the book.

Each chapter starts with a list of objectives

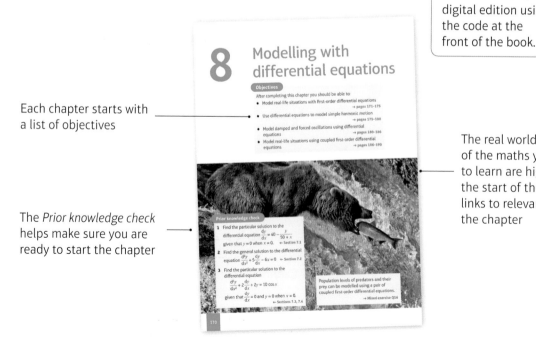

The real world applications of the maths you are about to learn are highlighted at the start of the chapter with links to relevant questions in the chapter

The *Prior knowledge check* helps make sure you are ready to start the chapter

Exercise questions are carefully graded so they increase in difficulty and gradually bring you up to exam standard

Exercises are packed with exam-style questions to ensure you are ready for the exams

Challenge boxes give you a chance to tackle some more difficult questions

Exam-style questions are flagged with 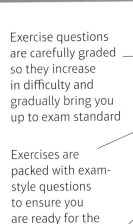 Ⓔ

Problem-solving questions are flagged with Ⓟ

Each section begins with explanation and key learning points

Each chapter ends with a *Mixed exercise* and a *Summary of key points*

Step-by-step worked examples focus on the key types of questions you'll need to tackle

Problem-solving boxes provide hints, tips and strategies, and *Watch out* boxes highlight areas where students often lose marks in their exams

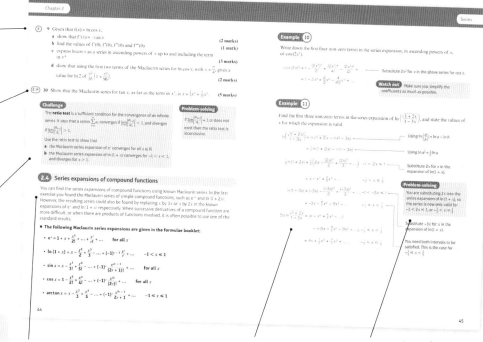

Every few chapters a *Review exercise* helps you consolidate your learning with lots of exam-style questions

Review exercise

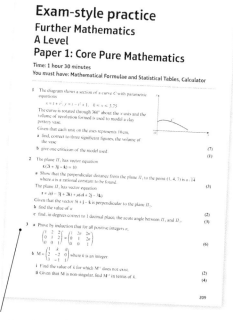

Exam-style practice
Further Mathematics
A Level
Paper 1: Core Pure Mathematics

Two A level practice papers at the back of the book help you prepare for the real thing.

Extra online content

Whenever you see an *Online* box, it means that there is extra online content available to support you.

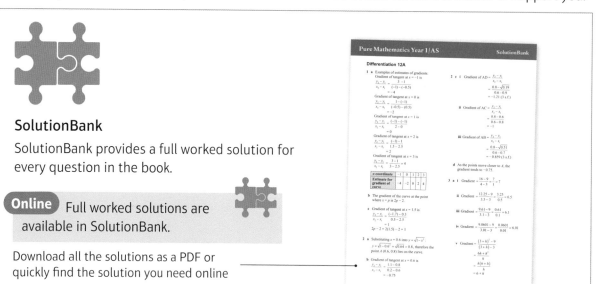

SolutionBank

SolutionBank provides a full worked solution for every question in the book.

Online Full worked solutions are available in SolutionBank.

Download all the solutions as a PDF or quickly find the solution you need online

Use of technology

Explore topics in more detail, visualise problems and consolidate your understanding using pre-made GeoGebra activities.

Online Find the point of intersection graphically using technology.

GeoGebra

GeoGebra-powered interactives

Interact with the maths you are learning using GeoGebra's easy-to-use tools

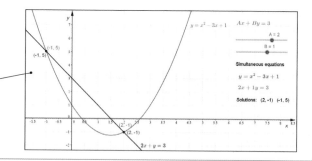

Access all the extra online content for free at:

www.pearsonschools.co.uk/cp2maths

You can also access the extra online content by scanning this QR code:

Complex numbers

1

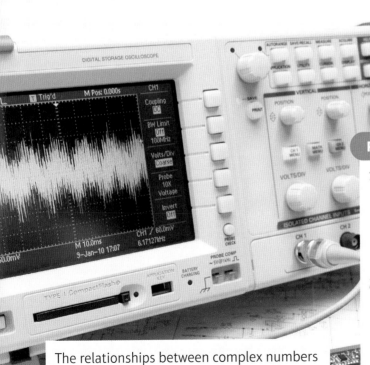

The relationships between complex numbers and trigonometric functions allow electrical engineers to analyse oscillations of voltage and current in electrical circuits more easily.

Prior knowledge check

1. $z = 4 + 4i\sqrt{3}$ and $w = 2\left(\cos\dfrac{\pi}{6} + i\sin\dfrac{\pi}{6}\right)$.
   Find:

   a $|z|$ **b** $\arg(z)$ **c** $|zw|$ **d** $\arg(zw)$

   e $\left|\dfrac{z}{w}\right|$ **f** $\arg\left(\dfrac{z}{w}\right)$ ← Book 1, Chapter 2

2. $f(z) = z^4 + 4z^3 + 9z^2 + 4z + 8$

   Given that $z = i$ is a root of $f(z) = 0$, show all the roots of $f(z) = 0$ on an Argand diagram.   ← Book 1, Chapters 1, 2

3. Use the binomial expansion to find the n^4 term in the expansion of $(2 + n)^9$.
      ← Pure Year 1, Chapter 8

1.1 Exponential form of complex numbers

You can use the modulus–argument form of a complex number to express it in the **exponential form**: $z = re^{i\theta}$.

You can write $\cos\theta$ and $\sin\theta$ as infinite series of powers of θ:

$$\cos\theta = 1 - \frac{\theta^2}{2!} + \frac{\theta^4}{4!} - \frac{\theta^6}{6!} + \ldots + \frac{(-1)^r\,\theta^{2r}}{(2r)!} + \ldots \quad (1)$$

$$\sin\theta = \theta - \frac{\theta^3}{3!} + \frac{\theta^5}{5!} - \frac{\theta^7}{7!} + \ldots + \frac{(-1)^r\,\theta^{2r+1}}{(2r+1)!} + \ldots \quad (2)$$

You can also write e^x, $x \in \mathbb{R}$, as a series expansion in powers of x.

$$e^x = 1 + x + \frac{x^2}{2!} + \frac{x^3}{3!} + \frac{x^4}{4!} + \frac{x^5}{5!} + \ldots + \frac{x^r}{r!} + \ldots$$

You can use this expansion to define the exponential function for complex powers, by replacing x with a complex number. In particular, if you replace x with the imaginary number $i\theta$, you get

$$e^{i\theta} = 1 + i\theta + \frac{(i\theta)^2}{2!} + \frac{(i\theta)^3}{3!} + \frac{(i\theta)^4}{4!} + \frac{(i\theta)^5}{5!} + \frac{(i\theta)^6}{6!} + \ldots$$

$$= 1 + i\theta + \frac{i^2\theta^2}{2!} + \frac{i^3\theta^3}{3!} + \frac{i^4\theta^4}{4!} + \frac{i^5\theta^5}{5!} + \frac{i^6\theta^6}{6!} + \ldots$$

$$= 1 + i\theta - \frac{\theta^2}{2!} - \frac{i\theta^3}{3!} + \frac{\theta^4}{4!} + \frac{i\theta^5}{5!} - \frac{\theta^6}{6!} + \ldots$$

$$= \left(1 - \frac{\theta^2}{2!} + \frac{\theta^4}{4!} - \frac{\theta^6}{6!} + \ldots\right) + i\left(\theta - \frac{\theta^3}{3!} + \frac{\theta^5}{5!} - \ldots\right)$$

By comparing this series expansion with (1) and (2), you can write $e^{i\theta}$ as

$$e^{i\theta} = \cos\theta + i\sin\theta$$

This formula is known as **Euler's relation**. It is important for you to remember this result.

- **You can use Euler's relation, $e^{i\theta} = \cos\theta + i\sin\theta$, to write a complex number z in exponential form:**

$$z = re^{i\theta}$$

where $r = |z|$ and $\theta = \arg z$.

Links The **modulus–argument** form of a complex number is $z = r(\cos\theta + i\sin\theta)$, where $r = |z|$ and $\theta = \arg z$.
← Book 1, Section 2.3

Links These are the Maclaurin series expansions of $\sin\theta$, $\cos\theta$ and e^x.
→ Chapter 2

Note Substituting $\theta = \pi$ into Euler's relation yields **Euler's identity**:

$$e^{i\pi} + 1 = 0$$

This equation links the five fundamental constants 0, 1, π, e and i, and is considered an example of mathematical beauty.

Example 1

Express the following in the form $re^{i\theta}$, where $-\pi < \theta \leqslant \pi$.

a $z = \sqrt{2}\left(\cos\dfrac{\pi}{10} + i\sin\dfrac{\pi}{10}\right)$ **b** $z = 5\left(\cos\dfrac{\pi}{8} - i\sin\dfrac{\pi}{8}\right)$

a $z = \sqrt{2}\left(\cos\dfrac{\pi}{10} + i\sin\dfrac{\pi}{10}\right)$ Compare with $r(\cos\theta + i\sin\theta)$.

So $r = \sqrt{2}$ and $\theta = \dfrac{\pi}{10}$

Therefore, $z = \sqrt{2}\,e^{\frac{\pi i}{10}}$ $z = re^{i\theta}$

b $z = 5\left(\cos\dfrac{\pi}{8} - i\sin\dfrac{\pi}{8}\right)$

$z = 5\left(\cos\left(-\dfrac{\pi}{8}\right) + i\sin\left(-\dfrac{\pi}{8}\right)\right)$

Problem-solving

Use $\cos(-\theta) = \cos\theta$ and $\sin(-\theta) = -\sin\theta$.

So $r = 5$ and $\theta = -\dfrac{\pi}{8}$ Compare with $r(\cos\theta + i\sin\theta)$.

Therefore, $z = 5e^{-\frac{\pi i}{8}}$ $z = re^{i\theta}$.

Example 2

Express $z = 2 - 3i$ in the form $re^{i\theta}$, where $-\pi < \theta \leqslant \pi$.

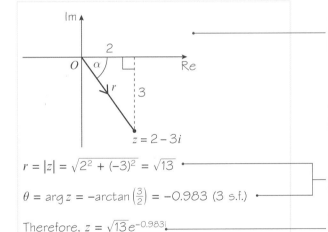

Sketch the Argand diagram, showing the position of the complex number.

Here z is in the fourth quadrant so the required argument is $-\alpha$.

$r = |z| = \sqrt{2^2 + (-3)^2} = \sqrt{13}$

$\theta = \arg z = -\arctan\left(\dfrac{3}{2}\right) = -0.983$ (3 s.f.)

Find r and θ.

Therefore, $z = \sqrt{13}\,e^{-0.983i}$ $z = re^{i\theta}$.

Example 3

Express $z = \sqrt{2}e^{\frac{3\pi i}{4}}$ in the form $x + iy$, where $x, y \in \mathbb{R}$.

$z = \sqrt{2}e^{\frac{3\pi i}{4}}$, so $r = \sqrt{2}$ and $\theta = \frac{3\pi}{4}$. ——— Compare with $re^{i\theta}$.

$z = \sqrt{2}\left(\cos\frac{3\pi}{4} + i\sin\frac{3\pi}{4}\right)$ ——— Write z in modulus–argument form.

$= \sqrt{2}\left(-\frac{1}{\sqrt{2}} + i\frac{1}{\sqrt{2}}\right)$

Therefore, $z = -1 + i$ ——— Simplify.

Example 4

Express $z = 2e^{\frac{23\pi i}{5}}$ in the form $r(\cos\theta + i\sin\theta)$, where $-\pi < \theta \leq \pi$.

$z = 2e^{\frac{23\pi i}{5}}$, so $r = 2$ and $\theta = \frac{23\pi}{5}$. ——— Compare with $re^{i\theta}$.

$\frac{23\pi}{5} - 2\pi = \frac{13\pi}{5}, \frac{13\pi}{5} - 2\pi = \frac{3\pi}{5}$

$\frac{3\pi}{5}$ is in the range $-\pi < \theta \leq \pi$

So $z = 2\left(\cos\frac{3\pi}{5} + i\sin\frac{3\pi}{5}\right)$

Problem-solving

$\cos\theta = \cos(\theta + 2\pi)$ and $\sin\theta = \sin(\theta + 2\pi)$.
Subtract multiples of 2π from $\frac{23\pi}{5}$ until you find a value in the range $-\pi < \theta \leq \pi$.

——— Write z in the form $r(\cos\theta + i\sin\theta)$.

Example 5

Use $e^{i\theta} = \cos\theta + i\sin\theta$ to show that $\cos\theta = \frac{1}{2}(e^{i\theta} + e^{-i\theta})$.

$e^{i\theta} = \cos\theta + i\sin\theta$ (1)

$e^{-i\theta} = e^{i(-\theta)} = \cos(-\theta) + i\sin(-\theta)$

So $e^{-i\theta} = \cos\theta - i\sin\theta$ (2) ——— Use $\cos(-\theta) = \cos\theta$ and $\sin(-\theta) = -\sin\theta$.

$e^{i\theta} + e^{-i\theta} = 2\cos\theta$ ——— Add (1) and (2).

$\Rightarrow \frac{e^{i\theta} + e^{-i\theta}}{2} = \cos\theta$ ——— Divide both sides by 2.

Hence, $\cos\theta = \frac{1}{2}(e^{i\theta} + e^{-i\theta})$, as required.

Exercise 1A

1 Express the following in the form $re^{i\theta}$, where $-\pi < \theta \leqslant \pi$. Use exact values of r and θ where possible, or values to 3 significant figures otherwise.

a -3

b $6i$

c $-2\sqrt{3} - 2i$

d $-8 + i$

e $2 - 5i$

f $-2\sqrt{3} + 2i\sqrt{3}$

g $\sqrt{8}\left(\cos\dfrac{\pi}{4} + i\sin\dfrac{\pi}{4}\right)$

h $8\left(\cos\dfrac{\pi}{6} - i\sin\dfrac{\pi}{6}\right)$

i $2\left(\cos\dfrac{\pi}{5} - i\sin\dfrac{\pi}{5}\right)$

2 Express the following in the form $x + iy$ where $x, y \in \mathbb{R}$.

a $e^{\frac{\pi i}{3}}$

b $4e^{\pi i}$

c $3\sqrt{2}\,e^{\frac{\pi i}{4}}$

d $8e^{\frac{\pi i}{6}}$

e $3e^{-\frac{\pi i}{2}}$

f $e^{\frac{5\pi i}{6}}$

g $e^{-\pi i}$

h $3\sqrt{2}e^{-\frac{3\pi i}{4}}$

i $8e^{-\frac{4\pi i}{3}}$

3 Express the following in the form $r(\cos\theta + i\sin\theta)$, where $-\pi < \theta \leqslant \pi$.

a $e^{\frac{16\pi i}{13}}$

b $4e^{\frac{17\pi i}{5}}$

c $5e^{-\frac{9\pi i}{8}}$

(P) 4 Use $e^{i\theta} = \cos\theta + i\sin\theta$ to show that $\sin\theta = \dfrac{1}{2i}\left(e^{i\theta} - e^{-i\theta}\right)$.

1.2 Multiplying and dividing complex numbers

You can apply the modulus–argument rules for multiplying and dividing complex numbers to numbers written in exponential form.

Recall that, for any two complex numbers z_1 and z_2,

- $|z_1 z_2| = |z_1||z_2|$

- $\arg(z_1 z_2) = \arg(z_1) + \arg(z_2)$

- $\left|\dfrac{z_1}{z_2}\right| = \dfrac{|z_1|}{|z_2|}$

- $\arg\left(\dfrac{z_1}{z_2}\right) = \arg(z_1) - \arg(z_2)$

Links These results can be proved by considering the numbers z_1 and z_2 in the form $r(\cos\theta + i\sin\theta)$ and using the addition formulae for cos and sin. ← **Book 1, Section 2.3**

Applying these results to numbers in exponential form gives the following result:

■ **If $z_1 = r_1 e^{i\theta_1}$ and $z_2 = r_2 e^{i\theta_2}$, then:**

- $z_1 z_2 = r_1 r_2 e^{i(\theta_1 + \theta_2)}$

- $\dfrac{z_1}{z_2} = \dfrac{r_1}{r_2} e^{i(\theta_1 - \theta_2)}$

Watch out You cannot automatically assume the laws of indices work the same way with complex numbers as with real numbers. This result only shows that they can be applied in these specific cases.

Example 6

a Express $2e^{\frac{\pi i}{6}} \times \sqrt{3}e^{\frac{\pi i}{3}}$ in the form $x + iy$.

b $z = 2 + 2i$, $\text{Im}(zw) = 0$ and $|zw| = 3|z|$

Use geometrical reasoning to find the two possibilities for w, giving your answers in exponential form.

a $2e^{\frac{\pi i}{6}} \times \sqrt{3}\,e^{\frac{\pi i}{3}} = (2 \times \sqrt{3})e^{i\left(\frac{\pi}{6} + \frac{\pi}{3}\right)}$ —————— $z_1z_2 = r_1r_2e^{i(\theta_1+\theta_2)}$

$\qquad = 2\sqrt{3}\,e^{\frac{\pi i}{2}}$ —————— Simplify.

$\qquad = 2\sqrt{3}\left(\cos\frac{\pi}{2} + i\sin\frac{\pi}{2}\right)$ —————— Convert the complex number to modulus–argument form.

$\qquad = 2\sqrt{3}(0 + i)$

$\qquad = 2i\sqrt{3}$

b $|zw| = 3|z| \Rightarrow |w| = 3$ —————— $|zw| = |z||w| = 3|z|$.

$\arg z = \arctan\left(\dfrac{2}{2}\right) = \dfrac{\pi}{4}$

$\text{Im}(zw) = 0$ so $\arg(zw) = 0$ or π

So $\arg w = \dfrac{3\pi}{4}$ or $-\dfrac{\pi}{4}$ —————— wz lies on the real axis, so z is rotated $\dfrac{3\pi}{4}$ clockwise or $\dfrac{\pi}{4}$ anticlockwise when multiplied by w.

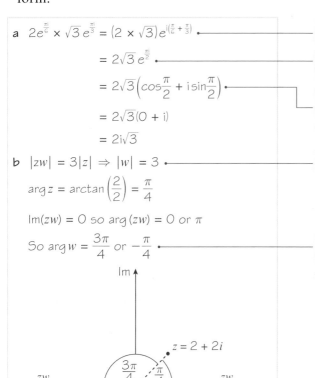

$w_1 = 3e^{-\frac{\pi i}{4}}$ and $w_2 = 3e^{\frac{3\pi i}{4}}$

Example 7

Express $\dfrac{2\left(\cos\dfrac{\pi}{12} + i\sin\dfrac{\pi}{12}\right)}{\sqrt{2}\left(\cos\dfrac{5\pi}{6} + i\sin\dfrac{5\pi}{6}\right)}$ in the form $re^{i\theta}$.

$\dfrac{2\left(\cos\dfrac{\pi}{12} + i\sin\dfrac{\pi}{12}\right)}{\sqrt{2}\left(\cos\dfrac{5\pi}{6} + i\sin\dfrac{5\pi}{6}\right)} = \dfrac{2e^{\frac{\pi i}{12}}}{\sqrt{2}e^{\frac{5\pi i}{6}}}$ —————— Convert the numerator and denominator to exponential form.

$\qquad = \dfrac{2}{\sqrt{2}}e^{i\left(\frac{\pi}{12} - \frac{5\pi}{6}\right)}$ —————— $\dfrac{z_1}{z_2} = \dfrac{r_1}{r_2}e^{i(\theta_1-\theta_2)}$

$\qquad = \sqrt{2}\,e^{-\frac{3\pi i}{4}}$ —————— Simplify.

Exercise **1B**

1 Express the following in the form $x + iy$, where $x, y \in \mathbb{R}$.

a $e^{\frac{\pi i}{3}} \times e^{\frac{\pi i}{4}}$

b $\sqrt{5}e^{i\theta} \times 3e^{3i\theta}$

c $\sqrt{2}e^{\frac{2\pi i}{3}} \times e^{-\frac{7\pi i}{3}} \times 3e^{\frac{\pi i}{6}}$

2 Express the following in the form $x + iy$ where $x, y \in \mathbb{R}$.

a $\dfrac{2e^{\frac{7\pi i}{2}}}{8e^{\frac{9\pi i}{2}}}$

b $\dfrac{\sqrt{3}e^{\frac{3\pi i}{7}}}{4e^{-\frac{2\pi i}{7}}}$

c $\dfrac{\sqrt{2}e^{-\frac{15\pi i}{6}}}{2e^{\frac{\pi i}{3}}} \times \sqrt{2}\,e^{\frac{19\pi i}{3}}$

3 Express the following in the form $re^{i\theta}$.

a $(\cos 2\theta + i\sin 2\theta)(\cos 3\theta + i\sin 3\theta)$

b $\left(\cos \dfrac{3\pi}{11} + i\sin \dfrac{3\pi}{11}\right)\left(\cos \dfrac{8\pi}{11} + i\sin \dfrac{8\pi}{11}\right)$

c $3\left(\cos \dfrac{\pi}{4} + i\sin \dfrac{\pi}{4}\right) \times 2\left(\cos \dfrac{\pi}{12} + i\sin \dfrac{\pi}{12}\right)$

d $\sqrt{6}\left(\cos \left(-\dfrac{\pi}{12}\right) + i\sin \left(-\dfrac{\pi}{12}\right)\right) \times \sqrt{3}\left(\cos \dfrac{\pi}{3} + i\sin \dfrac{\pi}{3}\right)$

4 Express the following in the form $re^{i\theta}$.

a $\dfrac{\cos 5\theta + i\sin 5\theta}{\cos 2\theta + i\sin 2\theta}$

b $\dfrac{\sqrt{2}\left(\cos \dfrac{\pi}{2} + i\sin \dfrac{\pi}{2}\right)}{\dfrac{1}{2}\left(\cos \dfrac{\pi}{4} + i\sin \dfrac{\pi}{4}\right)}$

c $\dfrac{3\left(\cos \dfrac{\pi}{3} + i\sin \dfrac{\pi}{3}\right)}{4\left(\cos \dfrac{5\pi}{6} + i\sin \dfrac{5\pi}{6}\right)}$

5 z and w are two complex numbers where $z = -9 + 3i\sqrt{3}$, $|w| = \sqrt{3}$ and $\arg w = \dfrac{7\pi}{12}$

Express the following in the form $re^{i\theta}$, where $-\pi < \theta \leqslant \pi$.

a z **b** w **c** zw **d** $\dfrac{z}{w}$

(P) **6** Use the exponential form for a complex number to show that

$$\dfrac{(\cos 9\theta + i\sin 9\theta)(\cos 4\theta + i\sin 4\theta)}{\cos 7\theta + i\sin 7\theta} \equiv \cos 6\theta + i\sin 6\theta$$

(E/P) **7** $z = 1 + i\sqrt{3}$, $\text{Re}\left(\dfrac{z^2}{w}\right) = 0$ and $\left|\dfrac{z^2}{w}\right| = |z|$

Use geometrical reasoning to find the two possibilities for w, giving your answers in exponential form. **(4 marks)**

(E/P) **8** **a** Evaluate $(1 + i)^2$, giving your answer in exponential form. **(2 marks)**

     b Use mathematical induction to prove that $(1 + i)^n = 2^{\frac{n}{2}} e^{\frac{n\pi i}{4}}$ for $n \in \mathbb{Z}^+$. **(4 marks)**

     c Hence find $(1 + i)^{16}$. **(1 mark)**

(P) **9** Use Euler's relation for $e^{i\theta}$ and $e^{-i\theta}$ to verify that $\cos^2 \theta + \sin^2 \theta \equiv 1$.

Challenge

a Given that n is a positive integer, prove by induction that
$$(r\mathrm{e}^{\mathrm{i}\theta})^n = r^n\mathrm{e}^{\mathrm{i}n\theta}$$

b Given further that $z^{-n} = \dfrac{1}{z^n}$ for all $z \in \mathbb{C}$, show that
$$(r\mathrm{e}^{\mathrm{i}\theta})^{-n} = r^{-n}\mathrm{e}^{-\mathrm{i}n\theta}$$

Watch out You cannot assume that the laws of indices will apply to complex numbers. Prove these results using only the properties

$$z_1 z_2 = r_1 r_2 \mathrm{e}^{\mathrm{i}(\theta_1 + \theta_2)}$$

$$\frac{z_1}{z_2} = \frac{r_1}{r_2}\mathrm{e}^{\mathrm{i}(\theta_1 - \theta_2)}$$

1.3 De Moivre's theorem

You can use Euler's relation to find powers of complex numbers given in modulus–argument form.

$$(r(\cos\theta + \mathrm{i}\sin\theta))^2 = (r\mathrm{e}^{\mathrm{i}\theta})^2$$
$$= r\mathrm{e}^{\mathrm{i}\theta} \times r\mathrm{e}^{\mathrm{i}\theta}$$
$$= r^2\mathrm{e}^{\mathrm{i}2\theta}$$
$$= r^2(\cos 2\theta + \mathrm{i}\sin 2\theta)$$

Similarly, $(r(\cos\theta + \mathrm{i}\sin\theta))^3 = r^3(\cos 3\theta + \mathrm{i}\sin 3\theta)$, and so on.

The generalisation of this result is known as **de Moivre's theorem**:

■ **For any integer n,**

$$(r(\cos\theta + \mathbf{i}\sin\theta))^n = r^n(\cos n\theta + \mathbf{i}\sin n\theta)$$

You can prove de Moivre's theorem quickly using Euler's relation.

$$(r(\cos\theta + \mathrm{i}\sin\theta))^n = (r\mathrm{e}^{\mathrm{i}\theta})^n$$
$$= r^n\mathrm{e}^{\mathrm{i}n\theta}$$
$$= r^n(\cos n\theta + \mathrm{i}\sin n\theta)$$

This step is valid for any integer exponent n. ← **Exercise 1B, Challenge**

You can also prove de Moivre's theorem for **positive integer exponents** directly from the modulus–argument form of a complex number using the addition formulae for sin and cos.

Links This proof uses the method of proof by induction.
← **Book 1, Chapter 8**

1. Basis step

$n = 1$; LHS $= (r(\cos\theta + \mathrm{i}\sin\theta))^1 = r(\cos\theta + \mathrm{i}\sin\theta)$

RHS $= r^1(\cos 1\theta + \mathrm{i}\sin 1\theta) = r(\cos\theta + \mathrm{i}\sin\theta)$

As LHS = RHS, de Moivre's theorem is true for $n = 1$.

2. Assumption step

Assume that de Moivre's theorem is true for $n = k$, $k \in \mathbb{Z}^+$:

$$(r(\cos\theta + \mathrm{i}\sin\theta))^k = r^k(\cos k\theta + \mathrm{i}\sin k\theta)$$

3. Inductive step

When $n = k + 1$,

$(r(\cos\theta + i\sin\theta))^{k+1} = (r(\cos\theta + i\sin\theta))^k \times r(\cos\theta + i\sin\theta)$

$\qquad = r^k(\cos k\theta + i\sin k\theta) \times r(\cos\theta + i\sin\theta)$ —— By assumption step

$\qquad = r^{k+1}(\cos k\theta + i\sin k\theta)(\cos\theta + i\sin\theta)$

$\qquad = r^{k+1}((\cos k\theta\cos\theta - \sin k\theta\sin\theta) + i(\sin k\theta\cos\theta + \cos k\theta\sin\theta))$

$\qquad = r^{k+1}(\cos(k\theta + \theta) + i\sin(k\theta + \theta))$ —— By addition formulae

$\qquad = r^{k+1}(\cos((k+1)\theta) + i\sin((k+1)\theta))$

Therefore, de Moivre's theorem is true when $n = k + 1$.

4. Conclusion step

If de Moivre's theorem is true for $n = k$, then it has been shown to be true for $n = k + 1$.

As de Moivre's theorem is true for $n = 1$, it is now proven to be true for all $n \in \mathbb{Z}^+$ by mathematical induction.

Links The corresponding proof for negative integer exponents is left as an exercise.
→ **Exercise 1C, Challenge**

Example 8

Simplify $\dfrac{\left(\cos\dfrac{9\pi}{17} + i\sin\dfrac{9\pi}{17}\right)^5}{\left(\cos\dfrac{2\pi}{17} - i\sin\dfrac{2\pi}{17}\right)^3}$

$\dfrac{\left(\cos\dfrac{9\pi}{17} + i\sin\dfrac{9\pi}{17}\right)^5}{\left(\cos\dfrac{2\pi}{17} - i\sin\dfrac{2\pi}{17}\right)^3}$

$= \dfrac{\left(\cos\dfrac{9\pi}{17} + i\sin\dfrac{9\pi}{17}\right)^5}{\left(\cos\left(-\dfrac{2\pi}{17}\right) + i\sin\left(-\dfrac{2\pi}{17}\right)\right)^3}$

$= \dfrac{\cos\dfrac{45\pi}{17} + i\sin\dfrac{45\pi}{17}}{\cos\left(-\dfrac{6\pi}{17}\right) + i\sin\left(-\dfrac{6\pi}{17}\right)}$

$= \cos\left(\dfrac{45\pi}{17} - \left(-\dfrac{6\pi}{17}\right)\right) + i\sin\left(\dfrac{45\pi}{17} - \left(-\dfrac{6\pi}{17}\right)\right)$

$= \cos\dfrac{51\pi}{17} + i\sin\dfrac{51\pi}{17}$

$= \cos 3\pi + i\sin 3\pi$

$= \cos\pi + i\sin\pi$

$= -1 + i(0)$

So $\dfrac{\left(\cos\dfrac{9\pi}{17} + i\sin\dfrac{9\pi}{17}\right)^5}{\left(\cos\dfrac{2\pi}{17} - i\sin\dfrac{2\pi}{17}\right)^3} = -1$

Problem-solving

You could also show this result by writing both numbers in exponential form:

$\dfrac{\left(e^{\frac{9\pi i}{17}}\right)^5}{\left(e^{-\frac{2\pi i}{17}}\right)^3} = \dfrac{e^{\frac{45\pi i}{17}}}{e^{-\frac{6\pi i}{17}}} = e^{i\left(\frac{45\pi}{17} - \left(-\frac{6\pi}{17}\right)\right)} = e^{3\pi i} = e^{\pi i} = -1$

$\cos(-\theta) = \cos\theta$ and $\sin(-\theta) = -\sin\theta$

Apply de Moivre's theorem to both the numerator and the denominator.

$\dfrac{z_1}{z_2} = \cos(\theta_1 - \theta_2) + i\sin(\theta_1 - \theta_2)$

Simplify.

Subtract 2π from the argument.

Example 9

Express $(1 + i\sqrt{3})^7$ in the form $x + iy$ where $x, y \in \mathbb{R}$.

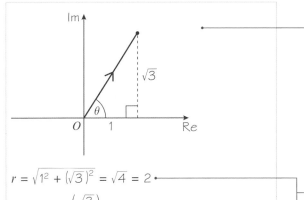

First, you need to find the modulus and argument of $1 + i\sqrt{3}$. You may want to draw an Argand diagram to help you.

$r = \sqrt{1^2 + (\sqrt{3})^2} = \sqrt{4} = 2$

$\theta = \arctan\left(\dfrac{\sqrt{3}}{1}\right) = \dfrac{\pi}{3}$

Find r and θ.

So $1 + i\sqrt{3} = 2\left(\cos\dfrac{\pi}{3} + i\sin\dfrac{\pi}{3}\right)$

Write $1 + i\sqrt{3}$ in modulus–argument form.

$(1 + i\sqrt{3})^7 = \left(2\left(\cos\dfrac{\pi}{3} + i\sin\dfrac{\pi}{3}\right)\right)^7$

$= 2^7\left(\cos\dfrac{7\pi}{3} + i\sin\dfrac{7\pi}{3}\right)$

Apply de Moivre's theorem.

$= 128\left(\cos\dfrac{\pi}{3} + i\sin\dfrac{\pi}{3}\right)$

Subtract 2π from the argument.

$= 128\left(\dfrac{1}{2} + i\left(\dfrac{\sqrt{3}}{2}\right)\right)$

Therefore, $(1 + i\sqrt{3})^7 = 64 + 64i\sqrt{3}$

Exercise 1C

1 Use de Moivre's theorem to express each of the following in the form $x + iy$, where $x, y \in \mathbb{R}$.

  a $(\cos\theta + i\sin\theta)^6$ **b** $(\cos 3\theta + i\sin 3\theta)^4$ **c** $\left(\cos\dfrac{\pi}{6} + i\sin\dfrac{\pi}{6}\right)^5$

  d $\left(\cos\dfrac{\pi}{3} + i\sin\dfrac{\pi}{3}\right)^8$ **e** $\left(\cos\dfrac{2\pi}{5} + i\sin\dfrac{2\pi}{5}\right)^5$ **f** $\left(\cos\dfrac{\pi}{10} - i\sin\dfrac{\pi}{10}\right)^{15}$

2 Express each of the following in the form $e^{in\theta}$.

  a $\dfrac{\cos 5\theta + i\sin 5\theta}{(\cos 2\theta + i\sin 2\theta)^2}$ **b** $\dfrac{(\cos 2\theta + i\sin 2\theta)^7}{(\cos 4\theta + i\sin 4\theta)^3}$ **c** $\dfrac{1}{(\cos 2\theta + i\sin 2\theta)^3}$

  d $\dfrac{(\cos 2\theta + i\sin 2\theta)^4}{(\cos 3\theta + i\sin 3\theta)^3}$ **e** $\dfrac{\cos 5\theta + i\sin 5\theta}{(\cos 3\theta - i\sin 3\theta)^2}$ **f** $\dfrac{\cos\theta - i\sin\theta}{(\cos 2\theta - i\sin 2\theta)^3}$

3 Evaluate the following, giving your answers in the form $x + iy$, where $x, y \in \mathbb{R}$.

a $\dfrac{\left(\cos\dfrac{7\pi}{13} - i\sin\dfrac{7\pi}{13}\right)^4}{\left(\cos\dfrac{4\pi}{13} + i\sin\dfrac{4\pi}{13}\right)^6}$

b $\dfrac{\left(\cos\dfrac{3\pi}{7} - i\sin\dfrac{11\pi}{7}\right)^3}{\left(\cos\dfrac{15\pi}{7} + i\sin\dfrac{\pi}{7}\right)^2}$

c $\dfrac{\left(\cos\dfrac{4\pi}{3} - i\sin\dfrac{2\pi}{3}\right)^7}{\left(\cos\dfrac{10\pi}{3} + i\sin\dfrac{4\pi}{3}\right)^4}$

4 Express the following in the form $x + iy$ where $x, y \in \mathbb{R}$.

a $(1 + i)^5$

b $(-2 + 2i)^8$

c $(1 - i)^6$

d $(1 - i\sqrt{3})^6$

e $\left(\dfrac{3}{2} - \dfrac{1}{2}i\sqrt{3}\right)^9$

f $(-2\sqrt{3} - 2i)^5$

(E) 5 Express $(3 + i\sqrt{3})^5$ in the form $a + bi\sqrt{3}$ where a and b are integers. **(2 marks)**

(E) 6 $w = 2\left(\cos\dfrac{\pi}{6} + i\sin\dfrac{\pi}{6}\right)$

Find the exact value of w^4, giving your answer in the form $a + ib$ where $a, b \in \mathbb{R}$. **(2 marks)**

(E) 7 $z = \sqrt{3}\left(\cos\dfrac{3\pi}{4} - i\sin\dfrac{3\pi}{4}\right)$

Find the exact value of z^6, giving your answer in the form $a + ib$ where $a, b \in \mathbb{R}$. **(3 marks)**

(E/P) 8 a Express $\dfrac{1 + i\sqrt{3}}{1 - i\sqrt{3}}$ in the form $re^{i\theta}$, where $r > 0$ and $-\pi < \theta \leqslant \pi$. **(3 marks)**

b Hence find the smallest positive integer value of n for which $\left(\dfrac{1 + i\sqrt{3}}{1 - i\sqrt{3}}\right)^n$ is real and positive. **(2 marks)**

(E/P) 9 Use de Moivre's theorem to show that $(a + bi)^n + (a - bi)^n$ is real for all integers n. **(5 marks)**

Challenge

Without using Euler's relation, prove that if n is a positive integer,
$(r(\cos\theta + i\sin\theta))^{-n} = r^{-n}(\cos(-n\theta) + i\sin(-n\theta))$

Problem-solving

You may assume de Moivre's theorem for positive integer exponents, but do not write any complex numbers in exponential form.

1.4 Trigonometric identities

You can use de Moivre's theorem to derive trigonometric identities.

Applying the binomial expansion to $(\cos\theta + i\sin\theta)^n$ allows you to express $\cos n\theta$ in terms of powers of $\cos\theta$, and $\sin n\theta$ in terms of powers of $\sin\theta$.

Links $(a + b)^n = a^n + {}^nC_1 a^{n-1}b + {}^nC_2 a^{n-2}b^2 + \ldots + {}^nC_r a^{n-r}b^r + \ldots + b^n, n \in \mathbb{N}$

where ${}^nC_r = \binom{n}{r} = \dfrac{n!}{r!(n-r)!}$

← Pure Year 1, Chapter 8

Example 10

Use de Moivre's theorem to show that
$$\cos 6\theta = 32\cos^6\theta - 48\cos^4\theta + 18\cos^2\theta - 1$$

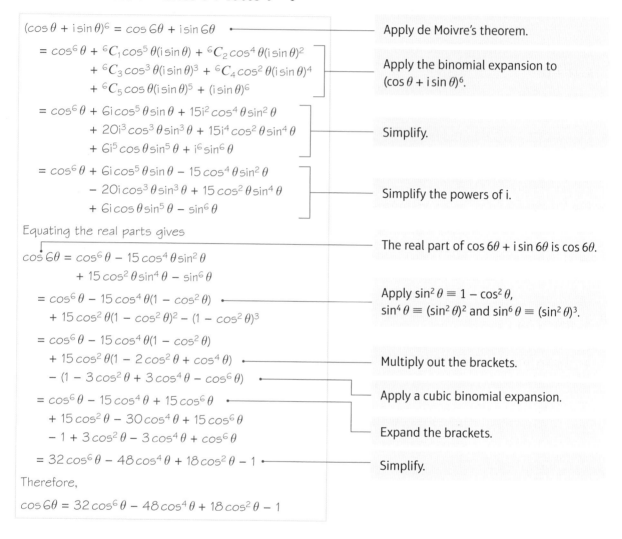

$(\cos\theta + i\sin\theta)^6 = \cos 6\theta + i\sin 6\theta$ ───── Apply de Moivre's theorem.

$= \cos^6\theta + {}^6C_1\cos^5\theta(i\sin\theta) + {}^6C_2\cos^4\theta(i\sin\theta)^2$
$\quad + {}^6C_3\cos^3\theta(i\sin\theta)^3 + {}^6C_4\cos^2\theta(i\sin\theta)^4$
$\quad + {}^6C_5\cos\theta(i\sin\theta)^5 + (i\sin\theta)^6$

Apply the binomial expansion to $(\cos\theta + i\sin\theta)^6$.

$= \cos^6\theta + 6i\cos^5\theta\sin\theta + 15i^2\cos^4\theta\sin^2\theta$
$\quad + 20i^3\cos^3\theta\sin^3\theta + 15i^4\cos^2\theta\sin^4\theta$
$\quad + 6i^5\cos\theta\sin^5\theta + i^6\sin^6\theta$

Simplify.

$= \cos^6\theta + 6i\cos^5\theta\sin\theta - 15\cos^4\theta\sin^2\theta$
$\quad - 20i\cos^3\theta\sin^3\theta + 15\cos^2\theta\sin^4\theta$
$\quad + 6i\cos\theta\sin^5\theta - \sin^6\theta$

Simplify the powers of i.

Equating the real parts gives

The real part of $\cos 6\theta + i\sin 6\theta$ is $\cos 6\theta$.

$\cos 6\theta = \cos^6\theta - 15\cos^4\theta\sin^2\theta$
$\quad + 15\cos^2\theta\sin^4\theta - \sin^6\theta$

$= \cos^6\theta - 15\cos^4\theta(1 - \cos^2\theta)$
$\quad + 15\cos^2\theta(1 - \cos^2\theta)^2 - (1 - \cos^2\theta)^3$

Apply $\sin^2\theta \equiv 1 - \cos^2\theta$, $\sin^4\theta \equiv (\sin^2\theta)^2$ and $\sin^6\theta \equiv (\sin^2\theta)^3$.

$= \cos^6\theta - 15\cos^4\theta(1 - \cos^2\theta)$
$\quad + 15\cos^2\theta(1 - 2\cos^2\theta + \cos^4\theta)$
$\quad - (1 - 3\cos^2\theta + 3\cos^4\theta - \cos^6\theta)$

Multiply out the brackets.

Apply a cubic binomial expansion.

$= \cos^6\theta - 15\cos^4\theta + 15\cos^6\theta$
$\quad + 15\cos^2\theta - 30\cos^4\theta + 15\cos^6\theta$
$\quad - 1 + 3\cos^2\theta - 3\cos^4\theta + \cos^6\theta$

Expand the brackets.

$= 32\cos^6\theta - 48\cos^4\theta + 18\cos^2\theta - 1$ ───── Simplify.

Therefore,
$\cos 6\theta = 32\cos^6\theta - 48\cos^4\theta + 18\cos^2\theta - 1$

You can also find trigonometric identities for $\sin^n\theta$ and $\cos^n\theta$ where n is a positive integer.
If $z = \cos\theta + i\sin\theta$, then

$$\frac{1}{z} = z^{-1} = (\cos\theta + i\sin\theta)^{-1}$$
$$= (\cos(-\theta) + i\sin(-\theta))$$ ───── Apply de Moivre's theorem.
$$= \cos\theta - i\sin\theta$$ ───── Use $\cos\theta = \cos(-\theta)$ and $-\sin\theta = \sin(-\theta)$.

It follows that

$$z + \frac{1}{z} = \cos\theta + i\sin\theta + \cos\theta - i\sin\theta = 2\cos\theta$$

$$z - \frac{1}{z} = \cos\theta + i\sin\theta - (\cos\theta - i\sin\theta) = 2i\sin\theta$$

Also,

$$z^n = (\cos \theta + i \sin \theta)^n = \cos n\theta + i \sin n\theta \quad \text{———— By de Moivre's theorem.}$$

$$\frac{1}{z^n} = z^{-n} = (\cos \theta + i \sin \theta)^{-n}$$

$$= (\cos(-n\theta) + i \sin(-n\theta)) \quad \text{———— Apply de Moivre's theorem.}$$

$$= \cos n\theta - i \sin n\theta \quad \text{———— Use } \cos \theta = \cos(-\theta) \text{ and } \sin(-\theta) = -\sin \theta.$$

It follows that

$$z^n + \frac{1}{z^n} = \cos n\theta + i \sin n\theta + \cos n\theta - i \sin n\theta = 2 \cos n\theta$$

$$z^n - \frac{1}{z^n} = \cos n\theta + i \sin n\theta - (\cos n\theta - i \sin n\theta) = 2i \sin n\theta$$

It is important that you remember and are able to apply these results:

- $z + \dfrac{1}{z} = 2 \cos \theta$
- $z^n + \dfrac{1}{z^n} = 2 \cos n\theta$

Notation In exponential form, these results are equivalent to:

$$\cos n\theta = \frac{1}{2}(e^{in\theta} + e^{-in\theta}) \qquad \sin n\theta = \frac{1}{2i}(e^{in\theta} - e^{-in\theta}).$$

- $z - \dfrac{1}{z} = 2i \sin \theta$
- $z^n - \dfrac{1}{z^n} = 2i \sin n\theta$

Example 11

Express $\cos^5 \theta$ in the form $a \cos 5\theta + b \cos 3\theta + c \cos \theta$, where a, b and c are constants.

Let $z = \cos \theta + i \sin \theta$

$$\left(z + \frac{1}{z}\right)^5 = (2 \cos \theta)^5 = 32 \cos^5 \theta \quad \text{———— Use } z + \frac{1}{z} = 2 \cos \theta.$$

$$= z^5 + {}^5C_1 z^4 \left(\frac{1}{z}\right) + {}^5C_2 z^3 \left(\frac{1}{z}\right)^2 + {}^5C_3 z^2 \left(\frac{1}{z}\right)^3$$

$$+ {}^5C_4 z \left(\frac{1}{z}\right)^4 + \left(\frac{1}{z}\right)^5 \quad \text{Apply the binomial expansion to } \left(z + \frac{1}{z}\right)^5.$$

$$= z^5 + 5z^4 \left(\frac{1}{z}\right) + 10z^3 \left(\frac{1}{z^2}\right) + 10z^2 \left(\frac{1}{z^3}\right)$$

$$+ 5z \left(\frac{1}{z^4}\right) + \left(\frac{1}{z^5}\right)$$

$$= z^5 + 5z^3 + 10z + \frac{10}{z} + \frac{5}{z^3} + \frac{1}{z^5} \quad \text{Simplify.}$$

$$= \left(z^5 + \frac{1}{z^5}\right) + 5\left(z^3 + \frac{1}{z^3}\right) + 10\left(z + \frac{1}{z}\right) \quad \text{Group } z^n \text{ and } \frac{1}{z^n} \text{ terms.}$$

$$= 2 \cos 5\theta + 5(2 \cos 3\theta) + 10(2 \cos \theta) \quad \text{Use } z^n + \frac{1}{z^n} = 2 \cos n\theta.$$

So, $32 \cos^5 \theta = 2 \cos 5\theta + 10 \cos 3\theta + 20 \cos \theta$

$$\Rightarrow \quad \cos^5 \theta = \frac{1}{16} \cos 5\theta + \frac{5}{16} \cos 3\theta + \frac{5}{8} \cos \theta \quad \text{This is in the required form with } a = \frac{1}{16}, \; b = \frac{5}{16} \text{ and } c = \frac{5}{8}$$

Example (12)

a Express $\sin^4 \theta$ in the form $d\cos 4\theta + e\cos 2\theta + f$, where d, e and f are constants.

b Hence find the exact value of $\displaystyle\int_0^{\frac{\pi}{2}} \sin^4 \theta \, d\theta$.

a Let $z = \cos\theta + i\sin\theta$

$\left(z - \dfrac{1}{z}\right)^4 = (2i\sin\theta)^4 = 16i^4\sin^4\theta = 16\sin^4\theta$ ⟵ Use $z - \dfrac{1}{z} = 2i\sin\theta$, noting that $i^4 = 1$

$= z^4 + {}^4C_1 z^3\left(-\dfrac{1}{z}\right) + {}^4C_2 z^2\left(-\dfrac{1}{z}\right)^2$

$+ {}^4C_3 z^1\left(-\dfrac{1}{z}\right)^3 + \left(-\dfrac{1}{z}\right)^4$ ⟵ Apply the binomial expansion to $\left(z - \dfrac{1}{z}\right)^4$

$= z^4 + 4z^3\left(-\dfrac{1}{z}\right) + 6z^2\left(\dfrac{1}{z^2}\right)$

$+ 4z\left(-\dfrac{1}{z^3}\right) + \left(\dfrac{1}{z^4}\right)$ ⟵ Simplify.

$= z^4 - 4z^2 + 6 - \dfrac{4}{z^2} + \dfrac{1}{z^4}$

$= \left(z^4 + \dfrac{1}{z^4}\right) - 4\left(z^2 + \dfrac{1}{z^2}\right) + 6$ ⟵ Group z^n and $\dfrac{1}{z^n}$ terms.

$= 2\cos 4\theta - 4(2\cos 2\theta) + 6$ ⟵ Use $z^n + \dfrac{1}{z^n} = 2\cos n\theta$.

So, $16\sin^4\theta = 2\cos 4\theta - 8\cos 2\theta + 6$

$\Rightarrow \quad \sin^4\theta = \tfrac{1}{8}\cos 4\theta - \tfrac{1}{2}\cos 2\theta + \tfrac{3}{8}$ ⟵ This is in the required form with $d = \tfrac{1}{8}$, $e = -\tfrac{1}{2}$ and $f = \tfrac{3}{8}$

b $\displaystyle\int_0^{\frac{\pi}{2}} \sin^4\theta \, d\theta = \int_0^{\frac{\pi}{2}} \left(\tfrac{1}{8}\cos 4\theta - \tfrac{1}{2}\cos 2\theta + \tfrac{3}{8}\right) d\theta$ ⟵ Use the answer from part **a**.

$= \left[\tfrac{1}{32}\sin 4\theta - \tfrac{1}{4}\sin 2\theta + \tfrac{3}{8}\theta\right]_0^{\frac{\pi}{2}}$ ⟵ $\cos k\theta$ integrates to $\dfrac{1}{k}\sin k\theta$.

$= \left(\tfrac{1}{32}\sin 2\pi - \tfrac{1}{4}\sin \pi + \tfrac{3}{8}\left(\dfrac{\pi}{2}\right)\right) - 0$

$= 0 - 0 + \dfrac{3\pi}{16}$

$= \dfrac{3\pi}{16}$

Exercise (1D)

Use de Moivre's theorem to prove the following trigonometric identities:

(P) **1 a** $\sin 3\theta \equiv 3\sin\theta - 4\sin^3\theta$ **b** $\sin 5\theta \equiv 16\sin^5\theta - 20\sin^3\theta + 5\sin\theta$

    c $\cos 7\theta \equiv 64\cos^7\theta - 112\cos^5\theta + 56\cos^3\theta - 7\cos\theta$ **d** $\cos^4\theta \equiv \tfrac{1}{8}(\cos 4\theta + 4\cos 2\theta + 3)$

    e $\sin^5\theta \equiv \tfrac{1}{16}(\sin 5\theta - 5\sin 3\theta + 10\sin\theta)$

E/P 2 a Use de Moivre's theorem to show that
$$\cos 5\theta \equiv 16\cos^5\theta - 20\cos^3\theta + 5\cos\theta$$ **(5 marks)**

b Hence, given also that $\cos 3\theta = 4\cos^3\theta - 3\cos\theta$, find all the solutions of $\cos 5\theta + 5\cos 3\theta = 0$ in the interval $0 \leqslant \theta < \pi$. Give your answers to 3 decimal places. **(6 marks)**

E/P 3 a Show that $32\cos^6\theta \equiv \cos 6\theta + 6\cos 4\theta + 15\cos 2\theta + 10$. **(6 marks)**

b Hence find $\displaystyle\int_0^{\frac{\pi}{6}} \cos^6\theta\, d\theta$ in the form $a\pi + b\sqrt{3}$ where a and b are rational constants to be found. **(3 marks)**

E/P 4 a Show that $32\cos^2\theta\sin^4\theta \equiv \cos 6\theta - 2\cos 4\theta - \cos 2\theta + 2$. **(6 marks)**

b Hence find the exact value of $\displaystyle\int_0^{\frac{\pi}{3}} \cos^2\theta\sin^4\theta\, d\theta$. **(3 marks)**

P 5 By using de Moivre's theorem, or otherwise, compute the following integrals.

a $\displaystyle\int_0^{\frac{\pi}{2}} \sin^6\theta\, d\theta$
b $\displaystyle\int_0^{\frac{\pi}{4}} \sin^2\theta\cos^4\theta\, d\theta$
c $\displaystyle\int_0^{\frac{\pi}{6}} \sin^3\theta\cos^5\theta\, d\theta$

E/P 6 a Use de Moivre's theorem to show that
$$\cos 6\theta \equiv 32\cos^6\theta - 48\cos^4\theta + 18\cos^2\theta - 1$$ **(5 marks)**

b Hence find the six distinct solutions of the equation
$$32x^6 - 48x^4 + 18x^2 - \frac{3}{2} = 0$$
giving your answers to 3 decimal places where necessary. **(5 marks)**

Problem-solving

Use the substitution $x = \cos\theta$ to reduce the equation to the form $\cos 6\theta = k$. Find as many values of θ as you need to find six distinct values of x.

E/P 7 a Use de Moivre's theorem to show that $\sin 4\theta \equiv 4\cos^3\theta\sin\theta - 4\cos\theta\sin^3\theta$. **(4 marks)**

b Hence, or otherwise, show that $\tan 4\theta \equiv \dfrac{4\tan\theta - 4\tan^3\theta}{1 - 6\tan^2\theta + \tan^4\theta}$ **(4 marks)**

c Use your answer to part b to find, to 2 decimal places, the four solutions of the equation
$x^4 + 4x^3 - 6x^2 - 4x + 1 = 0$. **(5 marks)**

1.5 Sums of series

You can use results about the sums of geometric series with complex numbers.

■ **For $w, z \in \mathbb{C}$,**

• $\displaystyle\sum_{r=0}^{n-1} wz^r = w + wz + wz^2 + \ldots + wz^{n-1} = \frac{w(z^n - 1)}{z - 1}$

• $\displaystyle\sum_{r=0}^{\infty} wz^r = w + wz + wz^2 + \ldots = \frac{w}{1 - z}, \; |z| < 1$

Links These results match the corresponding results for real numbers. The infinite series $\displaystyle\sum_{r=0}^{\infty} wz^r$ converges only when $|z| < 1$.

← Pure Year 2, Chapter 3

Example 13

Given that $z = \cos\dfrac{\pi}{n} + \mathrm{i}\sin\dfrac{\pi}{n}$, where n is a positive integer, show that

$$1 + z + z^2 + \ldots + z^{n-1} = 1 + \mathrm{i}\cot\left(\frac{\pi}{2n}\right)$$

$1 + z + z^2 + \ldots + z^{n-1} = \dfrac{z^n - 1}{z - 1}$

Use the result for $\displaystyle\sum_{r=0}^{n-1} wz^r$ with $w = 1$.

$= \dfrac{\left(e^{\frac{\pi i}{n}}\right)^n - 1}{e^{\frac{\pi i}{n}} - 1}$

Write z in exponential form as $z = e^{\frac{\pi i}{n}}$, and substitute.

$= \dfrac{e^{\pi i} - 1}{e^{\frac{\pi i}{n}} - 1}$

$\left(e^{\frac{\pi i}{n}}\right)^n = e^{\pi i} = -1$

$= \dfrac{-2}{e^{\frac{\pi i}{n}} - 1}$

$= \dfrac{-2e^{-\frac{\pi i}{2n}}}{e^{\frac{\pi i}{2n}} - e^{-\frac{\pi i}{2n}}}$

$= \dfrac{-2e^{-\frac{\pi i}{2n}}}{2\mathrm{i}\sin\dfrac{\pi}{2n}}$

$= \dfrac{\mathrm{i}e^{-\frac{\pi i}{2n}}}{\sin\dfrac{\pi}{2n}}$

Problem-solving

You know that $\sin n\theta = \dfrac{1}{2\mathrm{i}}(e^{\mathrm{i}n\theta} - e^{-\mathrm{i}n\theta})$. You can use this result to simplify an expression like $e^{\mathrm{i}\theta} - 1$ by writing it in the form $e^{\frac{\mathrm{i}\theta}{2}}\left(e^{\frac{\mathrm{i}\theta}{2}} - e^{-\frac{\mathrm{i}\theta}{2}}\right) = e^{\frac{\mathrm{i}\theta}{2}}\left(2\mathrm{i}\sin\dfrac{\theta}{2}\right)$. In this case this is equivalent to multiplying the top and bottom of the fraction by $e^{-\mathrm{i}\frac{\pi}{2n}}$.

$\dfrac{-2}{2\mathrm{i}} = \mathrm{i}$

$= \dfrac{\mathrm{i}\left(\cos\left(-\dfrac{\pi}{2n}\right) + \mathrm{i}\sin\left(-\dfrac{\pi}{2n}\right)\right)}{\sin\dfrac{\pi}{2n}}$

$= \dfrac{\mathrm{i}\left(\cos\left(\dfrac{\pi}{2n}\right) - \mathrm{i}\sin\left(\dfrac{\pi}{2n}\right)\right)}{\sin\dfrac{\pi}{2n}}$

$e^{-\mathrm{i}\theta} = \cos(-\theta) + \mathrm{i}\sin(-\theta)$
$= \cos\theta - \mathrm{i}\sin\theta$.

$= \dfrac{\sin\left(\dfrac{\pi}{2n}\right) + \mathrm{i}\cos\left(\dfrac{\pi}{2n}\right)}{\sin\dfrac{\pi}{2n}}$

$$= \frac{\sin\left(\frac{\pi}{2n}\right)}{\sin\left(\frac{\pi}{2n}\right)} + \frac{i\cos\left(\frac{\pi}{2n}\right)}{\sin\left(\frac{\pi}{2n}\right)}$$

$$= 1 + i\cot\left(\frac{\pi}{2n}\right) \text{ as required} \quad \longleftarrow \quad \text{Simplify.}$$

The series $e^{i\theta} + e^{2i\theta} + e^{3i\theta} + \dots + e^{ni\theta}$ is geometric with first term $e^{i\theta}$, common ratio $e^{i\theta}$ and n terms.

The sum of this series is given by $S_n = \dfrac{e^{i\theta}(e^{ni\theta} - 1)}{e^{i\theta} - 1}$

Converting the exponential form into modulus–argument form lets you consider the real and imaginary parts of the series separately.

$e^{i\theta} + e^{2i\theta} + e^{3i\theta} + \dots + e^{ni\theta}$

$\quad = (\cos\theta + i\sin\theta) + (\cos 2\theta + i\sin 2\theta) + (\cos 3\theta + i\sin 3\theta) + \dots + (\cos n\theta + i\sin n\theta)$

$\quad = (\cos\theta + \cos 2\theta + \cos 3\theta + \dots + \cos n\theta) + i(\sin\theta + \sin 2\theta + \sin 3\theta + \dots + \sin n\theta)$

Therefore,

$$\cos\theta + \cos 2\theta + \cos 3\theta + \dots + \cos n\theta = \text{Re}\left(\frac{e^{i\theta}(e^{ni\theta} - 1)}{e^{i\theta} - 1}\right)$$

$$\sin\theta + \sin 2\theta + \sin 3\theta + \dots + \sin n\theta = \text{Im}\left(\frac{e^{i\theta}(e^{ni\theta} - 1)}{e^{i\theta} - 1}\right)$$

Example 14

$S = e^{i\theta} + e^{2i\theta} + e^{3i\theta} + \dots + e^{8i\theta}$, for $\theta \neq 2n\pi$, where n is an integer.

a Show that $S = \dfrac{e^{\frac{9i\theta}{2}}\sin 4\theta}{\sin\dfrac{\theta}{2}}$

Let $P = \cos\theta + \cos 2\theta + \cos 3\theta + \dots + \cos 8\theta$ and $Q = \sin\theta + \sin 2\theta + \sin 3\theta + \dots + \sin 8\theta$

b Use your answer to part **a** to show that $P = \cos\dfrac{9\theta}{2}\sin 4\theta\,\text{cosec}\,\dfrac{\theta}{2}$ and find similar expressions for Q and $\dfrac{Q}{P}$

a $e^{i\theta} + e^{2i\theta} + e^{3i\theta} + \dots + e^{8i\theta} = \dfrac{e^{i\theta}((e^{i\theta})^8 - 1)}{e^{i\theta} - 1}$

S is the sum of a geometric series.

Use $\displaystyle\sum_{r=0}^{n-1} wz^r = \dfrac{w(z^n - 1)}{z - 1}$ with $w = z = e^{i\theta}$ and $n = 8$.

$\quad = \dfrac{e^{i\theta}(e^{8i\theta} - 1)}{e^{i\theta} - 1}$

$(e^{i\theta})^8 = e^{8i\theta}$

$\quad = \dfrac{e^{\frac{i\theta}{2}}(e^{8i\theta} - 1)}{e^{\frac{\theta}{2}} - e^{-\frac{\theta}{2}}}$

Multiply the numerator and denominator by $e^{-\frac{i\theta}{2}}$

$$= \frac{e^{\frac{i\theta}{2}}(e^{8i\theta} - 1)}{2i\sin\frac{\theta}{2}}$$

$e^{\frac{i\theta}{2}} - e^{-\frac{i\theta}{2}} = 2i\sin\frac{\theta}{2}$

$$= \frac{e^{\frac{i\theta}{2}}e^{4i\theta}(e^{4i\theta} - e^{-4i\theta})}{2i\sin\frac{\theta}{2}}$$

Use the relationship $e^{8i\theta} - 1 = e^{4i\theta}(e^{4i\theta} - e^{-4i\theta})$ to rewrite the numerator.

$$= \frac{e^{\frac{9\theta}{2}}(2i\sin 4\theta)}{2i\sin\frac{\theta}{2}}$$

$e^{4i\theta} - e^{-4i\theta} = 2i\sin 4\theta$

$$= \frac{e^{\frac{9\theta}{2}}\sin 4\theta}{\sin\frac{\theta}{2}}$$

Simplify.

b $P = \text{Re}(S) = \text{Re}\left(\frac{e^{\frac{9\theta}{2}}\sin 4\theta}{\sin\frac{\theta}{2}}\right)$

Problem-solving

By writing each term of S in modulus–argument form you can see that P is the real part of S and Q is the imaginary part of S.

$$= \frac{\cos\frac{9\theta}{2}\sin 4\theta}{\sin\frac{\theta}{2}}$$

$$= \cos\frac{9\theta}{2}\sin 4\theta \operatorname{cosec}\frac{\theta}{2}$$

$Q = \text{Im}(S) = \text{Im}\left(\frac{e^{\frac{9\theta}{2}}\sin 4\theta}{\sin\frac{\theta}{2}}\right)$

$$= \frac{\sin\frac{9\theta}{2}\sin 4\theta}{\sin\frac{\theta}{2}}$$

$$= \sin\frac{9\theta}{2}\sin 4\theta \operatorname{cosec}\frac{\theta}{2}$$

$$\frac{Q}{P} = \frac{\sin\frac{9\theta}{2}\sin 4\theta \operatorname{cosec}\frac{\theta}{2}}{\cos\frac{9\theta}{2}\sin 4\theta \operatorname{cosec}\frac{\theta}{2}} = \frac{\sin\frac{9\theta}{2}}{\cos\frac{9\theta}{2}} = \tan\frac{9\theta}{2}$$

Exercise 1E

P **1** Given $z = e^{\frac{\pi i}{n}}$, where n is a positive integer, show that:

a $1 + z + z^2 + \ldots + z^{2n-1} = 0$

b $1 + z + z^2 + \ldots + z^n = i\cot\left(\frac{\pi}{2n}\right)$

P **2** Show that if $z = e^{\frac{\pi i}{2}}$, then $\displaystyle\sum_{r=0}^{12} z^r = 1$.

P **3** Show that $\displaystyle\sum_{r=0}^{7}(1 + i)^r = -15i$.

E/P **4** The convergent infinite series C and S are defined as

$$C = 1 + \tfrac{1}{3}\cos\theta + \tfrac{1}{9}\cos 2\theta + \tfrac{1}{27}\cos 3\theta + \dots$$

$$S = \tfrac{1}{3}\sin\theta + \tfrac{1}{9}\sin 2\theta + \tfrac{1}{27}\sin 3\theta + \dots$$

Hint The sum of an infinite geometric series with first term a and common ratio r is $S_\infty = \dfrac{a}{1-r}$

← **Pure Year 2, Chapter 3**

a Show that $C + iS = \dfrac{3}{3 - e^{i\theta}}$ **(4 marks)**

b Hence show that $C = \dfrac{9 - 3\cos\theta}{10 - 6\cos\theta}$, and find a similar expression for S. **(4 marks)**

E/P **5** The series P and Q are defined for $0 < \theta < \pi$ as

$$P = 1 + \cos\theta + \cos 2\theta + \cos 3\theta + \dots + \cos 12\theta$$

$$Q = \sin\theta + \sin 2\theta + \sin 3\theta + \dots + \sin 12\theta$$

a Show that $P + iQ = \dfrac{e^{6i\theta}(e^{\frac{13i\theta}{2}} - e^{-\frac{13i\theta}{2}})}{e^{\frac{i\theta}{2}} - e^{-\frac{i\theta}{2}}}$ **(4 marks)**

b Deduce that $Q = \sin 6\theta \sin\dfrac{13\theta}{2}\operatorname{cosec}\dfrac{\theta}{2}$ and write down the corresponding expression for P.

You can assume the results $\sin\theta = \dfrac{e^{i\theta} - e^{-i\theta}}{2i}$ and $\cos\theta = \dfrac{e^{i\theta} + e^{-i\theta}}{2}$ **(4 marks)**

c Hence find the values of θ, in the range $0 < \theta < \pi$, for which $P + iQ$ is real. **(2 marks)**

E/P **6** Series C and S are defined as

$$C = 1 + \binom{n}{1}\cos\theta + \binom{n}{2}\cos 2\theta + \binom{n}{3}\cos 3\theta + \dots + \binom{n}{n}\cos n\theta$$

$$S = \binom{n}{1}\sin\theta + \binom{n}{2}\sin 2\theta + \binom{n}{3}\sin 3\theta + \dots + \binom{n}{n}\sin n\theta$$

a Show that $C = \left(2\cos\dfrac{\theta}{2}\right)^n \cos\dfrac{n\theta}{2}$ **(4 marks)**

b Show that $\dfrac{S}{C} = \tan\dfrac{n\theta}{2}$ **(3 marks)**

E/P **7** **a** Show that $(2 + e^{i\theta})(2 + e^{-i\theta}) = 5 + 4\cos\theta$. **(2 marks)**

The convergent infinite series C and S are defined by

$$C = 1 - \tfrac{1}{2}\cos\theta + \tfrac{1}{4}\cos 2\theta - \tfrac{1}{8}\cos 3\theta + \dots$$

$$S = \tfrac{1}{2}\sin\theta - \tfrac{1}{4}\sin 2\theta + \tfrac{1}{8}\sin 3\theta + \dots$$

b By considering $C - iS$, show that $C = \dfrac{4 + 2\cos\theta}{5 + 4\cos\theta}$ and write down the corresponding expression for S. **(4 marks)**

1.6 nth roots of a complex number

You can use de Moivre's theorem to solve an equation of the form $z^n = w$, where $z, w \in \mathbb{C}$.
This is equivalent to finding the nth roots of w.

Just as a real number, x, has two square roots, $\sqrt{x}$ and $-\sqrt{x}$, any complex number has n distinct nth roots.

■ **If z and w are non-zero complex numbers and n is a positive integer, then the equation $z^n = w$ has n distinct solutions.**

You can find the solutions to $z^n = w$ using
de Moivre's theorem, and by considering the fact
that the argument of a complex number is not unique.

Note $\cos(\theta + 2k\pi) = \cos\theta$ and
$\sin(\theta + 2k\pi) = \sin\theta$ for integer values of k.

■ **For any complex number $z = r(\cos\theta + i\sin\theta)$, you can write $z = r(\cos(\theta + 2k\pi) + i\sin(\theta + 2k\pi))$, where k is any integer.**

Example 15

a Solve the equation $z^3 = 1$.

b Represent your solutions to part **a** on an Argand diagram.

c Show that the three cube roots of 1 can be written as 1, ω and ω^2 where $1 + \omega + \omega^2 = 0$.

---

a $z^3 = 1$

$z^3 = \cos 0 + i\sin 0$ — Start by writing 1 in modulus–argument form.

$(r(\cos\theta + i\sin\theta))^3 =$
$\quad \cos(0 + 2k\pi) + i\sin(0 + 2k\pi), k \in \mathbb{Z}$ — Write z in modulus–argument form, and write the general form of the argument on the right-hand side by adding integer multiples of 2π.

$r^3(\cos 3\theta + i\sin 3\theta) =$
$\quad \cos(0 + 2k\pi) + i\sin(0 + 2k\pi), k \in \mathbb{Z}$ — Apply de Moivre's theorem to the left-hand side of the equation.

So $r = 1$

$3\theta = 2k\pi$ — Compare the modulus on both sides to get $r = 1$.

$k = 0 \Rightarrow \theta = 0$, so $z_1 = \cos 0 + i\sin 0 = 1$

$k = 1 \Rightarrow \theta = \dfrac{2\pi}{3}$ — Compare the arguments on both sides.

so $z_2 = \cos\left(\dfrac{2\pi}{3}\right) + i\sin\left(\dfrac{2\pi}{3}\right) = -\dfrac{1}{2} + i\dfrac{\sqrt{3}}{2}$

$k = -1 \Rightarrow \theta = -\dfrac{2\pi}{3}$

so $z_3 = \cos\left(-\dfrac{2\pi}{3}\right) + i\sin\left(-\dfrac{2\pi}{3}\right) = -\dfrac{1}{2} - i\dfrac{\sqrt{3}}{2}$

Therefore,

$z = 1, z = -\dfrac{1}{2} + i\dfrac{\sqrt{3}}{2}$ or $z = -\dfrac{1}{2} - i\dfrac{\sqrt{3}}{2}$ — These are the cube roots of unity.

Problem-solving

Choose values of k to find the three distinct roots. By choosing values on either side of $k = 0$ you can find three different arguments in the interval $[-\pi, \pi]$.

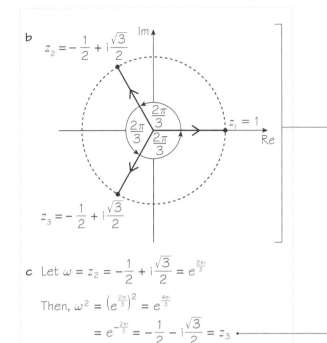

b $z_2 = -\frac{1}{2} + i\frac{\sqrt{3}}{2}$

$z_3 = -\frac{1}{2} + i\frac{\sqrt{3}}{2}$

Plot the points $z_1 = 1$, $z_2 = -\frac{1}{2} + i\frac{\sqrt{3}}{2}$ and $z_3 = -\frac{1}{2} - i\frac{\sqrt{3}}{2}$ on an Argand diagram:

The points z_1, z_2 and z_3 lie on a circle of radius 1 unit.

The angles between each of the vectors z_1, z_2 and z_3 are $\frac{2\pi}{3}$, as shown on the Argand diagram.

c Let $\omega = z_2 = -\frac{1}{2} + i\frac{\sqrt{3}}{2} = e^{\frac{2\pi i}{3}}$

Then, $\omega^2 = \left(e^{\frac{2\pi i}{3}}\right)^2 = e^{\frac{4\pi i}{3}}$

$= e^{-\frac{2\pi i}{3}} = -\frac{1}{2} - i\frac{\sqrt{3}}{2} = z_3$ ●——— Notice that $\omega^* = \omega^2$.

$1 + \omega + \omega^2 =$

$1 + \left(-\frac{1}{2} + i\frac{\sqrt{3}}{2}\right) + \left(-\frac{1}{2} - i\frac{\sqrt{3}}{2}\right) = 0$

Note It can be proved that the sum of the nth roots of unity is zero, for any positive integer $n \geqslant 2$.

■ **In general, the solutions to $z^n = 1$ are $z = \cos\left(\dfrac{2\pi k}{n}\right) + i\sin\left(\dfrac{2\pi k}{n}\right) = e^{\frac{2\pi i k}{n}}$ for $k = 1, 2, \ldots, n$ and are known as the nth roots of unity.**

If n is a positive integer, then there is an nth root of unity $\omega = e^{\frac{2\pi i}{n}}$ such that:

- **the nth roots of unity are $1, \omega, \omega^2, \cdots, \omega^{n-1}$**

- **$1, \omega, \omega^2, \cdots, \omega^{n-1}$ form the vertices of a regular n-gon**

- **$1 + \omega + \omega^2 + \ldots + \omega^{n-1} = 0$**

Example **16**

Solve the equation $z^4 = 2 + 2i\sqrt{3}$.

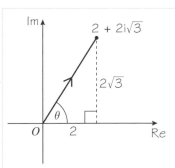

modulus $= \sqrt{2^2 + (2\sqrt{3})^2} = \sqrt{4 + 12} = 4$

argument $= \arctan\left(\dfrac{2\sqrt{3}}{2}\right) = \dfrac{\pi}{3}$

So $z^4 = 4\left(\cos\dfrac{\pi}{3} + i\sin\dfrac{\pi}{3}\right)$ •————

$(r(\cos\theta + i\sin\theta))^4$

$\quad = 4\left(\cos\left(\dfrac{\pi}{3} + 2k\pi\right) + i\sin\left(\dfrac{\pi}{3} + 2k\pi\right)\right), k \in \mathbb{Z}$ •————

$r^4(\cos 4\theta + i\sin 4\theta)$

$\quad = 4\left(\cos\left(\dfrac{\pi}{3} + 2k\pi\right) + i\sin\left(\dfrac{\pi}{3} + 2k\pi\right)\right), k \in \mathbb{Z}$ •————

So $r^4 = 4 \Rightarrow r = \sqrt[4]{4} = \sqrt{2}$ •————

$4\theta = \dfrac{\pi}{3} + 2k\pi$ •————

$k = 0 \Rightarrow \theta = \dfrac{\pi}{12},$ so $z_1 = \sqrt{2}\left(\cos\dfrac{\pi}{12} + i\sin\dfrac{\pi}{12}\right)$

$k = 1 \Rightarrow \theta = \dfrac{7\pi}{12},$ so $z_2 = \sqrt{2}\left(\cos\dfrac{7\pi}{12} + i\sin\dfrac{7\pi}{12}\right)$ •————

$k = -1 \Rightarrow \theta = -\dfrac{5\pi}{12},$ so $z_3 = \sqrt{2}\left(\cos\left(-\dfrac{5\pi}{12}\right) + i\sin\left(-\dfrac{5\pi}{12}\right)\right)$

$k = -2 \Rightarrow \theta = -\dfrac{11\pi}{12},$ so $z_4 = \sqrt{2}\left(\cos\left(-\dfrac{11\pi}{12}\right) + i\sin\left(-\dfrac{11\pi}{12}\right)\right)$

or $z = \sqrt{2}e^{\frac{\pi i}{12}}, z = \sqrt{2}e^{\frac{7\pi i}{12}}, z = \sqrt{2}e^{-\frac{5\pi i}{12}}$ or $z = \sqrt{2}e^{-\frac{11\pi i}{12}}$ •————

To solve an equation of the form $z^n = w$, start by writing w in modulus–argument form.

Now let $z = r(\cos\theta + i\sin\theta)$, and write the general form of the argument on the RHS by adding integer multiples of 2π.

Apply de Moivre's theorem to the LHS.

Compare the modulus on both sides to get $r = \sqrt{2}$.

Compare the arguments on both sides.

When $k = 1$, $4\theta = \dfrac{\pi}{3} + 2\pi$

$\Rightarrow \theta = \dfrac{\pi}{12} + \dfrac{2\pi}{4} = \dfrac{7\pi}{12}$

Watch out Make sure you choose n **consecutive** values of k to get n distinct roots. If an argument is not in the interval $[-\pi, \pi]$ you can add or subtract a multiple of 2π.

These are the solutions in the form $re^{i\theta}$.

You can also use the exponential form of a complete number when solving equations.

Example (17)

Solve the equation $z^3 + 4\sqrt{2} + 4i\sqrt{2} = 0$.

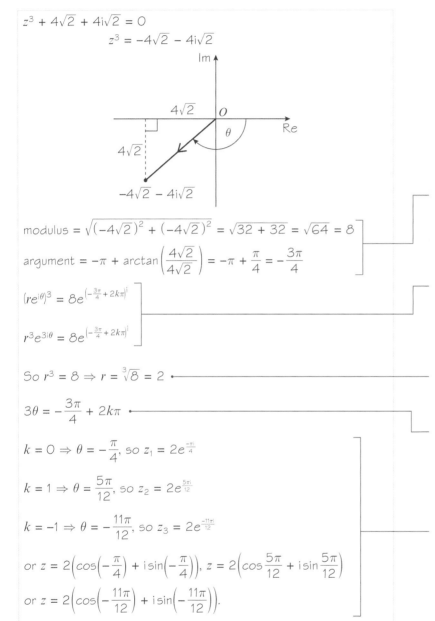

$z^3 + 4\sqrt{2} + 4i\sqrt{2} = 0$

$z^3 = -4\sqrt{2} - 4i\sqrt{2}$

$\text{modulus} = \sqrt{(-4\sqrt{2})^2 + (-4\sqrt{2})^2} = \sqrt{32 + 32} = \sqrt{64} = 8$

$\text{argument} = -\pi + \arctan\left(\dfrac{4\sqrt{2}}{4\sqrt{2}}\right) = -\pi + \dfrac{\pi}{4} = -\dfrac{3\pi}{4}$

Find the modulus and argument of $-4\sqrt{2} - 4i\sqrt{2}$.

$(re^{i\theta})^3 = 8e^{\left(-\frac{3\pi}{4} + 2k\pi\right)i}$

$r^3 e^{3i\theta} = 8e^{\left(-\frac{3\pi}{4} + 2k\pi\right)i}$

Write $z = re^{i\theta}$ and use $(re^{i\theta})n = r^n e^{in\theta}$. Remember to write the general form of the argument on the right-hand side by adding integer multiples of 2π.

So $r^3 = 8 \Rightarrow r = \sqrt[3]{8} = 2$

Compare the modulus on both sides to get $r = 2$.

$3\theta = -\dfrac{3\pi}{4} + 2k\pi$

Compare the arguments on both sides.

$k = 0 \Rightarrow \theta = -\dfrac{\pi}{4}$, so $z_1 = 2e^{\frac{-\pi i}{4}}$

$k = 1 \Rightarrow \theta = \dfrac{5\pi}{12}$, so $z_2 = 2e^{\frac{5\pi i}{12}}$

$k = -1 \Rightarrow \theta = -\dfrac{11\pi}{12}$, so $z_3 = 2e^{\frac{-11\pi i}{12}}$

or $z = 2\left(\cos\left(-\dfrac{\pi}{4}\right) + i\sin\left(-\dfrac{\pi}{4}\right)\right)$, $z = 2\left(\cos\dfrac{5\pi}{12} + i\sin\dfrac{5\pi}{12}\right)$

or $z = 2\left(\cos\left(-\dfrac{11\pi}{12}\right) + i\sin\left(-\dfrac{11\pi}{12}\right)\right)$.

Choose values of k to find three distinct roots. Either choose values that produce arguments in the interval $-\pi < \theta \leqslant \pi$, or add or subtract multiples of 2π as necessary.

Exercise 1F

1 Solve the following equations, expressing your answers for z in the form $x + iy$, where $x, y \in \mathbb{R}$.

  a $z^4 - 1 = 0$ **b** $z^3 - i = 0$ **c** $z^3 = 27$

  d $z^4 + 64 = 0$ **e** $z^4 + 4 = 0$ **f** $z^3 + 8i = 0$

2 Solve the following equations, expressing the roots in the form $r(\cos\theta + i\sin\theta)$, where $-\pi < \theta \leqslant \pi$.

  a $z^7 = 1$ **b** $z^4 + 16i = 0$ **c** $z^5 + 32 = 0$

  d $z^3 = 2 + 2i$ **e** $z^4 + 2i\sqrt{3} = 2$ **f** $z^3 + 32\sqrt{3} + 32i = 0$

3 Solve the following equations, expressing the roots in the form $re^{i\theta}$, where $r > 0$ and $-\pi < \theta \leqslant \pi$. Give θ to 2 decimal places.

  a $z^4 = 3 + 4i$ **b** $z^3 = \sqrt{11} - 4i$ **c** $z^4 = -\sqrt{7} + 3i$

(P) 4 **a** Find the three roots of the equation $(z + 1)^3 = -1$.
   Give your answers in the form $x + iy$, where $x, y \in \mathbb{R}$.

   b Plot the points representing these three roots on an Argand diagram.

   c Given that these three points lie on a circle, find its centre and radius.

(P) 5 **a** Find the five roots of the equation $z^5 - 1 = 0$.
   Give your answers in the form $r(\cos\theta + i\sin\theta)$, where $-\pi < \theta \leqslant \pi$.

   b Hence or otherwise, show that
   $$\cos\left(\frac{2\pi}{5}\right) + \cos\left(\frac{4\pi}{5}\right) = -\frac{1}{2}$$

> **Problem-solving**
>
> Use the fact that the sum of the five roots of unity is zero.

(E) 6 **a** Find the modulus and argument of $-2 - 2i\sqrt{3}$.   **(2 marks)**

   b Hence find all the solutions of the equation $z^4 + 2 + 2i\sqrt{3} = 0$.
   Give your answers in the form $re^{i\theta}$, where $r > 0$ and $-\pi < \theta \leqslant \pi$ and
   illustrate the roots on an Argand diagram.   **(4 marks)**

(E) 7 Find the four distinct roots of the equation $z^4 = 2(1 - i\sqrt{3})$ in exponential form, and show these roots on an Argand diagram.   **(7 marks)**

(E/P) 8 $z = \sqrt{6} + i\sqrt{2}$

   a Find the modulus and argument of z.   **(2 marks)**

   b Find the values of w such that $w^3 = z^4$, giving your answers in the form $re^{i\theta}$, where $r > 0$ and $-\pi < \theta \leqslant \pi$.   **(4 marks)**

(P) **9 a** Solve the equation

$$1 + z + z^2 + z^3 + z^4 + z^5 + z^6 + z^7 = 0$$

b Hence deduce that $(z^2 + 1)$ and $(z^4 + 1)$ are factors of

$$1 + z + z^2 + z^3 + z^4 + z^5 + z^6 + z^7.$$

Problem-solving

$1 + z + z^2 + z^3 + \ldots + z^7$ is the sum of a geometric series.

Challenge

a Find the six roots of the equation $z^6 = 1$ in the form $e^{i\theta}$, where $-\pi < \theta \leqslant \pi$.

b Hence show that the solutions to $(z + 1)^6 = z^6$ are

$$z = -\frac{1}{2} + \frac{1}{2}i \cot\left(\frac{k\pi}{6}\right), k = 1, 2, 3, 4, 5.$$

1.7 Solving geometric problems

You can use properties of complex nth roots to solve geometric problems.

- **The nth roots of any complex number a lie at the vertices of a regular n-gon with its centre at the origin.**

The orientation and size of the regular polygon will depend on a.

Notation The centre of a regular polygon is considered to be the centre of the circle that passes through all of its vertices.

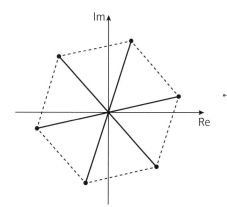

For example, the sixth roots of $7 + 24i$ form this regular hexagon. Each vertex of the hexagon is equidistant from the origin, which lies at the centre of the circle passing through all six vertices.

Online Explore nth roots of complex numbers in an Argand diagram using GeoGebra.

You can find the vertices of this regular polygon by finding a single vertex, and rotating that point around the origin. This is equivalent to multiplying by the nth roots of unity.

- **If z_1 is one root of the equation $z^n = s$, and $1, \omega, \omega^2, \ldots, \omega^{n-1}$ are the nth roots of unity, then the roots of $z^n = s$ are given by $z_1, z_1\omega, z_1\omega^2, \ldots, z_1\omega^{n-1}$.**

Example 18

The point $P(\sqrt{3}, 1)$ lies at one vertex of an equilateral triangle. The centre of the triangle is at the origin.

a Find the coordinates of the other vertices of the triangle.

b Find the area of the triangle.

Problem-solving

Consider the Cartesian coordinate plane as an Argand diagram. The vertices of the triangle will correspond to the cube roots of $(\sqrt{3} + i)^3$. You can find these roots by multiplying $\sqrt{3} + i$ by the cube roots of unity.

a The cube roots of unity are $1, \omega, \omega^2$ where $\omega = e^{\frac{2\pi i}{3}}$.

$\sqrt{3} + i = 2e^{\frac{\pi i}{6}}$

So the vertices are at:

$2e^{\frac{\pi i}{6}} = \sqrt{3} + i$

$2e^{\frac{\pi i}{6}}\left(e^{\frac{2\pi i}{3}}\right) = 2e^{\frac{5\pi i}{6}} = -\sqrt{3} + i$

$2e^{\frac{\pi i}{6}}\left(e^{\frac{2\pi i}{3}}\right)^2 = 2e^{\frac{\pi i}{6}}\left(e^{\frac{4\pi i}{3}}\right) = 2e^{\frac{9\pi i}{6}} = 2e^{-\frac{\pi i}{2}} = -2i$

So the coordinates of the vertices of the triangle are

$(\sqrt{3}, 1), (-\sqrt{3}, 1)$ and $(0, -2)$.

Use $\omega = e^{\frac{2\pi i}{n}}$ to write down the cube root of unity.

$|\sqrt{3} + i| = 2$ and $\arg(\sqrt{3} + i) = \dfrac{\pi}{6}$

You know that one cube root of $(\sqrt{3} + i)^3$ is $\sqrt{3} + i$. Multiply this by the cube roots of unity to find the other roots.

Write your answers as Cartesian coordinates.

b

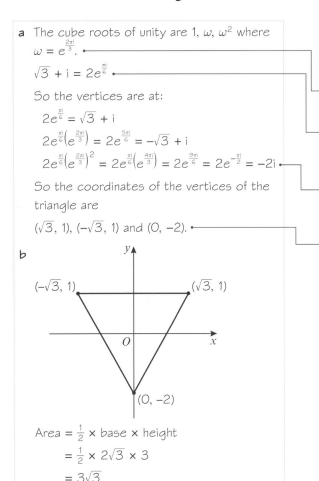

Area $= \dfrac{1}{2} \times$ base $\times$ height

$= \dfrac{1}{2} \times 2\sqrt{3} \times 3$

$= 3\sqrt{3}$

Exercise 1G

(P) **1** Find the coordinates of the vertices of the following regular polygons with centres at the origin.

    a Equilateral triangle with one vertex at $(0, 4)$

    b Square with one vertex at $(5, 0)$

    c Regular pentagon with one vertex at $(-1, \sqrt{3})$

    d Regular hexagon with one vertex at $(2, 2)$

(P) **2** Find the coordinates of the vertices of an equilateral triangle with centre $(2, 3)$ and one vertex at $(3, -2)$.

E/P **3** The triangle OAB in an Argand diagram is equilateral. O is the origin and A corresponds to the complex number $\sqrt{3}(1 - i)$. B is represented by the complex number b.

Find the two possibilities for b in the form $re^{i\theta}$. Illustrate the two possibilities for OAB in a sketch. **(5 marks)**

E/P **4 a** Find the 4th roots of $-12i$ in the form $re^{i\theta}$ where $r > 0$ and $-\pi < \theta \leqslant \pi$. Illustrate these roots on an Argand diagram. **(6 marks)**

Let the points representing these roots on an Argand diagram, taken in order of increasing θ, be A, B, C, D. The midpoints of the sides of $ABCD$ represent the 4th roots of a complex number w.

b Find w. **(4 marks)**

E/P **5** P is one vertex of a regular hexagon in an Argand diagram. The centre of the hexagon is at the origin. P corresponds to the complex number $8 + 8i$.

a Find, in the form $a + bi$, the complex numbers corresponding to the other vertices of the hexagon, and illustrate these on an Argand diagram. **(5 marks)**

b The six complex numbers corresponding to the vertices of the hexagon are squared to form the vertices of a new figure. Find, in the form $a + bi$, the complex numbers corresponding to the other vertices of the new figure. Find the area of the new figure. **(4 marks)**

E/P **6** An ant walks forward one unit and then turns to the right by $\dfrac{2\pi}{9}$. It repeats this a further

three times. Show that the distance of the ant from its initial position is $\dfrac{\sin\left(\dfrac{4\pi}{9}\right)}{\sin\left(\dfrac{\pi}{9}\right)}$ **(6 marks)**

Mixed exercise 1

P **1 a** Use $e^{i\theta} = \cos\theta + i\sin\theta$ to show that $\cos\theta = \frac{1}{2}(e^{i\theta} + e^{-i\theta})$.

b Hence prove that $\cos A \cos B \equiv \dfrac{\cos(A + B) + \cos(A - B)}{2}$

E/P **2** Given that $z = r(\cos\theta + i\sin\theta)$, $r \in \mathbb{R}$, prove by induction that $z^n = r^n(\cos n\theta + i\sin n\theta)$, $n \in \mathbb{Z}^+$. **(5 marks)**

3 Express $\dfrac{(\cos 3x + i\sin 3x)^2}{\cos x - i\sin x}$ in the form $\cos nx + i\sin nx$ where n is an integer to be determined.

4 Use de Moivre's theorem to evaluate:

a $(-1 + i)^8$ **b** $\dfrac{1}{\left(\frac{1}{2} - \frac{1}{2}i\right)^{16}}$

E/P **5 a** Given $z = \cos\theta + i\sin\theta$, use de Moivre's theorem to show that $z^n + \dfrac{1}{z^n} = 2\cos n\theta$. **(4 marks)**

b Express $\left(z^2 + \dfrac{1}{z^2}\right)^3$ in terms of $\cos 6\theta$ and $\cos 2\theta$. **(3 marks)**

c Hence, or otherwise, find constants a and b such that $\cos^3 2\theta = a\cos 6\theta + b\cos 2\theta$. **(3 marks)**

d Hence, or otherwise, show that $\displaystyle\int_0^{\frac{\pi}{6}} \cos^3 2\theta \, d\theta = k\sqrt{3}$, where k is a rational constant. **(4 marks)**

E/P **6 a** Show that

$$\cos^5\theta \equiv \tfrac{1}{16}(\cos 5\theta + 5\cos 3\theta + 10\cos\theta)$$ **(5 marks)**

The diagram shows the curve with equation $y = \cos^5 x$, $-\dfrac{\pi}{2} \leqslant x \leqslant \dfrac{\pi}{2}$. The finite region R is bounded by the curve and the x-axis.

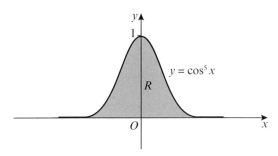

b Calculate the exact area of R. **(6 marks)**

E/P **7 a** Show that

$$\sin^6\theta \equiv -\tfrac{1}{32}(\cos 6\theta - 6\cos 4\theta + 15\cos 2\theta - 10)$$ **(5 marks)**

b Using the substitution $\alpha = \left(\dfrac{\pi}{2} - \theta\right)$, or otherwise, find a similar identity for $\cos^6\theta$. **(3 marks)**

c Given that $\displaystyle\int_0^a \cos^6\theta + \sin^6\theta\, d\theta = \dfrac{5\pi}{32}$, find the exact value of a. **(5 marks)**

E/P **8** Use de Moivre's theorem to show that

$$\sin 6\theta \equiv \sin 2\theta(16\cos^4\theta - 16\cos^2\theta + 3)$$ **(5 marks)**

E/P **9 a** Use de Moivre's theorem to show that

$$\cos 5\theta \equiv 16\cos^5\theta - 20\cos^3\theta + 5\cos\theta$$ **(5 marks)**

b Hence find all solutions to the equation

$$16x^5 - 20x^3 + 5x + 1 = 0$$

giving your answers to 3 decimal places where necessary. **(5 marks)**

E/P **10 a** Show that

$$\sin^5\theta \equiv \tfrac{1}{16}(\sin 5\theta - 5\sin 3\theta + 10\sin\theta)$$ **(5 marks)**

b Hence solve the equation

$$\sin 5\theta - 5\sin 3\theta + 9\sin\theta = 0 \text{ for } 0 \leqslant \theta < \pi$$ **(4 marks)**

E/P **11 a** Use de Moivre's theorem to show that $\cos 5\theta \equiv \cos\theta(16\cos^4\theta - 20\cos^2\theta + 5)$ **(5 marks)**

b By solving the equation $\cos 5\theta = 0$, deduce that $\cos^2\left(\dfrac{\pi}{10}\right) = \dfrac{5 + \sqrt5}{8}$ **(4 marks)**

c Hence, or otherwise, write down the exact values of $\cos^2\left(\dfrac{3\pi}{10}\right)$, $\cos^2\left(\dfrac{7\pi}{10}\right)$ and $\cos^2\left(\dfrac{9\pi}{10}\right)$. **(3 marks)**

(E/P) **12 a** Use de Moivre's theorem to find an expression for $\tan 3\theta$ in terms of $\tan\theta$. **(4 marks)**

b Deduce that $\cot 3\theta = \dfrac{\cot^3\theta - 3\cot\theta}{3\cot^2\theta - 1}$ **(2 marks)**

(E/P) **13** The infinite series C and S are defined as

$$C = 1 + k\cos\theta + k^2\cos 2\theta + k^3\cos 3\theta + \dots$$
$$S = k\sin\theta + k^2\sin 2\theta + k^3\sin 3\theta + \dots$$

where k is a real number and $|k| < 1$.

By considering $C + \mathrm{i}S$, show that $C = \dfrac{1 - k\cos\theta}{1 + k^2 - 2k\cos\theta}$ and write down the corresponding expression for S. **(8 marks)**

(E) **14 a** Express $4 - 4\mathrm{i}$ in the form $r(\cos\theta + \mathrm{i}\sin\theta)$, where $r > 0$, $-\pi < \theta \leqslant \pi$, where r and θ are exact values. **(2 marks)**

b Hence, or otherwise, solve the equation $z^5 = 4 - 4\mathrm{i}$, leaving your answers in the form $z = R\mathrm{e}^{\mathrm{i}k\pi}$, where R is the modulus of z and k is a rational number such that $-1 \leqslant k \leqslant 1$. **(4 marks)**

c Show on an Argand diagram the points representing the roots. **(2 marks)**

(E/P) **15 a** Find the cube roots of $2 - 2\mathrm{i}$ in the form $r\mathrm{e}^{\mathrm{i}\theta}$ where $r > 0$ and $-\pi < \theta \leqslant \pi$. **(5 marks)**

These cube roots are represented by points A, B and C in the Argand diagram, with A in the fourth quadrant and ABC going anticlockwise. The midpoint of AB is M, and M represents the complex number w.

b Draw an Argand diagram, showing the points A, B, C and M. **(2 marks)**

c Find the modulus and argument of w. **(2 marks)**

d Find w^6 in the form $a + b\mathrm{i}$. **(3 marks)**

(E/P) **16** An equilateral triangle has its centre at the origin and one vertex at the point $(2, 1)$.

a Find the coordinates of the other two vertices. **(4 marks)**

b Show that the length of one side of the triangle is $\sqrt{15}$. **(2 marks)**

Challenge

Show that the points on an Argand diagram that represent the roots

of $\left(\dfrac{z+1}{z}\right)^6 = 1$ lie on a straight line.

Summary of key points

1 You can use **Euler's relation**, $e^{i\theta} = \cos\theta + i\sin\theta$, to write a complex number z in exponential form:

$$z = re^{i\theta}$$

where $r = |z|$ and $\theta = \arg z$.

2 For any two complex numbers $z_1 = r_1 e^{i\theta_1}$ and $z_2 = r_2 e^{i\theta_2}$,

- $z_1 z_2 = r_1 r_2 e^{i(\theta_1 + \theta_2)}$

- $\dfrac{z_1}{z_2} = \dfrac{r_1}{r_2} e^{i(\theta_1 - \theta_2)}$

3 **De Moivre's theorem:**
For any integer n, $(r(\cos\theta + i\sin\theta))^n = r^n(\cos n\theta + i\sin n\theta)$

4
- $z + \dfrac{1}{z} = 2\cos\theta$
- $z^n + \dfrac{1}{z^n} = 2\cos n\theta$

- $z - \dfrac{1}{z} = 2i\sin\theta$
- $z^n - \dfrac{1}{z^n} = 2i\sin n\theta$

5 For $w, z \in \mathbb{C}$,

- $\displaystyle\sum_{r=0}^{n-1} wz^r = w + wz + wz^2 + \ldots + wz^{n-1} = \dfrac{w(z^n - 1)}{z - 1}$

- $\displaystyle\sum_{r=0}^{\infty} wz^r = w + wz + wz^2 + \ldots = \dfrac{w}{1 - z}$, $|z| < 1$

6 If z and w are non-zero complex numbers and n is a positive integer, then the equation $z^n = w$ has n distinct solutions.

7 For any complex number $z = r(\cos\theta + i\sin\theta)$, you can write

$$z = r(\cos(\theta + 2k\pi) + i\sin(\theta + 2k\pi))$$

where k is any integer.

8 In general, the solutions to $z^n = 1$ are $z = \cos\left(\dfrac{2\pi k}{n}\right) + i\sin\left(\dfrac{2\pi k}{n}\right) = e^{\frac{2\pi ik}{n}}$ for $k = 1, 2, \ldots, n$ and are known as the nth roots of unity.
If n is a positive integer, then there is an nth root of unity $\omega = e^{\frac{2\pi i}{n}}$ such that:
- The nth roots of unity are $1, \omega, \omega^2, \ldots, \omega^{n-1}$
- $1, \omega, \omega^2, \ldots, \omega^{n-1}$ form the vertices of a regular n-gon
- $1 + \omega + \omega^2 + \ldots + \omega^{n-1} = 0$

9 The nth roots of any complex number s lie on the vertices of a regular n-gon with its centre at the origin.

10 If z_1 is one root of the equation $z^n = s$, and $1, \omega, \omega^2, \ldots, \omega^{n-1}$ are the nth roots of unity, then the roots of $z^n = s$ are given by $z_1, z_1\omega, z_1\omega^2, \ldots, z_1\omega^{n-1}$.

Series

2

Objectives

After completing this chapter you should be able to:

● Understand and use the method of differences to sum finite series
→ **pages 32–37**

● Find and use higher derivatives of functions → **pages 38–39**

● Know how to express functions as an infinite series in ascending powers using Maclaurin series expansion → **pages 40–44**

● Be able to find the series expansions of compound functions
→ **pages 44–48**

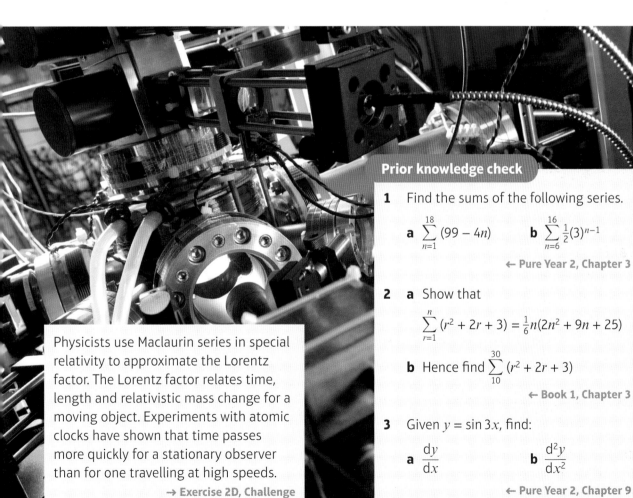

Physicists use Maclaurin series in special relativity to approximate the Lorentz factor. The Lorentz factor relates time, length and relativistic mass change for a moving object. Experiments with atomic clocks have shown that time passes more quickly for a stationary observer than for one travelling at high speeds.
→ **Exercise 2D, Challenge**

Prior knowledge check

1 Find the sums of the following series.

a $\sum_{n=1}^{18} (99 - 4n)$ **b** $\sum_{n=6}^{16} \frac{1}{2}(3)^{n-1}$

← **Pure Year 2, Chapter 3**

2 **a** Show that

$$\sum_{r=1}^{n} (r^2 + 2r + 3) = \frac{1}{6}n(2n^2 + 9n + 25)$$

b Hence find $\sum_{10}^{30} (r^2 + 2r + 3)$

← **Book 1, Chapter 3**

3 Given $y = \sin 3x$, find:

a $\frac{dy}{dx}$ **b** $\frac{d^2y}{dx^2}$

← **Pure Year 2, Chapter 9**

2.1 The method of differences

You can use the method of differences to find the sum of a finite series.

■ **If the general term, u_r, of a series can be expressed in the form**

$$f(r) - f(r + 1)$$

then $\displaystyle\sum_{r=1}^{n} u_r = \sum_{r=1}^{n} (f(r) - f(r + 1))$

so $u_1 = f(1) - f(2)$

$u_2 = f(2) - f(3)$

$u_3 = f(3) - f(4)$

$\vdots$

$u_n = f(n) - f(n + 1)$

Then adding $\displaystyle\sum_{r=1}^{n} u_r = f(1) - f(n + 1)$

You can also start with u_r written in the form $f(r + 1) - f(r)$. After adding and cancelling, you get $\displaystyle\sum_{r=1}^{n} u_r = f(n + 1) - f(1)$

$u_1 + u_2 = f(1) - f(2) + f(2) - f(3)$
$\qquad\quad = f(1) - f(3)$

The f(2) terms cancel.

By summing $u_1 + u_2 + \ldots + u_n$ all terms cancel except the very first term, f(1), and the very last term, f(n + 1).

Example 1

a Show that $4r^3 \equiv r^2(r + 1)^2 - (r - 1)^2 r^2$

b Hence prove, by the method of differences, that

$$\sum_{r=1}^{n} r^3 = \tfrac{1}{4}n^2(n + 1)^2$$

a $r^2(r + 1)^2 - (r - 1)^2 r^2$

$\equiv r^2(r^2 + 2r + 1) - (r^2 - 2r + 1)r^2$

$\equiv r^4 + 2r^3 + r^2 - r^4 + 2r^3 - r^2$

$\equiv 4r^3$

Start with the RHS.

Expand and simplify the brackets.

b Consider $\displaystyle\sum_{r=1}^{n} (r^2(r + 1)^2 - (r - 1)^2 r^2)$

Let $r = 1$: $1^2(2)^2 - (0)^2 1^2$

$r = 2$: $2^2(3)^2 - (1)^2 2^2$

$r = 3$: $3^2(4)^2 - (2)^2 2^3$

$\vdots$

$r = n$: $n^2(n + 1)^2 - (n - 1)^2 n^2$

Sum of terms $= n^2(n + 1)^2$

Then $4\displaystyle\sum_{r=1}^{n} r^3 = n^2(n + 1)^2$

So $\displaystyle\sum_{r=1}^{n} r^3 = \tfrac{1}{4}n^2(n + 1)^2$

All the terms cancel except the first and last.

Watch out When using the method of differences, be sure to write out enough terms to make it clear which terms cancel. When you cancel terms, make sure that they can still be clearly read. You could cross them out in pencil.

The same result could be proved by mathematical induction. ← **Book 1, Chapter 8**

Example 2

Verify that $\dfrac{1}{r(r+1)} \equiv \dfrac{1}{r} - \dfrac{1}{r+1}$ and hence find $\displaystyle\sum_{r=1}^{n} \dfrac{1}{r(r+1)}$ using the method of differences.

$\dfrac{1}{r} - \dfrac{1}{r+1} \equiv \dfrac{r+1-r}{r(r+1)}$ **Write as a single fraction.**

$\phantom{\dfrac{1}{r} - \dfrac{1}{r+1}} \equiv \dfrac{1}{r(r+1)}$ **Simplify.**

$\displaystyle\sum_{r=1}^{n} \dfrac{1}{r(r+1)} \equiv \sum_{r=1}^{n} \left(\dfrac{1}{r} - \dfrac{1}{r+1} \right)$

Let $r = 1$: $\dfrac{1}{1} - \dfrac{1}{\cancel{2}}$

$r = 2$: $\dfrac{1}{\cancel{2}} - \dfrac{1}{\cancel{3}}$

$r = 3$: $\dfrac{1}{\cancel{3}} - \dfrac{1}{\cancel{4}}$

$\vdots$

$r = n$: $\dfrac{1}{\cancel{n}} - \dfrac{1}{n+1}$

     All terms cancel except the first and last.

So $\displaystyle\sum_{r=1}^{n} \dfrac{1}{r(r+1)} = 1 - \dfrac{1}{n+1}$

$ = \dfrac{n+1-1}{n+1}$ **Put over a common denominator.**

$ = \dfrac{n}{n+1}$

Example 3

Find $\displaystyle\sum_{r=1}^{n} \dfrac{1}{4r^2 - 1}$ using the method of differences.

$\dfrac{1}{4r^2 - 1} \equiv \dfrac{1}{(2r+1)(2r-1)}$ **Use the difference of two squares to factorise the denominator.**

$\dfrac{1}{(2r+1)(2r-1)} \equiv \dfrac{A}{2r+1} + \dfrac{B}{2r-1}$ **Split the fraction into partial fractions.**

                          ← **Pure Year 2, Chapter 1**

$\phantom{\dfrac{1}{(2r+1)(2r-1)}} \equiv \dfrac{A(2r-1) + B(2r+1)}{(2r+1)(2r-1)}$ **Add the fractions.**

so $1 \equiv A(2r-1) + B(2r+1)$ **Set numerators of both sides equal to each other.**

Let $r = \frac{1}{2}$: $1 = 0 + B \times 2$

$\qquad\qquad B = \frac{1}{2}$

Let $r = -\frac{1}{2}$: $1 = A \times -2$

$\qquad\qquad A = -\frac{1}{2}$

— Put values of r in to find A and B.

So $\dfrac{1}{4r^2 - 1} \equiv \dfrac{-\frac{1}{2}}{2r + 1} + \dfrac{\frac{1}{2}}{2r - 1}$

$\qquad\qquad \equiv \frac{1}{2}\left(\dfrac{1}{2r - 1} - \dfrac{1}{2r + 1}\right)$

$\Rightarrow \displaystyle\sum_{r=1}^{n} \dfrac{1}{4r^2 - 1} = \frac{1}{2}\sum_{r=1}^{n} \left(\dfrac{1}{2r - 1} - \dfrac{1}{2r + 1}\right)$

Let $r = 1$: $\frac{1}{1} - \cancel{\frac{1}{3}}$

$\quad\ r = 2$: $\cancel{\frac{1}{3}} - \cancel{\frac{1}{5}}$

$\quad\ r = 3$: $\cancel{\frac{1}{5}} - \cancel{\frac{1}{7}}$

$\qquad\ \vdots$

$\quad\ r = n$: $\cancel{\dfrac{1}{2n - 1}} - \dfrac{1}{2n + 1}$

— All terms cancel except the first and last.
Substitute the values of r into $\dfrac{1}{2r - 1} - \dfrac{1}{2r + 1}$ only. The $\frac{1}{2}$ is only required later.

So $\displaystyle\sum_{r=1}^{n} \dfrac{1}{4r^2 - 1} = \frac{1}{2}\left(1 - \dfrac{1}{2n + 1}\right)$

$\qquad\qquad = \frac{1}{2}\left(\dfrac{2n + 1 - 1}{2n + 1}\right)$

$\qquad\qquad = \dfrac{n}{2n + 1}$

If the general term of the series is given in the form $f(r) - f(r + 2)$, you need to adapt the method of differences to consider the terms $f(1)$, $f(2)$, $f(n + 1)$ and $f(n + 2)$.

Example 4

a Express $\dfrac{2}{(r + 1)(r + 3)}$ in partial fractions.

b Hence prove by the method of differences that

$$\sum_{r=1}^{n} \dfrac{2}{(r + 1)(r + 3)} = \dfrac{n(an + b)}{6(n + 2)(n + 3)}$$

where a and b are constants to be found.

c Find the value of $\displaystyle\sum_{r=21}^{30} \dfrac{2}{(r + 1)(r + 3)}$ to 5 decimal places.

a $\dfrac{2}{(r+1)(r+3)} \equiv \dfrac{A}{r+1} + \dfrac{B}{r+3}$ •————————————— Split into partial fractions.

$\equiv \dfrac{A(r+3) + B(r+1)}{(r+1)(r+3)}$ •————————— Add the fractions.

$\Rightarrow \qquad 2 \equiv A(r+3) + B(r+1)$ •——————————— Compare numerators.

Let $r = -3$: $\quad 2 = -2B \Rightarrow B = -1$

Let $r = -1$: $\quad 2 = 2A \Rightarrow A = 1$

Therefore $\dfrac{2}{(r+1)(r+3)} \equiv \dfrac{1}{r+1} - \dfrac{1}{r+3}$

b Using the method of differences,

when $r = 1$: $\quad \frac{1}{2} - \frac{1}{4}$

$\quad r = 2$: $\quad \frac{1}{3} - \frac{1}{5}$

$\quad r = 3$: $\quad \frac{1}{4} - \frac{1}{6}$ ⎤
⎟———————————— Cancel terms.
$\qquad \vdots$ ⎟

$\quad r = n - 1$: $\quad \frac{1}{n} - \dfrac{1}{n+2}$ ⎟

$\quad r = n$: $\quad \dfrac{1}{n+1} - \dfrac{1}{n+3}$ ⎦

Problem-solving

$\sum_{r=1}^{n} (f(r) - f(r+2)) =$
$f(1) + f(2) - f(n+1) - f(n+2)$

So $\sum_{r=1}^{n} \dfrac{2}{(r+1)(r+3)} = \dfrac{5}{6} - \dfrac{1}{n+2} - \dfrac{1}{n+3}$ •——————— Put these four terms over a common denominator.

$= \dfrac{5(n+2)(n+3) - 6(n+3) - 6(n+2)}{6(n+2)(n+3)}$

$= \dfrac{5n^2 + 25n + 30 - 6n - 18 - 6n - 12}{6(n+2)(n+3)}$

$= \dfrac{5n^2 + 13n}{6(n+2)(n+3)}$

$= \dfrac{n(5n + 13)}{6(n+2)(n+3)}$ •——————————— Factorise.

So $a = 5$ and $b = 13$.

c $\sum_{r=21}^{30} \dfrac{2}{(r+1)(r+3)} = \sum_{r=1}^{30} \dfrac{2}{(r+1)(r+3)} - \sum_{r=1}^{20} \dfrac{2}{(r+1)(r+3)}$ •——— Subtract $\sum_{r=1}^{20}$ from $\sum_{r=1}^{30}$.

$= \dfrac{30(5 \times 30 + 13)}{6(30+2)(30+3)} - \dfrac{20(5 \times 20 + 13)}{6(20+2)(20+3)}$

$= \dfrac{815}{1056} - \dfrac{565}{759}$ •——————————— Evaluate.

$= \dfrac{665}{24\,288} = 0.02738$ to 5 d.p. •——————— Give answer to 5 d.p.

Exercise **2A**

1 a Show that $r \equiv \frac{1}{2}(r(r+1) - r(r-1))$.

b Hence show that $\sum_{r=1}^{n} r = \frac{n}{2}(n+1)$ using the method of differences.

(E) **2** Given $\dfrac{1}{r(r+1)(r+2)} \equiv \dfrac{1}{2r(r+1)} - \dfrac{1}{2(r+1)(r+2)}$

find $\displaystyle\sum_{r=1}^{n} \dfrac{1}{r(r+1)(r+2)}$ using the method of differences. **(5 marks)**

(E/P) **3 a** Express $\dfrac{1}{r(r+2)}$ in partial fractions. **(1 mark)**

b Hence find the sum of the series $\displaystyle\sum_{r=1}^{n} \dfrac{1}{r(r+2)}$ using the method of differences. **(5 marks)**

(E) **4 a** Express $\dfrac{1}{(r+2)(r+3)}$ in partial fractions. **(1 mark)**

b Hence find the sum of the series $\displaystyle\sum_{r=1}^{n} \dfrac{1}{(r+2)(r+3)}$ using the method of differences. **(5 marks)**

(E/P) **5 a** Show that $\dfrac{r}{(r+1)!} \equiv \dfrac{1}{r!} - \dfrac{1}{(r+1)!}$ **(2 marks)**

b Hence find $\displaystyle\sum_{r=1}^{n} \dfrac{r}{(r+1)!}$ **(5 marks)**

(E) **6** Given that $\dfrac{2r+1}{r^2(r+1)^2} \equiv \dfrac{1}{r^2} - \dfrac{1}{(r+1)^2}$, find $\displaystyle\sum_{r=1}^{n} \dfrac{2r+1}{r^2(r+1)^2}$ **(6 marks)**

(P) **7 a** Use the method of differences to prove that $\displaystyle\sum_{r=1}^{n} \dfrac{1}{2r+32r+5} = \dfrac{n}{an+b}$, where a and b are constants to be found.

b Prove your result from part **a** using mathematical induction.

(E/P) **8** Prove that $\displaystyle\sum_{r=1}^{n} \dfrac{8}{3r-23r+4} = \dfrac{n(an+b)}{(3n+1)(3n+4)}$, where a and b are constants to be found. **(6 marks)**

> **Hint** This question can be answered using either the method of differences or proof by induction. In the exam, either method would be acceptable. If you use proof by induction, you will need to substitute values of n to find the values of a and b.

(E/P) **9** Prove that $\displaystyle\sum_{r=1}^{n} (r+1)^2 - (r-1)^2 = an(n+1)$, where a is a constant to be found. **(4 marks)**

E/P **10 a** Prove that $\sum_{r=1}^{n} \dfrac{3}{(3r+1)(3r+4)} = \dfrac{an}{bn+c}$, where a, b and c are constants to be found. **(5 marks)**

b Hence, or otherwise, show that $\sum_{r=n}^{2n} \dfrac{3}{3r^2 + 13r + 4} = \dfrac{3(n+1)}{2(3n+1)(3n+2)}$ **(4 marks)**

E/P **11** Robin claims that $\sum_{r=1}^{n} \dfrac{2r+1}{r(r+1)} = 1 - \dfrac{1}{n+1}$

His workings are shown below. Explain the error that he has made.

Using partial fractions:

$$\dfrac{2r+1}{r(r+1)} \equiv \dfrac{A}{r} + \dfrac{B}{r+1}$$

Therefore $2r + 1 \equiv A(r+1) + Br$

So $A = 1$ and $B = 1$.

Using the method of differences,

$$f(1) = 1 + \tfrac{1}{2}$$
$$f(2) = \tfrac{1}{2} + \tfrac{1}{3}$$
$$f(3) = \tfrac{1}{3} + \tfrac{1}{4}$$
$$\vdots$$
$$f(n-1) = \dfrac{1}{n-1} + \dfrac{1}{n}$$

$$f(n) = \dfrac{1}{n} + \dfrac{1}{n+1}$$

Summing the differences: $\sum_{r=1}^{n} \dfrac{2r+1}{r(r+1)} = 1 - \dfrac{1}{n+1}$

(2 marks)

E/P **12** Show that $\dfrac{1}{1 \times 3} + \dfrac{1}{2 \times 4} + \dfrac{1}{3 \times 5} + \dots + \dfrac{1}{n(n+2)} = \dfrac{3}{4} - \dfrac{an+b}{2(n+1)(n+2)}$, where a and b are constants to be found. **(6 marks)**

E/P **13 a** Express $\dfrac{4}{(2r+1)(2r+5)}$ in partial fractions. **(3 marks)**

b Find the value of $\sum_{r=16}^{25} \dfrac{4}{(2r+1)(2r+5)}$ to 4 decimal places. **(5 marks)**

Challenge

a Given that $\sum_{r=1}^{30} \ln\left(1 + \dfrac{1}{r+2}\right) = \ln k$, where k is an integer, find k.

b Given that $\sum_{r=1}^{n} \dfrac{18}{r(r+3)} = \dfrac{n(an^2 + bn + c)}{(n+1)(n+3)(n+3)}$, find a, b and c.

2.2 Higher derivatives

You need to be able to find third, and higher, derivatives of given functions.
You already know how to find first and second derivatives.

If $y = f(x)$, the first derivative of $f(x)$ is given by $\dfrac{dy}{dx} = f'(x)$, and the second derivative of $f(x)$ is given by $\dfrac{d^2y}{dx^2} = \dfrac{d}{dx}\left(\dfrac{dy}{dx}\right) = f''(x)$.

Similarly, the third derivative is given by $\dfrac{d^3y}{dx^3} = \dfrac{d}{dx}\left(\dfrac{d^2y}{dx^2}\right) = f'''(x)$, and so on.

You can find the nth derivative of $f(x)$ by differentiating n times with respect to x.

Notation The nth derivative of $y = f(x)$ is written as $\dfrac{d^ny}{dx^n} = f^{(n)}(x)$.

Example 5

Given that $y = \ln(1 - x)$, find the value of $\dfrac{d^3y}{dx^3}$ when $x = \dfrac{1}{2}$

$\dfrac{dy}{dx} = \dfrac{1}{1 - x}\dfrac{d}{dx}(1 - x) = \dfrac{1}{1 - x} \times (-1) = -\dfrac{1}{1 - x}$

— Use the chain rule.
← **Pure Year 2, Section 9.3**

$\dfrac{d^2y}{dx^2} = \dfrac{d}{dx}\left(\dfrac{dy}{dx}\right) = \dfrac{d}{dx}(-(1 - x)^{-1}) = \dfrac{1}{(1 - x)^2} \times (-1) = -\dfrac{1}{(1 - x)^2}$

$\dfrac{d^3y}{dx^3} = \dfrac{d}{dx}\left(\dfrac{d^2y}{dx^2}\right) = \dfrac{d}{dx}(-(1 - x)^{-2}) = \dfrac{2}{(1 - x)^3} \times (-1) = -\dfrac{2}{(1 - x)^3}$

So when $x = \dfrac{1}{2}$, $\dfrac{d^3y}{dx^3} = \dfrac{-2}{\left(1 - \frac{1}{2}\right)^3} = -16$

— Substitute $x = \dfrac{1}{2}$

Example 6

$f(x) = e^{x^2}$

a Show that $f'(x) = 2xf(x)$.

b By differentiating the result in part **a** twice more with respect to x, show that:
  i $f''(x) = 2f(x) + 2xf'(x)$ **ii** $f'''(x) = 2xf''(x) + 4f'(x)$

c Deduce the values of $f'(0)$, $f''(0)$, and $f'''(0)$.

a $f'(x) = e^{x^2}\dfrac{d}{dx}(x^2) = 2xe^{x^2}$

— If $f(x) = e^u$, then $f'(x) = e^u\dfrac{du}{dx}$

$= 2xf(x)$

— $f(x) = e^{x^2}$

b i $f''(x) = 2f(x) + 2xf'(x)$

— Use the product rule.   ← **Pure Year 2, Section 9.4**

ii $f'''(x) = 2f'(x) + (2xf''(x) + 2f'(x))$

$= 2xf''(x) + 4f'(x)$

— Differentiate again.

c $f(0) = e^0 = 1$

   $f'(0) = 2 \times 0 \times e^0 = 0$

   $f''(0) = 2f(0) + 2 \times 0 \times f'(0)$ ←————————— Substitute $x = 0$ into $f''(x)$.

     $= 2f(0) = 2$

   $f'''(0) = 2 \times 0 \times f''(0) + 4f'(0)$ ←————————— Substitute $x = 0$ into $f'''(x)$.

     $= 4f'(0) = 0$

Exercise 2B

1 For each of the following functions, $f(x)$, find $f'(x)$, $f''(x)$, $f'''(x)$ and $f^{(n)}(x)$.

  a e^{2x} **b** $(1 + x)^n$ **c** xe^x **d** $\ln(1 + x)$

(P) 2 a Given that $y = e^{2+3x}$, find an expression, in terms of y, for $\dfrac{d^n y}{dx^n}$

  b Hence evaluate $\dfrac{d^6 y}{dx^6}$ when $x = \ln\left(\frac{1}{9}\right)$.

3 Given that $y = \sin^2 3x$,

  a show that $\dfrac{dy}{dx} = 3 \sin 6x$ **b** find expressions for $\dfrac{d^2 y}{dx^2}, \dfrac{d^3 y}{dx^3}$ and $\dfrac{d^4 y}{dx^4}$

  c Hence evaluate $\dfrac{d^4 y}{dx^4}$ when $x = \dfrac{\pi}{6}$

4 $f(x) = x^2 e^{-x}$.

  a Show that $f'''(x) = (6x - 6 - x^2)e^{-x}$.   **b** Show that $f''''(2) = 0$.

5 Given that $y = \sec x$,

  a show that $\dfrac{d^2 y}{dx^2} = 2 \sec^3 x - \sec x$

  b show that the value of $\dfrac{d^3 y}{dx^3}$ when $x = \dfrac{\pi}{4}$ is $11\sqrt{2}$.

(P) 6 Given that y is a function of x,

  a show that $\dfrac{d^2}{dx^2}(y^2) = 2y\dfrac{d^2 y}{dx^2} + 2\left(\dfrac{dy}{dx}\right)^2$

  b Find an expression, in terms of y, $\dfrac{dy}{dx}$, $\dfrac{d^2 y}{dx^2}$ and $\dfrac{d^3 y}{dx^3}$, for $\dfrac{d^3}{dx^3}(y^2)$.

7 Given that $f(x) = \ln\left(x + \sqrt{1 + x^2}\right)$, show that:

  a $\sqrt{1 + x^2}\, f'(x) = 1$ **b** $(1 + x^2) f''(x) + xf'(x) = 0$

  c $(1 + x^2) f'''(x) + 3xf''(x) + f'(x) = 0$ **d** Deduce the values of $f'(0)$, $f''(0)$ and $f'''(0)$.

2.3 Maclaurin series

Many functions can be written as an infinite sum of terms of the form ax^n. You may have already encountered series expansions like these:

$$\frac{1}{1-x} = 1 + x + x^2 + x^3 + \dots, \, |x| < 1$$

$$\sqrt{1+x} = 1 + \frac{x}{2} - \frac{x^2}{8} + \frac{x^3}{16} - \dots, \, |x| < 1$$

$$e^x = 1 + x + \frac{x^2}{2} + \frac{x^3}{6} + \frac{x^4}{24} + \dots, \, x \in \mathbb{R}$$

Links The first two series expansions shown here are examples of the binomial expansion. ← **Pure Year 2, Chapter 4**

Example 7

Given that f(x) can be differentiated infinitely many times and that it has a valid series expansion of the form f(x) = $a_0 + a_1 x + a_2 x^2 + a_3 x^3 + \dots + a_r x^r + \dots$, where the a_i are all real constants, show that the series expansion must be

$$f(x) = f(0) + f'(0)x + \frac{f''(0)x^2}{2!} + \dots + \frac{f^{(r)}(0)x^r}{r!} + \dots$$

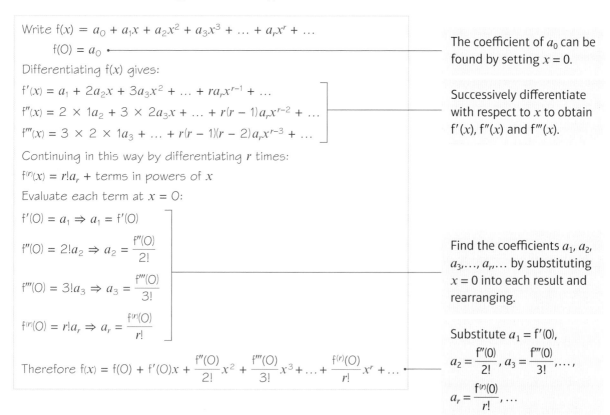

Write f(x) = $a_0 + a_1 x + a_2 x^2 + a_3 x^3 + \dots + a_r x^r + \dots$

    f(0) = a_0

The coefficient of a_0 can be found by setting $x = 0$.

Differentiating f(x) gives:

f'(x) = $a_1 + 2a_2 x + 3a_3 x^2 + \dots + ra_r x^{r-1} + \dots$

f''(x) = $2 \times 1a_2 + 3 \times 2a_3 x + \dots + r(r-1)a_r x^{r-2} + \dots$

f'''(x) = $3 \times 2 \times 1a_3 + \dots + r(r-1)(r-2)a_r x^{r-3} + \dots$

Successively differentiate with respect to x to obtain f'(x), f''(x) and f'''(x).

Continuing in this way by differentiating r times:

f$^{(r)}$(x) = $r!a_r$ + terms in powers of x

Evaluate each term at $x = 0$:

f'(0) = $a_1 \Rightarrow a_1 = $ f'(0)

f''(0) = $2!a_2 \Rightarrow a_2 = \dfrac{f''(0)}{2!}$

f'''(0) = $3!a_3 \Rightarrow a_3 = \dfrac{f'''(0)}{3!}$

f$^{(r)}$(0) = $r!a_r \Rightarrow a_r = \dfrac{f^{(r)}(0)}{r!}$

Find the coefficients a_1, a_2, a_3,..., a_r,... by substituting $x = 0$ into each result and rearranging.

Therefore f(x) = f(0) + f'(0)x + $\dfrac{f''(0)}{2!}x^2 + \dfrac{f'''(0)}{3!}x^3 + \dots + \dfrac{f^{(r)}(0)}{r!}x^r + \dots$

Substitute $a_1 = $ f'(0),

$$a_2 = \frac{f''(0)}{2!}, a_3 = \frac{f'''(0)}{3!}, \dots,$$

$$a_r = \frac{f^{(r)}(0)}{r!}, \dots$$

In this process, outlined in the worked example above, a polynomial in powers of x is being formed step by step. The process focuses on $x = 0$; substituting $x = 0$ into successive derivatives increases the power of the polynomial. For example, if you stop the process after finding f'(0) the polynomial is linear, $f(0) + f'(0)x$, after f"(0) it is quadratic, $f(0) + f'(0)x + \dfrac{f''(0)}{2!}x^2$, after f"'(0) it is cubic,

$f(0) + f'(0)x + \dfrac{f''(0)}{2!}x^2 + \dfrac{f'''(0)}{3!}x^3$ and so on.

The above argument assumes that the function can be written in the given form. This is only true if the given series converges. The above reasoning also only holds if the function can be differentiated an infinite number of times, and if $f^{(r)}(0)$ is always finite.

- **The Maclaurin series expansion of a function f(x) is given by**

$$f(x) = f(0) + f'(0)x + \frac{f''(0)}{2!}x^2 + \ldots + \frac{f^{(r)}(0)}{r!}x^r + \ldots$$

The series is valid provided that f(0), f'(0), f"(0), ... , $f^{(r)}(0)$, ... all have finite values.

The polynomial $f(0) + f'(0)x$ is a Maclaurin polynomial of degree 1.

The polynomial $f(0) + f'(0)x + \dfrac{f''(0)}{2!}x^2$ is a Maclaurin polynomial of degree 2.

The polynomial $f(0) + f'(0)x + \dfrac{f''(0)}{2!}x^2 + \ldots + \dfrac{f^{(r)}(0)}{r!}x^r$ is a Maclaurin polynomial of degree r.

Even when $f^{(r)}(0)$ exists and is finite for all r, a Maclaurin series expansion is only valid for values of x that give rise to a convergent series. For example, the Maclaurin series of $\dfrac{1}{1-x}$ is $1 + x + x^2 + x^3 + \ldots$.

But when $x = 2$, the series gives $1 + 2 + 4 + 8 + \ldots$ which does not converge to $\dfrac{1}{1-2} = -1$.

Note The range of validity for some individual Maclaurin series is given in the formulae booklet. If no range of validity is given in this chapter, you may assume that the expansion is valid for all $x \in \mathbb{R}$.

Example 8

a Express $\ln(1 + x)$ as an infinite series in ascending powers of x.

b Using only the first three terms of the series in part **a**, find estimates for:
  i $\ln 1.05$ **ii** $\ln 1.25$ **iii** $\ln 1.8$

Comment on the accuracy of the estimates.

a $f(x) = \ln(1 + x)$ $\Rightarrow$ $f(0) = \ln 1 = 0$

$f'(x) = \dfrac{1}{1+x} = (1 + x)^{-1} \Rightarrow$ $f'(0) = 1$

$f''(x) = -(1 + x)^{-2}$ $\Rightarrow$ $f''(0) = -1$

$f'''(x) = (-1)(-2)(1 + x)^{-3} \Rightarrow$ $f'''(0) = 2!$

$f^{(r)}(x) = (-1)(-2)(-3)\ldots(-(r-1))(1 + x)^{-r}$

               $\Rightarrow f^{(r)}(0) = (-1)^{r-1}(r - 1)!$

Problem-solving

The term $(-1)^r$ can be used in the general term of **alternating sequences**, in which the terms are alternately positive and negative.

So $\ln(1 + x) = 0 + 1x + \dfrac{-1}{2!}x^2 + \dfrac{(2!)}{3!}x^3 + \ldots$

$\qquad\qquad + \dfrac{(-1)^{r-1}(r-1)!}{r!}x^r + \ldots$

$\ln(1 + x) = x - \dfrac{x^2}{2} + \dfrac{x^3}{3} + \ldots + (-1)^{r-1}\dfrac{x^r}{r} + \ldots$

> Substitute the values for f(0), f'(0), f"(0) etc. into the Maclaurin series for f(x).

b i $\ln 1.05 = 0.05 - \dfrac{0.05^2}{2} + \dfrac{0.05^3}{3} - \ldots$

$\qquad\qquad \approx 0.0487916\ldots$ This is correct to 5 d.p.

ii $\ln 1.25 = 0.25 - \dfrac{0.25^2}{2} + \dfrac{0.25^3}{3} - \ldots$

$\qquad\qquad \approx 0.223958\ldots$ This is correct to 2 d.p.

iii $\ln 1.8 = 0.8 - \dfrac{0.8^2}{2} + \dfrac{0.8^3}{3} - \ldots$

$\qquad\qquad \approx 0.6506666\ldots$ This is not correct to 1 d.p.

> **Online** This expansion is valid for $-1 < x \leqslant 1$. If you use a computer to generate the graphs of the successive Maclaurin polynomials you will see that they converge to the graph of $\ln(1 + x)$ between $x = -1$ and $x = 1$, but outside that interval they diverge rapidly. Explore this using GeoGebra.

> The further away a value is from $x = 0$, the less accurate the approximation will be and the more terms of the series you need to take to maintain a required degree of accuracy.

Example 9

a Find the first four terms in the Maclaurin series of $\sin x$.

b Using the first two terms of the series find an approximation for $\sin 10°$.

a $f(x) = \sin x \qquad \Rightarrow \qquad f(0) = \sin 0 = 0$

$f'(x) = \cos x \qquad \Rightarrow \qquad f'(0) = \cos 0 = 1$

$f''(x) = -\sin x \qquad \Rightarrow \qquad f''(0) = -\sin 0 = 0$

$f'''(x) = -\cos x \qquad \Rightarrow \qquad f'''(0) = -\cos 0 = -1$

$f''''(x) = \sin x \qquad \Rightarrow \qquad f''''(0) = \sin 0 = 0$

> $f^{(n)} = 0$, if n is even, and the cycle of values 0, 1, 0, −1 repeats itself.

So $\sin x = x + \dfrac{-1}{3!}x^3 + \dfrac{1}{5!}x^5 + \dfrac{-1}{7!}x^7 + \ldots + \dfrac{(-1)^r}{(2r+1)!}x^{2r+1} + \ldots$

$\qquad = x - \dfrac{1}{3!}x^3 + \dfrac{1}{5!}x^5 - \dfrac{1}{7!}x^7 + \ldots$

> This expansion is valid for all values of x.

> **Watch out** x must be in radians in expansions of trigonometric functions.

b $\sin 10° = \sin\dfrac{\pi}{18} \approx \dfrac{\pi}{18} - \dfrac{1}{6}\left(\dfrac{\pi}{18}\right)^3$

$\qquad\qquad \approx 0.174532925 - 0.000886096$

$\qquad\qquad \approx 0.173646829$

> This estimate is correct to 5 decimal places; even using $\sin x \approx x$, the approximation is correct to 2 d.p.

Exercise 2C

1 Use the formula for the Maclaurin series and differentiation to show that:

a $(1 - x)^{-1} = 1 + x + x^2 + \dots + x^r + \dots$

b $\sqrt{1 + x} = 1 + \dfrac{x}{2} - \dfrac{x^2}{8} + \dfrac{x^3}{16} - \dots$

> **Hint** The binomial expansions of $(1 + x)^n$, where n is fractional or negative and $|x| < 1$, are the Maclaurin series of the function.

2 Use Maclaurin series and differentiation to show that the first three terms in the series expansion of $e^{\sin x}$ are $1 + x + \dfrac{x^2}{2}$

(P) 3 a Show that the Maclaurin series of $\cos x$ is $1 - \dfrac{x^2}{2!} + \dfrac{x^4}{4!} + \dots + (-1)^r \dfrac{x^{2r}}{(2r)!} + \dots$

b Using the first three terms of the series, show that it gives a value for $\cos 30°$ correct to 3 decimal places.

> **Hint** This expansion is valid for all values of x.

4 Using the series expansions for e^x and $\ln(1 + x)$ respectively, find, correct to 3 decimal places, the values of:

a e b $\ln\left(\dfrac{6}{5}\right)$

5 Use Maclaurin series and differentiation to expand, in ascending powers of x up to and including the term in x^4,

a e^{3x} b $\ln(1 + 2x)$ c $\sin^2 x$

(P) 6 Using the addition formula for $\cos(A - B)$ and the series expansions of $\sin x$ and $\cos x$, show that

$$\cos\left(x - \dfrac{\pi}{4}\right) = \dfrac{1}{\sqrt{2}}\left(1 + x - \dfrac{x^2}{2} - \dfrac{x^3}{6} + \dfrac{x^4}{24} + \dots\right)$$

(E) 7 Given that $f(x) = (1 - x)^2 \ln(1 - x)$,

a show that $f''(x) = 3 + 2\ln(1 - x)$ **(2 marks)**

b find the values of $f(0)$, $f'(0)$, $f''(0)$, and $f'''(0)$ **(1 mark)**

c express $(1 - x)^2 \ln(1 - x)$ in ascending powers of x up to and including the term in x^3.   **(3 marks)**

(E/P) 8 a Using the series expansions of $\sin x$ and $\cos x$, show that

$$3 \sin x - 4x \cos x + x = \dfrac{3}{2}x^3 - \dfrac{17}{120}x^5 + \dots$$ **(5 marks)**

b Hence, find the limit, as $x \to 0$, of $\dfrac{3 \sin x - 4x \cos x + x}{x^3}$ **(1 mark)**

9 Given that $f(x) = \ln \cos x$,

    a show that $f'(x) = -\tan x$ **(2 marks)**

    b find the values of $f'(0)$, $f''(0)$, $f'''(0)$ and $f''''(0)$ **(1 mark)**

    c express $\ln \cos x$ as a series in ascending powers of x up to and including the term in x^4 **(3 marks)**

    d show that using the first two terms of the Maclaurin series for $\ln \cos x$, with $x = \frac{\pi}{4}$, gives a value for $\ln 2$ of $\frac{\pi^2}{16}\left(1 + \frac{\pi^2}{96}\right)$.   **(2 marks)**

10 Show that the Maclaurin series for $\tan x$, as far as the term in x^5, is $x + \frac{1}{3}x^3 + \frac{2}{15}x^5$.   **(5 marks)**

Challenge

The **ratio test** is a sufficient condition for the convergence of an infinite series. It says that a series $\sum_{r=1}^{\infty} a_r$ converges if $\lim_{r \to \infty}\left|\dfrac{a_{r+1}}{a_r}\right| < 1$, and diverges if $\lim_{r \to \infty}\left|\dfrac{a_{r+1}}{a_r}\right| > 1$.

Use the ratio test to show that

a the Maclaurin series expansion of e^x converges for all $x \in \mathbb{R}$

b the Maclaurin series expansion of $\ln(1 + x)$ converges for $-1 < x < 1$, and diverges for $x > 1$.

Problem-solving

If $\lim_{r \to \infty}\left|\dfrac{a_{r+1}}{a_r}\right| = 1$ or does not exist then the ratio test is inconclusive.

2.4 Series expansions of compound functions

You can find the series expansions of compound functions using known Maclaurin series. In the last exercise you found the Maclaurin series of simple compound functions, such as e^{3x} and $\ln(1 + 2x)$. However, the resulting series could also be found by replacing x by $3x$ or x by $2x$ in the known expansions of e^x and $\ln(1 + x)$ respectively. When successive derivatives of a compound function are more difficult, or when there are products of functions involved, it is often possible to use one of the standard results.

■ **The following Maclaurin series expansions are given in the formulae booklet:**

- $e^x = 1 + x + \dfrac{x^2}{2!} + \ldots + \dfrac{x^r}{r!} + \ldots$ **for all x**

- $\ln(1 + x) = x - \dfrac{x^2}{2} + \dfrac{x^3}{3} - \ldots + (-1)^{r+1}\dfrac{x^r}{r} + \ldots$ **$-1 < x \leqslant 1$**

- $\sin x = x - \dfrac{x^3}{3!} + \dfrac{x^5}{5!} - \ldots + (-1)^r\dfrac{x^{2r+1}}{(2r+1)!} + \ldots$ **for all x**

- $\cos x = 1 - \dfrac{x^2}{2!} + \dfrac{x^4}{4!} - \ldots + (-1)^r\dfrac{x^{2r}}{(2r)!} + \ldots$ **for all x**

- $\arctan x = x - \dfrac{x^3}{3} + \dfrac{x^5}{5} - \ldots + (-1)^r\dfrac{x^{2r+1}}{2r+1} + \ldots$ **$-1 \leqslant x \leqslant 1$**

Example 10

Write down the first four non-zero terms in the series expansion, in ascending powers of x, of $\cos(2x^2)$.

$$\cos(2x^2) = 1 - \frac{(2x^2)^2}{2!} + \frac{(2x^2)^4}{4!} - \frac{(2x^2)^6}{6!} + \dots$$

Substitute $2x^2$ for x in the above series for $\cos x$.

$$= 1 - 2x^4 + \frac{2}{3}x^8 - \frac{4}{45}x^{12} + \dots$$

Watch out Make sure you simplify the coefficients as much as possible.

Example 11

Find the first three non-zero terms in the series expansion of $\ln\left(\frac{\sqrt{1+2x}}{1-3x}\right)$, and state the values of x for which the expansion is valid.

$$\ln\left(\frac{\sqrt{1+2x}}{1-3x}\right) = \ln\sqrt{1+2x} - \ln(1-3x)$$

Using $\ln\left(\frac{a}{b}\right) = \ln a - \ln b$

$$= \frac{1}{2}\ln(1+2x) - \ln(1-3x)$$

Using $\ln a^{\frac{1}{2}} = \frac{1}{2}\ln a$

$$\frac{1}{2}\ln(1+2x) = \frac{1}{2}\left(2x - \frac{(2x)^2}{2} + \frac{(2x)^3}{3} - \dots\right), \quad -1 < 2x \le 1$$

Substitute $2x$ for x in the expansion of $\ln(1+x)$.

$$= x - x^2 + \frac{4}{3}x^3 - \dots \qquad -\frac{1}{2} < x \le \frac{1}{2}$$

Problem-solving

You are substituting $2x$ into the series expansion of $\ln(1+x)$, so the series is now only valid for $-1 < 2x \le 1$, or $-\frac{1}{2} < x \le \frac{1}{2}$

$$\ln(1-3x) = (-3x) - \frac{(-3x)^2}{2} + \frac{(-3x)^3}{3} - \dots, \quad -1 < -3x \le 1$$

$$= -3x - \frac{9}{2}x^2 - 9x^3 - \dots \qquad -\frac{1}{3} \le x < \frac{1}{3}$$

Substitute $-3x$ for x in the expansion of $\ln(1+x)$.

$$\text{So } \ln\frac{\sqrt{1+2x}}{1-3x} = (x - x^2 + \frac{4}{3}x^3 - \dots)$$

$$- (-3x - \frac{9}{2}x^2 - 9x^3 - \dots), \quad -\frac{1}{3} \le x < \frac{1}{3}$$

$$= 4x + \frac{7}{2}x^2 + \frac{31}{3}x^3 + \dots, \qquad -\frac{1}{3} \le x < \frac{1}{3}$$

You need both intervals to be satisfied. This is the case for $-\frac{1}{3} \le x < \frac{1}{3}$

Example 12

Given that terms in x^n with $n > 4$ may be neglected, use the series expansions for e^x and $\sin x$ to show that

$$e^{\sin x} \approx 1 + x + \frac{x^2}{2} - \frac{x^4}{8}$$

$\sin x = x - \dfrac{x^3}{3!} + \dots$ — Only two terms are used as the next term is kx^5.

So $e^{\sin x} = e^{\left(x - \frac{x^3}{3!} + \dots\right)}$

$= e^x \times e^{-\frac{x^3}{6}} \times \dots$ — Use $e^{a-b} = e^a \times e^{-b}$

$= \left(1 + x + \dfrac{x^2}{2} + \dfrac{x^3}{6} + \dfrac{x^4}{24} + \dots\right)\left(1 + \left(-\dfrac{x^3}{6}\right) + \dots\right) \dots$ — Substitute $-\dfrac{x^3}{6}$ for x in the expansion of e^x.

$= 1 + x + \dfrac{x^2}{2} + \dfrac{x^3}{6} + \dfrac{x^4}{24} - \dfrac{x^3}{6} - \dfrac{x^4}{6} + \dots$

$\approx 1 + x + \dfrac{x^2}{2} - \dfrac{x^4}{8}$ — Simplify as much as possible.

Exercise 2D

(P) 1 Use the series expansions of e^x, $\ln(1 + x)$ and $\sin x$ to expand the following functions as far as the fourth non-zero term. In each case state the values of x for which the expansion is valid.

a $\dfrac{1}{e^x}$

b $\dfrac{e^{2x} \times e^{3x}}{e^x}$

c e^{1+x}

d $\ln(1 - x)$

e $\sin\left(\dfrac{x}{2}\right)$

f $\ln(2 + 3x)$

Hint For part **f**, write $2 + 3x$ as $2\left(1 + \dfrac{3x}{2}\right)$.

(E/P) 2 a Using the Maclaurin series of $\ln(1 + x)$, show that

$$\ln\left(\frac{1 + x}{1 - x}\right) = 2\left(x + \frac{x^3}{3} + \frac{x^5}{5} + \dots\right), \quad -1 < x < 1$$ **(4 marks)**

b Deduce the series expansion for $\ln\sqrt{\dfrac{1 + x}{1 - x}}$, $-1 < x < 1$ **(2 marks)**

c By choosing a suitable value of x, and using only the first three terms of the series from part **a**, find an approximation for $\ln\left(\frac{2}{3}\right)$, giving your answer to 4 decimal places. **(2 marks)**

d Show that the first three terms of your series from part **b**, with $x = \frac{3}{5}$, give an approximation for $\ln 2$, which is correct to 2 decimal places. **(2 marks)**

(E/P) 3 Show that, for small values of x, $e^{2x} - e^{-x} \approx 3x + \frac{3}{2}x^2$. **(4 marks)**

(E/P) 4 a Show that $3x \sin 2x - \cos 3x = -1 + \frac{21}{2}x^2 - \frac{59}{8}x^4 - \dots$ **(5 marks)**

b Hence find the $\lim\limits_{x \to 0}\left(\dfrac{3x \sin 2x - \cos 3x + 1}{x^2}\right)$ **(1 mark)**

P **5** Find the series expansions, up to and including the term in x^4, of:

  a $\ln(1 + x - 2x^2)$

  b $\ln(9 + 6x + x^2)$

Note Factorise the quadratic first.

  and in each case give the range of values of x for which the expansion is valid.

E/P **6 a** Write down the series expansion of $\cos 2x$ in ascending powers of x, up to and including the term in x^8. **(3 marks)**

  b Hence, or otherwise, find the first four non-zero terms in the series expansion for $\sin^2 x$. **(3 marks)**

E/P **7** Show that the first two non-zero terms of the series expansion, in ascending powers of x, of $\ln(1 + x) + (x - 1)(e^x - 1)$ are px^3 and qx^4, where p and q are constants to be found. **(6 marks)**

E/P **8 a** By considering the product of the series expansions of $\sin x$ and $(1 - x)^{-2}$, expand $\dfrac{\sin x}{(1 - x)^2}$ in ascending powers of x as far as the term in x^4. **(6 marks)**

  b Deduce the gradient of the tangent, at the origin, to the curve with equation $y = \dfrac{\sin x}{(1 - x)^2}$ **(3 marks)**

P **9** Use the Maclaurin series, together with a suitable substitution, to show that:

  a $(1 - 3x)\ln(1 + 2x) = 2x - 8x^2 + \dfrac{26}{3}x^3 - 12x^4 + \ldots$

  b $e^{2x}\sin x = x + 2x^2 + \dfrac{11}{6}x^3 + x^4 + \ldots$

  c $\sqrt{1 + x^2}\,e^{-x} = 1 - x + x^2 - \dfrac{2}{3}x^3 + \dfrac{1}{6}x^4 + \ldots$

E/P **10 a** Write down the first five non-zero terms in the series expansions of $e^{-\frac{x^2}{2}}$ **(3 marks)**

  b Using your result from part **a**, find an approximate value for $\displaystyle\int_{-1}^{1} e^{-\frac{x^2}{2}}\,dx$, giving your answer to 3 decimal places. **(3 marks)**

E/P **11 a** Show that $e^{px}\sin 3x = 3x + 3px^2 + \dfrac{3(p^2 - 3)}{2}x^3 + \ldots$ where p is a constant. **(5 marks)**

  b Given that the first non-zero term in the expansion, in ascending powers of x, of $e^{px}\sin 3x + \ln(1 + qx) - x$ is kx^3, where k is a constant, find the values of p, q and k. **(4 marks)**

E/P **12** $f(x) = e^{x - \ln x}\sin x$, $x > 0$

  a Show that, if x is sufficiently small, x^4 and higher powers of x may be neglected,

  $$f(x) \approx 1 + x + \frac{x^2}{3}$$ **(5 marks)**

  b Show that using $x = 0.1$ in the result from part **a** gives an approximation for $f(0.1)$ which is correct to 6 significant figures. **(2 marks)**

13 $y = \sin 2x - \cos 2x$

   a Show that $\dfrac{\mathrm{d}^4 y}{\mathrm{d}x^4} = 16y$ **(4 marks)**

   b Find the first five terms of the Maclaurin series for y, giving each coefficient in its simplest form.   **(4 marks)**

Challenge

The Lorentz factor of a moving object, λ, is given by the formula

$$\gamma = \frac{1}{\sqrt{1 - \beta^2}}$$

where $\beta = \dfrac{v}{c}$ is the ratio of v, the speed of the object, to c, the speed of light (3×10^8 m s^{-1}).

a Find the Maclaurin series expansion of $\gamma = \dfrac{1}{\sqrt{1 - \beta^2}}$ in ascending powers of β up to the term in β^4

The theory of special relativity predicts that a period of time observed as T within a stationary frame of reference will be observed as a period of time $\dfrac{T}{\gamma}$ in a moving frame of reference.

A spaceship travels from Earth to a planet 4.2 light years away. To an observer on Earth, the journey appears to take 20 years.

b Use your answer to part **a** to estimate the observed journey time for a person on the spaceship.

c Calculate the percentage error in your estimate.

d Comment on whether your approximation would be more or less accurate if the spaceship was travelling at three times the speed.

> **Note** A light year is the distance light travels in one year.

Mixed exercise 2

 1 a Express $\dfrac{2}{(r + 2)(r + 4)}$ in partial fractions.   **(1 mark)**

   b Hence show that $\displaystyle\sum_{r=1}^{n} \dfrac{2}{(r + 2)(r + 4)} = \dfrac{7n^2 + 25n}{12(n + 3)(n + 4)}$ **(5 marks)**

 2 a Express $\dfrac{4}{(4r - 1)(4r + 3)}$ in partial fractions.   **(2 marks)**

   b Using your answer to part **a** and the method of differences, show that

$$\sum_{r=1}^{n} \frac{4}{(4r - 1)(4r + 3)} = \frac{4n}{3(4n + 3)}$$ **(3 marks)**

   c Evaluate $\displaystyle\sum_{r=100}^{200} \dfrac{4}{(4r - 1)(4r + 3)}$ giving your answer to 3 significant figures.   **(2 marks)**

(E) 3 a Show that $(r + 1)^3 - (r - 1)^3 = 6r^2 + 2$. **(2 marks)**

   b Using the result from part **a** and the method of differences, show that

   $$\sum_{r=1}^{n} r^2 = \frac{1}{6}n(n + 1)(2n + 1)$$ **(5 marks)**

(E/P) 4 Prove that $\displaystyle\sum_{r=1}^{n} \frac{4}{(r + 1)(r + 3)} = \frac{n(an + b)}{3(n + 2)(n + 3)}$, where a and b are constants to be found. **(5 marks)**

(E/P) 5 Prove that $\displaystyle\sum_{r=n}^{2n}((r + 1)^3 - (r - 1)^3) = an^3 + bn^2 + cn + d$, where a, b, c and d are constants to be found. **(5 marks)**

6 a Given that $y = e^{1-2x}$, find an expression, in terms of y, for $\dfrac{d^n y}{dx^n}$

   b Hence show that $\dfrac{d^8 y}{dx^8}$ at $x = \ln 32$ is $\dfrac{e}{4}$

7 a For the function $f(x) = \ln(1 + e^x)$, find the values of $f'(0)$ and $f''(0)$.

   b Show that $f'''(0) = 0$.

   c Find the series expansion of $\ln(1 + e^x)$, in ascending powers of x up to and including the term in x^2.

(E/P) 8 a Write down the Maclaurin series of $\cos 4x$ in ascending powers of x, up to and including the term in x^6. **(3 marks)**

   b Hence, or otherwise, show that the first three non-zero terms in the series expansion of $\sin^2 2x$ are $4x^2 - \frac{16}{3}x^4 + \frac{128}{45}x^6$. **(3 marks)**

(E/P) 9 Given that terms in x^5 and higher powers may be neglected, use the Maclaurin series for e^x and $\cos x$, to show that $e^{\cos x} \approx e\left(1 - \dfrac{x^2}{2} + \dfrac{x^4}{6}\right)$. **(5 marks)**

(E/P) 10 Given that $|2x| < 1$, find the first two non-zero terms in the series expansion of $\ln((1 + x)^2(1 - 2x))$ in ascending powers of x. **(5 marks)**

(E/P) 11 Use differentiation and Maclaurin series, to express $\ln(\sec x + \tan x)$ as a series in ascending powers of x up to and including the term in x^3. **(5 marks)**

(P) 12 Show that the results of differentiating the standard series expansions of e^x, $\sin x$ and $\cos x$ agree with the following:

   a $\dfrac{d}{dx}(e^x) = e^x$ b $\dfrac{d}{dx}(\sin x) = \cos x$ c $\dfrac{d}{dx}(\cos x) = -\sin x$

E **13 a** Given that $\cos x = 1 - \dfrac{x^2}{2!} + \dfrac{x^4}{4!} - \ldots$, show that $\sec x = 1 + \dfrac{x^2}{2} + \dfrac{5}{24}x^4 + \ldots$. **(4 marks)**

  b Using the result found in part **a**, and given that $\sin x = x - \dfrac{x^3}{3!} + \dfrac{x^5}{5!} - \ldots$, find the first three non-zero terms in the series expansion, in ascending powers of x, for $\tan x$. **(4 marks)**

E/P **14** By using the series expansions of e^x and $\cos x$, or otherwise, find the expansion of $e^x \cos 3x$ in ascending powers of x up to and including the term in x^3. **(5 marks)**

E/P **15** Find the first three derivatives of $(1 + x)^2 \ln(1 + x)$. Hence, or otherwise, find the expansion of $(1 + x)^2 \ln(1 + x)$ in ascending powers of x up to and including the term in x^3. **(5 marks)**

E/P **16 a** Expand $\ln(1 + \sin x)$ in ascending powers of x up to and including the term in x^4. **(4 marks)**

  b Hence find an approximation for $\displaystyle\int_0^{\frac{\pi}{6}} \ln(1 + \sin x)\,dx$ giving your answer to 3 decimal places. **(3 marks)**

E/P **17 a** Using the first two terms, $x + \dfrac{x^3}{3}$, in the expansion of $\tan x$, show that
$$e^{\tan x} = 1 + x + \dfrac{x^2}{2} + \dfrac{x^3}{2} + \ldots$$ **(3 marks)**

  b Deduce the first four terms in the series expansion of $e^{-\tan x}$, in ascending powers of x. **(3 marks)**

P **18 a** Using Maclaurin series, and differentiation, show that $\ln \cos x = -\dfrac{x^2}{2} - \dfrac{x^4}{12} + \ldots$

  b Using $\cos x = 2\cos^2\left(\dfrac{x}{2}\right) - 1$, and the result in part **a**, show that
$$\ln(1 + \cos x) = \ln 2 - \dfrac{x^2}{4} - \dfrac{x^4}{96} + \ldots$$

E/P **19** $y = e^{3x} - e^{-3x}$

  a Show that $\dfrac{d^4y}{dx^4} = 81y$. **(4 marks)**

  b Find the first three non-zero terms of the Maclaurin series for y, giving each coefficient in its simplest form. **(3 marks)**

  c Find an expression for the nth non-zero term of the Maclaurin series for y. **(2 marks)**

Challenge

Given that the Maclaurin series of e^x is valid for all $x \in \mathbb{C}$, show, using series expansions, that $e^{ix} = \cos x + i \sin x$.

Summary of key points

1 If the general term, u_r, of a series can be expressed in the form $f(r) - f(r + 1)$

then $\sum_{r=1}^{n} u_r = \sum_{r=1}^{n} (f(r) - f(r + 1))$.

so $u_1 = f(1) - f(2)$

$u_2 = f(2) - f(3)$

$u_3 = f(3) - f(4)$

$\vdots$

$u_n = f(n) - f(n + 1)$

Then adding $\sum_{r=1}^{n} u_r = f(1) - f(n + 1)$

2 The **Maclaurin series** of a function $f(x)$ is given by

$$f(x) = f(0) + f'(0)x + \frac{f''(0)}{2!}x^2 + \ldots + \frac{f^{(r)}(0)}{r!}x^r + \ldots$$

The series is valid provided that $f(0)$, $f'(0)$, $f''(0)$, $\ldots$, $f^{(r)}(0)$, $\ldots$ all have finite values.

3 The following Maclaurin series are given in the formulae booklet:

$e^x = 1 + x + \frac{x^2}{2!} + \ldots + \frac{x^r}{r!} + \ldots$ for all x

$\ln(1 + x) = x - \frac{x^2}{2} + \frac{x^3}{3} - \ldots + (-1)^{r+1}\frac{x^r}{r} + \ldots$ $-1 < x \leqslant 1$

$\sin x = x - \frac{x^3}{3!} + \frac{x^5}{5!} - \ldots + (-1)^r \frac{x^{2r+1}}{(2r+1)!} + \ldots$ for all x

$\cos x = 1 - \frac{x^2}{2!} + \frac{x^4}{4!} - \ldots + (-1)^r \frac{x^{2r}}{(2r)!} + \ldots$ for all x

$\arctan x = x - \frac{x^3}{3} + \frac{x^5}{5} - \ldots + (-1)^r \frac{x^{2r+1}}{2r+1} + \ldots$ $-1 \leqslant x \leqslant 1$

3

Methods in calculus

Prior knowledge check

1 Find:

  a $\displaystyle\int \frac{5x}{\sqrt{3+x^2}}\,dx$ **b** $\displaystyle\int x^2 e^x\,dx$ **c** $\displaystyle\int \frac{\sin x \cos x}{1 + 3\sin^2 x}\,dx$

  ← Pure Year 2, Chapter 11

2 Find $\dfrac{dy}{dx}$ in terms of x and y for the following:

  a $x^2 + y^2 = 1$ **b** $5x^2 + xy + 2y^2 = 11$

  c $x = \tan y$ ← Pure Year 2, Chapter 9

3 Express in partial fractions:

  a $\dfrac{1}{x(x+1)}$ **b** $\dfrac{2x-1}{x^2-4}$ **c** $\dfrac{3x-2}{2x^2+3x+1}$

  ← Pure Year 2, Chapter 1

The lowest speed necessary for an object to escape from a gravitational field is called the escape velocity. You can use improper integrals to calculate escape velocities.

3.1 Improper integrals

If a function f(x) exists and is continuous for all values in the interval [a, b] then the definite integral $\int_a^b f(x)\,dx$ represents the area enclosed by the curve $y = f(x)$, the x-axis and the lines $x = a$ and $x = b$.

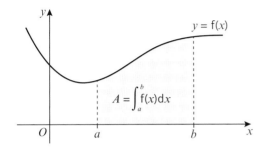

Notation The interval [a, b] is all the real numbers x satisfying the inequality $a \leqslant x \leqslant b$.

In this section you will consider integrals where one or both of the limits are **infinite**, or where the function is **not defined** at some point within the given interval. These are called **improper integrals**. In these cases it is still possible for the function to enclose a finite area.

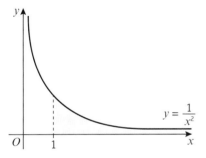

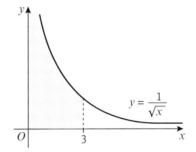

The area bounded by the curve $y = \dfrac{1}{x^2}$, the x-axis and the line $x = 1$ is finite. This area is represented by the improper integral $\int_1^\infty \dfrac{1}{x^2}\,dx$.

The function $f(x) = \dfrac{1}{\sqrt{x}}$ is not defined at $x = 0$. However, the area bounded by the curve $y = \dfrac{1}{\sqrt{x}}$, the coordinate axes and the line $x = 3$ is finite. This area is represented by the improper integral $\int_0^3 \dfrac{1}{\sqrt{x}}\,dx$.

- **The integral $\int_a^b f(x)\,dx$ is improper if either:**
  - **one or both of the limits is infinite**
  - **f(x) is undefined at $x = a$, $x = b$ or another point in the interval [a, b].**

Notation If an improper integral exists then it is said to be **convergent**. If it does not exist it is said to be **divergent**.

You can determine whether improper integrals are convergent, and evaluate them if so, by considering limits. To find $I = \int_0^\infty e^{-x}\,dx$, you need to consider the integral $\int_0^t e^{-x}\,dx$, for some finite value t. If this integral tends to a limit as $t \to \infty$ then I is convergent and equal to that limit. If it fails to tend to a limit, then I is divergent.

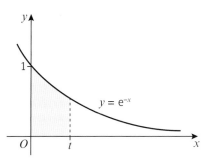

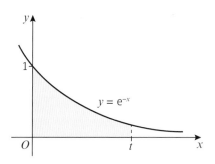

As $t \to \infty$,

$$\int_0^t e^{-x}\,dx \to \int_0^\infty e^{-x}\,dx$$

$$\int_0^t e^{-x}\,dx = [-e^{-x}]_0^t = -e^{-t} + 1$$

Since $e^{-t} \to 0$ as $t \to \infty$, the integral $\int_0^t e^{-x}\,dx \to 1$ as $t \to \infty$.

So $\int_0^\infty e^{-x}\,dx$ is convergent and equal to 1.

Notation You can use limit notation to write:

$$\int_0^\infty e^{-x}\,dx = \lim_{t \to \infty} \int_0^t e^{-x}\,dx = \lim_{t \to \infty}(-e^{-t} + 1) = 1$$

Example 1

Evaluate each improper integral, or show that it is not convergent.

a $\displaystyle\int_1^\infty \frac{1}{x^2}\,dx$ **b** $\displaystyle\int_1^\infty \frac{1}{x}\,dx$

a $\displaystyle\int_1^\infty \frac{1}{x^2}\,dx = \lim_{t \to \infty} \int_1^t \frac{1}{x^2}\,dx$

Replace the infinite limit by t, and take the limit as $t \to \infty$.

$$= \lim_{t \to \infty}\left[-\frac{1}{x}\right]_1^t$$

$$= \lim_{t \to \infty}\left(-\frac{1}{t} + 1\right)$$

$\dfrac{1}{t} \to 0$ as $t \to \infty$

$$= 1$$

So $\displaystyle\int_1^\infty \frac{1}{x^2}\,dx$ converges and $\displaystyle\int_1^\infty \frac{1}{x^2}\,dx = 1$

The area under the curve $y = \dfrac{1}{x^2}$ from 1 to infinity is finite and is exactly equal to 1.

b $\displaystyle\int_1^\infty \frac{1}{x}\,dx = \lim_{t \to \infty} \int_1^t \frac{1}{x}\,dx$

$$= \lim_{t \to \infty}[\ln x]_1^t$$

$$= \lim_{t \to \infty}(\ln t - \ln 1)$$

$$= \lim_{t \to \infty}(\ln t)$$

$\ln t \to \infty$ as $t \to \infty$, so $\displaystyle\int_1^\infty \frac{1}{x}\,dx$ does not converge.

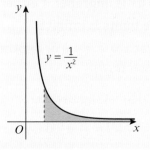

Online Explore the integral $\displaystyle\int_1^\infty \frac{1}{x^2}\,dx$ using GeoGebra.

Watch out Make sure you show the limiting process clearly in your working. You can't just write $\displaystyle\int_1^\infty \frac{1}{x}\,dx = \ln \infty = \infty$.

You need to use a similar limiting process if the function you are integrating is not defined at one or more points in the interval.

Example 2

Evaluate each integral, or show that it does not converge.

a $\displaystyle\int_0^1 \frac{1}{x^2}\,dx$ **b** $\displaystyle\int_0^2 \frac{x}{\sqrt{4-x^2}}\,dx$

a $\displaystyle\int_0^1 \frac{1}{x^2}\,dx = \lim_{t\to 0}\int_t^1 \frac{1}{x^2}\,dx$

$\qquad = \lim_{t\to 0}\left[-\frac{1}{x}\right]_t^1$

$\qquad = \lim_{t\to 0}\left(-1 + \frac{1}{t}\right)$

$-1 + \dfrac{1}{t} \to \infty$ as $t \to 0$, so $\displaystyle\int_0^1 \frac{1}{x^2}\,dx$ does not converge.

—— $y = \dfrac{1}{x^2}$ is undefined for $x = 0$, so replace the lower limit with t and take the limit as $t \to 0$.

—— $\dfrac{1}{t} \to \infty$ as $t \to 0$

b $\displaystyle\int_0^2 \frac{x}{\sqrt{4-x^2}}\,dx = \lim_{t\to 2}\int_0^t \frac{x}{\sqrt{4-x^2}}\,dx$

$\qquad = \lim_{t\to 2}\left[-\sqrt{4-x^2}\right]_0^t$

$\qquad = \lim_{t\to 2}\left(-\sqrt{4-t^2} - (-\sqrt{4})\right)$

$\qquad = \lim_{t\to 2}\left(2 - \sqrt{4-t^2}\right)$

$\qquad = 2$

So $\displaystyle\int_0^2 \frac{x}{\sqrt{4-x^2}}\,dx$ converges and

$\displaystyle\int_0^2 \frac{x}{\sqrt{4-x^2}}\,dx = 2$

—— $y = \dfrac{x}{\sqrt{4-x^2}}$ is not defined for $x = 2$, so replace the upper limit with t.

—— $\lim_{t\to 2}\left(\sqrt{4-t^2}\right) = 0$

If **both limits** of an integral are infinite, then you need to split the integral into the sum of two improper integrals. In other words, you write

$\displaystyle\int_{-\infty}^{\infty} f(x)\,dx = \int_{-\infty}^{c} f(x)\,dx + \int_{c}^{\infty} f(x)\,dx$ for some value c.

If both of these integrals converge, then the original integral converges, but if either diverges, then the original integral is also divergent.

Watch out Do not write $\displaystyle\int_{-\infty}^{\infty} f(x)\,dx$ as $\displaystyle\lim_{a\to\infty}\int_{-a}^{a} f(x)\,dx$. You must split it into two separate integrals to determine whether it converges.

→ **Review Exercise 1, Challenge Q3**

Example 3

a Find $\displaystyle\int x e^{-x^2}\,dx$.   **b** Hence show that $\displaystyle\int_{-\infty}^{\infty} x e^{-x^2}\,dx$ converges and find its value.

a Let $I = \displaystyle\int x e^{-x^2}\,dx$

Consider $y = e^{-x^2}$ —————————————— Try differentiating e^{-x^2}.

$\dfrac{dy}{dx} = -2x e^{-x^2}$ ———————————— The $-2x$ comes from differentiating $-x^2$.

So $I = -\dfrac{1}{2}e^{-x^2} + c$ ———————————— Use the reverse chain rule.

b Split $\displaystyle\int_{-\infty}^{\infty} x e^{-x^2}\,dx$ up as $\displaystyle\int_{-\infty}^{0} x e^{-x^2}\,dx + \int_{0}^{\infty} x e^{-x^2}\,dx$

Consider $\displaystyle\int_{-t}^{0} x e^{-x^2}\,dx$:

$$\int_{-t}^{0} x e^{-x^2}\,dx = \left[-\tfrac{1}{2}e^{-x^2}\right]_{-t}^{0} = -\tfrac{1}{2} + \tfrac{1}{2}e^{-t^2}$$

So $\displaystyle\lim_{t\to\infty}\int_{-t}^{0} x e^{-x^2}\,dx = \lim_{t\to\infty}\left(-\tfrac{1}{2} + \tfrac{1}{2}e^{-t^2}\right) = -\tfrac{1}{2}$

So $\displaystyle\int_{-\infty}^{0} x e^{-x^2}\,dx$ converges and $\displaystyle\int_{-\infty}^{0} x e^{-x^2}\,dx = -\tfrac{1}{2}$

Similarly, consider $\displaystyle\int_{0}^{t} x e^{-x^2}\,dx$:

$$\int_{0}^{t} x e^{-x^2}\,dx = \left[-\tfrac{1}{2}e^{-t^2}\right]_{0}^{t} = -\tfrac{1}{2}e^{-t^2} + \tfrac{1}{2}$$

So $\displaystyle\lim_{t\to\infty}\int_{0}^{t} x e^{-x^2}\,dx = \lim_{t\to\infty}\left(-\tfrac{1}{2}e^{-t^2} + \tfrac{1}{2}\right) = \tfrac{1}{2}$

So $\displaystyle\int_{0}^{\infty} x e^{-x^2}\,dx$ converges and $\displaystyle\int_{0}^{\infty} x e^{-x^2}\,dx = \tfrac{1}{2}$

Since both integrals converge, we know that

$\displaystyle\int_{-\infty}^{\infty} x e^{-x^2}\,dx$ converges and

$$\int_{-\infty}^{\infty} x e^{-x^2}\,dx = \int_{-\infty}^{0} x e^{-x^2}\,dx + \int_{0}^{\infty} x e^{-x^2}\,dx$$

$$= -\tfrac{1}{2} + \tfrac{1}{2} = 0$$

Problem-solving

You can choose any point at which to split the integral up, but choosing a special value like 0 will often make evaluating the integral easier.

To find the integral between $-\infty$ and 0, you should find the integral between $-t$ and 0 and then let $t \to \infty$.

Use $\int x e^{-x^2}\,dx = -\tfrac{1}{2}e^{-x^2} + c$

Watch out You need to check that **both** the integrals converge before you can determine that the original integral converges.

To find the integral between 0 and ∞, you should find the integral between 0 and t and then let $t \to \infty$.

Use $\int x e^{-x^2}\,dx = -\tfrac{1}{2}e^{-x^2} + c$

Apply $\displaystyle\int_{-\infty}^{\infty} f(x)\,dx = \int_{-\infty}^{c} f(x)\,dx + \int_{c}^{\infty} f(x)\,dx$

Exercise **3A**

1 Find the values of the following improper integrals.

a $\displaystyle\int_{1}^{\infty} \frac{1}{x^3}\,dx$

b $\displaystyle\int_{2}^{\infty} x^{-\frac{3}{2}}\,dx$

c $\displaystyle\int_{0}^{\infty} e^{-3x}\,dx$

2 For each of the following, show that the improper integral diverges.

a $\displaystyle\int_{0}^{\infty} e^{x}\,dx$

b $\displaystyle\int_{1}^{\infty} \frac{1}{\sqrt{x}}\,dx$

c $\displaystyle\int_{0}^{\infty} \frac{8x}{\sqrt{1 + x^2}}\,dx$

3 For each of the following, show that the improper integral converges and find its value.

a $\displaystyle\int_{0}^{1} \frac{1}{\sqrt{x}}\,dx$

b $\displaystyle\int_{0}^{\frac{2}{3}} \frac{1}{\sqrt{2 - 3x}}\,dx$

c $\displaystyle\int_{0}^{\ln 3} \frac{e^{x}}{\sqrt{e^{x} - 1}}\,dx$

(P) **4** For each of the following, determine whether the integral converges, and if so, find its value.

a $\displaystyle\int_{-1}^{2} \frac{1}{\sqrt{|x|}}\,dx$

b $\displaystyle\int_{-1}^{3} \frac{x - 1}{\sqrt{3 + 2x - x^2}}\,dx$

c $\displaystyle\int_{0}^{\pi} \tan x\,dx$

E **5 a** Find $\int \dfrac{1}{(7-3x)^2}\,dx$. **(2 marks)**

b Hence show that $\int_{-\infty}^{2} \dfrac{1}{(7-3x)^2}\,dx$ converges and find its value. **(3 marks)**

Watch out Make sure you show the limiting process clearly in your working.

E **6 a** Find $\int x^2 e^{x^3}\,dx$. **(2 marks)**

b Hence show that $\int_{-\infty}^{1} x^2 e^{x^3}\,dx$ converges and find its value. **(3 marks)**

E **7 a** Find $\int \dfrac{\ln x}{x}\,dx$. **(3 marks)**

b Hence show that $\int_{1}^{\infty} \dfrac{\ln x}{x}\,dx$ is divergent. **(3 marks)**

E **8 a** Find $\int (\ln x)^2\,dx$. **(2 marks)**
Hence show that:

b $\int_{0}^{1} (\ln x)^2\,dx$ is convergent. **(2 marks)**

c $\int_{0}^{\infty} (\ln x)^2\,dx$ is divergent. **(2 marks)**

E **9** Evaluate $\int_{0}^{2} \dfrac{6x}{\sqrt[3]{4-x^2}}\,dx$. **(4 marks)**

E/P **10** Evaluate $\int_{-2}^{2} \dfrac{\sqrt{2-x}-3\sqrt{2+x}}{\sqrt{4-x^2}}\,dx$. **(5 marks)**

E/P **11** The diagram shows the curve with equation $y = \ln x$.

Find the shaded area enclosed by the curve and the coordinate axes. You may assume that $x \ln x \to 0$ as $x \to 0$. **(5 marks)**

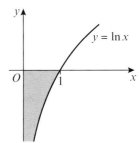

E **12 a** Explain why $\int_{0}^{\frac{\pi}{2}} \tan x\,dx$ is an improper integral. **(1 mark)**

b Show that $\int_{0}^{\frac{\pi}{2}} \tan x\,dx$ is divergent. **(3 marks)**

E/P **13** A student writes the following working to evaluate $\int_0^\pi \sec^2 x \, dx$.

$$\int_0^\pi \sec^2 x \, dx = [\tan x]_0^\pi$$
$$= \tan \pi - \tan 0$$
$$= 0 - 0 = 0$$

a Explain the mistake that the student has made. **(1 mark)**

b Show that $\int_0^\pi \sec^2 x \, dx$ is divergent. **(4 marks)**

E/P **14** Find all $a \in \mathbb{R}$ for which $\int_1^\infty \frac{1}{x^a} \, dx$ converges and find its value in the case when it converges. **(7 marks)**

E/P **15 a** Show that $\int_0^k \frac{1}{2x^2 + 3x + 1} \, dx = \ln\left(\frac{2k+1}{k+1}\right)$, where $k \geqslant 0$. **(4 marks)**

Problem-solving

When an integral is undefined at one or more points within the interval of integration, you need to split the integral and consider each part separately.

b Hence find the exact value of $\int_0^\infty \frac{1}{2x^2 + 3x + 1} \, dx$. **(3 marks)**

Challenge

Show that $\int_0^\infty e^{-x} \sin^2 x \, dx = \frac{2}{5}$

3.2 The mean value of a function

You can find the mean of a finite set of values by adding them up, and dividing by the number of values:

$$\bar{y} = \frac{1}{n}(y_1 + y_2 + y_3 + \dots + y_n)$$

You can extend this definition to evaluate the **mean value** (or **average value**) of a function on a given interval $[a, b]$. In this case, the function takes an infinite number of values, so you represent their sum by integrating the function between a and b, and you represent the 'number of values' by the width of the interval, $b - a$.

■ **The mean value of the function f(x) over the interval [a, b], is given by** $\dfrac{1}{b-a}\displaystyle\int_a^b \textbf{f}(x)\,\textbf{d}x.$

Notation The mean value of f(x) is sometimes written as $\bar{f}$, $\bar{y}$ or y_m.

You can think of the mean value geometrically by considering the area, A, bounded by the curve $y = f(x)$, the x-axis and the lines $x = a$ and $x = b$. If you were to draw a rectangle with its base on the interval $[a, b]$ and height $\bar{f}$, then the area of the rectangle would be equal to A.

The area of the rectangle is $(b - a)\bar{f}$. Setting this equal to the area under the curve gives:

$$(b - a)\bar{f} = \int_a^b f(x)\, dx$$

$$\Rightarrow \bar{f} = \frac{1}{b - a}\int_a^b f(x)\, dx$$

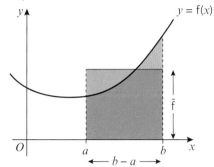

Example 4

Find the mean value of $f(x) = \dfrac{4}{\sqrt{2 + 3x}}$ over the interval $[2, 6]$.

$\displaystyle\int_2^6 \frac{4}{\sqrt{2 + 3x}}\, dx = 4\int_2^6 (2 + 3x)^{-\frac{1}{2}}\, dx$

$\qquad = \frac{8}{3}\left[(2 + 3x)^{\frac{1}{2}}\right]_2^6$ ──────── Using the reverse chain rule, if $y = (2 + 3x)^{\frac{1}{2}}$ then $\dfrac{dy}{dx} = \frac{3}{2}(2 + 3x)^{-\frac{1}{2}}$

$\qquad = \frac{8}{3}(\sqrt{20} - \sqrt{8})$

$\qquad = \frac{16}{3}(\sqrt{5} - \sqrt{2})$ ──────── Simplify.

So the mean value of $f(x)$ on $[2, 6]$ is

$\dfrac{1}{6 - 2}\displaystyle\int_6^2 \frac{4}{\sqrt{2 + 3x}}\, dx = \frac{1}{4}\left(\frac{16}{3}(\sqrt{5} - \sqrt{2})\right)$

$\qquad\qquad = \frac{4}{3}(\sqrt{5} - \sqrt{2})$ ──────── Apply $\dfrac{1}{b - a}\displaystyle\int_a^b f(x)\, dx$.

Example 5

$f(x) = \dfrac{4}{1 + e^x}$

a Show that the mean value of $f(x)$ over the interval $[\ln 2, \ln 6]$ is $\dfrac{4\ln\frac{9}{7}}{\ln 3}$

b Use the answer to part **a** to find the mean value over the interval $[\ln 2, \ln 6]$ of $f(x) + 4$.

c Use geometric considerations to write down the mean value of $-f(x)$ over the interval $[\ln 2, \ln 6]$.

a Integrate $\displaystyle\int_{\ln 2}^{\ln 6} \frac{4}{1 + e^x}\, dx$ using substitution.

Let $u = e^x$

$\dfrac{du}{dx} = e^x \Rightarrow dx = \dfrac{du}{u}$

$x = \ln 2 \Rightarrow u = e^{\ln 2} = 2$ ──────── Calculate the limits in the form $u = \ldots$

$x = \ln 6 \Rightarrow u = e^{\ln 6} = 6$

$$\int_{x=\ln2}^{x=\ln6} \frac{4}{1 + e^x}\,dx = \int_{u=2}^{u=6} \left(\frac{4}{1+u}\right)\left(\frac{du}{u}\right)$$

Transform the integral by substituting $u = e^x$ and $\frac{du}{dx} = e^x$ and substituting the limits.

$$= 4\int_2^6 \frac{1}{(1+u)u}\,du$$

Using partial fractions:

$$\frac{1}{u(1+u)} = \frac{A}{u} + \frac{B}{1+u}$$

To calculate $4\int_2^6 \frac{1}{(1+u)u}\,du$ it is necessary to use partial fractions.

So $A(1+u) + Bu = 1$

When $u = 0$, $A = 1$.

Equating u terms, $A + B = 0$, so $B = -1$.

Find the values of A and B.

$$4\int_2^6 \frac{1}{(1+u)u}\,du = 4\int_2^6 \left(\frac{1}{u} - \frac{1}{1+u}\right)du$$

$$= 4[\ln u - \ln(u + 1)]_2^6$$

Integrate with respect to u.

$$= 4((\ln 6 - \ln 7) - (\ln 2 - \ln 3))$$

Evaluate the integral using the limits.

$$= 4\ln\frac{18}{14}$$

$$= 4\ln\frac{9}{7}$$

Simplify using the laws of logarithms.

So the mean value of f on [ln 2, ln 6] is

$$\frac{1}{\ln 6 - \ln 2}\left(4\ln\frac{9}{7}\right) = \frac{4\ln\frac{9}{7}}{\ln 3}$$

Find $\frac{1}{b-a}\int_a^b f(x)\,dx$ and use the laws of logarithms to simplify.

b $\int_{\ln2}^{\ln6}\left(\frac{4}{1+e^x} + 4\right)dx = \int_{\ln2}^{\ln6} \frac{4}{1+e^x}\,dx + \int_{\ln2}^{\ln6} 4\,dx$

The original integral can be separated.

$$\int_{\ln2}^{\ln6} 4\,dx = [4x]_{\ln2}^{\ln6}$$

$$= 4(\ln 6 - \ln 2)$$

$$= 4\ln 3$$

Calculate the new integral.

Calculating the mean value,

$$\frac{1}{\ln3}\int_{\ln2}^{\ln6}\left(\frac{4}{1+e^x} + 4\right)dx$$

$$= \frac{1}{\ln3}\int_{\ln2}^{\ln6} \frac{4}{1+e^x}\,dx + \frac{1}{\ln3}\int_{\ln2}^{\ln6} 4\,dx$$

$$= \frac{4\ln\frac{9}{7}}{\ln 3} + \frac{1}{\ln3}(4\ln 3)$$

$$= \frac{4\ln\frac{9}{7}}{\ln 3} + 4$$

Problem-solving

Every value of f(x) in the interval has increased by 4, so the mean value has increased by 4.

c $-f(x)$ is a reflection in the x-axis of f(x).

The mean value of f(x) over the interval [ln 2, ln 6] was $\frac{4\ln\frac{9}{7}}{\ln 3}$

Therefore, the mean value of $-f(x)$ over the interval [ln 2, ln 6] is $-\frac{4\ln\frac{9}{7}}{\ln 3}$

In the example above, you saw that geometric considerations can be used to find mean values of transformed functions, if you already know the mean value of the original function on the same interval.

If the function f(x) has mean value $\bar{f}$ over the interval [a, b], and k is a real constant, then:

- f(x) + k has mean value $\bar{f}$ + k over the interval [a, b]
- kf(x) has mean value $k\bar{f}$ over the interval [a, b]
- −f(x) has mean value −$\bar{f}$ over the interval [a, b].

Watch out You cannot deduce the mean value of f(−x) or f(kx) in this way.

Exercise 3B

1 For each of the following functions f(x), find the mean value of f(x) on [0, 1].

   a f(x) = 1   **b** f(x) = $\dfrac{1}{x+1}$ **c** f(x) = e^x + 1

2 Find the exact mean value of f(x) over the given interval.

   a f(x) = $\dfrac{e^{3x}}{e^{3x}+1}$; [0, 2]   **b** f(x) = $\cos^3 x \sin^2 x$; $\left[0, \dfrac{\pi}{2}\right]$

   c f(x) = xe^{-x}; [1, 3]   **d** f(x) = $\dfrac{5}{(x+2)(2x+1)}$; [0, 3]

   e f(x) = $(\sec x - \cos x)^2$; $\left[0, \dfrac{\pi}{4}\right]$.

3 f(x) = $x^3 - 3x^2 - 24x + 100$

   a Find the coordinates of the turning points of f(x).

   b Sketch the graph of y = f(x).

   c Without calculation, state an upper and lower bound on the mean value of the function on the interval [−2, 4], giving a reason for your answer.

   d Calculate the exact mean value of f(x) over the interval [−2, 4].

(E) 4 Find the exact mean value of f(x) = $\dfrac{\sin x \cos x}{\cos 2x + 2}$ over the interval $\left[0, \dfrac{\pi}{2}\right]$. **(4 marks)**

(E) 5 Find the exact mean value of f(x) = $x\sqrt{x+4}$ over the interval [0, 5]. **(4 marks)**

(E) 6 Find the exact mean value of f(x) = $x \sin 2x$ over the interval $\left[0, \dfrac{\pi}{3}\right]$. **(4 marks)**

(E/P) 7 f(x) = $\dfrac{5x}{(2x-1)(x+2)}$

   a Show that the mean value of f(x) over the interval [1, 5] is $\frac{1}{4}\ln\frac{49}{3}$ **(4 marks)**

   b Hence, or otherwise, find the mean value over the interval [1, 5] of f(x) + ln k where k is a positive constant, giving your answer in the form $p \ln q$, where p and q are constants and q is in terms of k. **(2 marks)**

(E/P) 8 f(x) = $x(x^2 - 4)^4$

   a Show that the mean value of f(x) over the interval [0, 2] is $\frac{256}{5}$ **(3 marks)**

   b Use the answer to part **a** to find the mean value over the interval [0, 2] of −2f(x). **(2 marks)**

(E/P) 9 f(x) = $\ln(kx)$, where k is a positive constant.

   Given that the mean value of f(x) on the interval [0, 2] is −2, find the value of k. **(4 marks)**

(P) **10** Prove that if f(x) has mean value m on the interval [a, b], then f(x) + c has mean value m + c.

(E/P) **11** $f(x) = \dfrac{1}{\sqrt{2 - x}}$

Watch out This is an improper integral.

Find the exact mean value of f(x) on the interval [0, 2]. **(6 marks)**

(P) **12** Use geometric reasoning to explain why the mean value of f(x) = $\sin^5 x$ on the interval [0, 2π] is 0.

(E/P) **13** $f(x) = \dfrac{\cos x}{(2 + \sin x)^2}$

    a Find $\int f(x)\,dx$. **(4 marks)**

    b Hence show that the mean value of f(x) over the interval $\left[0, \dfrac{5\pi}{3}\right]$ is $-\dfrac{3}{130\pi}(3 + 4\sqrt{3})$. **(2 marks)**

    c Hence, or otherwise, find the mean value, over the interval $\left[0, \dfrac{5\pi}{3}\right]$, of f($x$) + 3$x$. **(3 marks)**

(P) **14 a** Sketch a graph of f(x) = 1 − 3x − 2x^2, finding the coordinates of any turning points.

    b Calculate $\displaystyle\int_a^{a+1} f(x)\,dx$ for $a \in \mathbb{R}$.

    c Find the maximum possible mean value of f(x) on any real interval of length 1.

3.3 Differentiating inverse trigonometric functions

You can differentiate the inverse trigonometric functions implicitly.

Example 6

Show that $\dfrac{d}{dx}(\arcsin x) = \dfrac{1}{\sqrt{1 - x^2}}$

Use $y = \sin(\arcsin x) = x$.

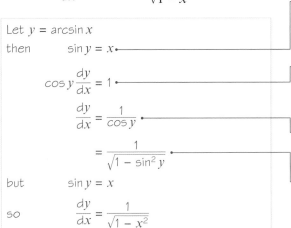

Let $y = \arcsin x$

then $\quad \sin y = x$

$\cos y \dfrac{dy}{dx} = 1$

$\dfrac{dy}{dx} = \dfrac{1}{\cos y}$

$= \dfrac{1}{\sqrt{1 - \sin^2 y}}$

but $\quad \sin y = x$

so $\quad \dfrac{dy}{dx} = \dfrac{1}{\sqrt{1 - x^2}}$

Differentiate implicitly. You could also differentiate $x = \sin y$ with respect to y then use $\dfrac{dy}{dx} = \dfrac{1}{\dfrac{dx}{dy}}$

← **Pure Year 2, Section 9.6**

Divide by $\cos y$.

Use $\cos^2 y = 1 - \sin^2 y$ and that $\cos y \geqslant 0$ when y is in the range of arcsin, i.e. $-\dfrac{\pi}{2} \leqslant y \leqslant \dfrac{\pi}{2}$

Problem-solving

Alternatively, since $\dfrac{dy}{dx} = \pm\dfrac{1}{\sqrt{1 - x^2}}$, you can conclude the sign is positive since the graph of $y = \arcsin x$ shows that the gradient is positive at all points x.

You can use similar methods to obtain the following standard results.

- $\dfrac{d}{dx}(\arcsin x) = \dfrac{1}{\sqrt{1 - x^2}}$

- $\dfrac{d}{dx}(\arccos x) = -\dfrac{1}{\sqrt{1 - x^2}}$

- $\dfrac{d}{dx}(\arctan x) = \dfrac{1}{1 + x^2}$

You should learn these results, but also be able to derive them as in the example above.

Notice that $\dfrac{d}{dx}(\arcsin x) = -\dfrac{d}{dx}(\arccos x)$.

Links Recall the domain and range of each of these inverse trigonometric functions:

Function	Domain	Range
$\arcsin x$	$[-1, 1]$	$\left[-\dfrac{\pi}{2}, \dfrac{\pi}{2}\right]$
$\arccos x$	$[-1, 1]$	$[0, \pi]$
$\arctan x$	$(-\infty, \infty)$	$\left(-\dfrac{\pi}{2}, \dfrac{\pi}{2}\right)$

← Pure Year 2, Chapter 6

Example 7

Given $y = \arcsin x^2$, find $\dfrac{dy}{dx}$

a using implicit differentiation

b using the chain rule and the formula for $\dfrac{d}{dx}\arcsin x$.

a $\sin y = x^2$ ——— Use $\sin(\arcsin x) = x$.

$\cos y \dfrac{dy}{dx} = 2x$ ——— Differentiate.

$\dfrac{dy}{dx} = \dfrac{2x}{\cos y}$ ——— Divide by $\cos y$.

$\dfrac{dy}{dx} = \dfrac{2x}{\sqrt{1 - \sin^2 y}}$ ——— Use $\cos^2 y = 1 - \sin^2 y$ and that $\cos y \geqslant 0$ when y is in the range of arcsin, i.e. $-\dfrac{\pi}{2} \leqslant y \leqslant \dfrac{\pi}{2}$

but $\sin y = x^2$

so $\dfrac{dy}{dx} = \dfrac{2x}{\sqrt{1 - x^4}}$

b Let $t = x^2$, then $y = \arcsin t$ ——— Substitute $t = x^2$ to get $\arcsin x^2$ in the form $\arcsin x$.

Then $\dfrac{dt}{dx} = 2x$ and $\dfrac{dy}{dt} = \dfrac{1}{\sqrt{1 - t^2}}$ ——— Differentiate t and y.

$\dfrac{dy}{dx} = \dfrac{dy}{dt} \times \dfrac{dt}{dx}$ ——— Use the chain rule.

$= \dfrac{2x}{\sqrt{1 - x^4}}$

Example **8**

Given $y = \arctan\left(\dfrac{1-x}{1+x}\right)$, find $\dfrac{dy}{dx}$

$$\tan y = \frac{1-x}{1+x}$$ ———— Use $\tan(\arctan x) = x$.

$$\sec^2 y \frac{dy}{dx} = \frac{-(1+x) - 1(1-x)}{(1+x)^2}$$ ———— Differentiate using the quotient rule on $\dfrac{1-x}{1+x}$

$$= -\frac{2}{(1+x)^2}$$ ———— Simplify.

So $$\frac{dy}{dx} = \frac{1}{\sec^2 y} \times \left(-\frac{2}{(1+x)^2}\right)$$ ———— Divide by $\sec^2 y$.

$$= \frac{1}{1 + \tan^2 y} \times \left(-\frac{2}{(1+x)^2}\right)$$ ———— Use $1 + \tan^2 y \equiv \sec^2 y$.

$$= \frac{1}{\left(1 + \dfrac{1-x}{1+x}\right)^2} \times \left(-\frac{2}{(1+x)^2}\right)$$ ———— Substitute $\tan y = \dfrac{1-x}{1+x}$

$$= \frac{(1+x)^2}{(1+x)^2 + (1-x)^2} \times \left(-\frac{2}{(1+x)^2}\right)$$ ———— Cancel $(1+x)^2$.

$$= -\frac{2}{2 + 2x^2}$$

$$= -\frac{1}{1 + x^2}$$

Problem-solving

You could also use the chain rule and the formula for $\dfrac{d}{dx}(\arctan x)$.

Exercise **3C**

1 Use implicit differentiation to differentiate the following functions.

   a $\arctan x$ **b** $\arccos x$

   c $\arccos x^2$ **d** $\arctan(x^3 + 3x)$

   e $\arcsin\left(\dfrac{1}{x}\right)$

Hint You can check your answers by using the chain rule as well as the results stated earlier in the section.

2 Differentiate $y = (\arccos x)(\arcsin x)$

E 3 Differentiate $y = \dfrac{1 + \arctan x}{1 - \arctan x}$ **(4 marks)**

E/P 4 $f(x) = \arccos x + \arcsin x$

    By considering $\int f'(x)\, dx$, prove that $f(x) = \dfrac{\pi}{2}$ for all values of x.   **(4 marks)**

5 Differentiate with respect to x:

   a $\arccos 2x$ **b** $\arctan \dfrac{x}{2}$ **c** $\arcsin 3x$ **d** $\operatorname{arccot}(x + 1)$

   e $\arcsin(1 - x^2)$ **f** $\arccos x^2$ **g** $e^x \arccos x$ **h** $\arcsin x \cos x$

   i $x^2 \arccos x$ **j** $e^{\arctan x}$

(E) **6** Given that $\tan y = x \arctan x$, find $\dfrac{\mathrm{d}y}{\mathrm{d}x}$ **(4 marks)**

(E) **7** Given that $y = \arcsin x$, prove that

$$(1 - x^2)\frac{\mathrm{d}^2 y}{\mathrm{d}x^2} - x\frac{\mathrm{d}y}{\mathrm{d}x} = 0$$ **(6 marks)**

8 Find an equation of the tangent to the curve with equation $y = \arcsin 2x$ at the point where $x = \frac{1}{4}$

9 Find the derivatives of the following functions.

  a $(\arctan x)^2$ **b** $\dfrac{1}{\arcsin x}$ **c** $\arctan(\arctan x)$

(P) **10** Sketch the graphs of the following:

  a $\arcsin(\arcsin x)$ **b** $\arccos(\arccos x)$ **c** $\arctan(\arctan x)$

(P) **11** Prove each of the following:

  a $\sin(\arccos x) = \sqrt{1 - x^2}$ **b** $\cos(\arctan x) = \dfrac{1}{\sqrt{1 + x^2}}$

  c $\sec(\arccos x) = \dfrac{1}{x}$ **d** $\sin(\text{arcsec } x) = \sqrt{1 - \dfrac{1}{x^2}}$

> **Hint** When taking a square root, you should consider the definitions or graphs of the inverse trigonometric functions to determine the sign.

3.4 Integrating with inverse trigonometric functions

You can use the results from the previous section to integrate functions of the forms $\dfrac{1}{a^2 + x^2}$ and $\dfrac{1}{\sqrt{a^2 - x^2}}$

Example 9

By using an appropriate substitution, show that $\displaystyle\int \frac{1}{\sqrt{a^2 - x^2}}\,\mathrm{d}x = \arcsin\left(\frac{x}{a}\right) + c$, where a is a positive constant and $|x| < a$.

$$\int \frac{1}{\sqrt{a^2 - x^2}}\,\mathrm{d}x = \int \frac{1}{\sqrt{a^2\left(1 - \left(\frac{x}{a}\right)^2\right)}}\,\mathrm{d}x$$

$$= \frac{1}{a}\int \frac{1}{\sqrt{1 - \left(\frac{x}{a}\right)^2}}\,\mathrm{d}x$$

$$= \int \frac{1}{\sqrt{1 - u^2}}\,\mathrm{d}u \quad\longleftarrow\quad \text{Use the substitution } u = \frac{x}{a} \text{ and } \mathrm{d}u = \frac{\mathrm{d}x}{a}$$

$$= \arcsin u + c \quad\longleftarrow\quad \text{Recall that } \frac{\mathrm{d}}{\mathrm{d}x}(\arcsin x) = \frac{1}{\sqrt{1 - x^2}}$$

$$= \arcsin\left(\frac{x}{a}\right) + c$$

The following two results are given in the formula booklet. You can quote them when calculating other integrals, but you should also be able to derive them using substitution as in the example above.

- $\int \dfrac{1}{a^2 + x^2}\,dx = \dfrac{1}{a}\arctan\left(\dfrac{x}{a}\right) + c,\ a > 0,\ |x| < a$

- $\int \dfrac{1}{\sqrt{a^2 - x^2}}\,dx = \arcsin\left(\dfrac{x}{a}\right) + c$

Example 10

Find $\displaystyle\int \dfrac{4}{5 + x^2}\,dx.$

$$\int \dfrac{4}{5 + x^2}\,dx = 4\int \dfrac{1}{5 + x^2}\,dx$$

$$= 4\left(\dfrac{1}{\sqrt{5}}\arctan\left(\dfrac{x}{\sqrt{5}}\right)\right) + c$$

Use $\int \dfrac{1}{a^2 + x^2}\,dx = \dfrac{1}{a}\arctan\left(\dfrac{x}{a}\right) + c$ with $a = \sqrt{5}$.

$$= \dfrac{4}{\sqrt{5}}\arctan\left(\dfrac{x}{\sqrt{5}}\right) + c$$

Example 11

a Find $\displaystyle\int \dfrac{1}{25 + 9x^2}\,dx.$

b Evaluate $\displaystyle\int_{-\frac{\sqrt{3}}{4}}^{\frac{\sqrt{3}}{4}} \dfrac{1}{\sqrt{3 - 4x^2}}$, leaving your answer in terms of π.

a $\displaystyle\int \dfrac{1}{25 + 9x^2}\,dx = \int \dfrac{1}{9\left(\frac{25}{9} + x^2\right)}\,dx$

You need to write $25 + 9x^2$ in the form $k(a^2 + x^2)$.

$$= \dfrac{1}{9}\left(\left(\dfrac{1}{\left(\frac{5}{3}\right)}\right)\arctan\left(\dfrac{x}{\left(\frac{5}{3}\right)}\right)\right) + c$$

Use $\int \dfrac{1}{a^2 + x^2}\,dx = \dfrac{1}{a}\arctan\left(\dfrac{x}{a}\right) + c$ with $a = \dfrac{5}{3}$.

$$= \dfrac{1}{15}\arctan\left(\dfrac{3x}{5}\right) + c$$

b $\displaystyle\int_{-\frac{\sqrt{3}}{4}}^{\frac{\sqrt{3}}{4}} \dfrac{1}{\sqrt{3 - 4x^2}}\,dx = \int_{-\frac{\sqrt{3}}{4}}^{\frac{\sqrt{3}}{4}} \dfrac{1}{\sqrt{4\left(\frac{3}{4} - x^2\right)}}\,dx$

Write $3 - 4x^2$ in the form $k(a^2 - x^2)$.

$$= \dfrac{1}{2}\int_{-\frac{\sqrt{3}}{4}}^{\frac{\sqrt{3}}{4}} \dfrac{1}{\sqrt{\left(\frac{3}{4} - x^2\right)}}\,dx$$

Use $\int \dfrac{1}{\sqrt{a^2 - x^2}}\,dx = \arcsin\left(\dfrac{x}{a}\right) + c$ with $a = \dfrac{\sqrt{3}}{2}$.

$$= \dfrac{1}{2}\left[\arcsin\left(\dfrac{2x}{\sqrt{3}}\right)\right]_{-\frac{\sqrt{3}}{4}}^{\frac{\sqrt{3}}{4}}$$

$$= \dfrac{1}{2}\arcsin\left(\dfrac{1}{2}\right) - \dfrac{1}{2}\arcsin\left(-\dfrac{1}{2}\right)$$

$$= \dfrac{\pi}{12} - \left(-\dfrac{\pi}{12}\right)$$

$-\dfrac{\pi}{2} \leqslant \arcsin x \leqslant \dfrac{\pi}{2}$

so $\arcsin\left(\dfrac{1}{2}\right) = \dfrac{\pi}{6}$ and $\arcsin\left(-\dfrac{1}{2}\right) = -\dfrac{\pi}{6}$

$$= \dfrac{\pi}{6}$$

Example **12**

Find $\int \dfrac{x+4}{\sqrt{1-4x^2}}\,dx$.

$\int \dfrac{x+4}{\sqrt{1-4x^2}}\,dx = \int \dfrac{x}{\sqrt{1-4x^2}}\,dx + 4\int \dfrac{1}{\sqrt{1-4x^2}}\,dx$

To calculate $\int \dfrac{x}{\sqrt{1-4x^2}}\,dx$ use the substitution

$u = 1 - 4x^2$

$du = -8x\,dx$

$\int \dfrac{x}{\sqrt{1-4x^2}}\,dx = -\dfrac{1}{8}\int \dfrac{1}{\sqrt{u}}\,du$

$\qquad\qquad = -\dfrac{1}{8}\int u^{-\frac{1}{2}}\,du$

$\qquad\qquad = -\dfrac{1}{4}u^{\frac{1}{2}} + c$

$\qquad\qquad = -\dfrac{1}{4}\sqrt{1-4x^2} + c$

$4\int \dfrac{1}{\sqrt{1-4x^2}}\,dx = 4\int \dfrac{1}{\sqrt{4\left(\frac{1}{4}-x^2\right)}}\,dx$

$\qquad\qquad = 2\int \dfrac{1}{\sqrt{\frac{1}{4}-x^2}}\,dx$

$\qquad\qquad = 2\arcsin 2x + c$

So $\int \dfrac{x+4}{\sqrt{1-4x^2}}\,dx = 2\arcsin 2x - \dfrac{1}{4}\sqrt{1-4x^2} + c$

Problem-solving

The integral can be split into a fraction which can be integrated using the 'reverse chain rule' and one that looks like those covered above.

Substitute for x and dx and adjust for the constant.

Rewrite in terms of x by resubstituting $u = 1 - 4x^2$.

Write $1 - 4x^2$ in the form $k(a^2 - x^2)$.

Use $\int \dfrac{1}{\sqrt{a^2 - x^2}}\,dx = \arcsin\left(\dfrac{x}{a}\right) + c$ with $a = \dfrac{1}{2}$

Exercise **3D**

1 Use the substitution $x = a\tan\theta$ to show that $\int \dfrac{1}{a^2 + x^2}\,dx = \dfrac{1}{a}\arctan\left(\dfrac{x}{a}\right) + c$.

2 Use the substitution $x = \cos\theta$ to show that $\int \dfrac{1}{\sqrt{1-x^2}}\,dx = -\arccos x + c$.

3 Find:

  a $\int \dfrac{3}{\sqrt{4-x^2}}\,dx$ **b** $\int \dfrac{4}{5+x^2}\,dx$ **c** $\int \dfrac{1}{\sqrt{25-x^2}}\,dx$ **d** $\int \dfrac{1}{\sqrt{x^2-2}}\,dx$

(E) **4** Find $\int \dfrac{1}{4 + 3x^2}\,dx$, giving your answer in the form $A\arctan(Bx) + c$ where c is an arbitrary constant and A and B are constants to be found. **(3 marks)**

(E) **5** Show that $\int \dfrac{1}{\sqrt{3-4x^2}}\,dx = P\arcsin(Qx) + c$ where c is an arbitrary constant and P and Q are constants to be found. **(3 marks)**

6 Evaluate:

   a $\displaystyle\int_1^3 \dfrac{2}{1+x^2}\,dx$ **b** $\displaystyle\int_1^2 \dfrac{3}{\sqrt{1+4x^2}}\,dx$ **c** $\displaystyle\int_{-1}^2 \dfrac{1}{\sqrt{21-3x^2}}\,dx.$

(E) **7** Show that $\displaystyle\int_{\sqrt{2}}^{\sqrt{3}} \dfrac{1}{\sqrt{4-x^2}}\,dx = \dfrac{\pi}{12}$ **(4 marks)**

(E/P) **8** $f(x) = \dfrac{2+3x}{1+3x^2}$

Show that $\int f(x)\,dx = A\arctan(\sqrt{3}x) + B\ln(1+3x^2) + c$ where c is an arbitrary constant and A and B are constants to be found. **(4 marks)**

> **Hint** Start by splitting the fraction into two separate integrals.

(E/P) **9** $f(x) = \dfrac{2x-1}{\sqrt{2-x^2}}$

Find $\int f(x)\,dx$, giving your answer in the form $A\arcsin\left(\dfrac{x}{\sqrt{2}}\right) + B\sqrt{2-x^2} + c$ where c is an arbitrary constant and A and

B are constants to be found. **(4 marks)**

(E/P) **10** $f(x) = \dfrac{8x-3}{4+x^2}$

Find $\int f(x)\,dx$, giving your answer in the form $A\ln(x^2+4) + B\arctan\left(\dfrac{x}{2}\right) + c$ where c is an arbitrary constant and A and B are constants to be found. **(4 marks)**

(E/P) **11** $f(x) = \dfrac{4x-1}{\sqrt{6-5x^2}}$

Show that $\int f(x)\,dx = P\sqrt{6-5x^2} + Q\arcsin\left(\sqrt{\tfrac{5}{6}}\,x\right) + c$ where c is an arbitrary constant and P and Q are constants to be found. **(4 marks)**

(E/P) **12** $f(x) = \dfrac{x+5}{x^2+16}$

   a Find $\int f(x)\,dx$, giving your answer in the form $A\ln(x^2+16) + B\arctan\left(\dfrac{x}{4}\right) + c$ where c is an arbitrary constant and A and B are constants to be found. **(4 marks)**

   b Hence show that the mean value of $f(x)$ over the interval $[0, 4]$ is $\dfrac{1}{4}\left(\dfrac{1}{2}\ln 2 + \dfrac{5\pi}{16}\right)$ **(3 marks)**

   c Hence write down the mean value of $-4f(x)$ over the interval $[0, 4]$. **(1 mark)**

P 13 Use the substitution $x = \frac{2}{3}\tan\theta$ to find $\int \frac{x^2}{9x^2 + 4}\,dx$.

P 14 By using the substitution $x = \frac{1}{2}\sin\theta$, show that $\int_0^{\frac{1}{4}} \frac{x^2}{\sqrt{1 - 4x^2}}\,dx = \frac{1}{192}(2\pi - 3\sqrt{3})$.

Challenge

Given that $x \geqslant 1$, use the substitution $x = \sec\theta$ to find:

a $\int \frac{1}{x\sqrt{x^2 - 1}}\,dx$ **b** $\int \frac{\sqrt{x^2 - 1}}{x}\,dx$

3.5 Integrating using partial fractions

In your A level course you used partial fractions to integrate some rational functions.

Example 13

Prove that

$$\int \frac{1}{a^2 - x^2}\,dx = \frac{1}{2a}\ln\left|\frac{a + x}{a - x}\right| + c$$

where a is a real constant.

Watch out Be careful not to confuse this result with $\int \frac{1}{a^2 + x^2}\,dx = \frac{1}{a}\arctan\left(\frac{x}{a}\right) + c$

$$\int \frac{1}{a^2 - x^2}\,dx = \int \frac{1}{(a + x)(a - x)}\,dx$$

Factorise the denominator in order to integrate using partial fractions. ← **Pure Year 2, Section 11.7**

$$\frac{1}{(a + x)(a - x)} = \frac{A}{a + x} + \frac{B}{a - x}$$

$$A(a - x) + B(a + x) = 1$$

$$x = -a \Rightarrow A = \frac{1}{2a}$$

$$x = a \Rightarrow B = \frac{1}{2a}$$

Split into partial fractions and calculate the values of A and B in terms of a.

$$\int \frac{1}{a^2 - x^2}\,dx = \frac{1}{2a}\int \frac{1}{a + x}\,dx + \frac{1}{2a}\int \frac{1}{a - x}\,dx$$

$$= \frac{1}{2a}\ln|a + x| - \frac{1}{2a}\ln|a - x| + c$$

Integrate using the reverse chain rule.

$$= \frac{1}{2a}\ln\left|\frac{a + x}{a - x}\right| + c$$

Simplify using the law of logarithms.

If the denominator of a partial fraction includes a quadratic factor of the form $(x^2 + c)$, $c > 0$, you cannot write it as a product of linear factors with real coefficients.

However, you can still write it in partial fractions, where the partial fraction corresponding to the quadratic factor has a linear numerator and quadratic denominator.

So $\dfrac{20}{(x + 3)(x^2 + 1)} = \dfrac{A}{x + 3} + \dfrac{Bx + C}{x^2 + 1}$

$20 = A(x^2 + 1) + (Bx + C)(x + 3)$ —————— Find the values of A, B and C by multiplying both sides by $(x + 3)(x^2 + 1)$.

Set $x = -3$: $20 = 10A \Rightarrow A = 2$ —————— Set $x = -3$ so that $(Bx + C)(x + 3) = 0$

$A + B = 0 \Rightarrow B = -2$ —————— Equate coefficients of x^2 on each side.

$3B + C = 0 \Rightarrow C = 6$ —————— Equate coefficients of x on each side.

So $\dfrac{20}{(x + 3)(x^2 + 1)} = \dfrac{2}{x + 3} + \dfrac{6 - 2x}{x^2 + 1}$

You can use the techniques from the previous section to integrate the second fraction on the right-hand side.

Example 14

Show that $\displaystyle\int \dfrac{1 + x}{x^3 + 9x}\, dx = A\ln\left(\dfrac{x^2}{x^2 + 9}\right) + B\arctan\left(\dfrac{x}{3}\right) + c$, where A and B are constants to be found.

$\displaystyle\int \dfrac{1 + x}{x^3 + 9x}\, dx = \int \dfrac{1 + x}{x(x^2 + 9)}\, dx = \int \left(\dfrac{A}{x} + \dfrac{Bx + C}{x^2 + 9}\right) dx$ —————— Separate into partial fractions to facilitate integration.

$A(x^2 + 9) + Bx^2 + Cx = x + 1$

Equate x^2 terms: $A + B = 0$

Equate x terms: $C = 1$ —————— Calculate the values of the coefficients by equating like terms.

Equate constant terms: $9A = 1 \Rightarrow A = \tfrac{1}{9}, B = -\tfrac{1}{9}$

$\displaystyle\int \dfrac{1 + x}{x^3 + 9x}\, dx = \int \left(\dfrac{1}{9x} + \dfrac{-\tfrac{1}{9}x + 1}{x^2 + 9}\right) dx$

$\displaystyle = \int \left(\dfrac{1}{9x} - \dfrac{x - 9}{9(x^2 + 9)}\right) dx$

$\displaystyle = \dfrac{1}{9}\int \dfrac{1}{x}\, dx - \dfrac{1}{9}\int \dfrac{x}{x^2 + 9}\, dx + \int \dfrac{1}{x^2 + 9}\, dx$ —————— Separate into 3 fractions and integrate each separately.

$\displaystyle = \dfrac{1}{9}\ln x - \dfrac{\tfrac{1}{9}\ln(x^2 + 9)}{2} + \dfrac{1}{3}\arctan\left(\dfrac{x}{3}\right) + c$ —————— Calculate the second integral using the reverse chain rule.

$\displaystyle = \dfrac{1}{9}\ln x - \dfrac{1}{18}\ln(x^2 + 9) + \dfrac{1}{3}\arctan\left(\dfrac{x}{3}\right) + c$ —————— Calculate the third integral using $\displaystyle\int \dfrac{1}{a^2 + x^2}\, dx = \dfrac{1}{a}\arctan\left(\dfrac{x}{a}\right) + c$ with $a = 3$.

$\displaystyle = \dfrac{1}{18}(2\ln x - \ln(x^2 + 9)) + \dfrac{1}{3}\arctan\left(\dfrac{x}{3}\right) + c$

$\displaystyle = \dfrac{1}{18}\ln\left(\dfrac{x^2}{x^2 + 9}\right) + \dfrac{1}{3}\arctan\left(\dfrac{x}{3}\right) + c$ —————— Simplify using the laws of logarithms.

Example 15

a Express $\dfrac{x^4 + x}{x^4 + 5x^2 + 6}$ as partial fractions.

b Hence find $\displaystyle\int \dfrac{x^4 + x}{x^4 + 5x^2 + 6}\,\mathrm{d}x$.

a $x^4 + 5x^2 + 6 = (x^2 + 2)(x^2 + 3)$

So $\dfrac{x^4 + x}{(x^2 + 2)(x^2 + 3)} \equiv A + \dfrac{Bx + C}{x^2 + 2} + \dfrac{Dx + E}{x^2 + 3}$

$x^4 + x \equiv A(x^2 + 2)(x^2 + 3)$
$\qquad + (Bx + C)(x^2 + 3) + (Dx + E)(x^2 + 2)$

$A = 1$

$B + D = 0$

$3B + 2D = 1$

So $B = 1$ and $D = -1$

$5A + C + E = 0$

$6A + 3C + 2E = 0$

So $C = 4$ and $E = -9$

So $\dfrac{x^4 + x}{x^4 + 5x^2 + 6} \equiv 1 + \dfrac{x + 4}{x^2 + 2} - \dfrac{x + 9}{x^2 + 3}$

Start by factorising the denominator. Since $x^4 + 5x^2 + 6$ does not contain an x^3 term or an x term, you can write it as $u^2 + 5u + 6$ where $u = x^2$.

The numerator and denominator both have degree 4, so this is an **improper fraction**. You will need a constant term, and terms with denominators $x^2 + 2$ and $x^2 + 3$.

Equate coefficients of x^4.

Equate coefficients of x^3 and x.

Equate coefficients of x^2 and constant terms, and use $A = 1$.

Problem-solving

There are other ways of determining the coefficients. You could find $A = 1$ by writing

$$\dfrac{x^4 + x}{x^4 + 5x^2 + 6} = \dfrac{(x^4 + 5x^2 + 6) - (5x^2 - x + 6)}{x^4 + 5x^2 + 6}$$

$$= 1 - \dfrac{5x^2 - x + 6}{x^4 + 5x^2 + 6}$$

Methods such as this are often quicker than using polynomial long division. You could also substitute $x = \mathrm{i}\sqrt{2}$ and $x = \mathrm{i}\sqrt{3}$ to eliminate terms.

b Using the partial fraction decomposition:

$$\int \frac{x^4 + x}{(x^2 + 2)(x^2 + 3)}\,dx = \int 1\,dx + \int \frac{x}{x^2 + 2}\,dx$$

$$+ \int \frac{4}{x^2 + 2}\,dx - \int \frac{x}{x^2 + 3}\,dx - \int \frac{9}{x^2 + 3}\,dx$$

Split the integral up into different parts that can be integrated using inverse trigonometric functions or the reverse chain rule.

$$= x + \frac{1}{2}\ln|x^2 + 2| + \frac{4}{\sqrt{2}}\arctan\left(\frac{x}{\sqrt{2}}\right)$$

$$- \frac{1}{2}\ln|x^2 + 3| - \frac{9}{\sqrt{3}}\arctan\left(\frac{x}{\sqrt{3}}\right) + c$$

Use $\int \frac{f'(x)}{f(x)}\,dx = \ln|f(x)| + c$ and $\int \frac{1}{x^2 + a^2}\,dx = \frac{1}{a}\arctan\left(\frac{x}{a}\right) + c$.

$$= x + \frac{1}{2}\ln\left|\frac{x^2 + 2}{x^2 + 3}\right| + 2\sqrt{2}\arctan\left(\frac{x}{\sqrt{2}}\right)$$

$$- 3\sqrt{3}\arctan\left(\frac{x}{\sqrt{3}}\right) + c$$

Simplify.

Exercise 3E

1 Express the following as partial fractions.

a $\dfrac{1}{(x^2 + 1)(x + 3)}$

b $\dfrac{1}{(x^2 + 2)(x - 1)}$

c $\dfrac{x - 4}{x(x^2 + 7)}$

(E/P) 2 Find $\displaystyle\int \frac{x^2 - 3x}{(x^2 + 6)(x + 2)}\,dx$, giving your answer in the form $A\ln|x + 2| + B\arctan\left(\dfrac{x}{\sqrt{6}}\right) + c$,

where A and B are constants to be found, and c is an arbitrary constant. **(4 marks)**

(E/P) 3 $f(x) = x^4 - x^3 - 4x^2 - 2x - 12$

a Given that $(x + 2)$ is a factor of $f(x)$, fully factorise $f(x)$. **(2 marks)**

b Hence find $\displaystyle\int \frac{x^3 - 20x^2 + 4x - 24}{x^4 - x^3 - 4x^2 - 2x - 12}\,dx$, giving your answer in the form

$\ln \dfrac{\cdot x + 2 \cdot^A}{\cdot x - 3 \cdot^B} + D\arctan\left(\dfrac{x}{\sqrt{2}}\right) + c$, where A, B and D are constants to be found,

and c is an arbitary constant. **(5 marks)**

(E/P) 4 Find $\displaystyle\int \frac{2 - x}{x^3 + 4x}\,dx$, giving your answer in the form $A\ln\left(\dfrac{x^2}{x^2 + 4}\right) + B\arctan\left(\dfrac{x}{2}\right) + c$,

where A and B are constants to be found, and c is an arbitrary constant. **(5 marks)**

(E/P) 5 Find $\displaystyle\int \frac{x^2 + 1}{4x^4 + 9x^2}\,dx$, giving your answer in the form $\dfrac{A}{x} + B\arctan\left(\dfrac{2x}{3}\right) + c$, where A

and B are constants to be found, and c is an arbitary constant. **(5 marks)**

E/P **6** Show that $\int \dfrac{x^3 + 9x^2 + x + 1}{x^4 - 1} \, dx = \ln \dfrac{|x - 1|^A}{|x + 1|^B} + D \arctan x + c$, where A, B and D are

constants to be found, and c is an arbitary constant. **(5 marks)**

E/P **7** $f(x) = x^3 - 4x^2 + 6x - 24$

    a Given that $f(4) = 0$, fully factorise $f(x)$. **(2 marks)**

    b Express $\dfrac{2x^2 - 3x + 24}{x^3 - 4x^2 + 6x - 24}$ in partial fractions. **(2 marks)**

    c Use your answer to part **b** and an appropriate substitution to calculate

    $\int \dfrac{2x^2 - 3x + 24}{x^3 - 4x^2 + 6x - 24} \, dx.$ **(4 marks)**

E/P **8** $f(x) = \dfrac{1}{(x - 2)(2x - 1)}$

    a Calculate $\int f(x) \, dx$. **(3 marks)**

    b Hence show that $\int_{\frac{1}{2}}^{2} \dfrac{1}{(x - 2)(2x - 1)} \, dx$ diverges. **(3 marks)**

E/P **9** **a** Express $\dfrac{x^4 + 5x^2 + 2x}{x^4 + 10x^2 + 24}$ as partial fractions. **(4 marks)**

    b Hence find $\int \dfrac{x^4 + 5x^2 + 2x}{x^4 + 10x^2 + 24} \, dx$. **(5 marks)**

E/P **10** Use the method of partial fractions to find $\int \dfrac{x^2 + 4x + 10}{x^3 + 5x} \, dx$, $x > 0$. **(4 marks)**

E/P **11** Show that $\int_{0}^{2} \dfrac{2}{(x + 1)(x^2 + 1)} \, dx = \frac{1}{4}(\pi + 2\ln 2)$. **(4 marks)**

E/P **12** **a** Express $\dfrac{x^4 + 1}{x(x^2 + 2)^2}$ as partial fractions. **(4 marks)**

    b Hence find $\int \dfrac{x^4 + 1}{x(x^2 + 2)^2} \, dx$. **(5 marks)**

Challenge

Find:

a $\displaystyle\int \dfrac{1}{x^2 - 8x + 8} \, dx$ **b** $\displaystyle\int \dfrac{1}{2x^2 + 4x + 11} \, dx$

Problem-solving

First complete the square in the denominator and then use an appropriate substitution.

Mixed exercise (3)

(E) **1 a** Using the substitution $u = e^x$, find $\int \dfrac{1}{e^x + e^{-x}}\, dx$. **(3 marks)**

   b Hence show that $\displaystyle\int_{-\infty}^{\infty} \dfrac{1}{e^x + e^{-x}}\, dx = \dfrac{\pi}{2}$ **(3 marks)**

(E) **2** Find the exact mean value of $f(x) = \dfrac{1 - \cos x}{\sin^2 x}$ over the interval $\left[\dfrac{\pi}{6}, \dfrac{\pi}{3}\right]$. **(4 marks)**

(E) **3** Show that the exact mean value of $f(x) = x \sin 2x$ over the interval $\left[0, \dfrac{\pi}{2}\right]$ is $\dfrac{1}{2}$ **(4 marks)**

(E) **4 a** Find the derivative of $\arccos x^2$. **(3 marks)**

   b Hence, or otherwise, calculate $\int \dfrac{3x}{\sqrt{16 - x^4}}\, dx$. **(1 mark)**

(E/P) **5** $f(x) = \arctan\left(\dfrac{2x + 3}{x - 1}\right)$

   a Show that $f'(x) = -\dfrac{1}{x^2 + 2x + 2}$ **(4 marks)**

   b Given that $-2 \leqslant x \leqslant 2$, show that $|f'(x)| \leqslant 1$ **(2 marks)**

(P) **6 a** Explain what it means for an integral to be improper.

   b Identify two features of $\displaystyle\int_{0}^{\infty} \dfrac{1}{(x + 1)\sqrt{x}}\, dx$ which make it an improper integral.

   c By differentiating $\arctan\sqrt{x}$, or otherwise, show that $\displaystyle\int_{0}^{\infty} \dfrac{1}{(x + 1)\sqrt{x}}\, dx$ is convergent and find its exact value.

(E/P) **7** $f(x) = \dfrac{1 + 5x}{\sqrt{1 - 5x^2}}$

   Find $\int f(x)\, dx$, giving your answer in the form $A\sqrt{1 - 5x^2} + B\arcsin\left(\sqrt{5}\, x\right) + c$ where c is an arbitrary constant and A and B are constants to be found. **(4 marks)**

(E) **8 a** Show that $\displaystyle\int_{0}^{t} \dfrac{1}{x^2 + 1}\, dx = \arctan t$. **(2 marks)**

   b Hence evaluate:

   i $\displaystyle\int_{0}^{\infty} \dfrac{1}{x^2 + 1}\, dx$ **(2 marks)**

   ii $\displaystyle\int_{-\infty}^{\infty} \dfrac{1}{x^2 + 1}\, dx$ **(2 marks)**

(E/P) **9** $f(x) = \dfrac{1 + 2x}{1 + 4x^2}$

     a Find $\int f(x)\,dx$, giving your answer in the form $A\ln(1 + 4x^2) + B\arctan(2x) + c$
     where c is an arbitrary constant and A and B are constants to be found.   **(4 marks)**

     b Hence find the exact value of $\displaystyle\int_0^{0.5} f(x)\,dx$ **(3 marks)**

(E) **10 a** Show that $\displaystyle\int \dfrac{1}{\sqrt{4 - 9x^2}}\,dx = P\arcsin Qx + c$ where c is an arbitrary constant and P and Q are
     constants to be found.   **(4 marks)**

     b Hence show that $\displaystyle\int_0^{\frac{2}{3}} \dfrac{1}{\sqrt{4 - 9x^2}}\,dx = \dfrac{\pi}{6}$ **(3 marks)**

(P) **11** Use the substitution $x = \sin\theta$ to show that $\displaystyle\int_0^{\frac{1}{2}} \dfrac{x^4}{\sqrt{1 - x^2}}\,dx = \dfrac{(4\pi - 7\sqrt{3})}{64}$

(E/P) **12** $f(x) = \dfrac{x}{1 + x^4}$

     a Use the substitution $u = x^2$ to calculate $\displaystyle\int_0^1 f(x)\,dx$.   **(4 marks)**

     b Hence show that $\displaystyle\int_0^{\infty} f(x)\,dx$ converges and state its value.   **(3 marks)**

(E/P) **13** Show that $\displaystyle\int \dfrac{2x^3 - 2x^2 + 18x + 9}{x^4 + 9x^2}\,dx = A\ln|x| - \dfrac{B}{x} + D\arctan\left(\dfrac{x}{3}\right) + c$, where A, B and D are
     constants to be found.   **(5 marks)**

(E/P) **14** $f(x) = \dfrac{x^2 - 3x + 14}{x^3 - 4x^2 + 2x - 8}$

     a Express $f(x)$ in the form $\dfrac{P}{x - 4} + \dfrac{Q}{x^2 + 2}$, where P and Q are constants to be found.   **(3 marks)**

     b Find $\int f(x)\,dx$, giving your answer in the form $A\ln|x - 4| + B\arctan\left(\dfrac{x}{\sqrt{2}}\right) + c$ where
     A and B are constants to be found.   **(4 marks)**

     c Hence show that $\displaystyle\int_4^{\infty} f(x)\,dx$ diverges.   **(2 marks)**

(E/P) **15** $f(x) = \dfrac{2}{x^3 + x}$

     a Find $\int f(x)\,dx$.   **(4 marks)**

     b Hence show that the mean value of $f(x)$ over the interval $[1, 2]$ is $\ln\dfrac{8}{5}$ **(2 marks)**

     c Hence, or otherwise, find the mean value, over the interval $[1, 2]$, of $2f(x) - \dfrac{6}{x}$
        (3 marks)

Challenge

A function is said to **attain its mean value** on the interval $[a, b]$ if there exists a value $c \in [a, b]$ such that $f(c) = \dfrac{1}{b-a} \displaystyle\int_a^b f(x)\, dx$.

a Show that the function $f(x) = x^3 - 2x + 4$ attains its mean value on the interval $[0, 2]$, and find the exact values of $c \in [0, 2]$ for which $f(c) = \dfrac{1}{2} \displaystyle\int_0^2 f(x)\, dx$.

b Give an example of a function which does not attain its mean value on the interval $[0, 2]$, fully justifying your answer.

Summary of key points

1 The integral $\displaystyle\int_a^b f(x)\, dx$ is **improper** if either:

- one or both of the limits is infinite

- $f(x)$ is undefined at $x = a$, $x = b$ or another point in the interval $[a, b]$.

2 The **mean value** of the function $f(x)$ over the interval $[a, b]$, is given by

$$\frac{1}{b-a} \int_a^b \mathbf{f(x)}\, \mathbf{dx}$$

3 If the function $f(x)$ has mean value $\bar{f}$ over the interval $[a, b]$, and k is a real constant, then:

- $f(x) + k$ has mean value $\bar{f} + k$ over the interval $[a, b]$

- $kf(x)$ has mean value $k\bar{f}$ over the interval $[a, b]$

- $-f(x)$ has mean value $-\bar{f}$ over the interval $[a, b]$.

4
- $\dfrac{d}{dx}(\arcsin x) = \dfrac{1}{\sqrt{1 - x^2}}$

- $\dfrac{d}{dx}(\arccos x) = -\dfrac{1}{\sqrt{1 - x^2}}$

- $\dfrac{d}{dx}(\arctan x) = \dfrac{1}{1 + x^2}$

5
- $\displaystyle\int \dfrac{1}{a^2 + x^2}\, dx = \dfrac{1}{a}\arctan\left(\dfrac{x}{a}\right) + c,\, a > 0,\, |x| < a$

- $\displaystyle\int \dfrac{1}{\sqrt{a^2 - x^2}}\, dx = \arcsin\left(\dfrac{x}{a}\right) + c$

Volumes of revolution

4

Objectives

After completing this chapter you should be able to:

* Find volumes of revolution around the x-axis → **pages 78–80**
* Find volumes of revolution around the y-axis → **pages 81–83**
* Find volumes of revolution for curves defined parametrically → **pages 83–87**
* Model real-life applications of volumes of revolution → **pages 87–89**

Prior knowledge check

1   Evaluate:

   a $\int_{0}^{3} x^2(3x^3 - 6)^2\,dx$

   b $\int_{\frac{\pi}{6}}^{\frac{\pi}{2}} \cos^2 x\,dx$

   c $\int_{0}^{2} x^2 e^{-2x}\,dx$ ← **Pure Year 2, Chapter 11**

2   Find the area of the region bounded by the curve $y = \frac{1}{2}\sec^4 x$, the x-axis, the y-axis and the line $x = 1$.

      ← **Pure Year 2, Chapter 11**

3   The region R is bounded by the curve $y = 4x^2 + 5$, the x-axis and the lines $x = 2$ and $x = 4$. The region is rotated through 2π radians about the x-axis. Find the volume of the object generated.

      ← **Book 1, Chapter 5**

Volumes of revolution can be used to model objects with circular cross-sections. By defining curves parametrically, you can find volumes of a wider range of objects.

→ **Exercise 4D Q4**

4.1 Volumes of revolution around the x-axis

You need to be able to find volumes of revolution of more complicated curves. In this chapter you might need to use any of the functions and integration techniques you encountered in your A level course.

Links You have already encountered volumes of revolution with simpler functions.
← Book 1, Section 5.1

- **The volume of revolution formed when $y = f(x)$ is rotated through 2π radians about the x-axis between $x = a$ and $x = b$ is given by**

  Volume $= \pi \int_a^b y^2 \, dx$

Online Explore volumes of revolution around the x-axis using GeoGebra.

Example 1

The region R is bounded by the curve with equation $y = \sin 2x$, the x-axis and the lines $x = 0$ and $x = \dfrac{\pi}{2}$. Find the volume of the solid formed when region R is rotated through 2π radians about the x-axis.

$V = \pi \int_0^{\frac{\pi}{2}} \sin^2 2x \, dx$ — Use $V = \pi \int_a^b y^2 \, dx$ with $a = 0$, $b \equiv \dfrac{\pi}{2}$ and $y^2 = \sin^2 2x$.

$= \pi \int_0^{\frac{\pi}{2}} \frac{1}{2}(1 - \cos 4x) \, dx$ — Use $\cos 2A \equiv 1 - 2\sin^2 A$
Rearrange to give $\sin^2 A = \ldots$
Note that $2 \times 2x$ gives $4x$ in the cos term.

$= \pi \left[\frac{1}{2}x - \frac{1}{8}\sin 4x \right]_0^{\frac{\pi}{2}}$

$= \left(\dfrac{\pi^2}{4} - 0 \right) - 0$

$= \dfrac{\pi^2}{4}$ — Multiply out and integrate.

Exercise 4A

1 Find the exact volume of the solid generated when each curve is rotated through 2π radians about the x-axis between the given limits.

a $y = \dfrac{2}{x + 1}$ between $x = 0$ and $x = 2$

b $y = \sqrt{\dfrac{4 \sin x}{1 + \cos x}}$ between $x = 0$ and $x = \dfrac{\pi}{2}$

c $y = \sqrt{x} \sec x$ between $x = 0$ and $x = \dfrac{\pi}{4}$

d $y = \sqrt{\dfrac{5x}{10x^2 + 1}}$ between $x = 0$ and $x = 2$

e $y = \dfrac{\sqrt{\ln x}}{x}$ between $x = 1$ and $x = 2$

f $y = \operatorname{cosec} x + \cot x$ between $x = \dfrac{\pi}{3}$ and $x = \dfrac{\pi}{2}$

(E/P) 2 The curve with equation $y = \cos x \sqrt{\sin 2x}$, $0 \leqslant x \leqslant \dfrac{\pi}{2}$ is shown in the diagram.

The finite region enclosed by the curve and the x-axis is shaded. The region is rotated about the x-axis to form a solid of revolution.
Find the volume of the solid generated. **(6 marks)**

$y = \cos x \sqrt{\sin 2x}$

(E/P) **3** The diagram shows the finite region R, which is bounded by the curve $y = \ln x$, the line $x = 3$ and the x-axis.

The region R is rotated through 2π radians about the x-axis. Use integration to find the exact volume of the solid generated. **(7 marks)**

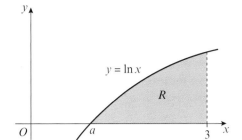

Problem-solving

You will need to find the value of a, where the curve crosses the x-axis

(E) **4 a** Using the substitution $x = 3\sin\theta$, or otherwise, find the exact value of

$$\int_{\frac{3}{2}}^{\frac{3\sqrt{2}}{2}} \frac{1}{x^2\sqrt{9 - x^2}}\,dx \qquad \textbf{(7 marks)}$$

The diagram shows a sketch of part of the curve with equation $y = \dfrac{9}{x(9 - x^2)^{\frac{1}{4}}}$

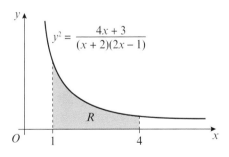

The shaded region R, shown in the diagram, is bounded by the curve, the x-axis and the lines with equations

$x = \dfrac{3}{2}$ and $x = \dfrac{3\sqrt{2}}{2}$. The shaded region R is rotated

through 2π radians about the x-axis to form a solid of revolution.

b Using your answer to part **a**, find the exact volume of the solid of revolution formed. **(2 marks)**

(E/P) **5** The curve with equation $y^2 = \dfrac{4x + 3}{(x + 2)(2x - 1)}$ is shown in the diagram.

The shaded region R, bounded by the lines $x = 1$, $x = 4$, the x-axis and the curve, is rotated $360°$ about the x-axis.

Use calculus to find the exact volume of the solid generated. **(6 marks)**

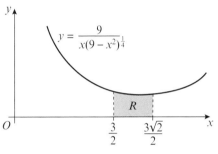

(E/P) **6** The curve shown in the diagram has equation $2y^2 = x\sin x + x$.

a Show that the coordinates of point A are

$\left(\dfrac{3\pi}{2}, 0\right)$. **(1 mark)**

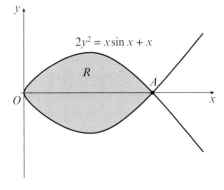

The shaded region R is rotated about the x-axis to generate a solid of revolution.

b Find the volume of the solid generated. **(5 marks)**

(E/P) 7 The curve with equation $y = \dfrac{10}{3(5 + 2x)}$ is shown in the diagram.

The region R bounded by the curve, the x-axis and the lines $x = -1$, $x = 2$ is shown in the diagram.
The region is rotated through $360°$ about the x-axis.

a Find the exact volume of the solid generated.

(6 marks)

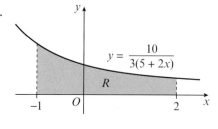

The region S, bounded by the curves $y = \dfrac{10}{3(5 + 2x)}$ and $y = \dfrac{20}{3(5 + 2x)}$, and the lines $x = -1$ and $x = 2$,

is shown in the diagram. The region is rotated through $360°$ about the x-axis.

b Find the exact volume of the solid generated.

(3 marks)

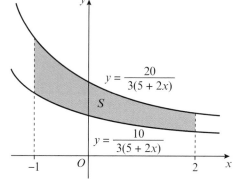

(E/P) 8 The region R is bounded by the curve with equation $y = xe^{-x}$ and the line with equation $y = \frac{1}{4}x$, as shown in the diagram.

The region is rotated through 2π radians about the x-axis.

Find the volume of the solid of revolution formed. Give your answer correct to 3 significant figures.

(8 marks)

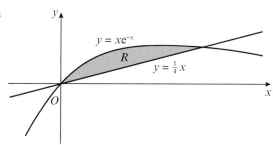

Challenge

The diagram shows the region R, which is bounded by the curve with equation $y = \sin x$, $0 \leqslant x \leqslant \pi$ and the line with equation $y = \dfrac{1}{\sqrt{2}}$.

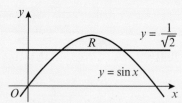

Region R is rotated through 2π radians about the line $y = \dfrac{1}{\sqrt{2}}$.

Show that the solid of revolution formed has area $\dfrac{\pi}{2}(\pi - 3)$.

4.2 Volumes of revolution around the y-axis

You can apply A level integration techniques to volumes of revolution formed when a curve is rotated about the y-axis.

- **The volume of revolution formed when $x = f(y)$ is rotated through 2π radians about the y-axis between $y = a$ and $y = b$ is given by**

  Volume $= \pi \int_a^b x^2 \, dy$

Links When you use this formula you are integrating with respect to y. You might need to rearrange functions to get an expression for x^2 in terms of y.   ← **Book 1, Section 5.2**

Online Explore volumes of revolution around the y-axis using GeoGebra.

Example 2

The diagram shows the curve with equation $y = 4\ln x - 1$. The finite region R, shown in the diagram, is bounded by the curve, the x-axis, the y-axis and the line $y = 4$. Region R is rotated by 2π radians about the y-axis. Use integration to show that the exact value of the volume of the solid generated is $2\pi\sqrt{e}(e^2 - 1)$.

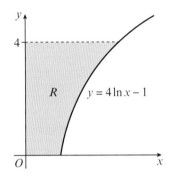

$y = 4\ln x - 1$

$\ln x = \dfrac{y + 1}{4}$

$x = e^{\frac{y+1}{4}} = e^{\frac{y}{4}} e^{\frac{1}{4}}$ ————————————— First rewrite x as a function of y.

$V = \pi \int_0^4 \left(e^{\frac{y}{4}} e^{\frac{1}{4}}\right)^2 dy = \pi e^{\frac{1}{2}} \int_0^4 e^{\frac{y}{2}} dy$ ———— Use $V = \pi \int_a^b x^2 \, dy$ with $a = 0$, $b = 4$ and $x = e^{\frac{y}{4}} e^{\frac{1}{4}}$.

$= 2\pi e^{\frac{1}{2}} \left[e^{\frac{y}{2}}\right]_0^4$ ——————————————— Integrate with respect to y.

$= 2\pi e^{\frac{1}{2}}(e^2 - e^0)$

$= 2\pi\sqrt{e}(e^2 - 1)$ ————————————— Simplify and leave in the correct form.

Exercise 4B

1 Find the exact volume of the solid generated when each curve is rotated through 2π radians about the y-axis between the given limits.

   a $x = e^{2y} - e^{-y}$ between $y = 0$ and $y = 1$

   b $x = \sqrt{y}\, e^{y^2}$ between $y = 0$ and $y = 1$

   c $x = \dfrac{\sqrt{5 - \ln y}}{y}$ between $y = 1$ and $y = 5$

   d $x = \dfrac{1}{\sqrt{y \ln y}}$ between $y = e^4$ and $y = e^9$

(P) 2 Find the exact volume of the solid generated when each curve is rotated through 2π radians about the y-axis between the given limits.

   a $y = \dfrac{1}{x} - 1$ between $y = 0$ and $y = 1$

   b $y = \dfrac{5 - 2x^2}{x^2 - 1}$ between $y = -1$ and $y = 1$

   c $y = 2e^{x^2}$ between $y = 2$ and $y = 4$

   d $y = \arccos \sqrt{x}$ between $y = 0$ and $y = \dfrac{\pi}{2}$

(E/P) **3** The diagram shows the curve with equation $x = \dfrac{1}{2y+1}$

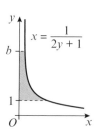

The finite region bounded by the curve, the y-axis and the lines $y = 1$ and $y = b$ is shown in the diagram. The region is rotated through 2π radians about the y-axis to generate a solid of revolution. Given that the volume of the solid generated is $\dfrac{\pi}{10}$, find the value of b. **(5 marks)**

(E/P) **4** The curve with equation $x = \sqrt{y}\sin y$ is shown in the diagram.

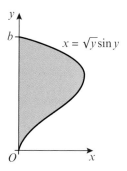

The finite region enclosed by the curve and the y-axis is shaded. The region is rotated through 2π radians about the y-axis.

a Find the value of b. **(1 mark)**

b Find the volume of the solid generated. **(6 marks)**

(E/P) **5** The diagram shows the curve with equation $y = 3\ln(x - 1)$.

The finite region R, shown shaded in the diagram, is bounded by the curve, the x-axis, the y-axis and the line $y = 5$. The region R is rotated by 2π radians about the y-axis. Use integration to find the exact value of the volume of the solid generated. **(5 marks)**

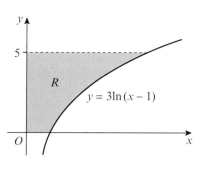

Watch out First rearrange the equation to make x the subject.

(E/P) **6 a** Express $\cos y + \sqrt{3}\sin y$ in the form $R\cos(y - \alpha)$, where $R > 0$ and α is acute. **(4 marks)**

The region R is bounded by the curve with equation $x = \dfrac{1}{\cos y + \sqrt{3}\sin y}$, the y-axis and the lines $y = 0$ and $y = \dfrac{\pi}{3}$

b Using your answer to part **a**, or otherwise, show that the volume of the solid formed when the region R is rotated through 2π radians about the y-axis is $\dfrac{\pi\sqrt{3}}{4}$ **(6 marks)**

(E/P) **7 a** Using the substitution $u = 2^y$, or otherwise, find the exact value of

$$\int_0^1 \frac{2^y}{(2^y + 1)^2}\,\mathrm{d}y \qquad \textbf{(6 marks)}$$

The diagram shows part of the curve with equation $x = \dfrac{\sqrt{2^y}}{2^y + 1}$

The shaded region R, shown in the diagram, is bounded by the curve, the y-axis and the lines $y = 0$ and $y = 1$. The region is rotated through 2π radians about the y-axis to form a solid of revolution.

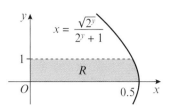

b Using your answer to part **a**, find the exact volume of solid of revolution formed. **(2 marks)**

(E/P) **8 a** By writing a suitable expansion for $\sin 5\theta$, or otherwise, show that

$$\sin^5 \theta \equiv \tfrac{1}{16}(10\sin\theta - 5\sin 3\theta + \sin 5\theta) \qquad \textbf{(3 marks)}$$

The curve shown in the diagram has equation $x = \sin^2 y \sqrt{\sin y}$.

The finite region bounded by the curve, the y-axis and the line $y = \dfrac{\pi}{4}$ is shown in the diagram.

The region is rotated through 2π radians about the y-axis to generate a solid of revolution.

b Show that the volume of the solid generated is $\dfrac{\pi}{15}\left(8 + \dfrac{43\sqrt{2}}{8}\right)$

(7 marks)

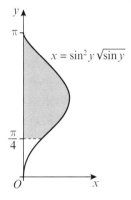

(4.3) ## Volumes of revolution of parametrically defined curves

When the equations of curves are given parametrically, you can adjust the formulae for volumes of revolution by using the chain rule.

Links For a parametric curve, x and y are each given as a function of a parameter, t.
← **Pure Year 2, Chapter 8**

■ **The volume of revolution formed when the parametric curve with equations $x = \mathbf{f}(t)$ and $y = \mathbf{g}(t)$ is rotated through 2π radians about the x-axis between $x = a$ and $x = b$ is given by**

$$\textbf{Volume} = \pi\int_{x=a}^{x=b} y^2\,\mathbf{d}x = \pi\int_{t=q}^{t=p} y^2\,\frac{\mathbf{d}x}{\mathbf{d}t}\,\mathbf{d}t$$

Watch out After you have used the chain rule, you are integrating with respect to the parameter, t. Generally if $x = a$, then $t \neq a$. You can evaluate the definite integral by rewriting the limits of the integral in terms of t.

■ **The volume of revolution formed by rotating the same curve through 2π radians about the y-axis between $y = a$ and $y = b$ is given by**

$$\textbf{Volume} = \pi\int_{y=a}^{y=b} x^2\,\mathbf{d}y = \pi\int_{t=q}^{t=p} x^2\,\frac{\mathbf{d}y}{\mathbf{d}t}\,\mathbf{d}t$$

Example 3

The curve C has parametric equations $x = t(1 + t)$, $y = \dfrac{1}{1 + t}$,

$t \geqslant 0$. The region R is bounded by C, the x-axis and the lines $x = 0$ and $x = 2$. Find the exact volume of the solid formed when R is rotated 2π radians about the x-axis.

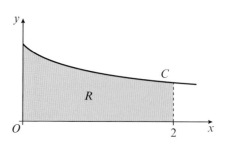

$y = \dfrac{1}{1 + t} \Rightarrow y^2 = \dfrac{1}{(1 + t)^2}$ — Find y^2 and $\dfrac{dx}{dt}$

$x = t + t^2 \Rightarrow \dfrac{dx}{dt} = 1 + 2t$

$x = 0 \Rightarrow t = 0$ — Find the limits in terms of t. You can ignore the second solution to each quadratic equation as the domain of t is given as $t \geqslant 0$.

$x = 2 \Rightarrow t = 1$

$V = \pi \displaystyle\int_0^1 \dfrac{1}{(1 + t)^2}(1 + 2t)\, dt$ — Use $V = \pi \displaystyle\int_p^q y^2 \dfrac{dx}{dt}\, dt$ with $p = 0$, $q = 1$,

$\dfrac{1 + 2t}{(1 + t)^2} \equiv \dfrac{A}{(1 + t)^2} + \dfrac{B}{1 + t}$ $y^2 = \dfrac{1}{(1 + t)^2}$ and $\dfrac{dx}{dt} = 1 + 2t$

$1 + 2t = A + B(1 + t)$

$\Rightarrow B = 2$ and $A = -1$ — Use partial fractions.

So $V = \pi \displaystyle\int_0^1 \left(\dfrac{2}{1 + t} - \dfrac{1}{(1 + t)^2} \right) dt$ — Substitute values of t or compare coefficients.

$= \pi \left[2\ln|1 + t| + \dfrac{1}{1 + t} \right]_0^1$

$= \pi\left((2\ln 2 + \tfrac{1}{2}) - (0 + 1) \right)$

$= \pi(2\ln 2 - \tfrac{1}{2})$

Exercise 4C

1 The curve C is given by the parametric equations $x = t^3$, $y = t^2$, $t \in \mathbb{R}$. The region R bounded by the curve, the coordinate axes and the line $x = 8$ is rotated through $360°$ about the x-axis. Find the volume of the solid of revolution formed.

2 The curve C is defined by parametric equations $x = e^t$, $y = \sqrt{t - 1}$, $t \geqslant 1$.

The finite region bounded by the curve, the x-axis and the lines $x = e^2$ and $x = e^3$ is rotated through 2π radians about the x-axis.

a Write down the values of t corresponding to $x = e^2$ and $x = e^3$.

b Find the volume of the solid of revolution formed.

c Show that a Cartesian equation of C is $y^2 = \ln x - 1$.

d Evaluate $\pi \displaystyle\int_{e^2}^{e^3} (\ln x - 1)\, dx$.

Hint Your answers to parts **b** and **d** should be the same. You can find a volume of revolution for a parametric curve by either integrating with respect to the parameter using $\pi \displaystyle\int y^2 \dfrac{dx}{dt}\, dt$, or by converting to Cartesian form and then using $\pi \displaystyle\int y^2\, dx$. If you convert to Cartesian form, you must remember to convert the limits of integration to values of x.

3 The curve C is defined by the parametric equations $x = \sqrt{1 - \sin\theta}$, $y = \cos\theta$, $0 \leqslant \theta \leqslant 2\pi$.

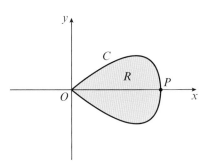

a Show that a Cartesian equation of the curve is $y^2 = 2x^2 - x^4$.

b Find the coordinates of the point P, where the curve intersects the x-axis.

The finite region bounded by the curve is rotated about the x-axis to form a solid of revolution.

c Find the volume of the solid formed.

4 The curve C is given by the parametric equations $x = \tan\theta$, $y = \sec^3\theta$, $0 \leqslant \theta < \dfrac{\pi}{2}$

The region R bounded by the curve, the y-axis and the lines $y = 1$ and $y = 8$ is rotated through 2π radians about the y-axis.

a Find the values of θ corresponding to $y = 1$ and $y = 8$.

b Find the volume of the solid of revolution formed.

c Show that a Cartesian equation of the curve is $x^2 = y^{\frac{2}{3}} - 1$.

d Use $\pi\displaystyle\int_a^b x^2 \, \mathrm{d}y$ to verify your answer to part **b**.

(P) 5 The curve C has parametric equations $x = \sin^4\theta\sqrt{\cos\theta}$, $y = \cos\theta$, $0 \leqslant \theta \leqslant \dfrac{\pi}{2}$

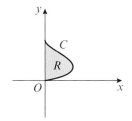

The finite region R bounded by the curve and the y-axis is rotated through $360°$ about the y-axis.

Find the volume of the solid of revolution formed.

(P) 6 The diagram shows the curve C with parametric equations $x = 2t$, $y = t^2$, $-2 \leqslant t \leqslant 2$. The points P and Q correspond to the points where $t = -2$ and 2 respectively.

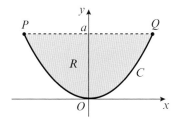

The region R is bounded by the curve and the line $y = a$. Region R is rotated about the y-axis to form a solid of revolution.

Use parametric integration to show that the volume of the solid formed is 32π.

(E/P) **7 a** Find $\int \cos^2\theta \, d\theta$ **(2 marks)**

The diagram shows part of the curve C with parametric

equations $x = \cot\theta$, $y = 4\sin 2\theta$, $0 \leqslant \theta < \dfrac{\pi}{2}$. The finite region

R shown in the diagram is bounded by C, the lines $x = \dfrac{1}{\sqrt{3}}$,

$x = \sqrt{3}$ and the x-axis. Region R is rotated through 2π
radians about the x-axis to form a solid of revolution.

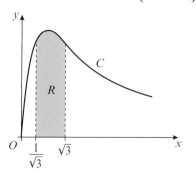

b Show that the volume of the solid of revolution formed
is given by the integral $k\displaystyle\int_a^b \cos^2\theta \, d\theta$, where a, b and k are
constants to be found. **(5 marks)**

c Hence find the exact value for this volume, giving your answer in the form $p\pi^2$,
where p is a constant to be found. **(3 marks)**

(E/P) **8** The curve C has parametric equations $x = \dfrac{1}{2t}$, $y = \ln 2t$, $t \geqslant \dfrac{1}{2}$

The finite region R, shown in the diagram, is bounded by C,
the x-axis, the y-axis and the line $y = a$. Region R is rotated
through 2π radians about the y-axis.

The solid of revolution formed has volume $\dfrac{24\pi}{49}$

Find the exact value of a. **(8 marks)**

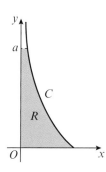

(E/P) **9** The curve C has parametric equations $x = 2\sin t$, $y = t^2$, $0 \leqslant t \leqslant \pi$.

The finite region R, shown in the diagram, is bounded by C and
the y-axis. The shaded region is rotated through 2π radians
about the y-axis. Use calculus to find the exact volume of the
solid generated. **(6 marks)**

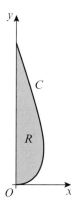

(E/P) **10** The diagram shows the curve C with parametric equations $x = t^2 - 2t$, $y = 1 - t^2$, $-1 \leqslant t \leqslant 1$.

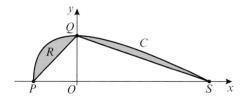

C intersects the coordinate axes at points P, Q and S as shown in the diagram.

The region R is bounded by the curve and the line segments PQ and QS.

Region R is rotated through 2π radians about the x-axis.

Find the exact volume of the solid of revolution. **(8 marks)**

11 The diagram shows part of the curve C with parametric equations $x = e^t$, $y = e^{-2t}$, $t \in \mathbb{R}$.

The region R is bounded by the curve, the y-axis and the lines $y = 1$ and $y = 6$. Region R is rotated through 2π radians about the y-axis.

a Use parametric integration to find the volume of the solid of revolution. **(6 marks)**

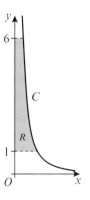

The tangent to the curve at the point $(1, 1)$ is shown on the diagram. The region S is bounded by this tangent, the curve, the y-axis and the line $y = 6$.

b Find the volume of the solid of revolution formed when the region S is rotated through 2π radians about the y-axis. **(3 marks)**

 Modelling with volumes of revolution

Volumes of revolution can be used to model real-life situations.

Example **4**

The diagram shows a model of a goldfish bowl. The cross-section of the model is described by the curve with parametric equations $x = 2\sin t$, $y = 2\cos t + 2$, $\dfrac{\pi}{6} \leqslant t \leqslant \dfrac{11\pi}{6}$, where the units of x and y are in cm. The goldfish bowl is formed by rotating this curve about the y-axis to form a solid of revolution.

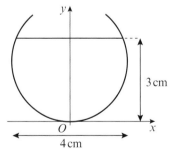

a Find the volume of water required to fill the model to a height of 3 cm.

The real goldfish bowl has a maximum diameter of 48 cm.

b Find the volume of water required to fill the real goldfish bowl to the corresponding height.

a $x = 2\sin t \Rightarrow x^2 = 4\sin^2 t$ — Find x^2 and $\dfrac{dy}{dt}$

$y = 2\cos t + 2 \Rightarrow \dfrac{dy}{dt} = -2\sin t$

$y = 0 \Rightarrow 2\cos t + 2 = 0 \Rightarrow t = \pi$ — Find the limits in terms of t.

$y = 3 \Rightarrow 2\cos t + 2 = 3 \Rightarrow t = \dfrac{\pi}{3}, \dfrac{5\pi}{3}$

Watch out The two possible values of t when $y = 3$ correspond to the two sides of the bowl. Choose one of these, as you need to rotate half of the bowl about the y-axis.

$V = \pi \displaystyle\int_{\pi}^{\frac{5\pi}{3}} 4\sin^2 t(-2\sin t)\,dt$

$= -8\pi \displaystyle\int_{\pi}^{\frac{5\pi}{3}} \sin^3 t\,dt$

Use $V = \pi \displaystyle\int_{p}^{q} x^2 \dfrac{dy}{dt}\,dt$ with $p = \pi$, $q = \dfrac{5\pi}{3}$, $x^2 = 4\sin^2 t$ and $\dfrac{dy}{dt} = -2\sin t$

$= -8\pi \displaystyle\int_{\pi}^{\frac{5\pi}{3}} \sin t(1 - \cos^2 t)\,dt$

$= -8\pi \displaystyle\int_{\pi}^{\frac{5\pi}{3}} (\sin t - \sin t\cos^2 t)\,dt$

Using the identity $\sin^2 t + \cos^2 t \equiv 1$ allows you to integrate $\sin^3 t$.

$= -8\pi \left[-\cos t + \dfrac{1}{3}\cos^3 t \right]_{\pi}^{\frac{5\pi}{3}}$

Integrate $\sin t\cos^2 t$ using the reverse chain rule.

$= -8\pi \left(\left(-\cos\dfrac{5\pi}{3} + \dfrac{1}{3}\cos^3\dfrac{5\pi}{3} \right) - \left(-\cos\pi + \dfrac{1}{3}\cos^3\pi \right) \right)$

$= -8\pi \left(\left(-\dfrac{1}{2} + \dfrac{1}{3}\left(\dfrac{1}{8}\right) \right) - \left(1 - \dfrac{1}{3} \right) \right)$

Substitute the limits.

$= -8\pi \left(-\dfrac{9}{8} \right) = 9\pi$ — Simplify.

b Linear scale factor = 12

Volume scale factor = 12^3 = 1728

Volume in actual tank = 1728 × 9π

= 48 900 cm³ (3 s.f.)

Exercise  4D

(E/P) **1** The diagram shows the curve with equation $x = \dfrac{2000}{20 + y}$, $y > 0$.

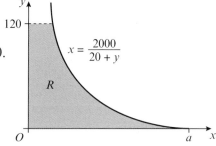

A volcano is modelled as the solid of revolution formed when the region R bounded by the x-axis, the y-axis, the line $y = 120$ and the curve is rotated about the y-axis. The units of x and y are metres.

a Write down the diameter of the base of the volcano according to this model. **(2 marks)**

b Use this model to estimate the volume of the volcano. **(6 marks)**

(E/P) **2** The diagram shows the cross-section of a vase, which has a height of 30 cm.

The vase is formed by rotating the curve C with equation $x^2 = \dfrac{100y}{10y^2 + 1}$,

$0 \leqslant y \leqslant 30$ through 360° about the y-axis. The vase is filled to a height of 20 cm with water. Find the exact volume of water in the vase in the form $p\pi \ln q$ cm³, where p and q are integers to be found. **(6 marks)**

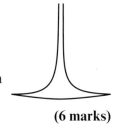

(E/P) **3 a** Prove that $\cos^3\theta \equiv \frac{3}{4}\cos\theta + \frac{1}{4}\cos 3\theta$ **(3 marks)**

The diagram shows the cross-section of a domed tent.
The tent can be modelled by a solid of revolution of a
curve C about the y-axis. Curve C has parametric
equations $x = 50\cos\theta$, $y = 30\sin\theta$, $0 \le \theta \le \dfrac{\pi}{2}$

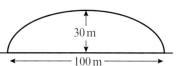

b Find the volume of the tent. **(5 marks)**

(E/P) **4** A scale model of a hot-air balloon is modelled as a solid of
revolution of a curve C about the y-axis. Curve C has

equation $x = \sin y\sqrt{\sin 2y}$, $0 \le y \le \dfrac{\pi}{2}$ where the units of x
and y are in metres.

a Find the volume of the model hot-air balloon. **(5 marks)**

b The real hot-air balloon has a height of 6π metres. Find the volume of this balloon. **(2 marks)**

(E/P) **5** The diagram shows the image of a silver earring, which has a height
of 3 mm. The earring is modelled by a solid of revolution of a curve C
about the y-axis. Curve C has parametric equations $x = 2\sin 2\theta$,
$y = 3\sin\theta$, $0 \le \theta \le \pi$.

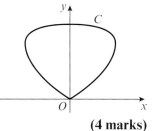

a Show that a Cartesian equation of the curve C is $x^2 = \dfrac{16}{81}y^2(9 - y^2)$ **(4 marks)**

Silver is melted down and cast into a mould to create each earring.

b Using the model, estimate the maximum number of earrings that can be manufactured from
300 mm³ of silver. **(6 marks)**

c Give one reason why this might be:
  i an underestimate
  ii an overestimate. **(2 marks)**

Mixed exercise ④

(E/P) **1 a** Find $\int x\cos 2x\,dx$. **(5 marks)**

b The diagram shows part of the curve C with
equation $y = 2x^{\frac{1}{2}}\sin x$. The shaded region in
the diagram is bounded by the curve, the x-axis
and the line with equation $x = \dfrac{\pi}{2}$. This shaded
region is rotated through 2π radians about the
x-axis to form a solid of revolution. Using
calculus, find the volume of the solid of
revolution formed, giving your answer in
terms of π. **(4 marks)**

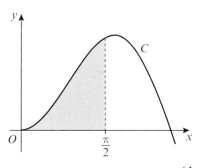

(E) **2 a** Use integration by parts to show that

$$\int_0^{\frac{\pi}{4}} x \sec^2 x \, dx = \frac{\pi}{4} - \frac{1}{2}\ln 2 \qquad \textbf{(5 marks)}$$

The finite region R, bounded by the curve with equation $y = x^{\frac{1}{2}} \sec x$, the line $x = \frac{\pi}{4}$ and the x-axis is shown. Region R is rotated through 2π radians about the x-axis.

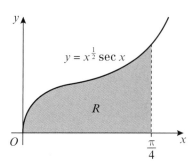

b Find the volume of the solid of revolution generated. **(2 marks)**

(E/P) **3** The diagram shows part of the curve C with equation $y = \dfrac{x+2}{x}$, $x > 0$.

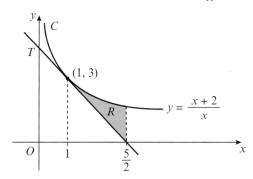

The tangent T to C at the point $(1, 3)$ meets the x-axis at the point $\left(\frac{5}{2}, 0\right)$. The shaded region is bounded by C, the line $x = \frac{5}{2}$ and T, as shown in the diagram.

The region is rotated by 2π radians about the x-axis to generate a solid of revolution.
Find the exact volume of thjis solid. **(10 marks)**

(E/P) **4** The shaded region R, shown in the diagram, is bounded by the curves $y = \sec x - \cos x$ and $y = \operatorname{cosec} x - \sin x$, and by the x-axis. The shaded region R is rotated through 2π radians about the x-axis to form a solid of revolution.

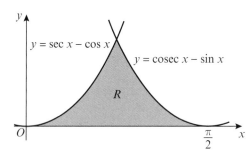

Find the exact volume of the solid. **(9 marks)**

(E/P) **5** The diagram shows part of the curve $x = e^{\frac{1}{2}y} - 2$

The region R is bounded by the curve, the y-axis and the lines $y = 2$ and $y = 4$, as shown in the diagram. Region R is rotated through 2π radians about the y-axis. Use integration to find the exact value of the volume of the solid formed. Leave your answer in the form $\pi(Ae^4 + Be^3 + Ce^2 + De + F)$. **(6 marks)**

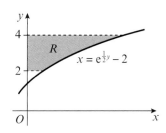

(P) **6** The diagram shows the region R that is bounded by the curve C and the line l.

Curve C has parametric equations $x = 2\sin^2 t, y = 2\cos t, 0 \leqslant t \leqslant \dfrac{\pi}{2}$

Line l is the tangent to the curve C at the point $P\left(\dfrac{3}{2}, 1\right)$.

a Find the Cartesian equation of the line l.

The region R is rotated through 2π radians about the y-axis.

b Find the volume of solid generated.

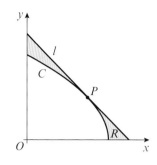

(E) **7** This graph shows, for $0 \leqslant t \leqslant 2$, the curve C with parametric equations

$x = (t + 1)^2, y = \dfrac{1}{2}t^3 + 3$.

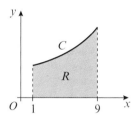

The shaded region R is bounded by curve C and the lines $x = 1$ and $x = 9$.

a Find the area of the region R. **(3 marks)**

The region R is rotated by 2π radians about the x-axis.

b Use integration to find the exact value of the volume of the solid formed. **(5 marks)**

(P) **8** A point on the unit circle has coordinates $(\cos t, \sin t)$. Use parametric integration to show that the volume of the unit sphere is $\dfrac{4\pi}{3}$

(E/P) **9 a** Prove the identity $\sin^3\theta \equiv \dfrac{3}{4}\sin\theta - \dfrac{1}{4}\sin 3\theta$. **(3 marks)**

The diagram shows a rugby ball, which has a length of $30\,\text{cm}$ and a height of $20\,\text{cm}$.

The curve C has parametric equations $x = 15\cos\theta, y = 10\sin\theta, 0 \leqslant \theta \leqslant \pi$

The rugby ball is modelled as the volume of revolution formed when the curve C is rotated by 2π radians about the x-axis.

b Find the exact volume of the rugby ball according to the model. **(6 marks)**

(E/P) **10** Part of the outline of a solid glass pendant is shown in the diagram. The outline is modelled by the curve with parametric equations

$x = 2\sin 2t, y = 4\cos t, 0 \leqslant t \leqslant \dfrac{\pi}{2}$. The piece of jewellery is

formed by rotating the shaded region through 2π radians about the y-axis.

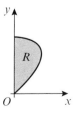

Use the model to estimate the volume of glass contained in the pendant. **(7 marks)**

Challenge

The curve C is defined by the parametric equations $x = t^2$, $y = 2t$, $t \in \mathbb{R}$. The diagram shows the finite region R bounded by the curve C and the line with equation $y = x$.

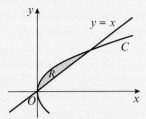

A solid of revolution is formed by rotating the region through 2π radians about the line $y = x$. Show that the volume of this solid is $\dfrac{32\pi}{15\sqrt{2}}$.

Summary of key points

1 The volume of revolution formed when $y = f(x)$ is rotated through 2π radians about the x-axis between $x = a$ and $x = b$ is given by
$$\textbf{Volume} = \pi \int_a^b y^2 \, \textbf{d}x$$

2 The volume of revolution formed when $x = f(y)$ is rotated through 2π radians about the y-axis between $y = a$ and $y = b$ is given by
$$\textbf{Volume} = \pi \int_a^b x^2 \, \textbf{d}y$$

• The volume of revolution formed when the parametric curve with equations $x = f(t)$ and $y = g(t)$ is rotated through 2π radians about the x-axis between $x = a$ and $x = b$ is given by
$$\textbf{Volume} = \pi \int_{x=a}^{x=b} y^2 \, \textbf{d}x = \pi \int_{t=q}^{t=p} y^2 \, \frac{\textbf{d}x}{\textbf{d}t} \, \textbf{d}t$$

• The volume of revolution formed by rotating the same curve through 2π radians about the y-axis between $y = a$ and $y = b$ is given by
$$\textbf{Volume} = \pi \int_{y=a}^{y=b} x^2 \, \textbf{d}y = \pi \int_{t=q}^{t=p} x^2 \, \frac{\textbf{d}y}{\textbf{d}t} \, \textbf{d}t$$

Review exercise

E **1** Show that
$$\frac{\cos 2x + i\sin 2x}{\cos 9x - i\sin 9x}$$
can be expressed in the form
$\cos nx + i\sin nx$, where n is an integer
to be found. **(4)**

← Section 1.2

E/P **2 a** Use de Moivre's theorem to show that
$\cos 5\theta = 16\cos^5\theta - 20\cos^3\theta + 5\cos\theta$. **(4)**

b Hence find 3 distinct solutions of the
equation $16x^5 - 20x^3 + 5x + 1 = 0$,
giving your answers to 3 decimal places
where appropriate. **(5)**

← Section 1.4

E/P **3 a** Use de Moivre's theorem to show that
$\sin 5\theta = \sin\theta(16\cos^4\theta - 12\cos^2\theta + 1)$ **(4)**

b Hence, or otherwise, solve, for
$0 \leqslant \theta < \pi$, $\sin 5\theta + \cos\theta\sin 2\theta = 0$. **(5)**

← Section 1.4

E/P **4 a** Use de Moivre's theorem to show that
$\sin^5\theta = \frac{1}{16}(\sin 5\theta - 5\sin 3\theta + 10\sin\theta)$. **(4)**

b Hence, or otherwise, show that
$$\int_0^{\frac{\pi}{2}} \sin^5\theta\, d\theta = \frac{8}{15}$$ **(6)**

← Section 1.4

E/P **5 a** Given that $z = \cos\theta + i\sin\theta$, show that
$z^n + z^{-n} = 2\cos n\theta$. **(2)**

b Express $\cos^6\theta$ in terms of cosines of
multiples of θ. **(4)**

c Hence show that
$$\int_0^{\frac{\pi}{2}} \cos^6\theta\, d\theta = \frac{5\pi}{32}$$ **(6)**

← Section 1.4

E/P **6** The convergent infinite series C and S are
defined as
$C = 1 + \cos\theta + \cos 2\theta + \ldots + \cos(n-1)\theta$
$S = \sin\theta + \sin 2\theta + \ldots \sin(n-1)\theta$
By considering $C + iS$, show that
$$C = \frac{1 - \cos\theta + \cos(n-1)\theta - \cos n\theta}{2 - 2\cos\theta}$$
and write down the corresponding
expression for S. **(4)**

← Section 1.5

E **7 a** Solve the equation
$$z^5 = 4 + 4i$$
giving your answers in the form
$z = re^{ik\pi}$, where r is the modulus of z
and k is a rational number such that
$0 \leqslant k \leqslant 2$. **(6)**

b Show on an Argand diagram the points
representing your solutions. **(2)**

← Section 1.6

E **8 a** Solve the equation
$$z^3 = 32 + 32\sqrt{3}i$$
giving your answers in the form $re^{i\theta}$,
where $r > 0$, $-\pi < \theta \leqslant \pi$. **(6)**

b Show that your solutions satisfy the
equation
$$z^9 + 2^k = 0$$
for an integer k, the value of which
should be stated. **(3)**

← Section 1.6

E **9** Solve the equation $z^5 = i$, giving your
answers in the form $\cos\theta + i\sin\theta$. **(6)**

← Section 1.6, 1.7

(E) **10 a** Find, in the form $re^{i\theta}$, the solutions to the equation
$$z^5 - 16 - 16i\sqrt{3} = 0 \qquad \textbf{(5)}$$

The solutions form the vertices of a polygon in the Argand diagram.

b State the name of the polygon formed.
(1)

← Section 1.7

(E/P) **11 a** Write down the five distinct solutions to $z^5 = 1$, giving your answers in exponential form, and show that their sum is 0. **(4)**

b The point $(3, 0)$ lies at one vertex of a regular pentagon. Given that the pentagon has its centre at the point $(2, 1)$, find the coordinates of the other vertices. **(4)**

← Section 1.8

(E/P) **12** Prove that
$$\sum_{r=1}^{n} \frac{2}{(r+1)(r+2)} = \frac{n}{n+2} \qquad \textbf{(5)}$$

← Section 2.1

(E/P) **13** Prove that
$$\sum_{r=1}^{n} \frac{2}{(r+1)(r+3)} = \frac{n(an+b)}{c(n+2)(n+3)}$$
where a, b and c are constants to be found. **(5)**

← Section 2.1

(E/P) **14 a** Show that
$$\frac{r+1}{r+2} - \frac{r}{r+1} \equiv \frac{1}{(r+1)(r+2)}, \, r \in \mathbb{Z}^+ \qquad \textbf{(2)}$$

b Hence, or otherwise, find
$$\sum_{r=1}^{n} \frac{1}{(r+1)(r+2)}, \text{ giving your answer}$$
as a single fraction in terms of n. **(3)**

← Section 2.1

(E/P) **15** $f(x) = \dfrac{2}{(x+1)(x+2)(x+3)}$

a Express $f(x)$ in partial fractions. **(2)**

b Hence find $\displaystyle\sum_{r=1}^{n} f(r)$. **(3)**

← Section 2.1

(E/P) **16 a** Express as a simplified single fraction
$$\frac{1}{(r-1)^2} - \frac{1}{r^2} \qquad \textbf{(2)}$$

b Hence prove, by the method of differences, that
$$\sum_{r=2}^{n} \frac{2r-1}{r^2(r-1)^2} = 1 - \frac{1}{n^2} \qquad \textbf{(3)}$$

← Section 2.1

(E/P) **17 a** Prove that
$$\sum_{r=1}^{n} \frac{4}{r(r+2)} = \frac{n(an+b)}{(n+1)(n+2)}$$
where a and b are constants to be found. **(5)**

b Find the value of $\displaystyle\sum_{r=50}^{100} \frac{4}{r(r+2)}$, to 4 decimal places. **(2)**

← Section 2.1

(E/P) **18 a** Prove that
$$\sum_{r=1}^{n} \frac{2}{4r^2 - 1} = 1 - \frac{1}{2n+1} \qquad \textbf{(5)}$$

b Hence find the exact value of
$$\sum_{r=11}^{20} \frac{2}{4r^2 - 1} \qquad \textbf{(2)}$$

← Section 2.1

(E) **19** Given that for all real values of r,
$$(2r+1)^3 - (2r-1)^3 = Ar^2 + B$$
where A and B are constants,

a find the value of A and the value of B. **(2)**

b Hence show that
$$\sum_{r=1}^{n} r^2 = \tfrac{1}{6}n(n+1)(2n+1) \qquad \textbf{(3)}$$

c Calculate $\displaystyle\sum_{r=1}^{40} (3r-1)^2$. **(2)**

← Section 2.1

(E/P) **20** Prove that
$$\sum_{r=1}^{2n} \frac{1}{r(r+1)(r+2)} = \frac{n(an+b)}{c(n+1)(2n+1)}$$
where a, b and c are constants to be found. **(6)**

← Section 2.1

(E) **21 a** Show that
$$\frac{r^3 - r + 1}{r(r+1)} \equiv r - 1 + \frac{1}{r} - \frac{1}{r+1}$$
for $r \neq 0, -1$. **(2)**

b Find $\sum_{r=1}^{n} \dfrac{r^3 - r + 1}{r(r+1)}$, expressing your answer as a single fraction in its simplest form. **(3)**

← Section 2.1

E/P **22** Find $\sum_{r=1}^{n} \dfrac{2r+3}{3^r(r+1)}$ **(5)**

← Section 2.1

E/P **23** Given that x is so small that terms in x^3 and higher powers of x may be neglected, show that

$$11 \sin x - 6 \cos x + 5 = A + Bx + Cx^2$$

stating the values of the constants A, B and C. **(6)**

← Sections 2.3, 2.4

E/P **24** Show that for $x > 1$,

$$\ln(x^2 - x + 1) + \ln(x + 1) - 3 \ln x$$
$$= \frac{1}{x^3} - \frac{1}{2x^6} + \dots + \frac{(-1)^{n-1}}{nx^{3n}} + \dots \quad \textbf{(6)}$$

← Sections 2.3, 2.4

E/P **25** Given that x is so small that terms in x^4 and higher powers of x may be neglected, find the values of the constants A, B, C and D for which

$$e^{-2x} \cos 5x = A + Bx + Cx^2 + Dx^3 \quad \textbf{(6)}$$

← Sections 2.3, 2.4

E/P **26 a** Find the first four terms of the expansion, in ascending powers of x, of

$$(2x + 3)^{-1}, \ |x| < \tfrac{2}{3} \quad \textbf{(3)}$$

b Hence, or otherwise, find the first four non-zero terms of the expansion, in ascending powers of x, of

$$\frac{\sin 2x}{2x + 3}, \ |x| < \tfrac{2}{3} \quad \textbf{(5)}$$

← Sections 2.3, 2.4

E/P **27 a** By using the Maclaurin series for $\cos x$ and $\ln(1 + x)$, find the series expansion for $\ln(\cos x)$ in ascending powers of x up to and including the term in x^4. **(6)**

b Hence, or otherwise, obtain the first two non-zero terms in the series expansion for $\ln(\sec x)$ in ascending powers of x. **(4)**

← Sections 2.3, 2.4

E **28** Given that

$$f(x) = \ln(1 + \cos 2x), \quad 0 \leqslant x < \frac{\pi}{2}$$

Show that:

a $f'(x) = -2 \tan x$ **(2)**

b $f''''(x) = -(f'''(x)\, f'(x) - (f''(x)^2))$ **(5)**

c Find the Maclaurin series expansion of $f(x)$, in ascending powers of x, up to and including the term in x^4. **(4)**

← Sections 2.2, 2.3, 2.4

E **29** Evaluate $\displaystyle\int_0^\infty e^{-x} \sin x \, dx$ **(5)**

← Section 3.1

E **30** Evaluate $\displaystyle\int_0^1 \frac{x^2}{\sqrt{1 - x^2}}\, dx$ **(5)**

← Section 3.1

E **31 a** Find $\displaystyle\int \frac{1}{x(x + 3)}\, dx$ **(3)**

b Hence show that $\displaystyle\int_3^\infty \frac{1}{x(x + 3)}\, dx$ converges and find its value. **(3)**

← Section 3.1

E **32** Show that $\displaystyle\int_1^\infty x^3 e^{-x^4}\, dx$ converges and find its exact value. **(5)**

← Section 3.1

E **33 a** Find $\displaystyle\int \frac{1}{(5 - 2x)^2}\, dx$ **(2)**

b Hence show that $\displaystyle\int_{-\infty}^3 \frac{1}{(5 - 2x)^2}\, dx$ diverges. **(4)**

← Section 3.1

E **34** Find the exact mean value of $f(x) = x \cos 2x$ over the interval $\left[0, \dfrac{\pi}{2}\right]$. **(4)**

← Section 3.2

(E) **35** $f(x) = \dfrac{3x}{(x-1)(2x-3)}$

    a Show that the mean value of f(x) over the interval [2, 5] is $\frac{1}{2}\ln\frac{343}{16}$ **(4)**

    b Use the answer to part **a** to find the mean value over the interval [2, 5] of f(x) + ln k where k is a positive constant, giving your answer in the form $p\ln q$, where p and q are constants and q is in terms of k. **(2)**

    ← Section 3.2

(E/P) **36** $f(x) = x^2(x^3 - 1)^3$

    a Show that the mean value of f(x) over the interval [1, 3] is $\frac{57122}{3}$ **(3)**

    b Use the answer to part **a** to find the mean value over the interval [1, 3] of -2f(x). **(2)**

    ← Section 3.2

(E/P) **37** $f(x) = \dfrac{1}{\sqrt{3-x}}$

    Find the exact mean value of f(x) on the interval [1, 3]. **(4)**

    ← Section 3.2

(E/P) **38** f(x) = ln kx, where k is a positive constant. Given that the mean value of f(x) on the interval [1, 5] is $\frac{1}{4}(9\ln 5 - 4)$, find the value of k. **(4)**

    ← Section 3.2

(E/P) **39** Given that $y = (\arcsin x)^2$,

    a prove that $(1 - x^2)\left(\dfrac{dy}{dx}\right)^2 = 4y$ **(4)**

    b deduce that $(1 - x^2)\dfrac{d^2y}{dx^2} - x\dfrac{dy}{dx} = 2.$ **(2)**

    ← Section 3.3

(E/P) **40 a** Given that $y = \arctan 3x$, and assuming the derivative of tan x, prove that

    $\dfrac{dy}{dx} = \dfrac{3}{1 + 9x^2}$ **(3)**

    b Show that

    $\displaystyle\int_0^{\frac{\sqrt{3}}{3}} 6x\arctan 3x = \frac{1}{9}(4\pi - 3\sqrt{3})$ **(4)**

    ← Sections 3.3, 3.4

(E/P) **41** f(x) = arcsin x

    a Show that f'(x) = $\dfrac{1}{\sqrt{1 - x^2}}$ **(3)**

    b Given that $y = \arcsin 2x$, obtain $\dfrac{dy}{dx}$ as an algebraic fraction. **(3)**

    c Using the substitution $x = \frac{1}{2}\sin\theta$, show that

    $\displaystyle\int_0^{\frac{1}{4}} \dfrac{x\arcsin 2x}{\sqrt{1 - 4x^2}}\, dx = \frac{1}{48}(6 - \pi\sqrt{3}).$ **(4)**

    ← Sections 3.3, 3.4

(E/P) **42** Show that

    $\displaystyle\int \dfrac{2x + 1}{x^3 + x}\, dx = A\arctan x + \ln x$
    $+ B\ln(x^2 + 1) + c$

    where A and B are constants to be found. **(5)**

    ← Section 3.5

(E/P) **43** $f(x) = \dfrac{3x^2 + 5x}{x^3 - 3x^2 + 5x - 15}$

    a Show that f(x) can be written in the form

    $\dfrac{A}{x - 3} + \dfrac{B}{x^2 + 5}$

    where A and B are constants to be found. **(2)**

    b Hence show that

    $\displaystyle\int f(x)\, dx = P\ln(x - 3) + Q\arctan Rx + c$

    where P, Q and R are constants to be found. **(4)**

    ← Section 3.5

(E) **44**

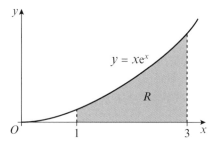

The figure shows the finite region R, which is bounded by the curve $y = xe^x$, the line $x = 1$, the line $x = 3$ and the x-axis.

The region R is rotated through 360° about the x-axis.

Use integration by parts to find the exact volume of the solid generated. **(8)**

← Section 4.1

(E) **45**

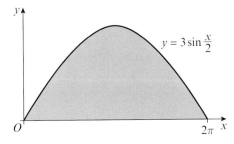

The curve with equation $y = 3\sin\frac{x}{2}$, $0 \leqslant x \leqslant 2\pi$, is shown in the figure. The finite region enclosed by the curve and the x-axis is shaded.

a Find, by integration, the area of the shaded region. **(4)**

This region is rotated through 2π radians about the x-axis.

b Find the volume of the solid generated. **(5)**

← Section 4.1

(E) **46**

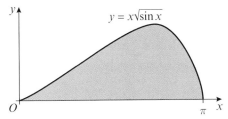

The figure shows a graph of $y = x\sqrt{\sin x}$, $0 < x < \pi$.

The finite region enclosed by the curve and the x-axis is shaded as shown in the figure. A solid body S is generated by rotating this region through 2π radians about the x-axis. Find the exact volume of S. **(8)**

← Section 4.1

(E/P) **47**

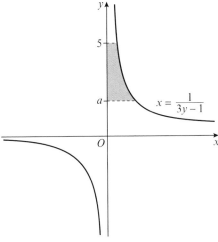

The curve shown has equation $x = \dfrac{1}{3y - 1}$

The finite region shaded is bounded by the y-axis, the line $y = 5$ and the line $y = a$. The region is rotated about the y-axis through 360°.

Given that the volume of the solid generated is $\dfrac{3\pi}{70}$, find the value of a. **(5)**

← Section 4.2

(E/P) **48**

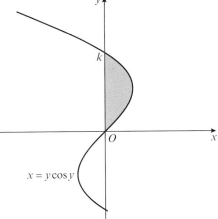

The curve shown has equation $x = y\cos y$. The finite region shaded is bounded by the curve and the y-axis. The curve intersects the positive y-axis at $(0, k)$.

a Show that $k = \dfrac{\pi}{2}$ **(2)**

The region is rotated through 2π radians about the y-axis.

b Show that the volume of the solid generated is $a\pi^4 + b\pi^2$ where a and b are constants to be found. **(6)**

← Section 4.2

(E) 49

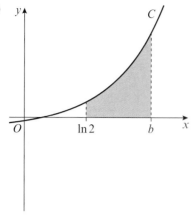

The diagram shows the curve C with parametric equations

$$x = \ln t, \ y = t^2 - 2, \ t > 0$$

The finite region shown shaded is bounded by the curve, the x-axis and the lines $x = \ln 2$ and $x = b$.

The region is rotated through 2π radians about the x-axis.

Given that the volume of the solid generated is $36\pi + 4\pi \ln 2$, find the value of b. **(6)**

← **Section 4.3**

(E/P) 50

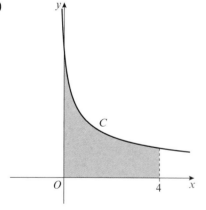

The shaded region above is formed by the x-axis, the lines $x = 0$ and $x = 4$ and the curve C where the equation of C is

$$y = \frac{5}{\sqrt{1 + 4x}}$$

A pottery vase is modelled by rotating the shaded region through $360°$ about the x-axis. Given that each unit on the axes represents $2\,\text{cm}$,

a show that the exact volume of the vase can be written in the form $a\pi \ln b$ where a and b are integers to be found. **(5)**

b Suggest a reason why the volume of the vase may actually be less than your answer to part **a**. **(1)**

← **Section 4.4**

(E/P) 51

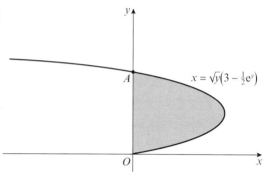

The diagram shows the curve with equation

$$x = \sqrt{y}\left(3 - \tfrac{1}{2}e^y\right)$$

a Show that the coordinates of the point marked A where the curve crosses the y-axis are $(0, \ln 6)$. **(2)**

The solid of revolution formed when the shaded region is rotated through $360°$ about the y-axis is used to model a prototype of a new type of orthopaedic cushion. The prototype is 3D printed using plastic filament.

Given that each unit on the axes is $1\,\text{cm}$,

b find, correct to 3 significant figures, the volume of the prototype. **(6)**

c Suggest a reason why the amount of filament used to print to model may exceed your answer to part **b**. **(1)**

← **Section 4.4**

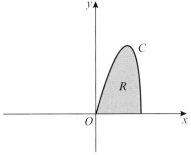

(E/P) 52

The diagram shows the curve C with parametric equations

$$x = 2\sin t, \ y = 3\sin 2t, \ 0 \leqslant t \leqslant \frac{\pi}{2}$$

A jewellery pendant is made in the shape of the solid of revolution formed when the region marked R is rotated through 2π radians about the x-axis. Each unit on the axes represents 0.5 cm.

a Show that the volume of the pendant can be found by evaluating the integral

$$\frac{9\pi}{4}\int_0^{\frac{\pi}{2}} \sin^2 2t \cos t \, dt \qquad \textbf{(4)}$$

b Hence show that the exact volume of the pendant is $\dfrac{6\pi}{5}$ cm³. **(6)**

← Section 4.4

Challenge

1 a Show that if $\omega = e^{\frac{2\pi i}{3}}$, then

$$\frac{1^n + \omega^n + (\omega^2)^n}{3} = \begin{cases} 1 & \text{if } n \text{ is zero or a multiple of 3} \\ 0 & \text{otherwise} \end{cases}$$

Let $f(x)$ be a finite polynomial whose largest power of x is a multiple of 3, so that

$$f(x) = a_0 + a_1x + a_2x^2 + \dots + a_{3k}x^{3k}$$

where $a_i \in \mathbb{R}, k \in \mathbb{N}$.
The sum S is given by

$$S = a_0 + a_3 + a_6 + \dots + a_{3k} = \sum_{r=0}^{k} a_{3r},$$

b By considering a general term of $f(x)$, show that $S = \dfrac{f(1) + f(\omega) + f(\omega^2)}{3}$

c Hence, by considering the binomial expansion of $(1 + x)^{45}$, show that

$$\sum_{r=0}^{15}\binom{45}{3r} = \frac{2^{45} - 2}{3}$$

← Section 1.6

2 The region bounded by the x-axis and the graph of the function

$$f(x) = \sqrt{\frac{x + 3}{x^3}}$$

on the interval $[2, \infty)$ is rotated through 360° about the x-axis.

Show that the volume of the described solid is finite and find its value.

← Sections 3.1, 4.1

3 A continuous random variable, X, has probability density function

$$f(x) = \frac{A}{1 + x^2}, \ x \in \mathbb{R}$$

where A is a constant.

a Given that $\int_{-\infty}^{\infty} f(x)\,dx = 1$, show that $A = \dfrac{1}{\pi}$

The variance of a continuous probability distribution which is defined over the real numbers and is symmetrical about $x = 0$ is given by

$$\int_{-\infty}^{\infty} x^2 f(x)\,dx$$

b Show that X has infinite variance.

The mean of a continuous probability distribution which is defined over the real numbers is given by $\int_{-\infty}^{\infty} xf(x)\,dx$.

c Show that

$$\lim_{a \to \infty}\int_{-a}^{a}\frac{x}{1 + x^2}\,dx \neq \lim_{a \to \infty}\int_{-a}^{2a}\frac{x}{1 + x^2}\,dx$$

and explain why the mean of X is undefined. ← Section 3.1

5 Polar coordinates

Objectives

After completing this chapter you should be able to:

- Understand and use polar coordinates   → pages 101–104
- Convert between polar and Cartesian coordinates → pages 102–104
- Sketch curves with r given as a function of θ → pages 104–109
- Find the area enclosed by a polar curve   → pages 109–112
- Find tangents parallel to, or at right angles to, the initial line
                                           → pages 113–116

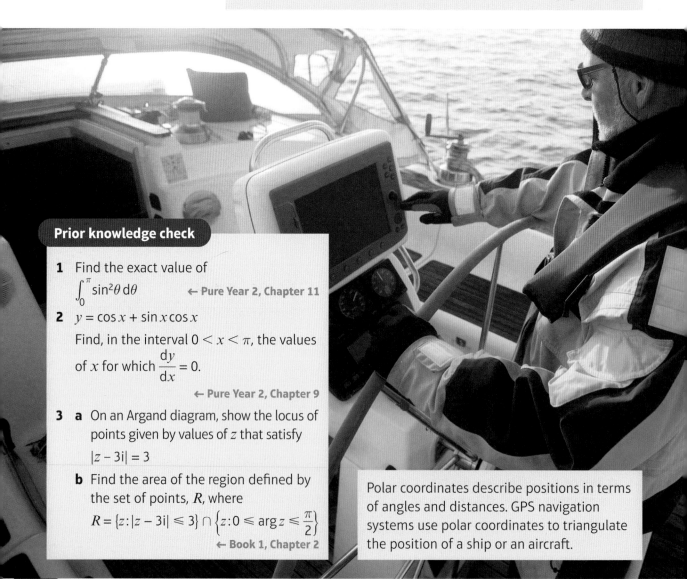

Prior knowledge check

1. Find the exact value of
   $$\int_0^{\pi} \sin^2\theta \, d\theta \qquad \text{← Pure Year 2, Chapter 11}$$

2. $y = \cos x + \sin x \cos x$

   Find, in the interval $0 < x < \pi$, the values of x for which $\dfrac{dy}{dx} = 0$.

   ← Pure Year 2, Chapter 9

3. **a** On an Argand diagram, show the locus of points given by values of z that satisfy
   $$|z - 3i| = 3$$

   b Find the area of the region defined by the set of points, R, where
   $$R = \{z : |z - 3i| \leqslant 3\} \cap \left\{z : 0 \leqslant \arg z \leqslant \frac{\pi}{2}\right\}$$

   ← Book 1, Chapter 2

Polar coordinates describe positions in terms of angles and distances. GPS navigation systems use polar coordinates to triangulate the position of a ship or an aircraft.

5.1 Polar coordinates and equations

Polar coordinates are an alternative way of describing the position of a point P in two-dimensional space. You need two measurements: firstly, the distance the point is from the **pole** (usually the origin O), r, and secondly, the angle measured anticlockwise from the **initial line** (usually the positive x-axis), θ. Polar coordinates are written as (r, θ).

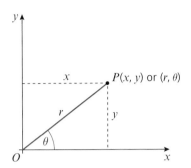

Notation When working in polar coordinates the axes might also be labelled like this:

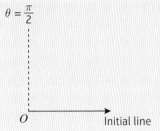

The coordinates of P can be written in either Cartesian form as (x, y) or in polar form as (r, θ).

You can convert between Cartesian coordinates and polar coordinates using right-angled triangle trigonometry.

From the diagram above you can see that:

■ $r\cos\theta = x$
  $r\sin\theta = y$

■ $r^2 = x^2 + y^2$
  $\theta = \arctan\left(\dfrac{y}{x}\right)$

Watch out Always draw a sketch diagram to check in which quadrant the point lies, and always measure the polar angle from the positive x-axis.

Example 1

Find polar coordinates of the points with the following Cartesian coordinates.

a $(3, 4)$ **b** $(5, -12)$ **c** $(-\sqrt{3}, -1)$

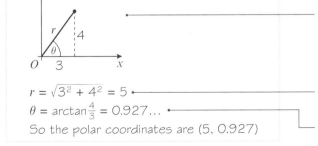

Draw a sketch.

$r = \sqrt{3^2 + 4^2} = 5$ — Use Pythagoras' theorem to find r.

$\theta = \arctan\dfrac{4}{3} = 0.927\ldots$ —

So the polar coordinates are $(5, 0.927)$

Use trigonometry to find θ. Give your answer in radians.

b

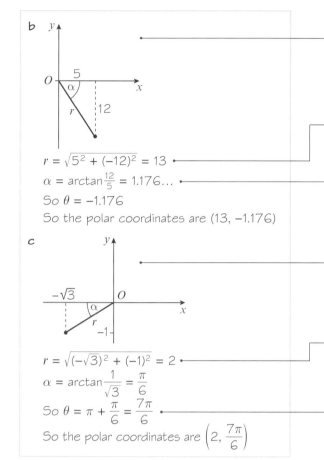

Draw a sketch.

$r = \sqrt{5^2 + (-12)^2} = 13$

Use Pythagoras' theorem to find r.

$\alpha = \arctan\frac{12}{5} = 1.176...$

So $\theta = -1.176$

So the polar coordinates are $(13, -1.176)$

Use trigonometry to find θ, taking care to ensure it is in the correct quadrant. You could also write this point as $(13, 5.107)$ since $-1.176 + 2\pi = 5.107$

c

The sketch shows that the point is in the 3rd quadrant.

$r = \sqrt{(-\sqrt{3})^2 + (-1)^2} = 2$

Use Pythagoras' theorem to find r.

$\alpha = \arctan\frac{1}{\sqrt{3}} = \frac{\pi}{6}$

So $\theta = \pi + \frac{\pi}{6} = \frac{7\pi}{6}$

So the polar coordinates are $\left(2, \frac{7\pi}{6}\right)$

The point is in the third quadrant so use $\theta = \frac{7\pi}{6}$

You could also use $\theta = \frac{7\pi}{6} - 2\pi = -\frac{5\pi}{6}$

Example **2**

Convert the following polar coordinates into Cartesian form. The angles are measured in radians.

a $\left(10, \frac{4\pi}{3}\right)$ **b** $\left(8, \frac{2\pi}{3}\right)$

a $x = r\cos\theta = 10\cos\frac{4\pi}{3} = -5$

$y = r\sin\theta = 10\sin\frac{4\pi}{3} = -5\sqrt{3}$

So the Cartesian coordinates are $(-5, -5\sqrt{3})$

b $x = r\cos\theta = 8\cos\frac{2\pi}{3} = -4$

$y = r\sin\theta = 8\sin\frac{2\pi}{3} = 4\sqrt{3}$

So the Cartesian coordinates are $(-4, 4\sqrt{3})$

Polar equations of curves are usually given in the form $r = f(\theta)$. For example,

$r = 2\cos\theta$

$r = 1 + 2\theta$

$r = 3$ — In this example r is constant.

You can convert between polar equations of curves and their Cartesian forms.

Example 3

Find Cartesian equations of the following curves.

a $r = 5$ **b** $r = 2 + \cos 2\theta$ **c** $r^2 = \sin 2\theta, \quad 0 < \theta \leqslant \dfrac{\pi}{2}$

---

a $r = 5$

Square both sides to get $r^2 = 25$

So a Cartesian equation is $x^2 + y^2 = 25$

> You need to replace r with an equation in x and y. Use $r^2 = x^2 + y^2$. So the equation $r = 5$ represents a circle with centre O and radius 5.

b $r = 2 + \cos 2\theta$

$r = 1 + (1 + \cos 2\theta)$

$r = 1 + 2\cos^2 \theta$

> You need an equation in x and y, so use $x = r\cos\theta$. This means first writing $\cos 2\theta$ in terms of $\cos\theta$.

Multiply by r^2:

$r^3 = r^2 + 2r^2 \cos^2 \theta$

$(x^2 + y^2)^{\frac{3}{2}} = x^2 + y^2 + 2x^2$

Or $(x^2 + y^2)^{\frac{3}{2}} = 3x^2 + y^2$

> Now use $x = r\cos\theta$ and $r^2 = x^2 + y^2$.

> **Watch out**   Polar coordinates often give rise to complicated Cartesian equations, which cannot be written easily in the form $y = \ldots$

c $r^2 = \sin 2\theta, \quad 0 < \theta \leqslant \dfrac{\pi}{2}$

$r^2 = 2\sin\theta\cos\theta$

Multiply by r^2:

$r^4 = 2 \times r\sin\theta \times r\cos\theta$

$(x^2 + y^2)^2 = 2xy$

> **Problem-solving**

> You need to use the substitutions $x = r\cos\theta$ and $y = r\sin\theta$. Use $\sin 2\theta \equiv 2\sin\theta\cos\theta$ and then multiply by r^2.

Example 4

Find polar equations for the following:

a $y^2 = 4x$ **b** $x^2 - y^2 = 5$ **c** $y\sqrt{3} = x + 4$

---

a $y^2 = 4x$

$r^2 \sin^2 \theta = 4r\cos\theta$

$r\sin^2 \theta = 4\cos\theta$

$r = \dfrac{4\cos\theta}{\sin^2 \theta} = 4\cot\theta\,\mathrm{cosec}\,\theta$

So a polar equation is $r = 4\cot\theta\,\mathrm{cosec}\,\theta$

> Substitute $x = r\cos\theta$ and $y = r\sin\theta$.

> Divide by r and simplify.

b $x^2 - y^2 = 5$

$r^2 \cos^2 \theta - r^2 \sin^2 \theta = 5$

$r^2 (\cos^2 \theta - \sin^2 \theta) = 5$

$r^2 \cos 2\theta = 5$

So a polar equation is $r^2 = 5\sec 2\theta$

> Substitute $x = r\cos\theta$ and $y = r\sin\theta$.

> Use $\cos 2\theta \equiv \cos^2 \theta - \sin^2 \theta$.

c $y\sqrt{3} = x + 4$

$r\sqrt{3}\sin\theta = r\cos\theta + 4$ •————— Substitute $x = r\cos\theta$ and $y = r\sin\theta$ and then try to simplify the trigonometric expression.

$r(\sqrt{3}\sin\theta - \cos\theta) = 4$

$r\left(\dfrac{\sqrt{3}}{2}\sin\theta - \dfrac{1}{2}\cos\theta\right) = \dfrac{4}{2}$

$r\sin\left(\theta - \dfrac{\pi}{6}\right) = 2$ •————— Use the $\sin(A - B)$ formula.

So a polar equation is $r = 2\csc\left(\theta - \dfrac{\pi}{6}\right)$

Exercise 5A

1 Find polar coordinates of the points with the following Cartesian coordinates.

  a $(5, 12)$ **b** $(-5, 12)$ **c** $(-5, -12)$

  d $(2, -3)$ **e** $(\sqrt{3}, -1)$

2 Convert the following polar coordinates into Cartesian form.

  a $\left(6, \dfrac{\pi}{6}\right)$ **b** $\left(6, -\dfrac{\pi}{6}\right)$ **c** $\left(6, \dfrac{3\pi}{4}\right)$

  d $\left(10, \dfrac{5\pi}{4}\right)$ **e** $(2, \pi)$

3 Find Cartesian equations for the following curves, where a is a positive constant.

  a $r = 2$ **b** $r = 3\sec\theta$ **c** $r = 5\csc\theta$

  d $r = 4a\tan\theta\sec\theta$ **e** $r = 2a\cos\theta$ **f** $r = 3a\sin\theta$

  g $r = 4(1 - \cos 2\theta)$ **h** $r = 2\cos^2\theta$ **i** $r^2 = 1 + \tan^2\theta$

4 Find polar equations for the following curves.

  a $x^2 + y^2 = 16$ **b** $xy = 4$ **c** $(x^2 + y^2)^2 = 2xy$

  d $x^2 + y^2 - 2x = 0$ **e** $(x + y)^2 = 4$ **f** $x - y = 3$

  g $y = 2x$ **h** $y = -\sqrt{3}x + a$ **i** $y = x(x - a)$

Challenge

Show that the distance, d, between the two points (r_1, θ_1) and (r_2, θ_2) in polar coordinates is

$d = \sqrt{r_1^2 + r_2^2 - 2r_1r_2\cos(\theta_1 - \theta_2)}$

5.2 Sketching curves

You can sketch curves given in polar form by learning the shapes of some standard curves.

- $r = a$ **is a circle with centre O and radius a.**
- $\theta = \alpha$ **is a half-line through O and making an angle α with the initial line.**
- $r = a\theta$ **is a spiral starting at O.**

Example 5

Sketch the following curves.

a $r = 5$ **b** $\theta = \dfrac{3\pi}{4}$ **c** $r = a\theta$

where a is a positive constant.

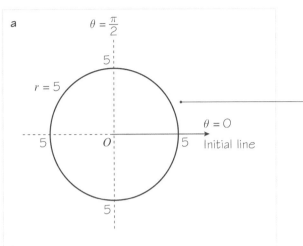

This is a standard curve: a circle with centre O and radius 5.

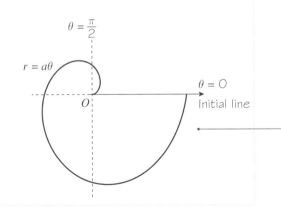

This is another standard graph: a half-line. Notice it is only 'half' of the line $y = -x$. The other half of the line would have equation $\theta = -\dfrac{\pi}{4}$ or $\theta = \dfrac{7\pi}{4}$

c

This is another standard curve: a spiral. It crosses the horizontal axis at $-a\pi$, 0 and $2a\pi$ and the vertical axis at $\dfrac{a\pi}{2}$ and $-\dfrac{3a\pi}{2}$. The curve here drawn for values of θ in the range $0 \leqslant \theta \leqslant 2\pi$.

You can also sketch curves by drawing up a table of values of r for particular values of θ. It is common to choose only values of θ that give positive values of r.

Watch out Some graph-drawing programs and graphical calculators will sketch polar curves for negative values of r so take care when using these tools to help you.

Example 6

Sketch the following curves.

a $r = a(1 + \cos\theta)$ **b** $r = a\sin 3\theta$ **c** $r^2 = a^2\cos 2\theta$

a $r = a(1 + \cos\theta)$

θ	0	$\dfrac{\pi}{2}$	π	$\dfrac{3\pi}{2}$	2π
r	$2a$	a	0	a	$2a$

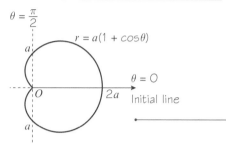

Problem-solving

When sketching polar curves it is useful to plot points for key values of θ. Make a table of values for θ at multiples of $\dfrac{\pi}{2}$ to determine the points at which the curve meets or intersects the coordinate axes.

This curve is 'heart' shaped and is known as a cardioid.

b $r = a\sin 3\theta$

Need to consider

$0 \leqslant \theta \leqslant \dfrac{\pi}{3}, \dfrac{2\pi}{3} \leqslant \theta \leqslant \pi$ and $\dfrac{4\pi}{3} \leqslant \theta \leqslant \dfrac{5\pi}{3}$

θ	0	$\dfrac{\pi}{6}$	$\dfrac{\pi}{3}$
r	0	a	0

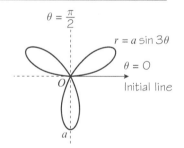

Since we only draw the curve when $r \geqslant 0$ you need to determine the values of θ required.

Choose values of θ which give exact values of r. The values shown here define the first loop of the curve. The values of r will be the same in the other two loops.

Problem-solving

The curve given by $r = a\sin 3\theta$ is typical of the patterns that arise in polar curves for equations of the form $r = a\cos n\theta$ or $r = a\sin n\theta$. They will have n loops symmetrically arranged around O.

c $r^2 = a^2\cos 2\theta$

You need values of θ in the ranges

$-\dfrac{\pi}{4} \leqslant \theta \leqslant \dfrac{\pi}{4}$ and $\dfrac{3\pi}{4} \leqslant \theta \leqslant \dfrac{5\pi}{4}$

Establish the values of θ for which the curve exists.

θ	$-\dfrac{\pi}{4}$	0	$\dfrac{\pi}{4}$	$\dfrac{3\pi}{4}$	π	$\dfrac{5\pi}{4}$
r	0	a	0	0	a	0

Draw up a table of values and sketch the curve.

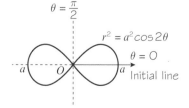

Online Explore curves given in polar form using GeoGebra.

Curves with equations of the form $r = a(p + q\cos\theta)$ are defined for all values of θ if $p \geqslant q$. An example of this, when $p = q$, was the cardioid seen in Example 6a. These curves fall into two types, those that are 'egg' shaped (i.e. a convex curve) and those with a 'dimple' (i.e. the curve is concave at $\theta = \pi$). The conditions for each type are given below:

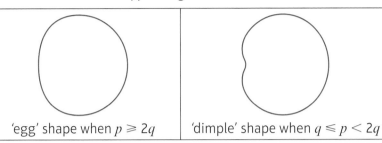

'egg' shape when $p \geqslant 2q$ | 'dimple' shape when $q \leqslant p < 2q$

Links You can prove these conditions by considering the number of tangents to the curve that are perpendicular to the initial line.

→ **Example 14**

Example (7)

Sketch the following curves.

a $r = a(5 + 2\cos\theta)$ **b** $r = a(3 + 2\cos\theta)$

a $r = a(5 + 2\cos\theta)$

θ	0	$\dfrac{\pi}{2}$	π	$\dfrac{3\pi}{2}$
r	$7a$	$5a$	$3a$	$5a$

Draw up a suitable table of values.

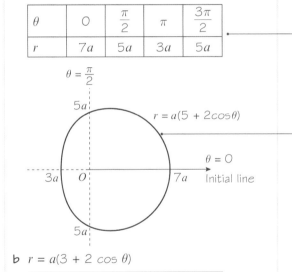

Since $5 > 2 \times 2$ there is no 'dimple'.

b $r = a(3 + 2\cos\theta)$

θ	0	$\dfrac{\pi}{2}$	π	$\dfrac{3\pi}{2}$
r	$5a$	$3a$	a	$3a$

Draw up a suitable table of values.

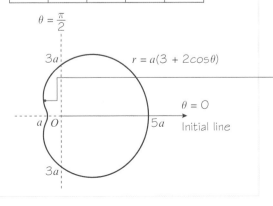

Since $3 < 2 \times 2$ there will be a 'dimple' for θ close to π.

You may also need to find a polar curve to represent a locus of points on an Argand diagram.

Links If the pole is taken as the origin, and the initial line is taken as the positive real axis, then the point (r, θ) will represent the complex number $re^{i\theta}$ ← **Section 1.1**

Example 8

a Show on an Argand diagram the locus of points given by the values of z satisfying $|z - 3 - 4i| = 5$

b Show that this locus of points can be represented by the polar curve $r = 6\cos\theta + 8\sin\theta$.

a

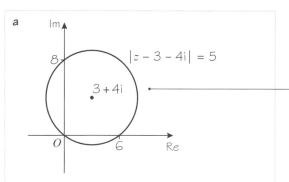

This locus is a circle with centre $3 + 4i$ and radius 5.

b In Cartesian form, $(x - 3)^2 + (y - 4)^2 = 25$

$(r\cos\theta - 3)^2 + (r\sin\theta - 4)^2 = 25$ — Substitute for x and y in polar form.

$r^2\cos^2\theta - 6r\cos\theta + 9 + r^2\sin^2\theta$
$\quad - 8r\sin\theta + 16 = 25$

$r^2(\cos^2\theta + \sin^2\theta) - 6r\cos\theta - 8r\sin\theta = 0$

$r^2 = 6r\cos\theta + 8r\sin\theta$

$r = 6\cos\theta + 8\sin\theta$

Exercise 5B

1 Sketch the following curves.

   a $r = 6$
           b $\theta = \dfrac{5\pi}{4}$
           c $\theta = -\dfrac{\pi}{4}$

   d $r = 2\sec\theta$
         e $r = 3\operatorname{cosec}\theta$
        f $r = 2\sec\left(\theta - \dfrac{\pi}{3}\right)$

   g $r = a\sin\theta$
         h $r = a(1 - \cos\theta)$
      i $r = a\cos 3\theta$

   j $r = a(2 + \cos\theta)$
     k $r = a(6 + \cos\theta)$
     l $r = a(4 + 3\cos\theta)$

   m $r = a(2 + \sin\theta)$
    n $r = a(6 + \sin\theta)$
    o $r = a(4 + 3\sin\theta)$

   p $r = 2\theta$
          q $r^2 = a^2\sin\theta$
       r $r^2 = a^2\sin 2\theta$

E **2** Sketch the graph with polar equation

$$r = k\sec\left(\dfrac{\pi}{4} - \theta\right)$$

where k is a positive constant, giving the coordinates of any points of intersection with the coordinate axes in terms of k. **(4 marks)**

(E) **3 a** Show on an Argand diagram the locus of points given by the values of z satisfying

$$|z - 12 - 5i| = 13$$ **(2 marks)**

b Show that this locus of points can be represented by the polar curve

$$r = 24\cos\theta + 10\sin\theta$$ **(4 marks)**

(E) **4 a** Show on an Argand diagram the locus of points given by the values of z satisfying

$$|z + 4 + 3i| = 5$$ **(2 marks)**

b Show that this locus of points can be represented by the polar curve

$$r = -8\cos\theta - 6\sin\theta$$ **(4 marks)**

5.3 Area enclosed by a polar curve

You can find areas enclosed by a polar curve using integration.

■ **The area of a sector bounded by a polar curve and the half-lines $\theta = \alpha$ and $\theta = \beta$, where θ is in radians, is given by the formula**

$$\textbf{Area} = \tfrac{1}{2}\int_{\alpha}^{\beta} r^2 \, \mathbf{d\theta}$$

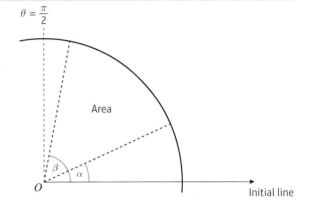

Example 9

Find the area enclosed by the cardioid with equation $r = a(1 + \cos\theta)$.

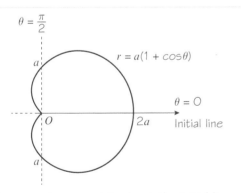

The curve is symmetric about the initial line and so finding the area above this line and doubling it gives:

Area $= 2 \times \dfrac{a^2}{2} \displaystyle\int_0^{\pi} (1 + \cos\theta)^2 \, d\theta$

$= a^2 \displaystyle\int_0^{\pi} (1 + 2\cos\theta + \cos^2\theta) \, d\theta$

$= a^2 \displaystyle\int_0^{\pi} \left(\tfrac{3}{2} + 2\cos\theta + \tfrac{1}{2}\cos 2\theta\right) d\theta$

$= a^2 \left[\tfrac{3}{2}\theta + 2\sin\theta + \tfrac{1}{4}\sin 2\theta\right]_0^{\pi}$

$= a^2 \left(\left(\tfrac{3}{2}\pi + 0 + 0\right) - 0\right)$

$= \dfrac{3a^2\pi}{2}$

Problem-solving

Start by sketching the curve. You can simplify your calculation by using the fact that the curve is symmetric about the initial line. Hence you can integrate from 0 to π and then double your answer.

Use the formula for area. Remember to square the expression for r.

You can use trigonometric identities for $\cos 2\theta$ to integrate terms in $\cos^2\theta$ or $\sin^2\theta$:

$$\cos^2\theta \equiv \dfrac{1 + \cos 2\theta}{2}$$ ← Pure Year 2, Chapter 11

Watch out Unlike Cartesian integration, areas in the third and fourth quadrants do not produce negative integrals. You could obtain the same result by integrating between 0 and 2π:

$$\tfrac{1}{2}\int_0^{2\pi} a^2(1 + \cos\theta)^2 \, d\theta = \dfrac{3a^2\pi}{2}$$

Example 10

Find the area of one loop of the curve with polar equation $r = a \sin 4\theta$.

$r = a \sin 4\theta$ will have one loop for
$$0 \le \theta \le \frac{\pi}{4}$$

Find the values of θ which will give the beginning and end of a loop by solving $r = 0$.

$$\text{Area} = \frac{1}{2} \int_0^{\frac{\pi}{4}} r^2 \, d\theta = \frac{a^2}{2} \int_0^{\frac{\pi}{4}} \sin^2 4\theta \, d\theta$$

Use the area formula.

$$= \frac{a^2}{4} \int_0^{\frac{\pi}{4}} (1 - \cos 8\theta) \, d\theta$$

Use the trigonometric identity for $\cos 2\theta$. In this case, $\sin^2 4\theta \equiv \dfrac{1 - \cos 8\theta}{2}$

$$= \frac{a^2}{4} \left[\theta - \frac{\sin 8\theta}{8} \right]_0^{\frac{\pi}{4}}$$

$$= \frac{a^2}{4} \left(\frac{\pi}{4} - \frac{\sin 2\pi}{8} \right) - 0$$

Remember $\sin 2\pi = 0$.

$$= \frac{a^2 \pi}{16}$$

Online Explore the area enclosed by a loop of the polar curve with the form $r = a \sin \theta$ using GeoGebra.

Watch out $r = \sin n\theta$ has n loops and so a simple way of finding the area of one loop would appear to be to find $\frac{1}{2} \int_0^{2\pi} r^2 \, d\theta$ and divide by n. This would give $\dfrac{a^2 \pi}{8}$

The reason why this is not the correct answer is because when you take r^2 in the integral you are also including the n loops given by $r < 0$. You need to choose your limits carefully so that $r \ge 0$ for all values within the range of the integral.

Example 11

a On the same diagram, sketch the curves with equations $r = 2 + \cos\theta$ and $r = 5\cos\theta$.

b Find the polar coordinates of the points of intersection of these two curves.

c Find the exact area of the region which lies within both curves.

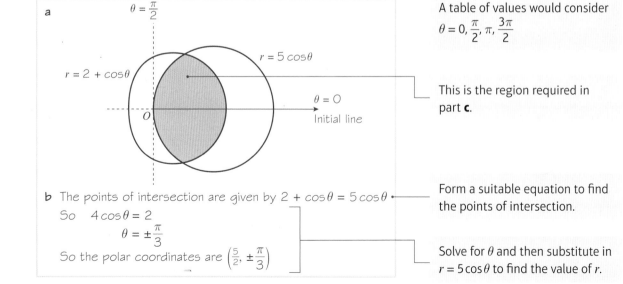

a

A table of values would consider $\theta = 0, \dfrac{\pi}{2}, \pi, \dfrac{3\pi}{2}$

This is the region required in part **c**.

b The points of intersection are given by $2 + \cos\theta = 5\cos\theta$

So $4\cos\theta = 2$

$$\theta = \pm\frac{\pi}{3}$$

So the polar coordinates are $\left(\frac{5}{2}, \pm\frac{\pi}{3} \right)$

Form a suitable equation to find the points of intersection.

Solve for θ and then substitute in $r = 5\cos\theta$ to find the value of r.

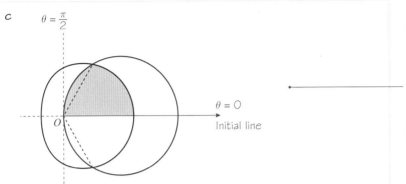

c

Remember that the area formula gives areas of *sectors*. So you need the sector formed by the purple curve and the sector formed by the blue curve. Again you can use symmetry about the initial line.

$$\text{Area} = 2 \times \frac{1}{2} \int_0^{\frac{\pi}{3}} (2 + \cos\theta)^2 \, d\theta + 2 \times \frac{1}{2} \int_{\frac{\pi}{3}}^{\frac{\pi}{2}} (5\cos\theta)^2 \, d\theta$$

$$= \int_0^{\frac{\pi}{3}} (4 + 4\cos\theta + \cos^2\theta) \, d\theta + \int_{\frac{\pi}{3}}^{\frac{\pi}{2}} 25\cos^2\theta \, d\theta$$

$$= \int_0^{\frac{\pi}{3}} \left(\frac{9}{2} + 4\cos\theta + \frac{\cos 2\theta}{2} \right) d\theta + \int_{\frac{\pi}{3}}^{\frac{\pi}{2}} \frac{25}{2} (1 + \cos 2\theta) \, d\theta$$

Square and use the trigonometric identity for $\cos 2\theta$.

$$= \left[\frac{9}{2}\theta + 4\sin\theta + \frac{\sin 2\theta}{4} \right]_0^{\frac{\pi}{3}} + \frac{25}{2} \left[\theta + \frac{\sin 2\theta}{2} \right]_{\frac{\pi}{3}}^{\frac{\pi}{2}}$$

$$= \left(\frac{3\pi}{2} + 2\sqrt{3} + \frac{\sqrt{3}}{8} \right) - (0) + \left(\frac{25\pi}{4} + 0 \right) - \left(\frac{25\pi}{6} + \frac{25\sqrt{3}}{8} \right)$$

Use the exact value of $\sin\frac{2\pi}{3}$

$$= \frac{43\pi}{12} - \sqrt{3}$$

Exercise 5C

1 Find the area of the finite region bounded by the curve with the given polar equation and the half-lines $\theta = \alpha$ and $\theta = \beta$.

  a $r = a\cos\theta$, $\alpha = 0$, $\beta = \frac{\pi}{2}$
  b $r = a(1 + \sin\theta)$, $\alpha = -\frac{\pi}{2}$, $\beta = \frac{\pi}{2}$
  c $r = a\sin 3\theta$, $\alpha = \frac{\pi}{6}$, $\beta = \frac{\pi}{4}$

  d $r^2 = a^2\cos 2\theta$, $\alpha = 0$, $\beta = \frac{\pi}{4}$
  e $r^2 = a^2\tan\theta$, $\alpha = 0$, $\beta = \frac{\pi}{4}$
  f $r = 2a\theta$, $\alpha = 0$, $\beta = \pi$

  g $r = a(3 + 2\cos\theta)$, $\alpha = 0$, $\beta = \frac{\pi}{2}$

2 Show that the area enclosed by the curve with polar equation $r = a(p + q\cos\theta)$ is $\dfrac{2p^2 + q^2}{2}\pi a^2$.

3 Find the area of a single loop of the curve with equation $r = a\cos 3\theta$.

(E) 4 A curve has equation $r = a + 5\sin\theta$, $a > 5$. The area enclosed by the curve is $\dfrac{187\pi}{2}$. Find the value of a. **(5 marks)**

(E/P) 5 The diagram shows the curves with equations $r = a\sin 4\theta$ and $r = a\sin 2\theta$ for $0 \leqslant \theta \leqslant \frac{\pi}{2}$

The finite region R is contained within both curves.

Find the area of R, giving your answer in terms of a. **(8 marks)**

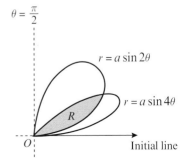

(E/P) 6 The diagram shows the curves with equations $r = 1 + \sin\theta$ and $r = 3\sin\theta$.

The finite region R is contained within both curves.

Find the area of R. **(8 marks)**

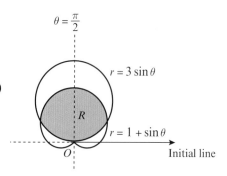

(E/P) 7 The set of points, A, is defined by
$$A = \left\{z : -\frac{\pi}{4} \leqslant \arg z \leqslant 0\right\} \cap \{z : |z - 4 + 3\mathrm{i}| \leqslant 5\}$$

a Sketch on an Argand diagram the set of points, A. **(4 marks)**

Given that the locus of points given by the values of z satisfying $|z - 4 + 3\mathrm{i}| = 5$ can be expressed in polar form using the equation $r = 8\cos\theta - 6\sin\theta$,

b find, correct to three significant figures, the area of the region defined by A. **(8 marks)**

(E/P) 8 The set of points, A, is defined by
$$A = \left\{z : \frac{\pi}{2} \leqslant \arg z \leqslant \pi\right\} \cap \{z : |z + 12 - 5\mathrm{i}| \leqslant 13\}$$

a Sketch on an Argand diagram the set of points, A. **(4 marks)**

b Find, correct to three significant figures, the area of the region defined by A. **(8 marks)**

(E/P) 9 The diagram shows the curve C with polar equation
$$r = 1 + \cos 3\theta, \ 0 \leqslant \theta \leqslant \frac{\pi}{3}$$

At points A and B, the value of r is $\dfrac{2 + \sqrt{2}}{2}$

Point A lies on C and point B lies on the initial line.

Find, correct to three significant figures, the finite area bounded by the curve, the line segment AB and the initial line, shown shaded in the diagram. **(9 marks)**

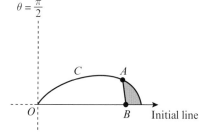

(E/P) 10 The diagram shows the curves $r = 1 + \sin\theta$ and $r = 3\sin\theta$.

Find the shaded area, giving your answer correct to two decimal places. **(8 marks)**

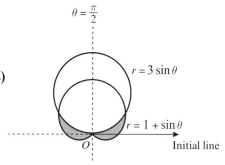

Challenge

The cross-section of a shell is modelled using the curve with polar equation $r = k\theta, \ 0 \leqslant \theta \leqslant 4\pi$, where k is a positive constant. The horizontal diameter of the shell, as shown in the diagram, is 3 cm.

a Find the exact value of k.

b Hence find the total shaded area of the cross-section.

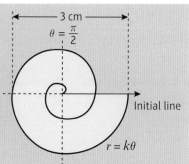

5.4 Tangents to polar curves

If you are given a curve $r = f(\theta)$ in polar form, you can write it as a parametric curve in Cartesian form, using θ as the parameter:

$$x = r\cos\theta = f(\theta)\cos\theta$$
$$y = r\sin\theta = f(\theta)\sin\theta$$

By differentiating parametrically, you can find the gradient of the curve at any point:

$$\frac{dy}{dx} = \frac{\dfrac{dy}{d\theta}}{\dfrac{dx}{d\theta}}$$

When $\dfrac{dy}{d\theta} = 0$, a tangent to the curve will be horizontal.

When $\dfrac{dx}{d\theta} = 0$, a tangent to the curve will be vertical.

You need to be able to find tangents to a polar curve that are **parallel** or **perpendicular** to the initial line.

- **To find a tangent parallel to the initial line set $\dfrac{dy}{d\theta} = 0$.**
- **To find a tangent perpendicular to the initial line set $\dfrac{dx}{d\theta} = 0$.**

Example 12

Find the coordinates of the points on $r = a(1 + \cos\theta)$ where the tangents are parallel to the initial line $\theta = 0$.

$y = r\sin\theta = a(\sin\theta + \sin\theta\cos\theta)$

$\dfrac{dy}{d\theta} = a(\cos\theta + \cos^2\theta - \sin^2\theta)$

Find an expression for y and then solve $\dfrac{dy}{d\theta} = 0$.

So $\quad 0 = 2\cos^2\theta + \cos\theta - 1$

$\qquad 0 = (2\cos\theta - 1)(\cos\theta + 1)$

$\qquad \cos\theta = \tfrac{1}{2} \ \Rightarrow \ \theta = \pm\dfrac{\pi}{3}$

So $\quad r = a(1 + \tfrac{1}{2}) = \dfrac{3a}{2}$

Solve the equations to find θ and then substitute back to find r.

$\cos\theta = -1 \ \Rightarrow \ \theta = \pi$, and so $r = 0$

So the tangents parallel to the initial line are at $\left(\dfrac{3a}{2}, \pm\dfrac{\pi}{3}\right)$ and $(0, \pi)$.

Problem-solving

You can see these tangents on a sketch of $y = a(1 + \cos\theta)$

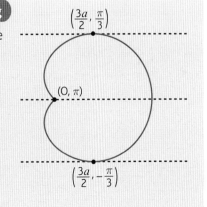

$\left(\dfrac{3a}{2}, \dfrac{\pi}{3}\right)$

$(0, \pi)$

$\left(\dfrac{3a}{2}, -\dfrac{\pi}{3}\right)$

Example 13

Find the equations and the points of contact of the tangents to the curve $r = a \sin 2\theta$, $0 \le \theta \le \dfrac{\pi}{2}$ that are:

a parallel to the initial line **b** perpendicular to the initial line.

Give answers to three significant figures where appropriate.

a $y = r \sin \theta = a \sin \theta \sin 2\theta$

$\dfrac{dy}{d\theta} = a(\cos \theta \sin 2\theta + 2 \cos 2\theta \sin \theta)$

$\quad = 2a \sin \theta (\cos^2 \theta + \cos^2 \theta - \sin^2 \theta)$

$\dfrac{dy}{d\theta} = 0 \Rightarrow \sin \theta = 0 \Rightarrow \theta = 0$

or $\quad 2\cos^2 \theta = \sin^2 \theta \Rightarrow \tan \theta = \pm \sqrt{2}$

$\quad\quad\quad\quad\quad\quad\quad \Rightarrow \theta = 0.955$

So $\quad \theta = 0$ or 0.955

and $\quad r = 0$ or $r = 2a \times \dfrac{\sqrt{2}}{\sqrt{3}} \times \dfrac{1}{\sqrt{3}}$

So the points are $(0, 0)$ and $\left(\dfrac{2a\sqrt{2}}{3}, 0.955 \right)$

The equation of the initial line is $\theta = 0$ and that is the tangent through $(0, 0)$.

The equation of the tangent through $\left(\dfrac{2a\sqrt{2}}{3}, 0.955 \right)$

is $y = \dfrac{2a\sqrt{2}}{3} \times \sin \theta = \dfrac{2a\sqrt{2}}{3} \times \dfrac{\sqrt{2}}{\sqrt{3}} = \dfrac{4a}{3\sqrt{3}}$

So the equation of the tangent is

$r = \dfrac{4a}{3\sqrt{3}} \operatorname{cosec} \theta$

b $x = r \cos \theta = a \cos \theta \sin 2\theta$

$\dfrac{dx}{d\theta} = -a \sin \theta \sin 2\theta + 2a \cos \theta \cos 2\theta$

$\quad = 2a \cos \theta (-\sin^2 \theta + \cos^2 \theta - \sin^2 \theta)$

$\dfrac{dx}{d\theta} = 0 \Rightarrow \cos \theta = 0 \Rightarrow \theta = \dfrac{\pi}{2}$

So the y-axis is a tangent.

Or $\quad \cos^2 \theta - 2 \sin^2 \theta = 0 \Rightarrow \tan \theta = \pm \dfrac{1}{\sqrt{2}}$

So $\quad \theta = 0.615$

and $r = 2a \times \dfrac{\sqrt{2}}{\sqrt{3}} \times \dfrac{1}{\sqrt{3}} = \dfrac{2a\sqrt{2}}{3}$

The tangent is at $\left(\dfrac{2a\sqrt{2}}{3}, 0.615 \right)$

$x = \dfrac{2a\sqrt{2}}{3} \times \cos \alpha = \dfrac{2a\sqrt{2}}{3} \times \dfrac{\sqrt{2}}{\sqrt{3}} = \dfrac{4a}{3\sqrt{3}}$

So the equation of the tangent is:

$r = \dfrac{4a}{3\sqrt{3}} \sec \theta$

Form an expression for y and differentiate using the product rule.

Use $\sin 2\theta \equiv 2 \sin \theta \cos \theta$ and then take out the common factor. Then use $\cos 2\theta \equiv \cos^2 \theta - \sin^2 \theta$

Choose values of θ within the range given in the question.

If $\tan a = \sqrt{2}$ then drawing a triangle shows that $\sin \alpha = \dfrac{\sqrt{2}}{\sqrt{3}}$ and $\cos \alpha = \dfrac{1}{\sqrt{3}}$
Use $\sin 2A \equiv 2 \sin A \cos A$ to find r.

Use $y = r \sin \theta$ to find the equation of the tangent and write it in polar form using $r = y \operatorname{cosec} \theta$.

Form an expression for x and differentiate using the product rule.

Use $\sin 2\theta = 2 \sin \theta \cos \theta$ and then take out the common factor. Then use a formula for $\cos 2\theta$.

If $\alpha = \dfrac{1}{\sqrt{2}}$ then drawing a triangle shows that $\cos \alpha = \dfrac{\sqrt{2}}{\sqrt{3}}$ and $\sin \alpha = \dfrac{1}{\sqrt{3}}$.
Use $\sin 2A \equiv 2 \sin A \cos A$ to find r.

Use $x = r \cos \theta$ to find the equation of the tangent in the form $r = x \sec \theta$.

Example 14

The curve C has equation $r = (p + q\cos\theta)$, where p and q are positive constants and $p > q$.
Prove that the curve is convex for $p \geqslant 2q$, and has a dimple for $p < 2q$.

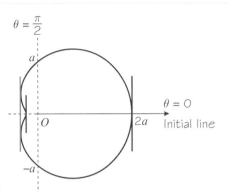

Problem-solving

If the curve is not convex then there will be more than two tangents to the curve that are perpendicular to the initial line.

$x = r\cos\theta = p\cos\theta + q\cos^2\theta$

$\dfrac{dx}{d\theta} = 0 \Rightarrow 0 = -p\sin\theta - 2q\cos\theta\sin\theta$

$\Rightarrow 0 = -\sin\theta(p + 2q\cos\theta)$

— Find an expression for x and differentiate.

This has solutions

$\sin\theta = 0$ when $\theta = 0$ or π

and $\cos\theta = -\dfrac{p}{2q}$

— Solve the equation and consider all possible cases.

If $p < 2q$ then there will be two solutions to this equation in the second and third quadrants (the green tangents). In this case the curve is not convex and has a dimple.

— The two tangents at the two points represented by these solutions have the same equation.

If $p = 2q$ then the solution is $\theta = \pi$ and so there are only two tangents (the blue ones). In this case the curve is convex.

If $p > 2q$ then there is no solution to this equation and only the two blue tangents are possible. In this case the curve is convex.

Hence the curve is convex for $p \geqslant 2q$, and has a dimple for $p < 2q$.

Exercise 5D

1 Find the points on the cardioid $r = a(1 + \cos\theta)$ where the tangents are perpendicular to the initial line.

2 Find the points on the spiral $r = e^{2\theta}$, $0 \leqslant \theta \leqslant \pi$, where the tangents are
   a perpendicular to the initial line   b parallel to the initial line.
   Give your answers to three significant figures.

3 a Find the points on the curve $r = a\cos 2\theta$, $-\frac{\pi}{4} \leqslant \theta \leqslant \frac{\pi}{4}$, where the tangents are parallel to the initial line, giving your answers to three significant figures where appropriate.

b Find the equations of these tangents.

(E) **4** Find the points on the curve with equation $r = a(7 + 2\cos\theta)$ where the tangents are parallel to the initial line. **(6 marks)**

(E) **5** Find the equations of the tangents to $r = 2 + \cos\theta$ that are perpendicular to the initial line. **(6 marks)**

(E) **6** Find the point on the curve with equation $r = a(1 + \tan\theta)$, $0 \leqslant \theta < \frac{\pi}{2}$, where the tangent is perpendicular to the initial line. **(6 marks)**

(E/P) **7** The curve C has polar equation

$$r = 1 + 3\cos\theta, \qquad 0 \leqslant \theta \leqslant \frac{\pi}{2}$$

The tangent to C at a point A on the curve is parallel to the initial line.

Point O is the pole.

Find the exact length of the line OA. **(7 marks)**

(E/P) **8** The diagram shows a cardioid with polar equation

$$r = 2(1 + \cos\theta)$$

The shaded area is enclosed by the curve and the vertical line segment which is tangent to the curve and perpendicular to the initial line.

Find the shaded area, correct to three significant figures. **(8 marks)**

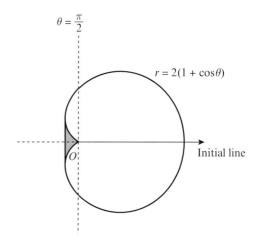

Mixed exercise 5

(E) **1** Determine the area enclosed by the curve with equation

$$r = a(1 + \tfrac{1}{2}\sin\theta), \quad a > 0, \quad 0 \leqslant \theta < 2\pi,$$

giving your answer in terms of a and π. **(6 marks)**

(E/P) **2 a** Sketch the curve with equation $r = a(1 + \cos\theta)$ for $0 \leqslant \theta \leqslant \pi$, where $a > 0$. **(2 marks)**

b Sketch also the line with equation $r = 2a\sec\theta$ for $-\frac{\pi}{2} < \theta < \frac{\pi}{2}$, on the same diagram. **(2 marks)**

c The half-line with equation $\theta = \alpha$, $0 < \alpha < \frac{\pi}{2}$, meets the curve at A and the line with equation $r = 2a\sec\theta$ at B. If O is the pole, find the value of $\cos\alpha$ for which $OB = 2OA$. **(5 marks)**

(E/P) **3** Sketch, in the same diagram, the curves with equations $r = 3\cos\theta$ and $r = 1 + \cos\theta$ and find the area of the region lying inside both curves. **(9 marks)**

(E) **4** Find the polar coordinates of the points on $r^2 = a^2 \sin 2\theta$ where the tangent is perpendicular to the initial line. **(7 marks)**

(E/P) **5 a** Shade the region R for which the polar coordinates r, θ satisfy

$$r \leqslant 4\cos 2\theta \quad \text{for} \quad -\frac{\pi}{4} \leqslant \theta \leqslant \frac{\pi}{4}$$ **(2 marks)**

  b Find the area of R. **(5 marks)**

(E) **6** Sketch the curve with polar equation $r = a(1 - \cos\theta)$, where $a > 0$, stating the polar coordinates of the point on the curve at which r has its maximum value. **(5 marks)**

(E/P) **7 a** On the same diagram, sketch the curve C_1 with polar equation

$$r = 2\cos 2\theta, \quad -\frac{\pi}{4} < \theta \leqslant \frac{\pi}{4}$$
  and the curve C_2 with polar equation $\theta = \frac{\pi}{12}$ **(3 marks)**

  b Find the area of the smaller region bounded by C_1 and C_2. **(6 marks)**

(E) **8 a** Sketch on the same diagram the circle with polar equation $r = 4\cos\theta$ and the line with polar equation $r = 2\sec\theta$. **(4 marks)**

  b State polar coordinates for their points of intersection. **(4 marks)**

(E/P) **9** The diagram shows a sketch of the curves with polar equations

$$r = a(1 + \cos\theta) \text{ and } r = 3a\cos\theta, a > 0$$

  a Find the polar coordinates of the point of intersection P of the two curves. **(4 marks)**

  b Find the area, shaded in the figure, bounded by the two curves and by the initial line $\theta = 0$, giving your answer in terms of a and π. **(7 marks)**

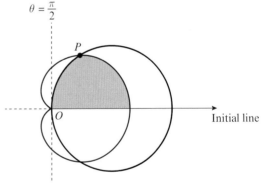

(E/P) **10** Obtain a Cartesian equation for the curve with polar equation

  a $r^2 = \sec 2\theta$ **(4 marks)**

  b $r^2 = \operatorname{cosec} 2\theta$ **(4 marks)**

(E/P) **11 a** Show on an Argand diagram the locus of points given by the values of z satisfying

$$|z - 1 - i| = \sqrt{2}$$ **(2 marks)**

  b Show that this locus of points can be represented by the polar curve

$$r = 2\cos\theta + 2\sin\theta$$ **(4 marks)**

  The set of points, A, is defined by

$$A = \left\{ z : \frac{\pi}{6} \leqslant \arg z \leqslant \frac{\pi}{2} \right\} \cap \left\{ z : |z - 1 - i| \leqslant \sqrt{2} \right\}$$

  c Show, by sketching on your Argand diagram, the set of points, A. **(2 marks)**

  d Find, correct to three significant figures, the area of the region defined by A. **(5 marks)**

(E) 12 The diagram shows the curve C with polar equation
$$r = 4\cos 2\theta, \qquad 0 \leqslant \theta \leqslant \frac{\pi}{4}$$

At point A the value of r is 2. Point A lies on C and point B lies on the initial line vertically below A.

Find, correct to three significant figures, the area of the finite region bounded by the curve, the line segment AB and the initial line, shown shaded in the diagram. **(9 marks)**

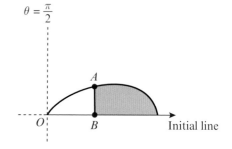

(E/P) 13 The diagram shows the curve with polar equation
$$r = 4\sin 2\theta, \qquad 0 \leqslant \theta \leqslant \frac{\pi}{2}$$

The shaded region is bounded by the curve, the initial line and the tangent to the curve which is perpendicular to the initial line.

Find, correct to two decimal places, the area of the shaded region. **(8 marks)**

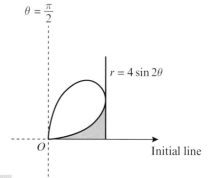

Challenge

The curve C has polar equation $r = \sqrt{2}\theta$.

Show that an equation for the tangent to the curve at the point where $\theta = \frac{\pi}{4}$ is $2(\pi - 4)y + 2(\pi + 4)x = \pi^2$

Summary of key points

1 For a point P with polar coordinates (r, θ) and Cartesian coordinates (x, y),
- $r\cos\theta = x$ and $r\sin\theta = y$
- $r^2 = x^2 + y^2$, $\theta = \arctan\left(\dfrac{y}{x}\right)$

Care must be taken to ensure that θ is in the correct quadrant.

2 • $r = a$ is a circle with centre O and radius a.
- $\theta = \alpha$ is a half-line through O and making an angle α with the initial line.
- $r = a\theta$ is a spiral starting at O.

3 The **area of a sector** bounded by a polar curve and the half-lines $\theta = \alpha$ and $\theta = \beta$, where θ is in radians, is given by the formula
$$\textbf{Area} = \tfrac{1}{2}\int_\alpha^\beta r^2 \, \mathbf{d}\theta$$

4 • To find a tangent parallel to the initial line set $\dfrac{\mathrm{d}y}{\mathrm{d}\theta} = 0$.
- To find a tangent perpendicular to the initial line set $\dfrac{\mathrm{d}x}{\mathrm{d}\theta} = 0$.

Hyperbolic functions

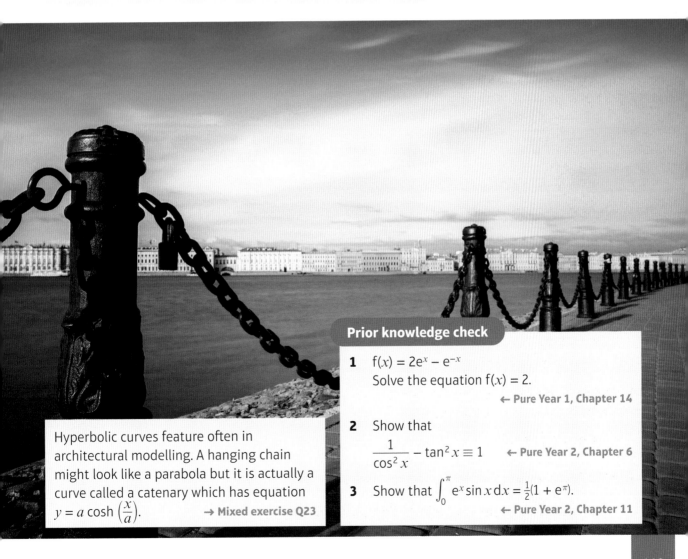

6

Objectives

After completing this chapter you should be able to:

● Understand the definitions of hyperbolic functions
→ pages 120–123

● Sketch the graphs of hyperbolic functions → pages 121–123

● Understand and use the inverse hyperbolic functions
→ pages 123–125

● Prove identities and solve equations using hyperbolic functions → pages 125–129

● Differentiate and integrate hyperbolic functions
→ pages 130–142

Hyperbolic curves feature often in architectural modelling. A hanging chain might look like a parabola but it is actually a curve called a catenary which has equation $y = a \cosh\left(\frac{x}{a}\right)$. → Mixed exercise Q23

Prior knowledge check

1   $f(x) = 2e^x - e^{-x}$
    Solve the equation $f(x) = 2$.
← Pure Year 1, Chapter 14

2   Show that
    $\dfrac{1}{\cos^2 x} - \tan^2 x \equiv 1$ ← Pure Year 2, Chapter 6

3   Show that $\displaystyle\int_0^\pi e^x \sin x \, dx = \tfrac{1}{2}(1 + e^\pi)$.
← Pure Year 2, Chapter 11

6.1 Introduction to hyperbolic functions

Hyperbolic functions have several properties in common with trigonometric functions, but they are defined in terms of exponential functions.

- **Hyperbolic sine (or sinh) is defined as** $\sinh x \equiv \dfrac{e^x - e^{-x}}{2}$

- **Hyperbolic cosine (or cosh) is defined as** $\cosh x \equiv \dfrac{e^x + e^{-x}}{2}$

- **Hyperbolic tangent (or tanh) is defined as** $\tanh x \equiv \dfrac{\sinh x}{\cosh x}$

You can use the definitions of $\sinh x$ and $\cosh x$ to write $\tanh x$ in exponential form.

$$\tanh x \equiv \frac{\sinh x}{\cosh x} \equiv \frac{e^x - e^{-x}}{2} \times \frac{2}{e^x + e^{-x}} \equiv \frac{e^x - e^{-x}}{e^x + e^{-x}}$$

Multiplying the numerator and denominator of the final expression through by e^x gives:

- $\tanh x \equiv \dfrac{e^{2x} - 1}{e^{2x} + 1}$

There are also hyperbolic functions corresponding to the reciprocal trigonometric functions:

$$\operatorname{cosech} x \equiv \frac{1}{\sinh x} \equiv \frac{2}{e^x - e^{-x}}$$

$$\operatorname{sech} x \equiv \frac{1}{\cosh x} \equiv \frac{2}{e^x + e^{-x}}$$

$$\coth x \equiv \frac{1}{\tanh x} \equiv \frac{e^{2x} + 1}{e^{2x} - 1}$$

Note You won't need to use these functions in your exam, but they are useful to know, and if you are confident with them you can use them to simplify your working.

Example 1

Find, to 2 decimal places, the values of:

a $\sinh 3$　　　　**b** $\cosh 1$　　　　**c** $\tanh 0.8$

a $\sinh 3 = \dfrac{e^3 - e^{-3}}{2} = 10.02$ (2 d.p.)

b $\cosh 1 = \dfrac{e^1 + e^{-1}}{2} = 1.54$ (2 d.p.)

c $\tanh 0.8 = \dfrac{e^{1.6} - 1}{e^{1.6} + 1} = 0.66$ (2 d.p.)

Example 2

Find the exact value of $\tanh(\ln 4)$.

$$\tanh(\ln 4) = \frac{e^{2\ln 4} - 1}{e^{2\ln 4} + 1} = \frac{e^{\ln 4^2} - 1}{e^{\ln 4^2} + 1} = \frac{e^{\ln 16} - 1}{e^{\ln 16} + 1}$$

$$= \frac{16 - 1}{16 + 1} = \frac{15}{17}$$

Use $e^{\ln k} = k$.

Example 3

Use the definition of $\sinh x$ to find, to 2 decimal places, the value of x for which $\sinh x = 5$.

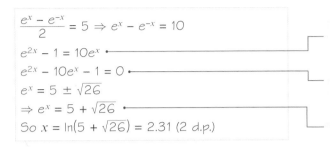

$\dfrac{e^x - e^{-x}}{2} = 5 \Rightarrow e^x - e^{-x} = 10$

$e^{2x} - 1 = 10e^x$

$e^{2x} - 10e^x - 1 = 0$

$e^x = 5 \pm \sqrt{26}$

$\Rightarrow e^x = 5 + \sqrt{26}$

So $x = \ln(5 + \sqrt{26}) = 2.31$ (2 d.p.)

— Multiply both sides by e^x.

— The substitution $u = e^x$ turns this into the quadratic equation $u^2 - 10u - 1 = 0$.

— e^x cannot be negative.

You can sketch the graphs of the hyperbolic functions by considering the graphs of $y = e^x$ and $y = e^{-x}$.

$$\sinh x = \frac{e^x - e^{-x}}{2} = \frac{e^x + (-e^{-x})}{2}$$

so the graph of $y = \sinh x$ is the 'average' of the graphs of $y = e^x$ and $y = -e^{-x}$.

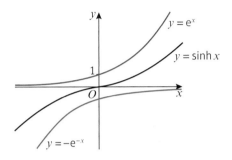

For the graph of $y = \sinh x$,

- when x is large and positive, e^{-x} is small, so $\sinh x \approx \frac{1}{2}e^x$
- when x is large and negative, e^x is small, so $\sinh x \approx -\frac{1}{2}e^{-x}$

- **For any value a, $\sinh(-a) = -\sinh a$**

> **Notation** $f(x) = \sinh x$ is an **odd** function since $f(-x) = -f(x)$.

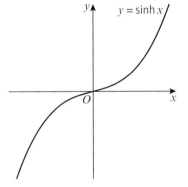

Consider the graphs of $y = e^x$ and $y = e^{-x}$.

$$\cosh x = \frac{e^x + e^{-x}}{2}$$

so the graph of $y = \cosh x$ is the 'average' of the graphs of $y = e^x$ and $y = e^{-x}$.

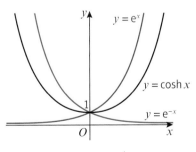

For the graph of $y = \cosh x$,

- when x is large and positive, e^{-x} is small, so $\cosh x \approx \frac{1}{2}e^x$
- when x is large and negative, e^x is small, so $\cosh x \approx \frac{1}{2}e^{-x}$

- **For any value a, $\cosh(-a) = \cosh a$**

> **Notation** $f(x) = \cosh x$ is an **even** function because $f(-x) = f(x)$.

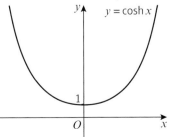

Example (4)

Sketch the graph of $y = \tanh x$.

$\tanh x = \dfrac{\sinh x}{\cosh x}$

When $x = 0$, $\tanh x = \frac{0}{1} = 0$

When x is large and positive, $\sinh x \approx \frac{1}{2}e^x$ and $\cosh x \approx \frac{1}{2}e^x$, so $\tanh x \approx 1$.

When x is large and negative, $\sinh x \approx -\frac{1}{2}e^{-x}$ and $\cosh x \approx \frac{1}{2}e^{-x}$, so $\tanh x \approx -1$.

As $x \to \infty$, $\tanh x \to 1$ and as $x \to -\infty$, $\tanh x \to -1$

For $f(x) = \tanh x$, $x \in \mathbb{R}$, the range of f is $-1 < f(x) < 1$

$y = -1$ and $y = 1$ are asymptotes to the curve.

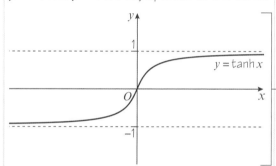

 Online Explore graphs of hyberbolic functions using GeoGebra.

Consider the graphs of $y = \sinh x$ and $y = \cosh x$ to work out the behaviour of $y = \tanh x$ as $x \to \infty$ and $x \to -\infty$.

You should always include any asymptotes on a sketch graph.

Exercise (6A)

1 Find, correct to 2 decimal places:

   a $\sinh 4$ **b** $\cosh \frac{1}{2}$ **c** $\tanh (-2)$

2 Write, in terms of e:

   a $\sinh 1$ **b** $\cosh 4$ **c** $\tanh 0.5$

3 Find the exact values of:

   a $\sinh (\ln 2)$ **b** $\cosh (\ln 3)$ **c** $\tanh (\ln 2)$

In questions **4** to **6**, use the definitions of the hyperbolic functions (in terms of exponentials) to find each answer, then check your answers using an inverse hyperbolic function on your calculator.

4 Find, to 2 decimal places, the values of x for which $\cosh x = 2$.

5 Find, to 2 decimal places, the values of x for which $\sinh x = 1$.

6 Find, to 2 decimal places, the values of x for which $\tanh x = -\frac{1}{2}$

7 On the same diagram, sketch the graphs of $y = \cosh 2x$ and $y = 2\cosh x$.

8 Find the range of each hyperbolic function.

   a $f(x) = \sinh x$, $x \in \mathbb{R}$

   b $f(x) = \cosh x$, $x \in \mathbb{R}$

   c $f(x) = \tanh x$, $x \in \mathbb{R}$

(E) 9 **a** Sketch the graph of $y = 3\tanh x + 2$. **(3 marks)**

      b Write down the equations of the asymptotes to this curve. **(2 marks)**

Challenge Sketch the graphs of:

   a $y = \operatorname{sech} x$ **b** $y = \operatorname{cosech} x$ **c** $y = \coth x$

6.2 Inverse hyperbolic functions

You can define and use the inverses of the hyperbolic functions.

If $f(x) = \sinh x$, the inverse function f^{-1} is called arsinh x.

The graph of $y = \operatorname{arsinh} x$ is the reflection of the graph of $y = \sinh x$ in the line $y = x$.

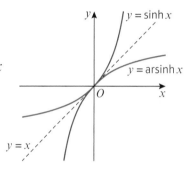

The inverse of a function is defined only if the function is one-to-one, so for $\cosh x$ the domain must be restricted in order to define an inverse.

For $f(x) = \cosh x$, $x \geq 0$, $f^{-1}(x) = \operatorname{arcosh} x$, $x \geq 1$

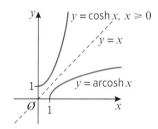

■ **The following table shows the inverse hyperbolic functions, with domains restricted where necessary.**

Hyperbolic function	Inverse hyperbolic function
$y = \sinh x$	$y = \operatorname{arsinh} x$
$y = \cosh x$, $x \geq 0$	$y = \operatorname{arcosh} x$, $x \geq 1$
$y = \tanh x$	$y = \operatorname{artanh} x$, $|x| < 1$

Notation arsinh, arcosh and artanh are sometimes written as $\sinh^{-1}$, $\cosh^{-1}$ and $\tanh^{-1}$.

You can express the inverse hyperbolic functions in terms of natural logarithms.

Example 5

Show that $\operatorname{arsinh} x = \ln\left(x + \sqrt{x^2 + 1}\right)$.

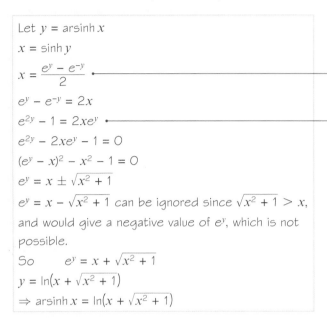

Use the definition of sinh.

Multiply by e^y.

Problem-solving

$e^{2y} - 2xe^y - 1 = 0$ is a quadratic in e^y.
You can write it as $(e^y)^2 - 2xe^y - 1 = 0$ and then complete the square.

Example 6

Show that $\operatorname{arcosh} x = \ln\left(x + \sqrt{x^2 - 1}\right)$, $x \geqslant 1$.

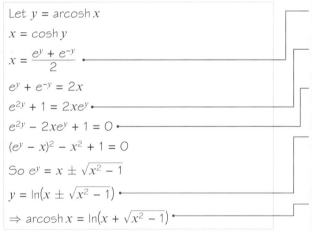

Use the definition of cosh.

Multiply by e^y.

Form and solve a quadratic in e^y.

Note that both $x + \sqrt{x^2 - 1}$ and $x - \sqrt{x^2 - 1}$ are positive.

arcosh x is always non-negative. For all values of $x > 1$, $x - \sqrt{x^2 - 1} < 1$ so the value of $\ln(x - \sqrt{x^2 - 1})$ is negative.

You can use a similar method to express artanh x in terms of natural logarithms.

The following formulae are provided in the formula booklet and can be used directly unless you are asked to prove them .

- **arsinh $x = \ln(x + \sqrt{x^2 + 1})$**   - **arcosh $x = \ln(x + \sqrt{x^2 - 1})$, $x \geqslant 1$**

- **artanh $x = \frac{1}{2}\ln\left(\dfrac{1 + x}{1 - x}\right)$, $|x| < 1$**

Example 7

Express as natural logarithms:

a arsinh 1   **b** arcosh 2   **c** artanh $\frac{1}{3}$

a $\text{arsinh } 1 = \ln\left(1 + \sqrt{1^2 + 1}\right) = \ln\left(1 + \sqrt{2}\right)$

b $\text{arcosh } 2 = \ln\left(2 + \sqrt{2^2 - 1}\right) = \ln\left(2 + \sqrt{3}\right)$

c $\text{artanh } \frac{1}{3} = \frac{1}{2}\ln\left(\dfrac{1 + \frac{1}{3}}{1 - \frac{1}{3}}\right) = \frac{1}{2}\ln 2 = \ln\sqrt{2}$ Use $a \ln x = \ln x^a$.

Exercise 6B

1 Sketch the graph of $y = \text{artanh } x$, $|x| < 1$.

(P) **2** Sketch the graph of $y = (\text{arsinh } x)^2$.

(E/P) **3** Prove that $\text{artanh } x = \frac{1}{2}\ln\left(\dfrac{1 + x}{1 - x}\right)$, $|x| < 1$.   **(5 marks)**

4 Express as natural logarithms:

     a arsinh 2   **b** arcosh 3   **c** artanh $\frac{1}{2}$

5 Express as natural logarithms:

     a arsinh $\sqrt{2}$ **b** arcosh $\sqrt{5}$ **c** artanh 0.1

6 Express as natural logarithms:

     a arsinh (-3) **b** arcosh $\frac{3}{2}$ **c** artanh $\dfrac{1}{\sqrt{3}}$

(E/P) **7** Given that $\text{artanh } x + \text{artanh } y = \ln\sqrt{3}$, prove that $y = \dfrac{2x - 1}{x - 2}$.   **(6 marks)**

6.3 Identities and equations

You can find and use identities for the hyperbolic functions that are similar to the trigonometric identities.

Example 8

Prove that $\cosh^2 A - \sinh^2 A \equiv 1$

$\text{LHS} \equiv \cosh^2 A - \sinh^2 A \equiv \left(\dfrac{e^A + e^{-A}}{2}\right)^2 - \left(\dfrac{e^A - e^{-A}}{2}\right)^2$ Use the definitions of cosh and sinh.

$\equiv \left(\dfrac{e^{2A} + 2 + e^{-2A}}{4}\right) - \left(\dfrac{e^{2A} - 2 + e^{-2A}}{4}\right)$

         $e^A \times e^{-A} = \dfrac{e^A}{e^A} = 1.$

$\equiv \dfrac{4}{4} \equiv 1 \equiv \text{RHS}$

- **$\cosh^2 A - \sinh^2 A \equiv 1$**

Example 9

Prove that $\sinh(A + B) \equiv \sinh A \cosh B + \cosh A \sinh B$

$\text{RHS} \equiv \sinh A \cosh B + \cosh A \sinh B$

$$\equiv \left(\frac{e^A - e^{-A}}{2}\right)\left(\frac{e^B + e^{-B}}{2}\right) + \left(\frac{e^A + e^{-A}}{2}\right)\left(\frac{e^B - e^{-B}}{2}\right)$$

$$\equiv \left(\frac{e^{A+B} + e^{A-B} - e^{-A+B} - e^{-A-B}}{4}\right) + \left(\frac{e^{A+B} - e^{A-B} + e^{-A+B} - e^{-A-B}}{4}\right)$$

$$\equiv \frac{2e^{A+B} - 2e^{-A-B}}{4} \equiv \frac{e^{A+B} - e^{-(A+B)}}{2} \equiv \sinh(A + B) \equiv \text{LHS}$$

You can prove other sinh and cosh addition formulae similarly, giving:

- **$\sinh(A \pm B) \equiv \sinh A \cosh B \pm \cosh A \sinh B$**
- **$\cosh(A \pm B) \equiv \cosh A \cosh B \pm \sinh A \sinh B$**

Example 10

Prove that $\cosh 2A \equiv 1 + 2\sinh^2 A$

$\text{RHS} \equiv 1 + 2\sinh^2 A$

$$\equiv 1 + 2\left(\frac{e^A - e^{-A}}{2}\right)\left(\frac{e^A - e^{-A}}{2}\right) \quad\longleftarrow\quad \text{Use the definition of sinh.}$$

$$\equiv 1 + 2\left(\frac{e^{2A} - 2 + e^{-2A}}{4}\right) \equiv 1 - 1 + \left(\frac{e^{2A} + e^{-2A}}{2}\right)$$

$$\equiv \cosh 2A \equiv \text{LHS}$$

Given a trigonometric identity, it is generally possible to write down the corresponding hyperbolic identity using what is known as **Osborn's rule**:

- Replace cos by cosh: $\cos A \rightarrow \cosh A$

- Replace sin by sinh: $\sin A \rightarrow \sinh A$

However ...

- replace any product (or implied product) of two sin terms by **minus** the product of two sinh terms:

    e.g. $\sin A \sin B \rightarrow -\sinh A \sinh B$

    $\tan^2 A \rightarrow -\tanh^2 A \quad\longleftarrow$ This is the implied product of two sin terms because

    $$\tan^2 A \equiv \frac{\sin^2 A}{\cos^2 A}$$

Example 11

Write down the hyperbolic identity corresponding to:

a $\cos 2A \equiv 2\cos^2 A - 1$ **b** $\tan(A - B) \equiv \dfrac{\tan A - \tan B}{1 + \tan A \tan B}$

> **a** $\cosh 2A \equiv 2\cosh^2 A - 1$
>
> **b** $\tanh(A - B) \equiv \dfrac{\tanh A - \tanh B}{1 - \tanh A \tanh B}$

Implied product of two sin terms because

$\tan A \tan B \equiv \dfrac{\sin A \sin B}{\cos A \cos B}$

Example 12

Given that $\sinh x = \frac{3}{4}$, find the exact value of:

a $\cosh x$ **b** $\tanh x$ **c** $\sinh 2x$

> **a** Using $\cosh^2 x - \sinh^2 x \equiv 1$,
>
> $\cosh^2 x - \frac{9}{16} = 1 \Rightarrow \cosh^2 x = \frac{25}{16}$
>
> $\Rightarrow \cosh x = \frac{5}{4}$
>
> **b** Using $\tanh x \equiv \dfrac{\sinh x}{\cosh x}$
>
> $\tanh x = \frac{3}{4} \div \frac{5}{4} = \frac{3}{5}$
>
> **c** Using $\sinh 2x \equiv 2\sinh x \cosh x$,
>
> $\sinh 2x = 2 \times \frac{3}{4} \times \frac{5}{4} = \frac{15}{8}$

$\cosh x \geqslant 1$, so $\cosh x = -\frac{5}{4}$ is not possible.

You can solve equations involving hyperbolic functions.

Example 13

Solve $6\sinh x - 2\cosh x = 7$ for real values of x.

> $6\left(\dfrac{e^x - e^{-x}}{2}\right) - 2\left(\dfrac{e^x + e^{-x}}{2}\right) = 7$
>
> $3e^x - 3e^{-x} - e^x - e^{-x} = 7$
>
> $2e^x - 7 - 4e^{-x} = 0$
>
> $2e^{2x} - 7e^x - 4 = 0$
>
> $(2e^x + 1)(e^x - 4) = 0$
>
> $e^x = -\frac{1}{2},\ e^x = 4$
>
> $e^x = 4$
>
> $x = \ln 4$

There is no hyperbolic identity that will easily transform the equation into an equation in just one hyperbolic function, so use the basic definitions.

There are no real values of x for which $e^x = -\frac{1}{2}$

Example 14

Solve $2\cosh^2 x - 5\sinh x = 5$, giving your answers as natural logarithms.

Using $\cosh^2 x - \sinh^2 x \equiv 1$, •————————— Use this identity to transform the equation into an equation in just one hyperbolic function.

$2(1 + \sinh^2 x) - 5\sinh x = 5$

$2\sinh^2 x - 5\sinh x - 3 = 0$

$(2\sinh x + 1)(\sinh x - 3) = 0$

So $\sinh x = -\dfrac{1}{2}$ or $\sinh x = 3$

Then,

$\quad x = \text{arsinh}\left(-\dfrac{1}{2}\right) \qquad$ or $x = \text{arsinh } 3$

$\Rightarrow x = \ln\left(-\dfrac{1}{2} + \sqrt{\dfrac{1}{4} + 1}\right)$ or $x = \ln(3 + \sqrt{9 + 1})$ •——— Use $\text{arsinh } x = \ln(x + \sqrt{x^2 + 1})$.

$\Rightarrow x = \ln\left(-\dfrac{1}{2} + \dfrac{\sqrt{5}}{2}\right) \qquad$ or $x = \ln(3 + \sqrt{10})$

Example 15

Solve $\cosh 2x - 5\cosh x + 4 = 0$, giving your answers as natural logarithms where appropriate.

Using $\cosh 2x \equiv 2\cosh^2 x - 1$, •————————— Use this identity to transform the equation into an equation in just one hyperbolic function.

$2\cosh^2 x - 1 - 5\cosh x + 4 = 0$

$\quad 2\cosh^2 x - 5\cosh x + 3 = 0$

$\quad (2\cosh x - 3)(\cosh x - 1) = 0$

So $\cosh x = \dfrac{3}{2}$ or $\cosh x = 1$

$\Rightarrow x = \ln\left(\dfrac{3}{2} \pm \sqrt{\dfrac{9}{4} - 1}\right)$ or $x = 0$•———

$\Rightarrow x = \ln\left(\dfrac{3}{2} \pm \dfrac{\sqrt{5}}{2}\right)$ or $x = 0$

You can use $\text{arcosh } x = \ln(x + \sqrt{x^2 - 1})$, but remember that both $\ln(x + \sqrt{x^2 - 1})$ and $\ln(x - \sqrt{x^2 - 1})$ are possible.

For any value of k greater than 1, $\cosh x = k$ will give two values of x, one positive and one negative.

Exercise 6C

1 Prove the following identities, using the definitions of $\sinh x$ and $\cosh x$.

   a $\sinh 2A \equiv 2\sinh A \cosh A$ **b** $\cosh(A - B) \equiv \cosh A \cosh B - \sinh A \sinh B$

   c $\cosh 3A \equiv 4\cosh^3 A - 3\cosh A$ **d** $\sinh A - \sinh B \equiv 2\sinh\left(\dfrac{A - B}{2}\right)\cosh\left(\dfrac{A + B}{2}\right)$

2 Use Osborn's rule to write down the hyperbolic identities corresponding to the following trigonometric identities.

   a $\sin(A - B) \equiv \sin A \cos B - \cos A \sin B$ **b** $\sin 3A \equiv 3\sin A - 4\sin^3 A$

   c $\cos A + \cos B \equiv 2\cos\left(\dfrac{A + B}{2}\right)\cos\left(\dfrac{A - B}{2}\right)$ **d** $\cos 2A \equiv \dfrac{1 - \tan^2 A}{1 + \tan^2 A}$

   e $\cos 2A \equiv \cos^4 A - \sin^4 A$

3 Given that $\cosh x = 2$, find the exact values of:

   a $\sinh x$ b $\tanh x$ c $\cosh 2x$

4 Given that $\sinh x = -1$, find the exact values of:

   a $\cosh x$ b $\sinh 2x$ c $\tanh 2x$

5 Solve the following equations, giving your answers as natural logarithms.

   a $3\sinh x + 4\cosh x = 4$ b $7\sinh x - 5\cosh x = 1$ c $30\cosh x = 15 + 26\sinh x$

   d $13\sinh x - 7\cosh x + 1 = 0$ e $\cosh 2x - 5\sinh x = 13$ f $3\sinh^2 x - 13\cosh x + 7 = 0$

   g $\sinh 2x - 7\sinh x = 0$ h $4\cosh x + 13e^{-x} = 11$ i $2\tanh x = \cosh x$

(E) 6 a Starting from the definitions of $\sinh x$ and $\cosh x$ in terms of exponentials, prove that

$$\cosh 2x \equiv 2\cosh^2 x - 1$$
                                                                                           (3 marks)

   b Solve the equation

$$\cosh 2x - 3\cosh x = 8$$

     giving your answers as exact logarithms.   **(5 marks)**

(E) 7 Solve the equation

$$2\sinh^2 x - 5\cosh x = 5$$

giving your answer in terms of natural logarithms in simplest form.   **(6 marks)**

(P) 8 Joshua is asked to prove the following identity:

$$\frac{1 + \tanh^2 x}{1 - \tanh^2 x} \equiv 2\cosh^2 x - 1$$

His answer is below.

$$\frac{1 + \tanh^2 x}{1 - \tanh^2 x} \equiv \frac{\text{sech}^2 x}{2 - \text{sech}^2 x} \quad (\text{using } \text{sech}^2 x \equiv 1 + \tanh^2 x: \text{ same identity as the trig one})$$

$$\equiv \frac{\text{sech}^2 x}{2} - 1 \quad (\text{splitting the fraction up and cancelling})$$

$$\equiv \frac{2}{\text{sech}^2 x} - 1 \quad (\text{taking the reciprocal of both terms})$$

$$\equiv 2\cosh^2 x - 1$$

Joshua has made three errors. Explain the errors and provide a correct proof.   **(6 marks)**

(E/P) 9 a Express $10\cosh x + 6\sinh x$ in the form $R\cosh(x + a)$ where $R > 0$. Give the value of a correct to 3 decimal places.   **(4 marks)**

> **Hint** Use the identity for $\cosh(A + B)$.

   b Write down the minimum value of $10\cosh x + 6\sinh x$.   **(1 mark)**

   c Use your answer to part **a** to solve the equation $10\cosh x + 6\sinh x = 11$. Give your answers to 3 decimal places.   **(4 marks)**

6.4 Differentiating hyperbolic functions

You can differentiate hyperbolic functions.

- $\dfrac{\mathrm{d}}{\mathrm{d}x}(\sinh x) = \cosh x$

- $\dfrac{\mathrm{d}}{\mathrm{d}x}(\cosh x) = \sinh x$

- $\dfrac{\mathrm{d}}{\mathrm{d}x}(\tanh x) = \operatorname{sech}^2 x$

Watch out The rules for $\sinh x$ and $\tanh x$ are the same as the corresponding rules for $\sin x$ and $\tan x$. However, the derivative of $\cosh x$ is **positive** $\sinh x$.

Example 16

Show that $\dfrac{\mathrm{d}}{\mathrm{d}x}(\cosh x) = \sinh x$.

$$\cosh x = \frac{e^x + e^{-x}}{2}$$ — Use the definition of $\cosh x$.

$$\text{So } \frac{\mathrm{d}}{\mathrm{d}x}(\cosh x) = \frac{\mathrm{d}}{\mathrm{d}x}\left(\frac{e^x + e^{-x}}{2}\right)$$

Differentiate with respect to x:

$$= \frac{e^x - e^{-x}}{2}$$ $\dfrac{\mathrm{d}}{\mathrm{d}x}(e^{-x}) = -e^{-x}$

$$\frac{e^x - e^{-x}}{2} = \sinh x$$ — By definition.

$$\text{So } \frac{\mathrm{d}}{\mathrm{d}x}(\cosh x) = \sinh x$$

Example 17

Differentiate $\cosh 3x$ with respect to x.

$$\frac{\mathrm{d}}{\mathrm{d}x}(\cosh 3x) = 3 \sinh 3x$$ — Use the chain rule.

Example 18

Differentiate $x^2 \cosh 4x$ with respect to x.

$$\frac{\mathrm{d}}{\mathrm{d}x}(x^2 \cosh 4x) = \frac{\mathrm{d}}{\mathrm{d}x}(x^2)\cosh 4x + x^2\frac{\mathrm{d}}{\mathrm{d}x}(\cosh 4x)$$ — Use the product rule.

$$= 2x \cosh 4x + x^2 \times 4 \sinh 4x$$

$$= 2x \cosh 4x + 4x^2 \sinh 4x$$

Example 19

Given that $y = A \cosh 3x + B \sinh 3x$, where A and B are constants, prove that $\dfrac{d^2y}{dx^2} = 9y$.

$\dfrac{dy}{dx} = 3A \sinh 3x + 3B \cosh 3x$ ———————— Differentiate y.

$\dfrac{d^2y}{dx^2} = 9A \cosh 3x + 9B \sinh 3x$ ———————— Differentiate again.

$= 9(A \cosh 3x + B \sinh 3x)$ ——————— Factorise.

$= 9y$ ———————————

$y = A \cosh 3x + B \sinh 3x$

You can also differentiate the inverse hyperbolic functions.

- $\dfrac{d}{dx} (\text{arsinh } x) = \dfrac{1}{\sqrt{x^2 + 1}}$

- $\dfrac{d}{dx} (\text{arcosh } x) = \dfrac{1}{\sqrt{x^2 - 1}}, \; x > 1$

- $\dfrac{d}{dx} (\text{artanh } x) = \dfrac{1}{1 - x^2}, \; |x| < 1$

Example 20

Given $y = x \, \text{arcosh } x$, find $\dfrac{dy}{dx}$

$\dfrac{dy}{dx} = \text{arcosh } x + x \times \dfrac{1}{\sqrt{x^2 - 1}}$ ——————— Use the product rule.

$= \text{arcosh } x + \dfrac{x}{\sqrt{x^2 - 1}}$

Example 21

Given $y = (\text{arcosh } x)^2$, prove that $(x^2 - 1) \left(\dfrac{dy}{dx}\right)^2 = 4y$.

$\dfrac{dy}{dx} = 2\,\text{arcosh } x \times \dfrac{1}{\sqrt{x^2 - 1}}$ ——————— Use the chain rule.

$\Rightarrow \sqrt{x^2 - 1} \dfrac{dy}{dx} = 2\,\text{arcosh } x$ ——————— Multiply by $\sqrt{x^2 - 1}$.

$\Rightarrow (x^2 - 1)\left(\dfrac{dy}{dx}\right)^2 = 4(\text{arcosh } x)^2$ ——————— Square both sides.

But $y = (\text{arcosh } x)^2$

so $(x^2 - 1)\left(\dfrac{dy}{dx}\right)^2 = 4y$

Example **22**

a Show that $\dfrac{d}{dx}(\text{arsinh}\,x) = \dfrac{1}{\sqrt{1 + x^2}}$

b Find the first two non-zero terms of the series expansion of $\text{arsinh}\,x$.

The general form for the series expansion of $\text{arsinh}\,x$ is given by

$$\text{arsinh}\,x = \sum_{r=0}^{\infty}\left(\frac{(-1)^n (2n)!}{2^{2n}(n!)^2}\right)\frac{x^{2n+1}}{2n+1}$$

c Find, in simplest terms, the coefficient of x^5.

d Use your approximation up to and including the term in x^5 to find an approximate value for $\text{arsinh}\,0.5$.

e Calculate the percentage error in using this approximation.

a Let $y = \text{arsinh}\,x$

then $\quad \sinh y = x$

$\qquad \Rightarrow \dfrac{dx}{dy} = \cosh y$ ————————— Differentiate.

$\qquad\qquad = \sqrt{\sinh^2 y + 1}$ ———————— Use $\cosh^2 x - \sinh^2 x \equiv 1$.

But $\sinh y = x$,

so $\qquad \dfrac{dx}{dy} = \sqrt{x^2 + 1}$ ———————— Take the reciprocal of both sides.

therefore $\dfrac{dy}{dx} = \dfrac{1}{\sqrt{x^2 + 1}}$

Find the second derivative using the chain rule or quotient rule.

b $f(x) = \text{arsinh}\,x \Rightarrow f(0) = 0$

$f'(x) = \dfrac{1}{\sqrt{1 + x^2}} \Rightarrow f'(0) = 1$

$f''(x) = -\dfrac{x}{(1 + x^2)^{\frac{3}{2}}} \Rightarrow f''(0) = 0$

Watch out You need to find the first two non-zero terms. $f(0) = 0$ and $f''(0) = 0$ so there is no constant term and no x^2 term. Differentiate again to find the x^3 term.

$f'''(x) = \dfrac{2x^2 - 1}{(1 + x^2)^{\frac{5}{2}}} \Rightarrow f'''(0) = -1$ ———— Find the third derivative using the quotient rule.

$\text{arsinh}\,x \approx x - \dfrac{x^3}{3!} = x - \dfrac{1}{6}x^3$ ———— Use the standard Maclaurin series expansion.

← **Chapter 2**

c The x^5 term will be when $n = 2$:

$\left(\dfrac{(-1)^2 4!}{2^4 (2!)^2}\right)\dfrac{x^5}{5} = \dfrac{1 \times 24}{16 \times 4} \times \dfrac{x^5}{5} = \dfrac{3}{40}x^5$

The coefficient of x^5 is $\dfrac{3}{40}$

Problem-solving

The general term contains $(-1)^n$ and a power of x^{2n+1}. The non-zero terms will all have odd powers of x and will alternate signs.

d $\text{arsinh}\,0.5 \approx 0.5 - \dfrac{1}{6}(0.5)^3 + \dfrac{3}{40}(0.5)^5$

$\qquad = 0.48151\ldots$

e $\%$ error $= \dfrac{0.48151\ldots - \text{arsinh}\,0.5}{\text{arsinh}\,0.5} \times 100$

$\qquad = 0.062\%$ (3 d.p.)

Exercise **6D**

1 Differentiate with respect to x:

    a $\sinh 2x$ **b** $\cosh 5x$ **c** $\tanh 2x$ **d** $\sinh 3x$

    e $\coth 4x$ **f** $\operatorname{sech} 2x$ **g** $e^{-x} \sinh x$

    h $x \cosh 3x$ **i** $\dfrac{\sinh x}{3x}$ **j** $x^2 \cosh 3x$

    k $\sinh 2x \cosh 3x$ **l** $\ln(\cosh x)$ **m** $\sinh x^3$

    n $\cosh^2 2x$ **o** $e^{\cosh x}$ **p** $\operatorname{cosech} x$

> **Hint** For part **e**, use $\coth x = \dfrac{1}{\tanh x}$
>
> For part **f**, use $\operatorname{sech} 2x = \dfrac{1}{\cosh 2x}$
>
> For part **p**, use $\operatorname{cosech} x = \dfrac{1}{\sinh x}$

(E) **2** If $y = a \cosh nx + b \sinh nx$, where a and b are constants, prove that $\dfrac{d^2y}{dx^2} = n^2y$. **(4 marks)**

(E/P) **3** Find the exact coordinates of the stationary point on the curve with equation
$y = 12 \cosh x - \sinh x$. **(7 marks)**

(E) **4** Given that $y = \cosh 3x \sinh x$, find $\dfrac{d^2y}{dx^2}$ **(6 marks)**

5 Differentiate:

    a $\operatorname{arcosh} 2x$ **b** $\operatorname{arsinh}(x + 1)$ **c** $\operatorname{artanh} 3x$

    d $\operatorname{arsech} x$ **e** $\operatorname{arcosh} x^2$ **f** $\operatorname{arcosh} 3x$

    g $x^2 \operatorname{arcosh} x$ **h** $\operatorname{arsinh} \dfrac{x}{2}$ **i** $e^{x^3} \operatorname{arsinh} x$

    j $\operatorname{arsinh} x \operatorname{arcosh} x$ **k** $\operatorname{arcosh} x \operatorname{sech} x$ **l** $x \operatorname{arcosh} 3x$

(P) **6** Prove that:

    a $\dfrac{d}{dx}(\operatorname{arcosh} x) = \dfrac{1}{\sqrt{x^2 - 1}}, \ x > 1$ **b** $\dfrac{d}{dx}(\operatorname{artanh} x) = \dfrac{1}{1 - x^2}, \ |x| < 1$

(E) **7** Given that $y = \operatorname{artanh}\left(\dfrac{e^x}{2}\right)$, prove that

$$(4 - e^{2x})\dfrac{dy}{dx} = 2e^x$$ **(6 marks)**

(E) **8** Given that $y = \operatorname{arsinh} x$, show that

$$(1 + x^2)\dfrac{d^3y}{dx^3} + 3x\dfrac{d^2y}{dx^2} + \dfrac{dy}{dx} = 0$$ **(7 marks)**

(E) **9** If $y = (\operatorname{arcosh} x)^2$, find $\dfrac{d^2y}{dx^2}$ **(6 marks)**

(E) **10** Find the equation of the tangent at the point where $x = \frac{12}{13}$ on the curve with equation
$y = \text{artanh}\, x$. **(3 marks)**

(E/P) **11** Show that the equation of the normal at the point where $x = 2$ on the curve with equation
$y = \text{arcosh}\, 2x$ can be written as $y = ax + b + \ln c$, where a, b and c are exact real numbers to
be found. **(5 marks)**

(E/P) **12 a** Find the first three non-zero terms of the Maclaurin series for $\cosh x$. **(5 marks)**

b Hence find the percentage error when this approximation is used to evaluate $\cosh 0.2$.
(3 marks)

(E/P) **13 a** Find the first three non-zero terms of the Maclaurin series for $\sinh x$. **(5 marks)**

b Hence find an expression for the nth non-zero term of the Maclaurin series
for $\sinh x$. **(2 marks)**

(E/P) **14** $y = \tanh x$

a Use a Maclaurin series expansion to show that $y \approx x - \frac{1}{3}x^3$. **(5 marks)**

b Find the percentage error when the approximation in **a** is used to evaluate $\tanh 0.8$. **(2 marks)**

(E/P) **15** $y = \text{artanh}\, x$

a Show that the first three non-zero terms of the Maclaurin series of y are
$x + \frac{1}{3}x^3 + \frac{1}{5}x^5$ **(6 marks)**

b Hence write down the general term for the nth non-zero term in the series expansion. **(1 mark)**

c Find the first two non-zero terms of the series expansion of $\cosh x\, \text{artanh}\, x$. **(5 marks)**

(E/P) **16** $y = \sinh x \cosh 2x$
Find the first three non-zero terms of the Maclaurin series for y, giving each coefficient in its
simplest form. **(7 marks)**

(E/P) **17** $y = \cos x \cosh x$

a Show that $\dfrac{d^4 y}{dx^4} = -4y$. **(4 marks)**

b Hence find the first three non-zero terms of the Maclaurin series for y, giving each
coefficient in its simplest form. **(4 marks)**

c Hence write the series expansion for y in the form $\displaystyle\sum_{r=0}^{\infty} f(r)x^{4r}$, where f is function to be
determined. **(2 marks)**

Challenge

Find the first three non-zero terms of the series expansion of $\text{sech}\, x$.

6.5 Integrating hyperbolic functions

You can integrate hyperbolic functions.

■ **You should be familiar with the following integrals:**

- $\int \sinh x \, dx = \cosh x + c$ since $\dfrac{d}{dx}(\cosh x) = \sinh x$

- $\int \cosh x \, dx = \sinh x + c$ since $\dfrac{d}{dx}(\sinh x) = \cosh x$

- $\int \dfrac{1}{\sqrt{1+x^2}} \, dx = \operatorname{arsinh} x + c$ since $\dfrac{d}{dx}(\operatorname{arsinh} x) = \dfrac{1}{\sqrt{1+x^2}}$

- $\int \dfrac{1}{\sqrt{x^2-1}} \, dx = \operatorname{arcosh} x + c, \ x > 1$ since $\dfrac{d}{dx}(\operatorname{arcosh} x) = \dfrac{1}{\sqrt{x^2-1}}, \ x > 1$

Example (23)

Find $\int \cosh(4x - 1) \, dx$.

$$\int \cosh(4x - 1)\,dx = \tfrac{1}{4}\sinh(4x - 1) + c$$

Example (24)

Find $\int \dfrac{2 + 5x}{\sqrt{x^2 + 1}} \, dx$.

$$\int \frac{2 + 5x}{\sqrt{x^2 + 1}}\,dx = \int \frac{2}{\sqrt{x^2 + 1}}\,dx + \int \frac{5x}{\sqrt{x^2 + 1}}\,dx$$

Splitting the numerator gives two recognisable integrals.

$$= 2\int \frac{1}{\sqrt{x^2 + 1}}\,dx + 5\int x(1 + x^2)^{-\frac{1}{2}}dx$$

This is the standard result for arsinh x.

$$= 2\operatorname{arsinh} x + 5\sqrt{1 + x^2} + c$$

This integral is of the form $k\int f'(x)(f(x))^n \, dx$.

← **Pure Year 2, Chapter 9**

Example (25)

Find:

a $\displaystyle\int \cosh^5 2x \sinh 2x \, dx$ **b** $\displaystyle\int \tanh x \, dx$

a $\displaystyle\int \cosh^5 2x \sinh 2x \, dx = \tfrac{1}{2}\int (\cosh 2x)^5 (2 \sinh 2x) \, dx$

Use $\displaystyle\int (f(x))^n f'(x)\,dx = \dfrac{(f(x))^{n+1}}{n+1} + c,$

$$= \tfrac{1}{12}\cosh^6 2x + c$$

with $f(x) = \cosh 2x$ and $n = 5$.

b $\int \tanh x \, dx = \int \frac{\sinh x}{\cosh x} \, dx$

$= \ln \cosh x + c$

Use $\int \frac{f'(x)}{f(x)} dx = \ln|f(x)| + c$,

with $f(x) = \cosh x$. Modulus signs are not necessary because $\cosh x > 0$, for all x.

- $\int \tanh x \, dx = \ln \cosh x + c$

Example 26

Find the following integrals.

a $\int \cosh^2 3x \, dx$ **b** $\int \sinh^3 x \, dx$

a $\int \cosh^2 3x \, dx = \int \frac{1 + \cosh 6x}{2} dx$

$= \frac{1}{2}\left(x + \frac{\sinh 6x}{6}\right) + c$

$= \frac{1}{2}x + \frac{1}{12}\sinh 6x + c$

Use $\cosh 2A \equiv 2\cosh^2 A - 1$ with $A \equiv 3x$.

b $\int \sinh^3 x \, dx = \int \sinh^2 x \sinh x \, dx$

$= \int (\cosh^2 x - 1)\sinh x \, dx$

$= \int \cosh^2 x \sinh x \, dx - \int \sinh x \, dx$

$= \frac{1}{3}\cosh^3 x - \cosh x + c$

Problem-solving

For small odd values of n, you can use $\int \sinh^n x \, dx = \int \sinh^{n-1} x \sinh x \, dx$.

$\int \cosh^n x \, dx$, for odd values of n, can be found similarly.

Sometimes the exponential definition of a hyperbolic function can be used to find a given integral.

Example 27

Find $\int e^{2x} \sinh x \, dx$.

$\int e^{2x}\sinh x \, dx = \int e^{2x}\left(\frac{e^x - e^{-x}}{2}\right) dx$

$= \frac{1}{2}\int (e^{3x} - e^x) \, dx$

$= \frac{1}{2}\left(\frac{e^{3x}}{3} - e^x\right) + c$

$= \frac{1}{6}(e^{3x} - 3e^x) + c$

Use the definition of $\sinh x$.

You need to be able to use hyperbolic substitutions to find the integrals of expressions of the forms

$\int \frac{1}{\sqrt{x^2 - a^2}} dx$ and $\int \frac{1}{\sqrt{x^2 + a^2}} dx$

Example 28

By using an appropriate substitution, find $\int \dfrac{1}{\sqrt{x^2 - a^2}}\, dx$, $x > a$.

As $\cosh^2 u - 1 \equiv \sinh^2 u$, it follows that

$a^2 \cosh^2 u - a^2 = a^2 \sinh^2 u$

Use the substitution $x = a \cosh u$,

$\dfrac{dx}{du} = a \sinh u$

so dx can be replaced by $a \sinh u\, du$.

$\int \dfrac{1}{\sqrt{x^2 - a^2}}\, dx = \int \dfrac{1}{\sqrt{a^2 \cosh^2 u - a^2}}\, a \sinh u\, du$

$= \int \dfrac{1}{a \sinh u} a \sinh u\, du$

$= u + c$

$= \operatorname{arcosh}\left(\dfrac{x}{a}\right) + c$

This is similar to using the substitution $x = a \sin u$ to integrate $\dfrac{1}{\sqrt{a^2 - x^2}}$ ← **Section 3.4**

$x = a \cosh u \Rightarrow \cosh u = \dfrac{x}{a} \Rightarrow u = \operatorname{arcosh}\left(\dfrac{x}{a}\right)$

■ $\int \dfrac{1}{\sqrt{a^2 + x^2}}\, dx = \operatorname{arsinh}\left(\dfrac{x}{a}\right) + c$

■ $\int \dfrac{1}{\sqrt{x^2 - a^2}}\, dx = \operatorname{arcosh}\left(\dfrac{x}{a}\right) + c,\ x > a$

Example 29

Show that $\displaystyle\int_5^8 \dfrac{1}{\sqrt{x^2 - 16}}\, dx = \ln\left(\dfrac{2 + \sqrt{3}}{2}\right)$

$\displaystyle\int_5^8 \dfrac{1}{\sqrt{x^2 - 16}}\, dx = \left[\operatorname{arcosh}\left(\dfrac{x}{4}\right)\right]_5^8$

Use the result for $\int \dfrac{1}{\sqrt{x^2 - a^2}}\, dx$ with $a = 4$.

$= \operatorname{arcosh} 2 - \operatorname{arcosh}\left(\dfrac{5}{4}\right)$

$= \ln(2 + \sqrt{3}) - \ln\left(\dfrac{5}{4} + \sqrt{\dfrac{9}{16}}\right)$

Use $\operatorname{arcosh} x = \ln(x + \sqrt{x^2 - 1})$.

$= \ln(2 + \sqrt{3}) - \ln 2$

$= \ln\left(\dfrac{2 + \sqrt{3}}{2}\right)$

Use $\ln a - \ln b = \ln\left(\dfrac{a}{b}\right)$

Example 30

Show that $\int \sqrt{1 + x^2}\, dx = \frac{1}{2}\operatorname{arsinh} x + \frac{1}{2}x\sqrt{1 + x^2} + c$.

$x = \sinh u \Rightarrow \dfrac{dx}{du} = \cosh u$

so dx can be replaced by $\cosh u\, du$

$\int \sqrt{1 + x^2}\, dx = \int \sqrt{1 + \sinh^2 u}\, \cosh u\, du$

$\qquad = \int \cosh^2 u\, du$

$\qquad = \frac{1}{2}\int (1 + \cosh 2u)\, du$ •————— Use $\cosh 2u \equiv 2\cosh^2 u - 1$.

$\qquad = \frac{1}{2}\left(u + \dfrac{\sinh 2u}{2}\right) + c$ ————— You need to be able to use $x = \sinh u$, so use $\sinh 2u \equiv 2\sinh u\cosh u$.

$\qquad = \frac{1}{2}(u + \sinh u\cosh u) + c$

$\qquad = \frac{1}{2}\operatorname{arsinh} x + \frac{1}{2}x\sqrt{1 + x^2} + c$ •————— $u = \operatorname{arsinh} x$ and $\cosh u \equiv \sqrt{1 + \sinh^2 u}$.

Example 31

By using a hyperbolic substitution, evaluate $\displaystyle\int_0^6 \dfrac{x^3}{\sqrt{x^2 + 9}}\, dx$.

Use the substitution $x = 3\sinh u$ •————— You need to reduce $x^2 + 9$ to a single term.
Using $x = 3\sinh u$ gives
$\dfrac{dx}{du} = 3\cosh u$

So dx can be replaced by $3\cosh u\, du$ $9\sinh^2 u + 9 = 9(\sinh^2 u + 1) = 9\cosh^2 u$

$\displaystyle\int_0^6 \dfrac{x^3}{\sqrt{x^2 + 9}}\, dx = \int_0^{\operatorname{arsinh} 2} \dfrac{27\sinh^3 u}{3\cosh u}\, 3\cosh u\, du$ •————— When $x = 6$, $\sinh u = 2 \Rightarrow u = \operatorname{arsinh} 2$.
When $x = 0$, $\sinh u = 0 \Rightarrow u = 0$.

$\qquad = 27\displaystyle\int_0^{\operatorname{arsinh} 2} \sinh^3 u\, du$ •————— Use the method from Example 26.

$\qquad = 27\left[\frac{1}{3}\cosh^3 u - \cosh u\right]_0^{\operatorname{arsinh} 2}$

$\qquad = 27\left(\dfrac{5\sqrt{5}}{3} - \sqrt{5}\right) - 27\left(\frac{1}{3} - 1\right)$ •————— As $\sinh u = 2$, $\cosh u = \sqrt{1 + 2^2} = \sqrt{5}$.

$\qquad = 18\sqrt{5} + 18$

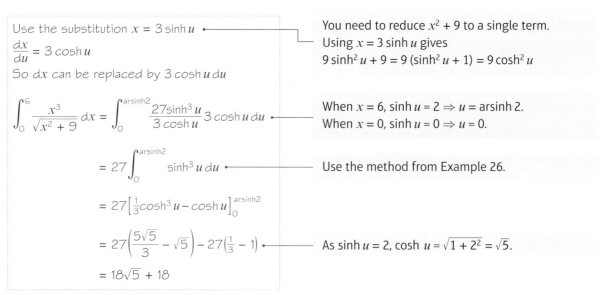

Example **32**

Find $\int \dfrac{1}{\sqrt{12x + 2x^2}}\,dx$.

$12x + 2x^2 = 2(x^2 + 6x)$
$\qquad\qquad = 2((x + 3)^2 - 9)$ — Complete the square.

So $\int \dfrac{1}{\sqrt{12x + 2x^2}}\,dx = \int \dfrac{1}{\sqrt{2((x + 3)^2 - 9)}}\,dx$

Let $u = x + 3$, then $du = dx$ — Choose the substitution.

$\int \dfrac{1}{\sqrt{12x + 2x^2}}\,dx = \dfrac{1}{\sqrt{2}} \int \dfrac{1}{\sqrt{u^2 - 9}}\,du$

$\qquad\qquad = \dfrac{1}{\sqrt{2}} \operatorname{arcosh}\left(\dfrac{u}{3}\right) + c$ — Select the standard form.

$\qquad\qquad = \dfrac{1}{\sqrt{2}} \operatorname{arcosh}\left(\dfrac{x + 3}{3}\right) + c$ — Rewrite the answer in terms of x.

Example **33**

Use the substitution $x = \tfrac{1}{2}(3 + 4\cosh u)$ to find $\int \dfrac{1}{\sqrt{4x^2 - 12x - 7}}\,dx$.

$x = \tfrac{1}{2}(3 + 4\cosh u) \Rightarrow \dfrac{dx}{du} = \tfrac{1}{2}(4\sinh u) = 2\sinh u$

so dx can be replaced by $2\sinh u\,du$

$4x^2 - 12x - 7 = 4\left(\tfrac{1}{2}(3 + 4\cosh u)\right)^2 - 6(3 + 4\cosh u) - 7$

$\qquad\qquad = 9 + 24\cosh u + 16\cosh^2 u - 18 - 24\cosh u - 7$

$\qquad\qquad = 16\cosh^2 u - 16$

$\qquad\qquad = 16\sinh^2 u$ — Use $\cosh^2 u - \sinh^2 u \equiv 1$

So $\int \dfrac{1}{\sqrt{4x^2 - 12x - 7}}\,dx = \int \dfrac{1}{4\sinh u} \times 2\sinh u\,du$

$\qquad\qquad = \tfrac{1}{2} \int 1\,du$

$\qquad\qquad = \tfrac{1}{2}u + c$

$\qquad\qquad = \tfrac{1}{2}\operatorname{arcosh}\left(\dfrac{2x - 3}{4}\right) + c$ — As $x = \tfrac{1}{2}(3 + 4\cosh u)$, $\cosh u = \left(\dfrac{2x - 3}{4}\right)$

Exercise 6E

1 Integrate the following with respect to x.

   a $\sinh x + 3\cosh x$
   b $\cosh x - \dfrac{1}{\cosh^2 x}$
   c $\dfrac{\sinh x}{\cosh^2 x}$

2 Find:

   a $\displaystyle\int \sinh 2x \, dx$
   b $\displaystyle\int \cosh\left(\dfrac{x}{3}\right) dx$

3 Find:

   a $\displaystyle\int \dfrac{1+x}{\sqrt{x^2-1}}\, dx$
   b $\displaystyle\int \dfrac{x-3}{\sqrt{1+x^2}}\, dx$

4 Find:

   a $\displaystyle\int \sinh^3 x \cosh x \, dx$
   b $\displaystyle\int \tanh 4x \, dx$
   c $\displaystyle\int \sqrt{\cosh 2x} \sinh 2x \, dx$

5 Find:

   a $\displaystyle\int \dfrac{\sinh x}{2+3\cosh x}\, dx$
   b $\displaystyle\int \dfrac{1+\tanh x}{\cosh^2 x}\, dx$
   c $\displaystyle\int \dfrac{5\cosh x + 2\sinh x}{\cosh x}\, dx$

6 Use integration by parts to find $\displaystyle\int x \sinh 3x \, dx$.

7 Find:

   a $\displaystyle\int e^x \cosh x \, dx$
   b $\displaystyle\int e^{-2x} \sinh 3x \, dx$
   c $\displaystyle\int \cosh x \cosh 3x \, dx$

8 Evaluate $\displaystyle\int_0^1 \dfrac{1}{\sinh x + \cosh x}\, dx$, giving your answer in terms of e.

9 Use appropriate identities to find:

   a $\displaystyle\int \sinh^2 x \, dx$
   b $\displaystyle\int \sinh^2 x \cosh^2 x \, dx$
   c $\displaystyle\int \cosh^5 x \, dx$

(E) 10 Show that $\displaystyle\int_0^{\ln 2} \cosh^2\left(\dfrac{x}{2}\right) dx = \frac{1}{8}(3 + \ln 16)$.
                                                                      (7 marks)

11 Use suitable substitutions to find:

   a $\displaystyle\int \dfrac{1}{\sqrt{x^2-9}}\, dx$
   b $\displaystyle\int \dfrac{1}{\sqrt{4x^2+25}}\, dx$

12 Write down the results for the following:

   a $\displaystyle\int \dfrac{3}{\sqrt{x^2+9}}\, dx$
   b $\displaystyle\int \dfrac{1}{\sqrt{x^2-2}}\, dx$

13 Find:

   a $\displaystyle\int \frac{1}{\sqrt{4x^2 - 12}}\,dx$ **b** $\displaystyle\int \frac{1}{\sqrt{9x^2 + 16}}\,dx$

14 Evaluate $\displaystyle\int_1^2 \frac{3}{\sqrt{1 + 4x^2}}\,dx$.

15 Evaluate, giving your answers as a single natural logarithms.

   a $\displaystyle\int_0^4 \frac{1}{\sqrt{x^2 + 16}}\,dx$ **b** $\displaystyle\int_{13}^{15} \frac{1}{\sqrt{x^2 - 144}}\,dx$

(E) **16** Use the substitution $x = \sinh^2 u$ to find $\displaystyle\int \sqrt{\frac{x}{x + 1}}\,dx$, $x > 0$.   **(6 marks)**

(E) **17** By using the substitution $u = x^2$, evaluate $\displaystyle\int_2^3 \frac{2x}{\sqrt{x^4 - 1}}\,dx$.   **(6 marks)**

(E) **18** Use the substitution $x = 2\cosh u$ to show that

   $\displaystyle\int \sqrt{x^2 - 4}\,dx = \tfrac{1}{2}x\sqrt{x^2 - 4} - 2\operatorname{arcosh}\left(\frac{x}{2}\right) + c$ **(6 marks)**

(E/P) **19 a** Show that $\displaystyle\int \frac{1}{2\cosh x - \sinh x}\,dx$ can be written as $\displaystyle\int \frac{2e^x}{e^{2x} + 3}\,dx$.   **(3 marks)**

   b Hence, by using the substitution $u = e^x$, find $\displaystyle\int \frac{1}{2\cosh x - \sinh x}\,dx$.   **(5 marks)**

(E/P) **20** Using the substitution $u = \tfrac{2}{3}\sinh x$, evaluate $\displaystyle\int_0^1 \frac{\cosh x}{\sqrt{4\sinh^2 x + 9}}\,dx$.   **(8 marks)**

(P) **21** Find the following:

Problem-solving

Complete the square in the denominator to identify a suitable substitution.

$$\frac{1}{\sqrt{x^2 - 4x - 12}} = \frac{1}{\sqrt{(x-2)^2 - 16}}$$ so the substitution $u = x - 2$ will reduce the integral in part **a** to a standard form.

   a $\displaystyle\int \frac{1}{\sqrt{x^2 - 4x - 12}}\,dx$ **b** $\displaystyle\int \frac{1}{\sqrt{x^2 + 6x + 10}}\,dx$

   c $\displaystyle\int \frac{1}{2x^2 + 4x + 7}\,dx$ **d** $\displaystyle\int \frac{1}{\sqrt{9x^2 - 8x + 1}}\,dx$

(P) **22** Find:

   a $\displaystyle\int \frac{1}{\sqrt{4x^2 - 12x + 10}}\,dx$ **b** $\displaystyle\int \frac{1}{\sqrt{4x^2 - 12x + 4}}\,dx$

(P) **23** Evaluate $\displaystyle\int_0^1 \frac{1}{\sqrt{x^2 + 2x + 5}}\,dx$

(E/P) **24** Evaluate $\displaystyle\int_1^3 \frac{1}{\sqrt{x^2 - 2x + 2}}\,dx$, giving your answer as a single natural logarithm. **(8 marks)**

(E/P) **25** Show that $\displaystyle\int_1^3 \frac{1}{\sqrt{3x^2 - 6x + 7}}\,dx = \frac{1}{\sqrt{3}}\ln(2 + \sqrt{3})$ **(8 marks)**

(E/P) **26** The curves shown have equations

$$y = 5\cosh x \text{ and } y = 7 - \sinh x.$$

a Using the definitions of $\sinh x$ and $\cosh x$ in terms of e^x, find exact values for the x-coordinates of the two points where the curves intersect. **(6 marks)**

b Use calculus to find the area of the finite region, R, between the two curves, giving your answer in the form $\ln a + b$ where a and b are integers. **(6 marks)**

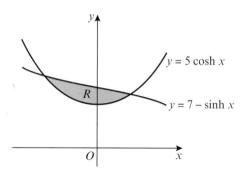

(E/P) **27** The region bounded by the curve $y = \sinh x$, the line $x = 1$ and the positive x-axis is rotated through 360° about the x-axis. Show that the volume of the solid of revolution formed is

$$\frac{\pi}{8e^2}(e^4 - 4e^2 - 1)$$ **(5 marks)**

Challenge

1 Using the substitution $x = 1 + \sinh\theta$, show that

$$\int \frac{1}{(x^2 - 2x + 2)^{\frac{3}{2}}}\,dx = \frac{x - 1}{\sqrt{x^2 - 2x + 2}} + c$$

2 By means of a suitable substitution, or otherwise, find:

a $\displaystyle\int x\cosh^2(x^2)\,dx$ **b** $\displaystyle\int \frac{x}{\cosh^2(x^2)}\,dx$

Mixed exercise 6

1 Find the exact value of: **a** $\sinh(\ln 3)$ **b** $\cosh(\ln 5)$ **c** $\tanh(\ln\frac{1}{4})$

2 Given that $\operatorname{artanh} x - \operatorname{artanh} y = \ln 5$, find y in terms of x.

(E/P) **3** Using the definitions of $\sinh x$ and $\cosh x$, prove that

$$\sinh(A - B) \equiv \sinh A \cosh B - \cosh A \sinh B$$ **(5 marks)**

(E/P) **4** Using definitions in terms of exponentials, prove that

$$\sinh x \equiv \frac{2\tanh\frac{1}{2}x}{1 - \tanh^2\frac{1}{2}x}$$

(5 marks)

(E) **5** Solve, giving your answers as natural logarithms

$9\cosh x - 5\sinh x = 15$

(6 marks)

(E) **6** Solve, giving your answers as natural logarithms

$23\sinh x - 17\cosh x + 7 = 0$

(6 marks)

(E) **7** Solve, giving your answers as natural logarithms

$3\cosh^2 x + 11\sinh x = 17$

(6 marks)

(E) **8 a** On the same diagram, sketch the graphs of $y = 6 + \sinh x$ and $y = \sinh 3x$. **(2 marks)**

    b Using the identity $\sinh 3x \equiv 3\sinh x + 4\sinh^3 x$, show that the graphs intersect where $\sinh x = 1$ and hence find the exact coordinates of the point of intersection. **(5 marks)**

(E/P) **9 a** Given that $13\cosh x + 5\sinh x = R\cosh(x + \alpha)$, $R > 0$, use the identity $\cosh(A + B) \equiv \cosh A\cosh B + \sinh A\sinh B$ to find the values of R and α, giving the value of α to 3 decimal places. **(4 marks)**

    b Write down the minimum value of $13\cosh x + 5\sinh x$. **(1 mark)**

(E/P) **10 a** Express $3\cosh x + 5\sinh x$ in the form $R\sinh(x + \alpha)$, where $R > 0$. Give α to 3 decimal places. **(4 marks)**

    b Use the answer to part **a** to solve the equation $3\cosh x + 5\sinh x = 8$, giving your answer to 2 decimal places. **(3 marks)**

    c Solve $3\cosh x + 5\sinh x = 8$ by using the definitions of $\cosh x$ and $\sinh x$. **(4 marks)**

11 Given $y = \cosh 2x$, find $\dfrac{dy}{dx}$

12 Differentiate with respect to x:

    a $\operatorname{arsinh} 3x$ **b** $\operatorname{arsinh}(x^2)$ **c** $\operatorname{arcosh}\dfrac{x}{2}$ **d** $x^2\operatorname{arcosh} 2x$

(E) **13** Given that $y = (\operatorname{arsinh} x)^2$, prove that

$$(1 + x^2)\frac{d^2y}{dx^2} + x\frac{dy}{dx} - 2 = 0$$

(5 marks)

(E/P) **14** Given that $f(x) = 5\cosh x - 3\sinh x$, find:

    a $f'(x)$ **(2 marks)**

    b the turning point on the curve $y = f(x)$ **(4 marks)**

(E) **15** Differentiate $\operatorname{arcosh}(\sinh 2x)$. **(4 marks)**

E/P **16** $y = \sin x \cosh x$

    a Show that $\dfrac{\mathrm{d}^4 x}{\mathrm{d}y^4} = -4y$.   **(4 marks)**

    b Hence find the first three non-zero terms of the Maclaurin series for y, giving each coefficient in its simplest form.   **(4 marks)**

E/P **17** $y = \sinh 2x \cosh x$

    Find the first three non-zero terms of the Maclaurin series for y, giving each coefficient in its simplest form.   **(7 marks)**

E/P **18** $4x^2 + 4x + 17 \equiv (ax + b)^2 + c,\ a > 0.$

    a Find the values of a, b and c.   **(3 marks)**

    b Find the exact value of $\displaystyle\int_{-\frac{1}{2}}^{\frac{3}{2}} \dfrac{1}{\sqrt{4x^2 + 4x + 17}}\,\mathrm{d}x$ **(6 marks)**

19 Find the following:

    a $\displaystyle\int \sinh 4x \cosh 6x\,\mathrm{d}x$ **b** $\displaystyle\int e^x \sinh x\,\mathrm{d}x$

E/P **20** The diagram shows the cross-section R of an artificial ski slope.

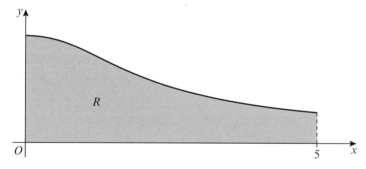

The slope is modelled by the curve with equation

$$y = \dfrac{10}{\sqrt{4x^2 + 9}},\ 0 \leqslant x \leqslant 5$$

Given that 1 unit on each axis represents 10 metres, use integration to calculate the area of R. Show your method clearly and give your answer to 2 significant figures.   **(6 marks)**

E/P **21** Find $\displaystyle\int \dfrac{1}{\sqrt{x^2 - 2x + 10}}\,\mathrm{d}x$ **(7 marks)**

E/P **22**   **a** Find $\displaystyle\int \dfrac{1}{\sinh x + 2\cosh x}\,\mathrm{d}x$ **(6 marks)**

    b Show that $\displaystyle\int_{1}^{4} \dfrac{3x - 1}{\sqrt{x^2 - 2x + 10}}\,\mathrm{d}x = 9(\sqrt{2} - 1) + 2\,\mathrm{arsinh}\,1$ **(6 marks)**

E/P **23** The diagram shows a hanging chain fixed to two vertical bollards fixed on horizontal ground 7 metres apart.

The chain is modelled by the curve $y = \cosh\dfrac{x}{3}$

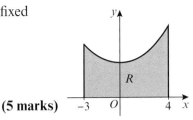

  a Find the acute angle that the chain makes with the right-hand bollard. Give your answer to 3 significant figures. **(5 marks)**

  b Use calculus to find, correct to 2 decimal places, the area of the finite region, R, enclosed by the bollards, the chain and the ground. **(5 marks)**

E **24** The curves shown have equations $y = 3\cosh 2x$ and $y = 8 + \sinh 2x$.

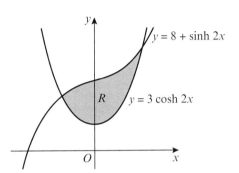

  a Using the definitions of $\sinh x$ and $\cosh x$ in terms of e^x, find exact values for the x-coordinates of the two points where the curves intersect. **(6 marks)**

  b Use calculus to find the area of the finite region, R, between the two curves, giving your answer correct to 3 significant figures. **(6 marks)**

E/P **25** The diagram shows the cross-section of a loaf of bread. Each unit on the axes represents 5 cm. The curved top of the loaf is modelled using the equation

$$y = \frac{5}{\sqrt{x^2 + 4}}$$

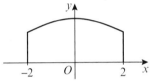

Given that the loaf can be modelled as a prism, with length 30 cm, find, correct to 3 significant figures, the volume of the loaf. **(8 marks)**

E **26** The diagram shows the curve $y = 3 - \sinh x$.

  a Find the exact coordinates of the point where the curve crosses the x-axis. **(3 marks)**

The shaded area is bounded by the curve, the y-axis and the x-axis.

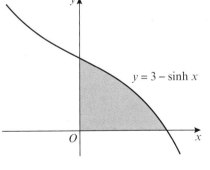

  b Find the volume of the solid of revolution formed when the shaded area is rotated through 360° about the x-axis. Give your answer correct to 3 significant figures. **(8 marks)**

Challenge

The diagram shows the graph of
$y = \operatorname{sech} x$.

Show that the area bounded by the curve and the x-axis is π.

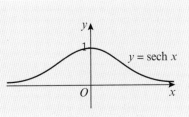

Summary of key points

1 · Hyperbolic sine (or **sinh**) is defined as $\sinh x \equiv \dfrac{e^x - e^{-x}}{2}$, $x \in \mathbb{R}$

· Hyperbolic cosine (or **cosh**) is defined as $\cosh x \equiv \dfrac{e^x + e^{-x}}{2}$, $x \in \mathbb{R}$

· Hyperbolic tangent (or **tanh**) is defined as $\tanh x \equiv \dfrac{\sinh x}{\cosh x} \equiv \dfrac{e^{2x} - 1}{e^{2x} + 1}$, $x \in \mathbb{R}$

2 · The graph of $y = \sinh x$:

· The graph of $y = \cosh x$:

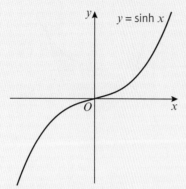

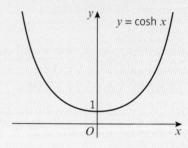

For any value a, $\sinh(-a) = -\sinh a$.

For any value a, $\cosh(-a) = \cosh a$.

3 The table shows the inverse hyperbolic functions, with domains restricted where necessary.

Hyperbolic function	Inverse hyperbolic function
$y = \sinh x$	$y = \operatorname{arsinh} x$
$y = \cosh x$, $x \geqslant 0$	$y = \operatorname{arcosh} x$, $x \geqslant 1$
$y = \tanh x$	$y = \operatorname{artanh} x$, $|x| < 1$

4 · $\operatorname{arsinh} x = \ln\left(x + \sqrt{x^2 + 1}\right)$ · $\operatorname{arcosh} x = \ln\left(x + \sqrt{x^2 - 1}\right)$, $x \geqslant 1$ · $\operatorname{artanh} x = \frac{1}{2}\ln\left(\dfrac{1 + x}{1 - x}\right)$, $|x| < 1$

5 $\cosh^2 A - \sinh^2 A \equiv 1$

6 · $\sinh(A \pm B) \equiv \sinh A \cosh B \pm \cosh A \sinh B$

· $\cosh(A \pm B) \equiv \cosh A \cosh B \pm \sinh A \sinh B$

7 · $\dfrac{\mathrm{d}}{\mathrm{d}x}(\sinh x) = \cosh x$ · $\dfrac{\mathrm{d}}{\mathrm{d}x}(\cosh x) = \sinh x$ · $\dfrac{\mathrm{d}}{\mathrm{d}x}(\tanh x) = \operatorname{sech}^2 x$

· $\dfrac{\mathrm{d}}{\mathrm{d}x}(\operatorname{arsinh} x) = \dfrac{1}{\sqrt{x^2 + 1}}$ · $\dfrac{\mathrm{d}}{\mathrm{d}x}(\operatorname{arcosh} x) = \dfrac{1}{\sqrt{x^2 - 1}}$ · $\dfrac{\mathrm{d}}{\mathrm{d}x}(\operatorname{artanh} x) = \dfrac{1}{1 - x^2}$

8 · $\displaystyle\int \sinh x \, \mathrm{d}x = \cosh x + c$ · $\displaystyle\int \cosh x \, \mathrm{d}x = \sinh x + c$

9 $\displaystyle\int \tanh x \, \mathrm{d}x = \ln \cosh x + c$

10 · $\displaystyle\int \dfrac{1}{\sqrt{a^2 + x^2}} \, \mathrm{d}x = \operatorname{arsinh}\left(\dfrac{x}{a}\right) + c$ · $\displaystyle\int \dfrac{1}{\sqrt{x^2 - a^2}} \, \mathrm{d}x = \operatorname{arcosh}\left(\dfrac{x}{a}\right) + c$, $x > a$

Methods in differential equations

Objectives

After completing this chapter you should be able to:

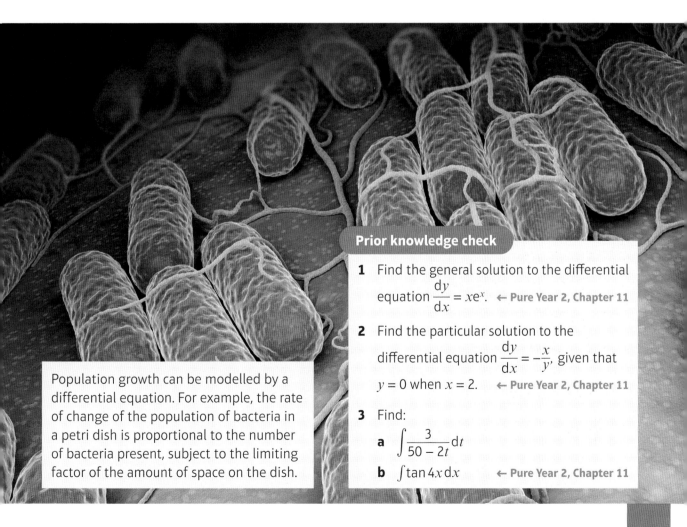

Population growth can be modelled by a differential equation. For example, the rate of change of the population of bacteria in a petri dish is proportional to the number of bacteria present, subject to the limiting factor of the amount of space on the dish.

Prior knowledge check

1 Find the general solution to the differential equation $\dfrac{dy}{dx} = xe^x$. ← **Pure Year 2, Chapter 11**

2 Find the particular solution to the differential equation $\dfrac{dy}{dx} = -\dfrac{x}{y}$, given that $y = 0$ when $x = 2$. ← **Pure Year 2, Chapter 11**

3 Find:

   a $\displaystyle\int \dfrac{3}{50 - 2t}\,dt$

   b $\displaystyle\int \tan 4x\,dx$ ← **Pure Year 2, Chapter 11**

7.1 First-order differential equations

If a first-order differential equation can be written in the form $\dfrac{dy}{dx} = f(x)g(y)$, then you can solve it by writing $\int \dfrac{1}{g(y)} dy = \int f(x) dx$.

Links This process is called **separating the variables**.

← Pure Year 2, Section 11.10

Example 1

Find the general solution to the differential equation

$$\frac{dy}{dx} = -\frac{y}{x}$$

and sketch members of the family of solution curves represented by the general solution.

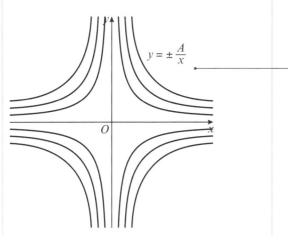

$\int \dfrac{1}{y} dy = -\int \dfrac{1}{x} dx$ — Separate the variables and integrate.

$\ln|y| = -\ln|x| + c$

$\ln|y| + \ln|x| = c$ — Collect the ln terms together and combine using the laws of logarithms.

$\ln|xy| = c$

$|xy| = e^c$

$y = \pm\dfrac{A}{x}$, where $A = e^c$

Some solution curves corresponding to different values of A are shown below.

$y = \pm\dfrac{A}{x}$

Problem-solving

If c is a constant of integration, then $A = e^c$ can also be used as a constant. Writing the equation in this form helps you determine the family of solution curves.

The graphs of $y = \pm\dfrac{A}{x}$ form the family of solution curves for this differential equation.

Online Explore families of solution curves using GeoGebra.

In this chapter, you will consider differential equations which cannot be solved by separating variables. The following example uses the product rule 'in reverse' to obtain a solution.

Example (2)

Find the general solution to the differential equation

$$x^3\frac{dy}{dx} + 3x^2y = \sin x$$

$$x^3\frac{dy}{dx} + 3x^2y = \sin x$$

You can use the product rule

$$u\frac{dv}{dx} + v\frac{du}{dx} = \frac{d}{dx}(uv), \text{ with } u = x^3 \text{ and } v = y, \text{ to}$$

recognise that $x^3\frac{dy}{dx} + 3x^2y = \frac{d}{dx}(x^3y)$.

$$\text{So } \frac{d}{dx}(x^3y) = \sin x$$

$$\Rightarrow x^3y = \int \sin x \, dx$$

Use integration as the inverse process of differentiation.

$$= -\cos x + c$$

$$\text{So } \quad y = -\frac{1}{x^3}\cos x + \frac{c}{x^3}$$

Integrate each side of the equation, including an arbitrary constant on the right-hand side.

Make y the subject by dividing each of the terms on the right-hand side by x^3.

One side of the differential equation in the example above is an exact derivative of a product in the form

$$f(x)\frac{dy}{dx} + f'(x)y = \frac{d}{dx}(f(x)y)$$

You can solve some first-order differential equations by turning them into equations of this form.

Consider the differential equation

$$\frac{dy}{dx} + \frac{3y}{x} = \frac{\sin x}{x^3}$$

The left-hand side is not a derivative of a product but if you multiply both sides by x^3 then the equation becomes the same as that in Example 2:

$$x^3\frac{dy}{dx} + 3x^2y = \sin x$$

Notation x^3 is called an **integrating factor**.

In general, if you can write a linear first-order differential equation in the form

$$\frac{dy}{dx} + P(x)y = Q(x)$$

where $P(x)$ and $Q(x)$ are functions of x, and the function $P(x)$ can be integrated, then it is possible to find an integrating factor which will convert the left-hand side of the equation into an exact derivative of a product. Suppose that the integrating factor has the form $f(x)$, then

$$f(x)\frac{dy}{dx} + f(x)P(x)y = f(x)Q(x)$$

Multiply the equation by the integrating factor $f(x)$.

In order for the left-hand side to be the derivative of the product $f(x)y$ it must have the form $f(x)\frac{dy}{dx} + f'(x)y$. You can see that $f(x)P(x)$ must be equal to $f'(x)$, so:

$$\int \frac{f'(x)}{f(x)}dx = \int P(x)dx$$

Divide both sides by $f(x)$ and integrate.

$$\Rightarrow \ln|f(x)| = \int P(x)dx$$

$$\Rightarrow \quad f(x) = e^{\int P(x)dx}$$

Multiplying every term in the original differential equation by this integrating factor,

$$e^{\int P(x)dx}\frac{dy}{dx} + e^{\int P(x)dx}P(x)y = e^{\int P(x)dx}Q(x)$$

So

$$\frac{d}{dx}\left(e^{\int P(x)dx}y\right) = e^{\int P(x)dx}Q(x) \quad\text{————} \quad \text{You can use the 'product rule in reverse' on the LHS.}$$

$$e^{\int P(x)dx}y = \int e^{\int P(x)dx}Q(x)\,dx \quad\text{————} \quad \text{The equation is now directly solvable by integrating both sides.}$$

Notice that the left-hand side is the integrating factor multiplied by y and the right-hand side is the integral of the integrating factor multiplied by $Q(x)$. This will always be the case.

- **You can solve a first-order differential equation of the form $\dfrac{dy}{dx} + P(x)y = Q(x)$ by multiplying every term by the integrating factor $e^{\int P(x)dx}$.**

Watch out You may write down this integrating factor without proof in your exam, but you must show all the subsequent stages of your working clearly.

Example 3

Find the general solution of the differential equation

$$\frac{dy}{dx} - 4y = e^x$$

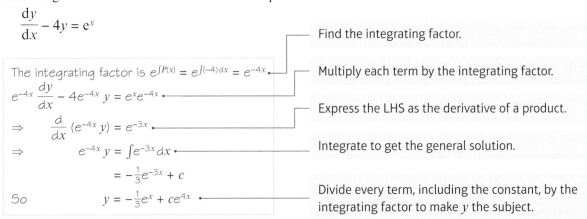

Find the integrating factor.

The integrating factor is $e^{\int P(x)} = e^{\int(-4)dx} = e^{-4x}$

$$e^{-4x}\frac{dy}{dx} - 4e^{-4x}y = e^x e^{-4x}$$

Multiply each term by the integrating factor.

$$\Rightarrow \quad \frac{d}{dx}(e^{-4x}y) = e^{-3x}$$

Express the LHS as the derivative of a product.

$$\Rightarrow \quad e^{-4x}y = \int e^{-3x}dx$$

Integrate to get the general solution.

$$= -\frac{1}{3}e^{-3x} + c$$

So $\quad y = -\frac{1}{3}e^x + ce^{4x}$

Divide every term, including the constant, by the integrating factor to make y the subject.

When you have integrated and found the general solution, you can let the arbitrary constant take different numerical values, thus generating particular solutions.

In some questions you will be given a boundary condition, such as $y = 1$ when $x = 0$. You can use this to find the value of the constant. Different boundary conditions will give rise to different particular solutions.

Example 4

a Find the general solution of the differential equation $\cos x \dfrac{dy}{dx} + 2y \sin x = \cos^4 x$.

b Find the particular solution which satisfies the condition that $y = 2$ when $x = 0$.

a Divide through by $\cos x$:
$$\frac{dy}{dx} + 2y\tan x = \cos^3 x \qquad (1)$$

The integrating factor is
$$e^{\int P(x)dx} = e^{\int 2\tan x\,dx} = e^{2\ln \sec x} = e^{\ln \sec^2 x}$$
$$= \sec^2 x$$

$$\sec^2 x \frac{dy}{dx} + 2y\sec^2 x\tan x = \sec^2 x\cos^3 x$$

So $\dfrac{d}{dx}(y\sec^2 x) = \cos x$

$\Rightarrow \qquad y\sec^2 x = \int\cos x\,dx$

$\Rightarrow \qquad y\sec^2 x = \sin x + c$

$\Rightarrow \qquad y = \cos^2 x(\sin x + c)$

b $2 = \cos^2 0(\sin 0 + c)$

$\Rightarrow c = 2$

$y = \cos^2 x(\sin x + 2)$ is the required particular solution.

Divide by $\cos x$ so that equation is in the form
$$\frac{dy}{dx} + P(x) = Q(x)$$

Use properties of ln to simplify the integrating factor.

Multiply equation (1) by the integrating factor and simplify the right-hand side.

Integrate to get the general solution and multiply through by $\cos^2 x$.

Substitute $y = 2$ and $x = 0$ into the general solution to find c.

Exercise 7A

1 For each of the following differential equations, find the general solution and sketch the family of solution curves.

a $\dfrac{dy}{dx} = 2x$

b $\dfrac{dy}{dx} = y$

c $\dfrac{dy}{dx} = \dfrac{2y}{x}$

d $\dfrac{dy}{dx} = \dfrac{x}{y}$

e $\dfrac{dy}{dx} = \cos x$

f $\dfrac{dy}{dx} = y\cot x, \quad 0 < x < \pi$

Hint You can solve all of these equations by separating variables.

2 Given that k is an arbitrary positive constant,

a show that $y^2 + kx^2 = 9k$ is the general solution to the differential equation
$$\frac{dy}{dx} = \frac{-xy}{9 - x^2}, \qquad |x| < 3$$

b find the particular solution, which passes through the point $(2, 5)$

c sketch the family of solution curves for $k = \frac{1}{9}, \frac{4}{9}, 1$ and include your particular solution in the diagram.

3 Find the general solutions to these differential equations.

a $x\dfrac{dy}{dx} + y = \cos x$

b $e^{-x}\dfrac{dy}{dx} - e^{-x}y = xe^x$

c $\sin x\dfrac{dy}{dx} + y\cos x = 3$

d $\dfrac{1}{x}\dfrac{dy}{dx} - \dfrac{1}{x^2}y = e^x$

e $x^2 e^y \dfrac{dy}{dx} + 2xe^y = x$

f $4xy\dfrac{dy}{dx} + 2y^2 = x^2$

(E) **4 a** Find the general solution to the differential equation $\dfrac{dy}{dx} + 2xy = e^{-x^2}$ **(4 marks)**

b Describe the behaviour of y as $x \to \infty$. **(1 mark)**

5 a Find the general solution to the differential equation

$$x^2 \frac{dy}{dx} + 2xy = 2x + 1$$

b Find the three particular solutions which pass through the points with coordinates $(-\frac{1}{2}, 0)$, $(-\frac{1}{2}, 3)$ and $(-\frac{1}{2}, 19)$ respectively and sketch their solution curves for $x < 0$.

6 a Find the general solution to the differential equation

$$\ln x \frac{dy}{dx} + \frac{y}{x} = \frac{1}{(x+1)(x+2)}, \qquad x > 1$$

b Find the particular solution which passes through the point $(2, 2)$.

7 Find the general solutions to these differential equations by using an integrating factor.

a $\dfrac{dy}{dx} + 2y = e^x$ 　　　　　　　　**b** $\dfrac{dy}{dx} + y \cot x = 1$

c $\dfrac{dy}{dx} + y \sin x = e^{\cos x}$ 　　　　**d** $\dfrac{dy}{dx} - y = e^{2x}$

e $\dfrac{dy}{dx} + y \tan x = x \cos x$ 　　　　**f** $\dfrac{dy}{dx} + \dfrac{y}{x} = \dfrac{1}{x^2}$

g $x^2 \dfrac{dy}{dx} - xy = \dfrac{x^3}{x+2}, x > -2$ 　　**h** $3x \dfrac{dy}{dx} + y = x$

i $(x+2) \dfrac{dy}{dx} - y = x + 2$ 　　　　**j** $x \dfrac{dy}{dx} + 4y = \dfrac{e^x}{x^2}$

(E) **8** Find y in terms of x given that $x \dfrac{dy}{dx} + 2y = e^x$ and that $y = 1$ when $x = 1$. **(8 marks)**

(E) **9** Solve the differential equation, giving y in terms of x, where $x^3 \dfrac{dy}{dx} - x^2 y = 1$ and $y = 1$ at $x = 1$. **(8 marks)**

(E) **10 a** Find the general solution to the differential equation

$$\left(x + \frac{1}{x}\right) \frac{dy}{dx} + 2y = 2(x^2 + 1)^2$$

giving y in terms of x. **(6 marks)**

b Find the particular solution which satisfies the condition that $y = 1$ at $x = 1$. **(2 marks)**

(E) **11 a** Find the general solution to the differential equation

$$\cos x \frac{dy}{dx} + y = 1, \quad -\frac{\pi}{2} < x < \frac{\pi}{2}$$ **(6 marks)**

b Find the particular solution which satisfies the condition that $y = 2$ at $x = 0$. **(2 marks)**

(E/P) **12** Find the general solution to the differential equation

$$\frac{dy}{dx} = x\sqrt{y^2 - 4}$$ **(5 marks)**

Problem-solving

You can use the substitution $y = 2\cosh u$ to integrate $\dfrac{1}{\sqrt{y^2 - 4}}$ ← Section 6.5

(E/P) 13 a Find the general solution to the differential equation

$$\frac{\mathrm{d}y}{\mathrm{d}x} = y \cosh x \qquad \textbf{(4 marks)}$$

b Find the particular solution which satisfies the condition that $y = \mathrm{e}$ when $x = 0$. **(2 marks)**

(E/P) 14 a Find the general solution to the differential equation

$$\frac{\mathrm{d}y}{\mathrm{d}x} = \sqrt{1 + y^2} \qquad \textbf{(4 marks)}$$

b Sketch the family of solution curves. **(3 marks)**

(E) 15 a Find the general solution to the differential equation

$$\cos x \frac{\mathrm{d}y}{\mathrm{d}x} + y \sin x = 1 \qquad \textbf{(6 marks)}$$

b Find the particular solution such that $y = 3$ when $x = \pi$. **(2 marks)**

c Show that the points $\left(\frac{\pi}{2}, 1\right)$ and $\left(\frac{3\pi}{2}, -1\right)$ lie on all possible solution curves. **(3 marks)**

(E/P) 16 Find a general solution to the equation $a\frac{\mathrm{d}y}{\mathrm{d}x} + by = 0$ in terms of a and b. **(6 marks)**

7.2 Second-order homogeneous differential equations

A second-order differential equation contains second derivatives.

Example 5

Find the general solution to the differential equation

$$\frac{\mathrm{d}^2 y}{\mathrm{d}x^2} = 12x$$

> **Watch out** The general solution to this second-order differential equation needs **two** arbitrary constants. If you wanted to find a particular solution you would need to know **two** boundary conditions.

$$\frac{\mathrm{d}y}{\mathrm{d}x} = 6x^2 + A$$

$$y = 2x^3 + Ax + B$$

In this section you will look at techniques for solving **linear** differential equations that are of the form

$$a\frac{\mathrm{d}^2 y}{\mathrm{d}x^2} + b\frac{\mathrm{d}y}{\mathrm{d}x} + cy = 0$$

where a, b and c are real constants. Equations of this form (with 0 on the right-hand side) are called **second-order homogeneous** differential equations with constant coefficients.

> **Notation** You sometimes see differential equations of this type written as
> $$ay'' + by' + cy = 0 \text{ where } y'' = \frac{\mathrm{d}^2 y}{\mathrm{d}x^2} \text{ and } y' = \frac{\mathrm{d}y}{\mathrm{d}x}$$

Using the techniques from the previous section, the general solution of $a\frac{\mathrm{d}y}{\mathrm{d}x} + by = 0$ is of the form $y = A\mathrm{e}^{kx}$, where $k = -\frac{b}{a}$. Notice that k is the solution to the equation $ak + b = 0$.

This suggests that an equation of the form $y = Ae^{kx}$ might also be a solution of the second-order differential equation $a\dfrac{d^2y}{dx^2} + b\dfrac{dy}{dx} + cy = 0$. But it cannot be the general solution, as it only contains one arbitrary constant. Since two constants are necessary for a second-order differential equation, you can try a solution of the form $y = Ae^{\lambda x} + Be^{\mu x}$, where A and B are arbitrary constants and λ and μ are constants to be determined.

$$\frac{dy}{dx} = A\lambda e^{\lambda x} + B\mu e^{\mu x}$$

$$\frac{d^2y}{dx^2} = A\lambda^2 e^{\lambda x} + B\mu^2 e^{\mu x}$$

Substituting these into the differential equation gives

$$a(A\lambda^2 e^{\lambda x} + B\mu^2 e^{\mu x}) + b(A\lambda e^{\lambda x} + B\mu e^{\mu x}) + c(Ae^{\lambda x} + Be^{\mu x}) = 0$$

$$aA\lambda^2 e^{\lambda x} + aB\mu^2 e^{\mu x} + bA\lambda e^{\lambda x} + bB\mu e^{\mu x} + cAe^{\lambda x} + cBe^{\mu x} = 0$$

$$Ae^{\lambda x}(a\lambda^2 + b\lambda + c) + Be^{\mu x}(a\mu^2 + b\mu + c) = 0$$

This shows that the equation $y = Ae^{\lambda x} + Be^{\mu x}$ will satisfy the original differential equation if both λ and μ are solutions to the quadratic equation $am^2 + bm + c = 0$.

The equation $am^2 + bm + c = 0$ is called the **auxiliary equation.**

- **The natures of the roots α and β of the auxiliary equation, $am^2 + bm + c = 0$ determine the general solution to the differential equation $a\dfrac{d^2y}{dx^2} + b\dfrac{dy}{dx} + cy = 0$.**
  You need to consider three different cases:

  - **Case 1: $b^2 > 4ac$**
    The auxiliary equation has two distinct real roots α and β. The general solution will be of the form $y = Ae^{\alpha x} + Be^{\beta x}$ where A and B are arbitrary constants.

  - **Case 2: $b^2 = 4ac$**
    The auxiliary equation has one repeated root α. The general solution will be of the form $y = (A + Bx)e^{\alpha x}$ where A and B are arbitrary constants.

  - **Case 3: $b^2 < 4ac$**
    The auxiliary equation has two complex conjugate roots α and β equal to $p \pm qi$. The general solution will be of the form $y = e^{px}(A\cos qx + B\sin qx)$ where A and B are arbitrary constants.

    Links Case 3 is equivalent to $y = Ae^{\alpha x} + Be^{\beta x}$ with complex α and β. → **Exercise 7B, Challenge**

    Note If the roots are purely imaginary ($p = 0$), the general solution reduces to $y = A\cos qx + B\sin qx$

Example 6

a Find the general solution to the equation $2\dfrac{d^2y}{dx^2} + 5\dfrac{dy}{dx} + 3y = 0$.

b Verify that your answer to part a satisfies the equation.

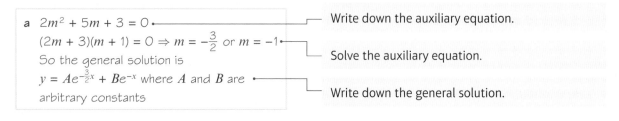

a $2m^2 + 5m + 3 = 0$ ———————————— Write down the auxiliary equation.
  $(2m + 3)(m + 1) = 0 \Rightarrow m = -\dfrac{3}{2}$ or $m = -1$ ——— Solve the auxiliary equation.
  So the general solution is
  $y = Ae^{-\frac{3}{2}x} + Be^{-x}$ where A and B are ——— Write down the general solution.
  arbitrary constants

b $y = Ae^{-\frac{3}{2}x} + Be^{-x}$

$\dfrac{dy}{dx} = -\dfrac{3}{2}Ae^{-\frac{3}{2}x} - Be^{-x}$

$\dfrac{d^2y}{dx^2} = \dfrac{9}{4}Ae^{-\frac{3}{2}x} + Be^{-x}$

$2(\dfrac{9}{4}Ae^{-\frac{3}{2}x} + Be^{-x}) + 5(-\dfrac{3}{2}Ae^{-\frac{3}{2}x} - Be^{-x})$
$\qquad\qquad\qquad + 3(Ae^{-\frac{3}{2}x} + Be^{-x})$

$= \dfrac{9}{2}Ae^{-\frac{3}{2}x} - \dfrac{15}{2}Ae^{-\frac{3}{2}x} + 3Ae^{-\frac{3}{2}x}$
$\qquad + 2Be^{-x} - 5Be^{-x} + 3Be^{-x}$

$= 0$ as required.

Write down expressions for the first and second derivatives.

Substitute your expressions for $\dfrac{d^2y}{dx^2}, \dfrac{dy}{dx}$ and y into the differential equation, expand and simplify.

Example 7

Show that $y = (A + Bx)e^{3x}$ satisfies the differential equation $\dfrac{d^2y}{dx^2} - 6\dfrac{dy}{dx} + 9y = 0$.

Let $y = Ae^{3x} + Bxe^{3x}$, then

$\dfrac{dy}{dx} = 3Ae^{3x} + 3Bxe^{3x} + Be^{3x}$

$\dfrac{d^2y}{dx^2} = 9Ae^{3x} + 9Bxe^{3x} + 3Be^{3x} + 3Be^{3x}$

$= 9Ae^{3x} + 9Bxe^{3x} + 6Be^{3x}$

Differentiate the expression for y twice.

$\dfrac{d^2y}{dx^2} - 6\dfrac{dy}{dx} + 9y = 9Ae^{3x} + 9Bxe^{3x} + 6Be^{3x}$

$\qquad\qquad - 6(3Ae^{3x} + 3Bxe^{3x} + Be^{3x})$
$\qquad\qquad + 9(Ae^{3x} + Bxe^{3x}) = 0$

So $y = (A + Bx)e^{3x}$ is a solution to the equation.

Substitute into the left-hand side of the differential equation and simplify to show that the result is zero.

Note The auxiliary equation $m^2 - 6m + 9 = 0$ has a repeated root at $m = 3$ so the general solution is in the form you expect.

Example 8

Find the general solution to the differential equation $\dfrac{d^2y}{dx^2} + 8\dfrac{dy}{dx} + 16y = 0$.

$m^2 + 8m + 16 = 0$

$(m + 4)^2 = 0 \Rightarrow m = -4$

So the general solution is $y = (A + Bx)e^{-4x}$.

Write down the auxiliary equation.

Solve the auxiliary equation. In this case there is a repeated root.

Example 9

Find the general solution to the differential equation $\dfrac{d^2y}{dx^2} - 6\dfrac{dy}{dx} + 34y = 0$.

$m^2 - 6m + 34 = 0 \Rightarrow m = 3 \pm 5i$

So the general solution is

$y = e^{3x}(A\cos 5x + B\sin 5x)$

Write down the auxiliary equation and solve it using the quadratic formula or by completing the square. In this case there are two complex conjugate roots.

Example **10**

Find the general solution to the differential equation $\dfrac{d^2y}{dx^2} + 16y = 0$.

$m^2 + 16 = 0 \Rightarrow m = \pm 4i$

So the general solution is

$y = A\cos 4x + B\sin 4x$

Write down the auxiliary equation and solve it. In this case there are two purely imaginary roots.

This is in the form $y = e^{px}(A\cos qx + B\sin qx)$ with $p = 0$.

Exercise **7B**

1 Find the general solution to each to the following differential equations.

a $\dfrac{d^2y}{dx^2} + 5\dfrac{dy}{dx} + 6y = 0$

b $\dfrac{d^2y}{dx^2} - 8\dfrac{dy}{dx} + 12y = 0$

c $\dfrac{d^2y}{dx^2} + 2\dfrac{dy}{dx} - 15y = 0$

d $\dfrac{d^2y}{dx^2} - 3\dfrac{dy}{dx} - 28y = 0$

e $\dfrac{d^2y}{dx^2} + 5\dfrac{dy}{dx} = 0$

f $3\dfrac{d^2y}{dx^2} + 7\dfrac{dy}{dx} + 2y = 0$

g $4\dfrac{d^2y}{dx^2} - 7\dfrac{dy}{dx} - 2y = 0$

h $15\dfrac{d^2y}{dx^2} - 7\dfrac{dy}{dx} - 2y = 0$

2 Find the general solution to each of the following differential equations.

a $\dfrac{d^2y}{dx^2} + 10\dfrac{dy}{dx} + 25y = 0$

b $\dfrac{d^2y}{dx^2} - 18\dfrac{dy}{dx} + 81y = 0$

c $\dfrac{d^2y}{dx^2} + 2\dfrac{dy}{dx} + y = 0$

d $\dfrac{d^2y}{dx^2} - 8\dfrac{dy}{dx} + 16y = 0$

e $16\dfrac{d^2y}{dx^2} + 8\dfrac{dy}{dx} + y = 0$

f $4\dfrac{d^2y}{dx^2} - 4\dfrac{dy}{dx} + y = 0$

g $4\dfrac{d^2y}{dx^2} + 20\dfrac{dy}{dx} + 25y = 0$

h $\dfrac{d^2y}{dx^2} + 2\sqrt{3}\dfrac{dy}{dx} + 3y = 0$

3 Find the general solution to each of the following differential equations.

a $\dfrac{d^2y}{dx^2} + 25y = 0$

b $\dfrac{d^2y}{dx^2} + 81y = 0$

c $\dfrac{d^2y}{dx^2} + y = 0$

d $9\dfrac{d^2y}{dx^2} + 16y = 0$

e $\dfrac{d^2y}{dx^2} + 8\dfrac{dy}{dx} + 17y = 0$

f $\dfrac{d^2y}{dx^2} - 4\dfrac{dy}{dx} + 5y = 0$

g $\dfrac{d^2y}{dx^2} + 20\dfrac{dy}{dx} + 109y = 0$

h $\dfrac{d^2y}{dx^2} + \sqrt{3}\dfrac{dy}{dx} + 3y = 0$

4 Find the general solution to each of the following differential equations.

a $\dfrac{d^2y}{dx^2} + 14\dfrac{dy}{dx} + 49y = 0$

b $\dfrac{d^2y}{dx^2} + \dfrac{dy}{dx} - 12y = 0$

c $\dfrac{d^2y}{dx^2} + 4\dfrac{dy}{dx} + 13y = 0$

d $16\dfrac{d^2y}{dx^2} - 24\dfrac{dy}{dx} + 9y = 0$

e $9\dfrac{d^2y}{dx^2} - 6\dfrac{dy}{dx} + 5y = 0$

f $6\dfrac{d^2y}{dx^2} - \dfrac{dy}{dx} - 2y = 0$

(E/P) **5** Given the differential equation $\dfrac{d^2x}{dt^2} + 2k\dfrac{dx}{dt} + 9x = 0$, where k is a real constant,

    a find the general solution to the differential equation in each of the following cases:

        i $|k| > 3$

        ii $|k| < 3$

        iii $|k| = 3$ **(8 marks)**

    b In the case where $k = 2$,

        i find the general solution

        ii describe what happens to x as $t \to \infty$.   **(4 marks)**

(P) **6** Given that $am^2 + bm + c = 0$ has equal roots $m = \alpha$, prove that $y = (A + Bx)e^{\alpha x}$ is a solution to the differential equation $a\dfrac{d^2y}{dx^2} + b\dfrac{dy}{dx} + c = 0$.

(P) **7** Given that $y = f(x)$ and $y = g(x)$ are both solutions to the second-order differential equation $a\dfrac{d^2y}{dx^2} + b\dfrac{dy}{dx} + cy = 0$,

Note This result is known as the **principle of superposition**.

prove that $y = Af(x) + Bg(x)$, where A and B are real constants, is also a solution.

Challenge

Let α and β be the roots of a real-valued quadratic equation, so that $\alpha = p + iq$ and $\beta = p - iq$, $p, q \in \mathbb{R}$. Show that it is possible to choose $A, B \in \mathbb{C}$ such that $Ae^{\alpha x} + Be^{\alpha x}$ can be written in the form $e^{px}(C\cos qx + D\sin qx)$ where C and D are arbitrary real constants.

7.3 Second-order non-homogeneous differential equations

Second-order differential equations of the form

$$a\dfrac{d^2y}{dx^2} + b\dfrac{dy}{dx} + cy = f(x)$$

Notation You sometimes see differential equations of this type written as

$ay'' + by' + cy = f(x)$ where $y'' = \dfrac{d^2y}{dx^2}$ and $y' = \dfrac{dy}{dx}$

are **non-homogeneous**.

To solve an equation of this type you first find the general solution of the corresponding homogeneous differential equation, $a\dfrac{d^2y}{dx^2} + b\dfrac{dy}{dx} + cy = 0$. This is called the **complementary function (C.F.)**.

You then need to find a **particular integral (P.I.)**, which is a function that satisfies the differential equation. The form of the particular integral depends on the form of f(x).

This table provides some particular integrals to try.

Form of f(x)	Form of particular integral
p	λ
$p + qx$	$\lambda + \mu x$
$p + qx + rx^2$	$\lambda + \mu x + \nu x^2$
pe^{kx}	λe^{kx}
$p\cos\omega x + q\sin\omega x$	$\lambda\cos\omega x + \mu\sin\omega x$

Use this form of the P.I. for functions such as $4x^2$ or $1 - x^2$.

Use this form of the P.I. for functions such as $\sin 2x$ or $5\cos x$.

- **A particular integral is a function which satisfies the original differential equation.**

Example 11

Find a particular integral of the differential equation $\dfrac{d^2y}{dx^2} - 5\dfrac{dy}{dx} + 6y = f(x)$ when f(x) is:

a 3 **b** $2x$ **c** $3x^2$ **d** e^x **e** $13\sin 3x$

a Let $y = \lambda$, then $\dfrac{dy}{dx} = 0$ and $\dfrac{d^2y}{dx^2} = 0$

Substitute into $\dfrac{d^2y}{dx^2} - 5\dfrac{dy}{dx} + 6y = 3$:

$0 - 5 \times 0 + 6\lambda = 3$

$\Rightarrow \lambda = \frac{1}{2}$

So a particular integral is $\frac{1}{2}$

When f(x) = 3, which is constant, choose P.I. = λ, which is also constant.

Differentiate twice and substitute the derivatives into the differential equation.

Solve equation to give the value of λ.

b Let $y = \lambda x + \mu$, then $\dfrac{dy}{dx} = \lambda$ and $\dfrac{d^2y}{dx^2} = 0$

Substitute into $\dfrac{d^2y}{dx^2} - 5\dfrac{dy}{dx} + 6y = 2x$:

$0 - 5 \times \lambda + 6(\lambda x + \mu) = 2x$

$\Rightarrow (6\mu - 5\lambda) + 6\lambda x = 2x$

$\Rightarrow 6\mu - 5\lambda = 0$ and $6\lambda = 2$

$\Rightarrow \lambda = \frac{1}{3}$ and $\mu = \frac{5}{18}$

So a particular integral is $\frac{1}{3}x + \frac{5}{18}$

When f(x) = $2x$, which is a linear function of x, choose P.I. = $\lambda x + \mu$.

Differentiate twice and substitute the derivatives into the differential equation.

Equate the constant terms and the coefficients of x to give simultaneous equations, which you can solve to find λ and μ.

c Let $y = \lambda x^2 + \mu x + \nu$

Then $\dfrac{dy}{dx} = 2\lambda x + \mu$ and $\dfrac{d^2y}{dx^2} = 2\lambda$

Substitute into $\dfrac{d^2y}{dx^2} - 5\dfrac{dy}{dx} + 6y = 3x^2$:

$2\lambda - 5(2\lambda x + \mu) + 6(\lambda x^2 + \mu x + \nu) = 3x^2$

$\Rightarrow (2\lambda - 5\mu + 6\nu) + (6\mu - 10\lambda)x + 6\lambda x^2 = 3x^2$

$\Rightarrow 2\lambda - 5\mu + 6\nu = 0, 6\mu - 10\lambda = 0$ and $6\lambda = 3$

$\Rightarrow \lambda = \frac{1}{2}, \mu = \frac{5}{6}$ and $\nu = \frac{19}{36}$

So a particular integral is $\frac{1}{2}x^2 + \frac{5}{6}x + \frac{19}{36}$

As f(x) = $3x^2$, which is a quadratic function of x let P.I. = $\lambda x^2 + \mu x + \nu$.

Equate the constant terms, the coefficients of x and the coefficients of x^2 to give simultaneous equations, which you can solve to find λ, μ and ν.

d Let $y = \lambda e^x$, then $\dfrac{dy}{dx} = \lambda e^x$ and $\dfrac{d^2y}{dx^2} = \lambda e^x$.

As $f(x) = e^x$, which is an exponential function of x let P.I. $= \lambda e^x$.

Substitute into $\dfrac{d^2y}{dx^2} - 5\dfrac{dy}{dx} + 6y = e^x$:

$\lambda e^x - 5\lambda e^x + 6\lambda e^x = e^x$

$\Rightarrow 2\lambda e^x = e^x$

$\Rightarrow \lambda = \tfrac{1}{2}$

Equate coefficients of e^x to find the value of λ.

So a particular integral is $\tfrac{1}{2}e^x$

e Let $y = \lambda \sin 3x + \mu \cos 3x$

As $f(x) = 13 \sin 3x$, which is a trigonometric function of x let P.I. $= \lambda \sin 3x + \mu \cos 3x$, also a similar trigonometric function.

Then $\dfrac{dy}{dx} = 3\lambda \cos 3x - 3\mu \sin 3x$

and $\dfrac{d^2y}{dx^2} = -9\lambda \sin 3x - 9\mu \cos 3x$

Substitute into $\dfrac{d^2y}{dx^2} - 5\dfrac{dy}{dx} + 6y = 13 \sin 3x$:

$-9\lambda \sin 3x - 9\mu \cos 3x - 5(3\lambda \cos 3x - 3\mu \sin 3x)$
$\quad + 6(\lambda \sin 3x + \mu \cos 3x) = 13 \sin 3x$

$\Rightarrow (-9\lambda + 15\mu + 6\lambda) \sin 3x +$
$\qquad (-9\mu - 15\lambda + 6\mu) \cos 3x = 13 \sin 3x$

$\Rightarrow -9\lambda + 15\mu + 6\lambda = 13$

and $-9\mu - 15\lambda + 6\mu = 0$

$\Rightarrow \lambda = -\tfrac{1}{6}$ and $\mu = \tfrac{5}{6}$

So a particular integral is $-\tfrac{1}{6} \sin 3x + \tfrac{5}{6} \cos 3x$

Problem-solving

Equate coefficients of $\sin 3x$ and of $\cos 3x$ and solve simultaneous equations.

- **To find the general solution to the differential equation** $a\dfrac{d^2y}{dx^2} + b\dfrac{dy}{dx} + cy = f(x)$,

  - **Solve the corresponding homogeneous equation** $a\dfrac{d^2y}{dx^2} + b\dfrac{dy}{dx} + cy = 0$ **to find the complementary function (C.F.)**

  - **Choose an appropriate form for the particular integral (P.I.) and substitute into the original equation to find the values of any coefficients.**

  - **The general solution is** $y = $ **C.F.** $+$ **P.I.**

Example **12**

Find the general solution to the differential equation $\dfrac{d^2y}{dx^2} - 5\dfrac{dy}{dx} + 6y = f(x)$ when $f(x)$ is:

a 3 **b** $2x$ **c** $3x^2$ **d** e^x **e** $13 \sin 3x$

$m^2 - 5m + 6 = 0$

$(m - 3)(m - 2) = 0 \Rightarrow m = 3$ or $m = 2$

Solve the auxiliary equation to find the values of m.

Hence the complementary function is

$y = Ae^{3x} + Be^{2x}$ where A and B are arbitrary constants.

The particular integrals were already found in example 11 so the general solutions are:

a $y = Ae^{3x} + Be^{2x} + \frac{1}{2}$

b $y = Ae^{3x} + Be^{2x} + \frac{1}{3}x + \frac{5}{18}$

c $y = Ae^{3x} + Be^{2x} + \frac{1}{2}x^2 + \frac{5}{6}x + \frac{19}{36}$

d $y = Ae^{3x} + Be^{2x} + \frac{1}{2}e^x$

e $y = Ae^{3x} + Be^{2x} - \frac{1}{6}\sin 3x + \frac{5}{6}\cos 3x$

— The general solution is $y = $ C.F. + P.I.

You need to be careful if the standard form of the particular integral contains terms which form part of the complementary function. If this is the case, you need to modify your particular integral so that no two terms in the general solution have the same form.

For example, this situation occurs when f(x) is of the form pe^{kx}, and k is one of the roots of the auxiliary equation. In this case you can try a particular integral of the form, λxe^{kx}.

Example 13

Find the general solution to the differential equation $\dfrac{d^2y}{dx^2} - 5\dfrac{dy}{dx} + 6y = e^{2x}$

As in Example 12, the complementary function is
$y = Ae^{3x} + Be^{2x}$.
The particular integral cannot be λe^{2x},
as this is part of the complementary function.

So let $y = \lambda xe^{2x}$

Then $\dfrac{dy}{dx} = 2\lambda xe^{2x} + \lambda e^{2x}$

and

$\dfrac{d^2y}{dx^2} = 4\lambda xe^{2x} + 2\lambda e^{2x} + 2\lambda e^{2x} = 4\lambda xe^{2x} + 4\lambda e^{2x}$

Substitute into $\dfrac{d^2y}{dx^2} - 5\dfrac{dy}{dx} + 6y = e^{2x}$:

$4\lambda xe^{2x} + 4\lambda e^{2x} - 5(2\lambda xe^{2x} + \lambda e^{2x}) + 6\lambda xe^{2x} = e^{2x}$

$\Rightarrow -\lambda e^{2x} = e^{2x}$

$\Rightarrow \lambda = -1$

So a particular integral is $-xe^{2x}$.
The general solution is $y = Ae^{3x} + Be^{2x} - xe^{2x}$. •

Watch out The function λe^{2x} is **part of the C.F.** and satisfies the differential equation
$\dfrac{d^2y}{dx^2} - 5\dfrac{dy}{dx} + 6y = 0$, so it cannot also satisfy
$\dfrac{d^2y}{dx^2} - 5\dfrac{dy}{dx} + 6y = e^{2x}$.

Let the P.I. be λxe^{2x} and differentiate, substitute and solve to find λ.

— The general solution is $y = $ C.F. + P.I.

When one of the roots of the auxiliary equation is 0, the complementary function will contain a constant term. If f(x) is a polynomial, you will need to multiply its particular integral by x to make sure the P.I. does not also contain a constant term.

Example 14

Find the general solution to the differential equation
$$\frac{d^2y}{dx^2} - 2\frac{dy}{dx} = 3$$

Find the complementary function by putting the right-hand side of the differential equation equal to zero, and solving this new equation.

First consider the equation $\dfrac{d^2y}{dx^2} - 2\dfrac{dy}{dx} = 0$

$m^2 - 2m = 0$

$m(m - 2) = 0$

$\Rightarrow m = 0$ or $m = 2$

So the complementary function is $y = A + Be^{2x}$.

The particular integral cannot be a constant, as this is part of the complementary function, so let $y = \lambda x$.

Then $\dfrac{dy}{dx} = \lambda$ and $\dfrac{d^2y}{dx^2} = 0$

Substitute into $\dfrac{d^2y}{dx^2} - 2\dfrac{dy}{dx} = 3$:

$0 - 2\lambda = 3$

$\Rightarrow \lambda = -\dfrac{3}{2}$

So a particular integral is $-\dfrac{3}{2}x$

The general solution is $y = A + Be^{2x} - \dfrac{3}{2}x$.

Write down and solve the auxiliary equation.

Try to find a particular integral. The right-hand side of the original equation was 3, which was a constant and usually this would imply a constant P.I.

As the C.F. includes a constant term 'A', the P.I. cannot also be constant. A value of λ would satisfy $\dfrac{d^2y}{dx^2} - 2\dfrac{dy}{dx} = 0$ rather than $\dfrac{d^2y}{dx^2} - 2\dfrac{dy}{dx} = 3$.

Multiply the 'expected' P.I. by x and try λx instead.

The general solution is $y = $ C.F. + P.I.

Exercise 7C

1 Solve each of the following differential equations, giving the general solution.

a $\dfrac{d^2y}{dx^2} + 6\dfrac{dy}{dx} + 5y = 10$

b $\dfrac{d^2y}{dx^2} - 8\dfrac{dy}{dx} + 12y = 36x$

c $\dfrac{d^2y}{dx^2} + \dfrac{dy}{dx} - 12y = 12e^{2x}$

d $\dfrac{d^2y}{dx^2} + 2\dfrac{dy}{dx} - 15y = 5$

e $\dfrac{d^2y}{dx^2} - 8\dfrac{dy}{dx} + 16y = 8x + 12$

f $\dfrac{d^2y}{dx^2} + 2\dfrac{dy}{dx} + y = 25\cos 2x$

g $\dfrac{d^2y}{dx^2} + 81y = 15e^{3x}$

h $\dfrac{d^2y}{dx^2} + 4y = \sin x$

i $\dfrac{d^2y}{dx^2} - 4\dfrac{dy}{dx} + 5y = 25x^2 - 7$

j $\dfrac{d^2y}{dx^2} - 2\dfrac{dy}{dx} + 26y = e^x$

(E) 2 a Find a particular integral for the differential equation
$$\frac{d^2y}{dx^2} - 5\frac{dy}{dx} + 4y = x^2 - 3x + 2$$
(6 marks)

b Hence find the general solution. **(3 marks)**

E/P **3** y satisfies the differential equation

$$\frac{d^2y}{dx^2} - 6\frac{dy}{dx} = 2x^2 - x + 1$$

    a Find the complementary function for this differential equation. **(3 marks)**

    b Hence find a suitable particular integral and write down the general solution to the differential equation. **(7 marks)**

> **Hint** Try a particular integral of the form $\lambda x + \mu x^2 + \nu x^3$.

E/P **4** Find the general solution to the differential equation

$$\frac{d^2y}{dx^2} + 4\frac{dy}{dx} = 24x^2$$

    (10 marks)

E/P **5** **a** Explain why $\lambda x e^x$ is not a suitable form for the particular integral for the differential equation

$$\frac{d^2y}{dx^2} - 2\frac{dy}{dx} + y = e^x$$

    (2 marks)

    b Find the value of λ for which $\lambda x^2 e^x$ is a particular integral for the differential equation.

    (5 marks)

    c Hence find the general solution. **(3 marks)**

E/P **6** $\dfrac{d^2y}{dt^2} + 4\dfrac{dy}{dt} + 3y = kt + 5$, where k is a constant and $t > 0$.

    a Find the general solution to the differential equation in terms of k. **(7 marks)**

    For large values of t, this general solution may be approximated by a linear function.

    b Given that $k = 6$, find the equation of this linear function. **(2 marks)**

Challenge

Find the general solution of the differential equation

$$\frac{d^2y}{dx^2} + y = 5xe^{2x}$$

7.4 Using boundary conditions

You can use given boundary conditions to find a particular solution to a second-order differential equation. Since there are two arbitrary constants, you will need two boundary conditions to determine the complete particular solution.

Example **15**

Find y in terms of x, given that $\dfrac{d^2y}{dx^2} - y = 2e^x$, and that $\dfrac{dy}{dx} = 0$ and $y = 0$ at $x = 0$.

First consider the equation $\dfrac{d^2y}{dx^2} - y = 0$.

$m^2 - 1 = 0 \Rightarrow m = \pm 1$

So the complementary function is $y = Ae^x + Be^{-x}$.

Solve the auxiliary equation to find the values of m.

The particular integral cannot be λe^x, as this is part of the complementary function, so let $y = \lambda x e^x$.

Then $\dfrac{dy}{dx} = \lambda x e^x + \lambda e^x$ and $\dfrac{d^2y}{dx^2} = \lambda x e^x + \lambda e^x + \lambda e^x$

Substitute into $\dfrac{d^2y}{dx^2} - y = 2e^x$:

$\lambda x e^x + \lambda e^x + \lambda e^x - \lambda x e^x = 2e^x$

$\Rightarrow \lambda = 1$

So a particular integral is $x e^x$.

The general solution is

$y = Ae^x + Be^{-x} + xe^x$

Since $y = 0$ at $x = 0$, $0 = A + B$

$\Rightarrow A + B = 0$

Differentiating $y = Ae^x + Be^{-x} + xe^x$ with respect to x gives

$\dfrac{dy}{dx} = Ae^x - Be^{-x} + e^x + xe^x$

Since $\dfrac{dy}{dx} = 0$ at $x = 0$, $0 = A - B + 1$

$\Rightarrow A - B = -1$

Solving the simultaneous equations gives

$A = -\frac{1}{2}$, and $B = \frac{1}{2}$

So $y = -\frac{1}{2}e^x + \frac{1}{2}e^{-x} + xe^x$ is the required solution.

As λe^x satisfies $\dfrac{d^2y}{dx^2} - y = 0$, it cannot also satisfy $\dfrac{d^2y}{dx^2} - y = 2e^x$.

Substitute the boundary condition, $y = 0$ at $x = 0$, into the general solution to obtain an equation relating A and B.

Substitute the second boundary condition, $\dfrac{dy}{dx} = 0$ at $x = 0$, into the derivative of the general solution, to obtain a second equation relating A and B.

Solve the two equations to find values for A and B.

Example 16

Given that a particular integral is of the form $\lambda \sin 2t$, find the solution to the differential equation $\dfrac{d^2x}{dt^2} + x = 3\sin 2t$, for which $x = 0$ and $\dfrac{dx}{dt} = 1$ when $t = 0$.

First consider the equation $\dfrac{d^2x}{dt^2} + x = 0$.

$m^2 + 1 = 0 \Rightarrow m = \pm i$

So, the complementary function is

$x = A\cos t + B\sin t$.

The particular integral is $\lambda \sin 2t$, so let $x = \lambda \sin 2t$.

Then $\dfrac{dx}{dt} = 2\lambda \cos 2t$ and $\dfrac{d^2x}{dt^2} = -4\lambda \sin 2t$

Substitute into $\dfrac{d^2x}{dt^2} + x = 3\sin 2t$:

$-4\lambda \sin 2t + \lambda \sin 2t = 3\sin 2t$

$\Rightarrow \lambda = -1$

Solve the auxiliary equation to find the values of m.

Watch out Normally you would need to try a particular integral of the form $\lambda \sin 2t + \mu \cos 2t$ for this equation. However, in this case you are told that there is a particular integral in the form $\lambda \sin 2t$.

So a particular integral is $-\sin 2t$.

The general solution is

$x = A \cos t + B \sin t - \sin 2t$

Since $x = 0$ at $t = 0$, $A = 0$.

Differentiating $x = B \sin t - \sin 2t$ with respect to t gives

$\dfrac{dx}{dt} = B \cos t - 2 \cos 2t$

Since $\dfrac{dx}{dt} = 1$ at $t = 0$, $1 = B - 2$

$\Rightarrow \quad B = 3$

And so $x = 3 \sin t - \sin 2t$ is the required solution.

Use general solution = complementary function + particular integral.

Substitute the initial condition, $x = 0$ at $t = 0$, into the general solution to obtain $A = 0$.

Substitute the second initial condition, $\dfrac{dx}{dt} = 1$ at $t = 0$, into the derivative of the general solution, to obtain a second equation leading to $B = 3$.

Exercise 7D

(E) 1 a Find the general solution to the differential equation

$$\frac{d^2y}{dx^2} + 5\frac{dy}{dx} + 6y = 12e^x$$ **(5 marks)**

b Hence find the particular solution that satisfies $y = 1$ and $\dfrac{dy}{dx} = 0$ when $x = 0$. **(4 marks)**

(E) 2 a Find the general solution to the differential equation

$$\frac{d^2y}{dx^2} + 2\frac{dy}{dx} = 12e^{2x}$$ **(5 marks)**

b Hence find the particular solution that satisfies $y = 2$ and $\dfrac{dy}{dx} = 6$ when $x = 0$. **(5 marks)**

(E) 3 Given that $y = 0$ and $\dfrac{dy}{dx} = \frac{1}{6}$ when $x = 0$, find the particular solution to the differential equation

$$\frac{d^2y}{dx^2} - \frac{dy}{dx} - 42y = 14$$ **(10 marks)**

(E) 4 a Find the general solution to the differential equation

$$\frac{d^2y}{dx^2} + 9y = 16\sin x$$ **(6 marks)**

b Hence find the particular solution that satisfies $y = 1$ and $\dfrac{dy}{dx} = 8$ when $x = 0$. **(6 marks)**

(E) 5 a Find the general solution to the differential equation

$$4\frac{d^2y}{dx^2} + 4\frac{dy}{dx} + 5y = \sin x + 4\cos x$$ **(6 marks)**

b Hence find the particular solution that satisfies $y = 0$ and $\dfrac{dy}{dx} = 0$ when $x = 0$. **(6 marks)**

(E/P) 6 a Find the general solution to the differential equation

$$\frac{d^2x}{dt^2} - 3\frac{dx}{dt} + 2x = 2t - 3$$ **(6 marks)**

b Given that $x = 1$ when $t = 0$, and $x = 2$ when $t = 1$, find a particular solution of this differential equation. **(6 marks)**

(E) **7** Find the particular solution to the differential equation

$$\frac{d^2x}{dt^2} - 9x = 10\sin t$$

that satisfies $x = 2$ and $\frac{dx}{dt} = -1$ when $t = 0$. **(10 marks)**

(E/P) **8 a i** Find the value of λ for which $y = \lambda t^3 e^{2t}$ is a particular solution to the differential equation

$$\frac{d^2x}{dt^2} - 4\frac{dx}{dt} + 4x = 3te^{2t}$$

    ii Hence find the general solution to the differential equation. **(6 marks)**

  b Find the particular solution that satisfies $x = 0$ and $\frac{dx}{dt} = 1$ when $t = 0$. **(6 marks)**

(E) **9** Find the particular solution to the differential equation

$$25\frac{d^2x}{dt^2} + 36x = 18$$

that satisfies $x = 1$ and $\frac{dx}{dt} = 0.6$ when $t = 0$. **(12 marks)**

(E) **10 a** Find the general solution to the differential equation

$$\frac{d^2x}{dt^2} - 2\frac{dx}{dt} + 2x = 2t^2$$ **(6 marks)**

  b Hence find the particular solution that satisfies $x = 1$ and $\frac{dx}{dt} = 3$ when $t = 0$. **(6 marks)**

(E/P) **11 a** Find the general solution to the differential equation

$$\frac{d^2y}{dx^2} - 3\frac{dy}{dx} + 2y = 3e^{2x}$$ **(7 marks)**

  b Hence find the particular solution that satisfies $y = 0$, $\frac{dy}{dx} = 0$ when $x = 0$. **(6 marks)**

(E/P) **12** Solve the differential equation

$$\frac{d^2y}{dx^2} + 9y = \sin 3x$$

subject to the boundary conditions $y = 0$, $\frac{dy}{dx} = 0$ when $x = 0$. **(14 marks)**

(E/P) **13** $\dfrac{d^2x}{dt^2} + 5\dfrac{dx}{dt} + 6x = 2e^{-t}$

Given that $x = 0$ and $\frac{dx}{dt} = 2$ at $t = 0$,

  a find x in terms of t. **(8 marks)**

  b Show that the maximum value of x is $\dfrac{2\sqrt{3}}{9}$ and justify that this is a maximum. **(7 marks)**

Mixed exercise 7

(E) **1** Find the general solution to the differential equation

$$\frac{dy}{dx} + y\tan x = 2\sec x$$

giving your answer in the form $y = f(x)$. **(7 marks)**

(E) **2** Find the general solution to the differential equation

$$(1 - x^2)\frac{dy}{dx} + xy = 5x, \quad -1 < x < 1$$

giving your answer in the form $y = f(x)$. **(7 marks)**

(E) **3** Find the general solution to the differential equation

$$x\frac{dy}{dx} + x + y = 0$$

giving your answer in the form $y = f(x)$. **(7 marks)**

(E) **4** y satisfies the differential equation

$$\frac{dy}{dx} + \frac{y}{x} = \sqrt{x}$$

Find y as a function of x. **(7 marks)**

(E) **5** y satisfies the differential equation

$$\frac{dy}{dx} + 2xy = x$$

Find y in terms of x. **(7 marks)**

(E/P) **6** Find the general solution to the differential equation

$$x(1 - x^2)\frac{dy}{dx} + (2x^2 - 1)y = 2x^3, \quad 0 < x < 1$$

giving your answer in the form $y = f(x)$. **(7 marks)**

(E/P) **7** Find the general solution to the equation $\frac{dy}{dx} - ay = Q(x)$, where a is a constant, giving your answer in terms of a, when

a $Q(x) = ke^{\lambda x}$ (k and λ are constants). **(6 marks)**

Given that $Q(x) = kx^n e^{ax}$, where k and n are constants,

b find the general solution to the differential equation. **(7 marks)**

(E/P) **8** Find, in the form $y = f(x)$, the general solution to the differential equation

$$\tan x \frac{dy}{dx} + y = 2\cos x \tan x, \, 0 < x < \frac{\pi}{2}$$ **(6 marks)**

(E) **9 a** Find the general solution to the differential equation

$$\frac{dy}{dx} + y \tan x = e^x \cos x, \, -\frac{\pi}{2} < x < \frac{\pi}{2}$$

giving your answer in the form $y = f(x)$. **(6 marks)**

b Find the particular solution for which $y = 1$ at $x = \pi$. **(3 marks)**

(E) **10** $\frac{dy}{dx} - 3y = \sin x$

Given that $y = 0$ when $x = 0$, find y in terms of x. **(7 marks)**

(E/P) **11 a** Find the general solution to the differential equation

$$\frac{dy}{dx} = y \sinh x$$ **(4 marks)**

b Find the particular solution which satisfies the condition that $y = 1$ when $x = 0$. **(2 marks)**

(E) **12** $\frac{dy}{dx} = x(4 - y^2)$

Given that $y = 1$ when $x = 0$, find y in terms of x. **(7 marks)**

(E) **13** Find the general solution to the differential equation $\frac{d^2y}{dx^2} + \frac{dy}{dx} + y = 0$ **(6 marks)**

(E) **14** Find the general solution to the differential equation $\frac{d^2y}{dx^2} - 12\frac{dy}{dx} + 36y = 0$ **(6 marks)**

(E) **15** Find the general solution to the differential equation $\frac{d^2y}{dx^2} - 4\frac{dy}{dx} = 0$ **(6 marks)**

(E/P) **16** Find y in terms of k and x, given that $\frac{d^2y}{dx^2} + k^2y = 0$ where k is a constant, and $y = 1$

and $\frac{dy}{dx} = 1$ at $x = 0$. **(8 marks)**

(E) **17** Find the solution to the differential equation $\frac{d^2y}{dx^2} - 2\frac{dy}{dx} + 10y = 0$ for which $y = 0$

and $\frac{dy}{dx} = 3$ at $x = 0$. **(8 marks)**

(E) **18 a** Find the value of k for which $y = ke^{2x}$ is a particular integral of the differential equation

$$\frac{d^2y}{dx^2} - 4\frac{dy}{dx} + 13y = e^{2x}$$ **(4 marks)**

b Using your answer to part **a**, find the general solution to the differential equation. **(5 marks)**

(E/P) **19** Find the general solution of the differential equation

$$\frac{d^2y}{dx^2} - y = 4e^x$$ **(7 marks)**

(E/P) **20** The differential equation $\frac{d^2y}{dx^2} - 4\frac{dy}{dx} + 4y = 4e^{2x}$ is to be solved.

a Find the complementary function. **(3 marks)**

b Explain why neither λe^{2x} nor $\lambda x e^{2x}$ can be a particular integral for this equation. **(2 marks)**

A particular integral has the form kx^2e^{2x}.

c Determine the value of the constant k and find the general solution of the equation. **(6 marks)**

(E/P) **21** Find the particular solution of the differential equation

$$\frac{d^2y}{dt^2} + 4y = 5\cos 3t$$

which satisfies the initial conditions that when $t = 0$, $y = 1$ and $\frac{dy}{dt} = 2$. **(12 marks)**

(E) **22 a** Find the values of λ, μ and k such that $y = \lambda + \mu x + kxe^{2x}$ is a particular integral of the differential equation

$$\frac{d^2y}{dx^2} - 3\frac{dy}{dx} + 2y = 4x + e^{2x}$$ **(5 marks)**

b Using your answer to part **a**, find the general solution of the differential equation. **(5 marks)**

(E/P) **23 a** Find the solution of the differential equation $16\frac{d^2y}{dx^2} + 8\frac{dy}{dx} + 5y = 5x + 23$ for which $y = 3$ and $\frac{dy}{dx} = 3$ at $x = 0$. **(8 marks)**

b Show that $y \approx x + 3$ for large values of x. **(2 marks)**

(E/P) **24** Find the solution of the differential equation $\frac{d^2y}{dx^2} - \frac{dy}{dx} - 6y = 3\sin 3x - 2\cos 3x$ for which $y = 1$ at $x = 0$ and for which y remains finite as $x \to \infty$. **(8 marks)**

(E/P) **25** x satisfies the differential equation

$$\frac{d^2x}{dt^2} + 8\frac{dx}{dt} + 16x = \cos 4t, \, t \geqslant 0$$

a Find the general solution of the differential equation. **(8 marks)**

b Find the particular solution of this differential equation for which, at $t = 0$, $x = \frac{1}{2}$ and $\frac{dx}{dt} = 0$. **(5 marks)**

c Describe the behaviour of the function for large values of t. **(2 marks)**

Challenge

1 Use the substitution $z = y^2$ to transform the differential equation

$$2(1 + x^2)\frac{dy}{dx} + 2xy = \frac{1}{y}$$

into a differential equation in z and x. By first solving the transformed equation,

a find the general solution of the original equation, giving y in terms of x.

b Find the particular solution for which $y = 2$ when $x = 0$.

2 a Find the general solution of the differential equation

$$x^2\frac{d^2y}{dx^2} + 4x\frac{dy}{dx} + 2y = \ln x, \qquad x > 0,$$

using the substitution $x = e^u$, where u is a function of x.

b Find the equation of the solution curve passing through the point $(1, 1)$ with gradient 1.

Summary of key points

1 You can solve a first-order differential equation of the form $\dfrac{\mathrm{d}y}{\mathrm{d}x} + \mathbf{P}(x)y = \mathbf{Q}(x)$ by multiplying every term by the **integrating factor** $\mathrm{e}^{\int P(x)\mathrm{d}x}$.

2 The natures of the roots α and β of the **auxiliary equation** determine the **general solution** to the second-order differential equation $a\dfrac{\mathrm{d}^2 y}{\mathrm{d}x^2} + b\dfrac{\mathrm{d}y}{\mathrm{d}x} + c = \mathbf{0}$.

   You need to consider three different cases:

   • **Case 1: $b^2 > 4ac$**

      The auxiliary equation has two real roots α and β ($\alpha \neq \beta$). The general solution will be of the form $y = A\mathrm{e}^{\alpha x} + B\mathrm{e}^{\beta x}$ where A and B are arbitrary constants.

   • **Case 2: $b^2 = 4ac$**

      The auxiliary equation has one repeated root α. The general solution will be of the form $y = (A + Bx)\mathrm{e}^{\alpha x}$ where A and B are arbitrary constants.

   • **Case 3: $b^2 < 4ac$**

      The auxiliary equation has two complex conjugate roots α and β equal to $p \pm q\mathrm{i}$. The general solution will be of the form $y = \mathrm{e}^{px}(A\cos qx + B\sin qx)$ where A and B are arbitrary constants.

3 A **particular integral** is a function which satisfies the original differential equation.

4 To find the general solution to the differential equation $a\dfrac{\mathrm{d}^2 y}{\mathrm{d}x^2} + b\dfrac{\mathrm{d}y}{\mathrm{d}x} + cy = \mathbf{f}(x)$,

   • Solve the corresponding homogeneous equation $a\dfrac{\mathrm{d}^2 y}{\mathrm{d}x^2} + b\dfrac{\mathrm{d}y}{\mathrm{d}x} + cy = 0$ to find the complementary function, C.F.

   • Choose an appropriate form for the particular integral, P.I., and substitute into the original equation to find the values of any coefficients.

   • The general solution is $y = $ C.F. + P.I.

Modelling with differential equations

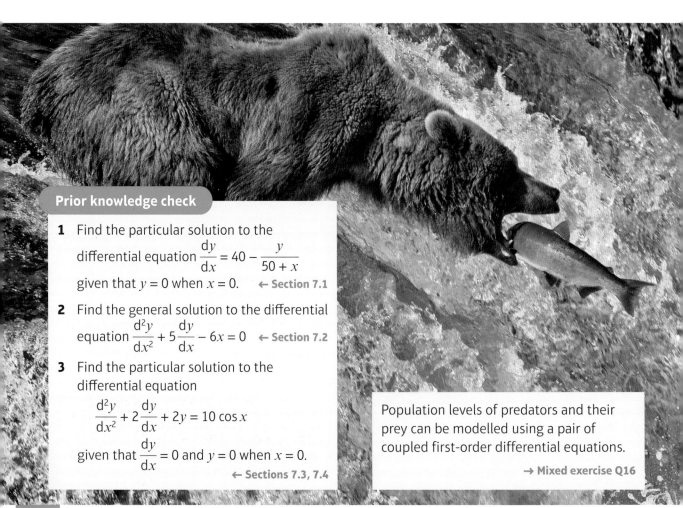

Population levels of predators and their prey can be modelled using a pair of coupled first-order differential equations.
→ **Mixed exercise Q16**

8.1 Modelling with first-order differential equations

First-order differential equations can be used to model problems in kinematics. You have covered some of these contexts in A level mathematics and you have learned the following relationships between displacement, velocity and acceleration:

$$v = \frac{ds}{dt} \qquad a = \frac{dv}{dt}$$

where s is the displacement of a particle, v is the velocity and a is the acceleration at time t.

You can use these relationships to construct first-order differential equations which you can solve using the standard methods of direct integration and separation of variables from A level mathematics, or the method of integrating factors covered in Chapter 7 of this book.

Example 1

A particle P starts from rest at a point O and moves along a straight line. At time t seconds the acceleration, $a\,\mathrm{m\,s^{-2}}$, of P is given by

$$a = \frac{6}{(t + 2)^2}, \, t \geqslant 0$$

a Find the velocity of P at time t seconds.

b Show that the displacement of P from O when $t = 6$ is $(18 - 12\ln 2)\,\mathrm{m}$.

a $\dfrac{dv}{dt} = \dfrac{6}{(t + 2)^2}$ — Write the given relationship as a first-order differential equation.

$v = \displaystyle\int \dfrac{6}{(t + 2)^2}\, dt = \int 6(t + 2)^{-2}\, dt$ — Integrate both sides with respect to t. Notice that this equation can be solved by direct integration.

$v = \dfrac{6(t + 2)^{-1}}{-1} + c$

$= c - \dfrac{6}{t + 2}$ — Remember to include the constant of integration.

When $t = 0$, $v = 0$:

$0 = c - \dfrac{6}{2} \Rightarrow c = 3$ — Use the initial conditions to find the value of c.

The velocity of P at time t seconds is

$\left(3 - \dfrac{6}{t + 2}\right)\mathrm{m\,s^{-1}}.$ — Set up another first-order differential equation using $\dfrac{ds}{dt} = v$.

b $\dfrac{ds}{dt} = 3 - \dfrac{6}{t + 2}$

$s = \displaystyle\int\left(3 - \dfrac{6}{t + 2}\right) dt$ — Solve this differential equation, again using standard methods, and include a second constant of integration. You are told that the particle starts from rest at the origin so your initial conditions are $s = 0$ when $t = 0$.

$= 3t - 6\ln(t + 2) + d$

When $t = 0$, $s = 0$:

$0 = -6\ln 2 + d \Rightarrow d = 6\ln 2$

$s = 3t - 6\ln(t + 2) + 6\ln 2$

When $t = 6$,
$$s = 18 - 6 \ln 8 + 6 \ln 2$$
$$= 18 - 6 \ln \left(\tfrac{8}{2}\right) = 18 - 6 \ln 4$$
$$= 18 - 12 \ln 2$$

The displacement of P from O when $t = 6$ is $(18 - 12 \ln 2)\,\text{m}$, as required.

Use the laws of logarithms to simplify your answer into the form asked for in the question. This can be done in more than one way. The working shown here uses
$$\ln 8 - \ln 2 = \ln \left(\tfrac{8}{2}\right) = \ln 4$$
and
$$\ln 4 = \ln 2^2 = 2 \ln 2.$$

Example 2

A particle P is moving along a straight line. At time t seconds, the acceleration of the particle is given by
$$a = t + \frac{3}{t} v, \ t \geq 0$$
Given that $v = 0$ when $t = 2$, show that the velocity of the particle at time t is given by the equation
$$v = c t^3 - t^2$$
where c is a constant to be found.

$$\frac{dv}{dt} - \frac{3}{t} v = t$$

Integrating factor $= e^{\int P dt} = e^{\int -\frac{3}{t} dt}$
$$= e^{-3 \ln t}$$
$$= e^{\ln t^{-3}}$$
$$= t^{-3}$$

So the original equation becomes

$$t^{-3} \frac{dv}{dt} - 3t^{-4} v = t^{-2}$$

$$\Rightarrow \quad \frac{d}{dt}(t^{-3} v) = t^{-2}$$

$$\Rightarrow \quad t^{-3} v = -t^{-1} + c$$

$$\Rightarrow v = -t^2 + c t^3$$

Since $v = 0$ when $t = 2$,

$$0 = -4 + 8c \Rightarrow c = \frac{1}{2}$$

So the velocity of the particle at time t is given by $v = \frac{1}{2} t^3 - t^2$

Write the differential equation in the form $\frac{dv}{dt} + Pv = Q$ where P and Q are functions of t. To solve this differential equation, you need to use the integrating factor method. ← **Section 7.1**

Find the integrating factor and use the standard method to find the general solution.

Multiply through by t^3 to find v.

First-order differential equations can also be used to model other real-life situations involving rates of change.

You might need to construct or analyse models based on situations other than kinematics in your exam.

Example 3

A storage tank initially contains 1000 litres of pure water. Liquid is removed from the tank at a constant rate of 30 litres per hour and a chemical solution is added to the tank at a constant rate of 40 litres per hour. The chemical solution contains 4 grams of copper sulphate per litre of water.

Given that there are x grams of copper sulphate in the tank after t hours and that the copper sulphate immediately disperses throughout the tank on entry,

a show that the situation can be modelled by the differential equation
$$\frac{\mathrm{d}x}{\mathrm{d}t} = 160 - \frac{3x}{100 + t}, t \geqslant 0$$

b Hence find the number of grams of copper sulphate in the tank after 6 hours.

c Explain how the model could be refined.

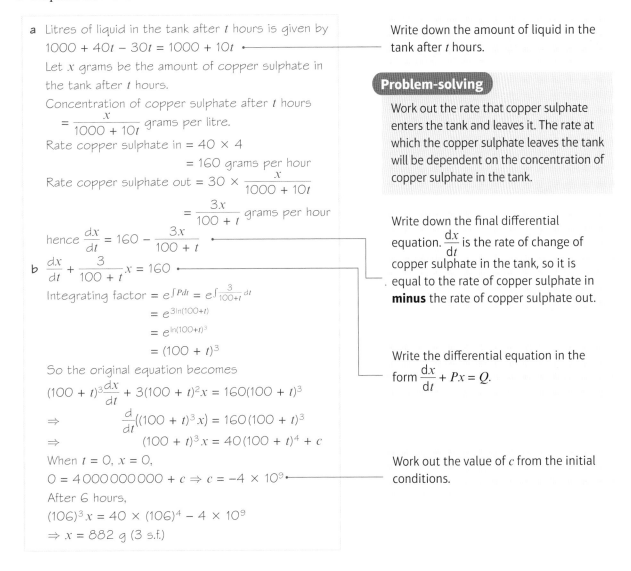

a Litres of liquid in the tank after t hours is given by
$1000 + 40t - 30t = 1000 + 10t$ ⟶ Write down the amount of liquid in the tank after t hours.

Let x grams be the amount of copper sulphate in the tank after t hours.

Concentration of copper sulphate after t hours
$= \dfrac{x}{1000 + 10t}$ grams per litre.

Problem-solving

Work out the rate that copper sulphate enters the tank and leaves it. The rate at which the copper sulphate leaves the tank will be dependent on the concentration of copper sulphate in the tank.

Rate copper sulphate in $= 40 \times 4$
$= 160$ grams per hour

Rate copper sulphate out $= 30 \times \dfrac{x}{1000 + 10t}$
$= \dfrac{3x}{100 + t}$ grams per hour

hence $\dfrac{\mathrm{d}x}{\mathrm{d}t} = 160 - \dfrac{3x}{100 + t}$ ⟶

Write down the final differential equation. $\dfrac{\mathrm{d}x}{\mathrm{d}t}$ is the rate of change of copper sulphate in the tank, so it is equal to the rate of copper sulphate in **minus** the rate of copper sulphate out.

b $\dfrac{\mathrm{d}x}{\mathrm{d}t} + \dfrac{3}{100 + t}x = 160$ ⟶

Integrating factor $= e^{\int P\mathrm{d}t} = e^{\int \frac{3}{100+t}\,\mathrm{d}t}$
$= e^{3\ln(100+t)}$
$= e^{\ln(100+t)^3}$
$= (100 + t)^3$

Write the differential equation in the form $\dfrac{\mathrm{d}x}{\mathrm{d}t} + Px = Q$.

So the original equation becomes
$(100 + t)^3\dfrac{\mathrm{d}x}{\mathrm{d}t} + 3(100 + t)^2 x = 160(100 + t)^3$

$\Rightarrow \qquad \dfrac{\mathrm{d}}{\mathrm{d}t}((100 + t)^3 x) = 160(100 + t)^3$

$\Rightarrow \qquad (100 + t)^3 x = 40(100 + t)^4 + c$

When $t = 0$, $x = 0$,
$0 = 4\,000\,000\,000 + c \Rightarrow c = -4 \times 10^9$ ⟶ Work out the value of c from the initial conditions.

After 6 hours,
$(106)^3 x = 40 \times (106)^4 - 4 \times 10^9$
$\Rightarrow x = 882$ g (3 s.f.)

c The model could be refined to take into account the fact that the copper sulphate does not disperse immediately on entering the tank.

You could give any sensible suggestion here, but make sure it is in the context of the model. For example, the rate at which liquid is removed could be made to vary with the volume of liquid in the tank.

Exercise 8A

1 A particle P is moving along the x-axis in the direction of x increasing. At time t seconds, the velocity of P is $(t \sin t)\,\text{m s}^{-1}$. When $t = 0$, P is at the origin. Show that when $t = \dfrac{\pi}{2}$, P is 1 metre from O.

2 A particle P is moving along a straight line. Initially P is at rest. At time t seconds P has velocity $v\,\text{m s}^{-1}$ and acceleration $a\,\text{m s}^{-2}$ where

$$a = \frac{6t}{(2 + t^2)^2}, \quad t \geqslant 0$$

Find v in terms of t.

(P) 3 A particle P is moving along the x-axis. At time t seconds P has velocity $v\,\text{m s}^{-1}$ in the direction x increasing and an acceleration of magnitude $4\mathrm{e}^{0.2t}\,\text{m s}^{-2}$ in the direction x decreasing. When $t = 0$, P is moving through the origin with velocity $20\,\text{m s}^{-1}$ in the direction x increasing. Find:

a v in terms of t

b the maximum value of x attained by P during its motion.

(P) 4 A particle, P, is moving along the x-axis. At time t seconds, the displacement of the particle from O is $x\,\text{m}$, and its velocity is $v\,\text{m s}^{-1}$, where

$$v = \mathrm{e}^{-\frac{x}{2}}$$

Given that the particle is initially at the origin, find x as a function of t.

(E/P) 5 A sports car moves along a horizontal straight road. At time t seconds the acceleration, in m s^{-2}, is modelled using the differential equation

$$\frac{\mathrm{d}v}{\mathrm{d}t} - 2vt = t$$

where v is the velocity of the car in m s^{-1}.

When $t = 0$, the car is travelling at $1\,\text{m s}^{-1}$.

a Show that the velocity of the car at time t seconds can be written as $v = \frac{1}{2}(3\mathrm{e}^{t^2} - 1)$. **(5 marks)**

b Find the velocity of the car after 2 seconds. **(2 marks)**

c State, with a reason, whether the model is suitable when $t = 4$ seconds. **(2 marks)**

(E/P) 6 A raindrop falls vertically from rest through mist. Water condenses on the raindrop as it falls. You are given that the motion of the raindrop may be modelled by the equation

$$(t + 4)\frac{\mathrm{d}v}{\mathrm{d}t} + 4v = 9.8(t + 4)$$

where t is the time in seconds and v is the velocity of the raindrop in m s^{-1}.

a Show that $v = \dfrac{49(t + 4)^5 - c}{25(t + 4)^4}$ where c is a constant to be found. **(6 marks)**

b Find the velocity of the raindrop after 5 seconds. **(2 marks)**

c By considering the velocity for large values of t, suggest one criticism of the model. **(1 mark)**

E/P **7** A gas storage tank initially contains $500\,\text{cm}^3$ of helium. The helium leaks out at a constant rate of $20\,\text{cm}^3$ per hour and a gas mixture is added to the tank at a constant rate of $50\,\text{cm}^3$ per hour. The gas mixture contains 5% oxygen and 95% helium.

Given that there is $x\,\text{cm}^3$ of oxygen in the tank after t hours and that the oxygen immediately mixes throughout the tank on entry,

a show that the situation can be modelled by the differential equation

$$\frac{\mathrm{d}x}{\mathrm{d}t} = 2.5 - \frac{2x}{50 + 3t}$$ **(4 marks)**

b Hence find the volume of oxygen in the tank after 4 hours. **(5 marks)**

c Explain how the model could be refined. **(1 mark)**

8.2 Simple harmonic motion

You can use second – order differential equations to model particles moving with **simple harmonic motion**.

- **Simple harmonic motion (S.H.M.) is motion in which the acceleration of a particle P is always towards a fixed point O on the line of motion of P. The acceleration is proportional to the displacement of P from O.**

The point O is called the **centre of oscillation**.

We write $\ddot{x} = -\omega^2 x$ •————————————

This can be shown on a diagram

The minus sign means that the acceleration is always directed towards O.

> **Links** The constant of proportionality in this equation is ω^2, where ω is the **angular velocity** of the particle.   → **FM2, Chapter 1**

Given that $\ddot{x} = \dfrac{\mathrm{d}v}{\mathrm{d}t}$ you can use the chain rule to derive a relationship between x, v and a which will allow you to solve the second-order differential equation for simple harmonic motion:

$$\ddot{x} = \frac{\mathrm{d}v}{\mathrm{d}t} = \frac{\mathrm{d}v}{\mathrm{d}x} \times \frac{\mathrm{d}x}{\mathrm{d}t}$$

Since $\dfrac{\mathrm{d}x}{\mathrm{d}t} = v$, you can write acceleration as follows:

- $\ddot{x} = v\dfrac{\mathrm{d}v}{\mathrm{d}x}$

> **Online** Explore simple harmonic motion using GeoGebra.

> **Notation** You can use 'dot' notation to indicate differentiation with respect to time.
> $\dot{x} = \dfrac{\mathrm{d}x}{\mathrm{d}t}$ and $\ddot{x} = \dfrac{\mathrm{d}^2 x}{\mathrm{d}t^2}$. So if x is used to denote displacement, then $\dot{x}$ represents velocity and $\ddot{x}$ represents acceleration.

Example 4

A particle P moves with simple harmonic motion about a point O. Given that the maximum displacement of the particle from O is a,

a show that $v^2 = \omega^2 (a^2 - x^2)$, where v is the velocity of the particle and ω^2 is a constant.

b show that $x = a \sin(\omega t + \alpha)$, where α is an arbitrary constant.

a $\ddot{x} = -\omega^2 x$ and $\ddot{x} = v\dfrac{dv}{dx}$

So $v\dfrac{dv}{dx} = -\omega^2 x$

$\int v\,dv = -\int \omega^2 x\,dx$

$\frac{1}{2}v^2 = -\frac{1}{2}\omega^2 x^2 + c$

$v = 0$ when $x = a$,

therefore $0 = -\frac{1}{2}\omega^2 a^2 + c \Rightarrow c = \frac{1}{2}\omega^2 a^2$

Hence $\frac{1}{2}v^2 = -\frac{1}{2}\omega^2 x^2 + \frac{1}{2}\omega^2 a^2$

$\Rightarrow\qquad v^2 = \omega^2(a^2 - x^2)$ as required.

b $\ddot{x} + \omega^2 x = 0$

$\dfrac{d^2x}{dt^2} + \omega^2 x = 0$

$m^2 + \omega^2 = 0 \Rightarrow m = \pm\omega i$

$x = A\cos\omega t + \beta\sin\omega t$

$\quad = R\sin(\omega t + \alpha)$

This has maximum amplitude R. Since the maximum amplitude of the particle is a:

$x = a\sin(\omega t + \alpha)$ as required.

Write down the equation for simple harmonic motion and use $\ddot{x} = v\dfrac{dv}{dx}$ to write a differential equation involving v and x only.

Separate the variables.

Integrate both sides and add a constant of integration.

The velocity of the particle will be zero when the particle is at maximum displacement.

This is a second-order linear differential equation. Write it in the form $a\dfrac{d^2x}{dt^2} + b\dfrac{dx}{dt} + cx = 0$ and then solve the corresponding auxiliary equation.

← Secton 7.2

Problem-solving

You are given information about the maximum displacement, so write the general solution in a form where you can determine the amplitude. The arbitrary constants become R and α, where $R^2 = A^2 + B^2$ and $\tan\alpha = \dfrac{A}{B}$

You can see from the above example that the path of a particle P under simple harmonic motion is a sine wave with period $\dfrac{2\pi}{\omega}$ and amplitude a.

Notation The **period** of the motion is the time the particle takes to complete one oscillation. The **amplitude** of the motion is the maximum displacement from the origin.

If the particle is at its equilibrium position at time $t = 0$, then $\alpha = 0$.

If the particle is at its stationary point, i.e. its maximum displacement, when $t = 0$, then $\alpha = \dfrac{\pi}{2}$.

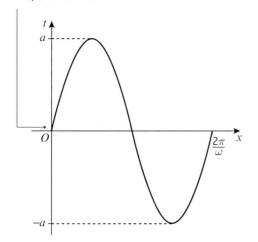

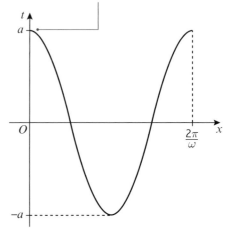

Example 5

A particle is moving along a straight line. At time t seconds its displacement, x m from a fixed point O is such that $\dfrac{d^2x}{dt^2} = -4x$.

Given that at $t = 0$, $x = 1$ and the particle is moving with velocity $4\,m\,s^{-1}$,

a find an expression for the displacement of the particle after t seconds

b hence determine the maximum displacement of the particle from O.

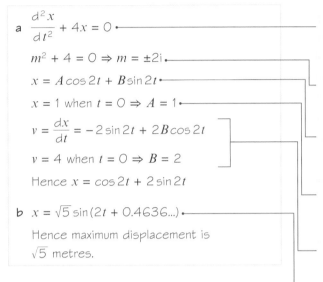

a $\dfrac{d^2x}{dt^2} + 4x = 0$

$m^2 + 4 = 0 \Rightarrow m = \pm 2i$

$x = A\cos 2t + B\sin 2t$

$x = 1$ when $t = 0 \Rightarrow A = 1$

$v = \dfrac{dx}{dt} = -2\sin 2t + 2B\cos 2t$

$v = 4$ when $t = 0 \Rightarrow B = 2$

Hence $x = \cos 2t + 2\sin 2t$

b $x = \sqrt{5}\sin(2t + 0.4636\ldots)$

Hence maximum displacement is $\sqrt{5}$ metres.

This is a second-order linear differential equation.
Write it in the form $a\dfrac{d^2y}{dx^2} + b\dfrac{dy}{dx} + c = 0$.

Write down and solve the auxiliary equation.

Write down the general solution. There are two purely imaginary roots so the general solution is in the form $y = A\cos qx + B\sin qx$ **← Section 7.2**

Substitute the initial condition for x:
$1 = A\cos(0) + B\sin(0)$

Differentiate x to find an expression for v and use the initial condition for v: $4 = -2\sin(0) + 2B\cos(0)$

Write your solution to **a** in the form $R\sin(\theta + \alpha)$.

Example 6

A particle, P, is attached to the ends of two identical elastic springs. The free ends of the springs are attached to two points A and B. The point C lies between A and B such that ABC is a straight line and $AC \neq BC$. The particle is held at C and then released from rest.

At time t seconds, the displacement of the particle from C is x m and its velocity is $v\,m\,s^{-1}$.

The subsequent motion of the particle can be described by the differential equation $\ddot{x} = -25x$.

a Describe the motion of the particle.

Given that $x = 0.4$ and $v = 0$ when $t = 0$,

b solve the differential equation to find x as a function of t

c state the period of the motion and calculate the maximum speed of P.

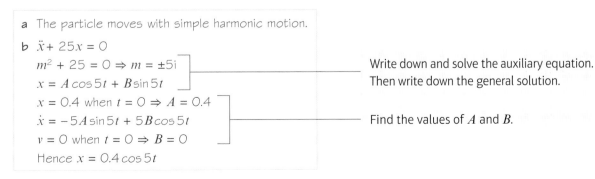

a The particle moves with simple harmonic motion.

b $\ddot{x} + 25x = 0$

$m^2 + 25 = 0 \Rightarrow m = \pm 5i$

$x = A\cos 5t + B\sin 5t$

$x = 0.4$ when $t = 0 \Rightarrow A = 0.4$

$\dot{x} = -5A\sin 5t + 5B\cos 5t$

$v = 0$ when $t = 0 \Rightarrow B = 0$

Hence $x = 0.4\cos 5t$

Write down and solve the auxiliary equation.
Then write down the general solution.

Find the values of A and B.

> **c** Period of motion is $\frac{2\pi}{5}$ seconds
>
> $\dot{x} = -2\sin 5t$, so maximum speed $= 2\,\text{m s}^{-1}$.

Exercise 8B

E **1** A particle is moving along a straight line. At time t seconds its displacement, x m, from a fixed point O is such that $\frac{d^2x}{dt^2} = -9x$.

   a Describe the motion of the particle. **(1 mark)**

   Given that at $t = 0$, $x = 2$ and the particle is moving with velocity $3\,\text{m s}^{-1}$,

   b find an expression for the displacement of the particle after t seconds. **(7 marks)**

   c Hence determine the maximum distance of the particle from O. **(2 marks)**

E **2** A particle is moving with simple harmonic motion. After t seconds its displacement, x m from a fixed point O is such that $\ddot{x} = -16x$.

   Given that at $t = 0$, $x = 5$ and $\dot{x} = 2$,

   a find an expression for the displacement of the particle after t seconds. **(7 marks)**

   b Hence determine the period of motion and the maximum distance of the particle from O. **(3 marks)**

E/P **3** A particle moves along a straight line. The particle moves such that its acceleration, in m s^{-2}, acts towards a fixed point O and is proportional to its distance, x m, from O.

   a Describe the motion of the particle. **(1 mark)**

   Given that the acceleration of the particle is $-5\,\text{m s}^{-2}$ when $x = 1$,

   b write down a differential equation to describe the motion of the particle. **(2 marks)**

   If the velocity and displacement of the particle at time $t = 0$ are $6\,\text{m s}^{-1}$ and 5 m respectively,

   c find an expression for the displacement of the particle after t seconds. **(7 marks)**

   d Hence find the maximum distance of the particle from O. **(2 marks)**

E/P **4** A particle moves along a straight line such that its acceleration, in m s^{-2}, acts towards a fixed point O and is proportional to its distance, x m, from O.

   The equation of motion is given as $\frac{d^2x}{dt^2} = -kx$, $t \geqslant 0$

   where k is a constant.

   Given that the acceleration is $-7\,\text{m s}^{-2}$ when $x = 2$,

   a write down the value of k. **(1 mark)**

   b Use your answer to part **a** to find x as a function of t given that $x = 6$ and $\dot{x} = 1$ at time $t = 0$. **(7 marks)**

   c Hence find, correct to 2 decimal places, the period of the motion. **(2 marks)**

E/P **5** A small rowing boat is floating on the surface of the sea, tied to a pier. The boat moves up and down in a vertical line, such that the vertical displacement, x m, from its equilibrium point satisfies the equation

$$\frac{d^2x}{dt^2} = -2.25x, \, t \geqslant 0$$

Given that the maximum displacement is 1.3 m and it occurs when $t = 2$ seconds,

a find an expression for x in terms of t in the form $x = A\sin\omega t + B\cos\omega t$ where A, B and ω are constants to be found. Give A and B correct to three decimal places. **(7 marks)**

b State the time elapsed between the boat being at its highest and lowest points. **(2 marks)**

c Criticise the model in terms of the motion of the boat for large values of t. **(1 mark)**

E/P **6** A particle P is attached to one end of a light elastic spring. The other end of the spring is fixed to a point A on the smooth horizontal surface on which P rests. The particle is held at rest with $AP = 0.9$ m and then released. At time t seconds the displacement of the particle from A is x m. The motion of the particle can be modelled using the equation $\ddot{x} = -200x$.

a State the type of motion exhibited by the particle P. **(1 mark)**

Given that $x = 0.3$ and the particle is at rest when $t = 0$,

b solve the differential equation to find x as a function of t **(7 marks)**

c find the period and amplitude of the motion **(3 marks)**

d calculate the maximum speed of P. **(2 marks)**

E **7** A particle P is attached to one end of a light elastic spring. The other end of the spring is fixed to a point O on the smooth horizontal surface on which P rests with $OP = 2.6$ m and then released. The motion of P can be described using the equation $\ddot{x} = -\frac{100}{0.64}x$, where x m is the displacement of P from O at time t seconds.

Given that $x = 1$ and the particle is at rest at time $t = 0$,

a solve the differential equation to find x as a function of t **(7 marks)**

b find the period of motion. **(2 marks)**

E **8** A smooth cylinder is fixed with its axis horizontal. A piston of mass 2.5 kg is inside the cylinder, attached to one end of the cylinder by a spring of natural length 50 cm. The piston is held at rest in the cylinder with the spring compressed to a length of 42 cm. The piston is then released. The spring can be modelled as a light elastic spring and the piston can be modelled as a particle.

The motion of P can be described using the equation $\ddot{x} = -320x$, where x cm is the compression of the spring from its natural length at time t seconds.

Given that $x = 8$ and $v = 0$ when $t = 0$,

a solve the differential equation to find x as a function of t **(7 marks)**

b find the period of the resulting oscillations. **(2 marks)**

E/P **9** A pendulum P is attached to one end of a light inextensible string. The other end of the string is attached to a fixed point A on a ceiling. The pendulum hangs in equilibrium at a point B vertically below A.

The pendulum is then moved through a horizontal distance of 15 cm and released from rest.

The subsequent motion can be modelled using the equation $\ddot{x} = -\frac{250}{3}x$ where x cm is the horizontal displacement from the vertical at time t seconds and $t \geqslant 0$.

a Solve the differential equation to find x as a function of t. **(7 marks)**

b Find the period and amplitude of the motion. **(3 marks)**

Anton says that since the pendulum describes simple harmonic motion, the model suggests that the pendulum will stay swinging forever.

c Suggest a refinement of the model in light of this statement. **(1 mark)**

8.3 Damped and forced harmonic motion

You can refine the model for simple harmonic motion by adding an additional force which is proportional to the velocity of the particle. When this force acts so as to slow the particle down it is known as a **damping force**, and the motion of the particle is known as **damped harmonic motion**.

- **For a particle moving with damped harmonic motion**

$$\frac{d^2x}{dt^2} + k\frac{dx}{dt} + \omega^2 x = 0$$

where x is the displacement from a fixed point at time t, and k and ω^2 are positive constants.

> **Notation** You could also write this as $\ddot{x} + k\dot{x} + \omega^2 x = 0$.

There are three separate cases corresponding to the auxiliary equation having distinct real, equal or complex roots.

> **Links** This is an example of a second-order homogeneous differential equation. You can solve equations like this by considering the auxiliary equation. ← Section 7.2

When $k^2 > 4\omega^2$ there are two distinct real roots for the auxiliary equation. This is known as **heavy damping**. In this case there will be no oscillations performed as the resistive force is large compared with the restoring force.

When $k^2 = 4\omega^2$ the auxiliary equation has equal roots. This is known as **critical damping**. Again there will be no oscillations performed.

When $k^2 < 4\omega^2$ the auxiliary equation has complex roots. This is known as **light damping** and is the only case where oscillations are seen. The amplitude of the oscillations will decrease exponentially over time.

For heavy and critical damping the exact nature of the motion will depend on the initial conditions given.

For light damping the period of the observed oscillations can be calculated.

Example 7

A particle P of mass 0.5 kg moves in a horizontal straight line. At time t seconds, the displacement of P from a fixed point, O, on the line is x m and the velocity of P is v m s^{-1}. A force of magnitude $8x$ N acts on P in the direction PO. The particle is also subject to a resistance of magnitude $4v$ N. When $t = 0$, $x = 1.5$ and P is moving in the direction of increasing x with speed 4 m s^{-1}.

a Show that $\dfrac{d^2x}{dt^2} + 8\dfrac{dx}{dt} + 16x = 0$ **b** Find the value of x when $t = 1$.

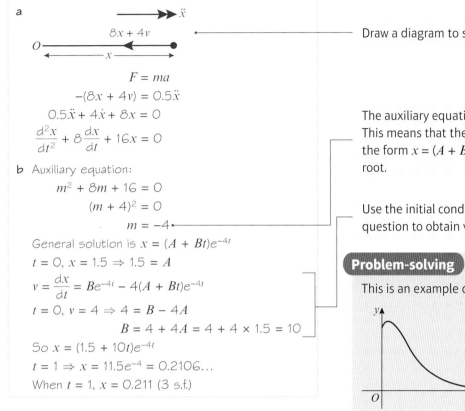

a

$$F = ma$$
$$-(8x + 4v) = 0.5\ddot{x}$$
$$0.5\ddot{x} + 4\dot{x} + 8x = 0$$
$$\frac{d^2x}{dt^2} + 8\frac{dx}{dt} + 16x = 0$$

b Auxiliary equation:
$$m^2 + 8m + 16 = 0$$
$$(m + 4)^2 = 0$$
$$m = -4$$

General solution is $x = (A + Bt)e^{-4t}$

$t = 0,\ x = 1.5 \Rightarrow 1.5 = A$

$v = \frac{dx}{dt} = Be^{-4t} - 4(A + Bt)e^{-4t}$

$t = 0,\ v = 4 \Rightarrow 4 = B - 4A$

$$B = 4 + 4A = 4 + 4 \times 1.5 = 10$$

So $x = (1.5 + 10t)e^{-4t}$

$t = 1 \Rightarrow x = 11.5e^{-4} = 0.2106...$

When $t = 1,\ x = 0.211$ (3 s.f.)

Draw a diagram to show the situation.

The auxiliary equation has equal roots. This means that the general solution is in the form $x = (A + Bt)e^{\alpha t}$, where α is the root. ← **Section 7.2**

Use the initial conditions given in the question to obtain values for A and B.

Problem-solving

This is an example of **critical damping**:

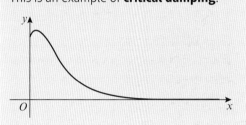

Online Explore damped harmonic motion using GeoGebra.

Example 8

A particle P hangs freely in equilibrium attached to one end of a light elastic string. The other end of the string is attached to a fixed point A. The particle is now pulled down and held at rest in a container of liquid which exerts a resistance to motion on P. P is then released from rest. While the string remains taut and the particle in the liquid, the motion can be modelled using the equation

$$\frac{d^2x}{dt^2} + 6k\frac{dx}{dt} + 5k^2x = 0, \text{ where } k \text{ is a positive real constant}$$

Find the general solution to the differential equation and state the type of damping that the particle is subject to.

Auxiliary equation: $m^2 + 6km + 5k^2 = 0$
$$(m + 5k)(m + k) = 0$$

$m = -5k$ or $-k$

General solution is $x = Ae^{-5kt} + Be^{-kt}$

The auxiliary equation has two distinct real roots so the particle is subject to heavy damping.

If the auxiliary equation has distinct real roots α and β, then the general solution is in the form $x = Ae^{\alpha t} + Be^{\beta t}$

Example 9

One end of a light elastic spring is attached to a fixed point A. A particle P is attached to the other end and hangs in equilibrium vertically below A. The particle is pulled vertically down from its equilibrium position and released from rest. A resistance proportional to the speed of P acts on P. The equation of motion of P is given as

$$\frac{d^2x}{dt^2} + 2k\frac{dx}{dt} + 2k^2x = 0$$

where k is a positive real constant and x is the displacement of P from its equilibrium position.

a Find the general solution to the differential equation.

b Write down the period of oscillation in terms of k.

a Auxiliary equation: $m^2 + 2km + 2k^2 = 0$

$$m = \frac{-2k \pm \sqrt{4k^2 - 4 \times 2k^2}}{2} = -k \pm ik$$

So $x = e^{-kt}(A\cos kt + B\sin kt)$

b Period $= \dfrac{2\pi}{k}$

If the auxiliary equation has complex roots $p \pm qi$, then the general solution is in the form
$x = e^{pt}(A\cos qt + B\sin qt)$

$(A\cos kt + B\sin kt)$ can be written as $R\cos(kt + e)$ to give a period of $\dfrac{2\pi}{k}$

Problem-solving

This is an example of **light damping**:

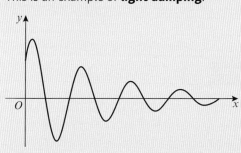

The displacement of the particle will oscillate with a reducing amplitude.

You can investigate the motion of a particle which is subject to the same two forces as above but is also forced to oscillate with a frequency other than its natural one. This type of motion is called **forced harmonic motion**.

- **For a particle moving with forced harmonic motion**

$$\frac{d^2x}{dt^2} + k\frac{dx}{dt} + \omega^2x = f(t)$$

where x is the displacement from a fixed point at time t, and k and ω^2 are positive constants.

Links This is an example of a second-order non-homogeneous differential equation. You will need to find the solution to the corresponding homogeneous equation, then add a **particular integral**, the form of which will depend on f(t).
← Section 7.3

Example **10**

A particle P of mass $1.5\,\text{kg}$ is moving on the x-axis. At time t the displacement of P from the origin O is x metres and the speed of P is $v\,\text{m\,s}^{-1}$. Three forces act on P, namely a restoring force of magnitude $7.5x\,\text{N}$, a resistance to the motion of P of magnitude $6v\,\text{N}$ and a force of magnitude $12\sin t\,\text{N}$ acting in the direction OP. When $t = 0$, $x = 5$ and $\dfrac{\mathrm{d}x}{\mathrm{d}t} = 2$.

a Show that $\dfrac{\mathrm{d}^2x}{\mathrm{d}t^2} + 4\dfrac{\mathrm{d}x}{\mathrm{d}t} + 5x = 8\sin t$. **b** Find x as a function of t.

c Describe the motion when t is large.

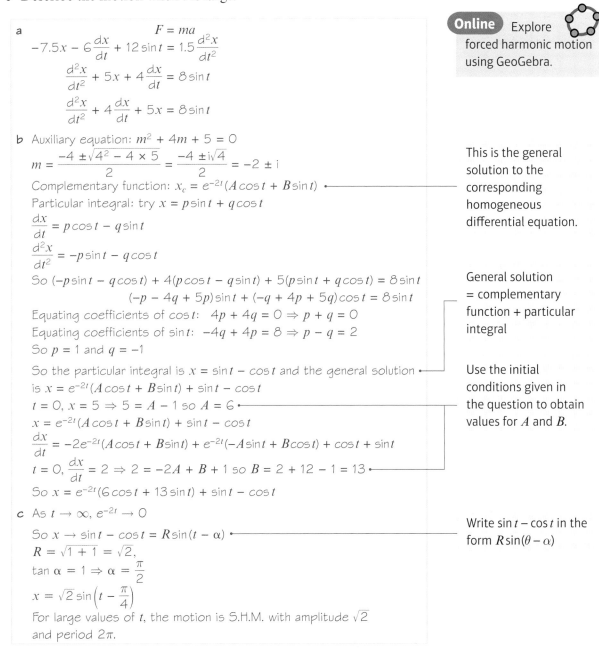

Online Explore forced harmonic motion using GeoGebra.

a
$$F = ma$$
$$-7.5x - 6\frac{\mathrm{d}x}{\mathrm{d}t} + 12\sin t = 1.5\frac{\mathrm{d}^2x}{\mathrm{d}t^2}$$
$$\frac{\mathrm{d}^2x}{\mathrm{d}t^2} + 5x + 4\frac{\mathrm{d}x}{\mathrm{d}t} = 8\sin t$$
$$\frac{\mathrm{d}^2x}{\mathrm{d}t^2} + 4\frac{\mathrm{d}x}{\mathrm{d}t} + 5x = 8\sin t$$

b Auxiliary equation: $m^2 + 4m + 5 = 0$
$$m = \frac{-4 \pm \sqrt{4^2 - 4 \times 5}}{2} = \frac{-4 \pm i\sqrt{4}}{2} = -2 \pm i$$
Complementary function: $x_c = e^{-2t}(A\cos t + B\sin t)$ ←

This is the general solution to the corresponding homogeneous differential equation.

Particular integral: try $x = p\sin t + q\cos t$
$$\frac{\mathrm{d}x}{\mathrm{d}t} = p\cos t - q\sin t$$
$$\frac{\mathrm{d}^2x}{\mathrm{d}t^2} = -p\sin t - q\cos t$$
So $(-p\sin t - q\cos t) + 4(p\cos t - q\sin t) + 5(p\sin t + q\cos t) = 8\sin t$
$$(-p - 4q + 5p)\sin t + (-q + 4p + 5q)\cos t = 8\sin t$$
Equating coefficients of $\cos t$: $4p + 4q = 0 \Rightarrow p + q = 0$
Equating coefficients of $\sin t$: $-4q + 4p = 8 \Rightarrow p - q = 2$
So $p = 1$ and $q = -1$

General solution = complementary function + particular integral

So the particular integral is $x = \sin t - \cos t$ and the general solution is $x = e^{-2t}(A\cos t + B\sin t) + \sin t - \cos t$
$t = 0$, $x = 5 \Rightarrow 5 = A - 1$ so $A = 6$ ←
$$x = e^{-2t}(A\cos t + B\sin t) + \sin t - \cos t$$
$$\frac{\mathrm{d}x}{\mathrm{d}t} = -2e^{-2t}(A\cos t + B\sin t) + e^{-2t}(-A\sin t + B\cos t) + \cos t + \sin t$$
$t = 0$, $\dfrac{\mathrm{d}x}{\mathrm{d}t} = 2 \Rightarrow 2 = -2A + B + 1$ so $B = 2 + 12 - 1 = 13$ ←
So $x = e^{-2t}(6\cos t + 13\sin t) + \sin t - \cos t$

Use the initial conditions given in the question to obtain values for A and B.

c As $t \to \infty$, $e^{-2t} \to 0$
So $x \to \sin t - \cos t = R\sin(t - \alpha)$ ←
$R = \sqrt{1 + 1} = \sqrt{2}$,
$\tan \alpha = 1 \Rightarrow \alpha = \dfrac{\pi}{2}$
$x = \sqrt{2}\sin\left(t - \dfrac{\pi}{4}\right)$
For large values of t, the motion is S.H.M. with amplitude $\sqrt{2}$ and period 2π.

Write $\sin t - \cos t$ in the form $R\sin(\theta - \alpha)$

Example 11

A particle P is attached to end A of a light elastic string AB. Initially the particle and the string lie at rest on a smooth horizontal plane. At time $t = 0$, the end B of the string is set in motion and moves with constant speed U in the direction AB, and the displacement of P from A is x. Air resistance acting on P is proportional to its speed. The subsequent motion can be modelled by the differential equation

$$\frac{d^2x}{dt^2} + 2k\frac{dx}{dt} + k^2x = 2kU$$

Find an expression for x in terms of U, k and t.

Auxiliary equation: $m^2 + 2km + k^2 = 0$

$\qquad\qquad\qquad (m + k)^2 = 0$

$\qquad\qquad\qquad m = -k$

Complementary function: $x = (A + Bt)e^{-kt}$ | The right–hand side of the differential equation is constant, so try a constant for the particular integral.

Particular integral: try $x = a$

$\dot{x} = \ddot{x} = 0$

So $k^2a = 2kU \Rightarrow a = \dfrac{2U}{k}$

General solution is $x = (A + Bt)e^{-kt} + \dfrac{2U}{k}$

$t = 0, \quad x = 0 \quad \Rightarrow 0 = A + \dfrac{2U}{k} \Rightarrow A = -\dfrac{2U}{k}$ | Use the initial conditions given in the question to obtain values for A and B.

$\dot{x} = -k(A + Bt)e^{-kt} + Be^{-kt}$

$t = 0 \Rightarrow \dot{x} = U$

$U = -kA + B$

$B = U + kA = -U$

So $x = \left(-\dfrac{2U}{k} - Ut\right)e^{-kt} + \dfrac{2U}{k}$

Exercise 8C

1 A particle P is moving in a straight line. At time t, the displacement of P from a fixed point on the line is x. The motion of the particle is modelled by the differential equation

$$\frac{d^2x}{dt^2} + 4\frac{dx}{dt} + 8x = 0$$

When $t = 0$, P is at rest at the point where $x = 2$.

a Find x as a function of t.

b Calculate the value of x when $t = \dfrac{\pi}{3}$

c State whether the motion is heavily, critically or lightly damped.

2 A particle P is moving in a straight line. At time t, the displacement of P from a fixed point on the line is x. The motion of the particle is modelled by the differential equation

$$\frac{d^2x}{dt^2} + 8\frac{dx}{dt} + 12x = 0$$

When $t = 0$, P is at rest at the point where $x = 4$.

Find x as a function of t.

E/P **3** A particle P is moving in a straight line. At time t, the displacement of P from a fixed point on the line is x. The motion of the particle is modelled by the differential equation

$$\frac{d^2x}{dt^2} + 2\frac{dx}{dt} + 6x = 0$$

When $t = 0$, P is at rest at the point where $x = 1$.

a Find x as a function of t. **(6 marks)**

The smallest value of t, $t > 0$, for which P is instantaneously at rest is T.

b Find the value of T. **(2 marks)**

E/P **4** A particle P is attached to one end of a light elastic spring. The other end of the spring is attached to a fixed point A and P hangs freely in equilibrium vertically below A. At time $t = 0$, P is projected vertically downwards with speed u. A resistance proportional to the speed of P acts on P. The motion of P can be modelled using the differential equation

$$\frac{d^2x}{dt^2} + 4k\frac{dx}{dt} + 4k^2x = 0$$

where x is the displacement of P from its equilibrium position at time t and k is a positive constant.

a Find an expression for x in terms of u, t and k. **(6 marks)**

b Find the time at which P comes to instantaneous rest. **(2 marks)**

E/P **5** A particle of mass $2\,\text{kg}$ moves in a horizontal straight line. At time t seconds, the displacement of P from a fixed point O is x metres and the speed of P is $v\,\text{m s}^{-1}$.

A force of magnitude $6x\,\text{N}$ acts on P in the direction PO. The particle is also subject to a resistance of magnitude $2v\,\text{N}$. When $t = 0$, $x = 1$ and P is moving in the direction of increasing x with speed $2\,\text{m s}^{-1}$.

a Show that $\ddot{x} + \dot{x} + 3x = 0$. **(2 marks)**

b Solve the differential equation in part **a** to find x as a function of t. **(8 marks)**

c Find the value of x when $t = 2$. **(2 marks)**

d Describe the motion of P for large values of t. **(1 mark)**

E/P **6** A particle P is attached to end A of a light elastic spring AB. The end B of the spring is oscillating. At time t the displacement of P from a fixed point is x. When $t = 0$, $x = 0$ and $\frac{dx}{dt} = \frac{k}{5}$ where k is a constant. Given that x satisfies the differential equation

$$\frac{d^2x}{dt^2} + 9x = k\cos t$$

find x as a function of t. **(8 marks)**

E/P **7** A particle P is attached to end A of a light elastic spring AB. Initially the spring and the particle lie at rest on a horizontal surface. The end B of the spring is then moved in a straight line in the direction AB with constant speed U. As P moves it is subject to a resistance proportional to its speed. The extension, x, in the spring can be modelled using the differential equation

$$\frac{d^2x}{dt^2} + 5k\frac{dx}{dt} + 6k^2x = 5kU$$

Find an expression in x in terms of t. **(8 marks)**

8 An engineering student is designing an oscillating piston that is attached to a vertical rod. The piston is to be released from rest from a point half way up the rod so that it oscillates in a vertical line. The vertical displacement, x metres, of the top of the piston below its initial position at time t seconds is modelled by the differential equation,

$$2\frac{d^2x}{dt^2} + 3\frac{dx}{dt} + x = 100\cos t, \; t \geqslant 0$$

a Show that a particular solution to the differential equation is $x = 30\sin t - 10\cos t$ **(3 marks)**

b Hence find the general solution to the differential equation. **(5 marks)**

c Use the model to find, to the nearest centimetre, the vertical distance of the top of the piston from its initial position 5 seconds after it is released. **(4 marks)**

8.4 Coupled first-order simultaneous differential equations

In some real-life situations rates of change of two variables are connected. For example, in a predator–prey model, the rate of change of the population of bears might be dependent on both the number of bears and the number of fish in a river. Simultaneously, the rate of change of the number of fish might be dependent on both the number of bears and the number of fish. In this case, you have two dependent variables, the number of bears and fish, and one independent variable, time. You can set up two first-order differential equations to model the rates of change of the numbers of bears and fish.

Letting the number of bears at time t be x and the number of fish at time t be y, you can write:

$$\frac{dx}{dt} = ax + by + f(t)$$

$$\frac{dy}{dt} = cx + dy + g(t)$$

> **Notation** If $f(t)$ and $g(t)$ are both zero, the system is said to be **homogenous**.

These equations are called **coupled first-order linear differential equations** and you can solve them simultaneously to find x and y as functions of t.

■ **You can solve coupled first-order linear differential equations by eliminating one of the dependent variables to form a second-order differential equation.**

Example 12

At the start of the year 2010, a survey began on the numbers of bears and fish on a remote island in Northern Canada. After t years the number of bears, x, and the number of fish, y, on the island are modelled by the differential equations

$$\frac{dx}{dt} = 0.3x + 0.1y \qquad (1)$$

$$\frac{dy}{dt} = -0.1x + 0.5y \qquad (2)$$

a Show that $\dfrac{d^2x}{dt^2} - 0.8\dfrac{dx}{dt} + 0.16x = 0$.

b Find the general solution for the number of bears on the island at time t.

c Find the general solution for the number of fish on the island at time t.

d At the start of 2010 there were 5 bears and 20 fish on the island.

Use this information to find the number of bears predicted to be on the island in 2020.

e Comment in the suitability of the model.

a $\quad y = 10\dfrac{dx}{dt} - 3x$ •————————————— Rearrange equation (1) to make y the subject.

$\dfrac{dy}{dt} = 10\dfrac{d^2x}{dt^2} - 3\dfrac{dx}{dt}$ •————————— Differentiate both sides with respect to t.

$10\dfrac{d^2x}{dt^2} - 3\dfrac{dx}{dt} = -0.1x + 0.5\left(10\dfrac{dx}{dt} - 3x\right)$•——— Substitute your expressions for y and $\dfrac{dy}{dt}$ into

$10\dfrac{d^2x}{dt^2} - 8\dfrac{dx}{dt} + 1.6x = 0$

$\dfrac{d^2x}{dt^2} - 0.8\dfrac{dx}{dt} + 0.16x = 0$ •

equation (2) to form a second–order differential equation in x and t.

Rearrange into the correct form.

b $\quad m^2 - 0.8m + 0.16 = 0 \Rightarrow m = 0.4$•

Hence $x = Ae^{0.4t} + Bte^{0.4t}$ •

Write down the auxiliary equation and solve it.

c $\quad \dfrac{dx}{dt} = 0.4Ae^{0.4t} + 0.4Bte^{0.4t} + Be^{0.4t}$

$y = 10\dfrac{dx}{dt} - 3x$ from equation (1)

$y = 10(0.4Ae^{0.4t} + 0.4Bte^{0.4t} + Be^{0.4t})$
$\quad - 3(Ae^{0.4t} + Bte^{0.4t})$

$y = Ae^{0.4t} + 10Be^{0.4t} + Bte^{0.4t}$

Use the general form of the solution of a differential equation with a repeated root.

Problem-solving

You do not need to go through the whole process to find an expression for y in terms of t. If you differentiate your answer to part **b** with respect to t you will have expressions for x and $\dfrac{dx}{dt}$ in terms of t only. You can substitute these into equation (1) and simplify to obtain the answer.

d At $t = 0$, $x = 5 \Rightarrow A = 5$

At $t = 0$, $y = 20 \Rightarrow B = 1.5$

$x = 5e^{0.4t} + 1.5te^{0.4t}$

At time $t = 10$: $x = 5e^4 + 15e^4 = 1092$•

The model predicts there will be 1092 bears on the island by 2020.

Use the initial conditions to find A and B.

e The model predicts the number of bears (and the number of fish) will grow without limit so it is unlikely to be realistic.

Substitute $t = 10$ into the equation for x. Round to the nearest whole number.

Example **13**

Two barrels contain contaminated water. At time t seconds, the amount of contaminant in barrel A is x ml and the amount of contaminant in barrel B is y ml. Additional contaminated water flows into barrel A at a rate of 5 ml per second. Contaminated water flows from barrel A to barrel B and from barrel B to barrel A through two connecting hoses, and drains out of barrel A to leave the system completely.

The system is modelled using the differential equations

$$\dfrac{dx}{dt} = 5 + \tfrac{4}{9}y - \tfrac{1}{7}x \qquad (1)$$

$$\dfrac{dy}{dt} = \tfrac{3}{70}x - \tfrac{4}{9}y \qquad (2)$$

Show that $630\dfrac{d^2y}{dt^2} + 370\dfrac{dy}{dt} + 28y = 135$.

$$\frac{dy}{dt} + \frac{4}{9}y = \frac{3}{70}x \text{ from equation } (2)$$

$$\frac{70}{3}\frac{dy}{dt} + \frac{280}{27}y = x \qquad (3)$$

Rearrange (2) to make x the subject.

$$\frac{dx}{dt} = \frac{70}{3}\frac{d^2y}{dt^2} + \frac{280}{27}\frac{dy}{dt} \qquad (4)$$

Differentiate (3) to find $\frac{dx}{dt}$.

$$\frac{70}{3}\frac{d^2y}{dt^2} + \frac{280}{27}\frac{dy}{dt} = 5 + \frac{4}{9}y - \frac{1}{7}\left(\frac{70}{3}\frac{dy}{dt} + \frac{280}{27}y\right)$$

$$70\frac{d^2y}{dt^2} + \frac{280}{9}\frac{dy}{dt} = 15 + \frac{4}{3}y - 10\frac{dy}{dt} - \frac{40}{9}y$$

$$630\frac{d^2y}{dt^2} + 280\frac{dy}{dt} = 135 + 12y - 90\frac{dy}{dt} - 40y$$

Substitute (3) and (4) into (1), simplify coefficients and remove fractions.

$$\Rightarrow 630\frac{d^2y}{dt^2} + 370\frac{dy}{dt} + 28y = 135 \text{ as required.}$$

Write your answer in the form required in the question.

Exercise 8D

(P) **1** Find the particular solutions to the differential equations

$$\frac{dx}{dt} = x + y$$

$$\frac{dy}{dt} = x - y$$

given that $x = 1$ and $y = 2$ at $t = 0$.

(P) **2 a** Find the general solutions to the differential equations

$$\frac{dx}{dt} = x + 5y$$

$$\frac{dy}{dt} = -3y - x$$

b Given that at time $t = 0$, $x = 1$ and $y = 2$, find the particular solutions.

(P) **3** A system of differential equations is given as

$$\frac{dx}{dt} = 2x - 3y - 2$$

$$\frac{dy}{dt} = x + y - 1$$

Given that $x = 0$ and $y = 1$ when $t = 0$, find the particular solutions to the system of differential equations.

(E/P) **4** At the start of 2012, a survey began on the number of sand foxes and the number of meerkats on a remote desert island. After t years, the number of sand foxes, x, and the number of meerkats, y, on the island are modelled by the differential equations

$$\frac{dx}{dt} = 0.2x + 0.2y$$

$$\frac{dy}{dt} = -0.5x + 0.4y$$

a Show that $\dfrac{d^2x}{dt^2} - 0.6\dfrac{dx}{dt} + 0.18x = 0$. **(3 marks)**

b Show that the general solution for the number of sand foxes at time t is

$x = e^{\alpha t}(A\cos\beta t + B\sin\beta t)$

where α and β are constants to be found. **(4 marks)**

c Find the general solution for the number of meerkats at time t.
Give your answer in the form $y = Pe^{\alpha t}(Q\cos\beta t + R\sin\beta t)$ where P is a constant to be found and Q and R are functions of A and B. **(3 marks)**

d Given that there were initially 3 sand foxes and 111 meerkats on the island, during which year does the model predict that the meerkats die out? **(5 marks)**

e How many sand foxes will there be when the meerkats die out? **(1 mark)**

f Use your answers to parts **d** and **e** to comment on the model. **(1 mark)**

(E/P) 5 A tank of water contains two different types of chemical that react with each other. The rates of change of each chemical can be modelled using the differential equations

$\dfrac{dx}{dt} = -3x + 2y$

$\dfrac{dy}{dt} = -2x + y$

where x is the number of litres of chemical X and y is the number of litres of chemical Y at time t hours.

Initially there is one litre of chemical X and two litres of chemical Y in the tank.

a Show that the solutions to the differential equations can be written as

$x = Pe^{-t}$

$y = Qe^{-t}$

where P and Q are functions of t to be found. **(8 marks)**

b Find, correct to three significant figures, the amount of each chemical at time $t = 2$ hours. **(2 marks)**

c Use the model to describe what happens to the amount of each chemical as t gets large. **(2 marks)**

(E/P) 6 A freely hanging pendulum oscillates in both the x and y directions. At time t, the rates of change of the x and y displacements are given by the differential equations

$\dfrac{dx}{dt} = -4y$

$\dfrac{dy}{dt} = 4x$

a Show that the pendulum describes simple harmonic motion in the y direction. **(3 marks)**

Given that the initial displacement of the pendulum is $x = 4$ and $y = 5$,

b find the particular solutions to the system of differential equations. **(6 marks)**

(E/P) 7 Joanna is investigating how a harmful substance from pollution is absorbed by the human body. She finds that the substance enters the body in the bloodstream and is transferred between the blood and the bodily organs. The harmful substance is then expelled from the body through, for example, sweat.

The amount of the substance in the blood, x mg, and the organs, y mg, at time t days, can be modelled using the differential equations

$$\frac{dx}{dt} = -0.03x + 0.01y + 50$$

$$\frac{dy}{dt} = 0.01x - 0.03y$$

a Show that $\dfrac{d^2x}{dt^2} + 0.06\dfrac{dx}{dt} + 0.0008x = 1.5$ **(6 marks)**

b Hence find the general solutions to the system of differential equations in the form

$$x = f(t)$$
$$y = g(t)$$ **(8 marks)**

c Describe what happens to the amount of the substance in the blood and the organs as t gets large. **(2 marks)**

(E/P) 8 A biologist is examining the rates of change of nutrients in both tree roots and the surrounding soil. Nutrients pass from the tree roots into the soil and from the soil into the tree roots. Nutrients also enter the system through both the roots and the soil and escape from the system in the same way.

The biologist believes that the amount of nutrients in the roots, x, and the amount of nutrients in the soil, y, at time t hours, can be modelled using the differential equations

$$\frac{dx}{dt} = -2x + y + 1$$

$$\frac{dy}{dt} = 4x + y + 2$$

a Show that $\dfrac{d^2x}{dt^2} + \dfrac{dx}{dt} - 6x = 1$. **(4 marks)**

b Find the general solutions to the system of differential equations. **(6 marks)**

c Using your answers to part **b**, comment on the suitability of the biologist's model. **(2 marks)**

Challenge

A closed environment supports populations of owls and field mice. At time t months, the sizes of each population are x and y respectively. The situation is modelled by the pair of differential equations

$$\frac{dy}{dt} = 2y - \frac{y^2}{6000} - 60x$$

$$\frac{dx}{dt} = 0.02y - x$$

Find the number of owls and the number of field mice such that the population of both is stable.

Hint A population is stable when its rate of growth is zero.

Mixed exercise **8**

E **1** A particle P moves along the x-axis in the direction of x increasing. At time t seconds, the velocity of P is $v\,\mathrm{m\,s^{-1}}$ and its acceleration is $20\,t\,\mathrm{e}^{-t^2}\,\mathrm{m\,s^{-2}}$. When $t = 0$ the velocity of P is $8\,\mathrm{m\,s^{-1}}$. Find:

a v in terms of t **(4 marks)**

b the limiting velocity of P. **(3 marks)**

E **2** A particle P moves along a straight line. Initially P is at rest at a point O on the line. At time t seconds, where $t \geqslant 0$, the acceleration of P is $\dfrac{18}{(2t+3)^3}\,\mathrm{m\,s^{-2}}$ directed away from O.

Find the value of t for which the speed of P is $0.48\,\mathrm{m\,s^{-1}}$. **(5 marks)**

E **3** A car moves along a horizontal straight road. At time t seconds the acceleration of the car is $\dfrac{100}{(2t+5)^2}\,\mathrm{m\,s^{-2}}$ in the direction of motion of the car. When $t = 0$, the car is at rest. Find:

a an expression for v in terms of t **(4 marks)**

b the distance moved by the car in the first 10 seconds of its motion. **(4 marks)**

E **4** A particle P is moving in a straight line with acceleration $\cos^2 t\,\mathrm{m\,s^{-2}}$ at time t seconds. The particle is initially at rest at a point O.

a Find the speed of P when $t = \pi$. **(4 marks)**

b Show that the distance of P from O when $t = \dfrac{\pi}{4}$ is $\frac{1}{64}(\pi^2 + 8)\,\mathrm{m}$. **(4 marks)**

E **5** A particle P is moving along the x-axis. At time t seconds, P has velocity $v\,\mathrm{m\,s^{-1}}$ in the direction x increasing and an acceleration of magnitude $\dfrac{2t+3}{t+1}\,\mathrm{m\,s^{-2}}$ in the direction x increasing.

When $t = 0$, P is at rest at the origin O. Find:

a v in terms of t **(4 marks)**

b the distance of P from O when $t = 2$. **(4 marks)**

E/P **6** A colony of bacteria reproduces in a laboratory jar. At time $t = 0$, the volume of bacteria is $1\,\mathrm{cm^3}$. Scientist Steve suggests that the rate of growth of the bacteria can be modelled using the differential equation

$$\frac{\mathrm{d}V}{\mathrm{d}t} = 2t + 3V + 5$$

where t is the time in hours and V is the volume in $\mathrm{cm^3}$.

a Show that $V = At + B + C\mathrm{e}^{3t}$ where A, B and C are exact constants to be found. **(6 marks)**

b Find the volume of bacteria after 2 hours. **(2 marks)**

c Give one criticism of Steve's model and suggest one refinement he could make. **(2 marks)**

E/P **7** A fluid reservoir initially contains 10 000 litres of unpolluted fluid.

The reservoir is leaking at a constant rate of 200 litres per day.

It is suspected that contaminated fluid flows into the reservoir at a constant rate of 300 litres per day and that the contaminated fluid contains 4 grams of contaminant in every litre of fluid.

It is assumed that the contaminant instantly disperses throughout the reservoir upon entry.

Given that there are x grams of contaminant in the reservoir after t days,

a Show that the situation can be modelled by the differential equation

$$\frac{dx}{dt} = 1200 - \frac{2x}{100 + t}$$

(4 marks)

b Hence find, correct to three significant figures, the number of grams of contaminant in the reservoir after 7 days. (5 marks)

c Explain how the model could be refined. (1 mark)

(E) **8** A particle P is attached to one end of a light elastic string of natural length 1.2 m. The other end of the string is attached to a fixed point A. The particle is hanging in equilibrium at the point O, which is vertically below A.

The particle is now displaced to a point B, vertically below A, and released from rest.

The subsequent motion while the string remains taut can be modelled using the equation $\ddot{x} = -49x$, where x m is the displacement of the particle from O at time t seconds.

a Describe the motion of the particle while the string remains taut. (1 mark)

b Solve the differential equation and hence find the period of the motion. (6 marks)

(E) **9** A particle P of mass 0.6 kg is attached to one end of a light elastic spring of natural length 2.5 m. The other end of the spring is attached to a fixed point A on the smooth horizontal table on which P lies. The particle is held at the point B where $AB = 4$ m and released from rest.

The motion of the particle can be described using the equation $\ddot{x} = -\frac{50}{3}x$, where x m is the displacement of the particle from A at time t seconds.

a Describe the motion of the particle. (1 mark)

b Solve the differential equation and hence find the period and amplitude of the motion. (7 marks)

(E/P) **10** A fisherman's float bobs up and down on the surface of the water. The float moves up and down in a vertical line, such that the vertical displacement, x cm, from its equilibrium point satisfies the equation

$$\frac{d^2x}{dt^2} = -0.25x, \ t \geqslant 0$$

Given that the maximum displacement is 4 cm and it occurs when $t = 2$ seconds,

a find an expression for x in terms of t in the form $x = A\sin\omega t + B\cos\omega t$ where A, B and ω are constants to be found. Give A and B correct to three decimal places. (7 marks)

b State the time elapsed between the float being at its highest and lowest points. (2 marks)

c Criticise the model in terms of the motion of the float. (1 mark)

(E/P) **11** A particle P of mass m is moving in a straight line. At time t the displacement of P from a fixed point O on the line is x. Given that x satisfies the differential equation

$$\frac{d^2x}{dt^2} + 2k\frac{dx}{dt} + n^2x = 0$$

where k and n are positive constants with $k < n$,

a find an expression for x in terms of k, n and t. (6 marks)

b Write down the period of the motion. (1 mark)

E/P **12** A particle P of mass m is attached to one end of light elastic spring. The other end of the spring is attached to a fixed point A and P is hanging in equilibrium with AP vertical.

The particle is now projected vertically downwards from its equilibrium position with speed U. A resistance of magnitude $2mkv$, where v is the speed of P, acts on P. At time t, $t > 0$, the displacement of P from its equilibrium position is x.

The motion of the particle is modelled by the differential equation

$$\frac{d^2x}{dt^2} + 2k\frac{dx}{dt} + 2k^2x = 0$$

a Show that P is instantaneously at rest when $kt = (n + \frac{1}{4})\pi$, where $n \in \mathbb{N}$. **(9 marks)**

b Sketch the graph of x against t. **(3 marks)**

E/P **13** A particle P of mass m is attached to one end of a light elastic spring. The other end of the spring is attached to the roof of a stationary lift. The particle is hanging in equilibrium with the spring vertical. At time $t = 0$ the lift starts to move vertically upwards with constant speed U. At time t, $t > 0$, the displacement of P from its initial position is x.

The motion of the particle is modelled by the differential equation

$$\frac{d^2x}{dt^2} + n^2x = n^2Ut$$

a find an expression for x in terms of t and n. **(8 marks)**

At time $t = T$, the particle is instantaneously at rest. Find:

b the smallest value of T **(3 marks)**

c the displacement of P from its initial position at this time. **(1 mark)**

E/P **14** A theme park ride designer is designing a new ride where the passengers will be in an enclosed car attached to a horizontal bar. The car will be released from rest from a point half way along the bar so that it oscillates in a horizontal line. The horizontal displacement, x metres, of the centre of the car relative to its initial position at time t seconds is modelled by the differential equation,

$$\frac{d^2x}{dt^2} + 4\frac{dx}{dt} + 3x = 150\cos t, \; t \geqslant 0$$

a Show that a particular solution to the differential equation is

$$x = 30\sin t + 15\cos t$$ **(3 marks)**

b Hence find the general solution to the differential equation. **(5 marks)**

c Use the model to find, to the nearest metre, the horizontal distance of the centre of the car from its initial position 10 seconds after it is released. **(4 marks)**

E/P **15 a** Find the general solution to the differential equation $\dfrac{d^2x}{dt^2} + 2\dfrac{dx}{dt} + 10x = 27\cos t - 6\sin t$. **(8 marks)**

The equation is used to model water flow in a reservoir. At time t days, the level of the water above a fixed level is x m. When $t = 0$, $x = 3$ and the water level is rising at 6 metres per day.

b Find an expression for x in terms of t. **(2 marks)**

c Show that after about a week, the difference between the lowest and highest water level is approximately 6 m. **(3 marks)**

E/P **16** At the start of 2008 a survey began on the number of hedgehogs and the number of slugs in a closed ecosystem. After t years, the number of hedgehogs, x, and the number of slugs, y, in the ecosystem are modelled by the differential equations

$$\frac{dx}{dt} = 2x + y$$

$$\frac{dy}{dt} = -2x + 4y$$

    a Show that $\dfrac{d^2 x}{d t^2} - 6\dfrac{dx}{dt} + 10x = 0$.   **(3 marks)**

    b Show that the general solution for the number of hedgehogs at time t is

        $x = e^{\alpha t}(A \cos \beta t + B \sin \beta t)$

        where α and β are constants to be found.   **(4 marks)**

    c Find the general solution for the number of slugs at time t.   **(3 marks)**

    d Given that there were initially 10 hedgehogs and 20 slugs in the ecosystem, during which year does the model predict that the slugs die out?   **(5 marks)**

    e How many hedgehogs will there be when the slugs die out?   **(1 mark)**

    f Use your answers to parts **d** and **e** to comment on the model.   **(1 mark)**

E/P **17** A sealed tank of bionutrient contains two different types of organism that interact with each other. The rates of change of each organism can be modelled using the differential equations

$$\frac{dx}{dt} = -4x + 3y$$

$$\frac{dy}{dt} = -3x + 2y$$

    where x is the number of organism M and y is the number of organism N at time t days. Initially $x = 10$ and $y = 20$.

    a Show that the solutions to the differential equations can be written as

        $x = Ate^{-t} + Be^{-t}$

        $y = Cte^{-t} + De^{-t}$

        where A, B, C and D are constants to be found.   **(8 marks)**

    b Find, correct to the nearest organism, the number of each organism at time $t = 2.1$ days.   **(2 marks)**

    c Use the model to describe what happens to the numbers of each type of organism as t gets large.   **(2 marks)**

18 An industrial process consists of two linked tanks, A and B, containing a chemical solution. The solution is free to pass between the tanks but it flows from A to B at a different rate than it flows from B to A. The solution also enters both tanks, and flows directly out of tank B. The situation is modelled using the differential equations

$$\frac{dx}{dt} = 2 + \frac{1}{3}y - \frac{1}{2}x \qquad (1)$$

$$\frac{dy}{dt} = 1 + \frac{1}{2}x - \frac{2}{3}y \qquad (2)$$

    where x litres is the amount of solution in tank A and y litres is the amount of solution in tank B at time t minutes.

    a Show that $6\dfrac{d^2 y}{dt^2} + 7\dfrac{dy}{dt} + y = 9$ **(6 marks)**

    b Given that both tanks initially contain 8 litres of solution, find x and y as functions of t.   **(7 marks)**

    c State, with a reason, the approximate amount of solution in each tank after the system has been running for a long time.   **(2 marks)**

Challenge

a Three water tanks are positioned as shown in the diagram. Water flows from tank X to tank Y, and from tank Y to tank Z, by means of identical taps. Each tap allows water to flow at a rate of r gallons/hour, where r is the amount of water in the corresponding tank in gallons.

Initially, tank X contains 300 gallons of water, tank Y contains 200 gallons of water, and tank Z contains 100 gallons of water. The taps are opened.

   i Show that after t hours have elapsed, the amount of water in tank X is $300e^{-t}$ gallons.

   ii Find the number of minutes after which tanks X and Y contain the same amount of water.

   iii Find an expression for the amount of water in tank Z after t hours.

b A second identical tap is attached to tank X, which is filled to the brim. Tanks Y and Z are emptied, and all three taps are opened.

   i Show that the amount of water in tank Y is at a maximum after 42 minutes have elapsed, to the nearest minute.

   ii Find the exact time elapsed before the amounts of water in tanks Y and Z are equal.

Summary of key points

1. **Simple harmonic motion** (S.H.M.) is motion in which the acceleration of a particle P is always towards a fixed point O on the line of motion of P. The acceleration is proportional to the displacement of P from O.

2. $\ddot{x} = v\dfrac{\mathrm{d}v}{\mathrm{d}x}$

3. For a particle moving with **damped harmonic motion**
   $$\frac{\mathrm{d}^2x}{\mathrm{d}t^2} + k\frac{\mathrm{d}x}{\mathrm{d}t} + \omega^2 x = 0$$
   where x is the displacement from a fixed point at time t, and k and ω^2 are positive constants.

4. For a particle moving with **forced harmonic motion**
   $$\frac{\mathrm{d}^2x}{\mathrm{d}t^2} + k\frac{\mathrm{d}x}{\mathrm{d}t} + \omega^2 x = \mathrm{f}(t)$$
   where x is the displacement from a fixed point at time t, and k and ω^2 are positive constants.

5. You can solve coupled first-order linear differential equations by eliminating one of the dependent variables to form a second-order differential equation.

2 Review exercise

(E) **1** Relative to the origin O as pole and initial line $\theta = 0$, find an equation in polar coordinate form for:

a a circle, centre O and radius 2 **(1)**

b a line perpendicular to the initial line and passing through the point with polar coordinates $(3, 0)$ **(2)**

c a straight line through the points with polar coordinates $(4, 0)$ and $\left(4, \frac{\pi}{3}\right)$. **(2)**

← Section 5.2

(E) **2 a** Sketch the curve with polar equation
$$r = a\cos 3\theta, \ 0 \leqslant \theta < 2\pi \quad \textbf{(2)}$$

b Find the area enclosed by one loop of this curve. **(6)**

← Sections 5.2, 5.3

(E/P) **3 a** Sketch the curve with polar equation
$$r = 3\cos 2\theta, \ -\frac{\pi}{4} \leqslant \theta < \frac{\pi}{4} \quad \textbf{(2)}$$

b Find the area of the smaller finite region enclosed between the curve and the half-line $\theta = \frac{\pi}{6}$ **(6)**

c Find the exact distance between the two tangents which are parallel to the initial line. **(6)**

← Sections 5.2, 5.3, 5.4

(E/P) **4 a** Sketch, on the same diagram, the curves defined by the polar equations $r = a$ and $r = a(1 + \cos\theta)$, where a is a positive constant and $-\pi < \theta \leqslant \pi$. **(4)**

b By considering the stationary values of $r\sin\theta$, or otherwise, find equations of the tangents to the curve $r = a(1 + \cos\theta)$ which are parallel to the initial line. **(6)**

c Show that the area of the region for which $a < r < a(1 + \cos\theta)$ is
$$\frac{(\pi + 8)a^2}{4} \quad \textbf{(6)}$$

← Sections 5.2, 5.3, 5.4

(E/P) **5** The curve C has polar equation $r = 3a\cos\theta, \ -\frac{\pi}{2} \leqslant \theta < \frac{\pi}{2}$. The curve D has polar equation $r = a(1 + \cos\theta), \ -\pi \leqslant \theta < \pi$. Given that a is positive,

a sketch, on the same diagram, the graphs of C and D, indicating where each curve cuts the initial line. **(4)**

The graphs of C and D intersect at the pole O and at the points P and Q.

b Find the polar coordinates of P and Q. **(3)**

c Use integration to find the exact value of the area enclosed by the curve D and the lines $\theta = 0$ and $\theta = \frac{\pi}{3}$. **(6)**

The region R contains all points which lie outside D and inside C.

Given that the value of the smaller area enclosed by the curve C and the line $\theta = \frac{\pi}{3}$ is
$$\frac{3a^2}{16}(2\pi - 3\sqrt{3}),$$

d show that the area of R is πa^2. **(6)**

← Sections 5.2, 5.3, 5.4

(E) **6 a** Show on an Argand diagram the locus of points given by the values of z satisfying
$$|z - 3 + 4i| = 5 \quad \textbf{(2)}$$

b Show that this locus of points can be represented by the polar curve
$$r = 6\cos\theta - 8\sin\theta. \quad \textbf{(4)}$$

The set of points A is defined by
$$A = \left\{z : -\frac{\pi}{2} \leqslant \arg z \leqslant 0\right\} \cap \{z : |z - 3 + 4i| \leqslant 5\}$$

c Find, correct to three significant figures, the area of the region defined by A. **(4)**

← Sections 5.2, 5.3

(E/P) **7 a** Sketch the curve with polar equation

$$r = \cos 2\theta, \ -\frac{\pi}{4} \leqslant \theta \leqslant \frac{\pi}{4} \qquad \textbf{(2)}$$

At the distinct points A and B on this curve, the tangents to the curve are parallel to the initial line, $\theta = 0$.

b Determine the polar coordinates of A and B, giving your answers to 3 significant figures. **(6)**

← Sections 5.2, 5.4

(E/P) **8 a** Sketch the curve with polar equation

$$r = \sin 2\theta, \ 0 \leqslant \theta \leqslant \frac{\pi}{2} \qquad \textbf{(2)}$$

At the point A, where A is distinct from O, on this curve, the tangent to the curve is parallel to $\theta = \frac{\pi}{2}$

b Determine the polar coordinates of the point A, giving your answer to 3 significant figures. **(6)**

← Sections 5.2, 5.4

(E) **9** The curve C has polar equation

$$r = 6\cos\theta, \ -\frac{\pi}{2} \leqslant \theta < \frac{\pi}{2}$$

and the line D has polar equation

$$r = 3\sec\left(\frac{\pi}{3} - \theta\right), \ -\frac{\pi}{6} \leqslant \theta < \frac{5\pi}{6}$$

a Find a Cartesian equation of C and a Cartesian equation of D. **(4)**

b Sketch on the same diagram the graphs of C and D, indicating where each cuts the initial line. **(4)**

The graphs of C and D intersect at the points P and Q.

c Find the polar coordinates of P and Q. **(3)**

← Sections 5.1, 5.2

(E) **10**

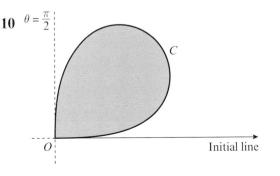

The figure shows a sketch of the curve C with polar equation

$$r^2 = a^2 \sin 2\theta, \ 0 \leqslant \theta \leqslant \frac{\pi}{2},$$

where a is a constant.

Find the area of the shaded region enclosed by C. **(6)**

← Section 5.3

(E/P) **11**

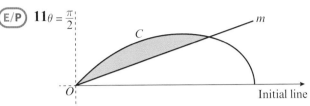

The figure shows a curve C with polar equation $r = 4a\cos 2\theta, \ 0 \leqslant \theta \leqslant \frac{\pi}{4}$, and a line m with polar equation $\theta = \frac{\pi}{8}$. The shaded region, shown in the figure, is bounded by C and m. Use calculus to show that the area of the shaded region is $\frac{1}{2}a^2(\pi - 2)$. **(6)**

← Section 5.3

(E/P) **12**

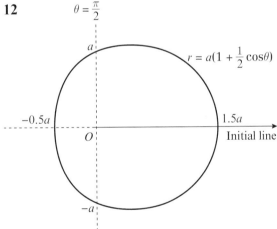

The curve shown in the figure has polar equation

$$r = a\left(1 + \tfrac{1}{2}\cos\theta\right), \ a > 0, \ 0 < \theta \leqslant 2\pi.$$

Determine the area enclosed by the curve, giving your answer in terms of a and π. **(6)**

← Section 5.3

E/P **13**

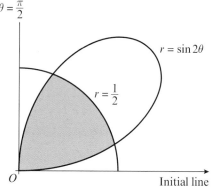

The figure show the half-lines $\theta = 0$, $\theta = \frac{\pi}{2}$, and the curves with polar equations

$r = \frac{1}{2}$, $0 \leqslant \theta \leqslant \frac{\pi}{2}$, and

$r = \sin 2\theta$, $0 \leqslant \theta \leqslant \frac{\pi}{2}$

a Find the exact values of θ at the two points where the curves cross. **(4)**

b Find by integration the area of the shaded region, shown in the figure, which is bounded by both curves. **(6)**

← Sections 5.2, 5.3

E/P **14**

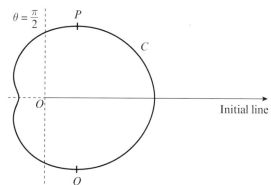

The curve C, shown in the figure, has polar equation

$r = a(3 + \sqrt{5} \cos \theta)$, $-\pi \leqslant \theta < \pi$

a Find the polar coordinates of the points P and Q where the tangents to C are parallel to the initial line. **(6)**

The curve C represents the perimeter of the surface of a swimming pool. The direct distance from P to Q is 20 m.

b Calculate the value of a. **(2)**

c Find the area of the surface of the pool. **(6)**

← Sections 5.2, 5.3, 5.4

E/P **15**

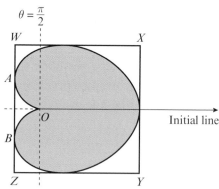

The figure shows a sketch of the cardioid C with equation $r = a(1 + \cos \theta)$, $-\pi < \theta \leqslant \pi$. Also shown are the tangents to C that are parallel and perpendicular to the initial line. These tangents form a rectangle $WXYZ$.

a Find the area of the finite region, shaded in the figure, bounded by the curve C. **(6)**

b Find the polar coordinates of the points A and B where WZ touches the curve C. **(6)**

c Hence find the length of WX. **(2)**

Given that the length of WZ is $\frac{3\sqrt{3}a}{2}$,

d find the area of the rectangle $WXYZ$. **(2)**

A heart-shape is modelled by the cardioid C, where $a = 10$ cm. The heart shape is cut from the rectangular card $WXYZ$, shown the figure.

e Find a numerical value for the area of card wasted in making this heart shape. **(3)**

← Sections 5.3, 5.4

E/P **16**

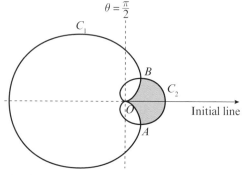

The figure is a sketch of two curves C_1 and C_2 with polar equations

$C_1 : r = 3a(1 - \cos \theta)$, $-\pi \leqslant \theta < \pi$

and $C_2 : r = a(1 + \cos \theta)$, $-\pi \leqslant \theta < \pi$

The curves meet at the pole O and at the points A and B.

a Find, in terms of a, the polar coordinates of the points A and B. **(2)**

b Show that the length of the line AB is $\dfrac{3\sqrt{3}}{2}a$. **(3)**

The region inside C_2 and outside C_1 is shaded in the figure.

c Find, in terms of a, the area of this region. **(6)**

A badge is designed which has the shape of the shaded region.

Given that the length of the line AB is 4.5 cm,

d calculate the area of this badge, giving your answer to 3 significant figures. **(3)**

← Sections 5.2, 5.3

 17

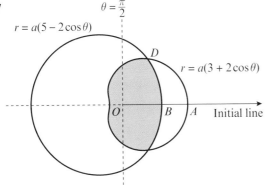

$\theta = \dfrac{\pi}{2}$

$r = a(5 - 2\cos\theta)$

D

$r = a(3 + 2\cos\theta)$

O B A Initial line

A logo is designed which consists of two overlapping closed curves.

The polar equations of these curves are
$$r = a(3 + 2\cos\theta), \quad 0 \leqslant \theta < 2\pi \quad \text{and}$$
$$r = a(5 - 2\cos\theta), \quad 0 \leqslant \theta < 2\pi$$

The figure is a sketch (not to scale) of these two curves.

a Write down the polar coordinates of the points A and B where the curves meet the initial line. **(2)**

b Find the polar coordinates of the points C and D where the two curves meet. **(4)**

c Show that the area of the overlapping region, which is shaded in the figure, is $\dfrac{a^2}{3}(49\pi - 48\sqrt{3})$ **(6)**

← Sections 5.2, 5.3

(E) **18** Find the value of x for which
$$2\tanh x - 1 = 0,$$
giving your answer in terms of a natural logarithm. **(4)**

← Section 6.1

(E) **19** Starting from the definition of $\cosh x$ in terms of exponentials, find, in terms of natural logarithms, the values of x for which $5 = 3\cosh x$. **(4)**

← Section 6.1

(E) **20** The curves with equations $y = 5\sinh x$ and $y = 4\cosh x$ meet at the point $A(\ln p, q)$. Find the exact values of p and q. **(4)**

← Section 6.3

(E) **21** Find the values of x for which
$$5\cosh x - 2\sinh x = 11,$$
giving your answers as natural logarithms. **(5)**

← Section 6.3

(E) **22** By expressing $\sinh 2x$ and $\cosh 2x$ in terms of exponentials, find the exact values of x for which
$$6\sinh 2x + 9\cosh 2x = 7,$$
giving each answer in the form $\frac{1}{2}\ln p$, where p is a rational number. **(5)**

← Section 6.3

(E) **23** Given that
$$\sinh x + 2\cosh x = k,$$
where k is a positive constant,

a find the set of values of k for which at least one real solution of this equation exists **(4)**

b solve the equation when $k = 2$. **(3)**

← Section 6.3

(E) **24** Using the definitions of $\cosh x$ and $\sinh x$ in terms of exponentials,

a prove that $\cosh^2 x - \sinh^2 x \equiv 1$ **(3)**

b solve the equation $\dfrac{1}{\sinh x} - \dfrac{2}{\tanh x} = 2$, giving your answer in the form $k\ln a$, where k and a are integers. **(5)**

← Section 6.3

(E) **25 a** From the definition of $\cosh x$ in terms of exponentials, show that
$$\cosh 2x \equiv 2\cosh^2 x - 1. \quad (3)$$

b Solve the equation
$$\cosh 2x - 5\cosh x = 2,$$
giving the answers in terms of natural logarithms. **(5)**

← Section 6.3

(E) **26 a** Using the definition of $\cosh x$ in terms of exponentials, prove that
$$4\cosh^3 x - 3\cosh x \equiv \cosh 3x. \quad (4)$$

b Hence, or otherwise, solve the equation
$$\cosh 3x = 5\cosh x,$$
giving your answer as natural logarithms. **(4)**

← Section 6.3

(E) **27 a** Starting from the definitions of $\cosh x$ and $\sinh x$ in terms of exponentials, prove that
$$\cosh(A - B) \equiv \cosh A \cosh B - \sinh A \sinh B. \quad (4)$$

b Hence, or otherwise, given that $\cosh(x - 1) = \sinh x$, show that
$$\tanh x = \frac{e^2 + 1}{e^2 + 2e - 1} \quad (5)$$

← Section 6.3

(E/P) **28 a** Starting from the definition
$$\sinh y = \frac{e^y - e^{-y}}{2},$$
prove that, for all real values of x,
$$\text{arsinh } x = \ln(x + \sqrt{(1 + x^2)}). \quad (4)$$

b Hence, or otherwise, prove that, for $0 < \theta < \pi$,
$$\text{arsinh}(\cot \theta) = \ln\left(\cot \frac{\theta}{2}\right). \quad (5)$$

← Sections 6.2, 6.3

(E/P) **29 a** Starting from the definition of $\tanh x$ in terms of e^x, show that
$$\text{artanh } x = \tfrac{1}{2}\ln\left(\frac{1 + x}{1 - x}\right), \ |x| < 1 \quad (5)$$

b Sketch the graph of $y = \text{artanh } x$. **(2)**

c Solve the equation $x = \tanh(\ln\sqrt{6x})$ for $0 < x < 1$. **(5)**

← Sections 6.2, 6.3

(E) **30 a** Show that, for $0 < x \le 1$,
$$\ln\left(\frac{1 - \sqrt{(1 - x^2)}}{x}\right) = -\ln\left(\frac{1 + \sqrt{(1 - x^2)}}{x}\right).$$
(2)

b Using the definitions of $\cosh x$ and $\sinh x$ in terms of exponentials, show that, for $0 < x \le 1$,
$$\text{arcosh}\left(\frac{1}{x}\right) = \ln\left(\frac{1 + \sqrt{1 - x^2}}{x}\right) \quad (3)$$

c Solve the equation
$$3\tanh^2 x - 4\,\text{sech } x + 1 = 0,$$
giving exact answers in terms of natural logarithms. **(4)**

← Sections 6.2, 6.3

(E/P) **31 a** Express $\cosh 3\theta$ and $\cosh 5\theta$ in terms of $\cosh \theta$. **(4)**

b Hence determine the real roots of the equation
$$2\cosh 5x + 10\cosh 3x + 20\cosh x = 243,$$
giving your answers to 2 decimal places. **(6)**

← Section 6.3

(E/P) **32 a** Show that, for $x = \ln k$, where k is a positive constant,
$$\cosh 2x = \frac{k^4 + 1}{2k^2} \quad (4)$$

b Given that $f(x) = px - \tanh 2x$, where p is a constant, find the value of p for which $f(x)$ has a stationary value at $x = \ln 2$, giving your answer as an exact fraction. **(6)**

← Sections 6.1, 6.4

(E) **33** The curve with equation
$$y = -x + \tanh 4x, \ x \ge 0,$$
has a maximum turning point A.

a Find, in exact logarithmic form, the x-coordinate of A. **(5)**

b Show that the y-coordinate of A is $\tfrac{1}{4}(2\sqrt{3} - \ln(2 + \sqrt{3}))$. **(3)**

← Section 6.4

(E) **34** $y = \sinh 2x \cosh 2x$

   a Find the first three non-zero terms of the Maclaurin series for y, giving each coefficient in its simplest form. **(7)**

   b Find an expression for the nth non-zero term of the Maclaurin series for y. **(2)**

       ← Section 6.4

(E) **35** $f(x) = \cos 2x \cosh x$

   a Find the first two non-zero terms of the Maclaurin series for $f(x)$, giving each coefficient in its simplest form. **(6)**

   b Hence find, correct to two significant figures, the percentage error when this approximation is used to evaluate $f(0.1)$. **(3)**

       ← Section 6.4

(E/P) **36** Use the substitution $x = \dfrac{a}{\sinh \theta}$, where a is a constant, to show that, for $x > 0$, $a > 0$,

$$\int \frac{1}{x\sqrt{x^2 + a^2}}\,dx = -\frac{1}{a}\operatorname{arsinh}\left(\frac{a}{x}\right) + \text{constant}.$$

                                    (6)

       ← Section 6.5

(E/P) **37** **a** Prove that the derivative of $\operatorname{artanh} x$, $-1 < x < 1$, is $\dfrac{1}{1 - x^2}$. **(4)**

   b Find $\displaystyle\int \operatorname{artanh} x\,dx$. **(4)**

       ← Sections 6.4, 6.5

(E/P) **38** **a** Starting from the definition of $\sinh x$ in terms of e^x, prove that

      $\operatorname{arsinh} x = \ln(x + \sqrt{x^2 + 1})$. **(2)**

   b Prove that the derivative of $\operatorname{arsinh} x$ is $(1 + x^2)^{-\frac{1}{2}}$. **(4)**

   c Show that the equation

$$(1 + x^2)\frac{d^2y}{dx^2} + x\frac{dy}{dx} - 2 = 0$$

     is satisfied when $y = (\operatorname{arsinh} x)^2$. **(4)**

   d Use integration by parts to find $\displaystyle\int_0^1 \operatorname{arsinh} x\,dx$, giving your answer in terms of a natural logarithm. **(5)**

       ← Sections 6.2, 6.4, 6.5

(E) **39** $4x^2 + 4x + 5 \equiv (px + q)^2 + r$

   a Find the values of the constants p, q and r. **(2)**

   b Hence, or otherwise, find

$$\int \frac{1}{4x^2 + 4x + 5}\,dx. \quad \textbf{(4)}$$

   c Show that

$$\int \frac{2}{\sqrt{4x^2 + 4x + 5}}\,dx$$
$$= \ln((2x + 1) + \sqrt{4x^2 + 4x + 5}) + k,$$

     where k is an arbitrary constant. **(5)**

       ← Section 6.5

(E) **40** Find $\displaystyle\int \frac{x + 2}{\sqrt{4x^2 + 9}}\,dx$ **(7)**

       ← Section 6.5

(E) **41** Show that $\displaystyle\int_2^5 \frac{1}{\sqrt{x^2 - 4x + 8}}\,dx = \operatorname{arsinh} k$, where k is a rational constant to be found. **(6)**

       ← Section 6.5

(E/P) **42**

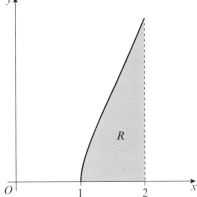

The figure above shows a sketch of the curve with equation

    $y = x \operatorname{arcosh} x$, $1 \le x \le 2$.

The region R, shaded in the figure, is bounded by the curve, the x-axis and the line $x = 2$.

Show that the area of R is

$$\frac{7}{4}\ln(2 + \sqrt{3}) - \frac{\sqrt{3}}{2} \quad \textbf{(8)}$$

       ← Section 6.5

E/P **43** The diagram shows the cross-section of a new greenhouse. Each unit on the axes represents 1 m.

The curved top of the roof of the greenhouse is modelled using the equation

$$y = \frac{10}{\sqrt{x^2 + 9}}$$

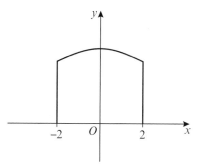

Given that the greenhouse can be modelled as a prism, length 55 m, find, correct to three significant figures, the volume of the greenhouse. **(8)**

← Section 6.5

E **44** Find, in the form $y = f(x)$, the general solution to the differential equation

$$\frac{dy}{dx} + \frac{4}{x} y = 6x - 5, \, x > 0$$ **(5)**

← Section 7.1

E **45** Solve the differential equation

$$\frac{dy}{dx} - \frac{y}{x} = x^2, \, x > 0$$

giving your answer for y in terms of x. **(5)**

← Section 7.1

E **46** Find the general solution to the differential equation

$$(x + 1)\frac{dy}{dx} + 2y = \frac{1}{x}, \, x > 0$$

giving your answer in the form $y = f(x)$. **(5)**

← Section 7.1

E **47** Obtain the solution to

$$\frac{dy}{dx} + y \tan x = e^{2x} \cos x, \, 0 \leqslant x < \frac{\pi}{2}$$

for which $y = 2$ at $x = 0$, giving your answer in the form $y = f(x)$. **(6)**

← Section 7.1

E **48** Find the general solution to the differential equation

$$\frac{dy}{dx} + 2y \cot 2x = \sin x, \, 0 < x < \frac{\pi}{2}$$

giving your answer in the form $y = f(x)$. **(5)**

← Section 7.1

E **49** Solve the differential equation

$$(1 + x) \frac{dy}{dx} - xy = xe^{-x}$$

given that $y = 1$ at $x = 0$. **(6)**

← Section 7.1

E **50** **a** Find the general solution to the differential equation

$$\cos x \frac{dy}{dx} + (\sin x)y = \cos^3 x$$ **(5)**

b Show that, for $0 \leqslant x \leqslant 2\pi$, there are two points on the x-axis through which all the solution curves for this differential equation pass. **(4)**

c Sketch the graph, $0 \leqslant x \leqslant 2\pi$, of the particular solution for which $y = 0$ at $x = 0$. **(3)**

← Section 7.1

E **51** **a** Find the general solution to the differential equation

$$\frac{dy}{dx} + 2y = x$$ **(5)**

Given that $y = 1$ at $x = 0$,

b find the exact values of the coordinates of the minimum point of the particular solution curve, **(3)**

c draw a sketch of the particular solution curve. **(2)**

← Section 7.1

E **52** **a** Find the general solution to the differential equation

$$\frac{dy}{dx} = y \sinh x$$ **(4)**

b Find the particular solution which satisfies the condition that $y = e^3$ when $x = 0$. **(2)**

← Section 7.1

E/P **53** Given that θ satisfies the differential equation

$$\frac{d^2\theta}{dt^2} + 4\frac{d\theta}{dt} + 5\theta = 0$$

and that, when $t = 0$, $\theta = 3$ and $\frac{d\theta}{dt} = -6$,

express θ in terms of t. **(8)**

← Sections 7.2, 7.4

E/P **54** Given that $3x\sin 2x$ is a particular integral of the differential equation

$$\frac{d^2y}{dx^2} + 4y = k\cos 2x$$

where k is a constant,

a calculate the value of k **(3)**

b find the particular solution of the differential equation for which at $x = 0$, $y = 2$, and for which at $x = \frac{\pi}{4}$, $y = \frac{\pi}{2}$ **(8)**

← Sections 7.3, 7.4

E/P **55** Given that $a + bx$ is a particular integral of the differential equation

$$\frac{d^2y}{dx^2} - 4\frac{dy}{dx} + 4y = 16 + 4x$$

a find the values of the constants a and b **(3)**

b find the particular solution to this differential equation for which $y = 8$ and $\frac{dy}{dx} = 9$ at $x = 0$. **(8)**

← Sections 7.3, 7.4

E/P **56** $\frac{d^2y}{dx^2} + 4\frac{dy}{dx} + 5y = 65\sin 2x$, $x > 0$

a Find the general solution to the differential equation. **(8)**

b Show that for large values of x this general solution may be approximated by a sine function and find this sine function. **(2)**

← Section 7.3

E/P **57** a Find the general solution to the differential equation

$$\frac{d^2y}{dt^2} + 2\frac{dy}{dt} + 2y = 2e^{-t}$$ **(8)**

b Find the particular solution to this differential equation for which $y = 1$ and $\frac{dy}{dt} = 1$ at $t = 0$. **(2)**

← Sections 7.3, 7.4

E/P **58** a Find the general solution to the differential equation

$$\frac{d^2x}{dt^2} + 2\frac{dx}{dt} + 5x = 0$$ **(8)**

b Given that $x = 1$ and $\frac{dx}{dt} = 1$ at $t = 0$,

find the particular solution to the differential equation, giving your answer in the form $x = f(t)$. **(2)**

c Sketch the curve with equation $x = f(t)$, $0 \leq t \leq \pi$, showing the coordinates, as multiples of π, of the points where the curve cuts the t-axis. **(2)**

← Sections 7.2, 7.4

E/P **59** a Find the general solution to the differential equation

$$2\frac{d^2y}{dt^2} + 7\frac{dy}{dt} + 3y = 3t^2 + 11t$$ **(8)**

b Find the particular solution to this differential equation for which $y = 1$ and $\frac{dy}{dt} = 1$ when $t = 0$. **(2)**

c For this particular solution, calculate the value of y when $t = 1$. **(2)**

← Sections 7.3, 7.4

E/P **60** a Find the value of λ for which $\lambda x\cos 3x$ is a particular integral of the differential equation

$$\frac{d^2y}{dx^2} + 9y = -12\sin 3x$$ **(3)**

b Hence find the general solution to this differential equation. **(6)**

The particular solution of the differential equation for which $y = 1$ and $\frac{dy}{dx} = 2$ at $x = 0$, is $y = g(x)$.

c Find $g(x)$. **(2)**

d Sketch the graph of $y = g(x)$, $0 \leq x \leq \pi$. **(2)**

← Sections 7.3, 7.4

Ⓔ **61** $\dfrac{d^2y}{dt^2} - 6\dfrac{dy}{dt} + 9y = 4e^{3t}$, $t \geqslant 0$

a Show that Kt^2e^{3t} is a particular integral of the differential equation, where K is a constant to be found. **(3)**

b Find the general solution to the differential equation. **(6)**

Given that a particular solution satisfies

$y = 3$ and $\dfrac{dy}{dt} = 1$ when $t = 0$,

c find this solution.

Another particular solution which satisfies

$y = 1$ and $\dfrac{dy}{dt} = 0$ when $t = 0$, has equation

$y = (1 - 3t + 2t^2)e^{3t}$ **(2)**

d For this particular solution, draw a sketch graph of y against t, showing where the graph crosses the t-axis. Determine also the coordinates of the minimum point on the sketch graph. **(4)**

← Sections 7.3, 7.4

Ⓔ/Ⓟ **62 a** Find the general solution to the differential equation

$2\dfrac{d^2x}{dt^2} + 5\dfrac{dx}{dt} + 2x = 2t + 9$ **(8)**

b Find the particular solution of this differential equation for which $x = 3$

and $\dfrac{dx}{dt} = -1$ when $t = 0$. **(2)**

The particular solution in part **b** is used to model the motion of the particle P on the x-axis. At time t seconds ($t \geqslant 0$), P is x metres from the origin O.

c Show that the minimum distance between O and P is $\frac{1}{2}(5 + \ln 2)$ m and justify that the distance is a minimum. **(4)**

← Sections 7.3, 7.4, 8.3

Ⓔ/Ⓟ **63** Given that $x = At^2e^{-t}$ satisfies the differential equation

$\dfrac{d^2x}{dt^2} + 2\dfrac{dx}{dt} + x = e^{-t}$,

a find the value of A. **(3)**

b Hence find the solution to the differential equation for which $x = 1$

and $\dfrac{dx}{dt} = 0$ at $t = 0$. **(7)**

c Use your solution to prove that for $t \geqslant 0$, $x \leqslant 1$. **(2)**

← Sections 7.3, 7.4

Ⓔ **64** Given that $y = kx$ is a particular solution of the differential equation

$\dfrac{d^2y}{dx^2} + y = 3x$,

a find the value of the constant k. **(3)**

b Find the most general solution to this differential equation for which $y = 0$ at $x = 0$. **(6)**

c Prove that all curves given by this solution pass through the point $(\pi, 3\pi)$ and that they all have equal gradients when $x = \dfrac{\pi}{2}$. **(3)**

d Find the particular solution to the differential equation for which $y = 0$ at $x = 0$ and at $x = \dfrac{\pi}{2}$. **(2)**

e Show that a local minimum value of the solution in part **d** is

$3\arccos\left(\dfrac{2}{\pi}\right) - \frac{3}{2}\sqrt{\pi^2 - 4}$ **(4)**

← Sections 7.3, 7.4

Ⓔ/Ⓟ **65** During an industrial process, the mass of salt, S kg, dissolved in a liquid, t minutes after the process begins, is modelled by the differential equation

$\dfrac{dS}{dt} + \dfrac{2S}{120 - t} = \frac{1}{4}$, $0 \leqslant t < 120$

Given that $S = 6$ when $t = 0$,

a find S in terms of t. **(6)**

b calculate the maximum mass of salt that the model predicts will be dissolved in the liquid at any one time during the process. **(3)**

← Section 8.1

E/P 66 A fertilized egg initially contains an embryo of mass m_0 together with a mass $100m_0$ of nutrient, all of which is available as food for the embryo. At time t, the embryo has mass m and the mass of nutrient which has been consumed is $5(m - m_0)$.

   a Show that, when three-quarters of the nutrient has been consumed, $m = 16m_0$. **(3)**

The rate of increase of the mass of the embryo is a constant μ multiplied by the product of the mass of the embryo and the mass of the remaining nutrient.

   b Show that $\dfrac{dm}{dt} = 5\mu m\,(21m_0 - m)$. **(4)**

The egg hatches at time T, when three-quarters of the nutrient has been consumed.

   c Show that $105\mu m_0 T = \ln 64$. **(5)**

               ← Section 8.1

E 67 **a** Find the general solution to the differential equation

$$t\frac{dv}{dt} - v = t,\ t > 0$$

      and hence show that the solution can be written in the form $v = t(\ln t + c)$, where c is an arbitrary constant. **(5)**

   b This differential equation is used to model the motion of a particle which has speed $v\,\mathrm{m\,s^{-1}}$ at time t seconds. When $t = 2$, the speed of the particle is $3\,\mathrm{m\,s^{-1}}$. Find, to 3 significant figures, the speed of the particle when $t = 4$. **(4)**

               ← Section 8.1

E/P 68 A particle P moves in a straight line. At time t seconds, the acceleration of P is $e^{2t}\,\mathrm{m\,s^{-2}}$, where $t \geqslant 0$. When $t = 0$, P is at rest. Show that the speed, $v\,\mathrm{m\,s^{-1}}$, of P at time t seconds is given by

$$v = \tfrac{1}{2}(e^{2t} - 1)$$ **(5)**

               ← Section 8.1

E/P 69 A particle P moves along the x-axis in the positive direction. At time t seconds, the velocity of P is $v\,\mathrm{m\,s^{-1}}$ and its acceleration is $\frac{1}{2}e^{-\frac{1}{6}t}\,\mathrm{m\,s^{-2}}$. When $t = 0$ the speed of P is $10\,\mathrm{m\,s^{-1}}$.

   a Express v in terms of t. **(4)**

   b Find, to 3 significant figures, the speed of P when $t = 3$. **(2)**

   c Find the limiting value of v. **(2)**

               ← Section 8.1

E/P 70 A particle P moves along the x-axis. At time t seconds its acceleration is $(-4e^{-2t})\,\mathrm{m\,s^{-2}}$ in the direction of x increasing. When $t = 0$, P is at the origin O and is moving with speed $1\,\mathrm{m\,s^{-1}}$ in the direction of x increasing.

   a Find an expression for the velocity of P at time t. **(4)**

   b Find the distance of P from O when P comes to instantaneous rest. **(2)**

               ← Section 8.1

E/P 71 A water droplet falls vertically from rest through low cloud. Water condenses on the droplet as it falls. You are given that the motion of the water droplet may be modelled by the equation

$$(t + 3)\frac{dv}{dt} + 3v = 9.8(t + 3)$$

where t is the time in seconds and v is the velocity of the droplet in $\mathrm{m\,s^{-1}}$.

   a Show that $v = \dfrac{49(t + 3)^4 + c}{20(t + 3)^3}$ where c is a constant to be found. **(6)**

   b Find the velocity of the water droplet after 6 seconds. **(2)**

   c By considering the velocity for large values of t, suggest one criticism of the model. **(1)**

               ← Section 8.1

(E/P) 72 A water bottle initially contains 400 ml of distilled water. The water leaks out at a constant rate of 30 ml per minute and a mixture is added to the bottle at a constant rate of 40 ml per minute. The mixture contains 10% acid and 90% distilled water.

Given that there is x ml of acid in the bottle after t minutes and that the acid immediately disperses on entry,

a show that the situation can be modelled by the differential equation

$$\frac{\mathrm{d}x}{\mathrm{d}t} = 4 - \frac{3x}{40 + t} \qquad \textbf{(4)}$$

b Hence find the amount of acid in the bottle after 7 minutes. **(5)**

c Explain how the model could be refined. **(1)**

← Section 8.1

(E/P) 73 A particle, P, is attached to the ends of two identical elastic springs. The free ends of the springs are attached to two points A and B. The point C lies between A and B such that ACB is a straight line and $AC \neq BC$. The particle is held at C and then released from rest.

The subsequent motion of the particle can be described by the differential equation $\ddot{x} = -49x$.

a Describe the motion of the particle. **(1)**

Given that $x = 0.3$ and $v = 0$ when $t = 0$,

b solve the differential equation to find x as a function of t. **(7)**

c State the period of the motion and calculate the maximum speed of P. **(2)**

← Section 8.2

(E/P) 74 A small boat is floating on the surface of a river, tied to a jetty. The boat moves up and down in a vertical line, such that the vertical displacement, x m, from its equilibrium point satisfies the equation

$$\frac{\mathrm{d}^2 x}{\mathrm{d}t^2} = -1.6x, \; t \geqslant 0$$

Given that the displacement is zero and the boat is moving at a velocity of $1\,\mathrm{m\,s}^{-1}$ at time $t = 0$ minutes,

a solve the differential equation and hence find, correct to three significant figures, the maximum displacement of the boat. **(7)**

b State the time elapsed between the boat being at its highest and lowest points. **(2)**

c Criticise the model in terms of the motion of the boat for large values of t. **(1)**

← Section 8.2

(E/P) 75 A particle P moves in a straight line. At time t seconds its displacement from a fixed point O on the line is x metres. The motion of P is modelled by the differential equation

$$\frac{\mathrm{d}^2 x}{\mathrm{d}t^2} + 2\frac{\mathrm{d}x}{\mathrm{d}t} + 2x = 12\cos 2t - 6\sin 2t$$

When $t = 0$, P is at rest at O.

a Find, in terms of t, the displacement of P from O. **(8)**

b Show that P comes to instantaneous rest when $t = \dfrac{\pi}{4}$ **(2)**

c Find, in metres to 3 significant figures, the displacement of P from O when $t = \dfrac{\pi}{4}$ **(2)**

d Find the approximate period of the motion for large values of t. **(2)**

← Section 8.3

E/P **76** A particle P of mass m is suspended from a fixed point by a light elastic spring. At time $t = 0$ the particle is projected vertically downwards with speed U from its equilibrium position.

At time t, the displacement of P downwards from its equilibrium position is x.

The motion of the particle can be modelled using the differential equation

$$\frac{d^2x}{dt^2} + 2\omega\frac{dx}{dt} + 2\omega^2x = 0$$

Given that the solution to this differential equation is $x = e^{-\omega t}(A\cos\omega t + B\sin\omega t)$, where A and B are constants,

a find A and B. **(8)**

b Find an expression for the time at which P first comes to rest. **(2)**

← Section 8.3

E/P **77** A particle P is attached to one end A of a light elastic string AB and is free to move on a horizontal table.

At time $t = 0$, P is at rest and the end B of the string is forced to move horizontally away from P with speed V. After t seconds the displacement of P from its initial position is x metres.

The motion of P can be modelled by the differential equation

$$\frac{d^2x}{dt^2} + 2k\frac{dx}{dt} + 10k^2x = 10k^2Vt$$

Find an expression for x in terms of t, k and V. **(8)**

← Section 8.3

E/P **78** A particle P is attached to one end of a light elastic string. The other end of the string is fixed to a point vertically above the surface of a liquid. The particle is held on the surface of the liquid and then released from rest. At time t seconds, the distance travelled down by P is x metres.

Given that the motion of P can be modelled using the differential equation

$$\frac{d^2x}{dt^2} + 6\frac{dx}{dt} + 8x = 2.4$$

a find x in terms of t **(8)**

b show that the particle continues to move down through the liquid throughout the motion. **(2)**

← Section 8.3

79 Colonies of angler fish and angel fish live in an ocean cave sealed off from the rest of the ocean by a thick wall of seaweed. After t years the number of angler fish, x, and the number of angel fish, y, in the cave are modelled by the differential equations

$$\frac{dx}{dt} = 0.1x + 0.1y \qquad (1)$$

$$\frac{dy}{dt} = -0.025x + 0.2y \qquad (2)$$

a Show that $\dfrac{d^2x}{dt^2} - 0.3\dfrac{dx}{dt} + 0.0225x = 0$ **(3)**

b Find the general solution for the number of angler fish in the cave at time t. **(4)**

c Find the general solution for the number of angel fish in the cave at time t. **(4)**

At the start of 2010 there were 20 angler fish and 100 angel fish in the cave.

d Use this information to find the number of angler fish predicted to be in the cave in 2017. **(4)**

e Comment in the suitability of the model. **(1)**

← Section 8.4

E/P **80** An industrial chemist is examining the rates of change of gases in two connected tanks, A and B. Gas passes between the two tanks. Gas also enters the system into both tanks and escapes from the system in the same way.

The chemist believes that the amount of gas in tank A, x litres, and the amount of gas in tank B, y litres, at time t hours, can be modelled using the differential equations

$$\frac{dx}{dt} = 2x + y + 1 \qquad (1)$$

$$\frac{dy}{dt} = 4x - y + 1 \qquad (2)$$

a Show that $\dfrac{d^2x}{dt^2} - \dfrac{dx}{dt} - 6x = 2$ **(4)**

b Given that tank A initially contains 20 litres of gas and tank B initially contains 60 litres of gas, find expressions for the amount of gas in each tank at time t hours. **(8)**

The tanks have a maximum capacity of 500 litres.

c Comment on the suitability of the model after one hour. **(2)**

← Section 8.4

Challenge

1 Given that $n \in \mathbb{Z}^+$, $x \in \mathbb{R}$ and
$$\mathbf{M} = \begin{pmatrix} \cosh^2 x & \cosh^2 x \\ -\sinh^2 x & -\sinh^2 x \end{pmatrix},$$
prove that $\mathbf{M}^n = \mathbf{M}$. ← Section 6.3

2 a A system of differential equations is given as
$$\frac{dy}{dt} = x, \quad \frac{dx}{dt} = y$$
Given that $y = 0$ and $x = 1$ when $t = 0$, show that $y = \sinh t$ and $x = \cosh t$.

b Another system of differential equations is given as
$$\frac{dp}{dt} = p - q$$
$$\frac{dq}{dt} = p + q$$
$$\frac{dr}{dt} = p + 2q + r$$
Given that $p = q = r = 1$ when $t = 0$, show that
$$r = e^t(3\sin t - \cos t + 2). \quad \leftarrow \text{Section 8.4}$$

3 The diagram shows the curve C with polar equation $r = f(\theta)$. The line l is a tangent to the curve at the point $P(r, \theta)$, and α is the acute angle between l and the radial line at P.

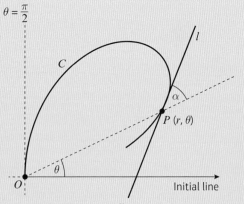

Show that $\tan \alpha = \dfrac{r}{\left(\dfrac{dr}{d\theta}\right)}$ ← Section 5.4

Exam-style practice

Further Mathematics
A Level
Paper 1: Core Pure Mathematics

Time: 1 hour 30 minutes

You must have: Mathematical Formulae and Statistical Tables, Calculator

1 The diagram shows a section of a curve C with parametric equations

$$x = t + t^2, y = t - t^2 + 1, \quad 0 \leqslant x \leqslant 3.75$$

The curve is rotated through 360° about the x-axis and the volume of revolution formed is used to model a clay pottery vase.

Given that each unit on the axes represents $10\,\text{cm}$,

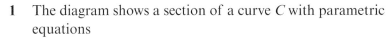

a find, correct to three significant figures, the volume of the vase **(7)**

b give one criticism of the model used. **(1)**

2 The plane Π_1 has vector equation

$$\mathbf{r}.(2\mathbf{i} + 3\mathbf{j} - \mathbf{k}) = 10$$

a Show that the perpendicular distance from the plane Π_1 to the point $(1, 4, 7)$ is $a\sqrt{14}$ where a is a rational constant to be found. **(3)**

The plane Π_2 has vector equation

$$\mathbf{r} = \lambda(\mathbf{i} - 3\mathbf{j} + 2\mathbf{k}) + \mu(a\mathbf{i} + 2\mathbf{j} - 3\mathbf{k})$$

Given that the vector $5\mathbf{i} + \mathbf{j} - \mathbf{k}$ is perpendicular to the plane Π_2,

b find the value of a **(2)**

c find, in degrees correct to 1 decimal place, the acute angle between Π_1 and Π_2. **(3)**

3 **a** Prove by induction that for all positive integers n,

$$\begin{pmatrix} 1 & 2 & 2 \\ 0 & 1 & 2 \\ 0 & 0 & 1 \end{pmatrix}^n = \begin{pmatrix} 1 & 2n & 2n^2 \\ 0 & 1 & 2n \\ 0 & 0 & 1 \end{pmatrix}$$ **(6)**

b $\mathbf{M} = \begin{pmatrix} 1 & k & 4 \\ 2 & -2 & 0 \\ 3 & -1 & 1 \end{pmatrix}$ where k is an integer.

  i Find the value of k for which $\mathbf{M}^{-1}$ does not exist. **(2)**

  ii Given that $\mathbf{M}$ is non-singular, find $\mathbf{M}^{-1}$ in terms of k. **(4)**

4 A complex number z has argument θ and modulus 1.

   a Show that $z^n - \dfrac{1}{z^n} = 2\mathrm{i}\sin n\theta$, $n \in \mathbb{Z}^+$ **(2)**

   b Hence, show that $8\sin^4\theta = \cos 4\theta - 4\cos 2\theta + 3$ **(5)**

5 An oil vat initially contains 500 litres of pure corn oil. The oil drains out at a constant rate of 15 litres per minute and a corn oil and sugar mixture is added to the vat at a constant rate of 30 litres per minute. The mixture contains 25 grams of sugar per litre of oil.

Given that there is x grams of sugar in the vat after t minutes and that the sugar immediately disperses throughout the vat on entry,

   a show that the situation can be modelled by the differential equation
$$\frac{\mathrm{d}x}{\mathrm{d}t} = 750 - \frac{3x}{100 + 3t}$$
     (4)

   b Hence find the number of grams of sugar in the vat after 10 minutes.   **(5)**

   c Explain how the model could be refined.   **(1)**

6   **a** Show that the locus of points given by the values of z satisfying
$$|z + 12 + 5\mathrm{i}| = 13$$
     can be represented by the polar curve with equation
$$r = -2(12\cos\theta + 5\sin\theta)$$
     (4)

   b Show on an Argand diagram the set of points A defined by
$$A = \{z : |z + 12 + 5\mathrm{i}| \leqslant 13\} \cap \{z : -\pi \leqslant \arg z \leqslant -\tfrac{3\pi}{4}\}$$
     (4)

   c Find, correct to three significant figures, the area of the region defined by A.   **(5)**

7 A scientific experiment looks at the concentration of glucose, dissolved in water, on either side of an osmotic membrane. The glucose solution passes through the membrane in both directions and also enters the system through a tube on the left side.

A researcher believes that the concentration of glucose on the left side of the membrane, x, and the concentration of glucose on the right side of the membrane, y, at time t hours, can be modelled by the differential equations
$$\frac{\mathrm{d}x}{\mathrm{d}t} = 0.3x + 0.2y + 1$$
$$\frac{\mathrm{d}y}{\mathrm{d}t} = -0.2x + 0.3y$$

   a Show that $100\dfrac{\mathrm{d}^2x}{\mathrm{d}t^2} - 60\dfrac{\mathrm{d}x}{\mathrm{d}t} + 13x + 30 = 0$.   **(3)**

   b Find the general solution for the concentration of glucose on the left side of the membrane at time t.   **(6)**

   c Hence find the general solution for the concentration of glucose on the right side of the membrane at time t.   **(3)**

At time $t = 0$, the concentration of glucose on the left side is 10 and on the right side is 5.

   d Find the particular solutions to the system of differential equations.   **(3)**

   e By considering the concentrations on each side on the membrane predicted by the model after 3 hours, comment on the suitability of the model.   **(2)**

Exam-style practice
Further Mathematics
A Level
Paper 2: Core Pure Mathematics

Time: 1 hour 30 minutes

You must have: Mathematical Formulae and Statistical Tables, Calculator

---

1 a Prove that

$$\sum_{r=1}^{n}\frac{1}{(r+2)(r+4)}=\frac{n(pn+q)}{24(n+3)(n+4)}$$

where p and q are constants to be found. **(5)**

b Prove that, for all positive integers n,

$$f(n) = 2^{n+2} + 3^{2n+1}$$

is divisible by 7. **(6)**

2 $f(x) = z^4 + az^3 + 30x^2 + bz + 85$

where a and b are real constants.

$z = 1 + 4i$ is a root of the equation $f(x) = 0$.

a Write down another root of the equation $f(x) = 0$. **(1)**

b Hence solve the equation $f(x)$ completely. **(6)**

c Show the roots of $f(x) = 0$ on a single Argand diagram. **(2)**

3 The diagram shows the curve C with polar equation

$$r = 6\sin 2\theta \quad 0 \leqslant \theta \leqslant \frac{\pi}{2}$$

The line segment AB is tangent to the curve at A and perpendicular to the initial line.

The finite region R, shown shaded in the diagram, is bounded by the curve, the initial line and the line segment AB.

Find, correct to three significant figures, the area of the shaded region R. **(9)**

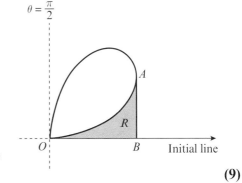

4 $f(x) = \cos x \sinh 2x$

a Find the first three non-zero terms of the Maclaurin series for $f(x)$, giving each coefficient in its simplest form. **(8)**

b Hence find, correct to four significant figures, the percentage error when the approximation is used to evaluate $f(0.1)$. **(2)**

211

5 Prove that $\displaystyle\int_0^\infty \frac{1}{x^2 + 4}\,dx = \frac{\pi}{4}$ **(5)**

6 A triangle T has vertices at $(0, 2)$, $(k, 0)$ and $(0, 8)$. Triangle T is transformed onto triangle T' by the matrix

$$\begin{pmatrix} 2 & 2 \\ -3 & 5 \end{pmatrix}$$

The area of triangle T' is 456 units², find the value of k. **(5)**

7 $\mathrm{f}(x) = \dfrac{1}{\sqrt{x^2 + 2x + 2}}$

  a Find the mean value of $\mathrm{f}(x)$ over the interval $[-1, 1]$, giving your answer correct to 3 decimal places. **(6)**

  b Hence find the mean value of $\mathrm{f}(x) + 2$ on the same interval. **(1)**

8 The line l_1 has equation $\dfrac{x - 3}{-1} = \dfrac{y - 2}{-2} = \dfrac{z - 1}{3}$

  The plane $\varPi$ has equation $2x - y + 3z = 4$.

  Point A on l_1 has x-coordinate $x = 4$.

  Line l_1 is reflected in the plane $\varPi$ and the image of point A is A'.

  Find the exact distance AA'. **(7)**

9 The differential equation

$$\frac{d^2x}{dt^2} + 2\frac{dx}{dt} + 3x = 21 + 15\cos t$$

is used to model the flow of water through a pump. x is the volume of water, in litres, at time t seconds.

  a Show that a particular solution to the differential equation is

$$x = 7 + \tfrac{15}{4}(\sin t + \cos t) \qquad \textbf{(3)}$$

  Given that the initial flow is two litres and the initial rate of change of flow is three litres per second,

  b Find the solution to the differential equation. **(8)**

  c State what happens to the flow of water as t gets large. **(1)**

Answers

CHAPTER 1

Prior knowledge check

1 a 8   b $\frac{\pi}{3}$ c 16

  d $\frac{\pi}{2}$ e 4   f $\frac{\pi}{6}$

2

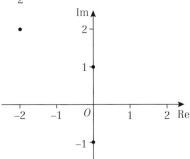

3 4032

Exercise 1A

1 a $3e^{\pi i}$ b $6e^{\frac{\pi i}{2}}$

  c $4e^{-\frac{5\pi}{6}i}$ d $\sqrt{65}\,e^{3.02i}$

  e $\sqrt{29}\,e^{-1.19i}$ f $2\sqrt{6}e^{\frac{3\pi i}{4}}$

  g $2\sqrt{2}e^{\frac{\pi i}{4}}$ h $8e^{-\frac{\pi i}{6}}$

  i $2e^{-\frac{\pi i}{5}}$

2 a $\frac{1}{2}+\frac{\sqrt{3}}{2}i$ b -4

  c $3+3i$ d $4\sqrt{3}+4i$

  e $-3i$ f $-\frac{\sqrt{3}}{2}+\frac{1}{2}i$

  g -1 h $-3-3i$

  i $-4+4i\sqrt{3}$

3 a $\cos\left(-\frac{10\pi}{13}\right)+i\sin\left(-\frac{10\pi}{13}\right)$

  b $4\left(\cos\left(-\frac{3\pi}{5}\right)+i\sin\left(-\frac{3\pi}{5}\right)\right)$

  c $5\left(\cos\left(\frac{7\pi}{8}\right)+i\sin\left(\frac{7\pi}{8}\right)\right)$

4 $e^{i\theta}=\cos\theta+i\sin\theta$ (1)

  $e^{-i\theta}=\cos(-\theta)+i\sin(-\theta)=\cos\theta-i\sin\theta$ (2)

  (1) – (2): $e^{i\theta}-e^{-i\theta}=2i\sin\theta$

  $\frac{1}{2i}(e^{i\theta}-e^{-i\theta})=\sin\theta$

  $\Rightarrow \sin\theta=\frac{1}{2i}(e^{i\theta}-e^{-i\theta})$ (as required)

Exercise 1B

1 a $\cos\frac{7\pi}{12}+i\sin\frac{7\pi}{12}$ b $3\sqrt{5}\cos4\theta+3i\sqrt{5}\sin4\theta$

  c $3i\sqrt{2}$

2 a $-\frac{1}{4}$ b $\frac{\sqrt{3}}{4}\cos\frac{5\pi}{7}+i\frac{\sqrt{3}}{4}\sin\frac{5\pi}{7}$

  c $-i$

3 a $e^{5i\theta}$ b $e^{\pi i}$ c $6e^{\frac{\pi i}{3}}$ d $3\sqrt{2}e^{\frac{\pi i}{4}}$

4 a $e^{3i\theta}$ b $2\sqrt{2}e^{\frac{\pi i}{4}}$ c $\frac{3}{4}e^{-\frac{\pi i}{2}}$

5 a $6\sqrt{3}e^{\frac{5\pi i}{6}}$ b $\sqrt{3}e^{\frac{7\pi i}{12}}$ c $18e^{-\frac{7\pi i}{12}}$ d $6e^{\frac{\pi i}{4}}$

6 $\dfrac{(\cos9\theta+i\sin9\theta)(\cos4\theta+i\sin4\theta)}{\cos7\theta+i\sin7\theta}=\dfrac{e^{9i\theta}e^{4i\theta}}{e^{7i\theta}}=e^{9i\theta+4i\theta-7i\theta}$

  $=e^{6i\theta}=\cos6\theta+i\sin6\theta$

7 $2e^{\frac{\pi}{6}i},\ 2e^{-\frac{5\pi}{6}i}$

8 a $2e^{\frac{\pi}{2}i}$

  b $n=1$: LHS $=(1+i)^1=1+i$

    RHS $=2^{\frac{1}{2}}e^{\frac{\pi i}{4}}=\sqrt{2}\left(\cos\frac{\pi}{4}+i\sin\frac{\pi}{4}\right)=\sqrt{2}\left(\frac{1}{\sqrt{2}}+i\frac{1}{\sqrt{2}}\right)$

    $=1+i$

    As LHS = RHS, the equation holds for $n=1$.

    Assume the equation holds for $n=k,\ k\in\mathbb{Z}^+$.

    i.e. $(1+i)^k=2^{\frac{k}{2}}e^{\frac{k\pi i}{4}}$

    With $n=k+1$, the equation becomes

    $(1+i)^{k+1}=(1+i)^k\times(1+i)=2^{\frac{k}{2}}e^{\frac{k\pi i}{4}}\times(1+i)$

    $=2^{\frac{k}{2}}e^{\frac{k\pi i}{4}}\times2^{\frac{1}{2}}e^{\frac{\pi i}{4}}$

    $=2^{\frac{k}{2}+\frac{1}{2}}e^{\frac{k\pi i}{4}+\frac{\pi i}{4}}=2^{\frac{k+1}{2}}e^{\frac{(k+1)\pi i}{4}}$

    Therefore, the equation holds when $n=k+1$.

    If the equation holds for $n=k$, then it has been shown to be true for $n=k+1$.

    As the equation holds for $n=1$, it is now also true for all $n\in\mathbb{Z}^+$ by mathematical induction.

  c 256

9 $e^{i\theta}=\cos\theta+i\sin\theta$, $e^{-i\theta}=\cos\theta-i\sin\theta$

  So $e^{i\theta}e^{-i\theta}=(\cos\theta+i\sin\theta)(\cos\theta-i\sin\theta)$

  LHS $=e^{i(\theta-\theta)}=e^0=1$

  RHS $=\cos^2\theta-i^2\sin^2\theta=\cos^2\theta+\sin^2\theta$

  Hence $\cos^2\theta+\sin^2\theta\equiv1$

Challenge

a $n=1$; LHS $=(re^{i\theta})^1=re^{i\theta}$

  RHS $=r^1e^{i\theta}=re^{i\theta}$

  As LHS = RHS, the equation holds for $n=1$.

  Assume the equation holds for $n=k,\ k\in\mathbb{Z}^+$.

  i.e. $(re^{i\theta})^k=r^ke^{ik\theta}$

  With $n=k+1$, the equation becomes

  $(re^{i\theta})^{k+1}=(re^{i\theta})^k\times re^{i\theta}=r^ke^{ik\theta}\times re^{i\theta}=r^{k+1}e^{i(k\theta+\theta)}=r^{k+1}e^{i(k+1)\theta}$

  Therefore, the equation holds when $n=k+1$.

  If the equation holds for $n=k$, then it has been shown to be true for $n=k+1$.

  As the equation holds for $n=1$, it is now also true for all $n\in\mathbb{Z}^+$ by mathematical induction.

b Given $n\in\mathbb{Z}^+$, we have: $(re^{i\theta})^{-n}=\dfrac{1}{(re^{i\theta})^n}=\dfrac{1}{r^ne^{in\theta}}=r^{-n}e^{-in\theta}$

Exercise 1C

1 a $\cos6\theta+i\sin6\theta$ b $\cos12\theta+i\sin12\theta$

  c $-\frac{\sqrt{3}}{2}+\frac{1}{2}i$ d $-\frac{1}{2}+\frac{\sqrt{3}}{2}i$

  e 1   f i

2 a $e^{i\theta}$ b $e^{2i\theta}$ c $e^{-6i\theta}$

  d $e^{-i\theta}$ e $e^{11i\theta}$ f $e^{5i\theta}$

3 a 1   b -1 c 1

4 a $(1+i)^5=-4-4i$ b $(-2+2i)^8=4096$

  c $(1-i)^6=8i$ d $(1-i\sqrt{3})^6=64$

  e $\left(\frac{3}{2}-\frac{1}{2}\sqrt{3}i\right)^9=81i\sqrt{3}$

  f $(-2\sqrt{3}-2i)^5=512\sqrt{3}-512i$

5 $(3+\sqrt{3}i)^5=-432+144i\sqrt{3}$

6 $-8+8i\sqrt{3}$

7 $-27i$

8 a $e^{\frac{2}{3}i}$ b 3

9 Write $a + bi$ and $a - bi$ as $r(\cos\theta + i\sin\theta)$ and $r(\cos\theta - i\sin\theta)$ respectively.

Then by de Moivre's theorem,

$$(a + bi)^n + (a - bi)^n = r^n(\cos n\theta + i\sin n\theta)$$
$$+ r^n(\cos n\theta - i\sin n\theta)$$
$$= 2r^n\cos n\theta$$

which is always real.

Challenge

Given $n \in \mathbb{Z}^+$, we have:

$$(r(\cos\theta + i\sin))^{-n} = \frac{1}{(r(\cos\theta + i\sin))^n} = \frac{1}{r^n(\cos n\theta + i\sin n\theta)}$$

by de Moivre's theorem for positive integer exponents.

$$= \frac{1}{r^n(\cos n\theta + i\sin n\theta)} \times \frac{\cos n\theta - i\sin n\theta}{\cos n\theta - i\sin n\theta}$$

$$= \frac{\cos n\theta - i\sin n\theta}{r^n(\cos^2 n\theta - i^2\sin^2 n\theta)} = \frac{\cos n\theta - i\sin n\theta}{r^n(\cos^2 n\theta + \sin^2 n\theta)}$$

$$= r^{-n}(\cos n\theta - i\sin n\theta) = r^{-n}(\cos(-n\theta) + i\sin(-n\theta))$$

Exercise 1D

1 a $(\cos\theta + i\sin\theta)^3 = \cos 3\theta + i\sin 3\theta$

$$= \cos^3\theta + 3i\cos^2\theta\sin\theta + 3i^2\cos\theta\sin^2\theta + i^3\sin^3\theta$$

$$= \cos^3\theta + 3i\cos^2\theta\sin\theta - 3\cos\theta\sin^2\theta - i\sin^3\theta$$

$$\Rightarrow \cos 3\theta + i\sin 3\theta = \cos^3\theta + 3i\cos^2\theta\sin\theta$$
$$- 3\cos\theta\sin^2\theta - i\sin^3\theta$$

Equating the imaginary parts:

$$\sin 3\theta = 3\cos^2\theta\sin\theta - \sin^3\theta$$
$$= 3\sin\theta(1 - \sin^2\theta) - \sin^3\theta$$
$$= 3\sin\theta - 4\sin^3\theta$$

b $(\cos\theta + i\sin\theta)^5 = \cos 5\theta + i\sin 5\theta$

$$= \cos^5\theta + 5i\cos^4\theta\sin\theta + 10i^2\cos^3\theta\sin^2\theta$$

$$+ 10i^3\cos^2\theta\sin^3\theta + 5i^4\cos\theta\sin^4\theta + i^5\sin^5\theta$$

$$\Rightarrow \cos 5\theta + i\sin 5\theta = \cos^5\theta + 5i\cos^4\theta\sin\theta$$
$$- 10\cos^3\theta\sin^2\theta - 10i\cos^2\theta\sin^3\theta$$
$$+ 5\cos\theta\sin^4\theta + i\sin^5\theta$$

Equating the imaginary parts:

$$\sin 5\theta = 5\cos^4\theta\sin\theta - 10\cos^2\theta\sin^3\theta + \sin^5\theta$$
$$= 5(1 - \sin^2\theta)^2\sin\theta - 10(1 - \sin^2\theta)\sin^3\theta + \sin^5\theta$$
$$= 16\sin^5\theta - 20\sin^3\theta + 5\sin\theta$$

c $(\cos\theta + i\sin\theta)^7 = \cos 7\theta + i\sin 7\theta$

$$= \cos^7\theta + 7i\cos^6\theta\sin\theta + 21i^2\cos^5\theta\sin^2\theta$$

$$+ 35i^3\cos^4\theta\sin^3\theta + 35i^4\cos^3\theta\sin^4\theta$$

$$+ 21i^5\cos^2\theta\sin^5\theta + 7i^6\cos\theta\sin^6\theta + i^7\sin^7\theta$$

$$\Rightarrow \cos 7\theta + i\sin 7\theta = \cos^7\theta + 7i\cos^6\theta\sin\theta$$
$$- 21\cos^5\theta\sin^2\theta - 35i\cos^4\theta\sin^3\theta + 35\cos^3\theta\sin^4\theta$$
$$+ 21i\cos^2\theta\sin^5\theta - 7\cos\theta\sin^6\theta - i\sin^7\theta$$

Equating the real parts:

$$\cos 7\theta = \cos^7\theta - 21\cos^5\theta\sin^2\theta + 35\cos^3\theta\sin^4\theta$$
$$- 7\cos\theta\sin^6\theta = \cos^7\theta - 21\cos^5\theta(1 - \cos^2\theta)$$
$$+ 35\cos^3\theta(1 - \cos^2\theta)^2 - 7\cos\theta(1 - \cos^2\theta)^3$$
$$= 64\cos^7\theta - 112\cos^5\theta + 56\cos^3\theta - 7\cos\theta$$

d Let $z = \cos\theta + i\sin\theta$

$$\left(z + \frac{1}{z}\right)^4 = (2\cos\theta)^4 = 16\cos^4\theta$$

$$= z^4 + 4z^3\left(\frac{1}{z}\right) + 6z^2\left(\frac{1}{z^2}\right) + 4z\left(\frac{1}{z^3}\right) + \frac{1}{z^4}$$

$$= \left(z^4 + \frac{1}{z^4}\right) + 4\left(z^2 + \frac{1}{z^2}\right) + 6$$

$$= 2\cos 4\theta + 4(2\cos 2\theta) + 6$$

$$16\cos^4\theta = 2\cos 4\theta + 4(2\cos 2\theta) + 6$$

$$= 2(\cos 4\theta + 4\cos 2\theta + 3)$$

$$\Rightarrow \cos^4\theta = \frac{1}{8}(\cos 4\theta + 4\cos 2\theta + 3)$$

e Let $z = \cos\theta + i\sin\theta$

$$\left(z - \frac{1}{z}\right)^5 = (2i\sin\theta)^5 = 32i^5\sin^5\theta = 32i\sin^5\theta$$

$$= z^5 + 5z^4\left(-\frac{1}{z}\right) + 10z^3\left(-\frac{1}{z}\right)^2 + 10z^2\left(-\frac{1}{z}\right)^3$$

$$+ 5z\left(-\frac{1}{z}\right)^4 + \left(-\frac{1}{z}\right)^5$$

$$= z^5 - 5z^3 + 10z - \frac{10}{z} + \frac{5}{z^3} - \frac{1}{z^5}$$

$$= \left(z^5 - \frac{1}{z^5}\right) - 5\left(z^3 - \frac{1}{z^3}\right) + 10\left(z - \frac{1}{z}\right)$$

$$= 2i\sin 5\theta - 5(2i\sin 3\theta) + 10(2i\sin\theta)$$

$$32i\sin^5\theta = 2i\sin 5\theta - 10i\sin 3\theta + 20i\sin\theta$$

$$\Rightarrow \sin^5\theta = \frac{1}{16}(\sin 5\theta - 5\sin 3\theta + 10\sin\theta)$$

2 a $(\cos\theta + i\sin\theta)^5 = \cos 5\theta + i\sin 5\theta$

$$= \cos^5\theta + {}^5C_1\cos^4\theta(i\sin\theta) + {}^5C_2\cos^3\theta(i\sin\theta)^2$$

$$+ {}^5C_3\cos^2\theta(i\sin\theta)^3 + {}^5C_4\cos\theta(i\sin\theta)^4 + (i\sin\theta)^5$$

$$= \cos^5\theta + 5i\cos^4\theta\sin\theta - 10\cos^3\theta\sin^2\theta$$

$$- 10i\cos^2\theta\sin^3\theta + 5\cos\theta\sin^4\theta + i\sin^5\theta$$

Equating the real parts gives

$$\cos 5\theta = \cos^5\theta - 10\cos^3\theta\sin^2\theta + 5\cos\theta\sin^4\theta$$
$$= \cos^5\theta - 10\cos^3\theta(1 - \cos^2\theta) + 5\cos\theta(1 - \cos^2\theta)^2$$
$$= \cos^5\theta - 10\cos^3\theta(1 - \cos^2\theta)$$
$$+ 5\cos\theta(1 - 2\cos^2\theta + \cos^4\theta)$$
$$= 16\cos^5\theta - 20\cos^3\theta + 5\cos\theta$$

b $0.475, 1.57, 2.67$ (3 s.f.)

3 a Let $z = \cos\theta + i\sin\theta$, then $2\cos\theta = z + \frac{1}{z}$

$$\left(z + \frac{1}{z}\right)^6 = (2\cos\theta)^6 = 64\cos^6\theta$$

$$= z^6 + 6z^5\left(\frac{1}{z}\right) + 15z^4\left(\frac{1}{z^2}\right) + 20z^3\left(\frac{1}{z^3}\right)$$

$$+ 15z^2\left(\frac{1}{z^4}\right) + 6z\left(\frac{1}{z^5}\right) + \left(\frac{1}{z^6}\right)$$

$$= \left(z^6 + \frac{1}{z^6}\right) + 6\left(z^4 + \frac{1}{z^4}\right) + 15\left(z^2 + \frac{1}{z^2}\right) + 20$$

$$= 2\cos 6\theta + 6(2\cos 4\theta) + 15(2\cos 2\theta) + 20$$

$$64\cos^6\theta = 2\cos 6\theta + 6(2\cos 4\theta) + 15(2\cos 2\theta) + 20$$

$$32\cos^6\theta = \cos 6\theta + 6\cos 4\theta + 15\cos 2\theta + 10$$

b $\int_0^{\frac{\pi}{6}}\cos^6\theta\,d\theta = \frac{5\pi}{96} + \frac{9}{64}\sqrt{3}$

4 a If $z = \cos\theta + i\sin\theta$, then $2\cos\theta = z + \frac{1}{z}$ and

$2i\sin\theta = z - \frac{1}{z}$

So, $2^2\cos^2\theta \times (2i)^4\sin^4\theta = \left(z + \frac{1}{z}\right)^2\left(z - \frac{1}{z}\right)^4$

$$= \left(\left(z + \frac{1}{z}\right)\left(z - \frac{1}{z}\right)\right)^2\left(z - \frac{1}{z}\right)^2 = \left(z^2 - \frac{1}{z^2}\right)^2\left(z - \frac{1}{z}\right)^2$$

$$= \left(z^4 - 2 + \frac{1}{z^4}\right)\left(z^2 - 2 + \frac{1}{z^2}\right)$$

$$= z^6 - 2z^4 - z^2 + 4 - \frac{1}{z^2} - \frac{2}{z^4} + \frac{1}{z^6}$$

$$= \left(z^6 + \frac{1}{z^6}\right) - 2\left(z^4 + \frac{1}{z^4}\right) - \left(z^2 + \frac{1}{z^2}\right) + 4$$

$$= 2\cos 6\theta - 2(2\cos 4\theta) - 2\cos 2\theta + 4$$

So, $64\cos^2\theta\sin^4\theta = 2\cos 6\theta - 4\cos 4\theta - 2\cos 2\theta + 4$

$$\Rightarrow 32\cos^2\theta\sin^4\theta = \cos 6\theta - 2\cos 4\theta - \cos 2\theta + 2$$

b $\frac{\pi}{48}$

5 a $\frac{5\pi}{32}$ **b** $\frac{\pi}{64} + \frac{1}{48}$ **c** $\frac{67}{6144}$

6 a $(\cos\theta + i\sin\theta)^6 = \cos 6\theta + i\sin 6\theta$

$$= \cos^6\theta + {}^6C_1\cos^5\theta(i\sin\theta) + {}^6C_2\cos^4\theta(i\sin\theta)^2$$

$$+ {}^6C_3\cos^3\theta(i\sin\theta)^3 + {}^6C_4\cos^2\theta(i\sin\theta)^4$$

$$+ {}^6C_5\cos\theta(i\sin\theta)^5 + (i\sin\theta)^6$$

$$= \cos^6\theta + 6i\cos^5\theta\sin\theta - 15\cos^4\theta\sin^2\theta$$

$$- 20i\cos^3\theta\sin^3\theta + 15\cos^2\theta\sin^4\theta$$

$$+ 6i\cos\theta\sin^5\theta - \sin^6\theta$$

Online Full worked solutions are available in SolutionBank.

Equating the real parts gives

$$\cos 6\theta = \cos^6\theta - 15\cos^4\theta\sin^2\theta + 15\cos^2\theta\sin^4\theta - \sin^6\theta$$
$$= \cos^6\theta - 15\cos^4\theta(1 - \cos^2\theta) + 15\cos^2\theta(1 - \cos^2\theta)^2$$
$$\quad - (1 - \cos^2\theta)^3$$
$$= \cos^6\theta - 15\cos^4\theta(1 - \cos^2\theta) + 15\cos^2\theta(1 - 2\cos^2\theta$$
$$\quad + \cos^4\theta) - (1 - 3\cos^2\theta + 3\cos^4\theta - \cos^6\theta)$$
$$= 32\cos^6\theta - 48\cos^4\theta + 18\cos^2\theta - 1$$

b $\cos\dfrac{\pi}{18} \approx 0.985$, $\cos\dfrac{5\pi}{18} \approx 0.643$, $\cos\dfrac{7\pi}{18} \approx 0.342$,

$\cos\dfrac{11\pi}{18} \approx -0.342$, $\cos\dfrac{13\pi}{18} \approx -0.643$, $\cos\dfrac{17\pi}{18} \approx -0.985$

7 a $\cos 4\theta + i\sin 4\theta = (\cos\theta + i\sin\theta)^4$
$$= \cos^4\theta + 4i\cos^3\theta\sin\theta + 6i^2\cos^2\theta\sin^2\theta$$
$$\quad + 4i^3\cos\theta\sin^3\theta + i^4\sin^4\theta$$
$$= \cos^4\theta + 4i\cos^3\theta\sin\theta - 6\cos^2\theta\sin^2\theta$$
$$\quad - 4i\cos\theta\sin^3\theta + \sin^4\theta$$

Equating the imaginary parts:

$$\sin 4\theta = 4\cos^3\theta\sin\theta - 4\cos\theta\sin^3\theta$$

b Equating the real parts:
$$\cos 4\theta = \cos^4\theta - 6\cos^2\theta\sin^2\theta + \sin^4\theta$$

$$\tan 4\theta = \frac{\sin 4\theta}{\cos 4\theta} = \frac{4\cos^3\theta\sin\theta - 4\cos\theta\sin^3\theta}{\cos^4\theta - 6\cos^2\theta\sin^2\theta + \sin^4\theta}$$

$$= \frac{\left(\dfrac{1}{\cos^4\theta}\right)(4\cos^3\theta\sin\theta - 4\cos\theta\sin^3\theta)}{\left(\dfrac{1}{\cos^4\theta}\right)(\cos^4\theta - 6\cos^2\theta\sin^2\theta + \sin^4\theta)}$$

$$= \frac{4\tan\theta - 4\tan^3\theta}{1 - 6\tan^2\theta + \tan^4\theta}$$

c $x = 0.20, 1.50, -5.03, -0.67$ (2 d.p.)

Exercise 1E

1 a $1 + z + \ldots + z^{2n-1} = \dfrac{z^{2n} - 1}{z - 1} = \dfrac{\left(e^{\frac{\pi i}{n}}\right)^{2n} - 1}{e^{\frac{\pi i}{n}} - 1}$

$= \dfrac{e^{2\pi i} - 1}{e^{\frac{\pi i}{n}} - 1} = \dfrac{1 - 1}{e^{\frac{\pi i}{n}} - 1} = 0$

b $1 + z + \ldots + z^n = \dfrac{z^{n+1} - 1}{z - 1} = \dfrac{\left(e^{\frac{\pi i}{n}}\right)^{n+1} - 1}{e^{\frac{\pi i}{n}} - 1}$

$= \dfrac{e^{\pi i + \frac{\pi i}{n}} - 1}{e^{\frac{\pi i}{n}} - 1} = \dfrac{-e^{\frac{\pi i}{n}} - 1}{e^{\frac{\pi i}{n}} - 1} = \dfrac{-e^{\frac{\pi i}{2n}} - e^{\frac{\pi i}{2n}}}{e^{\frac{\pi i}{2n}} - e^{\frac{\pi i}{2n}}} = \dfrac{-2\cos\dfrac{\pi}{2n}}{2i\sin\dfrac{\pi}{2n}}$

$= \dfrac{i\cos\dfrac{\pi}{2n}}{\sin\dfrac{\pi}{2n}} = i\cot\dfrac{\pi}{2n}$

2 $1 + z + \ldots + z^{12} = \dfrac{z^{13} - 1}{z - 1} = \dfrac{\left(e^{\frac{\pi i}{2}}\right)^{13} - 1}{e^{\frac{\pi i}{2}} - 1} = \dfrac{i - 1}{i - 1} = 1$

3 $z^8 = 2^{\frac{8}{2}}e^{\frac{8\pi i}{4}} = 2^4 e^{2\pi i} = 16$

$1 + z + \ldots + z^7 = \dfrac{z^8 - 1}{z - 1} = \dfrac{16 - 1}{(1 + i) - 1} = \dfrac{15}{i} = -15i$

4 a $C + iS = \left(1 + \dfrac{1}{3}\cos\theta + \dfrac{1}{9}\cos 2\theta + \ldots\right)$
$$\quad + i\left(\dfrac{1}{3}\sin\theta + \dfrac{1}{9}\sin 2\theta + \ldots\right)$$
$$= 1 + \dfrac{1}{3}(\cos\theta + i\sin\theta) + \dfrac{1}{9}(\cos 2\theta + i\sin 2\theta) + \ldots$$
$$= 1 + \dfrac{1}{3}e^{i\theta} + \dfrac{1}{3^2}e^{2i\theta} + \ldots = \dfrac{1}{1 - \dfrac{1}{3}e^{i\theta}} = \dfrac{3}{3 - e^{i\theta}}$$

b $\dfrac{3}{3 - e^{i\theta}} = \dfrac{3(3 - e^{-i\theta})}{(3 - e^{i\theta})(3 - e^{-i\theta})} = \dfrac{3(3 - e^{-i\theta})}{10 - 3(e^{i\theta} + e^{-i\theta})}$

$= \dfrac{3(3 - (\cos\theta - i\sin\theta))}{10 - 3(2\cos\theta)} = \dfrac{9 - 3\cos\theta + 3i\sin\theta}{10 - 6\cos\theta}$

So $C = \dfrac{9 - 3\cos\theta}{10 - 6\cos\theta}$ and $S = \dfrac{3\sin\theta}{10 - 6\cos\theta}$

5 a $P + iQ = (1 + \cos\theta + \cos 2\theta + \ldots + \cos 12\theta)$
$$\quad + i(\sin\theta + \sin 2\theta + \ldots + \sin 12\theta)$$
$$= 1 + (\cos\theta + i\sin\theta) + (\cos 2\theta + i\sin 2\theta) + \ldots$$
$$\quad + (\cos 12\theta + i\sin 12\theta)$$
$$= 1 + e^{i\theta} + e^{2i\theta} + \ldots + e^{12i\theta} = \dfrac{(e^{i\theta})^{13} - 1}{e^{i\theta} - 1}$$

$= \dfrac{e^{13i\theta} - 1}{e^{i\theta} - 1} = \dfrac{e^{\frac{13i\theta}{2}}\left(e^{\frac{13i\theta}{2}} - e^{-\frac{13i\theta}{2}}\right)}{e^{\frac{i\theta}{2}}\left(e^{\frac{i\theta}{2}} - e^{-\frac{i\theta}{2}}\right)} = \dfrac{e^{6i\theta}\left(e^{\frac{13i\theta}{2}} - e^{-\frac{13i\theta}{2}}\right)}{e^{\frac{i\theta}{2}} - e^{-\frac{i\theta}{2}}}$

b $\dfrac{e^{6i\theta}\left(e^{\frac{13i\theta}{2}} - e^{-\frac{13i\theta}{2}}\right)}{e^{\frac{i\theta}{2}} - e^{-\frac{i\theta}{2}}} = \dfrac{e^{6i\theta}\left(2i\sin\dfrac{13\theta}{2}\right)}{2i\sin\dfrac{\theta}{2}} = \dfrac{e^{6i\theta}\sin\dfrac{13\theta}{2}}{\sin\dfrac{\theta}{2}}$

$= \dfrac{(\cos 6\theta + i\sin 6\theta)\sin\dfrac{13\theta}{2}}{\sin\dfrac{\theta}{2}}$

$= \cos 6\theta\sin\dfrac{13\theta}{2}\operatorname{cosec}\dfrac{\theta}{2} + i\sin 6\theta\sin\dfrac{13\theta}{2}\operatorname{cosec}\dfrac{\theta}{2}$

So, $P = \cos 6\theta\sin\dfrac{13\theta}{2}\operatorname{cosec}\dfrac{\theta}{2}$, $Q = \sin 6\theta\sin\dfrac{13\theta}{2}\operatorname{cosec}\dfrac{\theta}{2}$

c $\dfrac{2\pi}{13}, \dfrac{\pi}{6}, \dfrac{4\pi}{13}, \dfrac{\pi}{3}, \dfrac{6\pi}{13}, \dfrac{\pi}{2}, \dfrac{8\pi}{13}, \dfrac{2\pi}{3}, \dfrac{10\pi}{13}, \dfrac{5\pi}{6}, \dfrac{12\pi}{13}$

6 a $C + iS = 1 + \dbinom{n}{1}(\cos\theta + i\sin\theta) + \dbinom{n}{2}(\cos 2\theta + i\sin 2\theta)$
$$\quad + \ldots + \dbinom{n}{n}(\cos n\theta + i\sin n\theta)$$
$$= 1 + \dbinom{n}{1}e^{i\theta} + \dbinom{n}{2}e^{2i\theta} + \ldots + \dbinom{n}{n}e^{ni\theta}$$
$$= 1 + \dbinom{n}{1}e^{i\theta} + \dbinom{n}{2}(e^{i\theta})^2 + \ldots + \dbinom{n}{n}(e^{i\theta})^n$$
$$= (1 + e^{i\theta})^n = \left(e^{\frac{i\theta}{2}}\left(e^{\frac{i\theta}{2}} + e^{-\frac{i\theta}{2}}\right)\right)^n = e^{\frac{ni\theta}{2}}\left(2\cos\dfrac{\theta}{2}\right)^n$$
$$= \left(2\cos\dfrac{\theta}{2}\right)^n\cos\dfrac{n\theta}{2} + i\left(2\cos\dfrac{\theta}{2}\right)^n\sin\dfrac{n\theta}{2}$$

So, $C = \left(2\cos\dfrac{\theta}{2}\right)^n\cos\dfrac{n\theta}{2}$

b $\dfrac{S}{C} = \dfrac{\left(2\cos\dfrac{\theta}{2}\right)^n\sin\dfrac{n\theta}{2}}{\left(2\cos\dfrac{\theta}{2}\right)^n\cos\dfrac{n\theta}{2}} = \dfrac{\sin\dfrac{n\theta}{2}}{\cos\dfrac{n\theta}{2}} = \tan\dfrac{n\theta}{2}$

7 a $(2 + e^{i\theta})(2 + e^{-i\theta}) = 4 + 2e^{i\theta} + 2e^{-i\theta} + 1 = 5 + 2(e^{i\theta} + e^{-i\theta})$
$$= 5 + 2(2\cos\theta) = 5 + 4\cos\theta$$

b $C - iS = 1 - \dfrac{1}{2}(\cos\theta + i\sin\theta) + \dfrac{1}{4}(\cos 2\theta + i\sin 2\theta)$
$$\quad - \dfrac{1}{8}(\cos 3\theta + i\sin 3\theta) + \ldots$$
$$= 1 - \dfrac{1}{2}e^{i\theta} + \dfrac{1}{4}e^{2i\theta} - \dfrac{1}{8}e^{3i\theta} + \ldots$$
$$= 1 - \dfrac{1}{2}e^{i\theta} + \dfrac{1}{2^2}(e^{i\theta})^2 - \dfrac{1}{2^3}(e^{i\theta})^3 + \ldots$$
$$= \dfrac{1}{1 + \dfrac{1}{2}e^{i\theta}} = \dfrac{2}{2 + e^{i\theta}} = \dfrac{2(2 + e^{-i\theta})}{(2 + e^{i\theta})(2 + e^{-i\theta})}$$
$$= \dfrac{2(2 + e^{-i\theta})}{5 + 4\cos\theta} = \dfrac{2(2 + (\cos\theta - i\sin\theta))}{5 + 4\cos\theta}$$
$$= \dfrac{4 + 2\cos\theta - 2i\sin\theta}{5 + 4\cos\theta}$$

So, $C = \dfrac{4 + 2\cos\theta}{5 + 4\cos\theta}$, $S = \dfrac{2\sin\theta}{5 + 4\cos\theta}$

Exercise 1F

1 a $z = 1, i, -1, -i$

b $z = \dfrac{\sqrt{3}}{2} + \dfrac{1}{2}i, -\dfrac{\sqrt{3}}{2} + \dfrac{1}{2}i, -i$

c $z = 3, -\dfrac{3}{2} + \dfrac{3\sqrt{3}}{2}i, -\dfrac{3}{2} - \dfrac{3\sqrt{3}}{2}i$

d $z = 2 + 2i, -2 + 2i, 2 - 2i, -2 - 2i$

e $z = 1 + i, -1 + i, 1 - i, -1 - i$

f $z = \sqrt{3} - i, 2i, -\sqrt{3} - i$

2 a $z = \cos 0 + i\sin 0, \cos\dfrac{2\pi}{7} + i\sin\dfrac{2\pi}{7},$

$\cos\dfrac{4\pi}{7} + i\sin\dfrac{4\pi}{7}, \cos\dfrac{6\pi}{7} + i\sin\dfrac{6\pi}{7}$

$\cos\left(-\dfrac{2\pi}{7}\right) + i\sin\left(-\dfrac{2\pi}{7}\right), \cos\left(-\dfrac{4\pi}{7}\right) + i\sin\left(-\dfrac{4\pi}{7}\right),$

$\cos\left(-\dfrac{6\pi}{7}\right) + i\sin\left(-\dfrac{6\pi}{7}\right)$

b $z = 2\left(\cos\left(-\dfrac{\pi}{8}\right) + i\sin\left(-\dfrac{\pi}{8}\right)\right),$

$2\left(\cos\left(\dfrac{3\pi}{8}\right) + i\sin\left(\dfrac{3\pi}{8}\right)\right), 2\left(\cos\left(\dfrac{7\pi}{8}\right) + i\sin\left(\dfrac{7\pi}{8}\right)\right),$

$2\left(\cos\left(-\dfrac{5\pi}{8}\right) + i\sin\left(-\dfrac{5\pi}{8}\right)\right)$

c $z = 2\left(\cos\dfrac{\pi}{5} + i\sin\dfrac{\pi}{5}\right), 2\left(\cos\dfrac{3\pi}{5} + i\sin\dfrac{3\pi}{5}\right),$

$2(\cos\pi + i\sin\pi), 2\left(\cos\left(-\dfrac{\pi}{5}\right) + i\sin\left(-\dfrac{\pi}{5}\right)\right),$

$2\left(\cos\left(-\dfrac{3\pi}{5}\right) + i\sin\left(-\dfrac{3\pi}{5}\right)\right)$

d $z = \sqrt{2}\left(\cos\dfrac{\pi}{12} + i\sin\dfrac{\pi}{12}\right), \sqrt{2}\left(\cos\dfrac{3\pi}{4} + i\sin\dfrac{3\pi}{4}\right),$

$\sqrt{2}\left(\cos\left(-\dfrac{7\pi}{12}\right) + i\sin\left(\dfrac{-7\pi}{12}\right)\right)$

e $z = \sqrt{2}\left(\cos\left(-\dfrac{\pi}{12}\right) + i\sin\left(-\dfrac{\pi}{12}\right)\right),$

$\sqrt{2}\left(\cos\left(\dfrac{5\pi}{12}\right) + i\sin\left(\dfrac{5\pi}{12}\right)\right), \sqrt{2}\left(\cos\left(\dfrac{11\pi}{12}\right) + i\sin\left(\dfrac{11\pi}{12}\right)\right),$

$\sqrt{2}\left(\cos\left(-\dfrac{7\pi}{12}\right) + i\sin\left(-\dfrac{7\pi}{12}\right)\right)$

f $z = 4\left(\cos\left(-\dfrac{5\pi}{18}\right) + i\sin\left(-\dfrac{5\pi}{18}\right)\right),$

$4\left(\cos\left(\dfrac{7\pi}{18}\right) + i\sin\left(\dfrac{7\pi}{18}\right)\right), 4\left(\cos\left(-\dfrac{17\pi}{18}\right) + i\sin\left(-\dfrac{17\pi}{18}\right)\right)$

3 a $z = 5^{\frac{1}{4}}e^{0.23i}, 5^{\frac{1}{4}}e^{1.80i}, 5^{\frac{1}{4}}e^{-1.34i}, 5^{\frac{1}{4}}e^{-2.91i}$

b $z = \sqrt{3}e^{-0.29i}, \sqrt{3}e^{1.80i}, \sqrt{3}e^{-2.39i}$

c $z = \sqrt{2}e^{0.57i}, z = \sqrt{2}e^{2.14i}, z = \sqrt{2}e^{-1.00i}, z = \sqrt{2}e^{-2.57i}$

4 a $z = -\dfrac{1}{2} + \dfrac{\sqrt{3}}{2}i, -2, -\dfrac{1}{2} - \dfrac{\sqrt{3}}{2}i$

b

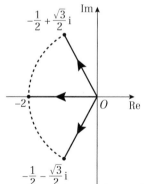

c centre $(-1, 0)$ radius 1

5 a $z = 1, \cos\left(\dfrac{2\pi}{5}\right) + i\sin\left(\dfrac{2\pi}{5}\right), \cos\left(\dfrac{4\pi}{5}\right) + i\sin\left(\dfrac{4\pi}{5}\right),$

$\cos\left(-\dfrac{2\pi}{5}\right) + i\sin\left(-\dfrac{2\pi}{5}\right), \cos\left(-\dfrac{4\pi}{5}\right) + i\sin\left(-\dfrac{4\pi}{5}\right)$

b $z_1 + z_2 + z_3 + z_4 + z_5 = 0$

$1 + \cos\dfrac{2\pi}{5} + i\sin\dfrac{2\pi}{5} + \cos\dfrac{4\pi}{5} + i\sin\dfrac{4\pi}{5} + \cos\left(-\dfrac{2\pi}{5}\right)$

$+ i\sin\left(-\dfrac{2\pi}{5}\right) + \cos\left(-\dfrac{4\pi}{5}\right) + i\sin\left(-\dfrac{4\pi}{5}\right) = 0$

$\Rightarrow 1 + \cos\dfrac{2\pi}{5} + i\sin\dfrac{2\pi}{5} + \cos\dfrac{4\pi}{5} + i\sin\dfrac{4\pi}{5}$

$+ \cos\left(\dfrac{2\pi}{5}\right) - i\sin\left(\dfrac{2\pi}{5}\right) + \cos\left(\dfrac{4\pi}{5}\right) - i\sin\left(\dfrac{4\pi}{5}\right) = 0$

$\Rightarrow 1 + 2\cos\dfrac{2\pi}{5} + 2\cos\dfrac{4\pi}{5} = 0$

$\cos\dfrac{2\pi}{5} + \cos\dfrac{4\pi}{5} = -\dfrac{1}{2}$

6 a $r = 4, \theta = -\dfrac{2\pi}{3}$

b $z = \sqrt{2}e^{-\frac{\pi i}{6}}, \sqrt{2}e^{\frac{\pi i}{3}}, \sqrt{2}e^{\frac{5\pi i}{6}}, \sqrt{2}e^{-\frac{2\pi i}{3}}$

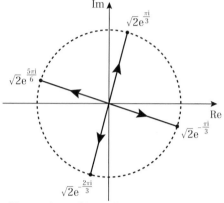

7 $\sqrt{2}e^{\frac{7\pi i}{12}}, \sqrt{2}e^{-\frac{\pi i}{12}}, \sqrt{2}e^{\frac{5\pi i}{12}}, \sqrt{2}e^{\frac{11\pi i}{12}}$

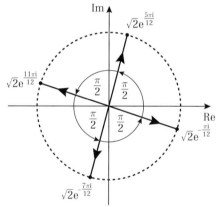

8 a $r = \sqrt{8}, \theta = \dfrac{\pi}{6}$

b $w = 4e^{\frac{2\pi i}{9}}, w = 4e^{\frac{8\pi i}{9}}, w = 4e^{-\frac{4\pi i}{9}}$

9 a $e^{\frac{\pi i}{4}}, i, e^{\frac{3\pi i}{4}}, -1, e^{\frac{5\pi i}{4}}, -i, e^{\frac{7\pi i}{4}}$

b Expressing as a product of the linear factors:

$(z + 1)(z - i)(z + i)\left(z - \dfrac{\sqrt{2}}{2} - \dfrac{\sqrt{2}}{2}i\right)\left(z - \dfrac{\sqrt{2}}{2} + \dfrac{\sqrt{2}}{2}i\right)$

$\left(z + \dfrac{\sqrt{2}}{2} + \dfrac{\sqrt{2}}{2}i\right)\left(z + \dfrac{\sqrt{2}}{2} - \dfrac{\sqrt{2}}{2}i\right)$

$= (z + 1)(z^2 + 1)(z^2 - \sqrt{2}z + 1)(z^2 + \sqrt{2}z + 1)$

$= (z + 1)(z^2 + 1)(z^4 + 1)$

Therefore $(z^2 + 1)$ and $(z^4 + 1)$ are factors.

Challenge

a $1, e^{\frac{\pi i}{3}}, e^{-\frac{\pi i}{3}}, e^{\frac{2\pi i}{3}}, e^{-\frac{2\pi i}{3}}, e^{\pi i}$

b Rewrite the equation as $\left(1 + \dfrac{1}{z}\right)^6 = 1$.

Then $1 + \dfrac{1}{z} = e^{\frac{k\pi i}{3}}$ for some $k \in \mathbb{Z}$, by **a**.

So, $\dfrac{1}{z} = e^{\frac{k\pi i}{3}} - 1$

$$z = \frac{1}{e^{\frac{k\pi i}{3}} - 1} = \frac{1}{e^{\frac{k\pi i}{6}}\left(e^{\frac{k\pi i}{6}} - e^{-\frac{k\pi i}{6}}\right)}$$

$$= \frac{1}{e^{\frac{k\pi i}{6}}\left(2i\sin\frac{k\pi}{6}\right)} = -\frac{ie^{-\frac{k\pi i}{6}}}{2\sin\frac{k\pi}{6}} = \frac{-i\left(\cos\frac{k\pi}{6} - i\sin\frac{k\pi}{6}\right)}{2\sin\frac{k\pi}{6}}$$

$$= -\frac{\sin\frac{k\pi}{6} + i\cos\frac{k\pi}{6}}{2\sin\frac{k\pi}{6}} = -\frac{1}{2} - \frac{1}{2}i\cot\frac{k\pi}{6}$$

$$= -\frac{1}{2} + \frac{1}{2}i\cot\left(-\frac{k\pi}{6}\right)$$

so take k to be $-1, -2, -3, -4, -5$.

Exercise 1G

1 a $(0,4), (-2\sqrt{3}, -2), (2\sqrt{3}, -2)$

  b $(5,0), (-5,0), (0,5), (0,-5)$

  c $\left(2\cos\frac{4\pi}{15}, 2\sin\frac{4\pi}{15}\right), (-1,\sqrt{3}), \left(2\cos\frac{16\pi}{15}, 2\sin\frac{16\pi}{15}\right),$
  $\left(2\cos\frac{22\pi}{15}, 2\sin\frac{22\pi}{15}\right), \left(2\cos\frac{28\pi}{15}, 2\sin\frac{28\pi}{15}\right)$

  d $(2, 2), \left(2\sqrt{2}\cos\frac{7\pi}{12}, 2\sqrt{2}\sin\frac{7\pi}{12}\right),$
  $\left(2\sqrt{2}\cos\frac{11\pi}{12}, 2\sqrt{2}\sin\frac{11\pi}{12}\right),$
  $\left(2\sqrt{2}\cos\frac{15\pi}{12}, 2\sqrt{2}\sin\frac{15\pi}{12}\right),$
  $\left(2\sqrt{2}\cos\frac{19\pi}{12}, 2\sqrt{2}\sin\frac{19\pi}{12}\right),$
  $\left(2\sqrt{2}\cos\frac{23\pi}{12}, 2\sqrt{2}\sin\frac{23\pi}{12}\right)$

2 $(3, -1), \left(\frac{1}{2}(3 + 5\sqrt{3}), \frac{1}{2}(11 + \sqrt{3})\right), \left(\frac{1}{2}(3 - 5\sqrt{3}), \frac{1}{2}(11 - \sqrt{3})\right)$

3 $\sqrt{6}\,e^{\frac{\pi i}{12}}, \sqrt{6}\,e^{\frac{7\pi i}{12}}$

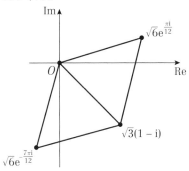

4 a $\sqrt[4]{12}\,e^{\frac{5\pi i}{8}}, \sqrt[4]{12}\,e^{-\frac{\pi i}{8}}, \sqrt[4]{12}\,e^{\frac{3\pi i}{8}}, \sqrt[4]{12}\,e^{\frac{7\pi i}{8}}$

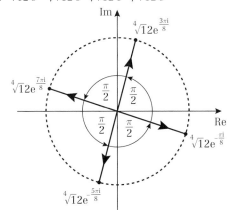

  b $3i$

5 a $-8 - 8i, 4(-1 + \sqrt{3}) - 4(1 + \sqrt{3})i,$
  $4(1 - \sqrt{3}) + 4(1 + \sqrt{3})i, 4(1 + \sqrt{3}) + 4(1 - \sqrt{3})i,$
  $-4(1 + \sqrt{3}) - 4(1 - \sqrt{3})i$

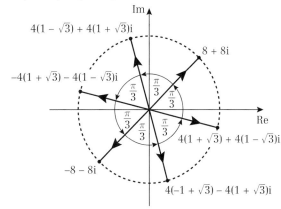

  b $128i, -64(\sqrt{3} + i), 64(\sqrt{3} - i),$ Area $= 12288\sqrt{3}$

6 Let the position of the ant be denoted by $a + bi$, where a in the number of units forward and b is the number of units to the right from its initial position.

In this notation, walking forwards one unit at an angle of θ to the right corresponds to adding $e^{i\theta}$ to its position.

Since the angles are $0, \frac{2\pi}{9}, \frac{4\pi}{9}$ and $\frac{6\pi}{9}$, the final position of the ant is:

$$1 + e^{\frac{2\pi i}{9}} + e^{\frac{4\pi i}{9}} + e^{\frac{6\pi i}{9}} = 1 + e^{\frac{2\pi i}{9}} + \left(e^{\frac{2\pi i}{9}}\right)^2 + \left(e^{\frac{2\pi i}{9}}\right)^3 = \frac{\left(e^{\frac{2\pi i}{9}}\right)^4 - 1}{e^{\frac{2\pi i}{9}} - 1}$$

$$= \frac{e^{\frac{8\pi i}{9}} - 1}{e^{\frac{2\pi i}{9}} - 1} = \frac{e^{\frac{4\pi i}{9}}\left(e^{\frac{4\pi i}{9}} - e^{-\frac{4\pi i}{9}}\right)}{e^{\frac{\pi i}{9}}\left(e^{\frac{\pi i}{9}} - e^{-\frac{\pi i}{9}}\right)} = \frac{e^{\frac{4\pi i}{9}}\left(2i\sin\frac{4\pi}{9}\right)}{e^{\frac{\pi i}{9}}\left(2i\sin\frac{\pi}{9}\right)} = \frac{\sin\frac{4\pi}{9}}{\sin\frac{\pi}{9}}e^{\frac{\pi i}{3}}$$

So the distance from its initial position is $\dfrac{\sin\frac{4\pi}{9}}{\sin\frac{\pi}{9}}$

Mixed exercise 1

1 a $e^{i\theta} = \cos\theta + i\sin\theta, e^{-i\theta} = \cos\theta - i\sin\theta$
  $e^{i\theta} + e^{-i\theta} = 2\cos\theta$, so $\cos\theta = \frac{1}{2}(e^{i\theta} + e^{-i\theta})$

  b $\cos A \cos B = \frac{1}{2}(e^{iA} + e^{-iA}) \times \frac{1}{2}(e^{iB} + e^{-iB})$
  $= \frac{1}{4}(e^{iA} + e^{-iA})(e^{iB} + e^{-iB})$
  $= \frac{1}{4}(e^{i(A+B)} + e^{i(A-B)} + e^{i(B-A)} + e^{-i(A+B)})$
  $= \frac{1}{4}((e^{i(A+B)} + e^{-i(A+B)}) + (e^{i(A-B)} + e^{-i(A-B)}))$
  $= \frac{1}{4}(2\cos(A + B) + 2\cos(A - B))$
  $= \frac{\cos(A + B) + \cos(A - B)}{2}$

2 $n = 1$; LHS $= r(\cos\theta + i\sin\theta)$
  RHS $= r^1(\cos\theta + i\sin\theta) = r(\cos\theta + i\sin\theta)$
  As LHS = RHS, the equation holds for $n = 1$.
  Assume the equation holds for $n = k, k \in \mathbb{Z}^+$.
  i.e. $z^k = r^k(\cos k\theta + i\sin k\theta)$
  With $n = k + 1$, the equation becomes:
  $z^{k+1} = z^k \times z$
  $= r^k(\cos k\theta + i\sin k\theta) \times r(\cos\theta + i\sin\theta)$
  $= r^{k+1}((\cos k\theta\cos\theta - \sin k\theta\sin\theta) + i(\sin k\theta\cos\theta + \cos k\theta\sin\theta))$
  $= r^{k+1}(\cos(k + 1)\theta + i\sin(k + 1)\theta)$
  by the addition formulae.
  Therefore, the equation holds when $n = k + 1$.

If the equation holds for $n = k$, then it has been shown to be true for $n = k + 1$.

As the equation holds for $n = 1$, it is now also true for all $n \in \mathbb{Z}^+$ by mathematical induction.

3 $\cos 7x + i \sin 7x$

4 a 16

  b 256

5 a Let $z = \cos \theta + i \sin \theta$

$z^n = (\cos \theta + i \sin \theta)^n = \cos n\theta + i \sin n\theta$

$\dfrac{1}{z^n} = z^{-n} = (\cos \theta + i \sin \theta)^{-n} = \cos(-n\theta) + i \sin(-n\theta)$

$\qquad = \cos n\theta - i \sin n\theta$

$\Rightarrow z^n + \dfrac{1}{z^n} = \cos n\theta + i \sin n\theta + \cos n\theta - i \sin n\theta = 2\cos n\theta$

  b $\left(z^2 + \dfrac{1}{z^2}\right)^3 = 2\cos 6\theta + 6\cos 2\theta$

  c $a = \dfrac{1}{4}, b = \dfrac{3}{4}$

  d $\displaystyle\int_0^{\frac{\pi}{6}} \cos^3 2\theta \, d\theta = \int_0^{\frac{\pi}{6}} \left(\dfrac{1}{4}\cos 6\theta + \dfrac{3}{4}\cos 2\theta\right) d\theta$

$\qquad = \left[\dfrac{1}{24}\sin 6\theta + \dfrac{3}{8}\sin 2\theta\right]_0^{\frac{\pi}{6}} = \dfrac{3}{16}\sqrt{3}$

6 a If $z = \cos \theta + i \sin \theta$, then $2\cos \theta = z + \dfrac{1}{z}$

So $2^5 \cos^5 \theta = \left(z + \dfrac{1}{z}\right)^5$

$= z^5 + {}^5C_1 z^4\left(\dfrac{1}{z}\right) + {}^5C_2 z^3\left(\dfrac{1}{z^2}\right) + {}^5C_3 z^2\left(\dfrac{1}{z^3}\right) + {}^5C_4 z\left(\dfrac{1}{z^4}\right) + \dfrac{1}{z^5}$

$= z^5 + 5z^3 + 10z + \dfrac{10}{z} + \dfrac{5}{z^3} + \dfrac{1}{z^5}$

$= \left(z^5 + \dfrac{1}{z^5}\right) + 5\left(z^3 + \dfrac{1}{z^3}\right) + 10\left(z + \dfrac{1}{z}\right)$

$= 2\cos 5\theta + 5(2\cos 3\theta) + 10(2\cos \theta)$

So $32\cos^5 \theta = 2\cos 5\theta + 10\cos 3\theta + 20\cos \theta$

$\cos^5 \theta = \dfrac{1}{16}(\cos 5\theta + 5\cos 3\theta + 10\cos \theta)$

  b $\dfrac{16}{15}$

7 a If $z = \cos \theta + i \sin \theta$, then $2i \sin \theta = z - \dfrac{1}{z}$

So $(2i)^6 \sin^6 \theta = \left(z - \dfrac{1}{z}\right)^6$

$= z^6 - {}^6C_1 z^5\left(\dfrac{1}{z}\right) + {}^6C_2 z^4\left(\dfrac{1}{z^2}\right) - {}^6C_3 z^3\left(\dfrac{1}{z^3}\right)$

$\quad + {}^6C_4 z^2\left(\dfrac{1}{z^4}\right) - {}^6C_5 z\left(\dfrac{1}{z^5}\right) + \dfrac{1}{z^6}$

$= z^6 - 6z^4 + 15z^2 - 20 + \dfrac{15}{z^2} - \dfrac{6}{z^4} + \dfrac{1}{z^6}$

$= \left(z^6 + \dfrac{1}{z^6}\right) - 6\left(z^4 + \dfrac{1}{z^4}\right) + 15\left(z^2 + \dfrac{1}{z^2}\right) - 20$

$= 2\cos 6\theta - 6(2\cos 4\theta) + 15(2\cos 2\theta) - 20$

So, $-64\sin^6 \theta = 2\cos 6\theta - 12\cos 4\theta + 30\cos 2\theta - 20$

  b $\cos^6 \theta \equiv \dfrac{1}{32}(\cos 6\theta + 6\cos 4\theta + 15\cos 2\theta + 10)$

  c $\dfrac{\pi}{4}$

8 $(\cos \theta + i \sin \theta)^6 = \cos 6\theta + i \sin 6\theta$

$= \cos^6 \theta + {}^6C_1 \cos^5 \theta(i \sin \theta) + {}^6C_2 \cos^4 \theta(i \sin \theta)^2$

$\quad + {}^6C_3 \cos^3 \theta(i \sin \theta)^3 + {}^6C_4 \cos^2 \theta(i \sin \theta)^4$

$\quad + {}^6C_5 \cos \theta(i \sin \theta)^5 + (i \sin \theta)^6$

$= \cos^6 \theta + 6i\cos^5 \theta \sin \theta - 15\cos^4 \theta \sin^2 \theta - 20i\cos^3 \theta \sin^3 \theta$

$\quad + 15\cos^2 \theta \sin^4 \theta + 6i\cos \theta \sin^5 \theta - \sin^6 \theta$

Equating imaginary parts gives

$\sin 6\theta = 6\cos^5 \theta \sin \theta - 20\cos^3 \theta \sin^3 \theta + 6\cos \theta \sin^5 \theta$

$= 2\sin \theta \cos \theta(3\cos^4 \theta - 10\cos^2 \theta \sin^2 \theta + 3\sin^4 \theta)$

$= \sin 2\theta(3\cos^4 \theta - 10\cos^2 \theta(1 - \cos^2 \theta) + 3(1 - \cos^2 \theta)^2)$

$= \sin 2\theta(3\cos^4 \theta - 10\cos^2 \theta(1 - \cos^2 \theta) + 3(1 - 2\cos^2 \theta + \cos^4 \theta))$

$= \sin 2\theta(16\cos^4 \theta - 16\cos^2 \theta + 3)$

9 a $(\cos \theta + i \sin \theta)^5 = \cos 5\theta + i \sin 5\theta$

$= \cos^5 \theta + {}^5C_1 \cos^4 \theta(i \sin \theta) + {}^5C_2 \cos^3 \theta(i \sin \theta)^2$

$\quad + {}^5C_3 \cos^2 \theta(i \sin \theta)^3 + {}^5C_4 \cos \theta(i \sin \theta)^4 + (i \sin \theta)^5$

$= \cos^5 \theta + 5i\cos^4 \theta \sin \theta - 10\cos^3 \theta \sin^2 \theta - 10i\cos^2 \theta \sin^3 \theta$

$\quad + 5\cos \theta \sin^4 \theta + i \sin^5 \theta$

Equating real parts gives

$\cos 5\theta = \cos^5 \theta - 10\cos^3 \theta \sin^2 \theta + 5\cos \theta \sin^4 \theta$

$= \cos^5 \theta - 10\cos^3 \theta(1 - \cos^2 \theta) + 5\cos \theta(1 - \cos^2 \theta)^2$

$= \cos^5 \theta - 10\cos^3 \theta(1 - \cos^2 \theta) + 5\cos \theta(1 - 2\cos^2 \theta + \cos^4 \theta)$

$= 16\cos^5 \theta - 20\cos^3 \theta + 5\cos \theta$

  b $-1, \dfrac{1}{4}(1 + \sqrt{5}) \approx 0.809, \dfrac{1}{4}(1 - \sqrt{5}) \approx -0.309$

10 a Let $z = \cos \theta + i \sin \theta$

$\left(z - \dfrac{1}{z}\right)^5 = (2i \sin \theta)^5 = 32i^5 \sin^5 \theta = 32i \sin^5 \theta$

$= z^5 + 5z^4\left(-\dfrac{1}{z}\right) + 10z^3\left(-\dfrac{1}{z}\right)^2$

$\quad + 10z^2\left(-\dfrac{1}{z}\right)^3 + 5z\left(-\dfrac{1}{z}\right)^4 + \left(-\dfrac{1}{z}\right)^5$

$= z^5 - 5z^3 + 10z - \dfrac{10}{z} + \dfrac{5}{z^3} - \dfrac{1}{z^5}$

$= \left(z^5 - \dfrac{1}{z^5}\right) - 5\left(z^3 - \dfrac{1}{z^3}\right) + 10\left(z - \dfrac{1}{z}\right)$

$= 2i \sin 5\theta - 5(2i \sin 3\theta) + 10(2i \sin \theta)$

So $32i \sin^5 \theta = 2i \sin 5\theta - 10i \sin 3\theta + 20i \sin \theta$

$\Rightarrow \sin^5 \theta = \dfrac{1}{16}(\sin 5\theta - 5\sin 3\theta + 10\sin \theta)$

  b $0, \dfrac{\pi}{6}, \dfrac{5\pi}{6}$

11 a $(\cos \theta + i \sin \theta)^5 = \cos 5\theta + i \sin 5\theta$

$= \cos^5 \theta + 5i\cos^4 \theta \sin \theta + 10i^2\cos^3 \theta \sin^2 \theta$

$\quad + 10i^3\cos^2 \theta \sin^3 \theta + 5i^4\cos \theta \sin^4 \theta + i^5 \sin^5 \theta$

$\Rightarrow \cos 5\theta + i \sin 5\theta = \cos^5 \theta + 5i\cos^4 \theta \sin \theta$

$\quad - 10\cos^3 \theta \sin^2 \theta - 10i\cos^2 \theta \sin^3 \theta$

$\quad + 5\cos \theta \sin^4 \theta - i \sin^5 \theta$

Equating the real parts:

$\cos 5\theta = \cos^5 \theta - 10\cos^3 \theta \sin^2 \theta + 5\cos \theta \sin^4 \theta$

$= \cos \theta(\cos^4 \theta - 10\cos^2 \theta(1 - \cos^2 \theta) + 5(1 - \cos^2 \theta)^2)$

$= \cos \theta(16\cos^4 \theta - 20\cos^2 \theta + 5)$

  b If $\cos 5\theta = 0$, then $\cos \theta(16\cos^4 \theta - 20\cos^2 \theta + 5) = 0$

If $x = \cos \theta$, then $x(16x^4 - 20x^2 + 5) = 0$ which has

solutions $x = 0$ and $x^2 = \dfrac{20 \pm \sqrt{80}}{32} = \dfrac{5 \pm \sqrt{5}}{8}$, by the

quadratic formula.

Since $\theta = \dfrac{\pi}{10}$ is a solution to $\cos 5\theta = 0$, $x = \cos\dfrac{\pi}{10}$

must be a solution to $x(16x^4 - 20x^2 + 5) = 0$.

Since $x \neq 0$, $\cos^2\left(\dfrac{\pi}{10}\right) = x^2 = \dfrac{5 \pm \sqrt{5}}{8}$, for some choice

of sign.

To find which, note that $\theta = \dfrac{3\pi}{10}$ gives another

solution and $\cos\dfrac{\pi}{10} > \cos\dfrac{3\pi}{10}$ by looking at the graph.

Hence $\theta = \dfrac{\pi}{10}$ corresponds to the larger of the two

solutions and $\cos^2\left(\dfrac{\pi}{10}\right) = \dfrac{5 + \sqrt{5}}{8}$

  c $\cos^2\left(\dfrac{3\pi}{10}\right) = \dfrac{5 - \sqrt{5}}{8}, \cos^2\left(\dfrac{7\pi}{10}\right) = \dfrac{5 - \sqrt{5}}{8},$

$\cos^2\left(\dfrac{9\pi}{10}\right) = \dfrac{5 + \sqrt{5}}{8}$

12 a $\tan 3\theta \equiv \dfrac{3\tan \theta - \tan^3 \theta}{1 - 3\tan^2 \theta}$

Online Full worked solutions are available in SolutionBank.

b $\cot 3\theta = \dfrac{1 - 3\tan^2\theta}{3\tan\theta - \tan^3\theta} = \dfrac{1 - 3\cot^{-2}\theta}{3\cot^{-1}\theta - \cot^{-3}\theta}$

$= \dfrac{\cot^3\theta - 3\cot\theta}{3\cot^2\theta - 1}$

13 $C + iS$

$= 1 + k(\cos\theta + i\sin\theta) + k^2(\cos 2\theta + i\sin 2\theta)$
$\quad + k^3(\cos 3\theta + i\sin 3\theta) + \ldots$

$= 1 + ke^{i\theta} + k^2e^{2i\theta} + k^3e^{3i\theta} + \ldots = 1 + ke^{i\theta} + (ke^{i\theta})^2$
$\quad + (ke^{i\theta})^3 + \ldots$

$= \dfrac{1}{1 - ke^{i\theta}}$, since $|ke^{i\theta}| = |k| < 1$.

$= \dfrac{1 - ke^{-i\theta}}{(1 - ke^{i\theta})(1 - ke^{-i\theta})} = \dfrac{1 - ke^{-i\theta}}{1 + k^2 - k(e^{i\theta} + e^{-i\theta})}$

$= \dfrac{1 - k(\cos\theta - i\sin\theta)}{1 + k^2 - 2k\cos\theta} = \dfrac{1 - k\cos\theta}{1 + k^2 - 2k\cos\theta}$

$\quad + i\dfrac{k\sin\theta}{1 + k^2 - 2k\cos\theta}$

So $C = \dfrac{1 - k\cos\theta}{1 + k^2 - 2k\cos\theta}$ and $S = \dfrac{k\sin\theta}{1 + k^2 - 2k\cos\theta}$

14 a $4\sqrt{2}\left(\cos\left(-\dfrac{\pi}{4}\right) + i\sin\left(-\dfrac{\pi}{4}\right)\right)$

b $z = \sqrt{2}e^{-\frac{\pi i}{20}}, \sqrt{2}e^{\frac{7\pi i}{20}}, \sqrt{2}e^{\frac{3\pi i}{4}}, \sqrt{2}e^{-\frac{9\pi i}{20}}, \sqrt{2}e^{-\frac{17\pi i}{20}}$

c

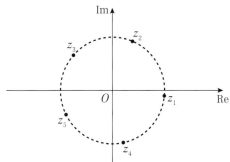

15 a $\sqrt{2}e^{-\frac{i\pi}{12}}, \sqrt{2}e^{\frac{7i\pi}{12}}, \sqrt{2}e^{-\frac{9i\pi}{12}}$

b

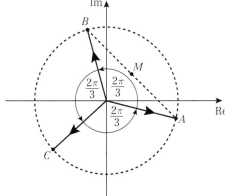

c $r = \dfrac{\sqrt{2}}{2}, \theta = \dfrac{\pi}{4}$

d $-\dfrac{i}{8}$

16 a $\left(-1 + \dfrac{\sqrt{3}}{2}, -\dfrac{1}{2} - \sqrt{3}\right), \left(-1 - \dfrac{\sqrt{3}}{2}, \sqrt{3} - \dfrac{1}{2}\right)$

b If z_1 and z_2 are the two vertices above respectively, then $z_1 - z_2 = \sqrt{3} - 2i\sqrt{3}$

So the length of this side of the triangle is

$|z_1 - z_2| = \sqrt{(\sqrt{3})^2 + (-2\sqrt{3})^2} = \sqrt{3 + 12} = \sqrt{15}$

Challenge

Rewrite the equation as $\left(1 + \dfrac{1}{z}\right)^6 = 1$.

Then $1 + \dfrac{1}{z} = e^{\frac{k\pi i}{3}}$ for some $k \in \mathbb{Z}$, since it is a sixth root of unity.

So $\dfrac{1}{z} = e^{\frac{k\pi i}{3}} - 1$

$z = \dfrac{1}{e^{\frac{k\pi i}{3}} - 1} = \dfrac{1}{e^{\frac{k\pi i}{6}}\left(e^{\frac{k\pi i}{6}} - e^{-\frac{k\pi i}{6}}\right)} = \dfrac{1}{e^{\frac{k\pi i}{6}}\left(2i\sin\dfrac{k\pi}{6}\right)} = -\dfrac{ie^{-\frac{k\pi i}{6}}}{2\sin\dfrac{k\pi}{6}}$

$= -\dfrac{i(\cos\dfrac{k\pi}{6} - i\sin\dfrac{k\pi}{6})}{2\sin\dfrac{k\pi}{6}} = -\dfrac{\sin\dfrac{k\pi}{6} + i\cos\dfrac{k\pi}{6}}{2\sin\dfrac{k\pi}{6}} = -\dfrac{1}{2} - \dfrac{1}{2}i\cot\dfrac{k\pi}{6}$

So the points lie on the straight line $z = -\dfrac{1}{2} + it$ for $t \in \mathbb{R}$.

CHAPTER 2
Prior knowledge check

1 a 1098 **b** 10761619.5

2 a Use the following:

$$\sum_{r=1}^{n} r^2 = \dfrac{n(n + 1)(2n + 1)}{6}$$

$$\sum_{r=1}^{n} r^2 = \dfrac{n(n + 1)}{2}$$

and simplify to get the answer.

  b 10073

3 a $\dfrac{dy}{dx} = 3\cos 3x$ **b** $\dfrac{d^2y}{dx^2} = -9\sin 3x$

Exercise 2A

1 a $\dfrac{1}{2}(r(r + 1) - r(r - 1)) = \dfrac{1}{2}(r^2 + r - r^2 + r) = \dfrac{1}{2}(2r) = r$

  b $\displaystyle\sum_{r=1}^{n} r = \dfrac{1}{2}\sum_{r=1}^{n} r(r + 1) - \dfrac{1}{2}\sum_{r=1}^{n} r(r - 1)$

    $r = 1$: $\dfrac{1}{2} \times 1 \times 2 - \dfrac{1}{2} \times 1 \times 0$

    $r = 2$: $\dfrac{1}{2} \times 2 \times 3 - \dfrac{1}{2} \times 2 \times 1$

    $r = 3$: $\dfrac{1}{2} \times 3 \times 4 - \dfrac{1}{2} \times 3 \times 2$

    $\vdots$

    $r = n - 1$: $\dfrac{1}{2} \times (n - 1)(n) - \dfrac{1}{2}(n - 1)(n - 2)$

    $r = n$: $\dfrac{1}{2}n(n + 1) - \dfrac{1}{2}n(n - 1)$

    When you add, all terms cancel except $\dfrac{1}{2}n(n + 1)$

    Hence $\displaystyle\sum_{r=1}^{n} r = \dfrac{1}{2}n(n + 1)$

2 $\dfrac{n(n + 3)}{4(n + 1)(n + 2)}$

3 a $\dfrac{1}{2r} - \dfrac{1}{2(r + 2)}$ **b** $\dfrac{n(3n + 5)}{4(n + 1)(n + 2)}$

4 a $\dfrac{1}{(r + 2)(r + 3)} = \dfrac{1}{r + 2} - \dfrac{1}{r + 3}$

  b $\dfrac{n}{3(n + 3)}$

5 a $\dfrac{1}{r!} - \dfrac{1}{(r + 1)!} \equiv \dfrac{(r + 1)! - r!}{r!(r + 1)!} \equiv \dfrac{r!(r + 1 - 1)}{r!(r + 1)!} \equiv \dfrac{r}{(r + 1)!}$

  b $1 - \dfrac{1}{(n + 1)!}$

6 $\dfrac{n(n + 2)}{(n + 1)^2}$

7 a Method of differences yields $\dfrac{1}{10} - \dfrac{1}{2(2n + 5)}$, which simplifies to $\dfrac{n}{10n + 25}$, so $a = 10$ and $b = 25$.

b For $n = 1$, $\dfrac{1}{5 \times 7} = \dfrac{1}{10 + 25}$. Assume true for $n = k$.

Let $n = k + 1$, then

$$\sum_{r=1}^{k+1} \frac{1}{(2r + 3)(2r + 5)} = \frac{k}{10k + 25} + \frac{1}{(2k + 5)(2k + 7)}$$

$$= \frac{2k^2 + 7k + 5}{(2k + 1)(2k + 7)} = \frac{k + 1}{10(k + 1) + 25}$$

Therefore true for all values of n.

8 Method of differences yields $\dfrac{4}{3}\left(\dfrac{1}{3r - 2} - \dfrac{1}{3r + 4}\right)$,

which simplifies to $\dfrac{n(15n + 17)}{(3n + 1)(3n + 4)}$, so $a = 15$ and $b = 17$.

9 Method of differences yields $(n + 1)^2 + n^2 - 1^2 - 0^2$
$= 2n^2 + 2n = 2n(n + 1)$ so $a = 2$.

10 a Method of differences yields $\dfrac{3n}{12n + 16}$,

so $a = 3$, $b = 12$ and $c = 16$.

b Simplify: $\dfrac{6n}{24n + 16} - \dfrac{3n - 3}{12n + 4}$

11 The general term $\dfrac{1}{r} + \dfrac{1}{r + 1}$ is a sum, not a difference,

so the terms will not cancel out, and the method of differences cannot be used in this case.

12 Recognise this is $\sum_{r=1}^{n} \dfrac{1}{r(r + 2)}$ and apply method of

differences. Simplify $\dfrac{1}{2} + \dfrac{1}{4} - \left(\dfrac{1}{2(n + 1)} + \dfrac{1}{2(n + 2)}\right)$ to

obtain $\dfrac{3}{4} - \dfrac{2n + 3}{2(n + 1)(n + 2)}$, stating $a = 2$ and $b = 3$.

13 a $\dfrac{1}{2r + 1} - \dfrac{1}{2r + 5}$

b 0.0218

Challenge

a $k = 11$ **b** $a = 11$, $b = 48$, $c = 49$

Exercise 2B

1 a $f'(x) = 2e^{2x}$, $f''(x) = 4e^{2x}$, $f'''(x) = 2^3 e^{2x} = 8e^{2x}$,
$f^{(n)}(x) = 2^n e^{2x}$

b $f'(x) = n(1 + x)^{n-1}$, $f''(x) = n(n - 1)(1 + x)^{n-2}$,
$f'''(x) = n(n - 1)(n - 2)(1 + x)^{n-3}$, $f^{(n)}(x) = n!$

c $f'(x) = e^x + xe^x$, $f''(x) = 2e^x + xe^x$, $f'''(x) = 3e^x + xe^x$,
$f^{(n)}(x) = ne^x + xe^x$

d $f'(x) = (1 + x)^{-1}$, $f''(x) = -(1 + x)^{-2}$, $f'''(x) = 2(1 + x)^{-3}$,
$f^{(n)}(x) = (-1)^{n-1}(n - 1)!(1 + x)^{-n}$

2 a $\dfrac{d^n y}{dx^n} = 3^n e^{2+3x} = 3^n y$ **b** e^2

3 a $\dfrac{dy}{dx} = 3 \times \cos 3x \times 2\sin 3x$

$= 6\sin x \cos x = 3\sin 6x$

b $\dfrac{d^2 y}{dx^2} = 18\cos 6x$, $\dfrac{d^3 y}{dx^3} = -108\sin 6x$, $\dfrac{d^4 y}{dx^4} = -648\cos 6x$

c 648

4 a $f'(x) = 2xe^{-x} - x^2 e^{-x}$
$f''(x) = (2e^{-x} - 2xe^{-x}) - (2xe^{-x} - x^2 e^{-x})$
$= e^{-x}(2 - 4x + x^2)$
$f'''(x) = e^{-x}(-4 + 2x) - e^{-x}(2 - 4x + x^2)$
$= e^{-x}(-6 + 6x - x^2)$

b $f''''(x) = e^{-x}(6 - 2x) - e^{-x}(-6 + 6x - x^2)$
$= e^{-x}(12 - 8x + x^2)$
so $f''''(2) = e^{-2}(12 - 16 + 4) = 0$

5 a Given that $y = \sec x$, $\dfrac{dy}{dx} = \sec x \tan x$

$\dfrac{d^2 y}{dx^2} = \sec x(\sec^2 x) + (\sec x \tan x)\tan x$

$= \sec x(\sec^2 x + \tan^2 x) = 2\sec^3 x - \sec x$

b $\dfrac{d^3 y}{dx^3} = 6\sec^2 x(\sec x \tan x) - \sec x \tan x$

$= \sec x \tan x(6\sec^2 x - 1)$

When $x = \dfrac{\pi}{4}$, $\dfrac{d^3 y}{dx^2} = (\sqrt{2})(1)(6(2) - 1) = 11\sqrt{2}$

6 a $\dfrac{d^2}{dx^2}(y^2) = \dfrac{d}{dx}\left(2y\dfrac{dy}{dx}\right) = 2y\dfrac{d^2 y}{dx^2} + 2\left(\dfrac{dy}{dx}\right)^2$

b $2\left(y\dfrac{d^3 y}{dx^3} + 3\dfrac{dy}{dx} \times \dfrac{d^2 y}{dx^2}\right)$

7 a $f'(x) = \dfrac{1}{x + \sqrt{1 + x^2}} \times \left(1 + \dfrac{x}{\sqrt{1 + x^2}}\right) = \dfrac{1}{\sqrt{1 + x^2}}$
So $\sqrt{1 + x^2}\, f'(x) = 1$

b Differentiating this equation w.r.t. x,
$\sqrt{1 + x^2}\, f''(x) + \dfrac{x}{\sqrt{1 + x^2}} f'(x) = 0$

$\Rightarrow (1 + x^2) f''(x) + xf'(x) = 0$

c Differentiating this equation w.r.t. x
$((1 + x^2) f'''(x) + 2xf''(x)) + (f'(x) + xf''(x)) = 0$
$\Rightarrow (1 + x^2) f'''(x) + 3xf''(x) + f'(x) = 0$

d $f'(0) = 1$, $f''(0) = 0$, $f'''(0) = -1$

Exercise 2C

1 a $f(x) = (1 - x)^{-1}$ $\Rightarrow f(0) = 1$
$f'(x) = -1(1 - x)^{-2}(-1) = (1 - x)^{-2}$ $\Rightarrow f'(0) = 1$
$f''(x) = -2(1 - x)^{-3}(-1) = 2(1 - x)^{-3}$ $\Rightarrow f''(0) = 2$
$f'''(x) = -(3 \times 2)(1 - x)^{-4}(-1) = (3 \times 2)(1 - x)^{-4}$
$\Rightarrow f'''(0) = 3!$
General term:
$f^{(r)}(x) = r(r - 1)\ldots 2(1 - x)^{-(r+1)} = r!(1 - x)^{-(r+1)}$
$\Rightarrow f^{(r)}(0) = r!$
Using $f(x) = f(0) + f'(0)x + \dfrac{f''(0)}{2!}x^2 + \ldots + \dfrac{f^{(r)}(0)}{r!}x^r + \ldots$

$(1 - x)^{-1} = 1 + x + \dfrac{2}{2!}x^2 + \ldots + \dfrac{r!}{r!}x^r + \ldots$

$= 1 + x + x^2 + \ldots + x^r + \ldots$

b $f(x) = \sqrt{1 + x} = (1 + x)^{\frac{1}{2}}$ $\Rightarrow f(0) = 1$
$f'(x) = \dfrac{1}{2}(1 + x)^{-\frac{1}{2}}$ $\Rightarrow f'(0) = \dfrac{1}{2}$
$f''(x) = \dfrac{1}{2}\left(-\dfrac{1}{2}\right)(1 + x)^{-\frac{3}{2}}$ $\Rightarrow f''(0) = -\dfrac{1}{4}$
$f'''(x) = \dfrac{1}{2}\left(-\dfrac{1}{2}\right)\left(-\dfrac{3}{2}\right)(1 + x)^{-\frac{5}{2}}$ $\Rightarrow f'''(0) = \dfrac{3}{8}$

Using Maclaurin's expansion,

$\sqrt{1 + x} = 1 + \dfrac{1}{2}x + \dfrac{\left(-\dfrac{1}{4}\right)}{2!}x^2 + \dfrac{\left(\dfrac{3}{8}\right)}{3!}x^3 - \ldots$

$= 1 + \dfrac{x}{2} - \dfrac{x^2}{8} + \dfrac{x^3}{16} - \ldots$

2 $f(x) = e^{\sin x}$ $\Rightarrow f(0) = 1$
$f'(x) = \cos x e^{\sin x}$ $\Rightarrow f'(0) = 1$
$f''(x) = \cos^2 x e^{\sin x} - \sin x e^{\sin x}$ $\Rightarrow f''(0) = 1$
Using Maclaurin's expansion,
$e^{\sin x} = 1 + x + \dfrac{1}{2!}x^2 + \ldots = 1 + x + \dfrac{1}{2}x^2\ldots$

3 a $f(x) = \cos x$ $\Rightarrow f(0) = 1$
$f'(x) = -\sin x$ $\Rightarrow f'(0) = 0$
$f''(x) = -\cos x$ $\Rightarrow f''(0) = -1$
$f'''(x) = \sin x$ $\Rightarrow f'''(0) = 0$
$f''''(x) = \cos x$ $\Rightarrow f''''(0) = 1$

The process repeats itself every 4th derivative. Using Maclaurin's expansion,

$$\cos x = 1 + \frac{-1}{2!}x^2 + \frac{1}{4!}x^4 + \ldots + \frac{(-1)^r}{(2r)!}x^{2r} + \ldots$$

$$= 1 - \frac{x^2}{2!} + \frac{x^4}{4!} + \ldots + \frac{(-1)^r}{(2r)!}x^{2r} + \ldots$$

b Using $\cos x \approx 1 - \frac{x^2}{2!} + \frac{x^4}{4!}$ with $x = \frac{\pi}{6}$,

$$\cos x \approx 1 - \frac{\pi^2}{72} + \frac{\pi^4}{31104} = 0.86605\ldots$$ which is correct to 3 d.p.

4 a $e = 2.718$ (3 d.p.)

b $\ln\left(\frac{6}{5}\right) = 0.182$ (3 d.p.)

5 a $1 + 3x + \frac{9}{2}x^2 + \frac{9}{2}x^3 + \frac{27}{8}x^4 + .$

b $2x - 2x^2 + \frac{8}{3}x^3 - 4x^4 + \ldots$

c $x^2 - \frac{x^4}{3} + \ldots$

6 $\cos\left(x - \frac{\pi}{4}\right) = \cos x \cos\frac{\pi}{4} + \sin x \sin\frac{\pi}{4}$

$$= \frac{1}{\sqrt{2}}(\cos x + \sin x)$$

$$= \frac{1}{\sqrt{2}}\left(\left(1 - \frac{x^2}{2!} + \frac{x^4}{4!} - \ldots\right) + \left(x - \frac{x^3}{3!} + \frac{x^5}{5!} - \ldots\right)\right)$$

$$= \frac{1}{\sqrt{2}}\left(1 + x - \frac{x^2}{2} - \frac{x^3}{6} + \frac{x^4}{24} - \ldots\right)$$

7 a $f(x) = (1-x)^2 \ln(1-x)$

$$f'(x) = (1-x)^2 \times \frac{-1}{1-x} + 2(1-x)(-1)\ln(1-x)$$

$$= x - 1 - 2(1-x)\ln(1-x)$$

$$f''(x) = 1 - 2\left((1-x) \times \frac{-1}{1-x} + (-1)\ln(1-x)\right)$$

$$= 3 + 2\ln(1-x)$$

b $f(0) = 0, f'(0) = -1, f''(0) = 3, f'''(0) = -2$

c $-x + \frac{3}{2}x^2 - \frac{1}{3}x^3$

8 a $\sin x = x - \frac{x^3}{3!} + \frac{x^5}{5!} - \ldots = x - \frac{1}{6}x^3 + \frac{1}{120}x^5 - \ldots$

$$\cos x = 1 - \frac{x^2}{2!} + \frac{x^4}{4!} - \ldots = 1 - \frac{1}{2}x^2 + \frac{1}{24}x^4 - \ldots$$

$$3\sin x - 4x\cos x + x$$

$$= 3\left(x - \frac{1}{6}x^3 + \frac{1}{120}x^5 - \ldots\right) - 4x\left(1 - \frac{1}{2}x^2 + \frac{1}{24}x^4 - \ldots\right) + x$$

$$= \frac{3}{2}x^3 - \frac{17}{120}x^5 + \ldots$$

b $\frac{3}{2}$

9 a $f'(x) = \frac{1}{\cos x} \times (-\sin x) = -\tan x$

b $f'(0) = 0, f''(0) = -1, f'''(0) = 0, f''''(0) = -2$

c $\frac{-x^2}{2} - \frac{x^4}{12}$

d $\ln\left(\cos\frac{\pi}{4}\right) = \ln(2^{-\frac{1}{2}}) = -\frac{1}{2}\ln 2$

And by the Maclaurin series we have also

$$\ln\left(\cos\frac{\pi}{4}\right) \approx -\frac{\left(\frac{\pi}{4}\right)^2}{2} - \frac{\left(\frac{\pi}{4}\right)^4}{12}$$

$$\ln 2 \approx \frac{\pi^2}{16}\left(1 + \frac{\pi^2}{96}\right)$$

10 $f(x) = \tan x \Rightarrow f(0) = 0$

$f'(x) = \sec^2 x \Rightarrow f'(0) = 1$

$f''(x) = 2\sec^2 x \tan x \Rightarrow f''(0) = 0$

$f'''(x) = 4\sec^2 x \tan^2 x + 2\sec^4 x = 6\sec^4 x - 4\sec^2 x$

$\quad = 2(\sec^4 x + 2\sec^2 x \tan^2 x) \Rightarrow f'''(0) = 2$

$f''''(x) = 24\sec^4 x \tan x - 8\sec^2 x \tan x \Rightarrow f''''(0) = 0$

$f'''''(x) = 24\sec^4 x \tan^2 x + 24\sec^6 x - 8\sec^2 x \tan^2 x$

$\quad - 8\sec^4 x \Rightarrow f'''''(0) = 16$

So the Maclaurin series is

$$0 + 1x + \frac{0}{2!}x^2 + \frac{2}{3!}x^3 + \frac{0}{4!}x^4 + \frac{16}{5!}x^5 + \ldots$$

$$= x + \frac{1}{3}x^3 + \frac{2}{15}x^5 + \ldots$$

Challenge

a $e^x = 1 + x + \frac{x^2}{2!} + \frac{x^3}{3!}\ldots + \frac{x^r}{r!} + \ldots$

$$a_r = \frac{x^r}{r!}; a_{r+1} = \frac{x^{r+1}}{(r+1)!}$$

$$\lim_{r \to \infty}\left|\frac{a_{r+1}}{a_r}\right| = \lim_{r \to \infty}\left|\frac{x^{r+1}}{(r+1)!} \times \frac{r!}{x^r}\right| = \lim_{r \to \infty}\left|\frac{|x|}{r+1}\right| < 1$$

b $\ln(1 + x) = x - \frac{x^2}{2} + \frac{x^3}{3} - \ldots + (-1)^{r+1}\frac{x^r}{r} + \ldots$

$$a_r = (-1)^{r+1}\frac{x^r}{r}; a_{r+1} = (-1)^{r+2}\frac{x^{r+1}}{r+1}$$

$$\lim_{r \to \infty}\left|\frac{a_{r+1}}{a_r}\right| = \lim_{r \to \infty}\left|\frac{(-1)^{r+2}x^{r+1}}{r+1} \times \frac{r}{(-1)^{r+1}x^r}\right| = \lim_{r \to \infty}\left|\frac{rx}{r+1}\right|$$

$$= \lim_{r \to \infty}\left|\frac{x}{1 + \frac{1}{r}}\right| = |x|$$

So $\ln(1 + x)$ converges for $-1 < x < 1$ and diverges for $x > 1$.

Exercise 2D

1 a $1 - x + \frac{x^2}{2} - \frac{x^3}{6} + \ldots$ valid for all values of x

b $1 + 4x + 8x^2 + \frac{32x^3}{3} + \ldots$ valid for all values of x

c $e\left(1 + x + \frac{x^2}{2} + \frac{x^3}{6} + \ldots\right)$ valid for all values of x

d $-x - \frac{x^2}{2} - \frac{x^3}{3} - \frac{x^4}{4} - \ldots \quad -1 \leq x < 1$

e $\frac{x}{2} - \frac{x^3}{48} + \frac{x^5}{3840} - \frac{x^7}{645120} + \ldots$ valid for all values of x

f $\ln 2 + \frac{3x}{2} - \frac{9x^2}{8} + \frac{9x^3}{8} + \ldots \quad -\frac{2}{3} < x \leq \frac{2}{3}$

2 a $\ln(1 + x) = x - \frac{x^2}{2} + \frac{x^3}{3} - \frac{x^4}{4} + \frac{x^5}{5} - \ldots, \quad -1 < x \leq 1$

$$\ln(1 - x) = -x - \frac{x^2}{2} - \frac{x^3}{3} - \frac{x^4}{4} + \frac{x^5}{5} - \ldots, \quad -1 \leq x < 1$$

$$\ln\left(\frac{1+x}{1-x}\right) = \ln(1 + x) - \ln(1 - x) = 2\left(x + \frac{x^3}{3} + \frac{x^5}{5} + \ldots\right)$$

As x must be in both the intervals $-1 < x \leq 1$ and $-1 \leq x < 1$, x must be in the interval $-1 < x < 1$.

b $\left(x + \frac{x^3}{3} + \frac{x^5}{5} + \ldots\right), \quad -1 < x < 1$

c $x = -\frac{1}{5}; -0.4055$ (4 d.p.)

d $\ln\left(\frac{1 + \frac{3}{5}}{1 - \frac{3}{5}}\right)^{\frac{1}{2}} = \frac{1}{2}\ln(4) = \ln(2)$

and the series from **b** gives

$$\frac{3}{5} + \frac{\left(\frac{3}{5}\right)^3}{3} + \frac{\left(\frac{3}{5}\right)^5}{5} + 0.69\ldots$$

Which is $\ln 2$ correct to 2 dp

3 $e^{2x} = 1 + 2x + \frac{(2x)^2}{2!} + \frac{(2x)^3}{3!} + \ldots = 1 + 2x + 2x^2 + \frac{4x^3}{3} + \ldots$

$$e^{-x} = 1 - x + \frac{(-x)^2}{2!} + \frac{(-x)^3}{3!} + \ldots = 1 - x + \frac{x^2}{2} - \frac{x^3}{6} + \ldots$$

So $e^{2x} - e^{-x} \approx 3x + \frac{3}{2}x^2$ if terms in x^3 and above may be neglected.

4 a $3x\sin 2x = 3x\left(2x - \dfrac{4x^3}{3} + \ldots\right)$

$\cos 3x = \left(1 - \dfrac{9x^2}{2} + \dfrac{27x^4}{8} - \ldots\right)$

So we get that

$3x\sin 2x - \cos 3x = 6x^2 - 4x^3 - \left(1 - \dfrac{9x^2}{2} + \dfrac{27x^4}{8}\right) + \ldots$

$= -1 + \dfrac{21}{2}x^2 - \dfrac{59}{8}x^4 + \ldots$

b $\dfrac{21}{2}$

5 a $x - \dfrac{5x^2}{2} + \dfrac{7x^3}{3} - \dfrac{17x^4}{4} + \ldots, \dfrac{1}{2} < x \leqslant \dfrac{1}{2}$

b $2\ln 3 + \dfrac{2x}{3} - \dfrac{x^2}{9} + \dfrac{2x^3}{81} - \dfrac{x^4}{162} + \ldots, -3 < x \leqslant 3$

6 a $1 - 2x^2 + \dfrac{2x^4}{3} - \dfrac{4x^6}{45} + \dfrac{2x^8}{315} - \ldots$

b $x^2 - \dfrac{x^4}{3} + \dfrac{2x^6}{45} - \dfrac{x^8}{315} + \ldots$

7 $p = \dfrac{2}{3}, q = -\dfrac{1}{8}$

8 a $x + 2x^2 + \dfrac{17x^3}{6} + \dfrac{11x^4}{3} + \ldots$

b 1

9 a $(1 - 3x)\ln(1 + 2x)$

$= (1 - 3x)\left(2x - 2x^2 + \dfrac{8x^3}{3} - 4x^4 + \ldots\right)$

$= 2x - 8x^2 + \dfrac{26}{3}x^3 - 12x^4 + \ldots$

b $e^{2x}\sin x$

$= \left(1 + 2x + \dfrac{(2x)^2}{2!} + \dfrac{(2x)^3}{3!} + \dfrac{(2x)^4}{4!} + \ldots\right)\left(x - \dfrac{x^3}{3!} + \ldots\right)$

$= \left(1 + 2x + 2x^2 + \dfrac{4x^3}{3} + \dfrac{2x^4}{3} + \ldots\right)\left(x - \dfrac{x^3}{6} + \ldots\right)$

$= x + 2x^2 + \dfrac{11}{6}x^3 + x^4 + \ldots$

c $\sqrt{1 + x^2}\, e^{-x} = (1 + x^2)^{\frac{1}{2}}\, e^{-x}$

$= \left(1 + \dfrac{1}{2}x^2 + \left(\dfrac{1}{2}\right)\left(-\dfrac{1}{2}\right)\dfrac{(x^2)^2}{2!} + \ldots\right)\left(1 - x + \dfrac{x^2}{2!} - \dfrac{x^3}{3!} + \dfrac{x^4}{4!} + \ldots\right)$

$= \left(1 + \dfrac{x^2}{2} - \dfrac{x^4}{8} + \ldots\right)\left(1 - x + \dfrac{x^2}{2} - \dfrac{x^3}{6} + \dfrac{x^4}{24} + \ldots\right)$

$= 1 - x + x^2 - \dfrac{2}{3}x^3 + \dfrac{1}{6}x^4 + \ldots$

10 a $1 - \dfrac{x^2}{2} + \dfrac{x^4}{8} - \dfrac{x^6}{48} + \dfrac{x^8}{384} - \ldots$

b 1.711 (3 d.p.)

11 a $e^{px}\sin 3x$

$= \left(1 + px + \dfrac{(px)^2}{2!} + \dfrac{(px)^3}{3!} + \ldots\right)\left(3x - \dfrac{(3x)^3}{3!} + \ldots\right)$

$= \left(1 + px + \dfrac{p^2x^2}{2} + \dfrac{p^3x^3}{6} + \ldots\right)\left(3x - \dfrac{9x^3}{2} + \ldots\right)$

$= 3x + 3px^2 + \dfrac{3(p^2 - 3)x^3}{2} + \ldots$

b $q = -2 \quad p = \dfrac{2}{3} \quad k = -\dfrac{13}{2}$

12 a $e^{x-\ln x} = e^x \times e^{-\ln x} = e^x \times e^{\ln x^{-1}} = \dfrac{e^x}{x}$

$\Rightarrow e^{x-\ln x}\sin x = \dfrac{e^x\sin x}{x}$

$f(x) = \dfrac{\left(1 + x + \dfrac{x^2}{2} + \dfrac{x^3}{6} + \ldots\right)\left(x - \dfrac{x^3}{6} + \ldots\right)}{x}, x > 0$

$= \left(1 + x + \dfrac{x^2}{2} + \dfrac{x^3}{6} + \ldots\right)\left(1 - \dfrac{x^2}{6} + \ldots\right)$

$= 1 + x + \dfrac{x^2}{3}$ ignoring terms in x^4 and above

b $f(0.1) = \dfrac{e^{0.1}\sin 0.1}{0.1} = 1.103329\ldots$

Using the approximation in part **a**,

$f(0.1) = 1 + 0.1 + 0.00333333 = 1.103333\ldots$

This result is correct to 6 s.f.

13 a $\dfrac{d^4y}{dx^4} = 16(\sin 2x - \cos 2x) = 16y$

b $y = -1 + 2x + 2x^2 - \dfrac{4}{3}x^3 - \dfrac{2}{3}x^4 + \ldots$

Challenge

a $\gamma = 1 + \dfrac{1}{2}\beta^2 + \dfrac{3}{8}\beta^4$

b 19.6 years (3 s.f.)   **c** 2%

d As β is larger, the error in γ is larger, so the approximation would be less accurate.

Mixed exercise 2

1 a $\dfrac{2}{(r + 2)(r + 4)} = \dfrac{1}{r + 2} - \dfrac{1}{r + 4}$

b $\displaystyle\sum_{r=1}^{n}\dfrac{2}{(r + 2)(r + 4)} = \sum_{r=1}^{n}\left(\dfrac{1}{r + 2} - \dfrac{1}{r + 4}\right)$

$= \dfrac{1}{3} + \dfrac{1}{4} - \dfrac{1}{n + 3} - \dfrac{1}{n + 4}$

$= \dfrac{7n^2 + 25n}{12(n + 3)(n + 4)}$

2 a $\dfrac{4}{(4r - 1)(4r + 3)} = \dfrac{1}{4r - 1} - \dfrac{1}{4r + 3}$

b $\displaystyle\sum_{r=1}^{n}\dfrac{4}{(4r - 1)(4r + 3)} = \dfrac{1}{3} - \dfrac{1}{4n + 3} = \dfrac{4n + 3 - 3}{3(4n + 3)}$

$= \dfrac{4n}{3(4n + 3)}$

c 0.00126

3 a $(r + 1)^3 - (r - 1)^3$

$= (r^3 + 3r^2 + 3r + 1) - (r^3 - 3r^2 + 3r - 1)$

$= 6r^2 + 2$

b $\displaystyle\sum_{r=1}^{n}(6r^2 + 2) = 6\sum_{r=1}^{n}r^2 + \sum_{r=1}^{n}2 = 2n^3 + 3n^2 + 3n$

So $6\displaystyle\sum_{r=1}^{n}r^2 + \sum_{r=1}^{n}2 = 6\sum_{r=1}^{n}r^2 + 2n = 2n^3 + 3n^2 + 3n$

So $6\displaystyle\sum_{r=1}^{n}r^2 = 2n^3 + 3n^2 + n = n(2n^2 + 3n + 1)$

$= n(n + 1)(2n + 1)$

So $\displaystyle\sum_{r=1}^{n}r^2 = \dfrac{1}{6}n(n + 1)(2n + 1)$

4 $\displaystyle\sum_{r=1}^{n}\dfrac{4}{(r + 1)(r + 3)} = \sum_{r=1}^{n}\left(\dfrac{2}{r + 1} - \dfrac{2}{r + 3}\right)$

$= \dfrac{2}{2} + \dfrac{2}{3} - \dfrac{2}{n + 2} - \dfrac{2}{n + 3} = \dfrac{n(5n + 13)}{3(n + 2)(n + 3)}$

5 $\displaystyle\sum_{r=1}^{n}((r + 1)^3 - (r - 1)^3) = n(2n^2 + 3n + 3)$

Calculate

$(2n)(2(2n)^2 + 3(2n) + 3) - (n - 1)(2(n - 1)^2 + 3(n - 1) + 3)$

Which gives that $a = 14, b = 15, c = 3, d = 2$

6 a $\dfrac{d^ny}{dx^n} = (-2)^n e^{1-2x}$

b $\dfrac{d^8y}{dx^8} = (-2)^8 e^{1-2\ln 32} = 256 e^{1+\ln 32^{-2}}$

$= 256(e^1)\left(e^{\ln\frac{1}{1024}}\right) = \dfrac{256}{1024}e^1 = \dfrac{e}{4}$

7 a $f'(0) = \dfrac{1}{2}, f''(0) = \dfrac{1}{4}$

b $f'''(x) = \dfrac{(1 + e^x)^2 e^x - e^x 2(1 + e^x)e^x}{(1 + e^x)^4} = \dfrac{e^x(1 - e^x)}{(1 + e^x)^3}$

$f'''(0) = 0$

c $\ln 2 + \dfrac{x}{2} + \dfrac{x^2}{8} + \ldots$

8 a $1 - 8x^2 + \frac{32}{3}x^4 - \frac{256}{45}x^6 + \dots$

b $\cos 4x = 1 - 2\sin^2 2x$

so $2\sin^2 2x = 1 - \cos 4x = 8x^2 - \frac{32}{3}x^4 + \frac{256}{45}x^6 + \dots$

so $\sin^2 2x = 4x^2 - \frac{16}{3}x^4 + \frac{128}{45}x^6 + \dots$

9 Using $e^x = 1 + x + \frac{x^2}{2} + \frac{x^3}{6} + \frac{x^4}{24} + \dots$ and

$\cos x = 1 - \frac{x^2}{2} + \frac{x^4}{24} - \dots$

$e^{\cos x} = e^{\left(1 - \frac{x^2}{2} + \frac{x^4}{24}\right)} = e \times e^{-\frac{x^2}{2}} \times e^{\frac{x^4}{24}}$

$= e\left(1 + \left(-\frac{x^2}{2}\right) + \frac{1}{2}\left(-\frac{x^2}{2}\right)^2 + \dots\right)\left(1 + \frac{x^4}{24} + \dots\right)$

$= e\left(1 - \frac{x^2}{2} + \frac{x^4}{8} + \frac{x^4}{24} + \dots\right) = e\left(1 - \frac{x^2}{2} + \frac{x^4}{6} + \dots\right)$

10 $-3x^2 - 2x^3 - \dots$

11 $x + \frac{x^3}{6} + \dots$

12 a $\frac{d}{dx}(e^x)$

$= \frac{d}{dx}\left(1 + x + \frac{x^2}{2!} + \frac{x^3}{3!} + \frac{x^4}{4!} + \dots + \frac{x^r}{r!} + \frac{x^{r+1}}{(r+1)!} + \dots\right)$

$= 0 + 1 + \frac{2x}{2!} + \frac{3x^2}{3!} + \frac{4x^3}{4!} + \dots + \frac{(r+1)x^r}{(r+1)!} + \dots$

$= 1 + x + \frac{x^2}{2!} + \frac{x^3}{3!} + \dots + \frac{x^r}{r!} + \dots = e^x$

b $\frac{d}{dx}(\sin x) = \frac{d}{dx}\left(x - \frac{x^3}{3!} + \frac{x^5}{5!} - \dots + (-1)^r\frac{x^{2r+1}}{(2r+1)!} + \dots\right)$

$= 1 - \frac{3x^2}{3!} + \frac{5x^4}{5!} - \dots + (-1)^r\frac{(2r+1)x^{2r}}{(2r+1)!} + \dots$

$= 1 - \frac{x^2}{2!} + \frac{x^4}{4!} - \dots + (-1)^r\frac{x^{2r}}{(2r)!}\dots = \cos x$

c $\frac{d}{dx}(\cos x) = \frac{d}{dx}\left(1 - \frac{x^2}{2!} + \frac{x^4}{4!} - \frac{x^6}{6!}\dots + (-1)^r\frac{x^{2r}}{(2r)!}\right.$

$\left. + (-1)^{r+1}\frac{x^{2r+2}}{(2r+2)!} + \dots\right)$

$= -\frac{2x}{2!} + \frac{4x^3}{4!} - \frac{6x^5}{6!}\dots + (-1)^r\frac{2rx^{2r-1}}{(2r)!}$

$+ (-1)^{r+1}\frac{(2r+2)x^{2r+1}}{(2r+2)!} + .$

$= -\left(x - \frac{x^3}{3!} + \frac{x^5}{5!} - \dots + (-1)^r\frac{x^{2r+1}}{(2r+1)!}\right) = -\sin x$

13 a $\cos x = 1 - \left(\frac{x^2}{2} - \frac{x^4}{24} + \dots\right)$

$\Rightarrow \sec x = \frac{1}{\cos x} = \left(1 - \left(\frac{x^2}{2} - \frac{x^4}{24} + \dots\right)\right)^{-1}$

$\sec x = 1 + (-1)\left(-\left(\frac{x^2}{2} - \frac{x^4}{24}\right)\right)$

$+ \frac{(-1)(-2)}{2!}\left(-\left(\frac{x^2}{2} - \frac{x^4}{24}\right)\right)^2 + \dots$

$= 1 + \frac{1}{2}x^2 + \frac{5}{24}x^4 + \dots$

b $x + \frac{x^3}{3} + \frac{2}{15}x^5 + \dots$

14 $1 + x - 4x^2 - \frac{13}{3}x^3 + \dots$

15 $f'(x) = (1 + x)(1 + 2\ln(1 + x))$

$f''(x) = 3 + 2\ln(1 + x)$

$f'''(x) = \frac{2}{1 + x}$

$(1 + x)^2\ln(1 + x) = x + \frac{3}{2}x^2 + \frac{1}{3}x^3 + \dots$

16 a $x - \frac{x^2}{2} + \frac{x^3}{6} - \frac{x^4}{12} + \dots$

b 0.116 (3 d.p.)

17 a $f(x) = e^{\tan x} = e^{x + \frac{x^3}{3} + \dots} = e^{x \dots} \times e^{\frac{x^3}{3}}$

$= \left(1 + x + \frac{x^2}{2!} + \frac{x^3}{3!} + \dots\right)\left(1 + \frac{x^3}{3} + \dots\right)$

$= 1 + x + \frac{x^2}{2} + \frac{x^3}{2} + \dots$

b $1 - x + \frac{x^2}{2} - \frac{x^3}{2} + \dots$

18 a

$f(x) = \ln\cos x$	$f(0) = 0$
$f'(x) = \frac{-\sin x}{\cos x} = -\tan x$	$f'(0) = 0$
$f''(x) = -\sec^2 x$	$f''(0) = -1$
$f'''(x) = -2\sec^2 x \tan x$	$f'''(0) = 0$
$f''''(x) = -2\sec^4 x - 4\sec^2 x\tan^2 x$	$f''''(0) = -2$

Substituting into Maclaurin,

$\ln\cos x = (-1)\frac{x^2}{2!} + (-2)\frac{x^4}{4!} + \dots = -\frac{x^2}{2} - \frac{x^4}{12} + \dots$

b Using $1 + \cos x = 2\cos^2\frac{x}{2}$,

$\ln(1 + \cos x) = \ln 2\cos^2\frac{x}{2} = \ln 2 + 2\ln\cos\frac{x}{2}$

so $\ln(1 + \cos x) = \ln 2 + 2\left(-\frac{1}{2}\left(\frac{x}{2}\right)^2 - \frac{1}{12}\left(\frac{x}{2}\right)^4 - \dots\right)$

$= \ln 2 - \frac{x^2}{4} - \frac{x^4}{96} - \dots$

19 a $\frac{dy}{dx} = 3(e^{3x} + e^{-3x}), \frac{d^2y}{dx^2} = 9(e^{3x} + e^{-3x}),$

$\frac{d^3y}{dx^3} = 27(e^{3x} + e^{-3x}), \frac{d^4y}{dx^4} = 81(e^{3x} - e^{-3x}) = 81y$

b $y = 6x + 9x^3 + \frac{81}{20}x^5 + \dots$

c $\frac{2(3)^{2n-1}x^{2n-1}}{(2n-1)!}$

Challenge

$e^x = 1 + x + \frac{x^2}{2} + \frac{x^3}{6} + \frac{x^4}{24} + \frac{x^5}{120}\dots$

$e^{ix} = 1 + (ix) + \frac{(ix)^2}{2} + \frac{(ix)^3}{6} + \frac{(ix)^4}{24} + \frac{(ix)^5}{120} + \dots$

$= 1 + ix - \frac{x^2}{2} - i\frac{x^3}{6} + \frac{x^4}{24} + i\frac{x^5}{120}\dots$

$\cos x = 1 - \frac{x^2}{2} + \frac{x^4}{24} - \dots$

$\sin x = x - \frac{x^3}{6} + \frac{x^5}{120} - \dots$

$i\sin x = i\left(x - \frac{x^3}{6} + \frac{x^5}{120} - \dots\right)$

Match up the items to show $e^{ix} = \cos x + i\sin x$

CHAPTER 3
Prior knowledge check

1 a $5\sqrt{3 + x^2} + c$ **b** $(x^2 - 2x + 2)e^x + c$

  c $\frac{1}{6}\ln(1 + 3\sin^2 x) + c$

2 a $-\frac{x}{y}$ **b** $-\frac{10x + y}{x + 4y}$ **c** $\frac{1}{\sec^2 y}$

3 a $\frac{1}{x} - \frac{1}{x + 1}$ **b** $\frac{5}{4(x + 2)} + \frac{3}{4(x - 2)}$ **c** $\frac{5}{x + 1} - \frac{7}{2x + 1}$

Exercise 3A

1 a $\frac{1}{2}$ **b** $\sqrt{2}$ **c** $\frac{1}{3}$

2 a $\int_0^\infty e^x\,dx = \lim_{t\to\infty}\int_0^t e^x\,dx = \lim_{t\to\infty}(e^t - 1)$

   and $e^t \to \infty$ as $t \to \infty$, so the integral diverges

b $\int_1^{\infty} \frac{1}{\sqrt{x}} \, dx = \lim_{t \to \infty} \int_1^t \frac{1}{\sqrt{x}} \, dx = \lim_{t \to \infty}(2\sqrt{t} - 2)$
and $\sqrt{t} \to \infty$ as $t \to \infty$, so the integral diverges

c $\int_0^{\infty} \frac{8x}{\sqrt{1 + x^2}} \, dx = \lim_{t \to \infty} \int_0^t \frac{8x}{\sqrt{1 + x^2}} \, dx = \lim_{t \to \infty}(8\sqrt{t^2 + 1} - 8)$
and $\sqrt{t^2 + 1} \to \infty$ as $t \to \infty$, so the integral diverges

3 a $\int_0^1 \frac{1}{\sqrt{x}} \, dx = \lim_{t \to 0} \int_t^1 \frac{1}{\sqrt{x}} \, dx = \lim_{t \to 0}\left[2\sqrt{x}\right]_t^1 = \lim_{t \to 0}\left(2 - 2\sqrt{t}\right) = 2$

b $\int_0^{\frac{2}{3}} \frac{1}{\sqrt{2 - 3x}} \, dx = \lim_{t \to \frac{2}{3}} \int_0^t \frac{1}{\sqrt{2 - 3x}} \, dx = \lim_{t \to \frac{2}{3}}\left[-\frac{2}{3}\sqrt{2 - 3x}\right]_0^t$
$= \lim_{t \to \frac{2}{3}}\left(\frac{2\sqrt{3}}{3} - \frac{2}{3}\sqrt{2 - 3t}\right) = \frac{2\sqrt{3}}{3}$

c $\int_0^{\ln 3} \frac{e^x}{\sqrt{e^x - 1}} \, dx = \lim_{t \to 0} \int_t^{\ln 3} \frac{e^x}{\sqrt{e^x - 1}} \, dx = \lim_{t \to 0}\left[2\sqrt{e^x - 1}\right]_t^{\ln 3}$
$= \lim_{t \to 0}(2\sqrt{2} - 2\sqrt{e^t - 1}) = 2\sqrt{2}$

4 a Integral converges; $2(1 + \sqrt{2})$
b Integral converges; 0
c Integral diverges

5 a $\frac{1}{3(7 - 3x)} + c$

b $\int_{-\infty}^2 \frac{1}{(7 - 3x)^2} \, dx = \lim_{r \to -\infty}\left[\frac{1}{3(7 - 3x)}\right]_r^2 = \lim_{r \to -\infty}\left(\frac{1}{3} - \frac{1}{21 - 9t}\right) = \frac{1}{3}$

6 a $\frac{1}{3}e^{x^3} + c$

b $\int_{-\infty}^1 x^2 e^{x^3} \, dx = \lim_{t \to -\infty}\left[\frac{1}{3}e^{x^3}\right]_t^1 = \lim_{t \to -\infty}\left(\frac{e}{3} - \frac{1}{3}e^{t^3}\right) = \frac{e}{3}$

7 a $\frac{(\ln x)^2}{2} + c$

b $\int_1^{\infty} \frac{\ln x}{x} \, dx = \lim_{t \to \infty} \int_1^t \frac{\ln x}{x} \, dx = \lim_{t \to \infty}\left(\frac{(\ln t)^2}{2}\right)$
and $(\ln t)^2 \to \infty$ as $t \to \infty$, so the integral diverges

8 a $x((\ln x)^2 - 2\ln x + 2) + c$
b $\int_0^1 (\ln x)^2 \, dx = \lim_{t \to 0} \int_t^1 (\ln x)^2 \, dx$
$= \lim_{t \to 0}(2 - t((\ln t)^2 - 2\ln t + 2)) = 2$
since $t(\ln t) \to 0$ and $t(\ln t)^2 \to 0$ as $t \to 0$, so the integral converges
c Split $\int_0^{\infty} (\ln x)^2 \, dx$ up as $\int_0^1 (\ln x)^2 \, dx + \int_1^{\infty} (\ln x)^2 \, dx$
and show the second integral diverges.
$\int_1^{\infty} (\ln x)^2 \, dx = \lim_{t \to \infty} \int_1^t (\ln x)^2 \, dx$
$= \lim_{t \to \infty}(t((\ln t)^2 - 2\ln t + 2) - 2)$
and $t(\ln t) \to \infty$, $t(\ln t)^2 \to \infty$ as $t \to \infty$, so the integral diverges

9 $9\sqrt[3]{2}$
10 -8
11 1
12 a $\tan x$ is undefined at the upper limit $x = \frac{\pi}{2}$
b $\int_0^{\frac{\pi}{2}} \tan x \, dx = \lim_{t \to \frac{\pi}{2}} \int_0^t \tan x \, dx = \lim_{t \to \frac{\pi}{2}}(-\ln \cos t)$ and
$\cos t \to 0$ as $t \to \frac{\pi}{2}$, so $-\ln \cos t \to \infty$ as $t \to \frac{\pi}{2}$,
so the integral diverges.

13 a $\sec^2 x$ is undefined at the point $x = \frac{\pi}{2}$ in the domain of the integral
b Split $\int_0^{\pi} \sec^2 x \, dx$ up as $\int_0^{\frac{\pi}{2}} \sec^2 x \, dx + \int_{\frac{\pi}{2}}^{\pi} \sec^2 x \, dx$ and show the first integral diverges.
$\int_0^{\frac{\pi}{2}} \sec^2 x \, dx = \lim_{t \to \frac{\pi}{2}} \int_0^t \sec^2 x \, dx = \lim_{t \to \frac{\pi}{2}}(\tan t)$
and $\tan t \to \infty$ as $t \to \frac{\pi}{2}$, so the integral diverges

14 The integral converges precisely when $a > 1$, in which case its value is $\frac{1}{a - 1}$

15 a $\frac{1}{2x^2 + 3x + 1} = \frac{1}{(2x + 1)(x + 1)} = \frac{2}{2x + 1} - \frac{1}{x + 1}$
in partial fractions.
So, $\int_0^k \frac{1}{2x^2 + 3x + 1} \, dx = [\ln|2x + 1| - \ln|x + 1|]_0^k$
$= \ln\left(\frac{2k + 1}{k + 1}\right)$

b $\ln 2$

Challenge

$\int e^{-x}\sin^2 x \, dx = \frac{1}{2}\int e^{-x}(1 - \cos 2x) \, dx$
$= -\frac{1}{2}e^{-x} + \frac{1}{10}e^{-x}(-2\sin 2x + \cos 2x) + c$,
where the last step is done by using repeated integration by parts.
So, $\int_0^{\infty} e^{-x}\sin^2 x \, dx = \lim_{t \to \infty} \int_0^t e^{-x}\sin^2 x \, dx$
$= \lim_{t \to \infty}\left[\frac{1}{10}e^{-x}(-2\sin 2x + \cos 2x - 5)\right]_0^t$
$= \lim_{t \to \infty}\left(\frac{1}{10}e^{-t}(-2\sin 2t + \cos 2t - 5) - \left(-\frac{2}{5}\right)\right)$
$= \frac{2}{5}$
since $e^{-t}\sin 2t \to 0$, $e^{-t}\cos 2t \to 0$ as $t \to \infty$

Exercise 3B

1 a 1 **b** $\ln 2$ **c** e
2 a $\frac{1}{6}\ln\left(\frac{1 + e^6}{2}\right)$ **b** $\frac{4}{15\pi}$ **c** $\frac{e^2 - 2}{e^3}$
   d $\frac{5}{9}\ln\frac{14}{5}$ **e** $\frac{5}{\pi} - \frac{3}{2}$

3 a $(-2, 128)$, $(4, 20)$
b

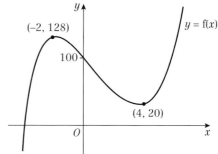

c A lower bound is 20 and a upper bound is 128, since these are the minimum and maximal values attained on $[-2, 4]$ respectively
d 74

4 $\frac{\ln 3}{2\pi}$

5 $\frac{506}{75}$

6 $\frac{1}{4} + \frac{3\sqrt{3}}{8\pi}$

7 a $\frac{5x}{(2x - 1)(x + 2)} = \frac{1}{2x - 1} + \frac{2}{x + 2}$ in partial fractions.
So, $\frac{1}{5 - 1}\int_1^5 \frac{5x}{(2x - 1)(x + 2)} \, dx = \frac{1}{4}\ln\frac{49}{3}$
b $\frac{1}{4}\ln\frac{49k^4}{3}$

8 a $\frac{1}{2}\int_0^2 x(x^2 - 4)^4 \, dx = \frac{1}{2}\left[\frac{1}{10}(x^2 - 4)^5\right]_0^2 = \frac{256}{5}$
b $-\frac{512}{5}$

9 $\frac{1}{2e}$

10 If $\dfrac{1}{b-a}\displaystyle\int_a^b f(x)\,dx = m$, then

$$\dfrac{1}{b-a}\int_a^b (f(x) + c)\,dx = \dfrac{1}{b-a}\left(\int_a^b f(x)\,dx + \int_a^b c\,dx\right)$$

$$= m + \dfrac{1}{b-a}(c(b-a)) = m + c$$

11 $\sqrt{2}$

12 The graph of f(x) between 0 and π is the negative of the graph between π and 2π and so the area under the graph between 0 and 2π must be zero.

13 a $-\dfrac{1}{2 + \sin x}$

b $\dfrac{3}{5\pi}\displaystyle\int_0^{\frac{5\pi}{3}}\dfrac{\cos x}{(2 + \sin x)^2}\,dx = \dfrac{3}{5\pi}\left[-\dfrac{1}{2 + \sin x}\right]_0^{\frac{5\pi}{3}}$

$= \dfrac{3}{5\pi}\left(\dfrac{1}{2} + \dfrac{2}{13}(4 + \sqrt{3})\right) = -\dfrac{3}{130\pi}(3 + 4\sqrt{3})$

c $\dfrac{5\pi}{2} - \dfrac{3}{130\pi}(3 + 4\sqrt{3})$

14 a Turning point is at $\left(-\dfrac{3}{4}, \dfrac{17}{8}\right)$

b $-2a^2 - 5a - \dfrac{7}{6}$

c $\dfrac{47}{24}$

Exercise 3C

1 a $\dfrac{1}{1 + x^2}$ **b** $-\dfrac{1}{\sqrt{1 - x^2}}$ **c** $-\dfrac{2x}{\sqrt{1 - x^4}}$

d $\dfrac{3(x^2 + 1)}{1 + (x^3 + 3x)^2}$ **e** $-\dfrac{1}{x\sqrt{x^2 - 1}}$

2 $\dfrac{\arccos x - \arcsin x}{\sqrt{1 - x^2}}$

3 $\dfrac{2}{(x^2 + 1)(1 - \arctan x)^2}$

4 $\dfrac{d}{dx}(\arccos x + \arcsin x) = -\dfrac{1}{\sqrt{1 - x^2}} + \dfrac{1}{\sqrt{1 - x^2}} = 0$

So f(x) = $\arccos x + \arcsin x$ is constant.

f(0) = $\dfrac{\pi}{2}$ + 0 = $\dfrac{\pi}{2}$, so f(x) = $\dfrac{\pi}{2}$ for all x

5 a $-\dfrac{2}{\sqrt{1 - 4x^2}}$ **b** $\dfrac{2}{4 + x^2}$

c $\dfrac{3}{\sqrt{1 - 9x^2}}$ **d** $-\dfrac{1}{1 + (x + 1)^2}$

e $-\dfrac{2x}{\sqrt{x^2(2 - x^2)}}$ **f** $-\dfrac{2x}{\sqrt{1 - x^4}}$

g $e^x\left(\arccos x - \dfrac{1}{\sqrt{1 - x^2}}\right)$ **h** $\dfrac{\cos x}{\sqrt{1 - x^2}} - \sin x \arcsin x$

i $x\left(2\arccos x - \dfrac{x}{\sqrt{1 - x^2}}\right)$ **j** $\dfrac{e^{\arctan x}}{1 + x^2}$

6 $\dfrac{x + (1 + x^2)\arctan x}{(1 + x^2)(1 + x^2(\arctan x)^2)}$

7 If $y = \arcsin x$, then $\dfrac{dy}{dx} = \dfrac{1}{\sqrt{1 - x^2}}$ and $\dfrac{d^2y}{dx^2} = \dfrac{x}{(1 - x^2)^{\frac{3}{2}}}$

So, $(1 - x^2)\dfrac{d^2y}{dx^2} - x\dfrac{dy}{dx} = 0$

8 $y = \dfrac{4\sqrt{3}}{3}x + \dfrac{\pi}{6} - \dfrac{\sqrt{3}}{3}$

9 a $\dfrac{2\arctan x}{1 + x^2}$ **b** $-\dfrac{1}{\sqrt{1 - x^2}(\arcsin x)^2}$

c $\dfrac{1}{(1 + x^2)(1 + (\arctan x)^2)}$

10 a

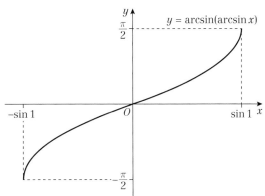

b

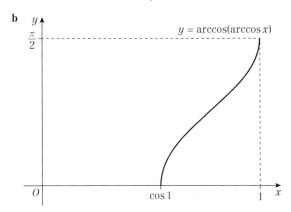

c

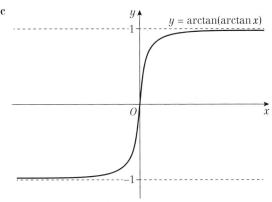

11 a If $y = \arccos x$, then $\sin y = \pm\sqrt{1 - \cos^2 y} = \pm\sqrt{1 - x^2}$. Since $\arccos x$ has range $[0, \pi]$ and $\sin y$ is positive on this domain, we must have $\sin y = \sqrt{1 - x^2}$

b If $y = \arctan x$, then

$$\cos y = \dfrac{1}{\sec y} = \pm\dfrac{1}{\sqrt{1 + \tan^2 y}} = \pm\dfrac{1}{\sqrt{1 + x^2}}$$

Since $\arctan x$ has range $\left(-\dfrac{\pi}{2}, \dfrac{\pi}{2}\right)$ and $\cos y$ is positive on this range, we must have $\cos y = \dfrac{1}{\sqrt{1 + x^2}}$

c If $y = \arccos x$, then $\sec y = \dfrac{1}{\cos y} = \dfrac{1}{x}$

d If $y = \text{arcsec}\,x$, then

$$\sin y = \pm\sqrt{1 - \cos^2 y} = \pm\sqrt{1 - \dfrac{1}{\sec^2 y}}$$

$$= \pm\sqrt{1 - \dfrac{1}{x^2}}$$

Since arcsec$x$ has range $\left(0, \frac{\pi}{2}\right) \cup \left(\frac{\pi}{2}, \pi\right)$ and $\sin y$ is positive on this domain, we must have

$$\sin y = \sqrt{1 - \frac{1}{x^2}}$$

Exercise 3D

1 $\displaystyle\int \frac{1}{a^2 + x^2}\,dx = \int \frac{a\sec^2\theta}{a^2 + (a\tan\theta)^2}\,d\theta = \frac{\theta}{a} + c = \frac{1}{a}\arctan\frac{x}{a} + c$

2 $\displaystyle\int \frac{1}{\sqrt{1 - x^2}}\,dx = \int \frac{-\sin\theta}{\sqrt{1 - \cos^2\theta}}\,d\theta = -\theta + c = -\arccos x + c$

3 a $3\arcsin\dfrac{x}{2} + c$ **b** $\dfrac{4\sqrt{5}}{5}\arctan\dfrac{x\sqrt{5}}{5} + c$

  c $\arcsin\dfrac{x}{5} + c$ **d** $\ln|x + \sqrt{x^2 - 2}| + c$

4 $\dfrac{\sqrt{3}}{6}\arctan\dfrac{x\sqrt{3}}{2} + c$

5 $\displaystyle\int \frac{1}{\sqrt{3 - 4x^2}}\,dx = \frac{1}{2}\int \frac{1}{\sqrt{\frac{3}{4} - x^2}}\,dx = \frac{1}{2}\arcsin\frac{2x}{\sqrt{3}} + c$

6 a $2\left(\arctan 3 - \dfrac{\pi}{4}\right)$

  b $\dfrac{3}{2}\ln\left(\dfrac{4 + \sqrt{17}}{2 + \sqrt{5}}\right)$

  c $\dfrac{\sqrt{3}}{3}\left(\arcsin\dfrac{1}{\sqrt{7}} + \arcsin\dfrac{2}{\sqrt{7}}\right)$

7 $\displaystyle\int_{\sqrt{2}}^{\sqrt{3}} \frac{1}{\sqrt{4 - x^2}}\,dx = \left[\arcsin\frac{x}{2}\right]_{\sqrt{2}}^{\sqrt{3}}$

    $= \arcsin\dfrac{\sqrt{3}}{2} - \arcsin\dfrac{\sqrt{2}}{2} = \dfrac{\pi}{3} - \dfrac{\pi}{4} = \dfrac{\pi}{12}$

8 $\displaystyle\int \frac{2 + 3x}{1 + 3x^2}\,dx = \int \frac{2}{1 + 3x^2}\,dx + \int \frac{3x}{1 + 3x^2}\,dx$

    $= \dfrac{2}{3}\displaystyle\int \frac{2}{\frac{1}{3} + x^2}\,dx + \frac{1}{2}\int \frac{1}{u}\,du$

    $= \dfrac{2\sqrt{3}}{3}\arctan(\sqrt{3}x) + \dfrac{1}{2}\ln(1 + 3x^2) + c$

9 $-\arcsin\dfrac{x}{\sqrt{2}} - 2\sqrt{2 - x^2} + c$

10 $4\ln(x^2 + 4) - \dfrac{3}{2}\arctan\dfrac{x}{2} + c$

11 $\displaystyle\int f(x)\,dx = \int \frac{4x}{\sqrt{6 - 5x^2}}\,dx - \int \frac{1}{\sqrt{6 - 5x^2}}\,dx$

    $= -\dfrac{2}{5}\displaystyle\int u^{-\frac{1}{2}}\,du - \frac{1}{\sqrt{5}}\int \frac{1}{\sqrt{\frac{6}{5} - x^2}}\,dx$

    $= -\dfrac{4}{5}\sqrt{6 - 5x^2} - \dfrac{1}{\sqrt{5}}\arcsin\left(\sqrt{\dfrac{5}{6}}x\right) + c$

12 a $\dfrac{1}{2}\ln(x^2 + 16) + \dfrac{5}{4}\arctan\dfrac{x}{4} + c$

  b $\dfrac{1}{4}\displaystyle\int_0^4 \frac{x + 5}{x^2 + 16}\,dx = \frac{1}{4}\left[\frac{1}{2}\ln(x^2 + 16) + \frac{5}{4}\arctan\frac{x}{4}\right]_0^4$

    $= \dfrac{1}{4}\left(\dfrac{1}{2}\ln 2 + \dfrac{5\pi}{16}\right)$

  c $-\dfrac{1}{2}\ln 2 - \dfrac{5\pi}{16}$

13 $\dfrac{x}{9} - \dfrac{2}{27}\arctan\dfrac{3x}{2} + c$

14 $\displaystyle\int_0^{\frac{1}{4}} \frac{x^2}{\sqrt{1 - 4x^2}}\,dx = \int_0^{\frac{\pi}{6}} \frac{1}{8}\sin^2\theta\,d\theta$

    $= \dfrac{1}{16}\displaystyle\int_0^{\frac{\pi}{6}} (1 + \cos 2\theta)\,d\theta = \frac{1}{16}\left[x + \frac{1}{2}\sin 2x\right]_0^{\frac{\pi}{6}}$

    $= \dfrac{1}{16}\left(\dfrac{\pi}{6} + \dfrac{\sqrt{3}}{4}\right) = \dfrac{1}{192}(2\pi - 3\sqrt{3})$

Challenge

a arcsec$x + c$

b $\sqrt{x^2 - 1} - \text{arcsec}\,x + c$

Exercise 3E

1 a $\dfrac{3 - x}{10(x^2 + 1)} + \dfrac{1}{10(x + 3)}$

  b $-\dfrac{x + 1}{3(x^2 + 2)} + \dfrac{1}{3(x - 1)}$

  c $\dfrac{4x + 7}{7(x^2 + 7)} - \dfrac{4}{7x}$

2 $\ln|x + 2| - \sqrt{\dfrac{3}{2}}\arctan\dfrac{x}{\sqrt{6}} + c$

3 a $(x + 2)(x - 3)(x^2 + 2)$

  b $\ln\dfrac{|x + 2|^4}{|x - 3|^3} - \sqrt{2}\arctan\left(\dfrac{x}{\sqrt{2}}\right) + c$

4 $\dfrac{1}{4}\ln\left(\dfrac{x^2}{x^2 + 4}\right) - \dfrac{1}{2}\arctan\dfrac{x}{2} + c$

5 $-\dfrac{6}{54x} + \dfrac{5}{54}\arctan\dfrac{2x}{3} + c$

6 $\displaystyle\int \frac{x^3 + 9x^2 + x + 1}{x^4 - 1}\,dx = \int \frac{3}{x - 1}\,dx - \int \frac{2}{x + 1}\,dx + \int \frac{4}{x^2 + 1}\,dx$

    $= 3\ln|x - 1| - 2\ln|x + 1| + 4\arctan x + c$

    $= \ln\dfrac{|x - 1|^3}{|x + 1|^2} + 4\arctan x + c$

7 a $(x - 4)(x^2 + 6)$ **b** $\dfrac{2}{x - 4} - \dfrac{3}{x^2 + 6}$

  c $2\ln|x - 4| - \sqrt{\dfrac{3}{2}}\arctan\dfrac{x}{\sqrt{6}} + c$

8 a $\dfrac{1}{3}\ln\left|\dfrac{x - 2}{2x - 1}\right| + c$

  b Split $\displaystyle\int_{\frac{1}{2}}^2 \frac{1}{(x - 2)(2x - 1)}\,dx$ up as

    $\displaystyle\int_{\frac{1}{2}}^1 \frac{1}{(x - 2)(2x - 1)}\,dx + \int_1^2 \frac{1}{(x - 2)(2x - 1)}\,dx$ and show the second integral diverges.

    $\displaystyle\int_1^2 \frac{1}{(x - 2)(2x - 1)}\,dx = \lim_{t \to 2}\int_1^t \frac{1}{(x - 2)(2x - 1)}\,dx$

    $= \left[\dfrac{1}{3}\ln\left|\dfrac{x - 2}{2x - 1}\right|\right]_1^t = \lim_{t \to 2}\left(\dfrac{1}{3}\ln\left|\dfrac{t - 2}{2t - 1}\right|\right) + \dfrac{1}{3}\ln 1$

    and $\ln\left|\dfrac{t - 2}{2t - 1}\right| \to -\infty$ as $t \to 2$, so the integral diverges

9 a $-\dfrac{x + 3}{x^2 + 6} + \dfrac{x - 2}{x^2 + 4} + 1$

  b $\dfrac{1}{2}\ln\left(\dfrac{x^2 + 4}{x^2 + 6}\right) + x - \arctan\dfrac{x}{2} - \sqrt{\dfrac{3}{2}}\arctan\dfrac{x}{\sqrt{6}} + c$

10 $\dfrac{1}{2}\ln\left(\dfrac{x^4}{x^2 + 5}\right) + \dfrac{4}{\sqrt{5}}\arctan\dfrac{x}{\sqrt{5}} + c$

11 $\dfrac{2}{(x + 1)(x^2 + 1)} = \dfrac{1 - x}{x^2 + 1} + \dfrac{1}{x + 1}$ in partial fractions.

  So, $\displaystyle\int_0^1 \frac{2}{(x + 1)(x^2 + 1)}\,dx$

    $= \displaystyle\int_0^1 \frac{1}{x^2 + 1}\,dx - \int_0^1 \frac{x}{x^2 + 1}\,dx + \int_0^1 \frac{1}{x + 1}\,dx$

    $= \left[\arctan x - \dfrac{1}{2}\ln(x^2 + 1) + \ln|x + 1|\right]_0^1 = \dfrac{\pi}{4} - \dfrac{1}{2}\ln 2 + \ln 2$

    $= \dfrac{1}{4}(\pi + 2\ln 2)$

Online Full worked solutions are available in SolutionBank.

12 a $\dfrac{3x}{4(x^2+2)} - \dfrac{5x}{2(x^2+2)^2} + \dfrac{1}{4x}$

b $\dfrac{1}{8}\left(\dfrac{10}{x^2+2} + 3\ln(x^2+2) + 2\ln|x|\right) + c$

Challenge

a $\dfrac{1}{4\sqrt2}\ln\left|\dfrac{x-4-2\sqrt2}{x-4+2\sqrt2}\right| + c$ **b** $\dfrac{1}{3\sqrt2}\arctan\dfrac{\sqrt2(x+1)}{3} + c$

Mixed exercise 3

1 a $\arctan e^x + c$

b Split $\displaystyle\int_{-\infty}^{\infty}\dfrac{1}{e^x+e^{-x}}\,dx$ up as

$\displaystyle\int_{-\infty}^{0}\dfrac{1}{e^x+e^{-x}}\,dx + \int_{0}^{\infty}\dfrac{1}{e^x+e^{-x}}\,dx$.

$\displaystyle\int_{-\infty}^{0}\dfrac{1}{e^x+e^{-x}}\,dx = \lim_{t\to-\infty}\int_{t}^{0}\dfrac{1}{e^x+e^{-x}}\,dx = \lim_{t\to-\infty}[\arctan e^x]_t^0$

$= \displaystyle\lim_{t\to-\infty}\left(\dfrac{\pi}{4} - \arctan e^t\right) = \dfrac{\pi}{4} - \arctan 0 = \dfrac{\pi}{4}$

Similarly $\displaystyle\int_{0}^{\infty}\dfrac{1}{e^x+e^{-x}}\,dx = \dfrac{\pi}{4}$, so $\displaystyle\int_{-\infty}^{\infty}\dfrac{1}{e^x+e^{-x}}\,dx = \dfrac{\pi}{2}$

2 $\dfrac{6}{\pi}\left(\dfrac{4}{\sqrt3} - 2\right)$

3 $\dfrac{2}{\pi}\displaystyle\int_{0}^{\frac{\pi}{2}} x\sin 2x\,dx = \dfrac{2}{\pi}\left[\dfrac{1}{4}(\sin 2x - 2x\cos 2x)\right]_0^{\frac{\pi}{2}} = \dfrac{1}{2}$

4 a $-\dfrac{2x}{\sqrt{1-x^4}}$ **b** $-\dfrac{3}{2}\arccos\dfrac{x^2}{4} + c$

5 a $f'(x) = \dfrac{1}{\left(\dfrac{2x+3}{x-1}\right)^2+1} \times \dfrac{-5}{(x-1)^2} = \dfrac{-5}{(2x+3)^2+(x-1)^2}$

$= -\dfrac{5}{5x^2+10x+10} = -\dfrac{1}{x^2+2x+2}$

b $x^2+2x+2 = (x+1)^2+1 \geqslant 1$,

so $|f'(x)| = \left|\dfrac{1}{x^2+2x+2}\right| \leqslant 1$

6 a We say an integral $\displaystyle\int_a^b f(x)\,dx$ is improper if one or both of the limits are infinite or if $f(x)$ is undefined at some point in $[a, b]$

b It in undefined at $x = 0$ and has upper limit ∞

c π

7 $-\sqrt{1-5x^2} + \dfrac{1}{\sqrt5}\arcsin\sqrt5 x + c$

8 a Use the substitution $x = \tan\theta$ and identify $\sec^2\theta \equiv 1 + \tan^2\theta$ so that the integral becomes

$\displaystyle\int_0^{\arctan t} 1\,d\theta = \arctan\theta$

b i $\dfrac{\pi}{2}$ **ii** π

9 a $\dfrac{1}{4}\ln(1+4x^2) + \dfrac{1}{2}\arctan 2x + c$

b $\dfrac{1}{8}(\pi + 2\ln 2)$

10 a $\displaystyle\int\dfrac{1}{\sqrt{4-9x^2}}\,dx = \dfrac{1}{3}\int\dfrac{1}{\sqrt{\frac{4}{9}-x^2}}\,dx = \dfrac{1}{3}\arcsin\left(\dfrac{3}{2}x\right) + c$

b $\displaystyle\int_0^{\frac{2}{3}}\dfrac{1}{\sqrt{4-9x^2}}\,dx = \left[\dfrac{1}{3}\arcsin\dfrac{3x}{2}\right]_0^{\frac{2}{3}} = \dfrac{\pi}{6}$

11 $\displaystyle\int_0^{\frac{1}{2}}\dfrac{x^4}{\sqrt{1-x^2}}\,dx = \int_0^{\frac{\pi}{6}}\sin^4\theta\,d\theta = \int_0^{\frac{\pi}{6}}\dfrac{1}{8}(3 - 4\cos 2x + \cos 4x)\,dx$

$= \dfrac{1}{8}\left[3x - 2\sin 2x + \dfrac{1}{4}\sin 4x\right]_0^{\frac{\pi}{6}} = \dfrac{1}{64}(4\pi - 7\sqrt3)$.

Here we know $\sin^4 x = \dfrac{1}{8}(3 - 4\cos 2x + \cos 4x)$ by de Moivre's theorem or by using the formula for $\sin^2 x$ twice.

12 a $\dfrac{\pi}{8}$

b $\displaystyle\int_0^{\infty} f(x)\,dx = \lim_{t\to\infty}\left[\dfrac{1}{2}\arctan x^2\right]_0^t = \lim_{t\to\infty}\left(\dfrac{1}{2}\arctan t^2 - 0\right) = \dfrac{\pi}{4}$

13 $\displaystyle\int f(x)\,dx = \int\dfrac{2}{x}\,dx + \int\dfrac{1}{x^2}\,dx - \int\dfrac{3}{x^2+9}\,dx$

$= 2\ln|x| - \dfrac{1}{x} - \arctan\left(\dfrac{x}{3}\right) + c$

14 a $\dfrac{1}{x-4} - \dfrac{3}{x^2+2}$ **b** $\ln|x-4| - \dfrac{3}{\sqrt2}\arctan\dfrac{x}{\sqrt2} + c$

c Split $\displaystyle\int_4^{\infty} f(x)\,dx$ up as $\displaystyle\int_4^5 f(x)\,dx + \int_5^{\infty} f(x)\,dx$ and show the first integral diverges.

$\displaystyle\int_4^5 f(x)\,dx = \lim_{t\to 4}\int_t^5 f(x)\,dx$

$= \displaystyle\lim_{t\to 4}\left(\ln|t-4| - \dfrac{3}{\sqrt2}\left(\arctan\dfrac{t}{\sqrt2} + \arctan\dfrac{5}{\sqrt2}\right)\right)$

and $\ln|t-4| \to -\infty$ as $t \to 4$, so the integral diverges

15 a $\ln\left|\dfrac{x^2}{x^2+1}\right| + c$

b $\displaystyle\int_1^2\dfrac{2}{x^3+x}\,dx = \left[\ln\left|\dfrac{x^2}{x^2+1}\right|\right]_1^2 = \ln\dfrac{8}{5}$

c $-2\ln 5$

Challenge

a $\dfrac{1}{2}\displaystyle\int_0^2 f(x)\,dx = \dfrac{1}{2}\left[\dfrac{1}{4}x^4 - x^2 + 4x\right]_0^2 = \dfrac{8}{2} = 4$

$f(c) = c^3 - 2c + 4 = 4 \Rightarrow c = 0$ or $c = \sqrt2$

b One example is $f(x) = 0$ for $x \leqslant 1$ and $f(x) = 1$ for $x > 1$. This has mean value $\dfrac{1}{2}$ on $[0,2]$ but the function only attains the values 0 and 1.

CHAPTER 4
Prior knowledge check

1 a $15\,633$ **b** $\dfrac{\pi}{6} - \dfrac{\sqrt3}{8}$ **c** $\dfrac{1-13e^{-4}}{4}$

2 1.41 (3 s.f.)

3 $\dfrac{59\,566\pi}{15}$

Exercise 4A

1 a $\dfrac{8\pi}{3}$ **b** $4\pi\ln 2$ **c** $\dfrac{\pi}{4}(\pi - \ln 4)$

d $\dfrac{\pi}{4}\ln 41$ **e** $\dfrac{\pi}{2}(1 - \ln 2)$ **f** $\pi\left(2\sqrt3 - 2 - \dfrac{\pi}{6}\right)$

2 $\dfrac{\pi}{2}$

3 $\pi(3(\ln 3)^2 - 6\ln 3 + 4)$

4 a $\dfrac{1}{9}(\sqrt3 - 1)$ **b** $9\pi(\sqrt3 - 1)$

5 $\pi\ln 14$

6 a $x = 0$ or $\sin x + 1 = 0 \Rightarrow x = 0$ or $\dfrac{3\pi}{2}$

b $\dfrac{\pi}{2}\left(\dfrac{9\pi^2}{8} - 1\right)$

7 a $\dfrac{100\pi}{81}$ **b** $\dfrac{100\pi}{27}$

8 0.237 (3 s.f.)

Challenge

$\pi\displaystyle\int_{\frac{\pi}{4}}^{\frac{3\pi}{4}}\left(\sin x - \dfrac{1}{\sqrt2}\right)^2 dx = \pi\int_{\frac{\pi}{4}}^{\frac{3\pi}{4}}\left(\dfrac{1}{2} - \dfrac{1}{2}\cos 2x - \sqrt2\sin x + \dfrac{1}{2}\right)dx$

$= \pi\left[x - \dfrac{1}{4}\sin 2x + \sqrt2\cos x\right]_{\frac{\pi}{4}}^{\frac{3\pi}{4}} = \dfrac{\pi}{2}(\pi - 3)$

Exercise 4B

1 a $\pi\left(\frac{1}{4}e^4 - 2e - \frac{1}{2}e^{-2} + \frac{9}{4}\right)$ **b** $\frac{1}{4}\pi(e^2 - 1)$

   c $\frac{\pi}{5}(\ln 5 + 16)$ **d** $\pi\ln\frac{9}{4}$

2 a $\frac{1}{2}\pi$ **b** $\pi(2 + 3\ln 3)$

   c $\pi(4\ln 2 - 2)$ **d** $\frac{3\pi^2}{16}$

3 $b = \frac{13}{4}$

4 a π **b** $\frac{\pi^3}{4}$

5 $\pi\left(\frac{3}{2}e^{\frac{10}{3}} + 6e^{\frac{5}{3}} - \frac{5}{2}\right)$

6 a $2\cos\left(y - \frac{\pi}{3}\right)$

   b $\pi\int_0^{\frac{\pi}{3}} \frac{1}{4}\sec^2\left(y - \frac{\pi}{3}\right)dy = \frac{\pi}{4}\left(\tan 0 - \tan\left(-\frac{\pi}{3}\right)\right) = \frac{\pi\sqrt{3}}{4}$

7 a $\frac{1}{6\ln 2}$ **b** $\frac{\pi}{6\ln 2}$

8 a By de Moivre's theorem,
$$\sin 3\theta = 3\cos^2\theta\sin\theta - \sin^3\theta = 3\sin\theta - 4\sin^3\theta$$
$$\sin 5\theta = 5\cos^4\theta\sin\theta - 10\cos^2\theta\sin^3\theta + \sin^5\theta$$
$$= 5\sin\theta - 20\sin^3\theta + 16\sin^5\theta$$
$$= 5\sin\theta - 5(3\sin\theta - \sin 3\theta) + 16\sin^5\theta$$
$$= -10\sin\theta + 5\sin 3\theta + 16\sin 5\theta$$
$$\Rightarrow \sin^5\theta = \frac{1}{16}(10\sin\theta - 5\sin 3\theta + \sin 5\theta)$$

   b $\pi\int_{\frac{\pi}{4}}^{\pi}\sin^5 y\,dy = \frac{\pi}{16}\int_{\frac{\pi}{4}}^{\pi}(10\sin y - 5\sin 3y + \sin 5y)\,dy$

$$= \frac{\pi}{16}\left[-10\cos y + \frac{5}{3}\cos 3y - \frac{1}{5}\cos 5y\right]_{\frac{\pi}{4}}^{\pi}$$

$$= \frac{\pi}{15}\left(8 + \frac{43\sqrt{2}}{8}\right)$$

Exercise 4C

1 $\frac{384\pi}{7}$

2 a $2, 3$

   b πe^3

   c $\ln x = t \Rightarrow y^2 = t - 1 = \ln x - 1$

   d πe^3

3 a $x^2 = 1 - \sin\theta \Rightarrow \sin\theta = 1 - x^2$,
     $y^2 = \cos^2\theta = 1 - \sin^2\theta = 1 - (1 - x^2)^2 = 2x^2 - x^4$

   b $(\sqrt{2}, 0)$

   c $\pi\left(\frac{8}{15}\sqrt{2}\right)$

4 a $0, \frac{\pi}{3}$ **b** $\frac{58\pi}{5}$

   c $\tan^2\theta = x^2$, $\sec^2\theta = y^{\frac{2}{3}}$
     so $\tan^2\theta \equiv \sec^2\theta - 1 \Rightarrow x^2 = y^{\frac{2}{3}} - 1$

   d $V = \pi\int_1^8 (y^{\frac{2}{3}} - 1)\,dy = \pi\left[\frac{3}{5}y^{\frac{5}{3}} - y\right]_1^8 = \frac{58\pi}{5}$

5 $\frac{1}{10}\pi$

6 $\pi\int_0^2 x^2\frac{dy}{dt}dt = \pi\int_0^2 4t^2 \times 2t\,dt = 8\pi\int_0^2 t^3\,dt = 32\pi$

7 a $\frac{1}{4}\sin 2\theta + \frac{1}{2}\theta + c$

   b $y = 4\sin 2\theta = 8\sin\theta\cos\theta \Rightarrow y^2 = 64\sin^2\theta\cos^2\theta$

     $\frac{dx}{d\theta} = -\text{cosec}^2\theta$

     $x = \frac{1}{\sqrt{3}} \Rightarrow \theta = \frac{\pi}{3}$, $x = \sqrt{3} \Rightarrow \theta = \frac{\pi}{6}$

     $\pi\int_{\frac{\pi}{3}}^{\frac{\pi}{6}} y^2\,dx/d\theta\,d\theta = -64\pi\int_{\frac{\pi}{3}}^{\frac{\pi}{6}}\cos^2\theta\,d\theta$

   c $\frac{16}{3}\pi^2$

8 $\ln 7$

9 $2\pi^3$

10 $\frac{4\pi}{5}$

11 a $\pi\ln 6$ **b** $\pi\left(\ln 6 - \frac{2}{3}\right)$

Exercise 4D

1 a $200\,\text{m}$ **b** $\frac{1\,200\,000\pi}{7}\,\text{m}^3$

2 $5\pi\ln 4001\,\text{cm}^3$

3 a $\cos 3\theta$
$$= \cos(2\theta + \theta)$$
$$= \cos 2\theta\cos\theta - \sin 2\theta\sin\theta$$
$$= (\cos^2\theta - \sin^2\theta)\cos\theta - 2\sin^2\theta\cos\theta$$
$$= \cos^3\theta - (1 - \cos^2\theta)\cos\theta - 2(1 - \cos^2\theta)\cos\theta$$
$$= 2\cos^3\theta - \cos\theta + \cos^3\theta - 2\cos\theta$$
$$= 4\cos^3\theta - 3\cos\theta$$
$$\Rightarrow \cos^3\theta = \frac{3}{4}\cos\theta + \frac{1}{4}\cos 3\theta$$

   b $50\,000\pi\,\text{m}^3$

4 a $\frac{\pi}{2}$ **b** $864\pi\,\text{m}^3$

5 a $x^2 = 16\sin^2\theta\cos^2\theta = 16\sin^2\theta(1 - \sin^2\theta)$
$$= 16\left(\frac{y}{3}\right)^2\left(1 - \left(\frac{y}{3}\right)^2\right) = \frac{16}{81}y^2(9 - y^2)$$

   b 14

   c i e.g. Patterned earring may mean that earring requires less material

     ii e.g. Wasted material upon transfer to mould

Mixed exercise 4

1 a $\frac{1}{2}x\sin 2x + \frac{1}{4}\cos 2x + c$ **b** $\pi\left(\frac{\pi^2}{4} + 1\right)$

2 a Use integration by parts with $u = x$ and $\frac{dv}{dx} = \sec^2 x$
     to get $\pi\int_0^{\frac{\pi}{4}} x\sec^2 x\,dx = \pi[x\tan x + \ln\cos x]_0^{\frac{\pi}{4}}$
$$= \pi\left(\frac{\pi}{4} - \frac{1}{2}\ln 2\right)$$

   b $\pi\left(\frac{\pi}{4} - \frac{1}{2}\ln 2\right)$

3 $\pi\left(4\ln\frac{5}{2} - \frac{3}{5}\right)$

4 $\frac{\pi}{4}(10 - 3\pi)$

5 $\pi(e^4 - 9e^2 + 8e + 8)$

6 a $y = -x + \frac{5}{2}$ **b** $\frac{113\pi}{120}$

7 a $\frac{172}{5}$ **b** $\frac{5584}{35}\pi$

8 $\pi\int_{-1}^1 x^2\,dy = \pi\int_{-\frac{\pi}{2}}^{\frac{\pi}{2}}\cos^3 t\,dt = \pi\int_{-\frac{\pi}{2}}^{\frac{\pi}{2}}\cos t(1 - \sin^2 t)\,dt$
   Using the substitution $u = \sin t$, this becomes
   $\pi\int_{-1}^1 (1 - u^2)\,du = \frac{4\pi}{3}$

9 a $\sin 3\theta = \sin(2\theta + \theta)$
$$= \sin 2\theta\cos\theta + \cos 2\theta\sin\theta$$
$$= (2\sin\theta\cos\theta)\cos\theta + (1 - 2\sin^2\theta)\sin\theta$$
$$= 2\sin\theta\cos^2\theta + \sin\theta - 2\sin^3\theta$$
$$= 2\sin\theta(1 - \sin^2\theta) + \sin\theta - 2\sin^3\theta$$
$$= 2\sin\theta - 2\sin^3\theta + \sin\theta - 2\sin^3\theta$$
$$= 3\sin\theta - 4\sin^3\theta$$
$$\Rightarrow \sin^3\theta = \frac{3}{4}\sin\theta - \frac{1}{4}\sin 3\theta$$

   b 2000π

10 $\frac{128\pi}{15}$

Online Full worked solutions are available in SolutionBank.

Challenge

Rotate C by $-\dfrac{\pi}{4}$ anticlockwise to the x-axis using the matrix

$$\begin{pmatrix} \cos\left(-\frac{\pi}{4}\right) & -\sin\left(-\frac{\pi}{4}\right) \\ \sin\left(-\frac{\pi}{4}\right) & \cos\left(-\frac{\pi}{4}\right) \end{pmatrix} = \begin{pmatrix} \frac{1}{\sqrt{2}} & \frac{1}{\sqrt{2}} \\ -\frac{1}{\sqrt{2}} & \frac{1}{\sqrt{2}} \end{pmatrix}$$

$$\begin{pmatrix} \frac{1}{\sqrt{2}} & \frac{1}{\sqrt{2}} \\ -\frac{1}{\sqrt{2}} & \frac{1}{\sqrt{2}} \end{pmatrix}\begin{pmatrix} t^2 \\ 2t \end{pmatrix} = \frac{1}{\sqrt{2}}\begin{pmatrix} t^2 + 2t \\ -t^2 + 2t \end{pmatrix}$$

So new parametric equations become

$x = \dfrac{1}{\sqrt{2}}(t^2 + 2t)$ and $y = \dfrac{1}{\sqrt{2}}(-t^2 + 2t)$

$y = 0 \Rightarrow \dfrac{1}{\sqrt{2}}(-t^2 + 2t) = 0 \Rightarrow t = 0, 2$

$V = \pi \displaystyle\int_0^2 \left(\dfrac{1}{\sqrt{2}}(-t^2 + 2t)\right)^2 \dfrac{\mathrm{d}x}{\mathrm{d}t}\,\mathrm{d}t$

$= \pi \displaystyle\int_0^2 \left(\dfrac{1}{\sqrt{2}}(-t^2 + 2t)\right)^2 \left(\dfrac{1}{\sqrt{2}}(2t + 2)\right)\mathrm{d}t$

$= \dfrac{\pi}{\sqrt{2}}\displaystyle\int_0^2 (t^5 - 3t^4 + 4t^2)\,\mathrm{d}t = \dfrac{\pi}{\sqrt{2}}\left[\dfrac{t^6}{6} - \dfrac{3t^5}{5} + \dfrac{4t^3}{3}\right]_0^2$

$= \dfrac{\pi}{\sqrt{2}}\left(\dfrac{32}{3} - \dfrac{96}{5} + \dfrac{16}{3}\right) - 0 = \dfrac{32\pi}{15\sqrt{2}}$

Review exercise 1

1 $\dfrac{\cos 2x + \mathrm{i}\sin 2x}{\cos 9x - \mathrm{i}\sin 9x} = \dfrac{\cos 2x + \mathrm{i}\sin 2x}{\cos(-9x) + \mathrm{i}\sin(-9x)}$

$= \dfrac{\mathrm{e}^{2x\mathrm{i}}}{\mathrm{e}^{-9x\mathrm{i}}} = \mathrm{e}^{11x\mathrm{i}} = \cos 11x + \mathrm{i}\sin 11x$

Hence $n = 11$

2 a $\cos 5\theta + \mathrm{i}\sin 5\theta = (\cos\theta + \mathrm{i}\sin\theta)^5$
$= \cos^5\theta + 5\mathrm{i}\cos^4\theta\sin\theta - 10\cos^3\theta\sin^2\theta$
$\quad - 10\mathrm{i}\cos^2\theta\sin^3\theta + 5\cos\theta\sin^4\theta + \mathrm{i}\sin^5\theta$
Equating real parts:
$\cos 5\theta = \cos^5\theta - 10\cos^3\theta\sin^2\theta + 5\cos\theta\sin^4\theta$
$= \cos^5\theta - 10\cos^3\theta(1 - \cos^2\theta) + 5\cos\theta(1 - \cos^2\theta)^2$
$= 16\cos^5\theta - 20\cos^3\theta + 5\cos\theta$

b $x = 0.809, -0.309, -1$

3 a $\cos 5\theta + \mathrm{i}\sin 5\theta = (\cos\theta + \mathrm{i}\sin\theta)^5$
$= \cos^5\theta + 5\mathrm{i}\cos^4\theta\sin\theta - 10\cos^3\theta\sin^2\theta$
$\quad - 10\mathrm{i}\cos^2\theta\sin^3\theta + 5\cos\theta\sin^4\theta + \mathrm{i}\sin^5\theta$
Equating imaginary parts:
$\sin 5\theta = 5\cos^4\theta\sin\theta - 10\cos^2\theta\sin^3\theta + \sin^5\theta$
$= \sin\theta(5\cos^4\theta - 10\cos^2\theta\sin^2\theta + \sin^4\theta)$
$= \sin\theta(5\cos^4\theta - 10\cos^2\theta(1 - \cos^2\theta) + (1 - \cos^2\theta)^2)$
$= \sin\theta(16\cos^4\theta - 12\cos^2\theta + 1)$

b $0, \dfrac{\pi}{4}, \dfrac{3\pi}{4}$, 1.209 (3 d.p.) and 1.932 (3 d.p)

4 a $\sin\theta = \dfrac{\mathrm{e}^{\mathrm{i}\theta} - \mathrm{e}^{-\mathrm{i}\theta}}{2\mathrm{i}}$, if $z = \mathrm{e}^{\mathrm{i}\theta}$, then $\sin\theta = \dfrac{z - z^{-1}}{2\mathrm{i}}$

$\sin^5\theta = \left(\dfrac{z - z^{-1}}{2\mathrm{i}}\right)^5$

$= \dfrac{1}{32\mathrm{i}}(z^5 - 5z^3 + 10z - 10z^{-1} + 5z^{-3} - z^{-5})$

$= \dfrac{1}{16}\left(\dfrac{z^5 - z^{-5}}{2\mathrm{i}} - \dfrac{5(z^3 - z^{-3})}{2\mathrm{i}} + \dfrac{10(z - z^{-1})}{2\mathrm{i}}\right)$

$= \dfrac{1}{16}(\sin 5\theta - 5\sin 3\theta + 10\sin\theta)$

b $\displaystyle\int_0^{\frac{\pi}{2}} \sin^5\theta\,\mathrm{d}\theta = \dfrac{1}{16}\displaystyle\int_0^{\frac{\pi}{2}}(\sin 5\theta - 5\sin 3\theta + 10\sin\theta)\mathrm{d}\theta$

$= \dfrac{1}{16}\left[-\dfrac{1}{5}\cos 5\theta + \dfrac{5}{3}\cos 3\theta - 10\cos\theta\right]_0^{\frac{\pi}{2}}$

$= \dfrac{1}{16}\left(0 - \left(-\dfrac{1}{5} + \dfrac{5}{3} - 10\right)\right) = \dfrac{8}{15}$

5 a $z^{-n} = \cos(-n\theta) + \mathrm{i}\sin(-n\theta) = \cos n\theta - \mathrm{i}\sin n\theta$
$z^n + z^{-n} = \cos n\theta + \mathrm{i}\sin n\theta + \cos n\theta - \mathrm{i}\sin n\theta = 2\cos n\theta$

b $\dfrac{1}{32}(\cos 6\theta + 6\cos 4\theta + 15\cos 2\theta + 10)$

c $\displaystyle\int_0^{\frac{\pi}{2}} \cos^6\theta\,\mathrm{d}\theta$

$= \dfrac{1}{32}\displaystyle\int_0^{\frac{\pi}{2}}(\cos 6\theta + 6\cos 4\theta + 15\cos 2\theta + 10)\mathrm{d}\theta$

$= \dfrac{1}{32}\left[\dfrac{1}{6}\sin 6\theta + \dfrac{6}{4}\sin 4\theta + \dfrac{15}{2}\sin 2\theta + 10\theta\right]_0^{\frac{\pi}{2}}$

$= \dfrac{1}{32}(5\pi - 0) = \dfrac{5\pi}{32}$

6 $C + \mathrm{i}S$

$= 1 + (\cos\theta + \mathrm{i}\sin\theta) + (\cos 2\theta + \mathrm{i}\sin 2\theta) + \dots$
$\quad + (\cos(n-1)\theta + \mathrm{i}\sin(n-1)\theta)$

$= \mathrm{e}^0 + \mathrm{e}^{\mathrm{i}\theta} + \mathrm{e}^{2\mathrm{i}\theta} + \dots + \mathrm{e}^{\mathrm{i}(n-1)\theta}$

Using the sum of a geometric series $S_n = \dfrac{a(1 - r^n)}{1 - r}$ and

$\cos\theta = \dfrac{\mathrm{e}^{\mathrm{i}\theta} + \mathrm{e}^{-\mathrm{i}\theta}}{2}$,

$C + \mathrm{i}S = \dfrac{1 - \mathrm{e}^{\mathrm{i}n\theta}}{1 - \mathrm{e}^{\mathrm{i}\theta}} = \dfrac{(1 - \mathrm{e}^{\mathrm{i}n\theta})(1 - \mathrm{e}^{-\mathrm{i}\theta})}{(1 - \mathrm{e}^{\mathrm{i}\theta})(1 - \mathrm{e}^{-\mathrm{i}\theta})}$

$= \dfrac{1 - \mathrm{e}^{\mathrm{i}n\theta} - \mathrm{e}^{-\mathrm{i}\theta} + \mathrm{e}^{\mathrm{i}(n-1)\theta}}{1 - \mathrm{e}^{\mathrm{i}\theta} - \mathrm{e}^{-\mathrm{i}\theta} + 1} = \dfrac{1 - \mathrm{e}^{\mathrm{i}n\theta} - \mathrm{e}^{-\mathrm{i}\theta} + \mathrm{e}^{\mathrm{i}(n-1)\theta}}{2 - 2\cos\theta}$

Equating real parts and using $\cos(-\theta) = \cos\theta$,

$C = \dfrac{1 - \cos n\theta - \cos(-\theta) + \cos(n-1)\theta}{2 - 2\cos\theta}$

$= \dfrac{1 - \cos\theta + \cos(n-1)\theta - \cos n\theta}{2 - 2\cos\theta}$

Equating imaginary parts and using $\sin(-\theta) = -\sin\theta$,

$S = \dfrac{-\sin n\theta - \sin(-\theta) + \sin(n-1)\theta}{2 - 2\cos\theta}$

$= \dfrac{\sin\theta + \sin(n-1)\theta - \sin n\theta}{2 - 2\cos\theta}$

7 a $z = \sqrt{2}\mathrm{e}^{\frac{\pi\mathrm{i}}{20}}, \sqrt{2}\mathrm{e}^{\frac{9\pi\mathrm{i}}{20}}, \sqrt{2}\mathrm{e}^{\frac{17\pi\mathrm{i}}{20}}, \sqrt{2}\mathrm{e}^{-\frac{7\pi\mathrm{i}}{20}}, \sqrt{2}\mathrm{e}^{-\frac{3\pi\mathrm{i}}{4}}$

b
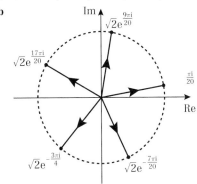

8 a $z = 4\mathrm{e}^{\mathrm{i}\frac{\pi}{9}}, 4\mathrm{e}^{\mathrm{i}\frac{7\pi}{9}}, 4\mathrm{e}^{-\mathrm{i}\frac{5\pi}{9}}$

b $z^9 = \left(4e^{i\frac{\pi}{9}}\right)^9, \left(4e^{i\frac{7\pi}{9}}\right)^9, \left(4e^{-i\frac{5\pi}{9}}\right)^9$

$= 4^9 e^{i\pi}, 4^9 e^{7i\pi}, 4^9 e^{-5i\pi}$

The value of all three of these expressions is
$-4^9 = -2^{18}$

Hence the solutions satisfy $z^9 + 2^k = 0$, where $k = 18$.

9 $z = \cos\theta + i\sin\theta$, where

$\theta = \dfrac{\pi}{10}, \dfrac{5\pi}{10}\left(=\dfrac{\pi}{2}\right), \dfrac{9\pi}{10}, -\dfrac{3\pi}{10}, -\dfrac{7\pi}{10}$

10 a $2e^{\frac{\pi i}{15}}, 2e^{\frac{7\pi i}{15}}, 2e^{\frac{13\pi i}{15}}, 2e^{-\frac{\pi i}{15}}, 2e^{-\frac{11\pi i}{15}}$

b Vertices of a regular pentagon, inscribed in a circle radius 2, centred on the origin.

11 a $e^{-\frac{4\pi i}{5}}, e^{-\frac{2\pi i}{5}}, 1, e^{\frac{2\pi i}{5}}, e^{\frac{4\pi i}{5}}$

$e^{-\frac{4\pi i}{5}} + e^{-\frac{2\pi i}{5}} + 1 + e^{\frac{2\pi i}{5}} + e^{\frac{4\pi i}{5}}$

$= e^{-\frac{4\pi i}{5}}\left(1 + e^{\frac{2\pi i}{5}} + e^{\left(\frac{2\pi i}{5}\right)^2} + e^{\left(\frac{2\pi i}{5}\right)^3} + e^{\left(\frac{2\pi i}{5}\right)^4}\right)$

$= e^{-\frac{4\pi i}{5}}\left(\dfrac{e^{\frac{10\pi i}{5}} - 1}{e^{\frac{2\pi i}{5}} - 1}\right) = e^{-\frac{4\pi i}{5}}\left(\dfrac{e^{2\pi i} - 1}{e^{\frac{2\pi i}{5}} - 1}\right) = e^{-\frac{4\pi i}{5}} \times 0 = 0$

b $(3.26, 1.64), (1.78, 2.40), (0.60, 1.22), (1.36, -0.26)$

12 Using partial fractions,

$\dfrac{2}{(r+1)(r+2)} = \dfrac{2}{r+1} - \dfrac{2}{r+2}$

Using the method of differences,

$\displaystyle\sum_{r=1}^{n}\dfrac{2}{(r+1)(r+2)} = \sum_{r=1}^{n}\left(\dfrac{2}{r+1} - \dfrac{2}{r+2}\right) = \dfrac{2}{2} - \dfrac{2}{n+2}$

$= 1 - \dfrac{2}{n+2} = \dfrac{n+2-2}{n+2} = \dfrac{n}{n+2}$

13 Using partial fractions,

$\dfrac{4}{(r+1)(r+3)} = \dfrac{1}{r+1} - \dfrac{1}{r+3}$

Using the method of differences,

$\displaystyle\sum_{r=1}^{n}\dfrac{4}{(r+1)(r+3)} = \sum_{r=1}^{n}\left(\dfrac{2}{r+1} - \dfrac{2}{r+3}\right)$

$= \dfrac{2}{2} + \dfrac{4}{3} - \dfrac{2}{n+2} - \dfrac{2}{n+3} = \dfrac{5}{3} - \dfrac{2}{n+2} - \dfrac{2}{n+3}$

$= \dfrac{5(n+2)(n+3) - 3(n+3) - 6(n+2)}{3(n+2)(n+3)}$

$= \dfrac{5n^2 + 25n + 30 - 6n - 18 - 6n - 12}{3(n+2)(n+3)}$

$= \dfrac{5n^2 + 13n}{3(n+2)(n+3)} = \dfrac{n(5n+13)}{3(n+2)(n+3)}$

Hence, $a = 5, b = 13, c = 3$

14 a $\dfrac{r+1}{r+2} - \dfrac{r}{r+1} = \dfrac{(r+1)(r+1) - r(r+2)}{(r+1)(r+2)}$

$= \dfrac{r^2 + 2r + 1 - r^2 - 2r}{(r+1)(r+2)} = \dfrac{1}{(r+1)(r+2)}$

b $\dfrac{n}{2(n+2)}$

15 a $f(x) = \dfrac{1}{x+1} - \dfrac{2}{x+2} + \dfrac{1}{x+3}$

b $\dfrac{1}{6} - \dfrac{1}{n+2} + \dfrac{1}{n+3}$

16 a $\dfrac{2r-1}{r^2(r-1)^2}$

b Using the method of differences,

$\displaystyle\sum_{r=2}^{n}\dfrac{2r-1}{r^2(r-1)^2} = \sum_{r=2}^{n}\left(\dfrac{1}{(r-1)^2} - \dfrac{1}{r^2}\right) = \dfrac{1}{1^2} - \dfrac{1}{n^2} = 1 - \dfrac{1}{n^2}$

17 a Using partial fractions,

$\dfrac{4}{r(r+2)} = \dfrac{2}{r} - \dfrac{2}{r+2}$

Using the method of differences,

$\displaystyle\sum_{r=1}^{n}\dfrac{4}{r(r+2)} = \sum_{r=1}^{n}\left(\dfrac{2}{r} - \dfrac{2}{r+2}\right) = \dfrac{2}{1} + \dfrac{2}{2} - \dfrac{2}{n+1} - \dfrac{2}{n+2}$

$= 3 - \dfrac{2}{n+1} - \dfrac{2}{n+2}$

$= \dfrac{3(n+1)(n+2) - 2(n+2) - 2(n+1)}{(n+1)(n+2)}$

$= \dfrac{3n^2 + 9n + 6 - 2n - 4 - 2n - 2}{(n+1)(n+2)}$

$= \dfrac{3n^2 + 5n}{(n+1)(n+2)} = \dfrac{n(3n+5)}{(n+1)(n+2)}$

Hence $a = 3, b = 5$

b 0.0398

18 a Using partial fractions,

$\dfrac{2}{4r^2 - 1} = \dfrac{1}{2r-1} - \dfrac{1}{2r+1}$

Using the method of differences,

$\displaystyle\sum_{r=1}^{n}\dfrac{2}{4r^2 - 1} = \sum_{r=1}^{n}\left(\dfrac{1}{2r-1} - \dfrac{1}{2r+1}\right) = 1 - \dfrac{1}{2n+1}$

b $\dfrac{20}{861}$

19 a $A = 24, B = 2$

b Using the identity from part **a**,

$\displaystyle\sum_{r=1}^{n}(24r^2 + 2) = \sum_{r=1}^{n}\left((2r+1)^3 - (2r-1)^3\right)$

$24\displaystyle\sum_{r=1}^{n}r^2 + \sum_{r=1}^{n}2 = \sum_{r=1}^{n}\left((2r+1)^3 - (2r-1)^3\right)$

Using the method of differences,

$24\displaystyle\sum_{r=1}^{n}r^2 = 8n^3 + 12n^2 + 6n + 1 - 1 - 2n$

$= 8n^3 + 12n^2 + 4n = 4n(n+1)(2n-1)$

$\displaystyle\sum_{r=1}^{n}r^2 = \dfrac{4n(n+1)(2n-1)}{24} = \dfrac{1}{6}n(n+1)(2n+1)$

c $194\,380$

20 Using partial fractions,

$\dfrac{1}{r(r+1)(r+2)} = \dfrac{1}{2r} - \dfrac{1}{r+1} + \dfrac{1}{2(r+2)}$

Using the method of differences,

$\displaystyle\sum_{r=1}^{2n}\dfrac{1}{r(r+1)(r+2)} = \sum_{r=1}^{2n}\left(\dfrac{1}{2r} - \dfrac{1}{r+1} + \dfrac{1}{2(r+2)}\right)$

$= \dfrac{1}{4} - \dfrac{1}{2(2n+1)} + \dfrac{1}{4(n+1)}$

$= \dfrac{(n+1)(2n+1) - 2(n+1) + (2n+1)}{4(n+1)(2n+1)}$

$= \dfrac{2n^2 + 3n + 1 - 2n - 2 + 2n + 1}{4(n+1)(2n+1)}$

$= \dfrac{2n^2 + 3n}{4(n+1)(2n+1)} = \dfrac{n(2n+3)}{4(n+1)(2n+1)}$

Hence $a = 2, b = 3, c = 4$

21 a RHS $= r - 1 + \dfrac{1}{r} - \dfrac{1}{r+1} = \dfrac{(r-1)r(r+1) + (r+1) - r}{r(r+1)}$

$= \dfrac{r(r^2 - 1) + 1}{r(r+1)} = \dfrac{r^3 - r + 1}{r(r+1)} = $ LHS

b $\dfrac{n(n^2 + 1)}{2(n+1)}$

Online Full worked solutions are available in SolutionBank.

22 $1 - \dfrac{1}{3^n(n+1)}$

23 $\cos x = 1 - \dfrac{x^2}{2!} + \dfrac{x^4}{4!} - \ldots = 1 - \dfrac{x^2}{2!}$, neglecting terms in x^3 and higher powers

$\sin x = x - \dfrac{x^3}{3!} + \dfrac{x^5}{5!} - \ldots = x$, neglecting terms in x^3 and higher powers

$11 \sin x - 6 \cos x + 5 = 11x - 6\left(1 - \dfrac{x^2}{2}\right) + 5$

$\qquad\qquad\qquad\qquad = -1 + 11x + 3x^2$

$A = -1, B = 11, C = 3$

24 LHS $= \ln(x^2 - x + 1) + \ln(x + 1) - 3\ln x$

$= \ln((x^2 - x + 1)(x + 1)) - \ln x^3$

$= \ln\left(\dfrac{x^3 + 1}{x^3}\right) = \ln\left(1 + \dfrac{1}{x^3}\right)$

Substituting $\dfrac{1}{x^3}$ for x and n for r in the series

$\ln(1 + x) = x - \dfrac{x^2}{2} + \dfrac{x^3}{3} + \ldots + \dfrac{(-1)^{r+1}x^r}{r} + \ldots$

LHS $= \dfrac{1}{x^3} - \dfrac{1}{2x^6} + \ldots + \dfrac{(-1)^{n-1}}{nx^{3n}} + \ldots$

25 $A = 1, B = -2, C = -\dfrac{21}{2}, D = \dfrac{71}{3}$

26 a $\dfrac{1}{3} - \dfrac{2}{9}x + \dfrac{4}{27}x^2 - \dfrac{8}{81}x^3 + \ldots$

b $\dfrac{2}{3}x - \dfrac{4}{9}x^2 - \dfrac{4}{27}x^3 + \dfrac{8}{81}x^4 + \ldots$

27 a $-\dfrac{x^2}{2} - \dfrac{x^4}{12} - \ldots$ **b** $\dfrac{x^2}{2} + \dfrac{x^4}{12} + \ldots$

28 a Let $u = 1 + \cos 2x$, then $f(x) = \ln u$

$\dfrac{du}{dx} = -2\sin 2x$

$f'(x) = f'(u)\dfrac{du}{dx} = \dfrac{1}{u}\dfrac{du}{dx} = \dfrac{1}{1 + \cos 2x} \times (-2\sin 2x)$

$= \dfrac{-4\sin x \cos x}{2\cos^2 x} = \dfrac{-2\sin x}{\cos x} = -2\tan x$

b $f''(x) = -2\sec^2 x$

$f'''(x) = -4\sec^2 x \tan x$

$f''''(x) = -8\sec x \sec x \tan x \tan x - 4\sec^2 x \sec^2 x$

$= -8\sec^2 x \tan^2 x - 4\sec^4 x$

c $\ln 2 - x^2 - \dfrac{1}{6}x^4 + \ldots$

29 $\dfrac{1}{2}$

30 $\dfrac{\pi}{4}$

31 a $\dfrac{1}{3}\ln\left(\dfrac{x}{x+3}\right) + c$

b $\displaystyle\int_3^\infty \dfrac{1}{x(x+3)}\,dx = \lim_{t\to\infty}\int_3^t \dfrac{1}{x(x+3)}\,dx = \lim_{t\to\infty}\left[\dfrac{1}{3}\ln\left(\dfrac{x}{x+3}\right)\right]_3^t$

$= \lim_{t\to\infty}\left(\dfrac{1}{3}\ln\left(\dfrac{t}{t+3}\right)\right) - \dfrac{1}{3}\ln\dfrac{1}{2}$

$= \lim_{t\to\infty}\left(\dfrac{1}{3}\ln\left(1 - \dfrac{3}{t+3}\right)\right) - \dfrac{1}{3}\ln\dfrac{1}{2}$

$= 0 - \dfrac{1}{3}\ln\dfrac{1}{2} = \dfrac{1}{3}\ln 2$

32 Using repeated integration by parts,

$\int x^3 e^{-x^4}\,dx = -\dfrac{1}{4}e^{-x^4} + c$

$\displaystyle\int_1^\infty x^3 e^{-x^4}\,dx = \lim_{t\to\infty}\int_1^t x^3 e^{-x^4}\,dx = \lim_{t\to\infty}\left[-\dfrac{1}{4}e^{-x^4}\right]_1^t$

$= \lim_{t\to\infty}\left(-\dfrac{1}{4}e^{-t^4}\right) - \left(-\dfrac{1}{4}e^{-1}\right) = 0 + \dfrac{1}{4e} = \dfrac{1}{4e}$

33 a $\dfrac{1}{2(5-2x)} + c$

b The integral is infinite at the end points and not defined at the point $x = \dfrac{5}{2}$, so split up the integral:

$\displaystyle\int_{-\infty}^3 \dfrac{1}{(5-2x)^2}\,dx = \int_{-\infty}^0 \dfrac{1}{(5-2x)^2}\,dx + \int_0^{\frac{5}{2}} \dfrac{1}{(5-2x)^2}\,dx$

$\qquad\qquad + \displaystyle\int_{\frac{5}{2}}^3 \dfrac{1}{(5-2x)^2}\,dx$

Consider the integral $I = \displaystyle\int_0^{\frac{5}{2}} \dfrac{1}{(5-2x)^2}\,dx$

$I = \displaystyle\int_0^{\frac{5}{2}} \dfrac{1}{(5-2x)^2}\,dx = \lim_{t\to\frac{5}{2}}\left[\dfrac{1}{2(5-2x)}\right]_0^t$

$= \lim_{t\to\frac{5}{2}}\left(\dfrac{1}{2(5-2t)} - \dfrac{1}{10}\right)$

As $t \to \dfrac{5}{2} \Rightarrow \dfrac{1}{2(5-2t)} - \dfrac{1}{10} \to \infty$

Therefore, I diverges, so $\displaystyle\int_{-\infty}^3 \dfrac{1}{(5-2x)^2}\,dx$ also diverges.

34 $-\dfrac{1}{\pi}$

35 a Mean value $= \dfrac{1}{5-2}\displaystyle\int_2^5 \dfrac{3x}{(x-1)(2x-3)}\,dx$

Using partial fractions,

$\dfrac{3x}{(x-1)(2x-3)} = \dfrac{9}{2x-3} - \dfrac{3}{x-1}$

Mean value $= \dfrac{1}{3}\displaystyle\int_2^5\left(\dfrac{9}{2x-3} - \dfrac{3}{x-1}\right)dx$

$= \displaystyle\int_2^5\left(\dfrac{3}{2x-3} - \dfrac{1}{x-1}\right)dx$

$= \left[\dfrac{3}{2}\ln(2x-3) - \ln(x-1)\right]_2^5$

$= \left(\dfrac{3}{2}\ln 7 - \ln 4\right) - \left(\dfrac{3}{2}\ln 1 - \ln 1\right)$

$= \left(\dfrac{3}{2}\ln 7 - \ln 4\right) - (0 - 0)$

$= \dfrac{1}{2}\ln 343 - \dfrac{1}{2}\ln 16 = \dfrac{1}{2}\ln\dfrac{343}{16}$

b $\dfrac{1}{2}\ln\dfrac{343\,k^2}{16}$

36 a Mean value $= \dfrac{1}{3-1}\displaystyle\int_1^3 x^2(x^3-1)^3\,dx$

$= \dfrac{1}{2}\left[\dfrac{1}{12}(x^3-1)^4\right]_1^3$

$= \dfrac{1}{24}\left[(x^3-1)^4\right]_1^3 = \dfrac{1}{24}((26)^4 - 0) = \dfrac{57122}{3}$

b $-\dfrac{114244}{3}$

37 $\sqrt{2}$

38 5

39 a $y = (\arcsin x)^2$

Let $u = \arcsin x$ and $y = u^2$

$\dfrac{dy}{du} = 2u$ and $\dfrac{du}{dx} = \dfrac{1}{\sqrt{1-x^2}}$

$\Rightarrow \dfrac{dy}{dx} = \dfrac{dy}{du} \times \dfrac{du}{dx} = 2u \times \dfrac{1}{\sqrt{1-x^2}} = \dfrac{2\arcsin x}{\sqrt{1-x^2}}$

$\sqrt{1-x^2}\dfrac{dy}{dx} = 2\arcsin x$

$(1-x^2)\left(\dfrac{dy}{dx}\right)^2 = 4(\arcsin x)^2 = 4y$

b Differentiating the results from part **a** implicitly with respect to x,

$$-2x\left(\frac{dy}{dx}\right)^2 + (1 - x^2)2\frac{dy}{dx}\frac{d^2y}{dx^2} = 4\frac{dy}{dx}$$

$$-x\frac{dy}{dx} + (1 - x^2)\frac{d^2y}{dx^2} = 2$$

$$(1 - x^2)\frac{d^2y}{dx^2} - x\frac{dy}{dx} = 2$$

40 a $y = \arctan 3x \Rightarrow \tan y = 3x$

Differentiating implicitly with respect to x,

$$\sec^2 y\frac{dy}{dx} = 3$$

$$\frac{dy}{dx} = \frac{3}{\sec^2 y} = \frac{3}{1 + \tan^2 y} = \frac{3}{1 + 9x^2}$$

b Using integration by parts and the result from part **a**,

$$\int_0^{\frac{\sqrt{3}}{3}} 6x\arctan 3x\,dx = 3x^2\arctan 3x - \int_0^{\frac{\sqrt{3}}{3}} 3x^2 \times \frac{3}{1 + 9x^2}\,dx$$

$$= 3x^2\arctan 3x - \int_0^{\frac{\sqrt{3}}{3}} 1\,dx + \int_0^{\frac{\sqrt{3}}{3}} \frac{1}{1 + 9x^2}\,dx$$

$$= 3x^2\arctan 3x - x + \frac{1}{3}\arctan 3x$$

$$\left[3x^2\arctan 3x - x + \frac{1}{3}\arctan 3x\right]_0^{\frac{\sqrt{3}}{3}} = \frac{4}{3}\arctan\sqrt{3} - \frac{\sqrt{3}}{3}$$

$$= \frac{1}{9}(4\pi - 3\sqrt{3})$$

41 a Let $y = f(x) = \arcsin x$, then $\sin y = x$

Differentiating implicitly with respect to x,

$$\cos y\frac{dy}{dx} = 1$$

$$\frac{dy}{dx} = \frac{1}{\cos y} = \frac{1}{\sqrt{1 - \sin^2 y}} = \frac{1}{\sqrt{1 - x^2}}$$

b $\dfrac{2}{\sqrt{1 - 4x^2}}$

c $x = \dfrac{1}{2}\sin\theta \Rightarrow \dfrac{dx}{d\theta} = \dfrac{1}{2}\cos\theta$

At $x = \dfrac{1}{4}$, $\dfrac{1}{4} = \dfrac{1}{2}\sin\theta \Rightarrow \theta = \dfrac{\pi}{6}$

At $x = 0$, $0 = \dfrac{1}{2}\sin\theta \Rightarrow \theta = 0$

$$\int_0^{\frac{1}{4}} \frac{x\arcsin 2x}{\sqrt{1 - 4x^2}}\,dx = \int_0^{\frac{\pi}{6}} \frac{\frac{1}{2}\sin\theta\arcsin(\sin\theta)}{\sqrt{1 - \sin^2\theta}}\frac{dx}{d\theta}\,d\theta$$

$$= \int_0^{\frac{\pi}{6}} \frac{\frac{1}{2}\sin\theta \times \theta}{\cos\theta}\left(\frac{1}{2}\cos\theta\right)d\theta = \frac{1}{4}\int_0^{\frac{\pi}{6}} \theta\sin\theta\,d\theta$$

$$= -\frac{1}{4}\theta\cos\theta + \frac{1}{4}\int_0^{\frac{\pi}{6}}\cos\theta\,d\theta = -\frac{1}{4}\theta\cos\theta + \frac{1}{4}\sin\theta$$

$$\Rightarrow \int_0^{\frac{1}{4}} \frac{x\arcsin 2x}{\sqrt{1 - 4x^2}}\,dx = \left[-\frac{1}{4}\theta\cos\theta + \frac{1}{4}\sin\theta\right]_0^{\frac{\pi}{6}}$$

$$= \left(-\frac{\pi}{24}\cos\frac{\pi}{6} + \frac{1}{4}\sin\frac{\pi}{6}\right) - 0 = \frac{1}{48}(6 - \pi\sqrt{3})$$

42 Using partial fractions, $\dfrac{2x + 1}{x^3 + x} = \dfrac{2x + 1}{x(x^2 + 1)} = \dfrac{2 - x}{x^2 + 1} + \dfrac{1}{x}$

$$\int \frac{2x + 1}{x^3 + x}\,dx = \int\left(\frac{2 - x}{x^2 + 1} + \frac{1}{x}\right)dx = \int\left(\frac{2}{x^2 + 1} - \frac{x}{x^2 + 1} + \frac{1}{x}\right)dx$$

$$= 2\arctan x - \frac{1}{2}\ln(x^2 + 1) + \ln x + c$$

Hence $A = 2$, $B = -\dfrac{1}{2}$

43 a $\dfrac{3x^2 + 5x}{x^3 - 3x^2 + 5x - 15} = \dfrac{3x^2 + 5x}{(x - 3)(x^2 + 5)} = \dfrac{A}{x - 3} + \dfrac{B}{x^2 + 5}$

$$\Rightarrow 3x^2 + 5x = A(x^2 + 5) + B(x - 3)$$

$x = 3: 42 = 14A \Rightarrow A = 3$

$x = 0: 0 = 15 - 3B \Rightarrow B = 5$

b $\displaystyle\int \frac{3x^2 + 5x}{x^3 - 3x^2 + 5x - 15}\,dx = \int\left(\frac{3}{x - 3} + \frac{5}{x^2 + 5}\right)dx$

$$= 3\ln(x - 3) + \sqrt{5}\arctan\frac{x}{\sqrt{5}} + c$$

Hence $P = 3$, $Q = \sqrt{5}$ and $R = \dfrac{1}{\sqrt{5}}$

44 $\dfrac{13}{4}\pi e^6 - \dfrac{\pi}{4}e^2$

45 a 12　　**b** $9\pi^2$

46 $\pi^3 - 4\pi$

47 $a = 2$

48 a $0 = y\cos y \Rightarrow 0 = \cos k \Rightarrow k = \dfrac{\pi}{2}$

b $V = \pi\displaystyle\int_0^{\frac{\pi}{2}} (y\cos y)^2\,dy = \pi\int_0^{\frac{\pi}{2}} y^2\cos^2 y\,dy$

$$= \frac{\pi}{2}\int_0^{\frac{\pi}{2}} y^2(\cos 2y + 1)\,dy$$

$$\int y^2\cos 2y\,dy = \frac{1}{2}y^2\sin 2y - \int y\sin 2y\,dy$$

$$= \frac{1}{2}y^2\sin 2y + \frac{1}{2}y\cos 2y - \int\frac{1}{2}\cos 2y\,dy$$

$$= \frac{1}{2}y^2\sin 2y + \frac{1}{2}y\cos 2y - \frac{1}{4}\sin 2y + c$$

$$V = \frac{\pi}{2}\left[\frac{1}{2}y^2\sin 2y + \frac{1}{2}y\cos 2y - \frac{1}{4}\sin 2y + \frac{1}{3}y^3\right]_0^{\frac{\pi}{2}}$$

$$= \frac{\pi}{2}\left(\left(0 - \frac{\pi}{4} - 0 + \frac{\pi^3}{24}\right) - 0\right) = \frac{1}{48}\pi^4 - \frac{1}{8}\pi^2$$

Hence $a = \dfrac{1}{48}$, $b = -\dfrac{1}{8}$

49 $\ln 4$

50 a Length scale factor $2 \Rightarrow$ volume scale factor 8

$$V = 8\pi\int_0^4\left(\frac{5}{\sqrt{1 + 4x}}\right)^2\,dx = 8\pi\int_0^4\frac{25}{1 + 4x}\,dx$$

$$= 8\pi\left[\frac{25}{4}\ln(1 + 4x)\right]_0^4$$

$$= 8\pi\left(\frac{25}{4}\ln 17 - 0\right) = 50\pi\ln 17$$

b The thickness of the vase has not been taken into account.

51 a $0 = \sqrt{y}\left(3 - \frac{1}{2}e^y\right) \Rightarrow 0 = 3 - \frac{1}{2}e^y \Rightarrow e^y = 6 \Rightarrow y = \ln 6$

b 9.65 cm^3

c e.g. Filament may be wasted, or the shape may not exactly match the model.

52 a Length scale factor $0.5 \Rightarrow$ volume scale factor 0.125

$$V = \frac{\pi}{8}\int_0^{\frac{\pi}{2}} (3\sin 2t)^2\frac{dx}{dt}\,dx = \frac{\pi}{8}\int_0^{\frac{\pi}{2}} 18\sin^2 2t\cos t\,dt$$

$$= \frac{9\pi}{4}\int_0^{\frac{\pi}{2}} \sin^2 2t\cos t\,dt$$

b $V = 9\pi\displaystyle\int_0^{\frac{\pi}{2}} \sin^2 t\cos^3 t\,dt$

$$= 9\pi\int_0^{\frac{\pi}{2}} \sin^2 t(1 - \sin^2 t)\cos t\,dt$$

$$= 9\pi\int_0^{\frac{\pi}{2}} (\cos t\sin^2 t - \cos t\sin^4 t)\,dt$$

$$= 9\pi\left[\frac{1}{3}\sin^3 t - \frac{1}{5}\sin^5 t\right]_0^{\frac{\pi}{2}} = 9\pi\left(\frac{1}{3} - \frac{1}{5}\right) = 9\pi\left(\frac{2}{15}\right) = \frac{6}{5}\pi\text{ cm}^2$$

Challenge

1 a n will be of one of the forms $3k$, $3k + 1$, $3k - 1$:

$n = 3k$:

$$\frac{1^{3k} + \left(e^{\frac{2\pi i}{3}}\right)^{3k} + \left(e^{\frac{2\pi i}{3}}\right)^{6k}}{3} = \frac{1 + e^{2\pi ki} + e^{4\pi ki}}{3} = \frac{1 + 1 + 1}{3} = 1$$

$n = 3k + 1$:

$$\frac{1^{3k+1} + \left(e^{\frac{2\pi i}{3}}\right)^{3k+1} + \left(e^{\frac{2\pi i}{3}}\right)^{6k+2}}{3} = \frac{1 + e^{2\pi ki + \frac{2\pi i}{3}} + e^{4\pi ki + \frac{4\pi i}{3}}}{3}$$

$$= \frac{1 + e^{\frac{2\pi i}{3}} + e^{\frac{4\pi i}{3}}}{3} = 0$$

$n = 3k - 1$:

$$\frac{1^{3k-1} + \left(e^{\frac{2\pi i}{3}}\right)^{3k-1} + \left(e^{\frac{2\pi i}{3}}\right)^{6k-2}}{3} = \frac{1 + e^{2\pi ki - \frac{2\pi i}{3}} + e^{4\pi ki - \frac{4\pi i}{3}}}{3}$$

$$= \frac{1 + e^{-\frac{2\pi i}{3}} + e^{-\frac{4\pi i}{3}}}{3} = 0$$

b Consider jth term of f(x), $a_j x^j$.

The corresponding terms in $\dfrac{f(1) + f(\omega) + f(\omega^2)}{3}$ are:

$$\frac{a_j(1)^j}{3} + \frac{a_j(\omega)^j}{3} + \frac{a_j(\omega^2)^j}{3}$$

From part **a**, this expression is equal to a_j if j is 0 or a multiple of 3, and 0 otherwise.

$\dfrac{f(1) + f(\omega) + f(\omega^2)}{3}$ is the sum of all such expressions for all terms in f(x), so is equal to the sum of all a_j where j is 0 or a multiple of 3, as required.

c $(1 + x)45 = \sum\limits_{r=0}^{45}\binom{45}{r}x^r$.

So the sum of the coefficients of powers of x that are 0 or multiples of 3 is $\sum\limits_{r=0}^{15}\binom{45}{3r}$.

From part **b**, this is equal to

$$\frac{(1 + 1)^{45} + (1 + \omega)^{45} + (1 + \omega^2)^{45}}{3}$$

$$= \frac{2^{45} + (-\omega^2)^{45} + (-\omega)^{45}}{3} = \frac{2^{45} - 2}{3}$$

2 $V = \pi \int_2^\infty \left(\sqrt{\dfrac{x+3}{x^3}}\right)^2 dx = \pi \int_2^\infty \dfrac{x+3}{x^3}dx = \pi \int_2^\infty \left(\dfrac{1}{x^2} + \dfrac{3}{x^3}\right)dx$

$= \lim\limits_{t\to\infty}\left(\pi\int_2^t \left(\dfrac{1}{x^2} + \dfrac{3}{x^3}\right)dx\right) = \lim\limits_{t\to\infty}\left(\pi\left[-\dfrac{1}{x} - \dfrac{3}{2x^2}\right]_2^t\right)$

$= \lim\limits_{t\to\infty}\left(\pi\left(-\dfrac{1}{t} - \dfrac{3}{2t^2}\right)\right) - \left(-\dfrac{1}{2} - \dfrac{3}{8}\right)$

As $t \to \infty$, $\dfrac{1}{t} \to 0$ and $\dfrac{1}{t^2} \to 0$, so $V = \dfrac{7\pi}{8}$

3 a $V = \int_{-\infty}^\infty \dfrac{A}{1+x^2}dx = \int_{-\infty}^0 \dfrac{A}{1+x^2}dx + \int_0^\infty \dfrac{A}{1+x^2}dx$

$= \lim\limits_{t\to\infty}\int_{-t}^0 \dfrac{A}{1+x^2}dx + \lim\limits_{t\to\infty}\int_0^t \dfrac{A}{1+x^2}dx$

$= A\left(\lim\limits_{t\to\infty}[\arctan x]^0_{-t} + \lim\limits_{t\to\infty}[\arctan x]^t_0\right)$

$= A\left(\arctan 0 - \lim\limits_{t\to\infty}\arctan(-t) + \lim\limits_{t\to\infty}\arctan t - \arctan 0\right)$

$= A\left(\lim\limits_{t\to\infty}\arctan t - \lim\limits_{t\to\infty}\arctan(-t)\right)$

As $t \to \infty$, $\arctan t \to \dfrac{\pi}{2}$ and $\arctan(-t) \to -\dfrac{\pi}{2}$

$V = A\left(\dfrac{\pi}{2} - \left(-\dfrac{\pi}{2}\right)\right) = A\pi$

Hence if $V = 1$, then $A = \dfrac{1}{\pi}$

b $\text{Var}(X) = \dfrac{1}{\pi}\int_{-\infty}^\infty \dfrac{x^2}{1+x^2}dx = \dfrac{1}{\pi}\int_{-\infty}^\infty\left(1 - \dfrac{1}{1+x^2}\right)dx$

$= \dfrac{1}{\pi}\int_{-\infty}^0\left(1 - \dfrac{1}{1+x^2}\right)dx + \dfrac{1}{\pi}\int_0^\infty\left(1 - \dfrac{1}{1+x^2}\right)dx$

Consider $I = \int_{-\infty}^0\left(1 - \dfrac{1}{1+x^2}\right)dx$

$I = \int_{-\infty}^0\left(1 - \dfrac{1}{1+x^2}\right)dx = \lim\limits_{t\to\infty}\int_{-t}^0\left(1 - \dfrac{1}{1+x^2}\right)dx$

$= \lim\limits_{t\to\infty}[x - \arctan x]^0_{-t}$

$= 0 - \arctan 0 - \lim\limits_{t\to\infty}(t - \arctan t)$

As $t \to \infty$, I diverges, so $\text{Var}(X)$ is infinite.

c $\int_{-a}^a \dfrac{x}{1+x^2}dx = \int_{-a}^0 \dfrac{x}{1+x^2}dx + \int_0^a \dfrac{x}{1+x^2}dx$

$\int_0^a \dfrac{x}{1+x^2}dx = \dfrac{1}{2}[\ln(1+x^2)]_0^a = \dfrac{1}{2}\ln(1+a^2)$

and similarly, $\int_0^{2a} \dfrac{x}{1+x^2}dx = \dfrac{1}{2}\ln(1+4a^2)$

So $\lim\limits_{a\to\infty}\left(\int_0^{2a}\dfrac{x}{1+x^2}dx - \int_0^a\dfrac{x}{1+x^2}dx\right)$

$= \dfrac{1}{2}\lim\limits_{a\to\infty}\left(\ln\dfrac{1+4a^2}{1+a^2}\right) = \dfrac{1}{2}\ln 4 \neq 0$

Therefore $\int_0^{2a}\dfrac{x}{1+x^2}dx \neq \int_0^a\dfrac{x}{1+x^2}dx$

$\Rightarrow \int_{-a}^{2a}\dfrac{x}{1+x^2}dx \neq \int_{-a}^a\dfrac{x}{1+x^2}dx$

$\lim\limits_{a\to\infty}\int_{-a}^0\dfrac{x}{1+x^2}dx = \dfrac{1}{2}\lim\limits_{a\to\infty}[\ln(1+x^2)]^0_{-a}$, which diverges

as $a \to \infty$, so the mean of X, $\lim\limits_{a\to\infty}\int_{-a}^a xf(x)\,dx$ is not defined.

CHAPTER 5
Prior knowledge check

1 0.5π

2 $\dfrac{\pi}{6}, \dfrac{5\pi}{6}$

3 a Circle centre $(0,3)$, radius 3

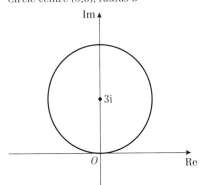

b $\dfrac{9\pi}{2}$

Exercise 5A

1 a $(13, 1.176)$ **b** $(13, 1.966)$

c $(13, -1.966)$ **d** $(\sqrt{13}, -0.983)$

e $\left(2, -\dfrac{\pi}{6}\right)$

2 a $(3\sqrt{3}, 3)$ **b** $(3\sqrt{3}, -3)$
  c $(-3\sqrt{2}, 3\sqrt{2})$ **d** $(-5\sqrt{2}, -5\sqrt{2})$
  e $(-2, 0)$

3 a $x^2 + y^2 = 4$ **b** $x = 3$
  c $y = 5$ **d** $x^2 = 4ay$ or $y = \dfrac{x^2}{4a}$
  e $x^2 + y^2 = 2ax$ or $(x - a)^2 + y^2 = a^2$
  f $x^2 + y^2 = 3ay$ or $x^2 + \left(y - \dfrac{3a}{2}\right)^2 = \dfrac{9a^2}{4}$
  g $(x^2 + y^2)^{\frac{3}{2}} = 8y^2$ **h** $(x^2 + y^2)^{\frac{3}{2}} = 2x^2$
  i $x^2 = 1$

4 a $r = 4$ **b** $r^2 = 8\operatorname{cosec} 2\theta$
  c $r^2 = \sin 2\theta$ **d** $r = 2\cos\theta$
  e $r^2 = \dfrac{4}{1 + \sin 2\theta}$ **f** $r = \dfrac{3}{\sqrt{2}}\sec\left(\theta + \dfrac{\pi}{4}\right)$
  g $\theta = \arctan 2$ **h** $r = \dfrac{a}{2}\operatorname{cosec}\left(\theta + \dfrac{\pi}{3}\right)$
  i $r = \tan\theta\sec\theta + a\sec\theta$

Challenge

Consider the triangle formed by the two points and the origin and use the cosine rule to find d.

Exercise 5B

1 a

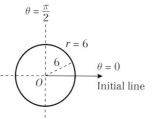

b

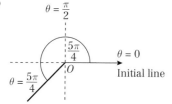

c

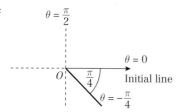

d

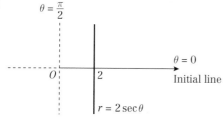

e

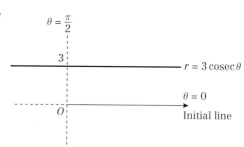

f

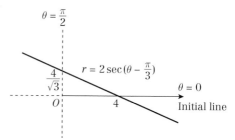

g

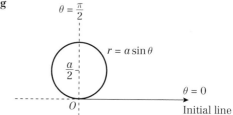

h

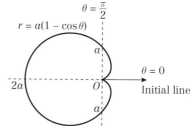

i

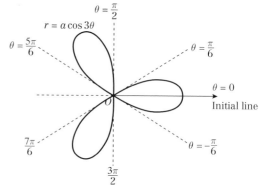

j

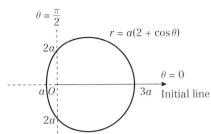

$\theta = \frac{\pi}{2}$

$r = a(2 + \cos\theta)$

$2a$

$\theta = 0$

a O $3a$ Initial line

$2a$

k

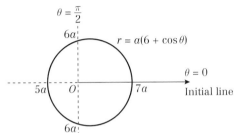

$\theta = \frac{\pi}{2}$

$6a$ $r = a(6 + \cos\theta)$

$\theta = 0$

$5a$ O $7a$ Initial line

$6a$

l

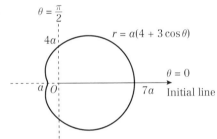

$\theta = \frac{\pi}{2}$

$4a$ $r = a(4 + 3\cos\theta)$

$\theta = 0$

a O $7a$ Initial line

m

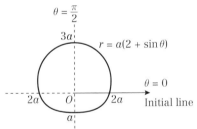

$\theta = \frac{\pi}{2}$

$3a$ $r = a(2 + \sin\theta)$

$\theta = 0$

$2a$ O $2a$ Initial line

a

n

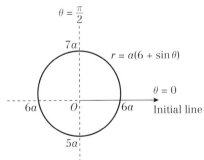

$\theta = \frac{\pi}{2}$

$7a$ $r = a(6 + \sin\theta)$

$\theta = 0$

$6a$ O $6a$ Initial line

$5a$

o

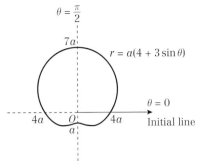

$\theta = \frac{\pi}{2}$

$7a$ $r = a(4 + 3\sin\theta)$

$\theta = 0$

$4a$ O $4a$ Initial line

a

p

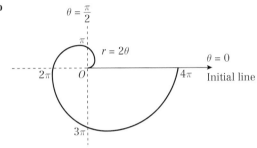

$\theta = \frac{\pi}{2}$

π $r = 2\theta$

$\theta = 0$

2π O 4π Initial line

3π

q

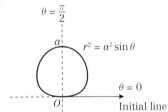

$\theta = \frac{\pi}{2}$

a $r^2 = a^2 \sin\theta$

$\theta = 0$

O Initial line

r

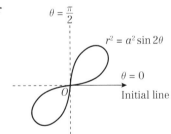

$\theta = \frac{\pi}{2}$

$r^2 = a^2 \sin 2\theta$

$\theta = 0$

O Initial line

2

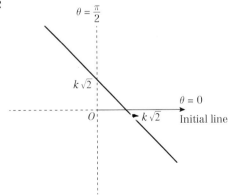

$\theta = \frac{\pi}{2}$

$k\sqrt{2}$

$\theta = 0$

O $k\sqrt{2}$ Initial line

3 a

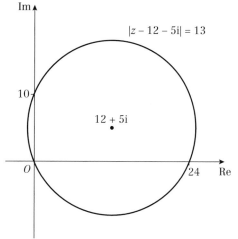

$|z - 12 - 5i| = 13$

$12 + 5i$

10

O 24 Re

b Cartesian equation is $(x - 12)^2 + (y - 5)^2 = 169$
Convert to polar coordinates:
$(r\cos\theta - 12)^2 + (r\sin\theta - 5)^2 = 169$
Then rearrange this to get $r = 24\cos\theta + 10\sin\theta$

4 a

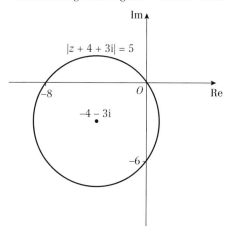

$|z + 4 + 3i| = 5$

-8 O Re

$-4 - 3i$

-6

b Cartesian equation is $(x + 4)^2 + (y + 3)^2 = 25$
Convert to polar coordinates:
$(r\cos\theta + 4)^2 + (r\sin\theta + 3)^2 = 25$
Then rearrange to get $r = -8\cos\theta - 6\sin\theta$

Exercise 5C

1 a $\dfrac{\pi a^2}{8}$ **b** $\dfrac{3\pi a^2}{4}$

   c $\dfrac{(\pi + 2)a^2}{48}$ **d** $\dfrac{a^2}{4}$

   e $\dfrac{a^2 \ln\sqrt{2}}{2}$ or $\dfrac{a^2 \ln 2}{4}$ **f** $\dfrac{2a^2\pi^3}{3}$

   g $\dfrac{a^2}{4}(11\pi + 24)$

2 Area $= 2 \times \dfrac{1}{2}\displaystyle\int_0^\pi a^2(p + q\cos\theta)^2 \, d\theta$

$= a^2\displaystyle\int_0^\pi (p^2 + 2pq\cos\theta + q^2\cos^2\theta) \, d\theta$

$= a^2[p^2\theta + 2pq\sin\theta]_0^\pi + \dfrac{a^2 q^2}{2}\displaystyle\int_0^\pi (\cos 2\theta + 1) \, d\theta$

$= a^2 p^2 \pi + \dfrac{a^2 q^2}{2}\left[\dfrac{1}{2}\sin 2\theta + \theta\right]_0^\pi$

$= a^2 p^2 \pi + \dfrac{a^2 q^2 \pi}{2} = \dfrac{2p^2 + q^2}{2}\pi a^2$

3 $\dfrac{\pi a^2}{12}$

4 $a = 9$

5 $\dfrac{a^2}{4}\left(\dfrac{\pi}{4} - \dfrac{3\sqrt{3}}{16}\right)$

6 $\dfrac{5\pi}{4}$

7 a

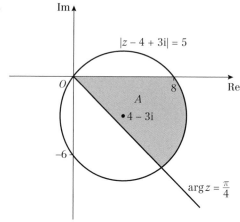

$|z - 4 + 3i| = 5$

O 8 Re

A

$\bullet\, 4 - 3i$

-6

$\arg z = \dfrac{\pi}{4}$

b 35.1

8 a

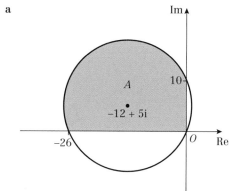

A 10

$\bullet$
$-12 + 5i$

-26 O Re

b 385

9 0.0966

10 0.79

Challenge

a $k = \dfrac{3}{7\pi}$ **b** $\dfrac{12\pi}{7}$

Exercise 5D

1 $(2a, 0)$, $\left(\dfrac{a}{2}, \dfrac{2\pi}{3}\right)$ and $\left(\dfrac{a}{2}, \dfrac{-2\pi}{3}\right)$

2 a $(9.15, 1.11)$ **b** $(212, 2.68)$

3 a $\left(\dfrac{2a}{3}, \pm 0.421\right)$ **b** $r = \pm\dfrac{a\sqrt{6}}{9}\operatorname{cosec}\theta$

4 $\left(\dfrac{15}{2}a, \pm 1.32\right)$

5 $r\cos\theta = 3$ $r\cos\theta = -1$ $r = 3\sec\theta$ $r = -\sec\theta$

6 $\left(2a, \dfrac{\pi}{4}\right)$

7 $\dfrac{3 + \sqrt{73}}{4}$

8 0.212

Mixed exercise 5

1 $\dfrac{9\pi a^2}{8}$

2 a, b

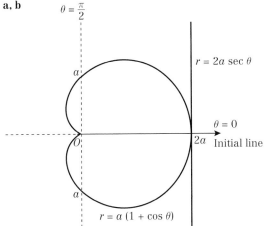
$$\theta = \frac{\pi}{2}$$
$r = 2a \sec \theta$
$r = a(1 + \cos\theta)$
$2a$ Initial line
$\theta = 0$

c $\cos\alpha = \dfrac{\sqrt{5}-1}{2}$

3

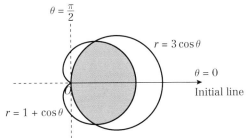
$$\theta = \frac{\pi}{2}$$
$r = 3\cos\theta$
$r = 1 + \cos\theta$
$\theta = 0$
Initial line

Area $= \dfrac{5\pi}{4}$

4 $\left(a\sqrt{\dfrac{\sqrt{3}}{2}}, \dfrac{\pi}{6}\right), \left(a\sqrt{\dfrac{\sqrt{3}}{2}}, \dfrac{7\pi}{6}\right)$ and $\left(0, \dfrac{\pi}{2}\right)$

5 a

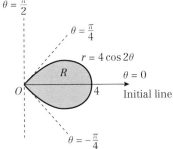
$$\theta = \frac{\pi}{2}$$
$\theta = \frac{\pi}{4}$
$r = 4\cos 2\theta$
R
$\theta = 0$
4 Initial line
$\theta = -\frac{\pi}{4}$

b 2π

6

$$\theta = \frac{\pi}{2}$$
$r = a(1 - \cos\theta)$
a
$\theta = 0$
$2a$ O Initial line
a

Maximum value at $(2a, \pi)$

7 a

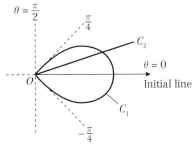
$$\theta = \frac{\pi}{2}$$
$\frac{\pi}{4}$
C_2
$\theta = 0$
Initial line
C_1
$-\frac{\pi}{4}$

b $\dfrac{\pi}{6} - \dfrac{\sqrt{3}}{8}$

8 a

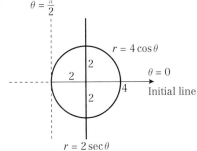
$$\theta = \frac{\pi}{2}$$
$r = 4\cos\theta$
2
2
$\theta = 0$
2 4 Initial line
2
$r = 2\sec\theta$

b $\left(2\sqrt{2}, \dfrac{\pi}{4}\right), \quad \left(2\sqrt{2}, -\dfrac{\pi}{4}\right)$

9 a $\left(\dfrac{3}{2}a, \dfrac{\pi}{3}\right)$ **b** $\dfrac{5\pi}{8}a^2$

10 a $y^2 = x^2 - 1$ **b** $y = \dfrac{1}{2x}$

11 a

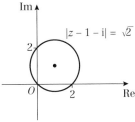
Im
$|z - 1 - i| = \sqrt{2}$
2
O 2 Re

b Cartesian equation is $(x-1)^2 - (y+1)^2 = 2$
Convert to polar coordinates:
$(r\cos\theta - 1)^2 + (r\sin\theta - 1)^2 = 2$
Then rearrange to get $r = 2\cos\theta + 2\sin\theta$

c

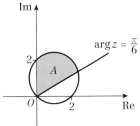
Im
$\arg z = \dfrac{\pi}{6}$
2
A
O 2 Re

d 3.59

12 2.09

13 1.52

Challenge

$x = r\cos\theta = \sqrt{2}\,\theta\cos\theta, \ y = r\sin\theta = \sqrt{2}\,\theta\sin\theta$

$\dfrac{dx}{d\theta} = \sqrt{2}\cos\theta - \sqrt{2}\,\theta\sin\theta, \dfrac{dy}{d\theta} = \sqrt{2}\sin\theta + \sqrt{2}\,\theta\cos\theta$

So $\dfrac{dy}{dx} = \dfrac{\sin\theta + \theta\cos\theta}{\cos\theta - \theta\sin\theta}$

At $\theta = \dfrac{\pi}{4}$ the gradient of the tangent is $\dfrac{1 + \dfrac{\pi}{4}}{1 - \dfrac{\pi}{4}} = \dfrac{4 + \pi}{4 - \pi}$

So the tangent is of the form $y = \left(\dfrac{4 + \pi}{4 - \pi}\right)x + c$

Substituting in the point $\left(\dfrac{\pi}{4}, \dfrac{\pi}{4}\right)$, $c = \dfrac{\pi^2}{2(\pi - 4)}$

So the equation for the tangent is
$y = \left(\dfrac{4 + \pi}{4 - \pi x}\right) + \dfrac{\pi^2}{(2\pi - 4)}$
Rearranging, this is $2(\pi - 4)y + 2(\pi + 4)x = \pi^2$

CHAPTER 6
Prior knowledge check

1 $\ln\left(\dfrac{1 + \sqrt{3}}{2}\right)$

2 $\dfrac{1}{\cos^2 x} - \tan^2 x \equiv \sec^2 x - \tan^2 x \equiv (1 + \tan^2 x) - \tan^2 x \equiv 1$

3 $\displaystyle\int_0^\pi e^x \sin x \, dx = [-e^x \cos x]_0^\pi + \int_0^\pi e^x \cos x \, dx$

$= [-e^x \cos x]_0^\pi + [e^x \sin x]_0^\pi - \int_0^\pi e^x \sin x \, dx$

$\Rightarrow \displaystyle\int_0^\pi e^x \sin x \, dx = \tfrac{1}{2}[-e^x \cos x + e^x \sin x]_0^\pi$

$= \tfrac{1}{2}((- e^\pi(-1) + e^\pi(0)) - (-1 + 0)) = \tfrac{1}{2}(1 + e^\pi)$

Exercise 6A

1 a 27.29 (2 d.p.) **b** 1.13 (2 d.p.) **c** −0.96 (2 d.p.)

2 a $\dfrac{e - e^{-1}}{2}$ **b** $\dfrac{e^4 + e^{-4}}{2}$ **c** $\dfrac{e - 1}{e + 1}$

3 a $\dfrac{3}{4}$ **b** $\dfrac{5}{3}$ **c** $\dfrac{3}{5}$

4 $x = 1.32$ (2 d.p.) $x = -1.32$ (2 d.p.)

5 $x = 0.88$ (2 d.p.)

6 $x = -0.55$ (2 d.p.)

7

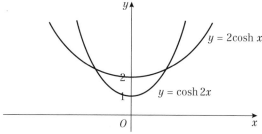

8 a $f(x) \in \mathbb{R}$ **b** $f(x) \geqslant 1$ **c** $-1 < f(x) < 1$

9 a

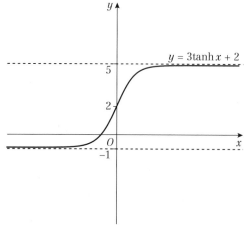

b $y = 5, y = -1$

Challenge

a

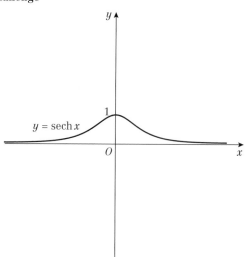

b

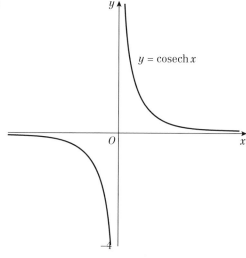

c

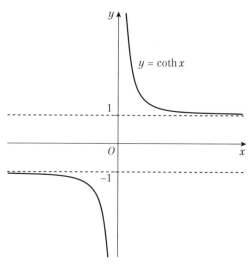

Exercise 6B

1

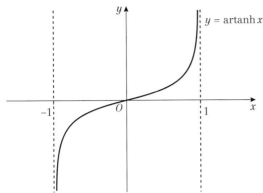

$y = \text{artanh}\,x$

2

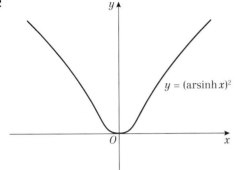

$y = (\text{arsinh}\,x)^2$

3 Let $y = \text{artanh}\,x$. Then $x = \tanh y = \dfrac{e^{2y} - 1}{e^{2y} + 1}$ and $|x| < 1$.

So $(e^{2y} + 1)x = e^{2y} - 1 \Rightarrow e^{2y}(1 - x) = 1 + x$

$\Rightarrow e^{2y} = \dfrac{1 + x}{1 - x} \Rightarrow y = \dfrac{1}{2}\ln\!\left(\dfrac{1 + x}{1 - x}\right)$ for $|x| < 1$.

4 a $\ln(2 + \sqrt{5})$ **b** $\ln(3 + 2\sqrt{2})$ **c** $\dfrac{1}{2}\ln 3$

5 a $\ln(\sqrt{2} + \sqrt{3})$ **b** $\ln(2 + \sqrt{5})$ **c** $\dfrac{1}{2}\ln\!\left(\dfrac{11}{9}\right)$

6 a $\ln(-3 + \sqrt{10})$ **b** $\ln\!\left(\dfrac{3 + \sqrt{5}}{2}\right)$ **c** $\dfrac{1}{2}\ln(2 + \sqrt{3})$

7 $\dfrac{1}{2}\ln\!\left(\dfrac{1 + x}{1 - x}\right) + \dfrac{1}{2}\ln\!\left(\dfrac{1 + y}{1 - y}\right) = \ln\sqrt{3}$

$\Rightarrow \ln\!\left(\sqrt{\dfrac{1 + x}{1 - x}} \times \sqrt{\dfrac{1 + y}{1 - y}}\right) = \ln\sqrt{3}$

$\Rightarrow (1 + x)(1 + y) = 3(1 - x)(1 - y) \Rightarrow xy - 2x - 2y + 1 = 0$

$\Rightarrow y(x - 2) = 2x - 1 \Rightarrow y = \dfrac{2x - 1}{x - 2}$

Exercise 6C

1 a RHS $\equiv 2\sinh A\cosh A$

$\equiv 2\!\left(\dfrac{e^A - e^{-A}}{2}\right)\!\left(\dfrac{e^A + e^{-A}}{2}\right)$

$\equiv \dfrac{1}{2}(e^{2A} - 1 + 1 - e^{-2A})$

$\equiv \dfrac{e^{2A} - e^{-2A}}{2}$

$\equiv \sinh 2A \equiv$ LHS

b RHS $\equiv \cosh A\cosh B - \sinh A\sinh B$

$\equiv \left(\dfrac{e^A + e^{-A}}{2}\right)\!\left(\dfrac{e^B + e^{-B}}{2}\right) - \left(\dfrac{e^A - e^{-A}}{2}\right)\!\left(\dfrac{e^B - e^{-B}}{2}\right)$

$\equiv \dfrac{e^{A+B} + e^{-A+B} + e^{A-B} + e^{-A-B}}{4} - \dfrac{e^{A+B} - e^{-A+B} - e^{A-B} + e^{-A-B}}{4}$

$\equiv \dfrac{2(e^{-A+B} + e^{A-B})}{4}$

$\equiv \dfrac{e^{A-B} + e^{-(A-B)}}{2}$

$\equiv \cosh(A - B) \equiv$ LHS

c RHS $\equiv 4\cosh^3 A - 3\cosh A$

$\equiv 4\!\left(\dfrac{e^A + e^{-A}}{2}\right)^3 - 3\!\left(\dfrac{e^A + e^{-A}}{2}\right)$

$(e^A + e^{-A})^3 \equiv e^{3A} + 3e^{2A}e^{-A} + 3e^A e^{-2A} + e^{-3A}$

$\equiv e^{3A} + 3e^A + 3e^{-A} + e^{-3A}$

RHS $\equiv \dfrac{e^{3A} + 3e^A + 3e^{-A} + e^{-3A}}{2} - \dfrac{3(e^A + e^{-A})}{2}$

$\equiv \dfrac{e^{3A} + e^{-3A}}{2} \equiv \cosh 3A \equiv$ LHS

d RHS $\equiv 2\sinh\!\left(\dfrac{A - B}{2}\right)\cosh\!\left(\dfrac{A + B}{2}\right)$

$\equiv 2\!\left(\dfrac{e^{\frac{A-B}{2}} - e^{\frac{-A+B}{2}}}{2}\right)\!\left(\dfrac{e^{\frac{A+B}{2}} + e^{\frac{-A-B}{2}}}{2}\right)$

$\equiv \dfrac{1}{2}\!\left(e^{\frac{A-B}{2} + \frac{A+B}{2}} - e^{\frac{-A+B}{2} + \frac{A+B}{2}} + e^{\frac{A-B}{2} + \frac{-A-B}{2}} - e^{\frac{-A+B}{2} + \frac{-A-B}{2}}\right)$

$\equiv \dfrac{1}{2}(e^A - e^B + e^{-B} - e^{-A})$

$\equiv \dfrac{1}{2}(e^A - e^{-A}) - \dfrac{1}{2}(e^B - e^{-B})$

$\equiv \sinh A - \sinh B$

$\equiv$ LHS

2 a $\sinh(A - B) \equiv \sinh A\cosh B - \cosh A\sinh B$

b $\sinh 3A \equiv 3\sinh A + 4\sinh^3 A$

c $\cosh A + \cosh B \equiv 2\cosh\!\left(\dfrac{A + B}{2}\right)\cosh\!\left(\dfrac{A - B}{2}\right)$

d $\cosh 2A \equiv \dfrac{1 + \tanh^2 A}{1 - \tanh^2 A}$

e $\cosh 2A \equiv \cosh^4 A - \sinh^4 A$

3 a $\sinh x \equiv \pm\sqrt{3}$ **b** $\tanh x \equiv \pm\dfrac{\sqrt{3}}{2}$ **c** $\cosh 2x \equiv 7$

4 a $\cosh x \equiv \sqrt{2}$ **b** $\sinh 2x \equiv -2\sqrt{2}$ **c** $\tanh 2x \equiv -\dfrac{2\sqrt{2}}{3}$

5 a $x = \ln\!\left(\dfrac{1}{7}\right), x = 0$ **b** $x = \ln 3$

   c $x = \ln\!\left(\dfrac{7}{2}\right), x = \ln 4$ **d** $x = \ln\!\left(\dfrac{5}{3}\right)$

   e $x = \ln\!\left(\dfrac{-3 + \sqrt{13}}{2}\right), x = \ln(4 + \sqrt{17})$

   f $x = \ln(4 \pm \sqrt{15})$ **g** $x = 0, x = \ln\!\left(\dfrac{7 \pm 3\sqrt{5}}{2}\right)$

   h $x = \ln\!\left(\dfrac{5}{2}\right), x = \ln 3$ **i** $x = \ln(1 + \sqrt{2})$

6 a RHS $\equiv 2\!\left(\dfrac{1}{4}(e^{2x} + 2 + e^{-2x})\right) - 1 \equiv \dfrac{1}{2}(e^{2x} + e^{-2x}) \equiv$ LHS

   b $\ln(3 \pm 2\sqrt{2})$

7 $\ln\!\left(\dfrac{7}{2} \pm \dfrac{3}{2}\sqrt{5}\right)$

8 He has not applied Osborn's rule in line 1 – correct identity should be $\text{sech}^2 x = 1 - \tanh^2 x$ since implied $\sin^2$ term; he has split the denominator of the fraction in line 2 which is invalid; he has taken the reciprocal of both terms in line 3 – this is mathematically incorrect.

Correct proof: $\dfrac{1 + \tanh^2 x}{1 - \tanh^2 x} \equiv \dfrac{2 - \text{sech}^2 x}{\text{sech}^2 x} \equiv \dfrac{2}{\text{sech}^2 x} - 1$

$\equiv 2\cosh^2 x - 1$

9 a $8\cosh(x + 0.693)$

   b 8

   c $0.148, -1.534$

Exercise 6D

1 a $2\cosh 2x$ **b** $5\sinh 5x$

   c $2\,\text{sech}^2 2x$ **d** $3\cosh 3x$

   e $-4\,\text{cosech}^2 4x$ **f** $-2\tanh 2x\,\text{sech}\,2x$

   g $e^{-x}(\cosh x - \sinh x)$ **h** $\cosh 3x + 3x\sinh 3x$

   i $\dfrac{x\cosh x - \sinh x}{3x^2}$ **j** $x(2\cosh 3x + 3x\sinh 3x)$

   k $2\cosh 2x\cosh 3x + 3\sinh 2x\sinh 3x$

   l $\tanh x$ **m** $3x^2\cosh x^3$

   n $4\cosh 2x\sinh 2x$ **o** $\sinh x\,e^{\cosh x}$

   p $-\coth x\,\text{cosech}\,x$

2 $y = a\cosh nx + b\sinh nx$

Differentiate with respect to x:

$\dfrac{dy}{dx} = an\sinh nx + nb\cosh nx$

$\dfrac{d^2y}{dx^2} = an^2\cosh nx + bn^2\sinh nx$

$\quad\ = n^2(a\cosh nx + b\sinh nx)$

$\dfrac{d^2y}{dx^2} = n^2 y$

3 $\left(\dfrac{1}{2}\ln\left(\dfrac{13}{11}\right), \dfrac{11\sqrt{\frac{13}{11}} + 13\sqrt{\frac{11}{13}}}{2}\right)$

4 $\dfrac{d^2y}{dx^2} = 2(5\cosh 3x\sinh x + 3\sinh 3x\cosh x)$

5 a $\dfrac{2}{\sqrt{4x^2 - 1}}$ **b** $\dfrac{1}{\sqrt{(x+1)^2 + 1}}$

   c $\dfrac{3}{1 - 9x^2}$ **d** $-\dfrac{1}{x^2\sqrt{\frac{1}{x^2} - 1}}$

   e $\dfrac{2x}{\sqrt{x^4 - 1}}$ **f** $\dfrac{3}{\sqrt{9x^2 - 1}}$

   g $2x\operatorname{arcosh} x + \dfrac{x^2}{\sqrt{x^2 - 1}}$ **h** $\dfrac{1}{\sqrt{x^2 + 4}}$

   i $3x^2 e^{x^3}\operatorname{arsinh} x + \dfrac{e^{x^3}}{\sqrt{x^2 + 1}}$

   j $\dfrac{1}{\sqrt{x^2 + 1}}\operatorname{arcosh} x + \dfrac{1}{\sqrt{x^2 - 1}}\operatorname{arsinh} x$

   k $\dfrac{\operatorname{sech} x}{\sqrt{x^2 - 1}} - \operatorname{arcosh} x\,\operatorname{sech} x\,\tanh x$

   l $\operatorname{arcosh} 3x + \dfrac{3x}{\sqrt{9x^2 - 1}}$

6 a $y = \operatorname{arcosh} x$, then $\cosh y = x$

$\dfrac{dx}{dy} = \sinh y = \sqrt{\cosh^2 y - 1} = \sqrt{x^2 - 1}$

So $\dfrac{d}{dx}(\operatorname{arcosh} x) = \dfrac{1}{\sqrt{x^2 - 1}}$

   b $y = \operatorname{artanh} x$, then $\tanh y = x$

$\dfrac{dx}{dy} = \operatorname{sech}^2 y = 1 - \tanh^2 y = 1 - x^2$

So $\dfrac{d}{dx}(\operatorname{artanh} x) = \dfrac{1}{1 - x^2}$

7 Using the chain rule, $\dfrac{dy}{dx} = \dfrac{e^x}{2}\left(\dfrac{1}{1 - \left(\frac{e^x}{2}\right)^2}\right) = \dfrac{2e^x}{4 - e^{2x}}$

So $(4 - e^{2x})\dfrac{dy}{dx} = 2e^x$, as required.

8 $\dfrac{dy}{dx} = (1 + x^2)^{-\frac{1}{2}}$, $\dfrac{d^2y}{dx^2} = 2x\left(-\dfrac{1}{2}\right)(1 + x^2)^{-\frac{3}{2}} = -x(1 + x^2)^{-\frac{3}{2}}$

$\dfrac{d^3y}{dx^3} = -x\left(2x\left(-\dfrac{3}{2}\right)(1 + x^2)^{-\frac{5}{2}}\right) - (1 + x^2)^{-\frac{3}{2}}$

$\quad\ = 3x^2(1 + x^2)^{-\frac{5}{2}} - (1 + x^2)^{-\frac{3}{2}}$

So $(1 + x^2)\dfrac{d^3y}{dx^3} + 3x\dfrac{d^2y}{dx^2} + \dfrac{dy}{dx}$

$\quad\ = 3x^2(1 + x^2)^{-\frac{3}{2}} - (1 + x^2)^{-\frac{1}{2}} - 3x^2(1 + x^2)^{-\frac{3}{2}} + (1 + x^2)^{-\frac{1}{2}} = 0$

9 $-\dfrac{2x\operatorname{arcosh} x}{(x^2 - 1)^{\frac{3}{2}}} + \dfrac{2}{x^2 - 1}$

10 $25y - 25\ln 5 = 169x - 156$

11 $\dfrac{dy}{dx} = \dfrac{2}{\sqrt{4x^2 - 1}} \Rightarrow y = -\dfrac{\sqrt{15}}{2}x + \sqrt{15} + \ln(4 + \sqrt{15})$

12 a $1 + \dfrac{1}{2}x^2 + \dfrac{1}{24}x^4$ **b** $8.7 \times 10^{-6}\%$

13 a $x + \dfrac{1}{6}x^3 + \dfrac{1}{120}x^5$ **b** $\dfrac{x^{2n+1}}{(2n+1)!}$

14 a $y = \tanh x$, $\tanh(0) = 0$

$\dfrac{dy}{dx} = \operatorname{sech}^2 x$, at $0\ \dfrac{dy}{dx} = 1$

$\dfrac{d^2y}{dx^2} = -2\operatorname{sech}^2 x\tanh x$, at $0\ \dfrac{d^2y}{dx^2} = 0$

$\dfrac{d^3y}{dx^3} = -2\operatorname{sech}^4 x + 4\operatorname{sech}^2 x\tanh^2 x$, at $0\ \dfrac{d^3y}{dx^3} = -2$

Now use a Maclaurin expansion to obtain the approximation

   b 5.23% (3 s.f.)

15 a $y = \operatorname{artanh} x$, $\operatorname{artanh} 0 = 0$

$\dfrac{dy}{dx} = (1 - x^2)^{-1}$, at $0\ \dfrac{dy}{dx} = 1$

$\dfrac{d^2y}{dx^2} = 2x(1 - x^2)^{-2}$, at $0\ \dfrac{d^2y}{dx^2} = 0$

$\dfrac{d^3y}{dx^3} = 2(1 - x^2)^{-2} + 8x^2(1 - x^2)^{-3}$, at $0\ \dfrac{d^3y}{dx^3} = 2$

$\dfrac{d^4y}{dx^4} = 8x(1 - x^2)^{-3} + 16x(1 - x^2)^{-3} + 48x^3(1 - x^2)^{-4}$,

at $0\ \dfrac{d^4y}{dx^4} = 0$

$\dfrac{d^5y}{dx^5} = 8(1 - x^2)^{-3} + 48x^2(1 - x^2)^{-4} + 16(1 - x^2)^{-3} + \dots$,

at $0\ \dfrac{d^5y}{dx^5} = 24$ since remaining terms all involve x

Now use a Maclaurin expansion to obtain the approximation

   b $\dfrac{x^{2n+1}}{2n+1}$ **c** $x + \dfrac{5}{6}x^3$

16 $x + \dfrac{13}{6}x^3 + \dfrac{121}{120}x^5$

17 a $\dfrac{dy}{dx} = \cos x\sinh x - \sin x\cosh x$

$\dfrac{d^2y}{dx^2} = -2\sin x\sinh x$

$\dfrac{d^3y}{dx^3} = -2\cos x\sinh x - 2\sin x\cosh x$

$\dfrac{d^4y}{dx^4} = -2y + 2\sin x\sinh x - 2\sin x\sinh x - 2y = -4y$

   b $1 - \dfrac{1}{6}x^4 + \dfrac{1}{2520}x^8$ **c** $(-4)^{n-1}\dfrac{x^{4n-4}}{(4n-4)!}$

Challenge

1 $-\dfrac{1}{2}x^2 + \dfrac{5}{24}x^4$

Exercise 6E

1 a $\cosh x + 3\sinh x + c$ **b** $\sinh x - \tanh x + c$

   c $-\operatorname{sech} x + c$

2 a $\dfrac{1}{2}\cosh 2x + c$

   b $3\sinh\left(\dfrac{x}{3}\right) + c$

3 a $\operatorname{arcosh} x + \sqrt{x^2 - 1} + c$ **b** $\sqrt{1 + x^2} - 3\operatorname{arsinh} x + c$

4 a $\dfrac{1}{4}\sinh^4 x + c$ **b** $\dfrac{1}{4}\ln\cosh 4x + c$

   c $\dfrac{1}{3}(\cosh 2x)^{\frac{3}{2}} + c$

5 a $\dfrac{1}{3}\ln(2 + 3\cosh x) + c$

   b $\tanh x + \dfrac{1}{2}\tanh^2 x + c$ or $\tanh x - \dfrac{1}{2}\operatorname{sech}^2 x + c$

   c $5x + 2\ln\cosh x + c$

6 $\dfrac{1}{3}x\cosh 3x - \dfrac{1}{9}\sinh 3x + c$

7 a $\dfrac{1}{4}e^{2x} + \dfrac{1}{2}x + c$

   b $\dfrac{1}{2}e^x + \dfrac{1}{10}e^{-5x} + c$

c $\frac{1}{16}e^{4x} - \frac{1}{16}e^{-4x} + \frac{1}{8}e^{2x} - \frac{1}{8}e^{-2x} + c$
or $\frac{1}{8}\sinh 4x + \frac{1}{4}\sinh 2x + c$

8 $1 - \frac{1}{e}$

9 a $\frac{1}{4}\sinh 2x - \frac{1}{2}x + c$

b $-\frac{1}{8}x + \frac{1}{32}\sinh 4x + c$

c $\sinh x + \frac{2}{3}\sinh^3 x + \frac{1}{5}\sinh^5 x + c$

10 $\int_0^{\ln 2} \cosh^2\left(\frac{x}{2}\right)dx = \frac{1}{2}\int_0^{\ln 2}(\cosh x + 1)\,dx = \frac{1}{2}\Big[\sinh x + x\Big]_0^{\ln 2}$

$= \left(\frac{e^{\ln 2} - e^{-\ln 2}}{2} + \ln 2 - (0 + 0)\right) = \frac{1}{2}\ln 2 + \frac{2 - \frac{1}{2}}{4}$

$= \frac{1}{8}(4\ln 2 + 3) = \frac{1}{8}(3 + \ln 16)$

11 a $\operatorname{arcosh}\left(\frac{x}{3}\right) + c$ **b** $\frac{1}{2}\operatorname{arsinh}\left(\frac{2x}{5}\right) + c$

12 a $3\operatorname{arsinh}\left(\frac{x}{3}\right) + c$ **b** $\operatorname{arcosh}\left(\frac{x}{\sqrt{2}}\right) + c$

13 a $\frac{1}{2}\operatorname{arcosh}\left(\frac{x}{\sqrt{3}}\right) + c$ **b** $\frac{1}{3}\operatorname{arsinh}\left(\frac{3x}{4}\right) + c$

14 0.977 (3 s.f.)

15 a $\ln(1 + \sqrt{2})$ **b** $\ln\left(\frac{4}{3}\right)$

16 $\sqrt{x}\sqrt{1 + x} - \operatorname{arsinh}\sqrt{x} + c$

17 0.824 (3 s.f.)

18 $\int\sqrt{x^2 - 4}\,dx = \int\sqrt{4\cosh^2 u - 4} \times 2\sinh u\,du$

$= 4\int\sinh^2 u\,du = 2\int(\cosh 2u - 1)\,du = 2\left(\frac{1}{2}\sinh 2u - u\right) + c$

$= 2\sinh u\cosh u - 2u + c = 2\cosh u\sqrt{\cosh^2 u - 1} - 2u + c$

$= \frac{1}{2}x\sqrt{x^2 - 4} - 2\operatorname{arcosh}\left(\frac{x}{2}\right) + c$

19 a $\int\frac{1}{2\cosh x - \sinh x}\,dx = \int\frac{1}{(e^x + e^{-x}) - \frac{1}{2}(e^x + e^{-x})}\,dx$

$= \int\frac{1}{\frac{1}{2}e^x + \frac{3}{2}e^{-x}}\,dx = \int\frac{2e^x}{e^{2x} + 3}\,dx$

LHS $= \frac{2}{2e^x + 2e^{-x} + e^{-x} - e^x} = \frac{2}{e^x + 3e^{-x}} = \frac{2e^x}{e^{2x} + 3}$ = RHS

b $\frac{2}{\sqrt{3}}\arctan\left(\frac{e^x}{\sqrt{3}}\right) + c$

20 0.360 (3 s.f.)

21 a $\operatorname{arcosh}\left(\frac{x - 2}{4}\right) + c$ **b** $\operatorname{arsinh}(x + 3) + c$

c $\frac{\sqrt{10}}{10}\arctan\left(\frac{\sqrt{2}\,(x + 1)}{\sqrt{5}}\right) + c$

d $\frac{1}{3}\operatorname{arcosh}\left(\frac{9x - 4}{\sqrt{7}}\right) + c$

22 a $\frac{1}{2}\operatorname{arsinh}(2x - 3) + c$ **b** $\frac{1}{2}\operatorname{arcosh}\left(\frac{2x - 3}{\sqrt{5}}\right) + c$

23 0.400 (3 s.f.)

24 $\ln(2 + \sqrt{5})$

25 $\int_1^3 \frac{1}{\sqrt{3x^2 - 6x + 7}}\,dx = \frac{1}{\sqrt{3}}\int_1^3 \frac{1}{\sqrt{(x - 1)^2 + \frac{4}{3}}}\,dx$

Using $u = x - 1$, this becomes

$\frac{1}{\sqrt{3}}\int_0^2 \frac{1}{\sqrt{u^2 + \frac{4}{3}}}\,du = \frac{1}{\sqrt{3}}\left[\operatorname{arsinh}\left(\frac{\sqrt{3}\,u}{2}\right)\right]_0^2$

$= \frac{1}{\sqrt{3}}\left[\ln\left(\frac{\sqrt{3}\,u}{2} + \sqrt{\frac{3u^2}{4} + 1}\right)\right]_0^2$

$= \frac{1}{\sqrt{3}}(\ln(\sqrt{3} + \sqrt{3 + 1}) - \ln(0 + 1)) = \frac{1}{\sqrt{3}}\ln(2 + \sqrt{3})$

26 a $-\ln 3, \ln 2$ **b** $\ln 279\,936 - 10$

27 Volume $= \pi\int_0^1 \sinh^2 x\,dx = \frac{\pi}{2}\int_0^1(\cosh 2x - 1)\,dx$

$= \frac{\pi}{2}\left[\frac{1}{2}\sinh 2x - x\right]_0^1 = \frac{\pi}{4}(\sinh 2 - 2 - \sinh 0 + 0)$

$= \frac{\pi}{4}\left(\frac{e^2 - e^{-2}}{2} - 2\right) = \frac{\pi}{8e^2}(e^4 - 4e^2 - 1)$

Challenge

1 $x^2 - 2x + 2 = 1 + \sinh^2\theta = \cosh^2\theta, \frac{dx}{d\theta} = \cosh\theta$

So $\int\frac{1}{(x^2 - 2x + 2)^{\frac{3}{2}}}\,dx = \int\frac{\cosh\theta}{\cosh^3\theta}\,d\theta$

$= \int\operatorname{sech}^2\theta\,d\theta = \tanh\theta + c = \frac{\sinh\theta}{\cosh\theta} + c$

$= \frac{x - 1}{\sqrt{x^2 - 2x + 2}} + c$

2 a $\frac{1}{8}\sinh(2x^2) + \frac{x^2}{4} + c$ **b** $\frac{1}{2}\tanh(x^2) + c$

Mixed exercise 6

1 a $\frac{4}{3}$ **b** $\frac{13}{5}$ **c** $-\frac{15}{17}$

2 $y = \frac{12 - 13x}{12x - 13}$

3 RHS $= \sinh A\cosh B - \cosh A\sinh B$

$= \left(\frac{e^A - e^{-A}}{2}\right)\left(\frac{e^B + e^{-B}}{2}\right) - \left(\frac{e^A + e^{-A}}{2}\right)\left(\frac{e^B - e^{-B}}{2}\right)$

$= \frac{e^{A+B} - e^{-A+B} + e^{A-B} - e^{-A-B}}{4} - \frac{e^{A+B} + e^{-A+B} - e^{A-B} - e^{-A-B}}{4}$

$= \frac{2(e^{A-B} - e^{-A+B})}{4} = \frac{e^{A-B} - e^{-(A-B)}}{2}$

$= \sinh(A - B) = $ LHS

4 RHS $= \frac{2\tanh\frac{1}{2}x}{1 - \tanh^2\frac{1}{2}x}$

$2\tanh\frac{1}{2}x = \frac{2(e^x - 1)}{e^x + 1}$

$1 - \tanh^2\frac{1}{2}x = 1 - \left(\frac{e^x - 1}{e^x + 1}\right)^2 = \frac{(e^x + 1)^2 - (e^x - 1)^2}{(e^x + 1)^2}$

$= \frac{4e^x}{(e^x + 1)^2}$

So RHS $= \frac{2(e^x - 1)}{e^x + 1} \times \frac{(e^x + 1)^2}{4e^x} = \frac{(e^x - 1)(e^x + 1)}{2e^x}$

$= \frac{e^{2x} - 1}{2e^x} = \frac{e^x - e^{-x}}{2} = \sinh x = $ LHS

5 $x = \ln\left(\frac{1}{2}\right), x = \ln 7$

6 $x = \ln\left(\frac{5}{3}\right)$

7 $x = \ln\left(\frac{-14 + \sqrt{205}}{3}\right)$

$x = \ln(1 + \sqrt{2})$

8 a

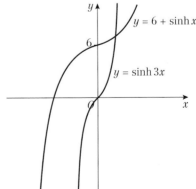

b $6 + \sinh x = 3\sinh x + 4\sinh^3 x \Rightarrow 2\sinh^3 x + \sinh x - 3 = 0$

$\Rightarrow \sinh x = 1 \Rightarrow x = \ln(1 + \sqrt{2})$

$\sinh(3\ln(1 + \sqrt{2})) = 7,$

so $(\ln(1 + \sqrt{2}), 7)$ is the point of intersection.

9 a $R = 12, \alpha = 0.405$ **b** 12

10 a $4\sinh(x + 0.693)$
b $x = 0.75$ (2 d.p.)
c 0.75 (2 d.p.)
11 $2\sinh 2x$
12 a $\dfrac{3}{\sqrt{9x^2 + 1}}$
b $\dfrac{2x}{\sqrt{x^4 + 1}}$
c $\dfrac{1}{\sqrt{x^2 - 4}}$
d $2x\left(\text{arcosh}\,2x + \dfrac{x}{\sqrt{4x^2 - 1}}\right)$

13 $\dfrac{dy}{dx} = \dfrac{2\text{arsinh}\,x}{\sqrt{1 + x^2}}, \dfrac{d^2y}{dx^2} = \dfrac{2}{1 + x^2} - \dfrac{2x\,\text{arsinh}\,x}{(\sqrt{1 + x^2})^3}$

So $(1 + x^2)\dfrac{d^2y}{dx^2} + x\dfrac{dy}{dx} - 2$

$= 2 - \dfrac{2x\,\text{arsinh}\,x}{\sqrt{1 + x^2}} + \dfrac{2x\,\text{arsinh}\,x}{\sqrt{1 + x^2}} - 2$

which cancels to 0.

14 a $\dfrac{dy}{dx} = 5\sinh x - 3\cosh x$
b $(\ln 2, 4)$

15 $\dfrac{2\cosh 2x}{\sqrt{\sinh^2 2x - 1}}$

16 a $\dfrac{dy}{dx} = \cos x \cosh x + \sin x \sinh x$

$\dfrac{d^2y}{dx^2} = 2\cos x \sinh x$

$\dfrac{d^3y}{dx^3} = 2\cos x \cosh x - 2\sin x \sinh x$

$\dfrac{d^4y}{dx^4} = 2\cos x \sinh x - 2\sin x \cosh x - 2\sin x \cosh x$
$\qquad\qquad - 2\cos x \sinh x = -4y$

b $x + \tfrac{1}{3}x^3 - \tfrac{1}{30}x^5$

17 $2x + \tfrac{7}{3}x^3 + \tfrac{61}{60}x^5$

18 a $a = 2, b = 1, c = 16$
b $\tfrac{1}{2}\ln(1 + \sqrt{2})$

19 a $\tfrac{1}{20}\cosh 10x - \tfrac{1}{4}\cosh 2x + c$
b $\tfrac{1}{4}e^{2x} - \tfrac{1}{2}x + c$

20 Area on graph is

$\displaystyle\int_0^5 \dfrac{10}{\sqrt{4x^2 + 9}}\,dx = 5\int_0^5 \dfrac{1}{\sqrt{x^2 + \frac{9}{4}}}\,dx = 5\left[\text{arsinh}\left(\dfrac{2x}{3}\right)\right]_0^5$

$= 5\,\text{arsinh}\,\tfrac{10}{3} - 5\,\text{arsinh}\,0 = 9.5944\ldots$

So area in real life is $960\,\text{m}^2$ (2 s.f.).

21 $\text{arsinh}\left(\dfrac{x - 1}{3}\right) + c$

22 a $\dfrac{2}{\sqrt{3}}\arctan(\sqrt{3}\,e^x) + c$

b Use substitution $x - 1 = 3\sinh u$.
Then integral becomes

$\displaystyle\int_0^{\text{arsinh}\,1} \dfrac{9\sinh u + 2}{\sqrt{9\cosh^2 u}} \times 3\cosh u\,du$

$= \displaystyle\int_0^{\text{arsinh}\,1} (9\sinh u + 2)\,du = [9\cosh u + 2u]_0^{\text{arsinh}\,1}$

$= (9\cosh(\text{arsinh}\,1) + 2\,\text{arsinh}\,1) - (9\cosh 0 + 0)$
Since $\text{arsinh}\,1 = \ln(1 + \sqrt{2})$,
$9\cosh(\text{arsinh}\,1) = 9\cosh(\ln(1 + \sqrt{2})$ and the integral
simplifies to
$9\sqrt{2} + 2\,\text{arsinh}\,1 - 9 = 9(\sqrt{2} - 1) + 2\,\text{arsinh}\,1$

23 a 59.5°
b $8.82\,\text{m}^2$
24 a $\tfrac{1}{2}\ln(4 \pm \sqrt{14})$
b 6.12
25 $6610\,\text{cm}^3$
26 a $(\ln(3 + \sqrt{10}), 0)$
b 22.7

Challenge

$\displaystyle\int_{-\infty}^{\infty} \text{sech}\,x\,dx = 2\int_0^{\infty} \text{sech}\,x\,dx = 2\lim_{t \to \infty}\int_0^t \dfrac{\text{sech}^2 x}{\text{sech}\,x}\,dx$

Using the substitution $u = \tanh x$, this becomes

$2\lim_{t \to \infty}\displaystyle\int_0^{\tanh t} \dfrac{1}{\sqrt{1 - u^2}}\,du = 2\lim_{t \to \infty}[\arcsin u]_0^{\tanh t}$

$= 2\lim_{t \to \infty}(\arcsin(\tanh t))$

$= 2\arcsin 1 = 2 \times \dfrac{\pi}{2} = \pi$

CHAPTER 7
Prior knowledge check
1 $y = (x - 1)e^x + c$
2 $y^2 = 4 - x^2$
3 a $-\tfrac{3}{2}\ln|50 - 2t| + c$
b $-\tfrac{1}{4}\ln|\cos(4x)| + c$

Exercise 7A
1 a $y = x^2 + c$ where c is constant

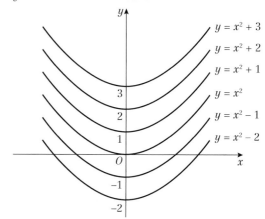

b $y = Ae^x$ where A is constant

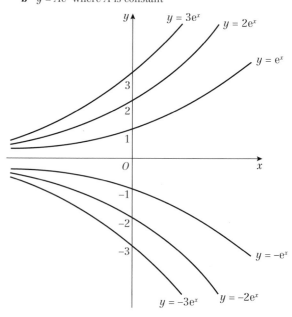

c $y = Ax^2$, where A is constant

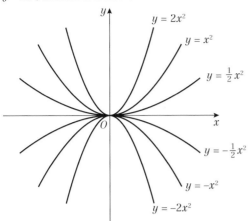

$y = 2x^2$
$y = x^2$
$y = \frac{1}{2}x^2$
$y = -\frac{1}{2}x^2$
$y = -x^2$
$y = -2x^2$

d $y^2 - x^2 = c$, where c is constant

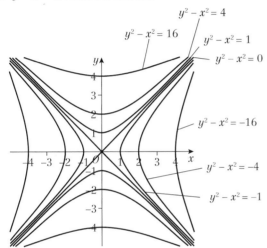

$y^2 - x^2 = 4$
$y^2 - x^2 = 16$
$y^2 - x^2 = 1$
$y^2 - x^2 = 0$
$y^2 - x^2 = -16$
$y^2 - x^2 = -4$
$y^2 - x^2 = -1$

e $y = \sin x + c$, where c is constant

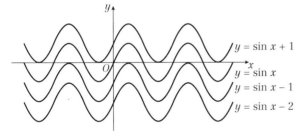

$y = \sin x + 1$
$y = \sin x$
$y = \sin x - 1$
$y = \sin x - 2$

f $y = A \sin x$, where A is constant

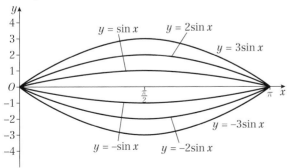

$y = \sin x$ $y = 2 \sin x$
$y = 3 \sin x$
$y = -\sin x$ $y = -2 \sin x$
$y = -3 \sin x$

2 a $\dfrac{dy}{y} = \dfrac{x\,dx}{x^2 - 9}$

$\displaystyle\int \frac{1}{y}\,dy = \frac{1}{2}\int \frac{2x}{x^2 - 9}\,dx$

$\ln y = \frac{1}{2}\ln(x^2 - 9) + c$

$y = e^c\sqrt{x^2 - 9}$

$y^2 = e^{2c}(x^2 - 9)$

Let $k = -e^{2c}$, then $y^2 + kx^2 = 9k$

b $y^2 + 5x^2 = 45$

c

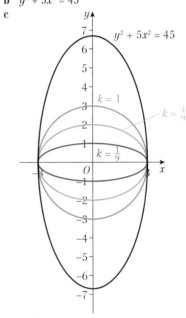

$y^2 + 5x^2 = 45$
$k = 1$
$k = \frac{4}{9}$
$k = \frac{1}{9}$

3 a $y = \dfrac{1}{x}\sin x + \dfrac{c}{x}$ **b** $y = xe^{2x} - e^{2x} + ce^x$

c $y = 3x\operatorname{cosec} x + c\operatorname{cosec} x$ **d** $y = xe^x + cx$

e $y = \ln\!\left(\dfrac{1}{2} + \dfrac{c}{x^2}\right)$ **f** $y = \pm\sqrt{\dfrac{1}{6}x^2 + \dfrac{c}{2x}}$

4 a $y = \dfrac{x + c}{e^{x^2}}$ **b** $y \to 0$

5 a $y = 1 + \dfrac{1}{x} + \dfrac{c}{x^2}$

b $1 + \dfrac{1}{x} + \dfrac{1}{4x^2}$

$1 + \dfrac{1}{x} + \dfrac{1}{x^2}$

$y = 1 + \dfrac{1}{x} + \dfrac{5}{x^2}$

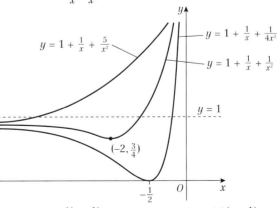

$y = 1 + \frac{1}{x} + \frac{5}{x^2}$
$y = 1 + \frac{1}{x} + \frac{1}{4x^2}$
$y = 1 + \frac{1}{x} + \frac{1}{x^2}$
$y = 1$
$(-2, \frac{3}{4})$
$-\frac{1}{2}$

6 a $y = \dfrac{\ln\dfrac{A(x+1)}{(x+2)}}{\ln x}$ **b** $y = \dfrac{\ln\dfrac{16}{3}\dfrac{(x+1)}{(x+2)}}{\ln x}$

7 a $y = \frac{1}{3}e^x + ce^{-2x}$ **b** $y = -\cot x + c\csc x$

c $y = xe^{\cos x} + ce^{\cos x}$ **d** $y = e^{2x} + ce^x$

e $y = \left(\frac{x^2}{2} + c\right)\cos x$ **f** $y = \frac{1}{x}\ln x + \frac{c}{x}$

g $y = x\ln(x + 2) + cx$ **h** $y = \frac{1}{4}x + cx^{-\frac{1}{3}}$

i $y = (x + 2)\ln(x + 2) + c(x + 2)$

j $y = \frac{1}{x^3}e^x - \frac{1}{x^4}e^x + \frac{c}{x^4}$

8 $y = \frac{1}{x}e^x - \frac{1}{x^2}e^x + \frac{1}{x^2}$

9 $y = -\frac{1}{3x^2} + \frac{4x}{3}$

10 a $y = \frac{1}{3}(x^2 + 1)^2 + \frac{c}{(x^2 + 1)}$

b $y = \frac{1}{3}(x^2 + 1)^2 - \frac{2}{3(x^2 + 1)}$

11 a $y = 1 + \frac{c}{\sec x + \tan x}$

b $y = 1 + \frac{1}{\sec x + \tan x}$ or $y = 1 + \frac{\cos x}{1 + \sin x}$

12 $y = 2\cosh\left(\frac{1}{2}x^2 + c\right)$

13 a $y = e^{\sinh x + c}$ **b** $y = e^{\sinh x + 1}$

14 a $y = \sinh(x + c)$

b

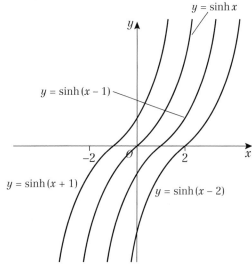

$y = \sinh x$

$y = \sinh(x - 1)$

$y = \sinh(x + 1)$

$y = \sinh(x - 2)$

15 a $y = A\cos x + \sin x$

b $y = -3\cos x + \sin x$

c $x = \frac{\pi}{2} \Rightarrow y = A \times 0 + 1 = 1$

$x = \frac{3\pi}{2} \Rightarrow y = A \times 0 - 1 = -1$

so $\left(\frac{\pi}{2}, 1\right)$ and $\left(\frac{3\pi}{2}, 1\right)$ lie on all possible solution

curves.

16 $y = e^{\frac{bx}{a}} + c$

Exercise 7B

1 a $y = Ae^{-3x} + Be^{-2x}$ **b** $y = Ae^{2x} + Be^{6x}$

c $y = Ae^{-5x} + Be^{3x}$ **d** $y = Ae^{7x} + Be^{-4x}$

e $y = A + Be^{-5x}$ **f** $y = Ae^{-\frac{1}{3}x} + Be^{-2x}$

g $y = Ae^{-\frac{1}{4}x} + Be^{2x}$ **h** $y = Ae^{-\frac{1}{5}x} + Be^{\frac{2}{3}x}$

2 a $y = (A + Bx)e^{-5x}$ **b** $y = (A + Bx)e^{9x}$

c $y = (A + Bx)e^{-x}$ **d** $y = (A + Bx)e^{4x}$

e $y = (A + Bx)e^{-\frac{1}{4}x}$ **f** $y = (A + Bx)e^{\frac{1}{2}x}$

g $y = (A + Bx)e^{-\frac{5}{2}x}$ **h** $y = (A + Bx)e^{-\sqrt{3}x}$

3 a $y = A\cos 5x + B\sin 5x$

b $y = A\cos 9x + B\sin 9x$

c $y = A\cos x + B\sin x$

d $y = A\cos\frac{4}{3}x + B\sin\frac{4}{3}x$

e $y = e^{-4x}(A\cos x + B\sin x)$

f $y = e^{2x}(A\cos x + B\sin x)$

g $y = e^{-10x}(A\cos 3x + B\sin 3x)$

h $y = e^{-\frac{3}{2}x}(A\cos\frac{3}{2}x + B\sin\frac{3}{2}x)$

4 a $y = (A + Bx)e^{-7x}$

b $y = Ae^{-4x} + Be^{3x}$

c $y = e^{-2x}(A\cos 3x + B\sin 3x)$

d $y = (A + Bx)e^{\frac{3}{4}x}$

e $y = e^{\frac{1}{3}x}(A\cos\frac{2}{3}x + B\sin\frac{2}{3}x)$

f $y = Ae^{\frac{2}{3}x} + Be^{-\frac{1}{2}x}$

5 a i $x = Ae^{(-k+\sqrt{k^2-9})t} + Be^{(-k-\sqrt{k^2-9})t}$

ii $x = e^{-t}(A\sin((\sqrt{9 - k^2})t) + B\cos((\sqrt{9 - k^2})t)$

iii $x = (A + Bt)e^{-kt}$

b i $x = e^{-2t}(A\cos(\sqrt{5}t) + B\sin(\sqrt{5}t))$

ii $x \to 0$

6 From auxiliary equation:

$\alpha = -\frac{b}{2a}$ (using quadratic formula)

$b^2 = 4ac$ (setting discriminant = 0)

$y = (A + Bx)e^{\alpha x}$

$\frac{dy}{dx} = \alpha e^{\alpha x}(A + Bx) + Be^{\alpha x}$

$\frac{d^2y}{dx^2} = B\alpha e^{\alpha x} + \alpha^2 e^{\alpha x}(A + Bx) + \alpha Be^{\alpha x}$

Substituting these 5 relationships into

$a\frac{d^2y}{dx^2} + b\frac{dy}{dx} + cy$

yields a result of 0, so $(A + Bx)e^{\alpha x}$ is a solution

7 Substitute $y = Af(x) + Bg(x)$ into differential equation:

$a(Af''(x) + Bg''(x)) + b(Af'(x) + Bg'(x)) + c(Af(x) + Bg(x))$

$= A(af''(x) + bf'(x) + cf(x)) + B(ag''(x) + bg'(x) + cg(x))$

$= A(0) + B(0)$

$= 0$

Challenge

$Ae^{\alpha x} + Be^{\beta x} = Ae^{px}e^{qix} + Be^{px}e^{-qix}$

$= e^{px}((A + B)\cos qx + i(A - B)\sin qx)$

Set $B = A^*$, so that $A = \lambda + \mu i$ and $B = \lambda - \mu i$, $\lambda, \mu \in \mathbb{R}$.

Then $A + B = 2\lambda$ and $i(A - B) = -2\mu$

Hence setting $\lambda = \frac{1}{2}C$ and $\mu = -\frac{1}{2}D$ gives the required result.

Exercise 7C

1 a $y = Ae^{-x} + Be^{-5x} + 2$

b $y = Ae^{6x} + Be^{2x} + 2 + 3x$

c $y = Ae^{-4x} + Be^{3x} - 2e^{2x}$

d $y = Ae^{-5x} + Be^{3x} - \frac{1}{3}$

e $y = (A + Bx)e^{4x} + 1 + \frac{1}{2}x$

f $y = (A + Bx)e^{-x} + 4\sin 2x - 3\cos 2x$

g $y = A\cos 9x + B\sin 9x + \frac{1}{6}e^{3x}$

h $y = A\cos 2x + B\sin 2x + \frac{1}{3}\sin x$

i $y = e^{2x}(A\cos x + B\sin x) + 3 + 8x + 5x^2$

j $y = e^x(A\cos 5x + B\sin 5x) + \frac{1}{25}e^x$

2 a $\frac{1}{4}x^2 - \frac{1}{8}x + \frac{7}{32}$

b $y = Ae^{4x} + Be^x + \frac{1}{4}x^2 - \frac{1}{8}x + \frac{7}{32}$

3 a $Ae^{6x} + B$

b $y = Ae^{6x} + B - \frac{1}{9}x^3 + \frac{1}{36}x^2 - \frac{17}{108}x$

4 $y = A + Be^{-4x} + 2x^3 - \frac{3}{2}x^2 - \frac{3}{4}x$

5 a C.F. contains a term in xe^x. Results in setting up equation in the form of $e^x = 0$. Not possible.

   b $\lambda = \frac{1}{2}$

   c $y = (A + Bx + \frac{1}{2}x^2)e^x$

6 a $y = Ae^{-t} + Be^{-3t} + \frac{5}{3} - \frac{4k}{9} + \frac{kt}{3}$

   b $y = 2t - 1$

Challenge

$y = A\cos x + B\sin x + \left(x - \frac{4}{5}\right)e^{2x}$

Exercise 7D

1 a $y = Ae^{-2x} + Be^{-3x} + e^x$ **b** $y = e^{-3x} - e^{-2x} + e^x$

2 a $y = A + Be^{-2x} + \frac{3}{2}e^{2x}$ **b** $y = 2 - \frac{3}{2}e^{-2x} + \frac{3}{2}e^{2x}$

3 $y = \frac{1}{6}e^{-6x} + \frac{1}{6}e^{7x} - \frac{1}{3}$

4 a $y = A\cos 3x + B\sin 3x + 2\sin x$

   b $y = \cos 3x + 2\sin 3x + 2\sin x$

5 a $y = e^{-\frac{1}{2}x}(A\cos x + B\sin x) + \sin x$

   b $y = \sin x(1 - e^{-\frac{1}{2}x})$

6 a $x = Ae^t + Be^{2t} + t$ **b** $x = e^t + e^{2t} + t$

7 $x = e^{3t} + e^{-3t} - \sin t$

8 a $x = Ae^{2t} + Bte^{2t} + \frac{1}{2}t^3e^{2t}$ **b** $x = (t + \frac{1}{2}t^3)e^{2t}$

9 $x = \frac{1}{2}(\cos\frac{6}{5}t + \sin\frac{6}{5}t + 1)$

10 a $x = e^t(A\cos t + B\sin t) + t^2 + 2t + 1$

   b $x = e^t\sin t + 1 + 2t + t^2$ or $x = e^t\sin t + (1 + t)^2$

11 a $y = Ae^x + Be^{2x} + 3xe^{2x}$ **b** $y = 3e^x - 3e^{2x} + 3xe^{2x}$

12 $y = \frac{1}{18}\sin 3x - \frac{x}{6}\cos 3x$

13 a $x = e^{-t} - e^{-3t}$

   b Setting $\frac{dx}{dt} = 0$ gives $t = \frac{1}{2}\ln 3$, then substituting this into $x = e^{-t} - e^{-3t}$ gives $x = \frac{2\sqrt{3}}{9}$

   Since $\frac{d^2x}{dt^2} < 0$, this is the maximum.

Mixed exercise 7

1 $y = 2\sin x + c\cos x$

2 $y = 5 + c(1 - x^2)^{\frac{1}{2}}$

3 $y = -\frac{x}{2} + \frac{c}{x}$

4 $y = \frac{2}{5}x^{\frac{3}{2}} + \frac{c}{x}$

5 $y = \frac{1}{2} + ce^{-x^2}$

6 $y = 2x + cx\sqrt{1 - x^2}$

7 a $y = \frac{ke^{\lambda x}}{\lambda - a} + ce^{ax}$ **b** $y = \frac{kx^{n+1}}{n + 1}e^{ax} + ce^{ax}$

8 $y = \sin x + A\cosec x$

9 a $y = e^x\cos x + A\cos x$

   b $y = e^x\cos x - (1 + e^\pi)\cos x$

10 $y = -\frac{1}{10}(3\sin x + \cos x) + \frac{1}{10}e^{3x}$

11 a $y = e^{\cosh x + c}$ **b** $y = e^{\cosh x - 1}$

12 $y = \frac{2(3e^{2x^2} - 1)}{3e^{2x^2} + 1}$

13 $y = e^{-\frac{1}{2}x}\left(A\cos\frac{\sqrt{3}}{2}x + B\sin\frac{\sqrt{3}}{2}x\right)$

14 $y = (A + Bx)e^{6x}$

15 $y = A + Be^{4x}$

16 $y = \cos kx + \frac{1}{k}\sin kx$

17 $y = e^x\sin 3x$

18 a $k = \frac{1}{9}$

   b $y = e^{2x}(A\cos 3x + B\sin 3x) + \frac{1}{9}e^{2x}$

19 $y = Ae^x + Be^{-x} + 2xe^x$

20 a $y = (A + Bx)e^{2x}$

   b They are part of the complementary function.

   c $k = 2$ and $y = (A + Bx + 2x^2)e^{2x}$

21 $y = \sin 2t + 2\cos 2t - \cos 3t$

22 a $k = 1, \mu = 2, \lambda = 3$

   b $y = Ae^x + Be^{2x} + xe^{2x} + 2x + 3$

23 a $y = 4e^{-\frac{1}{4}x}\sin\frac{1}{2}x + x + 3$

   b As $x \to \infty$, $e^{-\frac{1}{4}x} \to 0$, so $4e^{-\frac{1}{4}x}\sin\frac{1}{2}x \to 0$ and $y \approx x + 3$.

24 $y = \frac{5}{6}e^{-2x} + \frac{1}{6}(\cos 3x - \sin 3x)$

25 a $x = Ae^{-4t} + Bte^{-4t} + \frac{1}{32}\sin 4t$

   b $x = \frac{1}{2}e^{-4t} + \frac{15}{8}te^{-4t} + \frac{1}{32}\sin 4t$

   c Will oscillate as a sine wave with amplitude $\frac{1}{32}$ and period $\frac{\pi}{2}$

Challenge

1 a $y = \pm\sqrt{\frac{x + c}{1 + x^2}}$ **b** $y = \sqrt{\frac{x + 4}{1 + x^2}}$

2 a $y = \frac{A}{x} + \frac{B}{x^2} + \frac{1}{2}\ln x - \frac{3}{4}$ **b** $y = \frac{4}{x} - \frac{9}{4x^2} + \frac{1}{2}\ln x - \frac{3}{4}$

CHAPTER 8

Prior knowledge check

1 $y = \frac{20x^2 + 2000x}{x + 50}$

2 $y = Ae^{-6x} + B$

3 $y = 4\sin x + 2\cos x + e^{-x}(-2\cos x - 6\sin x)$

Exercise 8A

1 $s = -t\cos t + \sin t + c$

   When $t = 0$, $s = 0$, so $c = 0$.

   So $t = \frac{\pi}{2} \Rightarrow s = 0 + 1 = 1$ m

2 $v = \frac{3}{2} - \frac{3}{2 + t^2}$

3 a $v = 40 - 20e^{0.2t}$ **b** $200\ln 2 - 100$

4 $x = 2\ln\left(\frac{t}{2} + 1\right)$

5 a Integrating factor is e^{-t^2}, so equation becomes

   $ve^{-t^2} = \int te^{-t^2}\,dt \Rightarrow v = e^{t^2}(c - \frac{1}{2}e^{-t^2})$

   $v = 1$ when $t = 0 \Rightarrow c = \frac{3}{2}$, so $v = \frac{1}{2}(3e^{t^2} - 1)$

   b $81.4\,\text{m s}^{-1}$

   c No; velocity would be over 13 million m s^{-1}.

6 a Integrating factor is $(t + 4)^4$, so equation becomes

   $v(t + 4)^4 = 9.8\int(t + 4)^4\,dt = \frac{49}{25}(t + 4)^5 + b$

   $\Rightarrow \quad v = \frac{49(t + 4)^5 - c}{25(t + 4)^4}$

   $v = 0$ when $t = 0 \Rightarrow c = 50176$,

   so $\quad v = \frac{49(t + 4)^5 - 50176}{25(t + 4)^4}$

   b $17.3\,\text{m s}^{-1}$

   c Velocity will increase without limit – unlikely to be the case

7 a The 2.5 ($\text{cm}^3\,\text{hr}^{-1}$) comes from 5% of the 50 cm^3 gas mixture being added.

   The volume of the tank at time t is $(500 + 30t)\,\text{cm}^3$, so the amount of oxygen leaking out is

   $20 \times \dfrac{x}{500 + 30t}\,\text{cm}^3\,\text{hr}^{-1}$.

   b $9.34\,\text{cm}^3$

   c e.g. The model should take into account the fact that the oxygen does not mix throughout immediately on entering the tank

Exercise 8B

1 a Simple harmonic motion
b $x = 2\cos 3t + \sin 3t$ **c** $\sqrt{5}$

2 a $x = 5\cos 4t + \frac{1}{2}\sin 4t$ **b** $\frac{\pi}{2}, \frac{\sqrt{101}}{2}$

3 a Simple harmonic motion
b $\ddot{x} = -5x$
c $x = 5\cos(\sqrt{5}\,t) + \frac{6}{5}\sqrt{5}\sin(\sqrt{5}\,t)$
d $\frac{\sqrt{805}}{5}$

4 a $\frac{7}{2}$
b $x = 6\cos\left(\sqrt{\frac{7}{2}}\,t\right) + \sqrt{\frac{2}{7}}\sin\left(\sqrt{\frac{7}{2}}\,t\right)$
c 3.36 seconds

5 a $x = 0.183\sin\left(\frac{3}{2}t\right) - 1.287\cos\left(\frac{3}{2}t\right)$
b $\frac{2\pi}{3}$
c The model does not allow for any changes in amplitude over time.

6 a Simple harmonic motion
b $x = 0.3\cos(10\sqrt{2}t)$
c $\frac{\pi}{10}\sqrt{2}$s, 0.3m
d $4.24\,\text{m s}^{-1}$ (3 s.f.) or $3\sqrt{2}\,\text{m s}^{-1}$

7 a $x = \cos(12.5t)$ **b** $\frac{4\pi}{25}$

8 a $x = 8\cos(8\sqrt{5}t)$
b $0.351\,s$ (3 s.f.)

9 a $x = 15\cos\left(\frac{5}{3}\sqrt{10}\,t\right)$ cm
b $0.688\,$s, $15\,$cm
c Incorporate a damping effect, for example air resistance. This could take the form of a factor in the x formula which equals 1 at $t = 0$, and decreases down to zero as $t \to \infty$.

Exercise 8C

1 a $2e^{-2t}(\cos 2t + \sin 2t)$
b 0.0901 (3 s.f.)
c Lightly damped

2 $6e^{-2t} - 2e^{-6t}$

3 a $e^{-t}\left(\cos\sqrt{5}t + \frac{1}{\sqrt{5}}\sin\sqrt{5}t\right)$
b $\frac{\pi}{\sqrt{5}}$ or 1.40 (3 s.f.)

4 a $x = ut\,e^{-2kt}$ **b** $t = \frac{1}{2k}$

5 a $F = ma \Rightarrow -2v - 6x = 2a \Rightarrow \ddot{x} + \dot{x} + 3x = 0$
b $x = e^{-\frac{t}{2}}\left(\cos\left(\frac{\sqrt{11}}{2}t\right) + \frac{5}{11}\sqrt{11}\sin\left(\frac{\sqrt{11}}{2}t\right)\right)$
c $-0.459\,$m (3 s.f.)
d Maximum displacement will decrease exponentially (light damping).

6 $x = -\frac{k}{8}\cos 3t + \frac{k}{15}\sin 3t + \frac{k}{8}\cos t$

7 $x = \frac{2U}{3k}e^{-3kt} - \frac{3U}{2k}e^{-2kt} + \frac{5U}{6k}$

8 a $\frac{dx}{dt} = 30\cos t + 10\sin t, \frac{d^2x}{dt^2} = -30\sin t + 10\cos t$
$\Rightarrow 2\frac{d^2x}{dt^2} + 3\frac{dx}{dt} + x = 100\cos t$
b $x = Ae^{-\frac{1}{2}t} + Be^{-t} + 30\sin t - 10\cos t$
c $-34.55\,$m

Exercise 8D

1 $x = \frac{1}{4}(2 + 3\sqrt{2})e^{\sqrt{2}t} + \frac{1}{4}(2 - 3\sqrt{2})e^{-\sqrt{2}t}$
$y = \frac{1}{4}(4 - \sqrt{2})e^{\sqrt{2}t} + \frac{1}{4}(4 + \sqrt{2})e^{-\sqrt{2}t}$

2 a $x = e^{-t}(A\cos t + B\sin t)$
$y = \frac{1}{5}e^{-t}((B - 2A)\cos t - (A + 2B)\sin t)$
OR $y = e^{-t}(A\cos t + B\sin t)$
$x = -e^{-t}((2A + B)\cos t + (2B - A)\sin t)$
depending on your method
b $x = e^{-t}(\cos t + 12\sin t), y = e^{-t}(2\cos t - 5\sin t)$

3 $x = e^{\frac{3t}{2}}\left(\frac{-7}{\sqrt{11}}\sin\left(\frac{\sqrt{11}}{2}t\right) - \cos\left(\frac{\sqrt{11}}{2}t\right)\right) + 1$

$y = e^{\frac{3t}{2}}\left(\cos\left(\frac{\sqrt{11}}{2}t\right) - \frac{3}{\sqrt{11}}\sin\left(\frac{\sqrt{11}}{2}t\right)\right)$

4 a $y = 5\frac{dx}{dt} - x \Rightarrow \frac{dy}{dt} = 5\frac{d^2x}{dt^2} - \frac{dx}{dt}$
$\Rightarrow 5\frac{d^2x}{dt^2} - \frac{dx}{dt} = -0.5x + 0.4\left(5\frac{dx}{dt} - x\right)$
$\Rightarrow \frac{d^2x}{dt^2} - 0.6\frac{dx}{dt} + 0.18x = 0$
b $m^2 - 0.6m + 0.18 = 0 \Rightarrow m = 0.3 \pm 0.3i$
So $x = e^{0.3t}(A\cos 0.3t + B\sin 0.3t)$
c $y = 0.1e^{0.3t}((5A + 15B)\cos 0.3t + (5B - 15A)\sin 0.3t)$
d $t = 6.17...$, during 2018
e 441
f Model seems reasonable for the first few years, but becomes unsuitable in the longer term as x and y oscillate, sometimes giving negative values.

5 a $\frac{dy}{dt} = \frac{1}{2}\frac{d^2x}{dt^2} + \frac{3}{2}\frac{dx}{dt}$,
so $\frac{1}{2}\frac{d^2x}{dt^2} + \frac{3}{2}\frac{dx}{dt} = -2x + \frac{1}{2}\left(\frac{dx}{dt} + 3x\right)$
$\Rightarrow \frac{d^2x}{dt^2} + 2\frac{dx}{dt} + x = 0 \Rightarrow x = (A + Bt)e^{-t}$
$\frac{dx}{dt} = (B - A - Bt)e^{-t} \Rightarrow y = \left(\frac{1}{2}B + A + Bt\right)e^{-t}$
When $t = 0$, $x = A = 1$ and $y = \frac{1}{2}B + 1 = 2 \Rightarrow B = 2$
So $x = (1 + 2t)e^{-t}$ and $y = (2 + 2t)e^{-t}$.
b $x = 0.677$ litres, $y = 0.812$ litres
c The amount of both chemicals tends to zero

6 a $\frac{dx}{dt} = \frac{1}{4}\frac{d^2y}{dt^2} \Rightarrow \frac{1}{4}\frac{d^2y}{dt^2} = -4y \Rightarrow \frac{d^2y}{dt^2} = -16y$
$\Rightarrow \ddot{y} = -4^2y$. This is SHM in the y direction.
b $x = 4\cos 4t - 5\sin 4t, y = 4\sin 4t + 5\cos 4t$

7 a $y = 100\frac{dx}{dt} + 3x - 5000 \Rightarrow \frac{dy}{dt} = 100\frac{d^2x}{dt^2} + 3\frac{dx}{dt}$
$\Rightarrow 100\frac{d^2x}{dt^2} + 3\frac{dx}{dt} = 0.01x - 0.03\left(100\frac{dx}{dt} + 3x - 5000\right)$
$\Rightarrow \frac{d^2x}{dt^2} + 0.06\frac{dx}{dt} + 0.0008 = 1.5$
b $x = 1875 + Ae^{-\frac{1}{25}t} + Be^{-\frac{1}{50}t}, y = 625 - Ae^{-\frac{1}{25}t} + Be^{-\frac{1}{50}t}$
c x tends to a limiting value of 1875 and y tends to a limiting value of 625.

8 a $y = \frac{dx}{dt} + 2x - 1 \Rightarrow \frac{dy}{dt} = \frac{d^2x}{dt^2} + 2\frac{dx}{dt}$
So $\frac{d^2x}{dt^2} + 2\frac{dx}{dt} = 4x + \left(\frac{dx}{dt} + 2x - 1\right) + 2$
$\Rightarrow \frac{d^2x}{dt^2} + \frac{dx}{dt} - 6x = 1$
b $x = Ae^{2t} + Be^{-3t} - \frac{1}{6}, y = Ae^{2t} - 4Be^{-3t} + \frac{13}{6}$
c Model not suitable since for large values of t, the amount of nutrients grows exponentially without limit.

Online Full worked solutions are available in SolutionBank.

Challenge

96 owls and 4800 field mice.

Mixed exercise 8

1 a $v = 18 - 10e^{-t^2}$ b $18\,\mathrm{m\,s^{-1}}$

2 6

3 a $v = 10 - \dfrac{50}{2t + 5}$ b $(100 - 25\ln 5)\,\mathrm{m} \approx 59.8\,\mathrm{m}$

4 a $\dfrac{\pi}{2}\,\mathrm{m\,s^{-1}}$

   b $x = \dfrac{1}{4}t^2 - \dfrac{1}{8}\cos 2t + c.\ x = 0$ when $t = 0 \Rightarrow c = \dfrac{1}{8}$

   $t = \dfrac{\pi}{4} \Rightarrow x = \dfrac{\pi^2}{64} - 0 + \dfrac{1}{8} = \dfrac{1}{64}(\pi^2 + 8)$

5 a $v = 2t + \ln(t + 1)$ b $(2 + 3\ln 3)\,\mathrm{m}$

6 a Integrating factor is e^{-3t}, then solve the differential equation to get $V = -\dfrac{2}{3}t - \dfrac{17}{9} + \dfrac{26}{9}e^{3t}$

   b $1162.2\,\mathrm{cm^3}$

   c Bacteria will reproduce without limit – build in some limiting/decay factor

7 a The 1200 comes from 4g per incoming litre of water, per day. The fraction is from the leaking, which is the total grams x, times the proportion of the reservoir leaking out, which is $\dfrac{200}{10\,000 + 100t}$

   b $7860\,\mathrm{g}$

   c e.g. The model should take into account the fact that the contaminant does not mix throughout immediately on entry.

8 a Simple harmonic motion

   b General solution is $x = A\cos 7t + B\sin 7t$
   At rest at $t = 0$ gives $B = 0$, and A is the displacement of B from A. The period is then $\dfrac{2\pi}{7}$ (seconds)

9 a Simple harmonic motion

   b $x = 4\cos\!\left(5\sqrt{\dfrac{2}{3}}\,t\right)$
   Period is $1.54\,\mathrm{s}$ (3 s.f.)
   Amplitude is $(4 - 2.5)\,\mathrm{m} = 1.5\,\mathrm{m}$

10 a $x = 2.161\cos(\tfrac{1}{2}t) + 3.366\sin(\tfrac{1}{2}t)$

    b 2π

    c The model does not allow for any changes in amplitude over time or the effect of oscillations in the fisherman's line, for example.

11 a $x = e^{-kt}\!\left(A\cos(t\sqrt{n^2 - k^2}) + B\sin(t\sqrt{n^2 - k^2})\right)$

    b $\dfrac{2\pi}{\sqrt{n^2 - k^2}}$

12 a Solving the equation gives $x = e^{-kt}(A\cos kt + B\sin kt)$
    and $\dfrac{dx}{dt} = ke^{-kt}((-A + B)\cos kt + (-B - A)\sin kt)$
    When $t = 0$, $x = 0$ and $\dfrac{dx}{dt} = U$, so $A = 0$ and $B = \dfrac{U}{k}$
    So when P is instantaneously at rest,
    $\dfrac{dx}{dt} = Ue^{-kt}(\cos kt - \sin kt) = 0 \Rightarrow \tan kt = 1$
    $\Rightarrow kt = \left(n + \dfrac{1}{4}\right)\pi,\ n \in \mathbb{N}.$

    d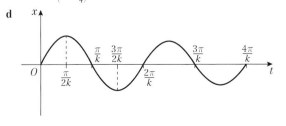

13 a $x = Ut - \dfrac{U}{n}\sin nt$ b $\dfrac{2\pi}{n}$ c $\dfrac{2U\pi}{n}$

14 a $\dfrac{dx}{dt} = 30\cos t - 15\sin t,\ \dfrac{d^2x}{dt^2} = -30\sin t - 15\cos t$
    So $\dfrac{d^2x}{dt^2} + 4\dfrac{dx}{dt} + 3x = 150\cos t$

    b $x = Ae^{-t} + Be^{-3t} + 30\sin t + 15\cos t$

    c $-29\,\mathrm{m}$

15 a $x = e^{-t}(A\cos 3t + B\sin 3t) + 3\cos t$

    b $x = 2e^{-t}\sin 3t + 3\cos t$

    c When $t = 7$, the first term in the expression for x is very small compared to the second, so can be ignored. So $x \approx 3\cos t$, which has a distance of 6 between maximum and minimum values.

16 a $y = \dfrac{dx}{dt} - 2x \Rightarrow \dfrac{dy}{dt} = \dfrac{d^2x}{dt^2} - 2\dfrac{dx}{dt}$
    So $\dfrac{d^2x}{dt^2} - 2\dfrac{dx}{dt} = -2x + 4\!\left(\dfrac{dx}{dt} - 2x\right)$
    $\Rightarrow \dfrac{d^2x}{dt^2} - 6\dfrac{dx}{dt} + 10x = 0$

    b Auxiliary equation has solutions $m = 3 \pm \mathrm{i}$, so the equation has solution $x = e^{3t}(A\cos t + B\sin t)$.

    c $y = e^{3t}((A + B)\cos t + (B - A)\sin t)$

    d 2009

    e 1113

    f The model predicts a huge amount of hedgehogs when the slugs die out so it might not be sensible.

17 a $3\dfrac{dy}{dt} = \dfrac{d^2x}{dt^2} + 4\dfrac{dx}{dt}$, so $\dfrac{d^2x}{dt^2} + 2\dfrac{dx}{dt} + x = 0$
    This has general solution $x = (A + Bt)e^{-t}$.
    $\dfrac{dx}{dt} = Be^{-t} - (A + Bt)e^{-t} \Rightarrow y = \dfrac{1}{3}((B + 3A) + 3Bt)e^{-t}$
    Using the initial conditions, $A = 10$ and $B = 30$, so
    $x = 30te^{-t} + 10e^{-t}$ and $y = 30te^{-t} + 20e^{-t}$.

    b 9 of organism M and 10 of organism N

    c The numbers of each organism tend to zero

18 a $\dfrac{1}{2}x = \dfrac{dy}{dt} + \dfrac{2}{3}y - 1 \Rightarrow \dfrac{dx}{dt} = 2\dfrac{d^2y}{dt^2} + \dfrac{4}{3}\dfrac{dy}{dt}$
    $2\dfrac{d^2y}{dt^2} + \dfrac{4}{3}\dfrac{dy}{dt} = 2 + \dfrac{1}{3}y - \left(\dfrac{dy}{dt} + \dfrac{2}{3}y - 1\right)$
    $\Rightarrow \dfrac{2d^2y}{dt^2} + \dfrac{7}{3}\dfrac{dy}{dt} + \dfrac{1}{3}y = 3$
    $6\dfrac{d^2y}{dt^2} + 7\dfrac{dy}{dt} + y = 9$

    b $x = -\dfrac{2}{5}e^{-t} - \dfrac{8}{5}e^{-\frac{t}{6}} + 10,\ y = \dfrac{3}{5}e^{-t} - \dfrac{8}{5}e^{-\frac{t}{6}} + 9$

    c As t becomes large $e^{-t} \to 0$, so there will be approximately 10 litres in tank A and 9 litres in tank B.

Challenge

a i $\dfrac{dX}{dt} = -X \Rightarrow \int\dfrac{dX}{X} = -\int dt \Rightarrow X = ce^{-t}$
      $X = 300$ when $t = 0 \Rightarrow c = 300$, so $X = 300e^{-t}$

   ii 20 minutes

   iii $600 - 100e^{-t}(3t + 5)$ or equivalent

b i $x' = -2x,\ y' = 2x - y,\ x(0) = V,\ y(0) = 0$
      $\Rightarrow x = Ve^{-2t},\ y = 2V(e^{-t} - e^{-2t}).$
      $y' = 0 \Rightarrow 2x = y \Rightarrow e^{-2t} = e^{-t} - e^{-2t}$
      $\Rightarrow t = \ln 2$ hours $= 42$ mins (nearest minute)

   ii $\ln 3$ hours

Review exercise 2

1 a $r = 2$ b $r = 3\sec\theta$

   c $r = 2\sqrt{3}\,\sec\!\left(\theta - \dfrac{\pi}{6}\right)$

2 a

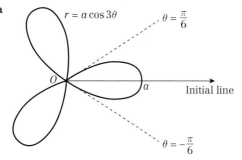

$r = a\cos 3\theta$

$\theta = \dfrac{\pi}{6}$

O a Initial line

$\theta = -\dfrac{\pi}{6}$

b $\dfrac{\pi}{12}a^2$

3 a

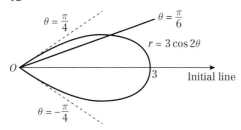

$\theta = \dfrac{\pi}{4}$ $\theta = \dfrac{\pi}{6}$

$r = 3\cos 2\theta$

O 3 Initial line

$\theta = -\dfrac{\pi}{4}$

b $\dfrac{3}{32}(2\pi - 3\sqrt{3})$ **c** $\dfrac{2\sqrt{6}}{3}$

4 a

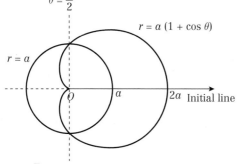

$\theta = \dfrac{\pi}{2}$

$r = a\,(1 + \cos\theta)$

$r = a$

O a $2a$ Initial line

b $r = \dfrac{3\sqrt{3}a}{4}\operatorname{cosec}\theta$

$r = -\dfrac{3\sqrt{3}a}{4}\operatorname{cosec}\theta$

$\theta = \pi$

c The circle and the cardioid meet when
$a = a(1 + \cos\theta) \Rightarrow \cos\theta = 0 \Rightarrow \theta = \pm\dfrac{\pi}{2}$

$A = 2 \times \dfrac{1}{2}\displaystyle\int_0^{\frac{\pi}{2}} r^2\,\mathrm{d}\theta$

$\displaystyle\int_0^{\frac{\pi}{2}} r^2\,\mathrm{d}\theta = \int_0^{\frac{\pi}{2}} a^2(1 + \cos\theta)^2\,\mathrm{d}\theta$

$\qquad = \displaystyle\int_0^{\frac{\pi}{2}} a^2(1 + 2\cos\theta + \cos^2\theta)\,\mathrm{d}\theta$

$\qquad = \displaystyle\int_0^{\frac{\pi}{2}} a^2\left(1 + 2\cos\theta + \dfrac{1}{2}\cos 2\theta + \dfrac{1}{2}\right)\mathrm{d}\theta$

$\qquad = a^2\displaystyle\int_0^{\frac{\pi}{2}}\left(2\cos\theta + \dfrac{1}{2}\cos 2\theta + \dfrac{3}{2}\right)\mathrm{d}\theta$

$\qquad = a^2\left[2\sin\theta + \dfrac{1}{4}\sin 2\theta + \dfrac{3\theta}{2}\right]_0^{\frac{\pi}{2}} = a^2\left(\dfrac{3\pi}{4} + 2\right)$

The required area is A less half the circle

$a^2\left(\dfrac{3\pi}{4} + 2\right) - \dfrac{1}{2}\pi a^2 = \left(\dfrac{\pi + 8}{4}\right)a^2$

5 a

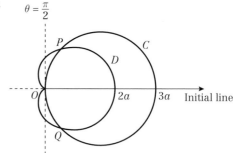

$\theta = \dfrac{\pi}{2}$

P C D

O $2a$ $3a$ Initial line

Q

b $P\left(\dfrac{3}{2}a, \dfrac{\pi}{3}\right), Q\left(\dfrac{3}{2}a, -\dfrac{\pi}{3}\right)$

c $\dfrac{a^2}{16}(4\pi + 9\sqrt{3})$

d Let the smaller area enclosed by C and the half-line $\theta = \dfrac{\pi}{3}$ be A_2:

$R = \pi\left(\dfrac{3a}{2}\right)^2 - 2A_1 - 2A_2$

$\quad = \dfrac{9a^2\pi}{4} - \dfrac{2a^2}{16}(4\pi + 9\sqrt{3}) - \dfrac{6a^2}{16}(2\pi - 3\sqrt{3})$

$\quad = \dfrac{9a^2\pi}{4} - \dfrac{a^2\pi}{2} - \dfrac{9\sqrt{3}a^2}{8} - \dfrac{3a^2\pi}{4} + \dfrac{9\sqrt{3}a^2}{8} = \pi a^2$

6 a

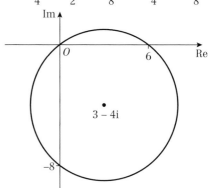

Im

O 6 Re

$3 - 4i$

-8

b In Cartesian form: $(x - 3)^2 + (y + 4)^2 = 25$
$\Rightarrow (r\cos\theta - 3)^2 + (r\sin\theta + 4)^2 = 25$
$\Rightarrow r^2\cos^2\theta - 6r\cos\theta + 9 + r^2\sin^2\theta + 8r\sin\theta$
$\qquad + 16 = 25$
$\Rightarrow r^2(\cos^2\theta + \sin^2\theta) - 6r\cos\theta + 8r\sin\theta = 0$
$\Rightarrow r^2(\cos^2\theta + \sin^2\theta) = r(6\cos\theta - 8\sin\theta)$
$\Rightarrow r = (6\cos\theta - 8\sin\theta)$

c 63.3

7 a

$\theta = \dfrac{\pi}{4}$ A $r = \cos 2\theta$

O 1 Initial line

$\theta = -\dfrac{\pi}{4}$ B

b $(0.667, 0.421)$ and $(0.667, -0.421)$

8 a

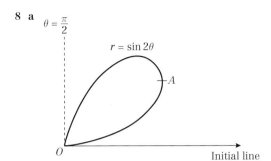

b $(0.943, 0.615)$

9 a $(x - 3)^2 + y^2 = 9$
$x + \sqrt{3}\,y = 6$

b

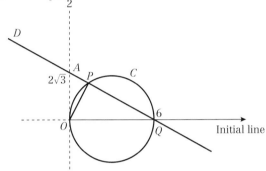

c $P\left(3, \frac{\pi}{3}\right), Q(6, 0)$

10 $\frac{1}{2}a^2$

11 $A = \frac{1}{2}\int_{\frac{\pi}{8}}^{\frac{\pi}{4}} r^2 \, d\theta = \frac{1}{2}\int_{\frac{\pi}{8}}^{\frac{\pi}{4}} 16\,a^2 \cos^2 2\theta \, d\theta$

$= 4\,a^2 \int_{\frac{\pi}{8}}^{\frac{\pi}{4}} (1 + \cos 4\theta)\,d\theta = 4\,a^2\left[\theta + \frac{1}{4}\sin 4\theta\right]_{\frac{\pi}{8}}^{\frac{\pi}{4}}$

$= 4\,a^2\left(\frac{\pi}{8} - \frac{1}{4}\right) = \frac{1}{2}a^2(\pi - 2)$

12 $\frac{9}{8}\pi a^2$

13 a $\theta = \frac{\pi}{12}, \frac{5\pi}{12}$ **b** $\frac{\pi}{12} - \frac{\sqrt{3}}{16}$

14 a $P(4a, 1.107), Q(4a, -1.107)$

b $\frac{5\sqrt{5}}{4}$ m

c $\frac{2875\pi}{32}$ m²

15 a $\frac{3}{2}\pi a^2$

b $A:\left(\frac{1}{2}a, \frac{2\pi}{3}\right), B:\left(\frac{1}{2}a, -\frac{2\pi}{3}\right)$

c $\frac{9}{4}a$

d $\frac{27\sqrt{3}}{8}a^2$

e 113 cm^2 (3 s.f.)

16 a $A:\left(\frac{3}{2}a, -\frac{\pi}{3}\right), B:\left(\frac{3}{2}a, \frac{\pi}{3}\right)$

b $AB = 2 \times \frac{3}{2}a \sin \frac{\pi}{3} = \frac{3\sqrt{3}}{2}a$

c $(9\sqrt{3} - 4\pi)a^2$

d 9.07 cm^2 (3 s.f.)

17 a $A:(5a, 0), B:(3a, 0)$

b $C:\left(4a, \frac{5\pi}{3}\right), D:\left(4a, \frac{\pi}{3}\right)$

c $A_1 = 2 \times \frac{1}{2}\int_{\frac{\pi}{3}}^{\pi} r^2 \, d\theta = \int_{\frac{\pi}{3}}^{\pi} a^2(3 + 2\cos\theta)^2 \, d\theta$

$= a^2 \int_{\frac{\pi}{3}}^{\pi} (9 + 12\cos\theta + 4\cos^2\theta)\,d\theta$

$= a^2 \int_{\frac{\pi}{3}}^{\pi} (11 + 12\cos\theta + 2\cos 2\theta)\,d\theta$

$= a^2[11\theta + 12\sin\theta + \sin 2\theta]_{\frac{\pi}{3}}^{\pi} = a^2\left(\frac{22\pi}{3} - \frac{13\sqrt{3}}{2}\right)$

$A_2 = 2 \times \frac{1}{2}\int_0^{\frac{\pi}{3}} a^2(5 - 2\cos\theta)^2 \, d\theta$

$= a^2 \int_0^{\frac{\pi}{3}} (25 - 20\cos\theta + 4\cos^2\theta)\,d\theta$

$= a^2 \int_0^{\frac{\pi}{3}} (27 - 20\cos\theta + 2\cos 2\theta)\,d\theta$

$= a^2\left[27\theta - 20\sin\theta + \sin 2\theta\right]_0^{\frac{\pi}{3}} = a^2\left(\frac{27\pi}{3} - \frac{19\sqrt{3}}{2}\right)$

$A_1 + A_2 = a^2\left(\frac{22\pi}{3} - \frac{13\sqrt{3}}{2}\right) + a^2\left(\frac{27\pi}{3} - \frac{19\sqrt{3}}{2}\right)$

$= \frac{a^2}{3}(49\pi + 48\sqrt{3})$

18 $\frac{1}{2}\ln 3$

19 $\ln\left(\frac{1}{3}\right), \ln 3$

20 $p = 3, q = \frac{20}{3}$

21 $\ln\frac{1}{3}, \ln 7$

22 $x = \frac{1}{2}\ln\frac{1}{3}, \frac{1}{2}\ln\frac{3}{5}$

23 a $k \geq \sqrt{3}$ **b** $0, -\ln 3$

24 a $\cosh^2 x - \sinh^2 x = \left(\frac{e^x + e^{-x}}{2}\right)^2 - \left(\frac{e^x - e^{-x}}{2}\right)^2$

$= \frac{e^{2x} + 2 + e^{-2x} - (e^{2x} - 2 + e^{-2x})}{4} = \frac{4}{4} = 1$

b $k = -1, a = 2$

25 a $2\cosh^2 x - 1 = 2\left(\frac{e^x + e^{-x}}{2}\right)^2 - 1 = \frac{e^{2x} + 2 + e^{-2x}}{2} - 1$

$= \frac{e^{2x} + e^{-2x}}{2} = \cosh 2x$

b $\pm\ln(3 + \sqrt{8})$

26 a $4\cosh^3 x - 3\cosh x = 4\left(\frac{e^x + e^{-x}}{2}\right)^3 - 3\left(\frac{e^x + e^{-x}}{2}\right)$

$= \frac{e^{3x} + 3e^x + 3e^{-x} + e^{-3x}}{2} - \frac{3e^x + 3e^{-x}}{2} = \frac{e^{3x} + e^{-3x}}{2}$

$= \cosh 3x$

b $\ln(\sqrt{2} \pm 1)$

27 a $\cosh A \cosh B - \sinh A \sinh B$

$= \left(\frac{e^A + e^{-A}}{2}\right)\left(\frac{e^B + e^{-B}}{2}\right) - \left(\frac{e^A - e^{-A}}{2}\right)\left(\frac{e^B - e^{-B}}{2}\right)$

$= \frac{1}{4}(e^{A+B} + e^{-A+B} + e^{A-B} + e^{-A-B} - e^{A+B} + e^{-A+B}$
$\quad + e^{A-B} - e^{-A-B})$

$= \frac{1}{4}(2e^{-A+B} + 2e^{A-B}) = \frac{e^{A-B} + e^{-(A-B)}}{2} = \cosh(A - B)$

b $\cosh x \cosh 1 - \sinh x \sinh 1 = \sinh x$
$\cosh x \cosh 1 = \sinh x(1 + \sinh 1)$

$\tanh x = \frac{\cosh 1}{1 + \sinh 1} = \frac{\dfrac{e + e^{-1}}{2}}{1 + \dfrac{e - e^{-1}}{2}} = \frac{e + e^{-1}}{2 + e - e^{-1}}$

$= \frac{e^2 + 1}{e^2 + 2e - 1}$

28 a Let $\operatorname{arsinh} x \Rightarrow x = \sinh y = \dfrac{e^y - e^{-y}}{2}$

$\Rightarrow 2x = e^y - e^{-y} \Rightarrow e^{2y} - 2x e^y - 1 = 0$

$\Rightarrow e^y = \dfrac{2x + \sqrt{4x^2 + 4}}{2} = x + \sqrt{x^2 + 1}$

$\Rightarrow y = \ln(x + \sqrt{x^2 + 1})$

b $\operatorname{arsinh}(\cot\theta) = \ln\left[\cot\theta + \sqrt{1 + \cot^2\theta}\right]$

$= \ln(\cot\theta + \operatorname{cosec}\theta)$

$= \ln\left(\dfrac{\cos\theta + 1}{\sin\theta}\right) = \ln\left|\dfrac{2\cos^2\dfrac{\theta}{2}}{2\sin\dfrac{\theta}{2}\cos\dfrac{\theta}{2}}\right| = \ln\left(\cot\dfrac{\theta}{2}\right)$

29 a Let $y = \operatorname{artanh} x$

$x = \tanh y = \dfrac{e^{2y} - 1}{e^{2y} + 1}$

$e^{2y} = \dfrac{1 + x}{1 - x} \Rightarrow 2y = \ln\left(\dfrac{1 + x}{1 - x}\right)$

$\Rightarrow y = \dfrac{1}{2}\ln\left(\dfrac{1 + x}{1 - x}\right)$ for $|x| < 1$

b

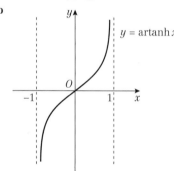

c $\dfrac{1}{2}, \dfrac{1}{3}$

30 a $\ln\left(\dfrac{1 - \sqrt{1 - x^2}}{x}\right) + \ln\left(\dfrac{1 + \sqrt{1 - x^2}}{x}\right)$

$= \ln\left(\dfrac{1 - \sqrt{1 - x^2}}{x}\right)\left(\dfrac{1 + \sqrt{1 - x^2}}{x}\right)$

$= \ln\left(\dfrac{1 - (1 - x^2)}{x^2}\right) = \ln\dfrac{x^2}{x^2} = \ln 1 = 0$

b $y = \operatorname{arcosh}\left(\dfrac{1}{x}\right) \Rightarrow \cosh y = \dfrac{1}{x} \Rightarrow \dfrac{e^y + e^{-y}}{2} = \dfrac{1}{x}$

$\Rightarrow x e^y + x e^{-y} - 2 = 0 \Rightarrow x e^{2y} - 2 e^y + x = 0$

$\Rightarrow e^y = \dfrac{2 \pm \sqrt{4 - 4x^2}}{2x} = \dfrac{1 \pm \sqrt{1 - x^2}}{x}$

$\Rightarrow y = \ln\left(\dfrac{1 + \sqrt{1 - x^2}}{x}\right)$

c $\pm\ln\left(\dfrac{3 + \sqrt{5}}{2}\right)$

31 a $\cosh 3\theta = 4\cosh^3\theta - 3\cosh\theta$
$\cosh 5\theta = 16\cosh^5\theta - 20\cosh^3\theta + 5\cosh\theta$

b ± 0.96

32 a $\cosh 2x = \dfrac{e^{2x} + e^{-2x}}{2} = \dfrac{e^{2\ln k} + e^{-2\ln k}}{2} = \dfrac{e^{\ln k^2} + e^{\ln\frac{1}{k^2}}}{2}$

$= \dfrac{1}{2}\left(k^2 + \dfrac{1}{k^2}\right) = \dfrac{k^4 + 1}{2k^2}$

b $\dfrac{128}{289}$

33 a $\dfrac{1}{4}\ln(2 + \sqrt{3})$

b $\tanh^2 4x = 1 - \operatorname{sech}^2 4x = 1 - \dfrac{1}{4} = \dfrac{3}{4}$

As $x \geqslant 0$, $\tanh 4x = \dfrac{\sqrt{3}}{2}$

At $x = \dfrac{1}{4}\ln(2 + \sqrt{3})$,

$y = -x + \tanh 4x = -\dfrac{1}{4}\ln(2 + \sqrt{3}) + \dfrac{\sqrt{3}}{2}$

$= \dfrac{1}{4}(2\sqrt{3} - \ln(2 + \sqrt{3}))$

34 a $2x + \dfrac{16}{3}x^3 + \dfrac{64}{15}x^5$

b $\dfrac{2^{4n-3}}{(2n - 1)!}x^{2n-1}$

35 a $1 - \dfrac{3}{2}x^2$ **b** 0.0029%

36 $x = \dfrac{a}{\sinh\theta} \Rightarrow \dfrac{dx}{d\theta} = -\dfrac{a\cosh\theta}{\sinh^2\theta}$

$\displaystyle\int \dfrac{1}{x\sqrt{x^2 + a^2}}\,dx = \int \dfrac{-\dfrac{a\cosh\theta}{\sinh^2\theta}}{\dfrac{a^2\sqrt{1 + \sinh^2\theta}}{\sinh^2\theta}}\,d\theta = -\dfrac{1}{a}\int 1\,d\theta$

$= -\dfrac{1}{a}\theta + c = -\dfrac{1}{a}\operatorname{arsinh}\left(\dfrac{a}{x}\right) + c$

37 a $y = \operatorname{artanh} x \Rightarrow \tanh y = x$

Differentiate implicitly with respect to x

$\operatorname{sech}^2 y\dfrac{dy}{dx} = 1 \Rightarrow \dfrac{dy}{dx} = \dfrac{1}{\operatorname{sech}^2 y} = \dfrac{1}{1 - \tanh^2 y} = \dfrac{1}{1 - x^2}$

b $x\operatorname{artanh} x + \dfrac{1}{2}\ln(1 - x^2) + A$

38 a Let $y = \operatorname{arsinh} x \Rightarrow x = \sinh y = \dfrac{e^y - e^{-y}}{2}$

$\Rightarrow 2x = e^y - e^{-y} \Rightarrow e^{2y} - 2x e^y - 1 = 0$

$\Rightarrow e^y = \dfrac{2x + \sqrt{4x^2 + 4}}{2} = x + \sqrt{x^2 + 1}$

$\Rightarrow y = \ln(x + \sqrt{x^2 + 1})$

b $y = \operatorname{arsinh} x \Rightarrow \sinh y = x$

Differentiating implicitly with respect to x

$\cosh y\dfrac{dy}{dx} = 1 \Rightarrow \dfrac{dy}{dx} = \dfrac{1}{\cosh y} = \dfrac{1}{\sqrt{1 + \sinh^2 y}} = \dfrac{1}{\sqrt{1 + x^2}}$

$\Rightarrow \dfrac{d}{dx}(\operatorname{arsinh} x) = (1 + x^2)^{-\frac{1}{2}}$

c $y = (\operatorname{arsinh} x)^2$, $\dfrac{dy}{dx} = 2\operatorname{arsinh} x(1 + x^2)^{-\frac{1}{2}}$

$\dfrac{d^2 y}{dx^2} = 2(1 + x^2)^{-1} - 2x\operatorname{arsinh} x(1 + x^2)^{-\frac{3}{2}}$

$\Rightarrow (1 + x^2)\dfrac{d^2 y}{dx^2} + x\dfrac{dy}{dx} - 2$

$= 2 - 2x\operatorname{arsinh} x(1 + x^2)^{-\frac{1}{2}} + 2x\operatorname{arsinh} x(1 + x^2)^{-\frac{1}{2}} - 2$

$= 0$

d $\ln(1 + \sqrt{2}) - \sqrt{2} + 1$

39 a $p = 2, q = 1, r = 4$

b $\dfrac{1}{4}\arctan\left(\dfrac{2x + 1}{2}\right) + c$

c $\displaystyle\int \dfrac{2}{\sqrt{4x^2 + 4x + 5}}\,dx = \int \dfrac{2}{\sqrt{(2x + 1)^2 + 4}}\,dx$

Let $2x + 1 = 2\sinh\theta \Rightarrow \dfrac{dx}{d\theta} = \cosh\theta$

$\displaystyle\int \dfrac{2}{\sqrt{(2x + 1)^2 + 4}}\,dx = \int \dfrac{2}{\sqrt{4\sinh^2\theta + 4}}\cosh\theta\,d\theta = \int 1\,d\theta$

$= \theta + c = \operatorname{arsinh}\left(\dfrac{2x + 1}{2}\right) + c$

Using $\operatorname{arsinh} x = \ln(x + \sqrt{x^2 + 1})$

$\int \dfrac{2}{\sqrt{4x^2 + 4x + 5}} \, dx = \ln\left(\dfrac{2x+1}{2} + \sqrt{\left(\dfrac{2x+1}{2}\right)^2 + 1}\right) + c$

$= \ln\left(\dfrac{2x+1}{2} + \dfrac{1}{2}\sqrt{4x^2 + 4x + 5}\right) + c$

$= \ln(2x + 1 + \sqrt{4x^2 + 4x + 5}) - \ln 2 + c$

$= \ln(2x + 1 + \sqrt{4x^2 + 4x + 5}) + k$

40 $\dfrac{\sqrt{4x^2 + 9}}{4} + \operatorname{arsinh}\left(\dfrac{2x}{3}\right) + c$

41 $\displaystyle\int_2^5 \dfrac{1}{\sqrt{x^2 - 4x + 8}} \, dx = \int_2^5 \dfrac{1}{\sqrt{(x-2)^2 + 2^2}} \, dx$

$= \left[\operatorname{arsinh}\left(\dfrac{x-2}{2}\right)\right]_2^5 = \operatorname{arsinh}\left(\dfrac{3}{2}\right) - \operatorname{arsinh} 0$

$= \operatorname{arsinh}\left(\dfrac{3}{2}\right)$, so $k = \dfrac{3}{2}$

42 $\displaystyle\int x \operatorname{arcosh} x \, dx = \dfrac{x^2}{2}\operatorname{arcosh} x - \int \dfrac{x^2}{2\sqrt{x^2 - 1}} \, dx$

Use integration by substitution to evaluate $\displaystyle\int \dfrac{x^2}{2\sqrt{x^2 - 1}} \, dx$

Let $x = \cosh\theta \Rightarrow \dfrac{dx}{d\theta} = \sinh\theta$

$\displaystyle\int \dfrac{x^2}{2\sqrt{x^2 - 1}} \, dx = \int \dfrac{(\cosh\theta)^2}{2\sqrt{(\cosh\theta)^2 - 1}} \sinh\theta \, d\theta$

$= \dfrac{1}{2}\int \cosh^2\theta \, d\theta = \dfrac{1}{4}\int (\cosh 2\theta + 1) \, d\theta$

$= \dfrac{\sinh 2\theta}{8} + \dfrac{\theta}{4} = \dfrac{\sinh\theta \cosh\theta}{4} + \dfrac{\theta}{4}$

$= \dfrac{x\sqrt{x^2 - 1}}{4} + \dfrac{1}{4}\operatorname{arcosh} x$

Area of $R = \left[\dfrac{x^2}{2}\operatorname{arcosh} x - \dfrac{x\sqrt{x^2 - 1}}{4} - \dfrac{1}{4}\operatorname{arcosh} x\right]_1^2$

$= \left(\dfrac{7}{4}\operatorname{arcosh} 2 - \dfrac{\sqrt{3}}{2}\right) - 0$

$= \dfrac{7}{4}\ln(2 + \sqrt{3}) - \dfrac{\sqrt{3}}{2}$

43 688 m^3

44 $y = x^2 - x + \dfrac{c}{x^4}$

45 $y = \dfrac{x^3}{2} + cx$

46 $y = \dfrac{x + \ln x + c}{(x + 1)^2}$

47 $y = \dfrac{1}{2}(e^{2x} + 3)\cos x$

48 $y = \dfrac{2\sin^3 x}{3\sin 2x} + \dfrac{c}{\sin 2x}$

49 $y = \dfrac{5e^x}{4(1 + x)} - \dfrac{xe^{-x}}{2(1 + x)} - \dfrac{e^{-x}}{4(1 + x)}$

50 a $y = \sin x \cos x + c \cos x$

b $\cos x = 0, 0 \leqslant x \leqslant 2\pi \Rightarrow x = \dfrac{\pi}{2}, \dfrac{3\pi}{2}$

The points $\left(\dfrac{\pi}{2}, 0\right)$ and $\left(\dfrac{3\pi}{2}, 0\right)$ lie on all of the solution curves for the differential equation.

c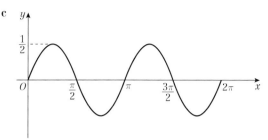

51 a $y = \dfrac{x}{2} - \dfrac{1}{4} + ce^{-2x}$ **b** $\left(\dfrac{1}{2}\ln 5, \dfrac{1}{4}\ln 5\right)$

c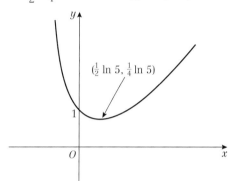

$\left(\dfrac{1}{2}\ln 5, \dfrac{1}{4}\ln 5\right)$

52 a $y = e^{\cosh x + c}$ **b** $y = e^{\cosh x + 2}$

53 $\theta = 3e^{-2t}\cos t$

54 a $k = 12$

b $y = 2\cos 2x - \dfrac{\pi}{4}\sin 2x + 3x\sin 2x$

55 a $a = 5, b = 1$

b $y = e^{2x}(3 + 2x) + 5 + x$

56 a $y = e^{-2x}(A\cos x + B\sin x) + \sin 2x - 8\cos 2x$

b As $x \to \infty$, $e^{-kx} \to 0 \Rightarrow y \to \sin 2x - 8\cos 2x$

Let $\sin 2x - 8\cos 2x = R\sin(2x - \alpha)$

$= R\sin 2x \cos\alpha - R\cos 2x \sin\alpha$

Equating the coefficients of $\cos 2x$ and $\sin 2x$

$\Rightarrow R = \sqrt{65}$, $\tan\alpha = 8$

Hence, for large x, y can be approximated by the sine function $\sqrt{65}\sin(2x - \alpha)$, where $\tan\alpha = 8$ ($\alpha \approx 82.9°$)

57 a $y = e^{-t}(A\cos t + B\sin t) + 2e^{-t}$

b $y = e^{-t}(2\sin t - \cos t) + 2e^{-t}$

58 a $x = e^{-t}(A\cos 2t + B\sin 2t)$

b $x = e^{-t}(\cos 2t + \sin 2t)$

c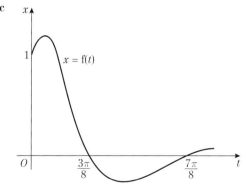

$x = f(t)$

59 a $y = Ae^{-\frac{1}{2}t} + Be^{-3t} + t^2 - t + 1$

b $y = \dfrac{4}{5}\left(e^{-\frac{1}{2}t} - e^{-3t}\right) + t^2 - t + 1$

c 1.45 (3 s.f.)

60 a $\lambda = 2$

b $y = A \cos 3x + B \sin 3x + 2x \cos 3x$

c $y = (1 + 2x) \cos 3x$

d

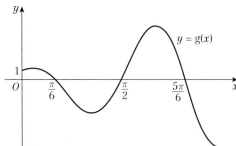

61 a $y = Kt^2 e^{3t}, \dfrac{dy}{dt} = 2Kt e^{3t} + 3Kt^2 e^{3t}, \dfrac{d^2y}{dt^2} = 2K e^{3t}$
$+ 12Kt e^{3t} + 9Kt^2 e^{3t}$

Substituting into the differential equation
$2K e^{3t} + 12Kt e^{3t} + 9Kt^2 e^{3t} - 12Kt e^{3t} - 18Kt^2 e^{3t}$
$+ 9Kt^2 e^{3t} = 4 e^{3t}$
$\Rightarrow 2K = 4 \Rightarrow K = 2$
$2t^2 e^{3t}$ is a particular integral of the differential equation

b $y = (A + Bt + 2t^2) e^{3t}$

c $y = (3 - 8t + 2t^2) e^{3t}$

d

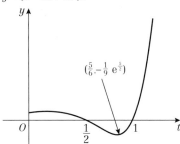

62 a $x = A e^{-\frac{1}{2}t} + B e^{-2t} + t + 2$

b $x = e^{-2t} + t + 2$

c $\dfrac{dx}{dt} = -2e^{-2t} + 1 = 0 \Rightarrow t = \dfrac{1}{2}\ln 2$

$\dfrac{d^2x}{dt^2} = 4e^{-2t} > 0$, for any real t

So stationary value is a minimum.

When $t = \dfrac{1}{2}\ln 2 \Rightarrow x = \dfrac{5}{2} + \dfrac{1}{2}\ln 2$

The minimum distance is $\dfrac{1}{2}(5 + \ln 2)$.

63 a $A = \dfrac{1}{2}$

b $x = \left(1 + t + \dfrac{1}{2}t^2\right)e^{-t}$

c $\dfrac{dx}{dt} = (1 + t)e^{-t} - \left(1 + t + \dfrac{1}{2}t^2\right)e^{-t} = -\dfrac{1}{2}t^2 e^{-t} \leqslant 0$,

for all real t
When $t = 0$, $x = 1$ and x has a negative gradient for all positive t, x is a decreasing function of t. Hence, for $t \geqslant 0$, $x \leqslant 1$.

64 a $k = 3$

b $y = A \sin x + 3x$

c At $x = \pi$, $y = A \sin \pi + 3\pi = 3\pi$
This is independent of the value of A. Hence, all curves given by the solution in part **a** pass through $(\pi, 3\pi)$.

$\dfrac{dy}{dx} = A \cos x + 3$

At $x = \dfrac{\pi}{2}$, $\dfrac{dy}{dx} = A \cos \dfrac{\pi}{2} + 3 = 3$

This is independent of the value of A. Hence, all curves given by the solution in part **a** have an equal gradient of 3 at $x = \dfrac{\pi}{2}$

d $y = 3x - \dfrac{3\pi}{2}\sin x$

e For a minimum $\dfrac{dy}{dx} = 3 - \dfrac{3\pi}{2}\cos x = 0$

$\cos x = \dfrac{2}{\pi} \Rightarrow x = \arccos \dfrac{2}{\pi}$

$\dfrac{d^2y}{dx^2} = \dfrac{3\pi}{2}\sin x$

In the interval $0 \leqslant x \leqslant \dfrac{\pi}{2}$, $\dfrac{d^2y}{dx^2} > 0 \Rightarrow$ minimum

$\sin^2 x = 1 - \cos^2 x = 1 - \dfrac{4}{\pi^2} = \dfrac{\pi^2 - 4}{\pi^2}$

In the interval $0 \leqslant x \leqslant \dfrac{\pi}{2}$, $\sin x = \dfrac{\sqrt{\pi^2 - 4}}{\pi^2}$

$y = 3 \arccos \dfrac{2}{\pi} - \dfrac{3}{2}\sqrt{\pi^2 - 4}$

65 a $S = \dfrac{120 - t}{4} - \dfrac{(120 - t)^2}{600}$ **b** $9\dfrac{3}{8}$ kg

66 a Three-quarters of the nutrient $= 75m_0$
At time t, the nutrient consumed is $5(m - m_0)$
$75m_0 = 5(m - m_0) \Rightarrow m = 16m_0$

b Rate of increase of mass $= \mu \times$ mass $\times$ mass of nutrient remaining
$\dfrac{dm}{dt} = \mu m(100m_0 - 5m + 5m_0) = 5\mu m(21m_0 - m)$

c $\dfrac{dm}{dt} = 5\mu m(21m_0 - m)$

$\int 5\mu \, dt = \int \dfrac{1}{m(21 m_0 - m)} \, dm$

Using partial fractions
$\dfrac{1}{m(21 m_0 - m)} = \dfrac{1}{21 m_0}\left(\dfrac{1}{m} + \dfrac{1}{21 m_0 - m}\right)$

$\Rightarrow 5\mu t = \int \dfrac{1}{21 m_0}\left(\dfrac{1}{m} + \dfrac{1}{21 m_0 - m}\right) dm$

$\Rightarrow 105\mu m_0 t = \ln m - \ln(21 m_0 - m) + c$

When $t = 0$, $m = m_0 \Rightarrow 0 = \ln m_0 - \ln 20m_0 + c$

$\Rightarrow c = \ln 20 m_0 - \ln m_0 = \ln \dfrac{20 m_0}{m_0} = \ln 20$

$\Rightarrow 105\mu m_0 t = \ln m - \ln(21 m_0 - m) + \ln 20$

$= \ln\left(\dfrac{20m}{21 m_0 - m}\right)$

From **a**, when $t = T$, $m = 16m_0$
$105\mu m_0 T = \ln\left(\dfrac{320 m_0}{5 m_0}\right) = \ln 64$

67 a $t\dfrac{dv}{dt} - v = t \Rightarrow \dfrac{dv}{dt} - \dfrac{v}{t} = 1$

Integrating factor is $e^{\int -\frac{1}{t}dt} = e^{-\ln t} = e^{\ln \frac{1}{t}} = \dfrac{1}{t}$

$\dfrac{1}{t}\dfrac{dv}{dt} - \dfrac{v}{t^2} = \dfrac{1}{t} \Rightarrow \dfrac{d}{dt}\left(\dfrac{v}{t}\right) = \dfrac{1}{t}$

$\Rightarrow \dfrac{v}{t} = \int \dfrac{1}{t} \, dt = \ln t + c$

$\Rightarrow v = t(\ln t + c)$

b 8.77 m s^{-1} (3 s.f.)

Online Full worked solutions are available in SolutionBank.

68 $a = \dfrac{dv}{dt} = e^{2t}$

$v = \int e^{2t}\, dt = \tfrac{1}{2}e^{2t} + A$

When $t = 0$, $v = 0 \Rightarrow 0 = \tfrac{1}{2} + A \Rightarrow A = -\tfrac{1}{2}$

Hence $v = \tfrac{1}{2}(e^{2t} - 1)$

69 a $v = 13 - 3e^{-\frac{1}{6}t}$ **b** $11.2\,\text{m s}^{-1}$ (3 s.f.)

   c 13

70 a $v = 2e^{-2t} - 1$ **b** $\tfrac{1}{2}(1 - \ln 2)\,\text{m}$

71 a $(t + 3)\dfrac{dv}{dt} + 3v = 9.8(t + 3) \Rightarrow \dfrac{dv}{dt} + \dfrac{3v}{t + 3} = \dfrac{49}{5}$

Integrating factor $e^{\int \frac{3}{t+3}\, dt} = e^{3\ln(t+3)} = e^{\ln(t+3)_3} = (t + 3)_3$

$\Rightarrow (t + 3)^3\dfrac{dv}{dt} + 3v(t + 3)^2 = \dfrac{49}{5}(t + 3)^3$

$\Rightarrow \dfrac{d}{dt}((t + 3)^3 v) = \dfrac{49}{5}(t + 3)^3$

$\Rightarrow (t + 3)^3 v = \dfrac{49}{20}(t + 3)^4 + c$

When $t = 0$, $v = 0 \Rightarrow 0 = \dfrac{49}{20} \times 3^4 + c \Rightarrow c = -\dfrac{3969}{20}$

$\Rightarrow (t + 3)^3 v = \dfrac{49}{20}(t + 4)^4 - \dfrac{3969}{20}$

$\Rightarrow (t + 3)^3 v = \dfrac{49(t + 4)^4 - 3969}{20}$

$\Rightarrow v = \dfrac{49(t + 4)^4 - 3969}{20(t + 3)^3}$, $c = -3969$

   b $21\tfrac{7}{9}\,\text{m s}^{-1}$

   c The speed continues to increase as t increases. This is unlikely to happen – terminal velocity, etc.

72 a Volume, ml of distilled water in the bottle after t minutes is given by $400 + 40t - 30t = 400 + 10t$

Concentration of acid after t minutes$= \dfrac{x}{400 + 10t}$

Rate acid in $= 4$ ml per minute

Rate acid out $= 30 \times \dfrac{x}{400 + 10t} = \dfrac{3x}{40 + t}$

Hence $\dfrac{dx}{dt} = 4 - \dfrac{3x}{40 + t}$

   b 22.3 ml (3 s.f.)

   c It is unlikely that the acid disperses immediately so this could be factored in.

73 a Simple harmonic motion

   b $x = 0.3\cos(7t)$

   c Period of motion $= \dfrac{2\pi}{7}$, Maximum speed $= 2.1\,\text{m s}^{-1}$

74 a $0.791\,\text{m}$

   b 2.48 minutes

   c Boat is unlikely to continue oscillating with such regularity.

75 a $3\sin 2t - 6e^{-t}\sin t$

   b $\dot{x} = 6e^{-t}\sin t - 6e^{-t}\cos t + 6\cos 2t$

$t = \dfrac{\pi}{4}$, $\dot{x} = 6\left(e^{-\frac{\pi}{4}}\sin\dfrac{\pi}{4} - e^{-\frac{\pi}{4}}\cos\dfrac{\pi}{4} + \cos\dfrac{\pi}{2}\right) = 0$

$\therefore P$ comes to instantaneous rest when $t = \dfrac{\pi}{4}$

   c $1.07\,\text{m}$ (3 s.f.)

   d π

76 a $A = 0$ $B = \dfrac{U}{\omega}$ **b** $\dfrac{\pi}{4\omega}$

77 $e^{-kt}\left(\dfrac{V}{5k}\cos 3kt - \dfrac{4V}{15k}\sin 3kt\right) + Vt - \dfrac{V}{5k}$

78 a $0.3e^{-4t} - 0.6e^{-2t} + 0.3$

   b $\dot{x} = -1.2e^{-4t} + 1.2e^{-2t} = 1.2e^{-4t}(e^{2t} - 1)$

$e^{2t} > 1$ for all $t > 0$

$\Rightarrow \dot{x} > 0$ throughout the motion (expect for $t = 0$) i.e. the particle continues to move down through the liquid throughout its motion.

79 a Differentiating (1) with respect to t:

$\dfrac{d^2x}{dt^2} = 0.1\dfrac{dx}{dt} + 0.1\dfrac{dy}{dt}$

Substituting (2): $\dfrac{d^2x}{dt^2} = 0.1\dfrac{dx}{dt} + 0.1(-0.025x + 0.2y)$

$\Rightarrow \dfrac{d^2x}{dt^2} = 0.1\dfrac{dx}{dt} - 0.0025x + 0.02y$

$\Rightarrow \dfrac{d^2x}{dt^2} = 0.1\dfrac{dx}{dt} - 0.0025x + 0.2\left(\dfrac{dx}{dt} - 0.1x\right)$

$\Rightarrow \dfrac{d^2x}{dt^2} = 0.1\dfrac{dx}{dt} - 0.0025x + 0.2\dfrac{dx}{dt} - 0.02x$

$\Rightarrow \dfrac{d^2x}{dt^2} - 0.3\dfrac{dx}{dt} + 0.0225x = 0$

   b $x = Ae^{0.15t} + Bte^{0.15t}$

   c $y = 0.5Ae^{0.15t} + 0.5Bte^{0.15t} + 10Be^{0.15t}$

   d 237

   e The number of angler fish and angel fish will both increase without limit so the model is unlikely to be suitable for large t.

80 a Differentiating (1) with respect to t: $\dfrac{d^2x}{dt^2} = 2\dfrac{dx}{dt} + \dfrac{dy}{dt}$

Substituting (2): $\dfrac{d^2x}{dt^2} = 2\dfrac{dx}{dt} + 4x - y + 1$

$\Rightarrow \dfrac{d^2x}{dt^2} = 2\dfrac{dx}{dt} + 4x - \left(\dfrac{dx}{dt} - 2x - 1\right) + 1$

$\Rightarrow \dfrac{d^2x}{dt^2} = \dfrac{dx}{dt} + 6x + 2$

$\Rightarrow \dfrac{d^2x}{dt^2} - \dfrac{dx}{dt} - 6x = 2$

   b $x = \dfrac{85}{3}e^{3t} - 8e^{-2t} - \dfrac{1}{3}$, $y = \dfrac{85}{3}e^{3t} + 32e^{2t} - \dfrac{1}{3}$

   c As t gets large, the e^{3t} term dominates and suggests the amount of gas increases without limit in both tanks. This is unlikely to be the case, for example size of tank will be a limiting factor.

Challenge

1 Let $n = 1$: The result $\mathbf{M}^n = \mathbf{M}$ becomes $\mathbf{M}^1 = \mathbf{M}$, which is true. Assume the result is true for $n = k$.

That is

$\mathbf{M}^k = \mathbf{M} = \begin{pmatrix} \cosh^2 x & \cosh^2 x \\ -\sinh^2 x & -\sinh^2 x \end{pmatrix}$

$\mathbf{M}^{k+1} = \mathbf{M}^k\mathbf{M} = \begin{pmatrix} \cosh^2 x & \cosh^2 x \\ -\sinh^2 x & -\sinh^2 x \end{pmatrix}\begin{pmatrix} \cosh^2 x & \cosh^2 x \\ -\sinh^2 x & -\sinh^2 x \end{pmatrix}$

$\mathbf{M}^k = \mathbf{M} = \begin{pmatrix} \cosh^4 x - \cosh^2 x\sinh^2 x & \cosh^4 x - \cosh^2 x\sinh^2 x \\ \sinh^4 x - \cosh^2 x\sinh^2 x & \sinh^4 x - \cosh^2 x\sinh^2 x \end{pmatrix}$

$= \begin{pmatrix} \cosh^2 x(\cosh^2 x - \sinh^2 x) & \cosh^2 x(\cosh^2 x - \sinh^2 x) \\ \sinh^2 x(-\cosh^2 x + \sinh^2 x) & \sinh^2 x(-\cosh^2 x + \sinh^2 x) \end{pmatrix}$

$= \begin{pmatrix} \cosh^2 x & \cosh^2 x \\ -\sinh^2 x & -\sinh^2 x \end{pmatrix}$

and this is the result for $n = k + 1$.

The result is true for $n = 1$, and if it is true for $n = k$, then it is true for $n = k + 1$.

By mathematical induction the result is true for all positive integers n.

2 a $\dfrac{dy}{dt} = \dfrac{d^2x}{dt^2} \Rightarrow \dfrac{d^2x}{dt^2} - x = 0$

$m^2 - 1 = 0 \Rightarrow m = \pm 1 \Rightarrow x = Ae^t + Be^{-t}$

$y = \dfrac{dx}{dt} = Ae^t - Be^{-t}$

When $t = 0$, $x = A + B = 1$ and $y = A - B = 0$, so $A = B = \frac{1}{2}$

So $x = \frac{1}{2}(e^t + e^{-t}) = \cosh t$ and $y = \frac{1}{2}(e^t - e^{-t}) = \sinh t$.

b $\dfrac{dq}{dt} = \dfrac{d^2p}{dt^2} + \dfrac{dp}{dt}$

$-\dfrac{d^2p}{dt^2} + \dfrac{dp}{dt} = p - \dfrac{dp}{dt} + p \Rightarrow \dfrac{d^2p}{dt^2} - 2\dfrac{dp}{dt} + 2p = 0$

$m^2 - 2m + 2 = 0 \Rightarrow m = 1 \pm i$ so $p = e^t(A \cos t + B \sin t)$

$\dfrac{dp}{dt} = e^t(A \cos t + B \sin t) + e^t(B \cos t - A \sin t)$

$q = p - \dfrac{dp}{dt} = e^t(-B \cos t + A \sin t)$

When $t = 0$, $p = A = 1$ and $q = -B = 1$, so $A = 1$ and $B = -1$.

$\dfrac{dr}{dt} - r = e^t(\cos t - \sin t) + 2e^t(\cos t + \sin t)$
$= e^t(3 \cos t + \sin t)$

Use integrating factor e^{-t},

$r = e^t \int (3 \cos t + \sin t) dt = e^t(3 \sin t - \cos t + C)$

When $t = 0$, $r = C - 1 = 1 \Rightarrow C = 2$ and so $r = e^t(3 \sin t - \cos t + 2)$

3 $x = r \cos\theta \Rightarrow \dfrac{dx}{d\theta} = -r \sin\theta + \dfrac{dr}{d\theta} \cos\theta$

$y = r \sin\theta \Rightarrow \dfrac{dy}{d\theta} = r \cos\theta + \dfrac{dr}{d\theta} \sin\theta$

So l has gradient $\dfrac{r \cos\theta + \dfrac{dr}{d\theta} \sin\theta}{-r \sin\theta + \dfrac{dr}{d\theta} \cos\theta} = \tan(\alpha + \theta)$

Thus $\dfrac{\tan\alpha + \tan\theta}{1 - \tan\alpha \tan\theta} = \dfrac{r \cos\theta + \dfrac{dr}{d\theta} \sin\theta}{-r \sin\theta + \dfrac{dr}{d\theta} \cos\theta}$

Rearrange and cancel to get

$-r \sin^2\theta + \dfrac{dr}{d\theta} \cos^2\theta \tan\alpha = r \cos^2\theta - \dfrac{dr}{d\theta} \tan\alpha \sin^2\theta$

$\Rightarrow \dfrac{dr}{d\theta} \tan\alpha = r \Rightarrow \tan\alpha = \dfrac{r}{\dfrac{dr}{d\theta}}$

Exam-style practice: Paper 1

1 a $11\,200\,cm^3$

b Does not take into account the thickness of the clay.

2 a $a = \dfrac{3}{14}$

$d = \dfrac{|2 \times 1 + 3 \times 4 + -1 \times 7 - 10|}{\sqrt{2^2 + 3^2 + (-1)^2}} = \dfrac{3\sqrt{14}}{14}$, $a = \dfrac{3}{14}$

b -1

c $43.9°$

3 a Let $n = 1$: $\begin{pmatrix} 1 & 2 & 2 \\ 0 & 1 & 2 \\ 0 & 0 & 1 \end{pmatrix} = \begin{pmatrix} 1 & 2 \times 1 & 2 \times 1^2 \\ 0 & 1 & 2 \times 1 \\ 0 & 0 & 1 \end{pmatrix}$,

which is true.

Assume the result is true for $n = k$.

$n = k$: $\begin{pmatrix} 1 & 2k & 2k^2 \\ 0 & 1 & 2k \\ 0 & 0 & 1 \end{pmatrix}$

$n = k + 1$: $\begin{pmatrix} 1 & 2 & 2 \\ 0 & 1 & 2 \\ 0 & 0 & 1 \end{pmatrix} \begin{pmatrix} 1 & 2k & 2k^2 \\ 0 & 1 & 2k \\ 0 & 0 & 1 \end{pmatrix}$

$= \begin{pmatrix} 1 & 2k+2 & 2k^2 + 4k + 2 \\ 0 & 1 & 2k + 2 \\ 0 & 0 & 1 \end{pmatrix}$

$= \begin{pmatrix} 1 & 2(k+1) & 2(k+1)^2 \\ 0 & 1 & 2(k+1) \\ 0 & 0 & 1 \end{pmatrix}$

and this is the result for $n = k + 1$.

The result is true for $n = 1$, and if it is true for $n = k$, then it is true for $n = k + 1$.

By mathematical induction the result is true for all positive integers n.

b i 7

ii $\dfrac{1}{14 - 2k} \begin{pmatrix} -2 & -(k+4) & 8 \\ -2 & -11 & 8 \\ 4 & 3k+1 & -2(k+1) \end{pmatrix}$

4 a $z = \cos\theta + i \sin\theta$

$z^n = (\cos\theta + i \sin\theta)^n$

$z^n = \cos n\theta + i \sin n\theta$

$\dfrac{1}{z^n} = \cos n\theta - i \sin n\theta$

$z^n - \dfrac{1}{z^n} = 2 \sin n\theta$

b $8 \sin^4\theta = \dfrac{1}{2}(2i \sin\theta)^4 = \dfrac{1}{2}\left(z - \dfrac{1}{z}\right)^4$

$= \dfrac{1}{2}\left(z^4 - 4z^2 + 6 - \dfrac{4}{z^2} + \dfrac{1}{z^4}\right)$

$= \dfrac{1}{2}(2 \cos 4\theta - 8 \cos 2\theta + 6)$

$= \cos 4\theta - 4 \cos 2\theta + 3$

5 a Volume $= 500 + 15t$

Concentration of sugar $= \dfrac{x}{500 + 15t}$

Rate of sugar into mixture $= 30 \times 25 = 750$

Lose sugar at rate $15 \dfrac{x}{500 + 15t} = \dfrac{3x}{100 + 3t}$

$\Rightarrow \dfrac{dx}{dt} = 750 - \dfrac{3x}{100 + 3t}$

b $6635\,g$

c Rate of leaking could vary with volume of oil, or model could take into account the fact that the sugar does not disperse throughout the vat on entry.

6 a $(x + 12)^2 + (y + 5)^2 = 169$

$(r \cos\theta + 12)^2 + (r \sin\theta + 5)^2 = 169$

$r^2 \cos^2\theta + 24r \cos\theta + 144 + r^2 \sin^2\theta + 10r \sin\theta + 25 = 169$

$r^2 = -24r \cos\theta - 10r \sin\theta$

$r = -2(12 \cos\theta + 5 \sin\theta)$

b

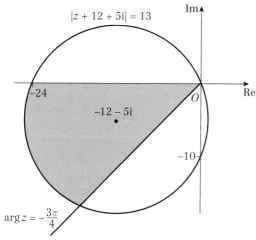

$|z + 12 + 5i| = 13$

-24

$-12 - 5i$

-10

$\arg z = -\dfrac{3\pi}{4}$

c 252

7 a $0.3 \times \dfrac{dx}{dt} - 0.2\dfrac{dy}{dt} = 0.3 \times 0.3x + 0.3 \times 0.2y + 0.3$
$\qquad\qquad\qquad\qquad\qquad + 0.2 \times 0.2x - 0.2 \times 0.3y$

$0.2\dfrac{dy}{dt} = 0.3\dfrac{dx}{dt} - (0.3^2 + 0.2^2)x - 0.3$

$\dfrac{d^2x}{dt^2} = 0.3\dfrac{dx}{dt} + 0.2\dfrac{dy}{dt} = 0.3\dfrac{dx}{dt} + 0.3\dfrac{dx}{dt}$
$\qquad\qquad\qquad\qquad\qquad - (0.3^2 + 0.2^2)x - 0.3$

$\dfrac{d^2x}{dt^2} - 0.6\dfrac{dx}{dt} + 0.13x + 0.3 = 0$

$100\dfrac{d^2x}{dt^2} - 60\dfrac{dx}{dt} + 13x + 30 = 0$

b $x = e^{0.3t}(A\cos 0.2t + B\sin 0.2t) - \dfrac{30}{13}$

c $y = e^{0.3t}(B\cos 0.2t - A\sin 0.2t) - \dfrac{20}{13}$

d $x = e^{0.3t}\left(\dfrac{160}{13}\cos 0.2t + \dfrac{85}{13}\sin 0.2t\right) - \dfrac{30}{13}$

$y = e^{0.3t}\left(\dfrac{85}{13}\cos 0.2t - \dfrac{160}{13}\sin 0.2t\right) - \dfrac{20}{13}$

e Concentration on right side predicted to be negative which isn't possible. Therefore, model is not suitable.

Exam-style practice: Paper 2

1 a $p = 7, q = 25$

Using partial fractions,

$\dfrac{1}{(r + 2)(r + 4)} = \dfrac{1}{2(r + 2)} - \dfrac{1}{2(r + 4)}$

Using the method of differences,

$\displaystyle\sum_{r=1}^{n}\dfrac{1}{(r + 2)(r + 4)} = \sum_{r=1}^{n}\dfrac{1}{2(r + 2)} - \dfrac{1}{2(r + 4)}$

$= \dfrac{1}{6} + \dfrac{1}{8} - \dfrac{1}{2(n + 3)} - \dfrac{1}{2(n + 4)} = \dfrac{n(7n + 25)}{24(n + 3)(n + 4)}$

b Let $n = 1 : f(1) = 2^3 + 3^3 = 35$ which is divisible by 7

Assume the result is true for $n = k$.

$n = k: f(k) = 2^{k+2} + 3^{2k+1}$ is divisible by 7

$n = k + 1 : f(k + 1) = 2^{k+3} + 3^{2k+3} = 2(2^{k+2}) + 3^2(3^{2k+1})$

$= 2(2^{k+2}) + 9(3^{2k+1})$

$= 2(2^{k+2}) + 2(3^{2k+1}) + 7(3^{2k+1})$

$= 2f(k) + 7(3^{2k+1})$ which is divisible by 7 and this is the result for $n = k + 1$.

The result is true for $n = 1$, and if it is true for $n = k$, then it is true for $n = k + 1$.

By mathematical induction the result is true for all positive integers n.

2 a $1 - 4i$

b $1 \pm 4i, 2 \pm i$

c

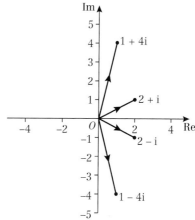

3 3.42 (3 s.f.)

4 a $2x + \dfrac{1}{3}x^3 - \dfrac{19}{60}x^5$ **b** $2.754 \times 10^{-6}\%$ (4 s.f.)

5 $\displaystyle\int_0^{\infty}\dfrac{1}{x^2 + 4}\,dx = \lim_{a\to\infty}\int_0^{a}\dfrac{1}{x^2 + 4}\,dx = \lim_{a\to\infty}\left[\dfrac{1}{2}\arctan\left(\dfrac{x}{2}\right)\right]_0^{a}$

$= \dfrac{1}{2}\lim_{a\to\infty}\arctan\dfrac{x}{2} = \dfrac{1}{2} \times \dfrac{\pi}{2} = \dfrac{\pi}{4}$

6 $k = 9.5$

7 a 0.722 **b** 2.722

8 $\dfrac{6\sqrt{14}}{7}$

9 a $(-B\sin t - C\cos t) + 2(B\cos t - C\sin t)$
$\quad + 3(A + B\sin t + C\cos t)$
$= 21 + 15\cos t$

$2(B - C)\sin t + 2(B + C)\cos t + 3A = 21 + 15\cos t$

$\left.\begin{array}{l} 3A = 21 \\ B - C = 0 \\ B + C = \dfrac{15}{2} \end{array}\right\} \Rightarrow A = 7, B = C = \dfrac{15}{4}$

$\Rightarrow x = 7 + \dfrac{15}{4}(\sin t + \cos t)$

b $x = 7 + \dfrac{15}{4}(\sin t + \cos t)$

$\quad - e^{-t}\left(\dfrac{19\sqrt{2}}{4}\sin(\sqrt{2}\,t) + \dfrac{35}{4}\cos(\sqrt{2}\,t)\right)$

c The flow will stabilise and oscillate evenly about $x = 7$.

Index